Islam and Society in Pakistan
Anthropological Perspectives

*Oxford in Pakistan Readings in Sociology
and Social Anthropology*

SERIES EDITOR: ALI KHAN

ISLAM AND SOCIETY IN PAKISTAN
Anthropological Perspectives

edited by
MAGNUS MARSDEN

OXFORD
UNIVERSITY PRESS

Oxford University Press is a department of the University of Oxford.
It furthers the University's objective of excellence in research, scholarship,
and education by publishing worldwide in

Oxford   New York

Auckland Cape Town Dar es Salaam Hong Kong Karachi
Kuala Lumpur Madrid Melbourne Mexico City Nairobi
New Delhi Shanghai Taipei Toronto

With offices in

Argentina Austria Brazil Chile Czech Republic France Greece
Guatemala Hungary Italy Japan Poland Portugal Singapore
South Korea Switzerland Turkey Ukraine Vietnam

Oxford is a registered trademark of Oxford University Press
in the UK and in certain other countries

Published in Pakistan by Oxford University Press

© Oxford University Press 2010

The moral rights of the author have been asserted

Database right Oxford University Press (maker)

First published 2010

All rights reserved. No part of this publication may be reproduced, translated,
stored in a retrieval system, or transmitted, in any form or by any means,
without the prior permission in writing of Oxford University Press.
Enquiries concerning reproduction should be sent to
Oxford University Press at the address below.

You must not circulate this work in any other form and you
must impose this same condition on any acquirer.

ISBN 978-0-19-547957-7

Second Impression 2013

Typeset in Adobe Garamond Pro
Printed in Pakistan by
Printech Quality Printers, Karachi.
Published by
Ameena Saiyid, Oxford University Press
No. 38, Sector 15, Korangi Industrial Area, PO Box 8214,
Karachi-74900, Pakistan.

Contents

Series Editor's Introduction — vii

Publisher's Acknowledgements — ix

Introduction: Anthropology, Islam, and Pakistan — xi
Magnus Marsden

1. Of Children and Jinns: An Enquiry into an Unexpected Friendship during Uncertain Times — 1
   Naveeda Khan

2. The Modern Businessman and the Pakistani Saint: The Interpenetration of Worlds — 34
   Katherine P. Ewing

3. Islamic Influences on Socio-legal Conditions of Pakistani Women — 52
   Anita M. Weiss

4. Religious Education and the Rhetoric of Reform: The Madrassahs in British India and Pakistan — 76
   Muhammad Qasim Zaman

5. Reforming Mysticism: Sindhi Separatist Intellectuals in Pakistan — 111
   Oskar Verkaaik

6. Flagellation and Fundamentalism: (Trans)forming Meaning, Identity, and Gender through Pakistani Women's Rituals of Mourning — 132
   Mary Elaine Hegland

7. The Sunni–Shia Conflict in Jhang (Pakistan) — 164
   Mariam Abou Zahab

8. Langar: Pilgrimage, Sacred Exchange, and Perpetual
   Sacrifice in a Sufi Saint's Lodge 177
   Pnina Werbner

9. All-Male Sonic Gatherings, Islamic Reform, and Masculinity
   in Northern Pakistan 201
   Magnus Marsden

10. Selves and Others: Representing Multiplicities of Difference
    in Gilgit and the Northern Areas of Pakistan 235
    Martin Sökefeld

11. Islam, the State, and Identity: The Zikris of Balochistan 259
    Inayatullah Baloch

12. Sakineh, the Narrator of Karbala: An Ethnographic
    Description of Women's Majles Ritual in Pakistan 283
    Shemeem Burney Abbas

13. Al-Huda: Of Allah and the Power-Point 299
    Sadaf Ahmad

14. The Rise of Sunni Militancy in Pakistan: The Changing
    Role of Islamism and the Ulama in Society and Politics 327
    S.V.R. Nasr

15. The Poetics of 'Sufi' Practice: Drumming, Dancing,
    and Complex Agency at Madho Lal Husain (and Beyond) 367
    Richard K. Wolf

Bibliography 404

Notes on Contributors 435

Index 441

Series Editor's Introduction

Mehrgarh, Harappa, Mohenjodaro—it begins here. Mehrgarh—located in Balochistan is the oldest known rural settlement dating from 7000 BCE. Harappa and Mohenjodaro, cities in the Indus Valley Civilisation, represent the most ancient of urban settlements dating back between 2800 BC–1800 BC.

These ancient cultures found their roots in the area that now encompasses modern day Pakistan. As time progressed through to the modern day more and more civilisations, each with their own unique influence, came and left their stamp. Multiple invasions—Persian, Greek, Turkic, Mongol, Arab, and later the British—led to the arrival of 'foreign' influences and populations, as migration (and trade) often followed conquests. Zoroastrianism, Buddhism, Hinduism, Sikhism, Islam—all flourished. The indigenous and the non-indigenous fused to produce a mosaic of ethnicities, religions and cultures. It also established the region as an area that has amongst the richest and most varied of legacies.

All of these influences continued to have a strong effect on the colonial and the post colonial state. Pakistan's subsequent 'development' after independence in 1947 and the problems associated with 'under-development'—widespread poverty, educating a rapidly expanding population, and uncontrolled urbanisation and migration, were all tinged with issues of regional identity, ethnicity, and religion. Today, in addition to these challenges, globalisation has brought entrenched 'traditions' into conflict with 'modernity', throwing newer issues such as the underpinning of modern day gender and labour relations on traditional 'hierarchical' foundations into the spotlight. Moreover, the transnational movement of Pakistanis has meant that as an area of study, Pakistan is part of a global culture rather than being confined solely to the physical boundaries of the nation state

But this rich melting pot of cultural nuances represents amongst the richest raw material for sociological and anthropological analysis. Yet, research on Pakistan in the field of anthropology and sociology—despite the potential of the area—has been scattered and limited in scale and scope. The Oxford University Press series is an attempt to try and fill this void. Firstly, by bringing together some of the best research on Pakistan which has to date remained spread across numerous journals and edited books; and secondly, by including fresh material, both by established academics and by researchers just starting their careers.

The strength of the series stems from this blend of older and newer articles and the fact that contributions have been made by both established and upcoming researchers. The common linkage, though, remains one of academic rigour and innovation.

The Reader in Anthropology and Sociology is aimed both at the serious Pakistan-focused academic as well as academics, students, and general readers who desire an introduction to the area as seen through a perspective that provides the kind of depth and intimacy of analysis that few disciplines can match.

This series of books would not have been possible without the support of the growing band of researchers involved in work on Pakistan and I am particularly thankful to all those who contributed to the different volumes. The Pakistan-focused researcher is a shy species but the level of support for this series has been overwhelming. From those who started writing on Pakistan decades ago to those who are busily exploring new frontiers today, all have gone out of their way with the aim of drawing attention to the richness of material available as well as the incredible potential that Pakistan holds for research in the fields of anthropology and sociology.

I would also like to thank the Oxford University Press for initiating this project. Ammara Maqsood, Maria Hasan, and Saad Siddiqui were my research assistants, and all three contributed to the quality of the end product. My final gratitude goes to my family who are my biggest support and especially my wife Mariyam and daughter Alena.

ALI KHAN

Publisher's Acknowledgements

The publisher acknowledges the following for permission to include articles in this volume. For some articles we have been unable to contact the copyright holder/s. If notified the publisher will be pleased to acknowledge the rights of the copyright holder/s and take any remedial action at the earliest opportunity.

Naveeda Khan, 'Of Children and Jinns: An Enquiry into an Unexpected Friendship during Uncertain Times.' Copyright © 2006 American Anthropological Association. Reprinted by permission from *Cultural Anthropology*, Vol. 21, No. 2.

Katherine Ewing, 'The Modern Businessman and the Pakistani Saint: The Interpenetration of Worlds' from *Manifestations of Sainthood in Islam* edited by Grace Martin Smith and Carl Ernst, Isis Press, Istanbul. Reprinted by permission.

Anita Weiss, 'Islamic Influences on Socio-legal Conditions of Pakistani Women.' Reprinted by permission. Courtesy of the *Islam in South Asia* monograph of Oriente Moderno (XXII, 2004), edited by Daniela Bredi.

Muhammad Qasim Zaman, 'Religious Education and the Rhetoric of Reform: The Madrassahs in British India and Pakistan' from *Comparative Study of Society and History*, Vol. 41, No. 2, April 1999, Cambridge University Press. Reprinted by permission.

Oskar Verkaaik, 'Reforming Mysticism: Sindhi Separatist Intellectuals in Pakistan' from *Popular Intellectuals and Social Movements: Framing Protests in Asia, Africa, and Latin America, International Review of Social History Supplements*, Baud and Rutten (eds.), No. 12 (2005).

Mary Elaine Hegland, 'Flagellation and Fundamentalism: Transforming Meaning, Identity, and Gender through Pakistani Women's Rituals of

Mourning.' Copyright © 1998 American Anthropological Association. Reprinted by permission from *American Ethnologist*, Vol. 25, No. 2.

Mariam Abou Zahab, 'The Sunni–Shia Conflict in Jhang' from *Islam in South Asia* edited by Imtiaz Ahmad and Helmut Reifeld, Social Science Press, New Delhi, 2004. Reprinted by permission.

Magnus Marsden, 'All-male Sonic Gatherings, Islamic Reform and Masculinity in Northern Pakistan.' Copyright © American Anthropological Association. Reprinted by permission from *American Ethnologist*, Vol. 34, No. 3.

Martin Sökefeld, *Selves and Others: Representing Multiplicities of Difference in Gilgit and the Northern Areas of Pakistan*. Reprinted by permission. Courtesy of the Oxford University Press, New Delhi, India.

Shemeem Burney Abbas, 'Sakineh, the Narrator of Karbala: An Ethnographic Description of Women's Majles Ritual in Pakistan' from *The Women of Karbala: Ritual Performance and Symbolic Discourses in Modern Shi'i Islam* edited by Kamran Scot Aghaie, Copyright © 2005. Courtesy of the University of Texas Press.

S.V.R. Nasr, 'The Rise of Sunni Militancy in Pakistan: The Changing Role of Islamism and the Ulama in Society and Politics.' Copyright © *Modern Asian Studies*, 34 (01). Reprinted by permission. The Cambridge University Press.

Richard K. Wolf, 'The Poetics of 'Sufi' Practice: Drumming, Dancing, and Complex Agency at Madho Lal Husain.' Copyright © American Anthropological Association. Reprinted by permission from *American Ethnologist*, Vol. 33, No. 2.

Pnina Werbner, 'Langar: Pilgrimage, Sacred Exchange, and Perpetual Sacrifice in a Sufi Saint's Lodge' from P. Werbner and H. Basu (eds.), *Embodying Charisma: Modernity, Locality and the Performance of Emotion in Sufi Cults*, Routledge. Reprinted by permission.

Introduction: Anthropology, Islam, and Pakistan

This book aims to bring together some of the most sophisticated recent anthropological works on the ways in which Pakistan's citizens from diverse social and regional backgrounds set to the task of being Muslim and contribute to the dynamic role played by Islam in the country's political and social life.

There is, of course, a long and important tradition of anthropological scholarship on Islam in Pakistan. Recent international events, moreover, have brought the analysis of Islam's place in Pakistani politics and society to the forefront of global debates about the state of the Muslim world. Whilst the expansion of ethnographic studies of Muslim everyday life in Pakistan is a welcome development in anthropological work on the country, the current focus on Islam in Pakistan also raises important problems. Above all else, there is a danger of Islam becoming what Appadurai has referred to as a gate-keeping concept (Appadurai 1986), leading to the assumption that the study of Islam and Pakistan are one and the same.

By addressing the diversity and complexity of the Islamic tradition in contemporary Pakistan and seeking to analyse this diversity from very different theoretical angles, the chapters in this book emphasise the multi-dimensionality of the varying ways in which Islam is an important part of the everyday life of Pakistani Muslims. The authors explore the vitality of Islam as a religious tradition in Pakistan both from the perspective of in-depth ethnographic fieldwork and historical research. They bring together ethnographic material from each of the country's five major provinces, as well as from a very wide spectrum of social settings within these, ranging from those of major cities to small towns and remote villages. In addition, several chapters have been included that are not anthropological in the strictest sense; these chapters provide the wider political and historical contexts within which many field-based studies of Muslim life in Pakistan have been framed, including, for example, the high-politics of sectarian violence and the colonial and postcolonial history of madrassah reform.

The book is divided into four main sections. These are: Islam and the state, local modes of being Muslim, Islam in Pakistan's diaspora, and sectarian violence. The division of the book thus reflects both the content of the chapters as well some of the central themes in anthropological work that focuses on Islam in Pakistan today. Whilst the individual chapters approach these issues from different ethnographic perspectives and in relationship to contrasting bodies of anthropological theory, they all challenge much that has been said and assumed about the contours of Muslim life in Pakistan in recent years. Since the 7 July 2005 attacks on London, most public discussion concerning Islam's place in Pakistan's society and political culture has focused on its 'radicalisation'; no longer seen as being peripheral to the wider Muslim world—a South Asian Islamic exception—Pakistan is now widely viewed as the key hub for so-called 'Islamic terrorists'. It is being seen as an international exporter of militancy and radicalism to neighbouring countries and Muslim communities elsewhere.

The chapters in this book challenge these popular stereotypes, which, as the Osellas have argued, pull categories such as 'reformism, Islamism and radicalism' 'together...as though generated exclusively within Islam itself, perhaps as an inevitable tradition of a religion which is essentially inimical—and militantly opposed—to modernity' (Osella and Osella 2007). As Mamdani has argued, Western stereotypes about Muslims have undergone important transformations in recent years; the demonization of Islam in its entirety remains powerful in the work of commentators such as Samuel Huntington, yet, new ways of locating Islam have emerged (Mamdani 2004). Prominent amongst these are attempts to define some Muslims as being inherently prone to violence and in need of extermination and others as being good, and more predisposed to tolerant and moderate attitudes to the world. This way of categorising good and bad Muslims appears in newspaper articles that depict particular Islamic 'movements' and 'sects' as being intimately connected to Islam's radicalisation.

Moreover, as events in Iraq and Afghanistan have shown, such stereotypes are not merely confined to the realm of Islam's representation—they are also central to the ways in which Western states interact with Muslims. From the streets of the United Kingdom to the villages of southern Afghanistan, Muslims are encouraged by the nation-states to which they belong to partake in what Mamdani calls a Western-directed civil war where good Muslims must exclude and isolate their bad co-religionists (Mamdani 2004). Such approaches always obscure the role played by Western politics and regimes in the production of apparently 'bad' ways of being Muslim. At the same time, they lead public commentators and policy makers to categorise Muslim groups, political parties, particular Islamic seminaries and whole schools of Islamic thinking according to simplistic, moralistic and often largely meaningless categories as 'radical', 'tolerant' and 'moderate'. Thus, Sufi-inspired forms of Islam in Pakistan tend to be represented in both the international print media and some scholarly writing as representing Pakistan's 'tolerant, plural, and authentic' side—it is Sufis, mostly gathered in shrines, who are wheeled out by journalists to give a glimpse into the more moderate side of Pakistani Islam. The good Sufi Muslim, however, is only ever made possible through a negative contrast with what Osella and Osella refer to as the 'maligned Other': reformist Islam (Osella and Osella 2007: 4). Thus, if ecstatic forms of worship are celebrated in the Western media as pointing towards a more authentic and more tolerant Islamic strain, then reform-minded schools of Islamic thought such as the South Asian Muslim school of thought known as the Deoband and the international preaching movement with which it is associated, the Tabligh-e Jama't, are routinely depicted as having been and continuing to be a key doctrinal and institutional force behind the radicalisation of South Asian Islam. As a journalist in a British newspaper recently commented with an alarming degree of confidence: 'if there are future problems with Islamic radicals in the world you can be sure they'll be associated with Pakistan and the Deoband.'

Both Sufism and reformism, however, are notoriously difficult terms to define—they reflect the form taken by Western scholarly attempts to order and understand the complexities of Islam and 'the Muslim world' as much as they point towards the realities of the thought processes, ritual practices, political strategies and modes of engagement with the wider world of those Muslims whom we are tempted to define as being reform-minded or Sufi (e.g. Soares 2005). For the sake of definition, however, reformism refers to projects that seek to bring Muslim thought and practice closer to Islamic doctrinal prescriptions. Sufism, in contrast, has often been described as Islam's 'mystical strain'; Sufi thought places greater emphasis on the possibility of there being a lived and experienced relationship between the believer and God.

The distinction between Sufi and reform-minded Islam also informs much writing on Pakistan. Pakistan's cities are home to some of the most vibrant Sufi shrines in the Muslim world and their annual gatherings that celebrate the death of the saint in whose name they are founded draw thousands of devotees, and increasingly, Western journalists. At the same time, Pakistan's madrassahs, or religious seminaries, form one of the most important networks for the transmission of reform-minded forms of Islamic thought and learning in the world today. As a number of Islam specialists have noted, distinguishing between these different ways of being Muslim as being good and bad ignores the complexity of the historical and ongoing interaction between reform-minded and Sufi-derived forms of Muslim thought and identity (e.g. Metcalf 2004). It also ignores the internal complexity, divisions, and conflicts within these different dimensions of the Islamic tradition: exploring the complexity of everyday Muslim life challenges the relevance of such modes of categorising Pakistan's Muslims. Yet, like the 'fundamentalists' they challenge, the policy makers who advance such simplistic understandings of the contours of Muslim thinking and identity in the world today remain resistant to having their grand schemes fractured by the complexity of the everyday.

A consideration of everyday Muslim life points towards the ways in which Pakistan's Muslims do not simply either conform to or resist pre-existing ways of being Muslim, be they reform-minded or Sufi-derived. Rather, Muslims deploy personal and collective forms of creative thought and reason in order to forge new and constantly emerging modes of being Muslim; these always reflect the particular circumstances of their daily lives and the dynamics of the diverse communities in which they live. My central consideration in bringing these chapters together has been to bring together as diverse an array of literature on Islam and Muslim life in Pakistan as possible. At one level, I have sought to include chapters which give ethnographically rich snapshots of Muslim life in Pakistan from across the country's linguistic and ethnic communities: I hope that the book will provide an accessible resource for the teaching of the complex ways in which Pakistan's cultural heterogeneity is played out and contested in the realm of religious life. I have also sought to include chapters that address shared themes from very different analytical perspectives. The nature and form of so-called 'sectarian violence' that has led to the killings of thousands of Muslims in Pakistan over the past two decades, for example, appears to change when it is considered from different places within the country, and again when explored from the perspective of villagers, town dwellers, committed members of movements of Islamic reform, and women. At another level, the chapters also engage with long running anthropological debates concerning, for example, the nature of distinctions between Sufi and reform-minded ways of being Muslim or 'local' and 'global Islam', as well as doctrinal differences between Sunni and Shi'a Muslims. They point both toward the ways in which Muslims undermine the analytical salience of such categories during the course of their everyday lives, but simultaneously also invest them with the power and influence to shape the nature of political and social dynamics at critical junctures in the country's history.

DIVERSITY AND UNITY

The chapters in this section address the diversity in the ways of being Muslim found in Pakistan today and focus on the ways in which both Pakistani Muslims themselves, and anthropologists, have sought to make sense of this diversity. As I have already noted, many popular works treat differences between Sufi and reform-minded Islam as marking distinctions between good and tolerant Muslims on the one hand, and those prone to terrorism and radicalisation on the other. Supposedly moderate forms of Sufi Islam are also widely held as being more authentically 'South Asian' than reform-minded schools of Islamic thought, which are depicted as having their roots in the Arab world and having been politicised by global Islamic influences and debates. There is also a tendency to assume that supposedly more moderate forms of Sufi Islam in Pakistan are currently on the back foot in an internal conflict with global forms of Muslim reformism, which are better organised and enjoy high levels of finance due to the thickness of their transnational links with Muslims beyond Pakistan. As the chapters in this section show, however, worship at Sufi shrines and adherence to Sufi saints remains a vital dimension of being Muslim for many Pakistanis, and so too are Sufi forms of Islam often expressed and injected with vitality in dense networks that join Sufi devotees not only across Pakistan, but also across the wider world. Such modes of religiosity are not merely important for Pakistan's villagers and small-town dwellers or its urban poor: educated persons and even elite professionals also often play an active role in organised movements of Sufi spirituality. Even more strikingly, the distinction between Sufi and reform-minded Islam often becomes irrelevant when the everyday lives of Muslims is considered in its full complexity. The chapters in this section, thus, point towards a complex spectrum of Sufi-influenced forms of Muslim thought and practice in Pakistan today and very often these are shaped by interactions with reform-minded ways of being Muslim. Ewing's chapter focuses on a type of person who might easily be assumed to treat Sufism either as an un-Islamic form of superstition or a marker of rural backwardness: the well educated, urban-based and highly trained businessman and professional. Yet Ewing explores the ways in which science-educated business people display a vital interest in Sufism in Pakistan. Sufism, moreover, is not merely just a romantic mode of escape from the material world. In contrast, the business people Ewing writes about consider affiliation to particular Sufi pirs (men of special spiritual insight and power) and the shrines of these men as having an important role in the strengthening of ties between colleagues and business associates. Sharing affiliation to a brotherhood or pir, moreover, also creates the possibility for imagining and creating relationships in the workplace that are not monolithically defined in terms of a hierarchy of 'organised seniority relationships', but rather, enriched by shared commitment to forms of Sufi devotion.

Marsden's Chitrali musicians and dancers demonstrate the vitality and relevance of Sufi-influenced but in no sense non-reformist, local ways of being Muslim in a very different Pakistani setting. The everyday importance of such ways of being Muslim persists, moreover, in the face of attacks made by Deobandi-educated and politically powerful men of piety on the local practices of music and dance with which they are associated. Marsden points to the complex ways in which Muslims in Pakistan's northernmost district, Chitral, receive and respond to the Islamising messages of the region's madrassah-educated mullahs. He challenges the notion that 'village Muslims' are passive and unthinking in the face of calls to commitment to reform their practices and everyday lives in line with Islamic doctrinal traditions. Moreover, he also points to the ways in which local, Sufi-derived ways of being Muslim have long been interacting with reform-minded Islamic doctrinal thought.

This interaction challenges the relevance of thinking about religious transformation in local settings in Pakistan or elsewhere in terms of the displacement of local modes of being Muslim by reform-minded or global forms of thought and identity. Rather, this interaction has led to the emergence of creative forms of Muslim life in Chitral and these bring together diverse and apparently incompatible influences in the thinking patterns of individual Muslims. In relation to the understanding of Sufism in Pakistan, Marsden's chapter illuminates that not all expressions of Sufi-derived thought and experience in the country are best understood in terms of a nexus between pirs, shrines and variously more or less ecstatic forms of devotional worship. In Chitral, Sufi concepts, such as those of intoxicating love, seep into the thinking of the region's Muslims through a regional tradition of poetic composition and performance: they are constantly injected with vitality by Chitrali Muslims through listening to cassette recordings of Chitrali-language ghazal (love) music, for example.

Introduction: Anthropology, Islam, and Pakistan   xvii

The lyrics of these ghazals point towards the ongoing significance of the Persianate Sufi canon to Chitrali Muslim life in a world where Islamist parties are powerful and influential and where there are no major shrine complexes.

In contrast, Wolf's chapter describes the type of ecstatic devotional practices that are not present in Chitral but that do continue to be central to religious experience in a major Sufi shrine in the Punjabi city of Lahore. Wolf is careful to recognise the dangers of treating shrine worship as an expression of 'popular religion', something that is the focus of devotion by the country's 'lower strata' and shunned by its educated, rational and reform-minded middle classes. Lahore's Islamising middle classes do often treat worship at the shrine as 'distasteful' and irrational; yet dancing at the shrine also holds a New Age appeal for Lahore's young elite. Wolf is concerned with the ways in which such 'processes of joining and division at encompassing geopolitical and religious levels' are enacted and conceptualised by worshipers at the shrine: shrine-goers include not only Lahore's rich and poor but also people who identify themselves as belonging to different ethnic groups. By considering the social poetics of dancing and the music at the shrine in relation to the ongoing negotiation of these varying axis of difference, Wolf explores the ways in which the feeling of a union with the saint that more 'engaged participants' seek to achieve at the shrine also becomes 'thoroughly implicated' in the politics of 'who gets included in the category of "Muslim" in Pakistan'. By furnishing insight into the ways in which shrine attendees manage processes of both coming together and drawing apart in relationship to the Sufi concepts of oneness, Wolf explores the ways in which Muslims themselves negotiate questions of unity and diversity in Islam and challenges the simplistic notion that Sufi forms of devotion and thought represent Islam's tolerant or inclusive strand.

As I have noted above there is a tendency to treat Sufism as South Asian Islam's more authentic and indigenous underbelly, and it is often defined in contrast to movements of piety and purification, which tend to be lumped together under the category of 'reformist'. These studies focus on the ways in which Islamisers seek to reform Sufism, arguing that it deviates from Islam's doctrinal traditions. Verkaaik's chapter, however, explores the ways in which Sufism, too, has undergone profound processes of reform and transformation. Pakistan's ruling elites and reform-minded Islamists have for long juxtaposed Sufi forms of Islam to more 'modern' and 'civilised' expressions of Islam that they advocate as being important building blocks for a shared Pakistani national identity. Likewise,

Pakistan's leaders today frequently talk of Sufi Islam as being moderate and a more authentic expression of Pakistani Islam then the country's Islamist parties. Verkaaik argues that in the course of being defined as the 'other' against which modern and reform-minded forms of Islam have been promoted, Sufism in Pakistan, too, is not merely an assemblage of religious practices or modes of devotion, but an 'object of intellectual enquiry'. The chapter focuses on the ways in which the idea of reformed Sufi Islam was central to the organic intellectuals who were central to the emergence of the Sindhi separatist movement in the 1960s and 1970s. In later years, an idea of reformed Sufism was also deployed by Prime Minister Zulfikar Ali Bhutto, who sought to stake his claims to political authority and influence by depicting himself as a kind of Sufi saint and devotee to the country's populace.

The chapters in this section introduce Sufism in Pakistan as it is practiced and experienced by educated business professionals, villages in the far north of the country's North-West Frontier Province, shrine devotees in Lahore, and nationalist intellectuals in Sindh. They point not only to the great diversity of Sufism in Pakistan, but also to the ways in which Sufism, just as much as reform-minded Islam, has undergone complex processes of reform and transformation and been implicated in Pakistan's divisive politics of inclusion and exclusion.

ISLAM, WOMEN, AND THE STATE

The state's role in the Islamisation of Pakistani society and political culture is the focus of much discussion amongst political scientists and historians. The country's successive military regimes have sought to use both Sufi shrines and the country's network of madrassahs to assert their authority and extend the webs of society across the country (e.g. Ewing 1982). Other rulers have also sought to more assertively Islamise society from top-down, by introducing versions of the Islamic legal code (Shariah) into the country's legal system, for example. General Zia's deployment of Islamic discourses, symbols and legislation during his period of rule have been interpreted by Pakistan specialists as a way of investing his military regime with popular legitimacy; they also facilitated the extension of intrusive state power into the intimate lives of the country's people, pointing towards a complex marriage between the Islamising social policies of Islamist political parties and the military's desire to extend the power of the state (Jalal 1995; Nasr 2002).

Introduction: Anthropology, Islam, and Pakistan

The chapters in this section explore the role played by 'the state' in the Islamisation of Pakistani society from an anthropological point of view. They enquire how different communities in Pakistan have experienced, negotiated and responded to 'top-down' Islamising legislation. At the same time, they challenge simplistic accounts that depict the Pakistani state as a reified actor, capable of only one-dimensionally imposing either Islamising or modernising legislation on the country's populace. The organs of the Pakistani state, rather, have needed to respond to the growing pressure of both civil society groups within the country and a wide range of increasingly influential international organisations. In particular, the status and nature of the version of 'Islamic law' the Pakistani state has sought to promote has been a hotly debated concern within and beyond the country over the past twenty years: some have called for its repeal, others for its further entrenchment, while still others have argued that it promotes majority Sunni forms of legal conventions and refuses to recognise the legal traditions of other Muslims in the country, notably Pakistan's Shi'a Muslim community.

These issues are explored in this section primarily through a consideration of the ways in which Pakistani women have responded and adapted to life under the conditions of state-led Islamisation. The lives of Pakistani women have been deeply affected by state-led forms of Islamic legislation in the country over the past three decades: the introduction of the Hudood ordinances, which made fornication a capital punishment being one particularly well-documented example. Yet, Pakistani women have responded to such forms of Islamising legislation in ways that reflect the particular socio-economic circumstances in which they live and the various ethnic and sectarian groups with whom they identify. In doing so, the chapters in this section question the idea that the expansion in public forms of Islam in Pakistan has lead to a one-dimensional reduction in the personal and collective agency of the country's women. Instead, the authors highlight the problems of applying Western notions of 'agency' to understand the complexity of women's lives in Pakistan at a time of heightened state-led Islamisation, or indeed, secularisation. Also, they explore the varying types of influence that women assert in the face of both newer and old constraints placed on their movement and speech. Others emphasise the problems with thinking about piety or reform-minded forms of Islam as a monolithic entity that poses further restrictions on women's lives by analysing the voices of women who have themselves sought to conform their behaviour according to Islamic doctrinal standards by becoming active participants in movements of Islamic reform.

Weiss' chapter offers the debates going on apace in Pakistan concerning 'women's rights'. The Pakistani state, she shows, is not a static, essential and unchanging monolith that lies beyond the influences of transformations both in Pakistani society and in the wider world. Weiss' chapter, rather, tracks the ways in which the Pakistani state has sought to 'articulate a definition of women's rights' in the context of a highly complex social and political climate within the country. At the same time, Weiss inserts these debates into a wider international arena: Pakistan's state authorities are increasingly finding themselves placed under pressure to become the signatories of global treaties concerning human, and particularly, women's rights, such as the Convention on the Elimination of All Forms of Discrimination against Women. To ignore such treaties has important ramifications. Development assistance, for example, is often tied to a country's 'human rights record' and international organisations may shy away from supporting states condemned internationally for their treatment of women. By exploring the complexity of these debates and the centrality of questions of gender to them, Weiss illuminates the problems and opportunities that discussions concerning Pakistani women's rights pose for the country's political, legal, and constitutional future.

The following two chapters also address questions concerning the status and rights of Pakistani women, yet from very different perspectives. Hegland's chapter explores the role played by Shi'a women in their community's mourning rituals in Peshawar, the administrative headquarters of the North-West Frontier Province. The chapter is based on research undertaken in the early 1990s, shortly after Pakistan's Shi'a Muslims had publicly mobilised themselves against the Islamising legislation of General Zia. Many Shi'a Muslims in the country interpreted Zia's legislation as being exclusively Sunni in its content and form. They claimed that it discriminated against the country's very significant Shi'a minority. Shia Muslims were involved, for example, in a collective march in Islamabad at which they demanded that they should be exempt from the payment of Islamic alms as required by the version of Shariah law introduced by Zia—Shi'as have their own legal norms for the collection and distribution of religious alms and they demanded that these should be recognised. These events contributed to a significant rise in so-called sectarian violence in Pakistan. Attacks on Shi'a places of worship increased and there was also an increase in the number of targeted assassinations of Shi'a professionals and religious scholars. At the same time, these national events were themselves located within a wider international realm: the early 1990s was also a period of increased sectarian violence in neighbouring Afghanistan—and Peshawar's Shi'a community with whom Hegland worked included significant numbers of Afghan refugees.

Hegland explores the ways in which Pakistani state legislation and the political climate contributed to an increasing sense amongst Shi'as in Peshawar that their community was a mistreated minority. Alongside the influence of an assertive model of Shi'a identity actively promoted and exported across the Muslim world by Iran in the wake of the revolution of 1979, Hegland suggests that this contributed to an increasingly 'fundamentalist' or doctrine-centred version of Shi'a identity being embraced by Peshawar's Shi'as. In an already conservative social setting where women rarely left their homes except for compelling reasons, it would be easy to assume that the growing strength of such a form of collective Shi'a Muslim identity would have resulted in the further attenuation of these women's capacity to act and exert agency in their wider world. Yet Hegland argues that even whilst women found it difficult to engage in 'direct, verbal confrontation', in this environment of religious reform and political uncertainty, they did play an active role in Shi'a mourning rituals, which have a significant role in the construction and experience of a sense of collective Shi'a identity in the city. Through their participation in these mourning rituals women contributed to community life in vital ways—they formed relationships between the community's very different ethno-linguistic members, for example. Hegland interprets the role played by women in Shi'a community identity as reflecting the importance of embodied and performance-centred modes of action to the understanding of women's agency, creativity and effort in a highly politically charged and gender-segregated public setting.

Ahmad's article extends Hegland's focus on the problems associated with conventional ways of thinking about the effects of the growing influence of reform-minded forms of Islam on women's agency. Her study provides an insight into the lives of women who actively seek to participate within movements of Islamic reform and piety. The all-women's piety movement with which Ahmad is concerned, Al Huda, has grown in strength and importance in Pakistan over recent years. It has been widely represented in the Western media as signalling the final stage of Pakistan's total Islamisation—unlike the women explored in Hegland's chapters, Al Huda members often identify themselves as belonging to Pakistan's English-language educated elite.

Building on an expanding body of anthropological work on women's Islamic piety groups elsewhere, Ahmad seeks to go beyond asking what the causes are behind the growth in support for Al Huda, by exploring the modes of religiosity and forms of ethical selfhood that such movements seek to inculcate in their followers. Ahmad documents the pedagogies deployed by Al Huda to transform the thinking and behaviour of its members, notably its focus on modes of learning Islamic doctrinal standards that emphasise the centrality of processes of self-reflection to the formation of a disciplined and ethical Muslim subject. Ahmad thus, identifies one important reason why Al Huda is attractive to Islamabad women: by defining itself as modern and disciplined in contrast to the unthinking and backward religiosity of the country's ulama, its content resonates with the thinking and attitudes of its elite and educated members.

What is especially important about Ahmad's account of women's experience as committed participants is her recognition that the movement's ideology does not shape the thoughts, attitudes and sensibilities of its members in any totalising or exceptionally coherent manner. Instead, Ahmad brings attention to the disruptions and inconsistencies in personal conduct and thinking of Al Huda members: women display photos in the intimate spaces of their houses, despite the fact that these are declared as *haram* and illegal according to the movement's understanding of Islamic legal requirements. Moreover, women justify this by drawing upon their own understanding of Islamic doctrine. Ahmad's observations are important: several studies of women's piety movements have emphasised the coherence and disciplinary power of such movements to shape the subjectivities and thoughts of their members, yet the everyday 'disruptions' that shatter the seamless relationship between discourse and practice are far rarely invested with importance in these works.

Ahmad's emphasis on the ways in which elite and middle class women distinguish themselves from the country's unkempt mullahs connects her contribution to Zaman's chapter. Zaman's focus is on the ways in which Pakistan's madrassah-educated ulama (trained men of Islamic piety) have had to respond to attempts both by the British colonial state and the modern Pakistani state to reform the organisation and teaching syllabi of the country's madrassahs. Both the colonial and postcolonial Pakistani state has frequently called for madrassahs to come in line with the requirements of modernity. Zaman documents how the Pakistani state has largely failed to bring madrassahs under its umbrella; he also shows that the ulama continue to hold and exert significant if not expanding political influence in the country today. Zaman considers some of the ways in which the colonial and postcolonial states have conceptualised the need for madrassah reform and actively sought to transform the role of madrassahs in Pakistani society. He emphasises that both the country's religious scholars and Pakistan's government officials have presented madrassahs as impervious to state policy. Yet what Zaman also illuminates is the extent to which attempts made by the ulama to maintain their role as the guardians of the place that madrassahs have in society, have themselves resulted in substantive redefinitions of 'what Islam means, where to locate it in society, and how best to serve its interests in Pakistan today'. He argues that the ulama, in the very act of seeking to locate religion in a distinct and autonomous sphere of society that is beyond the influence of the state and rather a sphere where their authority as the key interpreters of 'purely religious texts' is uncontested, have played a key role in the development of a modern notion of religion in Pakistan, i.e., something restricted to one sphere of life. This is despite the fact that Pakistan's ulama consistently challenge secular ideas that religion should be restricted to a specific sphere of life.

TRANSITIONAL FLOWS AND RELIGION IN PAKISTAN'S DIASPORA

Since the events of 7 July 2005, there has been an expanding interest in the modes of being Muslim and forms of Islam enacted and identified with, by Pakistanis living in the diaspora. Given the nature of the events that have propelled the nature of British–Pakistani Muslim thought and identity to the forefront of public debates about Islam in Europe, much recent work focuses on the emergence and growing importance of global and even radical ways of being Muslim amongst British Pakistani youth. Analytically, many commentators have emphasised the ways in which second and third-generation diaspora Muslims have come to increasingly identify with abstract and global forms of Islam, a project of identification often interpreted as a reflection of these young peoples' own experiences of globalising modernity, migration and attendant forms of cultural dislocation (Roy 2007). Others have sought to locate the shift to such ways of being Muslims as a response to the inability of madrassah-trained 'men of learning and authority' from Pakistan to understand the concerns of second and third generations in the Pakistani diaspora. What has become clear in these debates, however, is the extent to which the distinction between a good and bad Muslim so frequently used by analysts and influential policy-makers to think about the 'problems' posed by Islam in Pakistan is now increasingly also being deployed to understand the Muslim identities of Pakistanis living in countries such as the United Kingdom and the United States of America. Moreover, active attempts by governments to promote acceptable ways of being Muslim and urging the 'Muslim community' to exorcise 'bad Muslims' from within their midst are now a prominent dimension of the ways in which Western states engage with their own Muslim communities; religious spaces and discourses, thus, are playing an increasingly important role in the policing of community life and in determining the boundaries of acceptable modes of religiosity. Werbner's chapter is concerned with transnational connections between Britain's Pakistani diaspora and Muslims in Pakistan. What is distinctive about Werbner's ethnographic window into transnational forms of Muslim practice, thought and self-understanding is that she does not approach this complex nexus of issues through the study of a particular ethno-linguistic community. Rather, Werbner explores the connectedness of Muslim religious experience in Pakistan and the United Kingdom by means of an analysis of a site of particular religious importance to Muslims living in both countries—the shrine of a Sufi saint in Pakistan's North-West Frontier Province. Ethnographically, she explores the pilgrimages that Muslims make to the shrine, analysing also the ways in which it is also connected through movements of people, gifts and flows of religious grace to connected shrines in Britain. These connections illuminate the rich and complex connective webs that bring together Muslims both in Pakistan and the diaspora. Importantly, Werbner emphasises the significance of continuities in both religious discourse and practice displayed both by worshipers at the Sufi shrine in Pakistan and its branches in Britain. These forms of persistence, she suggests, underline the cult's transnational nature: in both Britain and Pakistan the cult's members observe the same religious festivals and send tribute to the same shaikh, or man of spiritual insight and power. Yet there is more to this Sufi cult than networks of religious affiliation that connect the saint's followers in Pakistan and Britain alone: the circuits of meaning, people and religious grace that energise the mundane world of the saint's followers are actively taken in other directions by the men and women of the cult: each year the saint and his followers converge in the holy shrine city of Makkah for the hajj. They descend, moreover, on Makkah not only from Britain and Pakistan, but also the Persian Gulf, where many of them work as labour migrants in cities such as Dubai.

This, then, Werbner argues, is a 'global regional cult', which has emerged from processes of international labour migration. It 'mediates between Islam's universalism and the particularistic nature of the migrants' networks of association'. Werbner's chapter, thus, notes the various levels at which transnational forms of Islam are imagined and experienced and her work serves as a very important corrective to more simplistic accounts that distinguish between bounded and inherently 'local forms of Islam' on the one hand, and more abstract, doctrinal and expansive expressions of 'global Islam' on the other.

SECTARIAN CONFLICT

Originally conceived of as an inclusive homeland for South Asia's diverse Muslim communities, Pakistan's recent history has witnessed the promotion and increasing power of a discourse of exclusion that seeks to deny membership within Pakistan's Muslim community on the basis of sectarian distinctions between the country's Muslims. Targeted shootings of Shi'a professionals and doctors and Sunni 'men of piety', 'small wars' between Sunni and Shi'a Muslims in the 'tribal areas' of Pakistan's North-West Frontier Province, and the bombing and mass slaughter of worshippers in mosques, moreover, have propelled the concept of 'sectarianism' to the forefront of the study of Pakistan and its representation in the world media. Anthropologists are now playing an increasingly important role in exploring the causes behind conflict between Pakistan's diverse doctrinal communities. Their work also addresses the degree to which such violence assumes very different forms across Pakistan's diverse regions and the ways in which during the course of everyday life Pakistani Muslims interact with people belonging to communities different than their own. The chapters in this section all seek to understand the history, development and everyday experience of sectarian difference and violent conflict in Pakistan. They place the emergence of sectarian conflict in the context of Pakistan's modern political history and provide vivid insights into the extent to which incidents of sectarian violence and tension in Pakistan involve a far more complex range of factors than a simple clash between Sunni and Shi'a Muslims alone. In so doing, they challenge the relevance of terms such as 'sect' and 'sectarianism' as totalising categories capable of describing the role played by doctrinal difference in shaping the self-understanding of Pakistan's Muslims or, indeed, as the best way of understanding the form taken by violent conflict between the country's Shi'a and Sunni Muslims.

Nasr's chapter deals with the modern history and politics of sectarianism in Pakistan. It is included in this volume because Nasr's work on sectarianism remains a point of departure for almost all scholars and students concerned with the understanding of sectarian conflict and violence in Pakistan today. Nasr focuses on the modern historical underpinnings of the conflict, challenging any temptation to see conflict between Sunni and Shi'a Muslims in the country as the product of the presence of unchanging 'sectarian communities' in terms of their unthinking allegiance to distinct bodies of doctrine and forms of religious practice. He explores the role played by religious parties, leaders and movements in the partition of the Indian subcontinent, arguing that some of the key dynamics and participants in sectarian conflict in recent years have their roots in the country's political history. In particular, Nasr explores the divisive legacies of the political divisions that emerged between Muslims during and after Partition. He emphasises the degree to which Muslim associations and political parties that opposed the creation of Pakistan and either moved to or continued to reside in the country after 1947 have played an especially significant role in the development of sectarian discourse in Pakistan's modern history. Nasr suggests that the leaders of these movements sought to depict themselves as the guardians of a pure Muslim Pakistan in the face of other public opinion forming figures who depicted them as traitors of the Pakistan cause. This, he argues, is what informs the attempts made by religious scholars who were initially opposed to the creation of Pakistan to vilify non-Sunni communities in the country—first the Ahmadiyyas, and in later years Shi'a Muslims—as a dangerous threat to Pakistan's Muslim purity. These discourses of sectarian difference emerged, moreover, alongside wider developments in the Muslim world. The Iranian revolution of 1979 played a significant role in fostering a worldwide sense of Shi'a assertiveness and Sunni states such as Saudi Arabia sought to challenge and limit growing Iranian influence through 'proxy wars' fought between Sunni and Shi'a Muslims in Pakistan.

The anthropological chapters in this section build on and problematise Nasr's insights, yet they do so both from specific regional perspectives and with very different analytical concerns in mind. Abou Zahab's chapter is the result of long-term fieldwork undertaken in Jhang—a city in central Punjab widely held to be one of the key crucibles of Shi'a–Sunni violence in the country over the past three decades. The militantly anti-Shi'a movement, the Sipah-e Sahaba Pakistan (SSP) was founded in Jhang in 1985, and the SSP has played a significant role in violence against Shi'as both in Jhang and elsewhere in the country. Rather than emphasising any fixed or primordial distinctions between Shi'a and Sunni Muslims in Jhang, or seeing conflict in the city in terms of the 'politics of identity' of two communities there, Zahab focuses on the complex, multiple and cascading social disputes that are central to everyday life in the city. She considers the connections between disputes reflecting tensions in the city's changing ethnic and class composition on the one hand, and the form taken by sectarian conflict and discourse in Jhang on the other. According to Zahab, sectarianism in Jhang reflects a multiple layered interworking of social, economic, status and ethnic tensions rather than being the one-dimensional product either of Shi'a assertiveness or Sunni majoritarianism.

Sökefeld, too, explores sectarian violence in relationship to interlinked forms of social, political, and cultural difference. Yet, his chapter is based on fieldwork in a very different setting: the city of Gilgit in Pakistan's mountainous Northern Areas. Gilgit's people, too, have witnessed and participated in spiralling levels of Shi'a–Sunni violence over the past twenty years—the city has seen both targeted shootings and riots, and the town's dwellers have lived under government imposed curfews for extended periods of time. It would be easy to assume that tensions between Sunni and Shi'a Muslims in Gilgit above all else reflect the gradual percolation of sectarian discourse and conflict from cities in the Punjab such as Jhang to the remote and mountainous towns of the Northern Areas. Sökefeld, however, focuses on the ways in which human identities are always characterised by their multiplicity, noting that these differences are not static and unchanging but 'relate to each other in specific and shifting ways'. This holds for both the ways in which different communities relate to one another and how difference within human selves is configured in terms of wider historical, political, and cultural contexts. Through in-depth ethnographic insights into everyday life in Gilgit, Sökefeld argues that movements of identity politics rarely have the capacity to 'stabilise a particular identity at the expense of another one'. For example, however influential Sunni movements that seek to generate a sense of homogenous Sunni identity imagined and enacted in opposition to Shia Muslims are within a particular social setting, their followers and adherents will always also have to negotiate other sources of identity difference in their personal and collective identities. Sökefeld traces the ways in which difference remains a vital feature of people's collective identities even in settings where distinctions between Sunni and Shi'a Muslims appear to have become ethnicised identity. Shi'a–Sunni differences in the Northern Areas are always invested with significance in relationship to other differences, notably those associated with markers of ethnicity and status. The Northern Areas, moreover, is a unique political space: constitutionally it is both 'part/not part' of Pakistan, having, at the time of Sökefeld's fieldwork, only been partially incorporated into the country's federal political system. Nationalist groups in the Northern Areas accuse the Pakistan state of seeking to dis-empower the region's people by refusing to confer upon them their full rights as citizens within Pakistan. Nationalists depicted sectarian violence in Gilgit as reflecting an attempt by the Pakistani state to further politically weaken through division the region's people by means of instrumentally creating conflict between its Sunni and Shi'a Muslims. For the nationalists, thus, Shi'a–Sunni violence did not reflect divisions between Muslims that were internal to the region. Rather, apparent divisions between Sunni and Shi'a Muslims were also deployed to reaffirm a nationalist identity in the face of the instrumental and divisive politics of the state of Pakistan.

Naveeda Khan also connects the study of sectarian conflict to the understanding of the ways in which multi-dimensional parts of a person's identity relate to one another through time in often very different ways. Her focus is on a family of Sunni Muslims in Lahore who identify themselves as being reform-minded Deobandi Sunni Muslims. Naveeda Khan argues for the need to understand sectarianism in Pakistan as being more than public conflict between ethnicised groups of Sunni and Shi'a Muslims. Rather, she seeks to raise broader anthropological questions concerning the multiplicity of selfhood and identity and the ways these should be understood in light of ethnographic enquiries into the nature of everyday life. At one level, to characterise sectarian conflict in Pakistan as being above all else about disputes between Shi'a and Sunni Muslims is also to ignore the importance of violent conflict between Sunnis, such as between Deobandi and Barelwi Sunni Muslims. At another level, Khan seeks to shift the analyses of sectarian violence in Pakistan away from impersonal, public arenas where largely all-male battles between Shi'a and Sunni Muslims are fought. Instead, she explores the ways in which religious differences are also 'worked into the weave of domesticity' and brought into the intimate domestic spaces and relationships of daily life. Sectarian differences take unexpected forms in the realm of the intimate, the site in which they may also become 'internal to being', rather than just unwelcome intrusions from the world of public politics beyond. Interpreting sectarian conflict merely as a negative influence that must either be wished away or violently exorcised by the state, Khan provocatively argues, ignores the complex processes through which sectarian disputes may simultaneously give and take away from 'voice'.

Pakistanis, Khan suggests, fear religious difference. At the same time, their recognition of differences not only between communities but also within their own selves is also a source of important personal-identity possibilities. Khan focuses on the complex texture taken by everyday life in the household of the Deobandi family with whom she worked when they said their home had come to be inhabited by spirits. This is a type of religious practice and belief not usually associated with Sunni Deobandis, many of whom talk about spirit possession as being an irrational and un-Islamic practice. Khan illustrates how this momentary seeping of religious difference into the Deobandi household challenged in powerful ways the nature of familial relationships within the home. At the same time, it also provided the possibility for some family members to recognise the transformations that their identities had undergone over the course of their lives, opening up spaces for the recognition and negotiation of multiplicity and difference in unexpected ways and amongst unexpected people.

Read side-by-side these four chapters offer a unique introduction into the form and study of sectarian violence in Pakistan today. They approach the issue from very different regional perspectives (southern Punjab, the Northern Areas, and Lahore), and also from very different perspectives. All of them emphasise the importance of the ways in which complex social and political conflicts in Pakistan have informed the shape taken by sectarian violence in the country. They explore the ways these conflicts intersect with movements of identity politics, and also come to enter intimate forms of everyday life and personal forms of self-understanding. In the light of their analysis, terms such as 'sectarianism' convey very little if anything about ways in which Muslims in the country confront and think about matters of sameness, difference, and heterogeneity on a day-to-day basis, or, indeed, the diverse forms taken by intra-Muslim conflict in the country in recent years.

MUSLIM SELFHOOD—INDIVIDUAL, MULTIPLE AND ON THE MOVE

To sum up, the chapters in this book explore Islam and Muslim life in Pakistan from the perspective of powerful opinion makers including government officials, middle-class Sindhi intellectuals, men of piety and learning trained in the country's Islamic seminaries, and well-educated elite businessmen. At the same time, they also furnish insights into a diverse range of religious practices and modes of religiosity including those enacted in Pakistan's Sufi shrines and their branches in Britain, elite study circles in Islamabad, musical gatherings in the supposedly 'Talibanised' North-West Frontier Province, Sufi *zikr* circles in Balochistan and in the mourning practices of Shi'a women in Peshawar. Together they provide an in-depth introduction through ethnographic case studies and comparative analysis into Muslim life in Pakistan and they do so from the perspective of persons, families, and communities who engage with diverse Islamic debates, practices, and conflicts within particular social and regional settings.

All the chapters included within this book have been written independently and many of them published previously; as such, they reflect the personal research projects and concerns of the authors. Nevertheless, I have sought to highlight in this introduction the degree to which they are connected by several strands of analysis and cross-cutting ethnographic themes. These include the role played by the state in shaping Pakistani people's experiences and conceptions of Islam, the various expressions of sectarian violence and difference that the country's Muslims experience and contribute to, and the complex interaction and engagement between reform-minded and Sufi-derived forms of Muslim thought and identity.

Several of the chapters in this book explore the ways in which Pakistani Muslims think about, judge, and evaluate the social and religious heterogeneity of everyday life in the country. These accounts stand in contrast to popular yet politically influential stereotypes that suggest that it is possible to distinguish between good and bad Muslims in the country. Instead, they provide on-the-ground ethnographic accounts of the diverse spectrum of ways of being Muslims actively enacted and cultivated by Muslims in Pakistan today. In so doing, they illuminate the danger of models of Muslim life in the country that seek to encourage moderate and tolerant Muslims to exorcise their co-religionists who are mostly just assumed to be inherently hostile to diversity. Moreover, the heterogeneity of Muslim life Pakistan with which all the chapters are concerned is not merely a reflection of the persistence of authentic local ways of being Muslim in the face of homogenising movements of reform or purification, or simply a result of the ongoing significance of archaic forms of doctrinal difference. Rather, this heterogeneity is something that is constantly remade and injected with wider political significance by Pakistan's Muslims; it also seeps inside the thought processes of individual Muslims who themselves openly reflect upon the diverse and multiple layered influences that shape their Muslim selves.

An especially interesting theme that emerges in several of the chapters in this book is the way in which the ethnographic recognition of the complex, multiple layered and often apparently contradictory influences that shape personal and collective forms of Muslim self-understanding in the country has led anthropologists working in the country to theorise the merits and demerits of the category of 'the self' for understanding Muslim identity in the country today. By way of conclusion, I want to highlight the very different understandings of Muslim selfhood that emerge from these chapters. In so doing, I hope to point towards the intense analytical debates taking place between anthropologists working in Pakistan and to point towards future anthropological research agendas in the country. Above all else, all the authors challenge simplistic distinctions that treat Pakistani Muslims as being either inherently tolerant or hostile towards diversity, depending on the type of Islamic dogma they have been schooled in or taught to identify with. Wolf demonstrates, for example, the problems with distinguishing between Sufis as moderate and tolerant, and reformists as intolerant and exclusive. Even participants in gatherings at Sufi shrines are clearly concerned by and involved in dynamic processes of joining and parting—the stakes of which in Pakistan today address issues concerning who may rightfully be identified as being Muslim.

All the authors also show that Pakistan's social and religious heterogeneity cannot be simply described and mapped in terms of 'grids of groups and identities' (Sökefeld). Instead, they depict social life in Pakistan as being made through processes of interaction between diverse status, ethnic, religious and political influences. Where the authors do differ, however, is with regard to the model of selfhood—collective and personal—that they deploy to understand this complexity. Ewing, for example, argues forcefully for the presence of multiple selves within an individual. She suggests that these different selves are called forth in specific contexts. In the face of this multiplicity, individuals must work hard psychologically and symbolically to maintain an illusion of wholeness or oneness, an illusion that is central to rendering life viable. Sökefeld, in contrast, argues a case for 'individuality', what he defines as the 'unique conditions of the human self'. He argues that different dimensions of a person's identity do not reflect the presence of 'multiple selves'. Rather, differences within selves always relate to one another and this is something that renders both attempts to categorise human beings as belonging to distinct groups or of being made-up of multiple and distinct selves as empirically false. Instead, each human being occupies a unique subject position within a grid of social identities, reflecting their own identity choices, always made in relationship to particular social contexts and the constraints these impose on choice-making processes. As a result, anthropologists should represent individuals as 'agents who more or less self-consciously and creatively act with the differences at hand within the constraints of historic and political setting'.

Khan's approach to the complex and inconsistent selves she encountered during fieldwork chimes with Sökefeld's, but with a significant twist: for Khan, the self is a realm of 'presubjective possibilities': these are activated by an individual one at a time, yet the activation of one never displaces the others entirely. Thus, as with Sökefeld, she claims that this coterminous presence of multiple types of differences in the self challenges the notion that individuals posses distinct, 'multiple identities'. In contrast, however, to Sökefeld who emphasises the role played by choice in determining where an individual is sited on a wider grid of identities, she suggests that individuals move constantly 'between these qualities without morphing into entirely different selves'; it is the movement along this series of differences or singularities that Khan defines as being 'difference internal to being'. In similar terms, Marsden emphasises the ways in which Chitralis switch between different registers of being Muslim in relationship to particular performative arenas: his model emphasises the degree to which contrasting forms of Chitrali-Muslim sociality adhere to particular types of social gatherings—movement through these different arenas stimulate people to switch between different modes of being Muslim. For Marsden, then, understanding the diverse ways in which Chitralis go about being Muslim requires a focus not so much on the interior dimensions of individual selfhood or on the ways in which persons choose which parts of their identities to highlight and which to subdue, but the social and political contexts of the arenas through which they move.

Finally, Ahmad's work builds on Mahmood's (2004) influential critique of Western conceptions of the autonomous subject. Mahmood argues Euro-American concepts of the autonomous self depends on a conception of agency that is enacted through resistance to social norms. Yet participants within the Cairo-based movement of Islamic piety that she studied worked hard to generate a pious self that was constituted by and emerged from a particular social norm, that of Islamic self-discipline. This is something they did through practices of Islamic self-making, enacted whilst they attended mosque gatherings and Qur'anic reading groups, for example. Ahmad also emphasises the ways in which Al Huda women sought to cultivate their selves as the embodiment of a model of Islamic ethical subjectivity. Yet what Ahmad also found herself having to address was the ways in which Al Huda women had to confront questions of heterogeneity and inconsistency—such as what they should do when they met a non-related Muslim male in a shopping centre in Islamabad, for example. Ahmad, thus, also explores the ways in which these women, despite seeking to enact a seamless type of subject tied to conceptions of Islamic self-discipline, were called upon to recognise the thought provoking power of 'disruptions' that challenged the totalising power of this model to shape their everyday lives.

CONCLUSION

The teaching of Pakistan-related material in undergraduate courses on the anthropology of South Asia often remains, unfortunately, a decidedly minor partner to the more expansive body of ethnographic material on India. The teaching of Pakistan in such courses is often confined to an occasional seminar on 'Islam in Pakistan' or a comparative discussion into Indian democracy and Pakistani military authoritarianism. As the chapters in this book richly demonstrate, however, anthropologists are currently posing complex and theoretically diverse questions about the nature of Islam and Muslim life in Pakistan. Their work is informed by a wide range of theoretical issues concerning the anthropological study of religion, politics, and personhood; and they are furnishing insights into dimensions of life in South Asia that have for too long been considered the preserve of India-specialists. Pakistan continues to be too often considered as an exceptional South Asian case located in the murky waters between Central Asia and the Middle East. As a result, anthropological work on Pakistan is all too easily called into action primarily to reflect either on the similarities or differences between Pakistan and India. Thus, whilst analytically models developed elsewhere in South Asia are frequently deployed, challenged and reformed in the light of ethnographic work in Pakistan, the obverse has rarely been the case. This book's chapters illuminate the ways in which scholars of the country and the world at large are now turning Pakistan's uneasy place in anthropological work on South Asia into a theoretical advantage. Above all else, perhaps, exploring Pakistan's social and religious heterogeneity has required them to generate new ways of thinking about and through diversity and difference at the interconnected levels of nation, community, and the person. By bringing together these chapters, I hope that more students and scholars will have access to the lively and stimulating body of anthropological work on Pakistan that was hitherto largely scattered in diverse scholarly journals. I also hope that those in the world beyond the academy will take notice of this ethnographically rich and theoretically lively body of literature and be encouraged to reflect on the issues raised by sophisticated anthropological debates about the interactions between Islam, politics, and society in Pakistan today.

CHAPTER 1

Of Children and Jinns: An Enquiry into an Unexpected Friendship during Uncertain Times

NAVEEDA KHAN

INTRODUCTION

Sectarianism in Pakistan, specifically the Shia–Sunni conflict, already analytically challenging (Zaman 2003) has taken on further complexity of late. Consider the intrusion of contemporary global political trends into national contexts and local worlds (see Devji 2005). In a recent incident of violence in a shrine outside Islamabad, suicide bombing left twenty dead amidst the mixed Shia–Sunni crowd gathered there to celebrate *urs* (ABC 27 May 2005). In the near past it may have been sufficient for scholars to wonder if the attack had arisen out of local tensions, or had been undertaken by Islamist parties, by Indian agents acting to provoke internal conflict, or even by agents of the Pakistani state seeking to create sympathy for Pakistan within the international community (Ahmad 1998; Ali 2000; Nasr 2000; Jaffrelot 2002). Now we have to wonder further if peoples associated or sympathetic to Al-Qaeda may not be responsible for the act to keep up the pressure on President Pervez Musharraf to retract his support to the United States in its unpopular global war on terrorism.

Within this landscape of ambiguity (Verkaaik 2001), I propose to attend to the register of everyday life in asking if scholars have done enough to understand the reach and scope of sectarianism in Pakistan. Specifically, do we know how sectarianism may extend out of or fold into everyday life? And, to what does sectarianism give expression? There exist long-standing religious differences between Shias and Sunnis that have been variously and violently mobilized at different moments in history with deleterious outcomes for life, in both its biological and social senses. Furthermore, there exist denominational differences among South Asian

Sunnis (Metcalf 1982; Sanyal 1996) that have more recently taken on violent tendencies in Pakistan (Nasr 2000). What I am interested in and take to be the predominant markers of the prevailing sectarian condition within Pakistan is how Shia–Sunni conflicts are reprised within Sunni–Sunni divides, while serving as a standing archive of attitudes and gestures for these divides, and how these conflicts and divides rest upon yet also inform everyday life as I found it in Lahore in the late 1990s. Based on the stories I heard and had a hard time assimilating into available narratives on sectarianism, I am suggesting that we move away from a purely negative casting of sectarianism in order to see how religious differences imply both threat and possibility for Pakistanis. Firstly, this move allows us to locate threat and possibility in ways in which malevolence and generosity rub up against one another within a family, suggesting how religious differences get folded into the weave of domesticity. In assuming that family, kinship, and domesticity bear a relation to sectarianism, I am striving to work beyond the public–private divide, specifically the exclusive focus on the public sphere, which implicitly informs much literature on sectarianism in Pakistan.[1] At the same time we capture something of the trancelike quality of everyday life in and through the tensions embedded within familial relations that animate religious differences in unanticipated ways.[2] Secondly, such an exploration shows how differences are internal to being. In other words, an exploration of such differences within everyday life may provide us a different picture of the pious self than that recently espoused by anthropologists of Islam and Muslim societies.[3]

In this chapter, I propose to attend to a mixed *muhajir*-Punjabi Sunni family with whom I was very close in Lahore, Pakistan, in particular their extended encounter with a *jinn* to show how the stories arising out of that relation are laced with a certain repulsion of the 'other', in particular the Shia other, that threaten the fragility of familial balances. Yet if one were to think how this repulsion opens up a place for a child to build conviviality with a creature made of smokeless fire and for a father to attend to the truths mediated by the child from another place one cannot but acknowledge how malevolence and a certain generosity go together, or how difficult it is to name something as sectarianism and to wish it away, as the Pakistani state would like. It is akin to saying that sectarianism gives voice. Here I am utilizing Veena Das's conceptualization of 'voice' in her article 'Voice as Birth of Culture' (1995) as not coinciding with 'speech' but with a certain movement beyond an impasse, a movement that she charts through the modality of 'hearing'.[4] It is my sense that unless we can hear the maelstrom out of which this voice arises and acknowledge the economy of gestures that comprises this voice, that is to say, that to which sectarianism gives expression, I fear that it will be hard to imagine how war *and* peace are equally possible within everyday life in Lahore.[5]

ONE SUMMER'S DAY

Let me now turn to the event that seemed to untether my fragile grasp on the fractured landscape in which I found myself. It was the year 2001 and I had been in and out of Lahore over two years already doing dissertation research on sectarianism in its urban spatial manifestations.[6] It was summer and my days of racing around the city, hanging out in *masjid*s, *madrassah*s, and *mazar*s, were coming to an end, stilled by the intensity of the heat and the sandstorms that sprang up unexpectedly making it hard for Farooq sahib, as I shall call him, my Urdu teacher and co-researcher, to navigate his scooter and for me to hold on to my seat on the pillion. Instead we would duck into a bank to pay a bill or linger at a bookstore to catch the cool waves of the air conditioner. Most afternoons, however, I spent at Farooq sahib's house, forever being vertically expanded, in Sandha, one of the many dense unauthorized urban settlements around the Mall in Lahore. I would trail his wife and daughters in their continual movements up and down their house and on their rare trips outside. On occasion I would take them to the local ice cream parlour so we could refresh ourselves with a *faluda* drink. I would also go to speak to the men of the house in the small, sparse room, decorated solely with a poster of the Prophet's mosque in Medina, allotted for their work on the two computers owned by the family. In addition to teaching me Urdu, assisting me in my research, and teaching Islamiyat at a local school, Farooq sahib ran a small business of what is commonly called 'composing' to make ends meet. Composing consists of typing handwritten Urdu texts, generally religious in Farooq sahib's case, into the computer before these texts go out for printing to the numerous small publishers crowding the Urdu bazaar in Anarkali. The nature of this work resonates with Farooq sahib's mode of self-fashioning, as will become clearer in the course of this chapter.

Our days were punctuated by the *azan* (the call to prayer), the men leaving for the mosque for each prayer and the women snatching time out of their schedules to go off to a quiet corner of the house to pray. I was, in a manner of speaking, in a powerhouse of religious rectitude, with everyone in the household a declared *Deobandi* (Metcalf 1982), the sons of the household being active members of the Tablighi Jamaat, the *dawa* arm of the Deobandi (Metcalf 1993; Masud 2000; Reetz 2002). They travelled regularly through mosques in and around the city preaching to Muslims to return to the right path, to expunge their religious practices of *bida,* the accretions of customs in the form of innovations or *shirk,* associating an object or person with God (Metcalf 1997; Shah Wali Allah 2003). Often times when I sat in a horse and buggy or a rickshaw with Adeeb, one of Farooq sahib's two sons, en-route to an interview, he would strike up a conversation with the driver that would end by Adeeb urging him to go to his local mosque. 'You will find solace there from your daily life,' Adeeb would say quietly.

Imagine my surprise when Farooq sahib and Rahima *baji*, his wife, walked in one afternoon into the room in which I lay dozing, speaking between themselves about the ants they had seen on the steps of the house. I wasn't paying attention. 'Ants?' I asked, half asleep. Farooq sahib, putting on that voice of his that always indicated to me that I ought to be taking notes, declared,

> Naveeda, did we ever tell you that we had jinns living with us? We got them from an acquaintance who had inherited a group of jinns from his father, a famous *amil*. But he has no use for these jinns so he gives them to whomever he thinks will benefit from them. But the recipients have to be good Muslims. Each of the men in this family was given a jinn. Hostile jinns once attacked our house posing as ants. We knew they could not be just ants because they would bleed when we killed them whereas ants do not bleed. Thankfully, our jinns helped us to get rid of them.

By this time I was sitting up. At my look of shock at what I was hearing he assured me that the jinns had since returned to their original guardian.[7] He had made no effort to bring them back as he felt that they were leading his family astray, that is, his family had ceased to make entreaties directly to Allah through their growing reliance upon the jinns. 'Our *aqida* had become weak and our *ibadat* was suffering.' However, he continued exasperatedly,

> For a while we were the most harangued house in this neighbourhood, with the women dropping by all the time to ask us to locate lost keys, secure marriages, get their husbands' jobs, like we were *amils* or something. If the women could, they would have the jinns undertake *ibadat* on their behalf.

Mildly intrigued by my interest, Farooq sahib's family related stories upon stories to me about the jinns who had shared their home with them. 'Oh, we hadn't told you about them,' they said. Over the next two days their interest began to wane. 'Naveeda, better get back to your research,' Farooq sahib declared.

JINNS IN CONTEXT

The most important verification of jinns is to be found in the Holy Quran in Surat 72, titled Al-Jinn, which opens thus:

> Say: It has been
> Revealed to me that
> A company of jinns
> Listened (to the Quran).
> They said, 'We have
> Really heard a wonderful Recital

And, further on,

> There were some foolish ones
> Among us, who used
> To utter extravagant lies
> Against Allah;
> But we think
> That no man or jinn
> Should say aught that is
> Untrue against Allah (The Holy Quran:1830–31)

The most cited *hadith* in support of jinns is the one in which the Prophet Muhammad (PBUH) asked his assembled companions who among them would come with him to a gathering of jinns. When none volunteered he pressed one among them into service. The two walked till they had left the human settlement far behind and found themselves in a desolate area. There in an open field stood tall figures who struck fear in the heart of the companion. The Prophet recited the Quran to the silent receptive crowd after which he turned back towards the settlement. When he was a little way away from the figures he picked up a piece of bone and dung from the ground and flung it at them. He told his companion that he had asked God that the jinns be able to get sustenance from wood and dung during their travels. In other words, he had interceded on their behalf to God (El-Zein 1996:332).

The above have provided the two strongest textual verifications of the existence of jinns within Islam. It has been said that the belief in the existence of jinns is one with that of the existence of angels, which is within the primary articles of faith in Islam, and consequently, it is heretical to disbelieve in them (El-Zein).[8] I provide here a few commonly known characteristics of jinns from the enormous archive of religious commentary, prophetic tales, magicians' manuals, folklore, and ethnography that has emerged around them in order to facilitate our acquaintance of the jinns who came to live in Farooq sahib's house.

The majority of Muslims believe jinns to be a species of spiritual beings created by God out of smokeless fire, long before he created humans out of clay, and to whom he gave the earth to inhabit. By constitution they are drawn to both good and evil. That is, they are unlike angels who were created out of pure light, hence incapable of evil, and who were given the heavens to inhabit (Hughes 1885; entry under Djinn in Encyclopaedia of Islam 2003). In many ways jinns are the equivalent of humans in that they are endowed with passions, rational faculties, and responsibility for their own actions (El-Zein 1996). Biologically, they eat, grow, procreate, and die much like humans. Socially, they organize themselves also much like humans (Westermarck 1926). However, unlike humans, jinns are capable of shape shifting, fast movement, great acts of strength, long lives, and are also known to eavesdrop upon the angels in the lower reaches of heaven thereupon acquiring limited knowledge of the future (Hughes 1885; Westermarck 1926; El-Zein 1996; Encyclopaedia of Islam [EI] 2003). These two species, humans and jinns, co-inhabit the earth, although jinni haunts are primarily desolate places, such as, forests, ruins, and graveyards. Their inter-relations range from mutual indifference to wars between collectivities in the distant past, relations of love and guardianship between individuals of both species, and the disruption of one another's lives most visibly manifest in spirit possessions (see Crapanzano 1980; Boddy 1889; Bowen 1993; El-Zein 1996; Rotherberg 1998; Pandolfo 2000; Seigel 2003). And it is to harness the powers of jinns that humans have long struggled to bring jinns within their possession. However, as we shall see, these relations between humans and jinns are constantly evolving. I offer my study as the latest instalment in the story of humans and jinns.

The word of Islam was sent to jinns as to men through the Prophet Muhammad (PBUH). After the introduction of Islam, this species became divided between those who became Muslims and those who did not. But a more distinctive shift in the concept of the jinn from pre-Islam to Islam was that the jinn began to be much more unequivocally associated with evil whereas previously both good and bad had been ascribed to their constitution. There is an early theological debate, as yet unresolved, as to whether the devil, more specifically, Iblis, originates from this species (Hughes 1885; El-Zein 1996; EI 2003). Some claim that he was allowed among the ranks of angels because of his immense devotion to God and was later banished from the heavens after his refusal to kneel before Adam. This possible association with Iblis hints at the anxiety that currently attends to the existence and disruptive tendencies of jinns. Another classical theological debate that continues into the present deliberates whether jinns are indeed a different category of being from humans, or whether they are forces of nature or projections of human interiority, in the Muslim sense, notably of the little mischievous *nafs* that make up a self (Bowen 1993; El-Zein 1996; see Metcalf 1997 on *nafs*).

However, I have generally found an acceptance of the anthropomorphic existence of jinns in South Asia, intermixed with a wariness that this acknowledgement of alternative worlds should not be seen as yet another marker of Muslim irrationality. Be that as it may, I do not here attend to this sense of insecurity that arises from an almost quotidian acceptance of jinns nor do I do justice to the rich anthropological and psychological literature that sees in the belief of jinns complex arrangements of cultural memory, political strategy, mental illness, and individual subjectivity (see Crapanzano 1980; Boddy 1889; Bowen 1993; El-Zein 1996; Rotherberg 1998; Pandolfo 2000; Seigel 2003). Rather, I simply accept the jinn as a being in its given-ness. In my argument, the appearance of the jinn within a family provides insight into the tensions that under-gird everyday life within which religious differences are feared and embodied by a single self.

MARYAM THE MEDIUM

Besides his wife and himself, Farooq sahib's immediate family comprised of his two sons and three daughters (born in that order) at the time the jinns came to be with them some seven years prior to my initial acquaintance with them in 1999. At that time, Maryam, the second of Farooq sahib's daughters, was an eight-year-old girl and had been their conduit to the jinns. By the time that I met Maryam, she was fifteen, and had ceased her education at a private school for girls after passing her matric examinations. Her elder sister, who was sixteen, was to be married shortly, so Maryam had assumed many of the household duties she once shared with her sister. Even at this more advanced age Maryam was viewed as the most spiritual of the girls, akin to her eldest brother Adeeb who had gained a reputation for great piety from an early age.[9]

Although I did not observe Maryam's transition from childhood to adulthood, I imagined how it must have been for her by observing the family's treatment of their youngest daughter, Farah, who was eight at the time I met her. At that age Farah did not as yet observe *purdah*, frisked around in frocks and high heels, and even occasionally dabbed some lipstick. Previously readily held and kissed, indulged, and asked to perform in public (*naat*), by the end of my stay, when she was almost ten, she was already being pulled out of her sleep, protesting, to say her prayers with the family since she would soon be accountable.

To clarify this in brief, according to Islamic principles, children, although born free of sin and with the ability to communicate with divine beings (Das 1989), are considered beings without *aql*, that is, they carry the threat of being easily led astray (Lapidus 1976; Aijaz 1989; Devji 1994). Consequently, Islamic and Quranic instruction has to begin as early as four to ensure that children are provided guidance from early in their lives. However, the age at which Muslim parents are urged by the *ulama* (religious scholars) to hold their children responsible for any missed religious duties, notably the reading of the Quran, prayers, and fasting, is ten as by that time they are considered to have reached the age of sexual maturation. According to a hadith quoted in a manual titled *Muslim Children—How to Bring up?*, 'the Prophet (PBUH) has said that we should call upon our children to offer prayers when they are seven years old and when they are ten years they should be punished for missing prayer and should have separate beds' (Aijaz 1989: 32). By this time parental entreaties may be replaced by punishment if children have not formed the habit of prayer and fasting (30).[10]

It was Maryam who would communicate between the jinns and her family. As an eight-year-old, she had a window into the spirit world. While at times she would look into the palms of her hands to see what the jinns would have her see, at others, the stories seemed to suggest, she was attuned to the ways in which this world and the jinn world, a mirror of this one, were intertwined. She saw jinns interspersed among her family members. She relayed the requests of the human world to the jinns, bringing forth advice, instructions, and sometimes expressions of desire from the jinns. For instance, one day she told her father that one of the jinns wanted to taste human food and with her father's permission she instructed the jinn that he could enter her father's body. That day, as Farooq sahib related to me, he had an appetite that frightened him with its enormity. He felt if the food had not finished he would have stayed rooted to his seat on the floor and continued eating through the night.[11]

When the jinns first came to Farooq sahib's house, the family's curiosity would compel them to spend long hours conversing with the jinns about their lives in their world. It was in the course of these initial introductions that it emerged that one among the jinns was a *sahaba* jinn. The title *sahaba* refers to a close companion of the Prophet or at least one who was alive at the time of the Prophet, thus having the opportunity to see him and to relay his teachings. Moreover, certain *ahadith* attests to the Prophet Muhammad's (PBUH) conversion of tribes of both people and jinns to Islam. Given the long life attributed to jinns, it was conceivable to have a sahaba jinn alive today.[12]

THE SAHABA IN PERSPECTIVE

However, the title of sahaba had acquired other resonances in Pakistan since the early 1990s. Here is an account of one such resonance of that time. It was a moment of tremendous political tensions as Benazir Bhutto and Nawaz Sharif fought each other to be the leader of the nation. It was the period following the death of General Ziaul Huq who had ruled with an iron hand and in whose time and under whose influence the Shia–Sunni conflict had emerged in its current configuration (Zaman 2002). Largely centred in Punjab, the conflict between Shias and Sunnis was at its height. At the same time, the ethnic battles in Sindh between Sindhis and muhajirs, those who had migrated from India at the time of Partition, was on the decline. One modality of violence replaced another (Tambiah 1996; Verkaaik 2004). Instead of riots in mixed neighbourhoods and public battles among competing political groups, there were bloody shootouts in mosques, shrines, and at religious processions, and public assassinations by people unseen, most often masked men on motorbikes. Within this context, even a pious reference to the sahaba or concern for their reputation weighed in against the Shias.

Three of the four caliphs, the original sahaba, were considered by the Shias to have wrongfully deprived the Prophet's cousin Ali (RA), the fourth caliph, of his right to assume the mantle of leadership of the Muslim community after the Prophet's death. The Shias have developed a ritual denunciation, or *tabarra* of the first three caliphs in retaliation to the Omayyad practice of cursing Ali from the pulpit after his martyrdom. This is usually undertaken in the Islamic month of Muharram, when the Shias mourn the martyrdom of Ali's son, Hussein, in the Battle of Karbala, in modern day Iraq, at the hands of Yazid, the seventh caliph. The practice of *tabarra*, already documented in the ascendant during colonial times (Cole 1988; Freitag 1989), began to be protested again in the early 1990s with the Sunnis insisting that Shias be apostasized for defaming the sahaba. Scholars of Pakistan, such as Christophe Jaffrelot (2002) and Mukhtar Ahmad Ali (2000), have argued persuasively if not a little reductively that anti-Shia rhetoric provided the muhajirs in Punjab a new way to locate themselves within a political field largely monopolized by Shia landowning families. The few ulama within Pakistan's National Assembly unsuccessfully tried to pass an amendment to the infamous Blasphemy Law in the Penal Code, Section 295, to include the sahaba as sacred religious personages second only to the Prophet. Hagiographic books and tracts on known and unknown sahaba, including prophets prior to Muhammad (PBUH), started to circulate in unprecedented numbers to inform Sunni Muslims about their venerable precursors.

By the time I began my fieldwork in Lahore in 1999, these books had clearly helped to provide alternative ways to appropriate calendrical days ritually significant to the Shias. So, for instance, one Sunni family with whom I worked insisted on sending around sweets to their friends and family in celebration of Adam and Eve's birthday, which happened to fall on *Ashura*, the tenth day of Muharram that marks the culmination of Shia mourning. Some families had even begun to hold weddings in this month whereas in the past Muharram was considered an inauspicious time to undertake celebrations. Even name giving had taken on a poisonous edge as people had started to name their children Yazid, after the much-hated Sunni caliph who is held responsible for killing Hussein in the Battle of Karbala. The intensity of this hatred made the month of Muharram, which I twice spent in Lahore, a tense time, a mood that the state attempted to assuage by having open-topped trucks, with standing soldiers displaying machine guns, make the rounds of the city.[13]

So although to them it seemed it was pure chance that led Farooq sahib's family to have in their control a jinn who had had direct contact with the Prophet, it was a chance not un-free of a certain vindication for Farooq sahib. From an early conversation with Farooq sahib I already knew that although he did not provide any assistance to the Sipah-e-Sahaba, the modern day warriors of the sahaba, who were responsible for assassinating many important Pakistani Shias and Iranians (see Zaman 2002), he supported them in spirit. Once, while driving around with Farooq sahib's son Adeeb before a meeting with a Shia *alim*, I was warned by him to not be taken in by Shia good looks as it was used to disarm people into lapsing into Shiism. When I asked him if it wasn't God that gave us our visages, he replied that this was why Shias lost their good looks so early in life, as their internal corruption came to the fore.

Within this situation it was with the sahaba jinn with whom the family was most taken. In fact, Maryam would spend most of her time describing Sulayman, as this jinn was called.[14] He was tall, I was told.[15] He had a long beard that he kept well groomed. He was always dressed in spotlessly clean clothes. He kept his face arranged in a serious expression, careful not to indulge in loud outbursts of laughter. Although he looked stern, he smiled easily. He would sit down to drink his water or to partake in food. And he was very gentle with Maryam. She said she never felt frightened in his presence. And she rewarded him by claiming him as her friend. The family was captivated by these details about Sulayman's comportment, much more so than of the extensive physical landscape and social structure of the world of jinns also available to them. In fact, father and sons would attend to Maryam's descriptions taking them as examples of the correct way to imitate the Prophet's example.

PIOUS IMITATION

I understood Farooq sahib's preoccupation with the Prophet's example. From the beginning of my research Farooq sahib had been integral to the picture of religious differences I was putting together. It was he amongst my various Urdu teachers who had taken it upon himself to teach me the nuances of the theological aspects of religious conflict. He would not let me slip into a comfortable modernist pose of dismissing these differences as the political expressions of the *petit bourgeoisie*, as identity politics. It was through his very confident articulations and his heated conversations with others that I understood how ontological these differences were, how they expressed different lived relations to the time and personality of the Prophet, to nature, and to creation.

Farooq sahib was by no means a religious scholar but he took such scholarship seriously. He was from the *ashraf*. He was a calligrapher by training, a teacher of Urdu and Islamiyat by vocation, and a composer of computer generated religious texts by profession. For him calligraphy in the Islamic tradition was the textual expression of that which is enjoined upon every Muslim, *imatio Muhammadi*. Just as the calligrapher, now composer, seeks to make the most perfect copy of a text without introducing any novelty into it, so too did Farooq sahib and his sons struggle to make themselves the perfect imitation of the Prophet, to uphold his *sunnah* without introducing any innovation into it.[16]

By the time I met Farooq sahib he had already tried out another mode of imitating the Prophet, different from the Deobandi path and yet still within Sunni Islam in Pakistan, through passionate love for and ecstatic identification with the Prophet. This was the Barelwi path (see Sanyal 1996; Buehler 1998), into which he was born, which is generally recognized as infused with Sufism. In this path the Prophet was immanent in the world, present everywhere, of course with the permission of God so as not to grant God's powers to another even if it were the Prophet himself, the most beloved of God. Farooq sahib's own family, that is, his parents and sisters and brothers, who had stayed behind in Delhi, India at the time of the Partition of 1947, had remained Barelwi. Farooq sahib moved to Lahore in part so that his wife could be closer to her own family and in part so that he could ply his profession as calligrapher, later composer, in a place where Urdu would be the *lingua franca* of the nation. However, through his ceaseless copying of religious texts, old and new, authentic and inauthentic, in the new nation of Pakistan in which flourished much experimentation with Muslim identities, Farooq sahib had come to realize that this was not the correct path through which to experience the Prophet.[17] Although he neglected to mention this to me, Rahima baji, his wife, drew to my attention that she was also instrumental in Farooq sahib's conversion to Deobandism as her own family is of this path. This detail is important in opening up a space to consider a family, in particular, a woman's place in the experience and expression of religious differences.[18]

Now Farooq sahib was persuaded by the Deobandi path, also within Sunni Islam, in which the Prophet called forth a love, not *fana-e rasul* as in Barelwism in which one was oblivious to one's being in the world in one's passionate embrace of the Prophet (see Ernst 1985), but rather a love that compelled one to literally embody the Prophet in this world. It was the imagination of simultaneously seeing the Prophet in one's mind's eye and imitating him. In it the Prophet was not immanent in the world although he was alive in his grave in Medina wherein he was witness to the world, once again by God's permission. Thus, although one could legitimately dream of the Prophet, if the Prophet so wished to bless one with his presence, one could never call him forth, as Barelwis believed of prayers in a mosque. Both these paths accepted jinns as having a dynamic if disruptive presence within the human world, alongside those of angels and saints (*wali-ullah,* literally friends of Allah) whose shrines were scattered across the country. Deobandis, however, felt that Muslims risked angering God with their excessive reliance upon jinns, angels, and saints for it was God who alone ought to be relied upon (see Metcalf 1997).

I will further distinguish the Deobandi imagination from that of a third path, by which to imitate the Prophet within Sunni Islam in Pakistan. Followers of this third path, the Ahl-i Hadith, state that the Prophet, as a man, albeit a great man, demands of us not love but respect (see Metcalf 1982; Brown 1996). So when one imagines the Prophet, as Akbar, a librarian, a friend and a self-identified Ahl-i Hadith, once described to me, one imagines oneself riding behind the Prophet as though on horseback, being led by him. The ahadith intermixed by *sirah* were the only legitimate means to access the Prophetic will. That is, there could be no other experience of the Prophet other than through the record of his words and deeds simply because, in Akbar's words, he was quite dead and turned to dust. So for instance, dreaming of the Prophet, for the stricter Ahl-i Hadith, was sheer fancy. Every time I mentioned the topic of jinns to my Ahl-i Hadith acquaintances they would repress superior smiles although I knew that a few of them were not averse to activating these forces when they had the need.[19]

Thus it was in and through these varied affective relations (ecstatic love, reverential love, respect) to the Prophet that the variations among the Sunni paths became a little clearer to me. But the enmity that had developed between the two major Muslim sects, Sunnis and Shias in the early 1990s was also part of the relations among the travellers of these three paths within Sunni Islam in South Asia, although, as I have tried to show above, this enmity did not take the form of a unified Sunni versus static Shia conflict. So, for instance, at one point Adeeb contemptuously referred to the Sunni Barelwi practice of celebrating the Prophet's birthday (*Milad-un Nabi*) by taking out processions of models of the Prophet's Mosque in Medina as repressed Shiism ('they just want to be like the Shias') for it was not unlike the procession of Shia *taziya*s during Muharram. Another time Akbar, my Ahl-i Hadith friend, commented that the Sunni Barelwi and Deobandi belief that the Prophet was alive in his grave was akin to Shia notions of the hidden Imam,[20] giving his Barelwi and Deobandi friends in the library in which they all worked, a real fright. This one comment generated one of the bitterest conversations I heard in my time in Pakistan. Thus, even within the daily struggle to feel the presence of the Prophet with a certainty that only a faithful imitation could provide, there were considerable concerns on how to ground this imitation in proper religious authority. The Barelwi, Deobandi, or Ahl-i Hadith, each of the Sunni paths had evolved complex procedures to buttress its individual modes of *imatio Muhammadi*. For the Deobandi this involved face-to-face relations with the *ulama-e salih*, the rightful scholars of Islam, for only through their teachings and behaviour could one have concrete examples of how to imitate the Prophet.[21]

Given the Deobandi emphasis on face-to-face learning from the ulama, what rattled me was that Farooq sahib would take his cues on the Prophet's example from a faceless and voiceless jinn with his child serving as its ventriloquist. One way to approach this would be to say that Farooq sahib was doing what many others do in activating several, even competing, bodies of knowledge and sets of relations in the hope that one of them will pay off (see Ewing 1996). However, I had gotten to know Farooq sahib quite well by this point and I knew of his insistence upon a modicum of consistency in his life. I knew, for instance, that he struggled with the fact that he did not like to keep a beard although he was strongly urged by his sons to do so as it was a practice of the Prophet. And given his disapproval of over-reliance upon jinns to get things done, it seemed strange to me that he would allow jinns into his home in the first place. Let me simply flag this discrepancy in Farooq sahib's actions, postponing my interpretations of it for the end of the chapter. I now move on to how the introduction of the jinns into the household brought to the fore the frayed ties within the extended family. Conversely, I explore how religious differences got a fillip from these very same ties.

RELIGIOUS DIFFERENCES IN THE WEAVE OF DOMESTICITY

As I have mentioned earlier, Farooq sahib's immediate family consisted of himself, his wife, and five children. Although this was not a joint family arrangement, that is to say, only one family ever resided in the house in Sandha, the exact number of inhabitants remained in flux.[22] Relatives came and went as the family retained close ties with its extended family as far a-field as Multan, Karachi, and even Delhi in India. Furthermore, there was an expectation of future growth, as the adult sons would soon have their families within this household.

However, over the time I was in Lahore (1999–2001), the unproductiveness of the sons was a continual source of tension within the family. While Farooq sahib toiled at numerous paying jobs, Adeeb spent much of his time undertaking pious, but unremunerated work, taking private lessons with a well known *alim*; doing *gasht* of the neighbourhood, that is, inviting male members of households to come pray in the mosque; preparing *dars* with his Tablighi *sathi*s in their *markaz* in Lahore; going on *chilla* to convert errant Muslims in other parts of the country and abroad; and even on occasion, sitting *ihtekaf,* that is, retreating to the mosque for fasting, prayer and contemplation, for the Islamic month of Ramzan (see Metcalf 1993; Masud 2000; Reetz 2002). While the family, in particular Rahima baji, was very proud of him, they also felt his meagre contributions to the family coffers very keenly. Of late, Adeeb had gained a lot of weight, which, combined with his beard, head cap and loose flowing *shalwar kameez*, made him look older than his twenty years. People had started to teasingly refer to him as a mullah, once a title of respect but by now a derogatory term for a religious personage who is seen to mostly sit around the mosque (see Ewing 1999; Khan 2003).

His younger brother, Ali, was not doing much better. At the beginning of our acquaintance he was ambivalent about being openly pious, preferring to spend his free time hanging out with his friends, watching pirated Hindi films, and generally exploring avenues to quit Pakistan entirely. When, by the end of my trip, he turned more strongly towards his faith, he tended to be drawn to the more strident aspects of the Deobandi path that sought to keep a watchful eye on members of the other Sunni paths for their misuse of *fiqh-e Hanafiya*.[23] Fashioning themselves on the Sipah-e-Sahaba, the incipient group called themselves Sipah-e Hanafiya. One time, disgusted by Adeeb and Ali's meagre financial support of the family, Farooq sahib spat out at them, 'why don't you call up jinn *bhoots* to make some money'. In other words, if they considered themselves too superior to take up regular jobs then why didn't they simply resort to being amils to make some money? By this time the jinns had come and gone from the family, and from what I could make out, the family saw it beneath themselves to profit monetarily from them. Although Adeeb had shown some talent in the profession, chalked up to his piety, to turn to *amiliyat* now would be a considerable step down for these *sharif* boys.

By the end of my stay, in 2001, Rahima's sister died young and quite unexpectedly in nearby Multan. Rahima's family grieved her loss. She had left behind two young children, a boy and a girl, who came to live with Farooq sahib and Rahima baji shortly after their mother's death. Farooq sahib, in keeping with his generosity, agreed to keep them and even adopt them if necessary. From what I gathered in conversation with them, the children pined for their father. At the same time there was some concern: how would Farooq sahib manage financially if they did come to live with him permanently? No one dared approach the children's father about this matter. Instead they sat around speculating whether he planned to remarry and forever abandon his children.

To remind the reader, by this time (2001) the jinns had returned to their original guardian (the amil who had entrusted Farooq sahib's family with them) and Maryam had ceased to be of the correct age to serve as a medium. However, in discussion the family struck upon the idea of speaking to Sulayman the jinn about what lay ahead for the young children. The family decided to take Farah, Farooq sahib's youngest daughter, to speak to Sulayman, to transmigrate to Multan with him if necessary, to see what was in the absent father's mind. However, Farah did not fare as well as Maryam. She was alternatively frightened of the jinns and upset at them for not taking her to Makkah as they had earlier promised. Amidst much regrets that Maryam was no longer capable of serving as a medium, the family sent the two children with Sulayman. When they returned to their bodies, (can we call this act very matter-of-factly stated metempsychosis?), they described how they had seen their father in their house packing his bag. This was followed by an exuberant hope that he was packing to come pick them up, as indeed he did shortly afterwards, but then just as quickly sent them back. Through the time that I was there, the children remained in limbo among several households.

Keeping this unresolved tension of the children's fate in mind and the challenge their possible integration offered to the straitened state of finances within the family, I turn briefly to a third story, that of the withholding of forgiveness. Rahima's mother, Farooq's mother-in-law, became the *de facto* guardian of the children I spoke of above. A beautiful old woman quite untouched by the ravages of time, she had returned to mothering, she said, when she ought to be knitting sweaters. Her own arrangement was a continuing source of tension within Farooq sahib's household. She lived in Lahore with her eldest son while her husband, whom she only referred to as 'he' and never by his name, lived with Farooq sahib and Rahima baji in whose house he generally kept to a dark corner. He would only emerge to go to the mosque to pray. The husband and wife were estranged and had been so for almost a decade. Farooq sahib's mother-in-law refused to speak to 'him' for whatever untold miseries he had heaped on her. As he got older, and apparently more

Of Children and Jinns: An Enquiry into an Unexpected Friendship 17

concerned with his mortality, he felt the need to reconcile with his wife before he died. Of late he had developed a cough that racked his body and he sensed that he might die soon. He had sought out his wife on several of her visits to Farooq sahib's house but, as she told me, although she wanted to do the right thing by him his presence made her sick. Spurred on by Rahima baji, Farooq sahib attempted to reconcile the two. When all the stories of the jinn were being told to me, Rahima's mother came up and said almost ruefully, 'Naveeda, I too was offered a jinn once. Now what is a jinn but a man. And I don't want to have a relationship with a man ever again.'

The above stories, of parental disappointment with sons, of children's possible abandonment by their father, and of a wife's estrangement from her dying husband, hint at the tensions that tear at families, even one as close knitted as Farooq sahib's, of the ambiguities that under-gird lived relations. A final story suggests how these familial tensions and the tensions between Shias and Sunnis or among Sunnis, graft onto one another, or how religious differences receive a fillip from familial tensions. What is particularly noteworthy is how familial modes of relating provide a figuration of the vague threat of religious differences within the domestic sphere, which now takes shape as a malevolent witch.

The following story pertains to the time when Maryam still served as the family's medium, long before I came into the picture. Farooq sahib had traveled to India to spend time with the Barelwi side of his family there. Maryam remained restless the entire time he was away, scared that he might never come back. She asked her mother to take her to their amil friend almost every day so that she might speak with Sulayman the jinn. Every day she would whisper something to him. Meanwhile, Farooq sahib tried to get his Indian visa extended to allow him to spend more time with his family in Delhi. However, it seemed to him, particularly in retrospect, that his every attempt failed. Dejected he had to return on the very day that his original visa expired. Maryam rushed to greet him at the door of the house but then she fell back screaming. Apparently a 30 feet *churail*[24] had followed Farooq sahib back from India. Farooq sahib immediately dropped his bags at the doorstep and without pausing rushed to the mosque to say his prayers. When he returned home Maryam assured him that the witch had left him. If at that time Maryam had still been frightened, he said, he would have had to tear up the city looking for someone to rid him of the witch but thankfully prayers had done the trick. When I asked Maryam why she did not want her father to stay on in India, she replied that his family there was not going to let him go and that they had literally bewitched him because they were jealous he was returning to his other family. When I asked Farooq sahib what he thought of this suggestion, he shrugged and thought it genuinely possible that his Barelwi family would pull such a prank because they did not take his being a Deobandi seriously enough. I pushed him on this statement. After all, it was a grave accusation to make against one's own brothers and sisters. 'Jealousy is a strong force. Sometimes those who are jealous do not even know how they bind others up,' he replied.

Similarly, the attack on the family by jinns posing as ants, with which Farooq sahib and Rahima baji had begun telling these stories to me, was taken as another indication of the force of jealousy, this time emanating from their Barelwi neighbours who wished to test the truth of the Deobandi family's claim to having jinns in their possession.

DIFFERENCE INTERNAL TO BEING

So, to return to our deferred line of inquiry, what then do we make of Farooq sahib's impulsive gesture of bringing the jinns into his home in the first place? In all the anthropological literature, occult manuals, and encyclopaedic entries I have read on jinns, sustained contact with jinns augurs madness. The average amil undergoes considerable pain and deprivation to be able to lay claim upon a particular force, and undertakes continual exercises of the body and mind to control it (see Shurreef 1823).[25] However, Farooq sahib did not train himself to be an amil, in fact, he still retained his sense of distance and disdain of the profession. He allowed the entry of jinns into his home without the armature of the average amil. He appeared to have knowingly risked the potential disruption of his family, their flight to madness if you will, or, at the very least, the possibility of his family being permanently affected by this encounter.

One way to read his actions is to acknowledge the casualness with which he took on the jinns. It was nothing special, speaking to the ordinariness of jinns within the landscape of Lahore in the late 1990s. The mainstream Urdu Press carried stories of jinn sightings and abductions interspersed with their gory stories of family feuds, political rivalries, and sectarian violence. Often, to caricature the gullibility of the ordinary Pakistani and to make fun of the Urdu Press, the English Press, the exclusive preserve of a cosmopolitan Pakistani elite, would plant stories in their pages about their correspondents attending jinn weddings.

A second, more productive way to read Farooq sahib's decision is to see it as enmeshed within a certain unintentional malevolence existing alongside generosity. Let me say that by 'malevolence' I mean the quality of being harmful rather than being productive of evil. By 'generosity' I mean the willingness to concede to others rather than a nobility of character. These qualifications are necessary as they are more honest to the actions and dispositions of those of whom I speak. If, in the story immediately above of Maryam and the witch, the threat of religious differences is materialized as the malevolent witch, here we see how Farooq sahib may be reasonably seen as malevolent arising out of the ethical dilemma inherent in the act of introducing the jinns and 'exposing' his children to their disruptive yet generative powers. After all, in exposing his daughter to the jinns, he had allowed her to become enthralled with them, in a manner of speaking, in order to better serve his preoccupation with getting closer to the Prophetic way.

To complicate this thought I have found very useful Pamela Reynold's (1996) concern with the 'exposure of children to evil' in her own work on the Zezuru in Zimbabwe whose perspectives she brings to bear upon Henry James's infamous novella *The Turn of the Screw* (1971). In his story, James wrote about a young governess who is given 'supreme authority' over her two charges. She comes to suspect that the two are haunted by two dead servants who have returned to take possession of the children's souls. The governess takes it upon herself to expunge this scourge by seeking the children out whilst in the company of the dead spirits and making the children confess to the presence of the spirits. The young girl denies being so possessed, then falls ill and takes a dislike to the governess. On the other hand, the young boy confesses to being in the presence of a ghost and promptly dies in the arms of the triumphant governess.

Felman (1980) has written how the controversy surrounding the novella has long centred on whether to believe the governess or not, or whether to see her as mentally sick projecting her forceful fantasies upon the children. Reynolds proposes a different interpretation. I follow only two of the myriad lines of thought running through her chapter titled 'Zezuru Turn of the Screw: On Children's Exposure to Evil'. She writes if the Zezuru were asked to comment upon James' story they would fault the governess for assuming too much upon herself, arrogantly thinking herself spiritually and physically prepared to take on the spirits alone, whereas 'she is, according to Zezuru ethics, without direction, lost without a code of behaviour, and wrong in abrogating the role of the ancestors, relying rather on her own will' (1996:83–4). Secondly, they would fault the story for neglecting the innate resources of children, 'for Zezuru, children are pure: they represent nonevil. They belong to the shades. Their innocence does not imply a state of passivity. Rather, children's own resources are bolstered by the protection afforded by living and dead kin' (71).[26]

In effect, Reynolds is saying that a guardian, even a parent, cannot know in advance to what regions of experience and expression the child has access or of what s/he is capable. Nor are guardians everywhere compelled to protect children from evil in the same way. Children in the Islamic context, as I have written earlier, are free of religious obligations up to a certain age until they are seen as maturing. However, they are not seen as innocent creatures to be protected until this age. Rather they are considered to have a certain strength and prescience, which is what makes them effective as conduits to the world of spirits. And one's protection of them can only extend so far beyond which they have to fight their own battles. In the case of spirit possession of children, they may be buttressed by counter charms and buffeted by exorcism, but ultimately that fight is their own (see Magoe and Howard 1996). The innate strength attributed to children is indicated by the following hadith of the Prophet:

> I swear by that Pure Being in whose power is my life that the child who is miscarried will take the mother by the umbilical cord and pull her in the direction of paradise if the mother's object (*niyat*) has been to seek reward (Quoted in Metcalf 1997: 210).

Within this view of children, it is not inconceivable that Farooq sahib trusted Maryam more so than he did any jinn. He could have felt that she would guide their family through this world, rejecting it if it posed any overt danger to them. It was just as conceivable that she could have a privileged access to truth and could be trusted to communicate it faithfully. To recognize the truth as such she must have been formed in the light of her father's beliefs so that she could in turn be his light. Thus, religious difference, first materialized as a threat in the form of a malevolent witch, then in a father's malevolent instrumentalization of his daughter, is seen to also imply the possibility for generosity, which I see in Farooq sahib abdicating his position of authority within his family to attend to his daughter's words of guidance.[27]

Let us briefly take note of how Farooq sahib's turn towards Maryam may be taken to be a turn away from the present, from a particular experience of everyday life. I have suggested above how ambiguity plagues daily struggles to ground the pious imitation of the Prophet in proper religious authority within each of the Sunni paths. Modern politics of the copy/copying/even the copyright intrude into these struggles making more tenuous any textual or extra-textual claims to authenticity (see Khan 2003, 2005). One may develop a sensibility finely attuned to theological differences so one may ascertain whether claims to authenticity are from within one's particular path, over those of others. But there are such claims, within the rubric of one's path, that are more productive of *shak-o-shubha* (doubts) over satisfactory certainty, if not resolute certainty. Farooq sahib was fully sensitive to this problem. Together he and I had mulled over many 'authorized' posters affixed to Deobandi mosques, which left us worried about their possible reception. In turning towards Maryam, Farooq sahib's action appeared to be giving expression to his sense of the illusory quality of everyday life, where things were not as they appeared to be. In such a situation, guidance may well come from an unexpected source from an unexpected place and one had to know enough to accept and acknowledge it.[28]

Let me now rehearse the various moves Farooq sahib makes in his family's encounter with jinns before I attend to Maryam's relationship with Sulayman the jinn. Farooq sahib appears to stand beside himself, to be quite otherwise than the reformed Muslim he claims to be, when he first brings the jinns into his family's life after espousing derision for those who do so. Then he moves again from his position as a certain kind of pedagogical figure as father to become a pupil to his daughter, newly moved herself by the force of the jinn. He returns to a position of authority when he decides not to attempt to bring back the jinns after they return to their guardian. But it is no longer the position he occupied before the jinns came. He has had an encounter out of the ordinary with the world. He has moved through positions unfamiliar to him. The genetic elements in his milieu and within him have reorganized around him. He senses the block of becoming jinn that has asserted itself into this milieu/within him expressed in his deferral that 'Our *aqida* had become weak and our *ibadat* was suffering.' There was something of the quality of becoming mad in that time in his and his family's life. This was communicated to me through my conversations with Farooq sahib's colleagues who also taught and befriended me. They told me that they steered clear of him during this time, scared that their previous light teasing of him on account of his religiosity may bring forth a vengeful response from him.

Yet in Farooq sahib's moves next to himself, I choose not to see contradictory positions to be resolved in a final form but rather difference internal to his being. Farooq sahib is different from himself, beside himself, next to himself, at various points in the stories he and his family tell me. Through his moves he makes manifest possibilities immanent within himself and his milieu. Furthermore, his wry acknowledgement of difference speaks to the possibility of a generous relationship to himself. So in an interesting way a space opens up alongside a forcefield of malevolence to be generous to oneself and another.

The title of this chapter speaks tantalizingly about the friendship between a child and a jinn. Thus far we have mulled on familial and kinship relations. Let us mull over friendship as one more element of this universe. Unquestionably, friendship has a place of privilege within the Islamic tradition. One cannot control the family into which one is born or the family one begets. Earlier I cited an injunction in which the author claimed that it is best to disown one's children if they continue to resist parental authority to mould them into pious Muslims (Aijaz 1989). However, good friends aid one in the pursuit of piety. In his commentary on the ahadith collection, *Mishkat-ul-Masabih*, Maulana Fazlul Karim writes that,

> a trusted friend is a safe treasure in the world and his companionship is to be greatly valued. This is possible only in good fellowship for good and pious works (1989:549).

Certainly, friendship nourished Adeeb, providing a resolution to a standing tension within Farooq sahib's family over his sons' unproductiveness. It opened up a future for him to continue to be pious in the way he desired. After I left in 2001, he met and befriended a young industrialist in his travels with his Tablighi *sathi*s who recently gave him a job as the *imam* of a mosque on his industrial estate on the fringes of Lahore. There Adeeb finally accepted his talents as an amil and began to dispense cures and spells to the workers in the estate. He married the younger sister of the industrialist. He secured a marriage for Maryam with another of his Tablighi sathis. Maryam now has a child and the two often return home to stay with her parents for extended periods of time while her husband travels to spread the word of Islam.

But what nature of friendship did Maryam share with Sulayman the jinn? Maryam did not seem to remember much, busy donning the role of the only grown-up daughter in her parents' home at the time I left in

2001, now busy donning the role of a wife and mother. Yet here too something has changed. When I last spoke to her about her experiences on my last visit to Pakistan in the winter of 2004, she readily claimed a friendship with Sulayman, thankful that he never frightened her in their many interactions. She missed him when he left. Farooq sahib and Rahima baji recall her crying herself to sleep for weeks after. She claimed to have had dreams, such dreams, but she cannot recall them now. She just recalled the sense of those dreams with a shiver, while busy making us tea.[29]

Did Sulayman simply aid her in the family's pursuit of piety? In place of her words, I imagine a certain friendship, derived in part from my own readings of the *Arabian Nights* tales and from the insight that perhaps she herself was not unfamiliar with these stories. As in the famous tale of Aladdin and the magic lamp, familiar to the contemporary imagination through the Disney cartoon, a child finds a genie and can be literally pulled out of a certain existence to soar the skies. She shares in his joy of discovering human food. She gets to whisper her secrets into his ears and to make him complicit in her projects. She gets to go to places with him, although Sulayman said that he would not go to the United States. She gets to help out her family and her neighbours. And, she gets to take leave of her body that is changing beyond her control. Pretty soon she would not be able to access this spirit world anymore and I imagine her father was not averse to the jinns leaving before she was faced with a sense of loss. Is Sulayman then an arc of a certain line of flight for Maryam through this family in this country?[30] I am not saying that hers is a miserable existence from which Sulayman, or even the idea of Sulayman, provided her certain escape. Instead, I am suggesting that a friendship between a human and a non-human, within the context of malevolence and generosity that enables and even nurtures this friendship, is a productive movement within a field of negativity and therefore a means of gaining voice. Have we thus understood what it is to which sectarianism gives expression?

GLOSSARY

amil	magician
aqida	faith
aql	reason,
ashraf	noble-born, those who claim descent from the Prophet.
bhoots	ghosts

chilla	trips; forty days of retreat to undertake austerities
churail	witch
dars	lessons
dawa	missionary
Deobandi	a *masliq* [path] affiliated with the Sunni reformist movement dating from nineteenth century colonial India
gasht	the beat
hadith	Prophetic tradition
ibadat	obligatory worship
ijaza	permission
imam	prayer leader
Islamiyat	the fundamentals of Islam and Islamic history
jinn	genie
madrassahs	religious seminaries
Mahdi	the Awaited or Expected One,
markaz	centre
masjids	mosques
mazars	shrines
muakkals	a minor form of jinns
mufti	legal scholar
muhajir	migrant
naat	a form of poetry in praise of the Prophet
nafs	spirits
sathis	companions
sharif	noble born
Sipah-e Hanafiya	warriors of Hanafiya
Sipah-e-Sahaba	warriors of the Sahaba,
sirah	biographies of the Prophet
sunnah	his manner of life
taqlid	imitation
taziyas	models of the tomb of Hussein in Karbala
urs	the birthday of the saint

NOTES

1. See Malik (1996), Ahmad (1998), Nasr (2000), Zaman (2002), Jaffrelot (2002). See Ring (2003) for a useful corrective of this tendency although for the field of ethnic violence rather than sectarianism in Pakistan.
2. Here I draw my inspiration from Stanley Cavell (1982, 1988, 1989, and 1990) who has written extensively on Ludwig Wittgenstein to show how the latter understood scepticism to be a standing threat within ordinary language. See Das (1998) for a fuller exploration of Wittgenstein's possible reception via Cavell within anthropology. Her concurrent critique of anthropologists of everyday life is particularly pertinent for me. Das writes: 'The problem is that the notion of the everyday is too easily secured in these ethnographies because they hardly ever consider the temptations and

threats of scepticism as part of the lived reality and hence do not tell us what is the stake in the everyday that they discovered. In Cavell's rendering of Wittgenstein's appeal to the everyday, it is found to be a pervasive scene of illusion and trance and artificiality of need' (183). I take Das to be saying that in finding the everyday so, its importance for the continuation of life as such becomes simultaneously clearer and more opaque. Thus, anthropologists must redouble their efforts to understand what is at stake within the everyday, what jeopardizes it internally and externally and how, and what work goes into securing it.

3. Although such writings are by now legion, I draw from them two recent books which provide relatively different renditions of the formation of selves within contemporary Muslim societies, notably Ewing's *Arguing Sainthood: Modernity, Psychoanalysis and Islam* (1997), and Mahmood's *The Politics of Piety: The Islamic Revival and the Feminist Subject* (2005). Ewing (1997, also see 1990b) argues for the existence of multiple selves within an individual, each context dependent and inter-subjective. Even though an individual may espouse different self representations at different moments these are not viewed as inconsistent to the illusion of wholeness that Ewing claims each individual must maintain of necessity. Mahmood (2003) is much less concerned with inconsistencies within her subjects, being more interested in how each subject comes to inhabit norms in such a manner as to make it appear that the norm is working on the subject, that is, the subject acts on herself in such a way as to make the norm constitute her as a pious self. This is not an abnegation of the self in the service of a higher ideal but rather a self that is generated through its particular emergence from, and interpenetration, with the norm.

I take distance from both pictures of the self in that I am neither satisfied with a finalist account of a self nor with a picture of multiple selves. Rather I am much more interested in the self as the realm of pre-subjective possibilities. These possibilities, in Gilles Deleuze's words in *Logic of Sense* 'impersonal and pre-individual singularities,' (1990:103) exist within a plane of immanence. 'Far from being individual or personal, singularities preside over the genesis of individuals and persons; they are distributed in a 'potential' which admits neither Self nor I, but which produces them by actualizing or realizing itself, although the figures of this actualization do not at all resemble the realized potential' (1990:103). In this picture, an individual actualizes only one of these possibilities/singularities/potential. However, despite his individuation, these other singularities exist within him, they are his link to this plane of immanence. Again in Deleuze's words 'The problem is therefore one of knowing how the individual would be able to transcend his form and his syntactical link with a world, in order to attain to the universal communication of events' (1990:178). In other words, there exists a multiplicity within the individual but one cannot call these multiple selves (*pace* Ewing). Rather the multiplicity retains its pre-individual, impersonal qualities, it is marked by irreducible singularities, and these singularities distinguish themselves from one another not by negation but by affirmation. A given individual moves between these qualities without necessarily morphing into different selves. This multiplicity or rather singularities in a given series within an individual, and the movement within this series of singularities, is what I mean by difference internal to being.

The questions of interest to me are: what brings about a movement internal to self, what is the nature of this movement, and what is this movement towards? In *Difference and Repetition* Deleuze writes that movement is brought on by encounter, a shock to thought. 'Something in the world forces us to think. This something is an object not of recognition but of a fundamental *encounter*. What is encountered may be Socrates, a temple, or a demon. In whichever tone, its primary characteristic is that it can only be sensed' (1994:139).

The movement is not one of negation but of affirmation. Quoting Deleuze again, 'Instead of something distinguished from something else, imagine something which distinguishes itself—and yet that from which it distinguishes itself does not distinguish itself from it. Lightning, for example, distinguishes itself from the black sky but must also trail behind it, as though it were distinguishing itself from that which does not distinguish itself from it' (1994:28). In other words, a given singularity may individualize within a person but never at the expense of the other singularities. These other possibilities crowd around the person, perhaps never to be actualized but to be differentially sensed by the person at various moments of encounter between the person and something in the world. That is, the person is in perpetual movement between these singularities.

Finally, this movement between singularities is one of never arriving at one. It is that of becoming, or rather, continual becoming. In Deleuze and Guattari's words in *A Thousand Plateaus: Capitalism and Schizophrenia*, 'A becoming is not a correspondence between relations. But neither is it a resemblance, an imitation, or, at the limit, an identification. The whole structuralist critique of the series seems irrefutable. To become is not to progress or regress along a series. Above all, becoming does not occur in the imagination.... What is real is the becoming itself, the block of becoming, not the supposedly fixed terms through which that which becomes passes' (1987:237–8).

Now I am not suggesting that we do away with all theories of subject formation. Clearly Ewing and Mahmood each write with deep conviction against dominant images of Muslims, be that of Pakistani Muslims as inconsistent in their religiosity or Egyptian Muslim women as willing participants in their own subjugation respectively. There is a need and a place for such analysis. However, I am arguing for the need to also attend to the plane of immanence as it cuts through beings, humans or otherwise, organic or inorganic, within everyday life. Only then can we generate more robust pictures of selves, be they pious Muslim selves or otherwise, in the process of continually becoming other, with its attendant threats and promises (see Khan 2005). It opens up regions of experience and expressions of creativity within life, a necessary corrective to the exhausted feel of everyday life of recent years.

4. 'From being a dead shell, culture comes to be born paradoxically at this juncture when a different relationship between the articulation of voice and hearing is established' (Das 1995:167). It is an ongoing challenge for me to try to bring Cavellian insights into everyday life as one of existence under continual threat in line with Deleuzian insights into living as one of joyful becoming other. See Singh (2005) for a sustained effort to find convergences between their respective lines of inquiry. For me it has been a question of the vastly different affects espoused by the two authors, one of melancholia and the other of joy, even joy taking in cruelty, respectively. However, Veena Das's writings provide a possible link between Cavell and Deleuze in line with my particular interest. As I have outlined above in endnote No. 3 it is through Das (1998) that we get an exploration of Wittgenstein, and therefore, Cavell's possible reception within anthropology. In particular, we receive their sense of everyday life as one fraught with risks. Again, it is through Das (1995) that we get an exploration of a self who betrays the immediate norms of her family in order to ensure her continued relationship with that family. In effect, she moves to a next self before her family is willing to allow her to do so, so as to keep alive the self she used to be in relation to this family. It seems to me that Das, *pace* Cavell,

captures full well the risks inherent in this movement as well as the joyful aspect of the movement to which Deleuze is referring manifest in the woman's return to these old relationships that sustain her. Might one then think of difference as movement entailing the risks of everyday life and the joy of becoming the other?

5. Most recently Charles Hirschkind (2001) has written about the 'ethics of listening' within the Islamic tradition and as practiced by Egyptian Muslims attending religious sermons, whereby Muslims train their bodies to hear sermons in such a manner as to bring about the appropriate affective and mental responses in line with the normative picture of the pious self. In other words a certain work on the body elicits a specific mode of listening. I would distinguish my understanding of 'gestures' and its relationship to 'hearing' from Hirschkind's of 'body' to 'listening' very simply. In my case gestures and their hearing do not necessarily happen to/within the same body, although it may, as much as between bodies. Furthermore, the challenge for me, as one of those bodies, is to listen to gestures, that is, not read them as a cultural text *pace* Clifford Geertz nor assume therein lies the code to crack the regulative mechanisms of a society *pace* Pierre Bourdiou, but rather to draw out how thinking proceeds apace with gestures, how gestures gather thought, sounded and the unsounded, within themselves, how voice is incorporative of these gestures. Here I am drawing upon lines of thought more fully developed in Martin Heidegger's *What is Called Thinking?* (1968). In his extended inquiry into what is this thing called thinking, Heidegger says that if we are to learn thinking then we must learn to listen and listen to, say, the gestures of the hand: 'the hand's gestures run everywhere through language, in their most perfect purity precisely when man speaks by being silent. And only when man speaks, does he think—not the other way around, as metaphysics still believes' (16). These words are very resonant with Veena Das's in 'Wittgenstein and Anthropology' (1998) in which she writes: 'Now if I am correct that the inner is not like a distinct state that can be projected to the outer world through language in Wittgenstein but rather like something that lines the outer, then language and the world (including the inner world) are learned simultaneously' (190). Or further on, 'That is not to say that we do not *read* the body but rather that we depend on grammar to tell us what kind of an object something is. Inserting the centrality of the body in human society is important not in inferring internal states of mind but in the intuition of language as a bodying forth...' (191). If I am correct in my intuition that Heidegger's understanding of thinking is like Wittgenstein's understanding of language bodying forth, gestures are a mode of thinking/language bodying forth, which is precisely why they call for a hearing/listening.

6. See Khan (2003).

7. Let me just say at the outset that I was not surprised at the claimed existence of jinns. I had been told of alternative worlds to the human one and of the material and spiritual negotiations that humans entered into with the inhabitants of these worlds. What shocked me was that I had understood Farooq sahib's family to only accept ibadat as the legitimate way to approach God having heard only their derision of other intercessionary modes in the two years I had known them. Yet here I was at the last leg of my research learning that they had once had jinns in their possession. It raises an interesting question about the temporality of memory, that is, why did it take this family almost two years to remember to tell me this experience? Or is it a question of trust?

8. Even the Mutazilates, early Muslim materialists, dared not discount the existence of jinns although on the few occasions they spoke of them they referred to jinns as uncivilized tribes inhabiting the world (El-Zein 1996).

9. As a young boy Adeeb had seen the Prophet Muhammad (PBUH) twice in his dreams. According to the Islamic tradition, one cannot be deluded about seeing the Prophet in one's dreams as Iblis/Satan cannot take the Prophet's form. Adeeb's piety is both a source of pride and tension within the family as we will see later. It is also the reason why the jinns associated with him, first Sulayman (see below), and later many others given to him by his friends and well wishers, are seen to be particularly efficacious.

10. In the interest of brevity I present here simply the most basic duties incumbent upon parents to raise their children to be proper Muslims in accordance with the Islamic tradition. However, the importance of the child for the Muslim family cannot be emphasized enough. In the introduction to her edited book, *Children in the Muslim Middle East*, Fernea writes that 'In the Middle East, the child is seen as the crucial generational link in the family unit, the key to its continuation, the living person that ties the present to the past and to the future' (1995:4). In addition to the socio-biological significance of children, the burden of raising them as good Muslims rests heavily upon parents not only in the interests of grounding Islamic society but also in ensuring parents' standing before God. As a child I was often urged to attend to my Arabic lessons and prayers with seriousness so that my parents might meet their maker without shame or fear of retribution on the Day of Judgment. In the manual translated by Aijaz it is written, 'It is hoped that the parents will resolve to train and educate their children according to the Islamic principles as their primary obligation. If they fail in their duty they will have to bear the entire responsibility of children's deviation from the moral principles' (1989:162). Furthermore, 'if one's offspring and close relatives obdurately stick to infidelity then faith demands that they should be disowned and all kinds of relationship with them should be cut off' (34). Unfortunately, it is beyond the scope of my ethnography to speak of the societal construction of childhood (see James and Prout 1997; Gupta 2002) or attempt a child centred ethnography (see Das 1989; Reynolds 1989, 1996) to flesh out the picture I have provided above.

11. To highlight the singular nature of Maryam's relationship with the jinns it is necessary to sketch a field of the documented states of possession in the literature on jinns and other spirits in Muslim societies. The reader should be warned that this is a very schematic sketch. To be a victim of possession is to be struck by any number of somatic illnesses or psychic effects of mysterious origins (Bowen 1993; Seigel 2003). For instance, under the description of demonical possession in Jaffur Shurreef's *Qanoon-e Islam*, a nineteenth century text, the author writes that the symptoms of this state are as follows: 'Some are struck dumb; others shake their heads; others grow mad and walk about naked; they feel no inclination to pursue their usual avocations; but lie down and are inactive (1832/1973: 218).' However, the expectation affixed to attempts to cure this state is that it is temporary, eased by the interventions of healers/magicians, or by medical experts in the last resort (Pandolfo 2000). On the other hand, one may be permanently possessed, as in the case of Tuhami in Vincent Crapanzano's ethnography by that name (1980). He was enslaved by a female jinni by the name of Aisha Qandisha and could not easily shake off his state of enslavement. In both of these instances we have a picture of possession which comes from outside the self and over which the self appears to exert little control. In contrast to the victim, a healer/magician's state of possession is much more of his/her own doing. Such a person may have jinns or related spirits in his/her possession and it is a matter of undertaking the correct discipline and ritual activity to ensure the presence of this jinn. Although one would not strictly call this state one of possession as described by Shurreef, the healer/magician does leave himself/herself vulnerable to the jinn's

intrusion into his/her body or mind or s/he may even encourage such an intrusion to facilitate communication and negotiations with the spirit in question (Shurreef 1832; Bowen 1993; Seigel 2003). In this picture the self maintains some control over the scene of possession. There are instances in which the healer/magician may utilize a child to presence/communicate with the spiritual being. However, the child is only seen as a conduit for the jinns being thoroughly guided in this process by the healer/magician. In other words the subjectivity of the child is never brought into focus although of course s/he must meet the objective criteria for being a medium and is known to be effective as one. With these few, granted impoverished, pictures of possession, let us turn to Maryam's. She cannot be called possessed either in the sense that Shurreef describes or that provided by Crapanzano. In other words, the control over possession does not lie outside of herself. Nor is she a trained healer/magician to control the scene of possession. Rather, unguided by any healer magician, she presences the jinn on her own volition and participates in or comments on their sociality as a matter of course. In the literature on jinns, there is a category of spirits called *qarin* or *qarina* which is the evil double of the individual which is born with him or her and stays with him or her their entire life (see Zwemer 1939). I have also heard references to children having *hamzard*s (familiars) who do not appear innately evil as in the case of *qarin/qarinas* but as we know in this instance the jinns were given to this family and therefore cannot be grouped under these other categories. I will later have more opportunity to speculate what manner of relation Maryam bore to the jinns and what it says about Maryam, her family, and her milieu but for now I simply want to bring into focus the unusualness of the arrangement before us.

12. In the following story quoted by El-Zein (1996) we have reference to a sahaba jinn:

    Shibli said: 'Some people left for Makkah. They lost their way and felt that they were about to die, so they put on their shrouds and lay down waiting for death to come. Then a jinn came from the trees and said: "I am one of the jinn who listened to the Prophet. I heard him saying: 'The believer is like a brother to the believer. He is his eye and his guide and never forsakes him. This is the water and this is the way." Then he guided them to the water and showed them the way' (313).

13. The following story relates how the jinns come to give expression to the myriad ways Shia–Sunni tensions fold into everyday life. Around the time I first learnt about the jinns in Farooq sahib's life (2001), I met Farooq sahib one day looking utterly frantic. He had lost the registration papers of his motorbike. As Shia–Sunni tensions were particularly intense in those days with police at checkpoints everywhere stopping men on motorbikes, he was frightened that he would be thrown into jail if caught without his papers. He was even more frightened that someone involved in sectarian activities might use his papers, might leave them at the scene of violence, to throw the police off their tracks. He rushed to his friend the amil to get his help in tracking down the papers to see if the jinns could give him some rough idea of where to look for them. After extensive searching he later found them in a garbage can outside his house.

14. While I have changed the names of all my subjects in this chapter, I have left the original name of the favoured jinn. This is because I want to draw attention to the significance of the name Sulayman to the history of jinns. In the Quran, Sulayman is mentioned as the prophet and the king to whom God gave the power to discourse with animals and jinns, whose powers Sulayman in turn harnessed to construct the Temple named after him. In Surat Saba of the Quran, it is elaborated that the jinns continued to build the Temple after Sulayman died and only realized that he was dead when the staff upon which his body had been leaning crumbled, having been

eaten by termites, and the body fell over. In *Muhammad and the Golden Bough* (1996), Stetkevych writes that the mythopoetic registers of the Quran have been neglected within the field of Islamic studies. One could make a similar argument for the mythopoetic registers of everyday life within Muslim societies. As a corrective, it may be speculated how Sulayman the jinn introduces a mythic moment in the Islamic tradition in which man, beasts, and jinns lived in close communication and cooperation into a present in which prophets, kings, and caliphs are activated to express difference and dissonance among men. Furthermore, Das has made the interesting argument that children take 'frequent recourse to the mythic' in making sense of their oftentime violently changing social reality (1989: 288). This leads me to speculate further upon the (unintended?) agency of Maryam in mediating King Sulayman's claim upon this violent present, as a different modality of being with difference.

15. Now it is known that jinns are creatures of smokeless fire, that is, they do not have a fixed form. However, if they show themselves in one particular form to humans, they remain in that form as long as that very same human's eyes are fixed upon them. The only way they can change forms is if they can trick the humans into looking at a copy of them, which then frees them to take another form or to escape into formlessness (El-Zein 1996). This suggests something of the coercive force humans may exert upon jinns, fixing them to a form when they may wish to be other. In this instance, however, the jinns left the family after the men were forced into dancing the traditional *bhangra* dance at a cousin's wedding. The jinns condemned this as immoral behaviour which they did not wish to condone through their continued existence as part of this family. See Rothenberg (1998) for another instance of how jinns provide a barometer of everyday morality.

Interestingly, Farooq sahib said that he was very embarrassed to face his neighbours after the jinns left his family. Although he did not provide any explanation for his embarrassment one can guess that it looked bad on the family to be judged so by jinns and to suffer a loss of power/status after the jinns withdrew from them. However, Farooq sahib said that he quickly got over the loss as he realized that one risked one's faith in God through reliance upon supernatural forces. 'Our *aqida* had become weak and our ibadat was suffering.' That is, he came to espouse the normative Deobandi position on jinns. Clearly, he must have held to this view before the jinns came into his life so his later espousal of this norm raises an interesting problem for anthropologists as to whether we ought to be attentive to the myriad ways people re-experience and re-express a norm? And, if we are to be attentive to these micro-processes then we cannot take people's expression of a norm as their first and last word. We have to attend to how they come to speak/re-speak those words. Although Mahmood (2005) speaks of how selves are produced in the interpenetration of bodily practices and norms, I feel that she emphasizes too much how a self came to be expressive of norms once and for all without attending to how these norms are continually re-signified for that self,

16. I elect to call Farooq sahib's relation to the Prophet one of pious imitation rather than copying so as not to introduce modern anxieties over the loss of aura attending copies into a time honoured practice of embodying and transmitting the Islamic tradition. However, this is not to say that such modern anxieties do not come to haunt this practice. See Khan (2005) in which I discuss contemporary legal discussions in Pakistan over copyrighting aspects of the Islamic tradition and its attendant anxieties.

17. See Khan (2001) for a brief exploration of the citational insecurity that attends to textual production in the religious publishing world in Pakistan.
18. As Devji (1994) has shown, since the nineteenth century women in South Asian Islam have been largely portrayed as constitutionally and customarily impious, a portrayal which has helped make them the natural subject of various reform efforts. However, not enough attention has gone to show how they are constituted as pious subjects and have aided in the making of Muslim piety. See Mahmood (2005) for a study of this in the Egyptian context.
19. Another family with whom I was close was closely allied with the Ahl-i Hadith path. Although they routinely disparaged the reliance upon amils they were themselves very close to a self-professed Ahl-i Hadith amil who went by the name of Baba. Although he travelled widely visiting people afflicted by illnesses and spells at their own homes, an Ahl-i Hadith mosque was known to be his favourite place of worship and for the dispensation of advice and medicine. During one of our few conversations in the mosque Baba related a dream of his, which came to him in the mosque, and which he took to be the authoritative statement on the tense Shia–Sunni relations prevailing in the country. He said that he had long wondered about the truth of *Zuljinah*, the famed white horse of Imam Hussein, who had stood by the wounded men during the Battle of Karbala and who had carried the news of their demise to the Prophet's family, his face marked by the martyrs' blood. Baba had often wondered whether such a horse wasn't more myth than reality, one more emotional crutch for the Shias. However, in his dream he saw himself praying in the mosque when the sounds of a procession floated to his ears. Upon completing his prayers he looked out of the window to see Imam Hussein astride a beautiful white horse riding through a cheering crowd. He was moved to tears by the sight of the Imam on his horse. And from that day hence he has been convinced that Sunnis do great wrong to mock Shia beliefs and that each has to seek his own way to God. Coming as this did from a man who was very careful to keep his reputation free of any association with the Shias (his continued use of a strict Ahl-i Hadith mosque being a testimony to this) hints at the availability of dreaming as a mode of living religious differences. See von Grunebaum and Caillos (1966) and Ewing (1990) for the particular significance given to dreaming as a fraction of revelation (*wahy*) within the Islamic tradition.
20. This is a reference to the majority Twelver Shia belief that the twelfth of their twelve divinely inspired leaders (*imam*s) had gone into occultation/concealment, who was expected to return in the figure of the *Mahdi*, and whose return would signal the nearing of the Day of Judgment. While Sunni Muslims also believe in the return of the Mahdi at end time they do not subscribe to the idea of his previous appearance and subsequent occultation (see Cole 1988).
21. In Khan (2001) I discuss a book of religious instruction by a well-known contemporary Deobandi *mufti*, Dr Mufti Abdul Wahid of Jammiya Madania, Lahore, in which the topics are easily laid out to enable individual perusal of the contents of the book. However, the mufti warns against self-education despite his book lending itself to such. Instead, he advises that the interested buyer seek out a good alim to teach him the contents of the book and indicates how he is to be taught, how many chapters per day, for what length of time, the means of testing his knowledge acquisition, the total time required to complete the entire curriculum (six months for the book), etc. In other words, authoritative books require authoritative transmitters to ensure that the student comes to be a Muslim correctly. Authorized textual instructions in themselves do not ensure their correct transmission.

22. See Das (1970) for a detailed account of Indian Punjabi kinship. Note that this family was a mixed muhajir-Punjabi family.
23. South Asian Sunnis of the Deobandi and Barelwi paths do *taqlid* of *fiqh-e Hanafiya*, one of the four major schools of Islamic jurisprudence extant. However, the Ahl-i Hadith only support the Quran and the Ahadith as legitimate textual sources for guidance and advocate an esoteric blend of all four schools in the making of legal opinions, although they too tend to largely rely upon fiqh-e Hanafiya. See Anderson (1959), Schacht (1964), or Coulson (1969) for an introduction to the four fields of Islamic jurisprudence in the modern world; see Fyzee (1974), Metcalf (1982), Sanyal (1996) and Brown (1996) for the specificities of conflicts over fiqh-e Hanafiya among Sunnis in South Asia.
24. Informally a witch but to speak more specifically it is the ghost of a woman who has died during childbirth, a very inauspicious, likely a vengeful figure.
25. Let me draw the example of the Ahl-i Hadith amil, Baba, with whom I had a brief acquaintanceship. He related how he had to track down magicians of note to get their *ijaza* to use Quranic verses for talismanic purposes. Some of the verses were associated with jinni power and he had to undertake *chilla* to conquer their forces, to bring them under his possession. He had to carry out many more prayers than the five obligatory ones to continue to maintain his powers over both verses and jinns, which took up most of his days. Nonetheless, despite all his work to possess jinns he was much more comfortable utilizing *muakkal*s to carry out his wishes because he feared jinns and their inherent capacity for evil.
26. These perspectives resonate with Das who writes in another context, 'In the Indian case…the child is seen as already being a full person in domains to which the mother does not have access' (1989:268). And further on, 'the world of children and the world of adults meet on many points. They have a kind of floating relationship which cannot be described through analogy or polarity alone. Children's play reproduces the world of adults in some contexts and transforms it in others' (279).
27. In making explicit his trust in his daughter, a trust that he does not readily articulate in relation to his wife Rahima who claims herself responsible for Farooq sahib's conversion to the Deobandi *masliq* in an earlier period in their life, nor does he ever explicitly articulate in relation to his son Adeeb who later deepens Farooq sahib's association with the masliq through his own relations with the Tablighi Jamaat, the missionary arm of the Deobandis, is Farooq sahib giving expression to a permissible, possibly gendered love for one's daughter? Certainly there is something specific about that relation within South Asia. See Veena Das' 'Language and Body' in which she writes how 'fathers willed their daughters to die for family honour rather than live with bodies that had been violated by other men' (1997:77) in the aftermath of the violence of Partition. Yet, in the story by Sadat Hasan Manto that Das analyzes, a father shouts in joy 'my daughter is alive' upon recovering her violated and possibly dead body. Here then that specificity of gendered love, of a father's love for his daughter, gets a unique articulation: 'To be masculine when death was all around was to be able to hand death to your violated daughter without flinching…In the background of such stories, a single sentence of joy uttered by old Sarajjudin transforms the meaning of being a father' (77).
28. In exploring how everyday life may be a place of trance and illusion, I am taking my inspiration from Cavell (see footnote no. 3). For Cavell this quality of everyday life, its ability to withdraw from us, is a standing threat. However, this perspective does not necessarily line up with the Islamic injunction that one should treat this world as a temporary way station on the path to God, that one strike a balance between

participation in the world so as to enable life and keep a discrete distance from this world so that we do not become attached to it. Islam condemns asceticism, that is, excessive withdrawal from the world, as strongly as it does excessive attachment to it. Consequently, striking this balance is most difficult because it effectively entails keeping up the illusory nature of everyday life while participating in it. Another way to look at the incident of Farooq sahib turning towards Maryam for guidance is to see him in mid-attempt towards striking this balance. Taking another place to be more real than this one, it makes illusory this everyday life. Yet by making the words from another place come to bear upon his behaviour within this place he also attempts to ensure his continued participation within this everyday life. How this Islamic injunction links up with Cavellian understanding of the everyday is up for further exploration.

29. See Lambek (1980) for an account of how spirits who possess women strike up friendships/relationships with their spouses, relationships which endure even after the spirit leaves the woman's mind and body or even in the instances in which the spouses leave the possessed women.
30. If we think of my descriptions of the Shia–Sunni conflict and the differences within Sunni Islam as being at the level of the *molar,* and what happens to Farooq sahib as being at the level of the *molecular,* then what Maryam, with her encounter with Sulayman the jinn, brings to the picture is a possible *line of flight* into the plane of immanence. See Deleuze's 'Many Politics' in Deleuze and Parnet (2002).

CHAPTER 2

The Modern Businessman and the Pakistani Saint: The Interpenetration of Worlds

KATHERINE P. EWING

INTRODUCTION

There have been pressures in Pakistan toward both modernization and the reform of religious practice in the direction of a 'purer' Islam. But both trends in their most extreme forms reject the legitimacy of saints and shrines as part of traditional 'folk' Islam. Politically active fundamentalist reformists such as Maulana Maududi, for instance, sought to 'shun the language and terminology of the Sufis, their mystical allusions and metaphoric references, their dress and etiquette, the Saint-disciple institutions and all other things associated with it,'[1] attributing the decline in Muslim political power in South Asia to a 'chronic ailment' associated with the attachment of a follower to the personality of his spiritual guide. Those who have assumed that modernization must be accompanied by secularization have also equated backward ignorance with a devotion to Sufi pirs, an equation reflected in accounts such as that of The Lahore District Census Report for 1961:

> Pirs are held in esteem and respect by villagers.... Besides the living Pirs, the people have great faith in the Pirs who died centuries ago and attend their shrines at the time of their annual *Urs*. The hold of the Pirs is gradually dying away.[2]

Researchers have repeatedly demonstrated in recent years that modernization theories misjudged the persistence of traditional cultural orientations. In Pakistan, despite forces discouraging adherence to Sufism and pirs, many people continue to display a strong and vital interest in Sufism and associated activities at shrines. As yet another affirmation of the inadequacy of modernization theories, this continuing interest is particularly notable among Pakistani businessmen and professionals. These men are not ignorant peasants under the thrall of a hereditary pir who simply collects their money in the perpetuation of a feudal-type relationship. Many of them, on the contrary, are highly educated, often in the sciences, with extensive exposure to European ideas, and for some, even extended residence abroad. Yet they encompass in their lives both a professional orientation and a Sufi orientation. Western observers had assumed that such professionals were becoming secularized, found it difficult to reconcile their modern orientation with Sufism, or had lost interest in such traditional pursuits.[3] Largely because of such assumptions, Western observers were surprised by the intense resurgence of Islam in recent years. At this point, therefore, the interesting question is not whether traditional cultural forms and orientations survive, which has already been well demonstrated, but rather how Sufis can also be business and professional men in an industrializing economy.

For certain radical Muslims, Islamic resurgence has involved an active rejection of Western values and social forms. Many Muslims, however, are integrating their experiences in an international working world that is based on Western organizational models with their experiences of growing up in a Muslim cultural environment. Judging from their activities, it appears that Pakistani professionals do not consider training in the sciences and modern technology incompatible with their involvement in Sufi activities. If we look at the ways in which Pakistani professional and business men interact with their Pakistani colleagues in office settings, for instance, it appears that, in practice, many do not find it necessary to firmly separate their professional activities from their involvement in Sufism, even to the extent that Westerners typically compartmentalize their own activities. This interweaving of contexts is particularly evident in the overlapping of interpersonal networks in business and Sufi activities.[4] There is little to suggest that professionals and businessmen who are also Sufis experience radical discontinuities in frames of reference or maintain sharply bounded spheres of activity.[5]

In this chapter I investigate how Pakistani business and professional men integrate these two worlds of experience by considering what they are seeking in their relationships with Sufi pirs, and how these relationships may shape their approach to the working world.[6] With the Sufi pir, the Pakistani professional man maintains a characteristically South Asian hierarchical authority relationship that is essentially congruent with his childhood experiences in the extended family. But paradoxically, I argue, he is often able to use this relationship to avoid becoming helplessly trapped in conflicts in the workplace between the demands of a bureaucratic organization based on Western models of competence and the perpetuation of familiar authority relationships by his superiors, thus enabling him to act with what to the Western observer appears to be autonomy and independence. I will demonstrate that the intrapsychic underpinnings or sources of this autonomy and independence are characteristically South Asian, and thus, very different from their usual sources among Westerners.

Though there are many living Sufi pirs in Pakistan with whom individuals interact in specific social relationships, I will focus here not on how these individuals actually interact with their pirs as people, but on how the Sufi pir functions as a kind of 'personal symbol'[7] for Pakistanis of this particular socio-cultural background. Examination of a symbol such as this may proceed in two directions. A personal symbol has both socio-cultural and personal psychological referents and affords at a symbolic level the resolution of opposition and conflict. One may focus on the intrapsychic significance of the symbol for a particular individual, tracing the associative links between specific uses of the symbol and events in the individual's past. Alliteratively, one may examine the ways in which such symbols are used in communication, as the basis of culturally shared understandings with others. Though the two chains of meaning need not necessarily overlap, there is no sharp boundary between them; and there may be many aspects of personal meaning that are also shared, suggesting the cultural patterning of certain aspects of personality or emotional structure.

In this chapter I highlight the cultural components of the pir as a personal symbol and develop a model of the culturally shaped aspects of intrapsychic organization that accounts for many of the communications and activities of business and professional men who are also Sufis.[8] As a clue to what is going on intrapsychically, I focus particularly on the characteristic ways in which these men talk about their emotional reactions to the pir, exploring central concepts such as 'longing' and 'love' and tracing their possible psychological roots from a developmental perspective.

JUXTAPOSITION OF THE SUFI–DISCIPLE RELATIONSHIP AND RELATIONSHIPS IN THE WORLD

As others have observed,[9] in South Asia work relationships tend to replicate hierarchical authority relationships within the family and are frequently conceptualized in familial terms. Kakar has argued that this organizational model is inappropriate in modern institutions whose purpose is scientific inquiry or technological development: 'Such organizations require a more egalitarian structure in which competence rather than age legitimates authority, and in which capacity for initiative as well as seniority governs role relationships.' In such a setting, he argues, younger professionals, in whom the hierarchical tradition has been thoroughly internalized, are psychologically unable to confront or critically question their elders about discrepancies they perceive between the criteria of professional performance and the prevailing mores of the organization: 'Instead, the conflict between intellectual conviction and developmental "fate" manifests itself in a vague sense of helplessness and impotent rage.'[10]

This conflict is pervasive among Pakistanis, who complain about bureaucratic corruption but also feel that they are trapped by the system. They frequently articulate their frustration and rage in conversation. Yet the very man who extols the virtues of being a proper Muslim and denounces corruption will attempt to rig exam results for a son or for a friend's son, and then say with some self-disparagement, 'That's the way we Pakistanis are'. Among professionals and the educated elite, frustration and disillusionment may further derive from the sense that even men at the top of their profession are subordinate to their Western counterparts, because the professional world in which they operate is organized in terms of Western models. In most offices and businesses, there is the pervasive sense that Pakistanis are inefficient, that Pakistani products are inferior to Western products, that Pakistani education is a pale imitation of British or American education. University students are often critical of their professors because they feel that the professors' knowledge and research are derivative and far inferior to the academic pursuits of their Western counterparts. Just as many Muslims attributed the fall of the Mughal Empire in the face of the onslaught of the West to their own failure to adhere to the principles of Islam,[11] many see bureaucratic corruption in similar terms. People are acutely aware of this tension. For many, living with such tension creates a nagging sense of discontent and may stimulate a quest for meaning. This quest often takes the form of a renewed interest in Islam, particularly Sufism, and the search for spiritual guidance from a pir.

A fundamental aspect of the socio-cultural meaning of the pir which facilitates characteristic personal uses of the pir as a symbol is his spirituality, which is typically conceptualized as a detachment from or transcendence of normal bodily appetites and needs. (It may be claimed that even a rather portly pir subsists on nothing but water and spices, for instance.) The relationship with the pir can thus be experienced as a kind of haven from the corrupting influences of the world. Disciples draw sharp contrasts between the behaviour and expectations of the pir and the standards for behaviour in the everyday world. Descriptions of the pir typically contrast him with the orientations that characterize worldly relationships: 'I have seen a lot but what I found in my shaikh [pir] is purity, freedom from hypocrisy, cant, and prejudice, and a knowledge and love for all humanity. Everyone finds in him solace, and comfort, and a spirit of humility.' The relationship with the pir is a relationship with an idealized other.

Despite the contrasts that informants draw between relationships in the everyday world and a relationship with a pir, the latter can be understood as a distillation of what they seek in other social relationships. For instance, a university graduate student articulated what he was searching for in a Sufi pir by focusing on what he found disappointing in his university professors. Like many other people I met in Pakistan, he was not seeking autonomy, but rather the perfect elder, the perfect authority figure, and he felt that whatever difficulties and frustrations he was experiencing came from the inadequacies of his elders. He juxtaposed his experience of his university professors with his idea of what a teacher should be like. He complained that there was no real relationship between teacher and student, and that his teachers had nothing to offer but rote and were devoid of any kind of experiential knowledge or wisdom. In contrast, he was seeking a university mentor. He described how he had found a Sufi mentor and had been his follower for the past five years. It was evident from his disappointment that he expected a profound congruence between his experience with a Sufi and his university education. He was inspired by this mentor, in contrast to his teachers. He described his pir in terms reminiscent of the descriptions of the perfect Master that abound in Sufi literature.[12]

Given this young man's juxtaposition of the image of the pir with his image of his teachers, how did his Sufi involvement affect his way of managing the university world? His relationship with a Sufi pir served as a model for worldly activity. From his perspective, any discontinuities between the two stemmed from inadequacies in the university rather than from any basic inconsistency in frames of references. This young man was fearful of making overt criticisms of his teachers and allowed himself to do so with me only under the assurance of complete confidentiality. But once he felt assured that his defiance would not be discovered, he expounded at great length about the inadequacies of his teachers. Over time, as he gradually told me more about his family relationships, he expressed similar feelings of criticism and disillusionment about his authoritarian grandfather and his father. In our relationship, too, he developed manifestations of a transference[13] that oscillated between deferential respect and a kind of defiance in which he constantly tested my knowledge and 'wisdom'. At the most superficial level, this transference was shaped by his identification of me with his teachers on the one hand (our meetings occurred in a university setting), and with his pir on the other (he knew that I had done research on pirs, and had come to me because of this), although clearly the transference had roots in his childhood experience. The extent of my observations of this young man does not permit complete interpretations of his psychological organization, but it was evident that his idealization of the pir provided him with a safe anchor that enabled him to challenge other authority figures in his life. It allowed him to establish a measure of independence from the authority structure of his family without throwing him into a position of absolute isolated autonomy.

In another case, a well-educated senior officer in a government office described a moment when a junior officer violated the hierarchical authority relationship that existed between them in order to maintain the explicit (but often disregarded) operating rules of the organization. The case even more clearly illustrates how, with the support of the internalized image of the pir, a young man can act with what appears to be independence and autonomy. As the senior officer told it, he experienced a moment of discontinuity, because the hierarchical power relations in his office (which at one level he perceived as corrupt) were juxtaposed, not against the explicit rules of proper procedure for a modern office, but rather against the principles of Islam. Islam was thus being used in the service of the explicit bureaucratic rules of the organization. The experience of discontinuity precipitated a spiritual transformation in the senior officer, whom I shall call Suhrawardi Sahib:

> I became a Suhrawardi because of the present *sajjāda nishin* of Faiz Qalandar's shrine, who is the son of Faiz Qalandar. He works in the same office with me in WAPDA. Once a friend of mine had done some work for WAPDA and submitted a bill for payment. My friend asked me if I could arrange that he be paid right away. I went to the man in the office who was authorized to write cheques for WAPDA. I asked him to do me a favour and write the cheque immediately. But there was some outstanding work still to be done by

my friend, so the man refused. He said, 'If I do anything like that then my pir-father would get angry.' I was a senior officer and he was a junior officer in the company. In an office, a junior officer cannot refuse a senior officer anything. I was so impressed. I said to myself, 'Here is a real Muslim. Though he lives an ordinary life and does not sit at a grave, even so he has fear of his pir.' We became friends because of this. He said to me, 'If you wish to come to my father's shrine, I can take you there and show you how you'll feel there.' From the time I went to the shrine and prayed [*du'ā karnā*], I have felt a change in my life.

Suhrawardi Sahib experienced a moment of inconsistency between the principles of Islam and his professional life, but the discord was not between a religious, spiritual orientation and a rational, scientific point of view. Rather, there was a juxtaposition of a traditional, hierarchical assumption about power and influence and the principles of Islam. Suhrawardi Sahib had enacted two fundamental operating principles of the traditional order: (1) one has obligations to one's friends, and (2) seniors have authority over juniors. In this case, Suhrawardi Sahib had been trying to fulfil an obligation to a friend by using his authority as a senior officer to oblige a junior officer to pay prematurely for work not yet completed.

Suhrawardi Sahib described a moment of being brought up short, a moment when he was forced to confront an inconsistency. Though he expressed the inconsistency in terms of a conflict between his identity as a Muslim and his social and professional selves, the principles of Islam, at least in a very general sense, were actually being used to reinforce a principle consistent with a Western model of rational bureaucratic procedures. Suhrawardi Sahib described the social, pragmatic significance of the junior officer's actions: the junior officer had risked arousing his ire, perhaps even putting his career on the line. By creating such a confrontation, the junior risks shaming the senior, because both know that the requested procedures are improper. As Suhrawardi Sahib stated clearly, most young Pakistani men would be incapable of violating hierarchical authority relationships in this way.

Interestingly, the junior officer justified his reactions not by simply saying that it would be improper, illegal, or even against Islam, but rather by saying that his pir-father would be angry—that there is another elder that takes precedence, regardless of social context. Thus, it is not the case that the junior officer was able to stand up to a person in authority because he had embraced an ethic of egalitarian independence and autonomous decision-making, as a Western observer might expect but, rather because he was able to rely on an idealized elder whom he experienced as an absolute authority in all spheres of activity. Suhrawardi Sahib attributed the strength he recognized in the junior man to the spiritual strength of his pir, and this experience in turn stirred up deep-seated expectations and a sense of longing in him.

The examples of the university student and the senior government officer suggest that a reliance on the strategy of achieving some independence of an authority hierarchy and its perceived inadequacies or 'worldly corruption' by idealizing another elder (the pir) is an aspect of intrapsychic organization that is culturally shared. A closer examination of what this idealization involves will allow us to specify some of its intrapsychic components as well as the cultural forms in which it is expressed. Furthermore, correspondences can be demonstrated between specific aspects of this form of idealization and characteristic forms of relationship in the South Asian extended family, suggesting that such idealizations have their roots in early childhood experience.

THE EXPERIENCE OF LONGING AND THE SEARCH FOR A PIR

Many business and professional men described their experience of a state of longing (*shauq*) that characterized their lives before they met their pir. Others were still in that state when I met them. The idea of longing is important in Sufi literature, but it also represents a powerful emotional state for those who reported their experiences to me. It thus points to psychological roots that may be revealed by closely examining the concept and how these men used it.

A state of longing was particularly characteristic of men who had lived for extended periods of time in the West, though it was not limited to them. Several of the professional men who had become or were seeking to become Sufi disciples experienced a particular intensity of longing shortly after a return from a prolonged stay in England or the United States. One man, for instance, had an initiation dream[14] which triggered an intense search for a pir after spending the war years in England, at a time in his life when he seriously had to face the issue of reconciling two very different cultural traditions and orientations to life. The dream intensified his conscious feeling of longing and crystallized his image of the object of his search.

Similarly, I saw an instance of this expression of longing in my first encounter with a psychiatrist who had recently returned after ten years of training and practice in England and was just establishing a private practice in Lahore. In this case, my own narration of a dream triggered a moment of intense, vicarious longing in this professional man, who up to that point in our conversation had been extremely guarded about his own feelings about Sufism and pirs. I had contacted him because I was interested in learning whether he had encountered much involvement with pirs among his Pakistani patients. When he found out that I was studying Sufism and pirs, he declared that there was no relationship between the two and that the system of pirs was a complete fraud, a common complaint among Pakistanis. After expounding on this for several minutes, he asked me if I could tell him which pirs are frauds and which are not. When, in a half-joking manner, I told him about a dream I had had after several meetings with one pir, he listened to my story wide-eyed, to my surprise. Still not sure how to interpret his response, I talked about coincidence and discounted any belief in the story myself, and went on to talk about the followers of that pir who believe similar miracles about him. But the psychiatrist had suddenly become very intent. He asked me if I had asked the pir for any more demonstrations of his spiritual power. I laughed and said 'No'. He replied, 'You should'. He even wanted me to take him to see the pir so that he could determine for himself whether he was a fraud or not. There was a sad longing evident in the psychiatrist's face. Since he had finally communicated his attitude unambiguously, I was then able to ask him if he had met anyone with real spiritual power, and he said, 'No, but I'm looking. I feel a great longing'.

I had encountered this man in his professional identity, which was reinforced by the fact that I had begun by asking him about his patients. Much of the tension that was evident in the early part of our conversation may be attributed to my identity as an American, in conjunction with his extensive contact with Westerners in England, when he had undoubtedly experienced the expectation that he maintain a sharp differentiation between his professional identity and his personal concerns. Aside from this awkwardness, he did not appear to experience any discontinuity between his professional orientation and an interest in Sufism. I found that despite many years of professional life in England, he displayed an intense interest and potential emotional investment in Sufism. He clearly expected to experience an overwhelming emotional reaction when he did finally meet the right pir, elements of which were already present in his reaction to my description of my experience. Descriptions of such states and of the image of the pir who is the object of that longing, are instances of the convergence in an individual of deep-seated intrapsychic issues with culturally patterned expressions of shared understandings that also have social referents and encompass a range of domains of experience.

Is it possible to specify what these men are seeking? There are characteristic ways that Pakistanis use to describe the intensity of longing when one is seeking a pir, as well as the experience of a first encounter with one's true pir. One man described the experience of meeting his pir for the first time in the following terms: 'When I looked at him, I knew that this was my pir. He looked at me and smiled. Then I felt my life start to ebb out of me, starting from my toes. I felt I was going to die.' This man's account followed a typical pattern of restless searching, dissatisfaction, and longing that culminated in an overwhelming emotional reaction when he finally encountered 'his' pir for the first time.

Sufi literature is replete with depictions of the state of longing. Though most expressions of longing are stated in terms of a desire for union with God, devotion to one's Sufi master may be expressed in similar terms, particularly among Persian and South Asian Sufis. As Nasr explains a verse of the Persian Sun poet Tabriz, 'To behold the perfect master is to regain the ecstasy and joy of the spring of life and to be separated from the master is to experience the sorrow of old age.'[15]

The psychiatrist described above raised an issue that was uppermost in the minds of almost every Pakistani I talked with about Sufism and pirs: that of determining whether or not one has found the right pir, or more bluntly, whether the pir is a fraud. Just as the authority relationship between disciple and pir parallels relationships in daily life, concerns about corruption, so prevalent in attitudes about the working world, also pervade expectations about pirs. Shaikh Sharfuddin Maneri, a fifteenth-century Indian Sufi of Bihar, posed and answered this very question: 'It is not meet for a beginner to weigh Divine Men with the balance of his little intellect and to look at them with his limited vision. Nor is it meet to follow another on his mere assertion. Then how to know if such a one is a genuine Teacher or a mere pretender?' He replies: 'There is no sign or mood, the presence or absence of which alone would mark a Teacher or a pretender. In short, one blessed with Divine Grace should set his feet on the Path, turn away from sensual pleasures and passional gratifications, and fix his attention on God. Then the glance of some Perfect Teacher will shine in the mirror of the heart.... When a true disciple catches such a glance, he instantly contacts a love for the Beauty of His Godly Strength, becomes restless and uneasy, and comes to the Path.'[16] Similarly, though the men who told me about their experience of longing and love for a pir often listed a series of characteristics and qualifications of the perfect Sufi pir, the crucial factor in becoming a follower is typically the emotional reaction a disciple experiences toward his pir.

Furthermore, as Nasr, writing about Persian Sufism, has said, 'not every shaykh is a master for every disciple. The disciple must seek and find the master who conquers his soul and dominates him as an eagle or falcon pounces upon a sparrow in the air.'[17] A Pakistani disciple made this point in imagery readily comprehensible to an American: 'When you see someone, a pir who is tuned to the same frequency, the hearts respond—they respond to the vibrations. I visited other pirs, but I already had the image of my sheikh [whom he had not yet found] in my heart, and we didn't "click".'

Many Sufi business and professional men commented that, to find your true pir, you just have to go to different pirs and see what you feel, further confirming that an aspect of the experience of longing that people describe is a search for an overwhelming emotional reaction when meeting a pir for the first time. Aspects of this reaction include the feeling that the pir can see right through you and knows everything about you without any overt verbal communication being necessary, a kind of union between the disciple and his pir.

Though extreme love for the Sufi master and the attempt to become annihilated in him are not unique to South Asian Sufism, Hindu authors studying the phenomenon have equated it with the typical Hindu love for the *guru*.[18] The Pakistani poet, Muhammad Iqbal, was highly critical of the state of union and resulting stagnation that he thought the Indian Muslim typically feels with his pir. Iqbal criticized the spiritual role of the pir in the lives of South Asian Muslims, seeing it as a source of thraldom—a replacement of Muslim democracy with a 'spiritual Aristocracy'.[19] Nevertheless, Iqbal did not deny the importance of spiritual longing. In his philosophy, longing is the highest state the soul can reach. In contrast to the state of union, which results in silence and annihilation, a state of longing stimulates creativity.[20] Iqbal's sensitivity to this phenomenon may have been coloured by what he saw as a particularly South Asian emphasis on union as a positive goal.

What, then, is expected of the relationship between pir and disciple? Maneri, the fifteenth century Bihari Sufi, repeats a familiar Sufi image: 'It is indispensable for a Disciple to put off his desires and protests, and place himself before the Teacher as a dead body before the washer of the dead, so that he may deal with him as he likes.'[21] In other words, the disciple is expected to be passive and unquestioning of his pir. Pakistani disciples struggle with this expectation, as did Iqbal. One professional man, a former accountant who had worked for an American government office in Lahore, discussed his own failure to achieve this passive, accepting state:

> You see, my only fault was that I always tried to analyze what he said. I don't know why. Because you see, I had been a student of science also. I studied; I have a master of sciences, a master of social sciences also. He treated me as his confidential secretary. But I had my shortcomings.[22] I questioned some of his acts. I tried to differ with him. These were my faults.

Though this disciple expressed his inability in terms of a tension between his Sufi and professional orientations, he did not see 'science' as potentially threatening to a Sufi frame of reference, but rather as a device that he, in his weakness, had used to distance himself from his pir. The juxtaposition of science, or rational knowledge, and Sufi insight (gnosis) has always been a popular topic of Sufi poets. This man was thus echoing the perspective of an alleged hadith that calls '*ilm*', the 'greatest veil' separating man from God.

Evidence from Sufi literature suggests that there are a variety of images of longing and of the pir, which thus may also vary considerably in intrapsychic significance. For instance, the relationship between the disciple and pir may be one in which the disciple is considered to be a 'part of' the pir, as 'son is part of the father' or the pir may be thought to nourish him 'with spiritual milk like a mother'.[23]

But certain imagery is distinctive of South Asian Sufism and is not shared by Sufi literature from other areas. The extent to which such distinctive imagery is congruent with characteristic aspects of psychological development within the South Asian family may be particularly suggestive of the extent of overlap between culturally shared understandings and the intrapsychic significance of such imagery for Pakistani Sufi disciples, and may form the basis for hypotheses about aspects of psychological organization that are prominent among Pakistani Sufi disciples.

Specifically, a component of the relationship expected between pir and disciple is suggested by a characteristic of Sindhi and Punjabi poetry that Schimmel argues is typical of Indian Sufi poetry more generally: the longing soul is always depicted as a woman. She suggests that this distinctive feature was directly inherited from Hinduism.[24] The image of the longing soul as a woman and the goal of union with the pir are culturally specified aspects of the meaning of the pir. In conjunction with other imagery that is characteristic of Sufism more generally, the feminine image may be particularly significant in the use of the pir as a personal symbol by Pakistani disciples.

THE INTRAPSYCHIC SIGNIFICANCE OF LONGING FOR UNION WITH THE PIR

It may be useful to summarize the images that are prominent in disciples' descriptions of their expectations concerning a pir before going on to construct a model of how such images may be linked to intrapsychic constellations organized during the course of childhood development. We have identified an experience of intense longing for union with the pir, accompanied by a fear that such a union will be stifling and annihilating. The longing is also thought to be like that of a woman for her lover. Disciples expect to experience an intense, overwhelming emotional reaction to the pir at their first meeting. Typically, the pir has been 'expecting' the disciple, and there is wordless, complete communication and understanding at the moment of that first meeting. The image of the disciple as a corpse in the hands of the washer suggests a passive acceptance of this idealized authority. The pir is thought to nourish the disciple with spiritual milk, like a mother. But the pir is also a father to the disciple, who becomes a 'part' of him.

Though rather diverse with respect to their probable association with specific developmental issues, these images do clearly echo aspects of early childhood experience, some explicitly so. On the one hand, the range of culturally shared imagery provides disciples with options for expressing their personal experiences in ways that most closely reflect their specific intrapsychic conflicts and concerns. On the other hand, when these images are examined as a cluster, they can be used to specify a pattern of idealization that is remarkably consistent with psychoanalytically inspired observations and hypotheses concerning the typical resolution of developmental issues in the South Asian extended family.

Drawing on both cultural and psychoanalytic clinical data, Kakar has developed a model articulating the culturally characteristic ways in which the Indian male resolves developmental issues such as separation-individuation and the resolution of the Oedipus complex. He highlights certain typical defensive strategies and solutions that are strikingly congruent with aspects of the idealization of the pir as evidenced by imagery in Sufi literature and informants' accounts. This cluster of features can thus be explained in terms of a particular developmental sequence.

According to Kakar, in the Indian family, the oedipal boy typically experiences a prolonged narcissistic merger with a mother who is nurturing and closely attuned to his nonverbally expressed needs; yet she is also threatening in her efforts to engulf him because of his importance for satisfying her own needs as a young wife in her husband's extended family.[25] As a way of avoiding annihilation, the son forms a lasting feminine identification with her. We can see possible echoes of this in the Sufi imagery of the longing soul as a woman. In situations of stress, the Indian male is thus liable to a kind of psychological self-castration, leading to a state of passivity congruent with the Sufi idea of 'the corpse in the hands of the washer'. As a way of escaping from merger with the mother and asserting his masculine identity, the son turns to the father in a way that overshadows oedipal competition and rivalry.[26] Kakar associates this path of development with what Fenichel has identified as the 'apprentice complex, a temporary feminine submission to the father in order to prepare oneself for a later masculine competition with him'.[27] The outcome of this course of psychological development is that the growing male experiences a compelling need for merger with powerful authority figures.

The pir represents the nurturing but potentially engulfing mother, with whom union will result in stifling annihilation. The disciple re-experiences the wordless communication of preverbal experience, when the mother was attuned to the child's needs. But the pir is also the father to whom the oedipal son turns as a way of affirming his masculine identity. The disciple becomes a 'part of' this father, another form of merger and submission, with the hope of eventually taking the place of this pir as his successor.

The merger of the personalities of the disciple and the pir is given vivid cultural expression in stories such as the following, which was narrated to me by a disciple who was also a businessman. In this story, the oral-incorporative imagery and the theme of annihilation are explicit:

> When a sheikh is about to die, he may decide to pass on his spirituality to someone. He calls this person, takes his face between his hands, puts his lips on the lips of that person, inserts his tongue into this person's mouth, and embraces him. It happens so quickly—it changes a person completely. All veils are lifted completely and spiritual enlightenment comes. Whatever a sheikh has, this person has it, too. For example, my *dādā murshid* had a disciple, not a learned person, but a man who served him faithfully, giving him his hookah, getting groceries, sweeping the floor. He served with the utmost devotion for several years. One day the *murshid* was in a kind mood and promised to pray

to God to give him anything he wanted.... The disciple asked, 'Honoured master, make me like yourself.' When he said that, an expression of sorrow flitted across the murshid's face, and he said, 'Don't ask me for this.' But the disciple held him to his promise, so they went alone into a room. My murshid and *pīr-bhā'īs* waited outside for fifteen minutes. Suddenly the door opened. We thought that our sheikh was standing in the doorway, but we looked closely and found that it was the disciple'. But there was a radiance about him he looked like our sheikh.... He stepped across the threshold, and then he heaved one long sigh and fell dead. We ran to pick him up, but he was dead.... The sheikh said, 'I tried to dissuade him. I told him he wasn't ready for it. But he wouldn't listen, so I put myself into him, and he couldn't bear it.' This is what happens; this is how a transfer takes place. So before he transfers this spirituality, the pir prepares the person for it.

This story suggests that for the Pakistani male the route to maturity is perceived to be through the incorporation of the power and authority of the male elder. Once this internalization is firmly established, he is able to act with authority himself.

DISCUSSION

Many Pakistani business and professional men display a tendency to seek an intense attachment with an authority figure in the form of a pir. Though I have not included extensive clinical and developmental data on the intrapsychic constellations of the specific individuals discussed above, their strategies for handling conflicts in the workplace suggest that the developmental model described is applicable and helps to explain their actions and concerns. Their accounts of themselves demonstrate a capacity to draw upon the relationship with the pir in order to resolve conflicts in the workplace between traditional authority relationships and the principles of bureaucratic organization. The disciple becomes more independent of an existing authority structure by relying on his image of the pir as an alternative source of authority. As the disciple matures, he internalizes this image, until he reaches a point when he himself is endowed with power and authority.

Many Pakistani men are able to operate in a business and professional world which is infused with Western values and language, while simultaneously maintaining public reputations to Sufis. Given the widespread acceptance of Sufism and pir–disciple relationships in the Pakistani business and professional worlds, such an identity as a Sufi need not create any major disjunctures in the life of a new disciple. Instead, it may solidify social ties with office associates and other friends who share an interest in a particular pir or in Sufism more generally. Furthermore, this network creates the potential for role relationships that are not solely dependent on hierarchical organized seniority relationships.

The specific teachings of the pir which the disciple carries with him into his professional world are themselves typically consistent with the principles of decision-making that characterize institutions based on professional competence and the goals of innovation and productivity. These teachings typically stress such principles as the equality of all men and the evils of corruption. The outcome may even include phenomena such as 'whistle-blowing' which superficially resemble manifestations of what Americans consider to be the virtues of autonomy and independence. But for the Pakistani professional, the intrapsychic underpinnings of such phenomena are likely to be fundamentally different from those of his Western counterparts. Psychoanalytic techniques and concepts provide a way of identifying the strategies individuals actually use to integrate their diverse experiences, and thus are an important avenue of research for understanding Muslim perceptions of their participation in educational, economic, and professional activities, as well as in Sufism. Such perceptions have implications for the evolving role of the Muslim world in a global society.

GLOSSARY

pirs	saints
Urs	death anniversary festival
Suhrawardi	a member of one of the four major Sufi orders in South Asia
sajjāda nishin	successor; descendents of the Sufi pirs entombed at many of the major shrines in the area
WAPDA	Water and Power Development Authority
ilm	knowledge
dādā murshid	literally, 'grandfather teacher,' i.e., the pir of one's pir
pīr-bhā'īs	literally 'pir-brothers,' disciples of the same pir

NOTES

1. Sayyid Abul A'la Maududi, *A Short History of the Revivalist Movement in Islam,* trans. Al Ash'ari (Lahore: Islamic Publications, 1963), p. 106.
2. Pakistan, *Population Census: The Lahore District Census Report,* Part I (Karachi: Government of Pakistan, 1961), p. 22.

3. With respect to Sufism in Pakistan, such an impression was reinforced by the observation that many young hereditary *sajjāda nishins* have gone into occupations such as engineering or medicine. Many sajjāda nishins have also become actively involved in politics, but this may best be seen as a continuation of one of the traditional activities of pirs in a modern political setting rather than an abandonment of the traditional role of pir.
4. Frequently, a man may first visit a pir at the suggestion of an office associate or professional acquaintance. This professional friend may accompany him on his visits to the pir or shrine. As a result, a pir may develop a wide following of people from the same office. A justice of the Lahore High Court, for instance, persuaded several of his colleagues to become followers of a pir who had established a Sufi centre in a rural area near Lyallpur (see Katherine P. Ewing, 'The Politics of Sufism: Redefining the Saints of Pakistan,' *Journal of Asian Studies* 42 [1983], pp. 251–265). These judges also frequently travelled together to the annual celebration ('urs) at major shrines, becoming involved in ritual activities and meditation together at the shrine.
5. Compare Singer's discussion of Hindu strategies for managing the relationship between ritual and the industrial workplace in the context of a consideration of modernization and secularization. See Milton Singer, *When a Great Tradition Modernizes* (New York: Praeger Publishers, 1972), pp. 320–331.
6. Data for this chapter were collected during the course of fieldwork in Lahore, Pakistan, during 1975–77 and in 1984–85. Research was funded by grants from the American Institute of Pakistan Studies.
7. See Gannanath Obeyesekere, *Medusa's Hair: An Essay on Personal Symbols and Religious Experience* (Chicago: University of Chicago Press, 1981). My use of the term is not identical with Obeyesekere's. I do not distinguish personal and psychogenetic symbols, though I agree with his point that what may look like a particular type of psychological symbol to a psychoanalyst may not have that meaning for any particular individual. This is true, I argue, of any symbol.
8. Spiro maintains that this type of cultural data can be used to make inferences about intrapsychic, unconscious structures. I would agree that, though this type of data is valuable for hypothesizing about psychological organization, specific data about individuals, gathered using methods such as psychoanalytic interviewing, are necessary to test such hypotheses. Frequently, similar affective and symbolic expressions may have very different psychological roots. See Melford Spiro, *Oedipus in the Trobriands* (Chicago: University of Chicago Press, 1982).
9. For example, Sudhir Kakar, *The Inner World: A Psychoanalytical Study of Childhood and Society in India* (2nd ed., Delhi: Oxford University Press, 1981); Alan Roland, 'Toward a Psychoanalytical Psychology of Hierarchical Relationships in Hindu India,' Ethos 10 (1982), pp. 232–253; Carol Prindle, 'Occupation and Orthopraxy in Bengali Muslim Rank,' in *Shari'at and Ambiguity in South Asian Islam*, ed. Katherine P. Ewing (Berkley: University of Chicago Press, 1988).
10. Kakar, *The Inner World*, p. 120.
11. See Peter Hardy, *The Muslims of British India* (Cambridge: Cambridge University Press, 1972).
12. For example, Shaikh Sharfuddin Maneri, *Letters from a Sufi Teacher,* trans. Baijnath Singh (New York: Sameul Weiser, 1974).
13. Transference may be defined as 'the displacement of patterns of feelings and behaviour, originally experienced with significant figures of one's childhood, to individuals in one's current relationships' (Burness E. Moore and Bernard D. Fine,

A Glossary of Psychoanalytic Terms and Concepts [New York: The American Psychoanalytic Association, 1967], p. 89). Moore and Fine distinguish intra-analytic and extra-analytic transference, the latter potentially developing in any relationship between human beings. I am using the concept of transference in this most general sense.

14. See Katherine P. Ewing, 'The Dream of Spiritual Initiation: and the Organization of Self Representations among Pakistani Sufis,' *American Ethnologist* 17, p. 60.
15. Seyyed Hossain Nasr, *Sufi Essays* (New York, 1972; reprint ed., New York: Schocken Books, 1977)
16. Maneri, *Letters from a Sufi Teacher*, pp. 13–14.
17. Nasr, *Sufi Essays*, p. 61.
18. Annemarie Schimmel, *Mystical Dimensions of Islam* (Chapel Hill: University of North Carolina Press, 1975), p. 387.
19. Muhammad Iqbal, 'Islam and Mysticism,' in *Thoughts and Reflections of Iqbal*, ed. Syed Abdul Vahid (Lahore: Sh. Muhammad Ashraf, 1964), p. 82.
20. Schimmel, *Mystical dimensions of Islam*, p. 307.
21. Maneri, *Letters from a Sufi Teacher*, p. 38
22. Schimmel, *Mystical Dimensions of Islam,* p. 140.
23. Ibid., p. 103.
24. Ibid., pp. 389, 434
25. Kakar, *The Inner World*, p. 89.
26. Ibid., pp 109, 131.
27. Otto Fenichel, *The Psychoanalytic Theory of Neurosis* (New York: W.W. Norton, 1954), p. 89.

CHAPTER 3

Islamic Influences on Socio-legal Conditions of Pakistani Women[1]

ANITA M. WEISS

The very concept 'women's rights' elicits disparate, conflicting images in contemporary Pakistan. What constitutes women's rights, who is to define what these rights are, and where responsibility lies for ensuring these rights is hotly discussed in Pakistan, though rarely actually debated. The various contending viewpoints hardly recognize other perspectives as even existing, let alone legitimate enough to debate. Where these issues are being debated is *within* each larger viewpoint either to convince sympathetic contestants of one's stance or, less often, to find common ground within a given perspective. The state, virtually by default so as to keep the varying camps at bay, has undertaken the difficult task to construct culturally appropriate definitions of women's rights as well as culturally acceptable mechanisms to implement them.

Indeed, the effort to find and articulate culturally appropriate definitions of women's rights is not just an issue in Pakistan but is a contentious one worldwide. While we must be wary of essentializing Muslim women and hence, their human rights challenges, in Pakistan, as in much of the Muslim world, culture and religion are inextricably intertwined and both Islamic laws and codified traditions play powerful roles in how Muslim states govern themselves and define their jurisdictions. A critical question in a social environment such as Pakistan's is that while what is acceptable within Islam—especially pertaining to women and their rights—may not be acceptable within prevailing cultural constructs, which arena will 'win out' as the defining social construct and be acceptable to all? The process of responding to this question, replete with its own contradictions, is still evolving.

It would be easy to assign rudimentary labels to the three principal sentiments—Islamist, secular/progressive and traditional—and then discuss the vision each holds of women's rights in contemporary Pakistan. Easy, but grossly inaccurate. To initiate the discourse on women's rights in Pakistan as seen from the vantage points of three distinct viewpoints would be to slip into the temptation to essentialize them into monolithic groupings. The enormous degree of diversity within each of these camps forces us to question the utility of using such kinds of categories at all. The way in which the state has interacted with the first two groups, in some cases appropriating their philosophy and language for its own ends, has also contributed to fissures within them. In addition, as culture and religion have become inextricably intertwined in many areas of Pakistan, there exists substantial confusion over where the lines are drawn between what is Islamic, what is codified tradition, and how (if at all) to delineate their separate jurisdictions. We have seen in the past few months, for example, members of the Sipah-e-Sahaba, the Jama'at-i-Islami and of many *madrassahs* experience their identity as Muslims as inseparable from other component parts of their culture, and often confuse those things that are not in accordance with cultural norms, values or practices as being in contradiction with Islam. Alternatively, various women's rights groups such as AGHS, the Aurat Foundation, Bedari, Pattan, Shirkat Gah and Simorgh, engaged in activist research addressing such themes as the rise in domestic violence, female education, and women's political participation, question Islam's jurisdictional space in the contemporary political sphere and whether women's rights need necessarily be limited at all by Islamic injunctions.

There are two principle reasons why the question of women's rights has become an important issue today in the Muslim world, and particularly in Pakistan. The first is that the engendering of Muslim civil society is raising profound questions regarding women's social roles and essential human rights in the public arena of their societies. Concurrently, greater pressure exists within the international arena for asserting women's human rights at the level of states becoming parties to international human rights treaties. Development assistance—aid—is often tied to human rights records, and both donors and Western governments shy away from supporting those states which global popular culture condemns in their treatment of women and their treading on their human rights. The 'Report of the Commission of Inquiry for Women in Pakistan', released in August 1997 (p. xi), clarifies what these pressures are:

> No community or nation is an island anymore, and Pakistan cannot remain unwashed by the rising global currents. It needs to address its domestic issues

in ways that are in some harmony with the international perspective and universally accepted norms. If it does not do it now, it will be compelled to do it later, after much damage.

How the state has endeavoured to articulate a definition of women's rights becomes even more compelling when we consider this prevailing social climate, particularly as the state has set the discourse within an Islamic framework. This chapter, therefore, focuses on the Pakistani state's efforts to create an understanding of what constitutes women's rights in this Islamic context, the ongoing and at times contentious debate to define those rights, and what the state is proposing to do to ensure them. These actions underscore the state's professed commitment to improve the status, condition and circumstances of women as well as the persistent challenges to creating a popular, legitimate vision of women's rights in Pakistan.

While many Muslim states have voiced concerns that certain elements of some of the global human rights treaties are contradictory to Islamic tenets, they have also acknowledged that most are not. The most important of these international human rights treaties regarding women today is CEDAW, the Convention on the Elimination of All Forms of Discrimination against Women. Twenty of the thirty-two Muslim states which are UN members have ratified CEDAW thus far; Pakistan did so in March 1996. I will turn, towards the end of this chapter, to the example of Pakistan's efforts to implement CEDAW as a means by which we can see how the state and local civil society groups are grappling with clarifying the domains of what constitutes women's human rights, and the dilemmas the state then faces in securing these rights. While Pakistan has sought to clarify or adapt its national laws, planning processes and related institutions to conform to CEDAW's requirements, it has also sought to clarify arenas where it cannot conform. What is emerging are abundant views and opinions on Islam and its conceptions of women's human rights. I.A. Rehman, chairperson of the Human Rights Commission of Pakistan, once said to me that 'there is no Islamic discourse in the country.' While I have found such markedly different views in Pakistan on the issue—and vision—of women's rights, the process of articulating what this vision is has not undergone any kind of internal debate although the government of Pakistan has ratified CEDAW. Now, due to these external pressures, it is searching for a workable way of enforcing the Convention.

THE INWARD-LOOKING STATE: ISLAMIC INFLUENCE ON LAWS AFFECTING WOMEN'S RIGHTS

What happens at the level of the state, whether domestically or in its international negotiations, is little known nor understood by most women within the country. They are instead bound by traditional views on and customary practices towards women, most of which are commonly perceived as being derived from Islamic norms. In most instances and under most circumstances, any effort by a woman to transgress these boundaries may well result in her death. In that event, it is unlikely her murderer (or murderers) will be arrested or convicted, for honour killings remain culturally sanctioned, albeit they are not officially nor legally sanctioned.

An event in Lahore in 1999 highlights women's greatest fears in asserting their legitimate rights. A 29-year old woman from Peshawar, Samia Sarwar, contacted a lawyer in late March 1999 and asked for assistance in divorcing her husband of ten years. Women in Pakistan are entitled to the right of divorce under Hanafi interpretations of *shariah*. She alleged that she had been physically abused and tortured by her addict husband, her maternal aunt's son. Four years earlier, she had moved into her parents' home after her husband had thrown her down some stairs when she was pregnant with her second child. Her parents, however, refused to help her get a divorce, citing that to do so would bring dishonour to her and her family. She finally fled to Lahore and moved into DASTAK, a shelter set up by the law firm, AGHS, to aid victims of domestic violence. She did not want to meet anyone from her family as she feared for her life. But her family countered her claims and said that they wanted to avoid a court case, and her mother agreed to meet with her, alone, in the safety of the lawyer's office. Though the 6 April meeting at AGHS's office was to be attended solely by Samia and her mother, Samia's paternal uncle and another man (later identified as Habibur Rehman, a driver) arrived with her mother. When Hina Jilani, Samia's lawyer, tried to get them to leave, the driver pulled out a gun, shot Samia through the temple and nearly killed her lawyer as well. Despite the efforts of local human rights activists, it remains questionable if Samia's killers and abettors will ever be penalized. On the contrary, her family is claiming the murder was justified as it is a tribal custom, what is characterized as an 'honour killing,' and that instead lawyers who take up such cases should 'be hanged as they are showing Pakistani women a Western path.' Notwithstanding this statement, murdering a woman because she is seeking a divorce is indeed against Pakistani civil law and Islamic shariah.

In Pakistan, judicial decisions concerning Islam are based, by and large, on Hanafi interpretations, though on occasion the state has turned to decisions based on other schools of *fiqh* as well. The Muslim Personal Law of Shariat (1948), passed a year after the country gained its independence from Britain, recognized a woman's right to inherit all forms of property, consistent with local interpretations of women's rights in Islam but not consistent with common, local practices. This was followed by a futile attempt to have the government include a Charter of Women's Rights in the 1956 Constitution. Considered amongst the most socially progressive legislation Pakistan has ever passed, the 1961 Muslim Family Laws Ordinance transformed the institution of marriage by requiring the registration of all marriages, the written permission of a man's wife (or wives) before an arbitration council decides if he may marry again, the abolition of divorce by repudiation (*talaq*), and instituted other safeguards for women in the event of a divorce. Twelve years later, the 1973 Constitution further advanced women's legal rights in the country.

Pakistan's constitutional framework is not consistent on women's rights. The 1973 Constitution further advanced women's legal rights in the country on a number of fronts. In the section on Fundamental Rights and Principles, Article 3 affirms that the state is committed to eliminating exploitation and to guarantee 'the gradual fulfilment of the fundamental principle, from each according to his ability, to each according to his work'.[2] Article 8 (1), the first in the Chapter on Fundamental Rights, states:

> Any law, or any custom or usage having the force of law, in so far as it is inconsistent with the rights conferred by this Chapter, shall, to the extent of such inconsistency, be void.[3]

Article 25 (1) guarantees that all citizens are equal under the law and are entitled to equal protection of law; Article 25 (2) adds 'There shall be no discrimination on the basis of sex alone.' Article 27 prohibits discrimination on the basis of sex, race, religion or caste for government employment. Finally, in the Principles of Policy section, Article 34 states that 'steps shall be taken to ensure full participation of women in all spheres of national life;' and Article 38(a) adds that it is the responsibility of the state to 'secure the well-being of the people, irrespective of sex, caste, creed or race, by raising their standard of living.'

However, when most people think of the issue of women's rights in Pakistan, they think of the controversy surrounding General Ziaul Haq's 1979 Islamisation programme, of the Hudood Ordinances and the Law of Evidence (*Qanoon-e-Shahadat*). The resultant Islamisation programme, particularly the Hudood Ordinances, that was initiated by the government in 1979 has been highly controversial.[4] In particular, the Zina Ordinance does not make a legal distinction between adultery (*zina*) and rape (*zina-bil-jabr*). Its enforcement has been discriminatory: a man must actually be observed committing *zina* to be convicted, while a woman can also be convicted if she becomes pregnant (i.e., pregnancy is allowable as admissible evidence). Four years later, Zia's government promulgated the highly debatable Qanoon-e-Shahadat (Law of Evidence). This disallowed women from testifying in certain kinds of *hudood* cases at all and caused their testimony in other matters to become irrelevant unless corroborated by another woman. While Pakistani case law has since held this up only in matters pertaining to economic transactions, the resultant effect, however, is discriminatory towards women as they are not equal economic actors with men in the eyes of the law.

In 1984, various groups launched a campaign against the proposed Qisas and Diyat Ordinance. If the interpretation being promoted at the time had passed, this ordinance would have promoted even greater inequity in the value placed on women as the amount of compensation given to a female victim or a female victim's family for effecting injury or death by the perpetrator of a crime would have been about half than if the victim were a male. The bill, finally passed into law in 1990, just over a year after democracy had returned to Pakistan, did not include the gender-discriminatory clause.

Casual observers of Pakistan might, however, also be aware of the establishment of the Women's Division, also in 1979; of the efforts of its successor, the Ministry for Women's Development, in preparing Pakistan's National Report for the 1995 Beijing conference; and its follow-up project to implement the promises made in Beijing, the 'National Plan of Action', issued in 1998.

When Pakistan was preparing its National Report in 1994, the Senate decided to establish a 'high-powered commission' to review the country's laws as 'a step toward ending the grosser iniquities against women.' The resultant 'Report of the Commission of Inquiry for Women' states that

> There is a widespread misconception about the place Islam accords to women, which is not just a distortion spread in the West but it exists even among the

intelligentsia in the Muslim World, including Pakistan. It is believed that Islam relegates women to an inferior status; it confines them inside the four walls of their homes; and it restrains them from taking up employment outside their homes or running their own business. This is wholly contrary to fact. Muslim scholars are agreed that Islam accords women virtually the whole gamut of rights, including the rights to property, to work and wages, to choice of spouse, to divorce if marriage does not prosper, to education and to participation in economic, social and political activity. These are guaranteed to Muslim women by Shariat.[5]

It continues by noting that many of the derogatory laws and customs in Pakistan are, unfortunately,

justified in the name of Islam or have been introduced as Islamic laws when clearly they are retrograde customs and traditions, or ill-informed interpretations that bear no relation to the divine design. This distinction has to be clarified once and for all. Ambiguity allows obscurantist elements to re-open debate on settled fundamental principles, and gives rise to insecurity among women within Pakistan and to an extremely adverse image abroad.[6]

Pakistan's efforts to integrate women's rights issues into the national planning structure began with the Seventh Five-Year Plan (1988–93) as part of the PPP's efforts to design cross-cutting social initiatives. In the Eighth Plan (1993–98), the succeeding PML (Pakistan Muslim League) government enlisted representatives from women's groups for feedback on a range of important areas affecting women, resulting in a Plan that ostensibly supported rural democratization, community development, and targeting affirmative action for women while working in tandem with the short-lived Social Action Programme. The Ninth (1998–2003) and Tenth (2001–04) Plans go even further in addressing social conditions—and particularly the conditions of women—though we must remember that scant resources have been dedicated in the past to implementing similar proposals, hence reflecting their lower priority.

With the dissolution of extended families concomitant with high rates of inflation, more and more urban women are engaged in working for remuneration, although only 28 per cent of Pakistani women are counted as part of the formal labour force (World Bank 2001: 279). Amartya Sen (1999: 3) would argue that these economic challenges are part of the process of expanding real freedoms for both men and women, requiring the elimination of 'major sources of unfreedom including poor economic opportunities' for women. In Pakistan, however, this has not necessarily been the case, for despite prevailing arduous economic conditions, restrictions on women's mobility have resulted in highly limited ways for a woman to earn an income and still retain her *izzat* and *sharafat* within her family and local community. In addition, concerns over traditional notions of propriety still often prevent women and their families from admitting that women are working and that a family is living off the labour of its women.[7] Such restrictions often force women to seek employment in the informal sector where working conditions are unregulated and income far lower than in the formal sector of the economy. Indeed, there remains a great deal of confusion regarding the work which women actually do. On the basis of the predominant fiction that most women do not labour outside of their domestic chores, past governments have been hesitant to adopt deliberate policies increasing women's employment options and to provide for legal support for women's labour force participation.

Culturally sanctioned violence against women is pervasive in Pakistan, and the implicit threat of gender-based violence is particularly acute within the household in the form of domestic violence. However, domestic violence is seen as a private matter and therefore beyond the concern of the public spheres of policy making and legislation. Laws enforced during Ziaul Haq's Islamisation programme exacerbate prevailing culturally sanctioned violence. Marital rape is not a punishable crime under Pakistani law at this time. Due to the tendency to censure the victims of domestic abuse, women are often reluctant to discuss violent acts of abuse. Indeed, in Pakistan today, a woman who claims to be a victim of rape but is unable to prove it can be charged with adultery (*zina*) and imprisoned. A common fear among women is that if they flee from their homes (as victims of abuse), they may be charged with *zina*. Additionally, they fear they will be separated from their children who, by law, are to be remanded to a father's custody under most circumstances, another reminder of their sense of powerlessness. The law has been subsequently amended but not to the extent of alleviating the concern of women.

Violence against women within their homes is an extension of the subordination of women in the larger society, reinforced by religious beliefs, cultural norms, traditional practices, and—as seen in the example of allegations of adultery—actual laws. It is likely exacerbated by changing roles and expectations which men and women are experiencing along with the social expectation held by men that they exert control over the actions of 'their women'. The cultural structure of the family not only places women in a subordinate role, but also fosters gender-based violence and coercion. The prevailing family structure—particularly prevalent in Pakistan where a new bride moves into her husband's home with all his relatives—coupled with perceptions of women's dependent roles within the family and in society, create an atmosphere conducive to violence against women.

Population planning, growing numbers of educated women, and the nuclearisation of previously extended families have brought about important changes in the family as an institution in Pakistan. While the family still plays an essential role, its nature is rapidly changing as Pakistan moves from a culture based largely on ascription to one based more on achievement. Men's power within the family, once absolute in its control over women's mobility, is declining. Many women feel they can no longer rely on the men of their family as securely as they had in the past. They have seen men abandon their wives, go abroad to work leaving the wife virtually on her own, and increased drug addiction among men. Many feel that the education and work opportunities now available to women can help them take a tentative step towards independence. However, when a woman becomes the primary economic support of her household, while she gains a stronger voice in influencing important family events, by no means does she become an independent agent. In nearly all instances, she must still ultimately defer to men either from her natal family or her in-laws when faced with major decisions, such as arranging marriages for her children.[8]

Importantly, negotiations of gendered power within families do not consistently result in spiralling domestic violence. An alternative result is the family encouraging a girl's empowerment, the path towards which is seen to be the acquisition of a good education. The lack of others physically present within a household leaves open the heightened possibility of escalated domestic violence. Increasingly, however, the absence of close extended family members coupled with the rise of female primary education is resulting in a significant shift to school friends becoming a replacement support system. However, while a school friend may have become a fictive kin for a woman, the friend cannot wield the same degree of influence over a woman's husband that a member of his extended family can. There is no longer any viable social control over men's attempts to subdue their wives by the use of physical (and/or psychological) force. Often, this fear of domestic violence has replaced the former willing acquiescence by women to male and familial control.

Indeed, *family* control over female mobility has lessened significantly, particularly in urban areas. Power issues between spouses are constantly being renegotiated: in many cases, women have indeed gained power by now having the right to make some of their own choices. In other cases—whose ranks are steadily shrinking—rigid tradition-based restrictions still apply to women. But in seemingly more and more instances, an ambiguity is now prevailing where before there was more clarity. Ambiguity, however, can be empowering in the family, especially if it means that it is a move away from a previous rigid conformity to norms.

While laws can do little to mitigate disputes over gender roles within the family, legal reforms can create the potential for a more open, adaptive society. Today, there are a number of efforts underway to change laws that will affect women's rights. These include attempts to refine the National Plan of Action (NPA), develop microcredit plans and enhance the Khushal Bank's scope, place greater importance on the mandate and work of the National Commission on the Status of Women, articulate and institutionalize a National Policy on Women, implement the UN Convention on the Elimination of all forms of Discrimination Against Women (CEDAW), and finalize Pakistan's CEDAW report. Indeed, the current Plan states that the 'Enhancement of the status of women is essential not only on grounds of equity and human rights *but also to meet the goal of sustained growth, human resource development and poverty alleviation*' [emphasis mine].[9]

THE OUTWARD-LOOKING STATE: UNITED NATIONS' HUMAN RIGHTS INSTRUMENTS

Pakistan has become a State Party to a number of gender-focused UN human rights instruments, beginning with its endorsement of the 1953 Convention on the Political Rights of Women. However, instead of ratifying the Convention on the Consent to Marriage, Minimum Age for Marriage and Registration of Marriage, the state promulgated the 1961 Muslim Family Laws Ordinance. While it doesn't go as far as the UN Convention in empowering women in the context of marriage, it does provide additional economic and legal protection to women in its regulation of divorce and restraint of polygamy. Pakistan then became a State Party to the UN Convention on the Rights of the Child in 1990, the 1993 Vienna Declaration 'which recognized women's rights as human rights' (*Report*, p. xi), the 1994 Cairo Population and Development conference's Programme of Action, and the 1995 'Platform for Action' in Beijing.

Government officials often invoke Article 227 of the Constitution to explain why Pakistan has not acceded to the two major human rights accords—the International Covenant on Civil and Political Rights and the International Covenant on Economic, Social and Cultural Rights (both adopted by the UN in December 1966)—as it states,

> All existing laws shall be brought in conformity with the Injunctions of Islam as laid down in the Holy Quran and Sunnah...and no law shall be enacted which is repugnant to such Injunctions. (National Assembly of Pakistan 1993: 137)[10]

The interpretation, at least in the past, was that at least some of the components of the human rights covenants were incompatible with Islamic law. However, officials in the Ministry of Foreign Affairs told me that the government of Pakistan is revisiting its prior stance on these covenants as some other Muslim states, including Egypt, Morocco, and Tunisia, have acceded to them.

When the 1993 United Nations' Conference on Human Rights in Vienna declared that women's rights were unequivocal human rights, Pakistan was at the forefront of the Muslim states which declared that this should be judged on the basis of equity, not equality. The following year, discussions at the UNDP Population and Development Conference in Cairo connected the question of engendered human rights with women's participation in family planning decisions. However, the contradictory stance of Benazir Bhutto, then prime minister of Pakistan, at the Cairo conference is a cogent example of the contradictions confronting Pakistan on changing notions of gendered ethics and human rights. In particular, it reveals the dilemma the state faces when it, on the one hand, wants to portray itself on the global stage as an important, innovative contender while, on the other hand, it must also be attentive to how its international positions are understood by local political constituencies and employees within the state's own bureaucracies. We must remember, too, how divided those local visions of women's rights are within Pakistan.

At the urging of many local groups and international donor agencies, the PPP government decided it would send a strong delegation to the Cairo Population and Development conference. When Benazir decided that she would personally participate, she came under attack by Islamist opposition leaders in Pakistan for attending the conference at all and giving credibility to what, they argued, was an anti-Muslim event. A key theme which emerged at the Cairo conference was that the single-most viable method to contain population growth rates was to raise the status of women, which resonated with stances which had been central to the PPP's own election platforms for some time. However, in the speech Benazir gave in Cairo, she instead emphasized Islamic tenets and asserted Islam's opposition to abortion on the basis that Allah has promised to provide for however many children are born in the world. Her government claimed that Bhutto's participation facilitated reshaping the discourse to include 'the religious and ethical values and standards of member states' to bring about important amendments in the suggested Programme of Action, paving the way for its final adoption by the Conference.[11]

This stance indeed gave her heightened credibility and popularity amongst certain groups in Pakistan, particularly those which had not been in favour of the prime minister even attending the conference. However, it alienated others, especially many women who were otherwise more inclined to support the PPP's more liberal stance on social issues than the opposition's.

Benazir was elected to chair the meeting of Muslim Women Parliamentarians held in Islamabad in August 1995. In front of 120 women delegates from 35 Muslim countries, she inaugurated the meeting by declaring that,

> Many of us face challenges from obscurantist groups, which declare that women should not leave their home. Such views are a direct contradiction to the message of liberation contained in Islam.[12]

The resultant document, the Islamabad Declaration, called on Muslim states to abolish discriminatory legislation and help women combat illiteracy, deprivation, bias and violence. It pledged to promote and protect human rights of women 'at all stages of their life cycle in the true spirit of Islam,' to strive to eradicate illiteracy in Islamic societies, and to work for laws supportive of women's positive role and rights in society. The final statement in the Islamabad Declaration upheld Islam as a religion of tolerance and blamed widespread discrimination against women on archaic traditions and ignorance.

Perhaps buoyed by the widespread support from the Muslim women parliamentarians at the Islamabad conference, Benazir took a more activist, progressive stance at the UN Fourth World Conference for

Women in Beijing than she had taken in Cairo a year earlier. She began her Beijing speech by declaring:

> There is a moral crisis engulfing the world as we speak, a crisis of injustice and inaction, a crisis of silence and acquiescence. The crisis is caused by centuries and generations of oppression and repression. This conference, therefore, transcends politics and economics. We are dealing with a fundamental moral issue.[13]

She declared that Muslim women have a special responsibility to help distinguish between actual Islamic teachings and what may popularly be assumed to be Islamic but are instead social taboos spun by the traditions of a patriarchal society. She continued by vowing to prioritize educating women and getting them jobs, though acknowledging that not all Muslim leaders agreed with her position:

> The holding of this conference makes us determined to contribute each in our own way, in any manner we can, to lessen the oppression, repression and discrimination against women.... As women, we draw satisfaction from the Beijing Platform for Action which encompasses a comprehensive approach towards the empowerment of women.... Today in this world, in the fight for the liberation of women, there can be no neutrality.[14]

She declared that Pakistan would do all it could to promote the empowerment of its women. Besides becoming a signatory to the 'Platform for Action' which emerged from that meeting, she vowed to ratify CEDAW, which finally occurred the following spring.

PAKISTAN'S EFFORTS AT IMPLEMENTING CEDAW

CEDAW was introduced as part of the United Nations' global efforts to empower the world's women. It builds on former international agreements, treaties and instruments and is clearly rooted in the spirit of the United Nations' Charter, as the Preamble of the Convention states that it 'reaffirms faith in fundamental human rights, in the dignity and worth of the human person and in the equal rights of men and women.' CEDAW's essence is summarized in Article 3 of the Convention:

> State parties shall take in all fields, in particular in the political, social, economic and cultural fields, all appropriate measures, including legislation, to ensure the full development and advancement of women, for the purpose

of guaranteeing them the exercise and enjoyment of human rights and fundamental freedoms on a basis of equality with men.

It is important to remember that CEDAW is unique in a variety of ways, both in the requirement to submit periodic reports that indicate the measures that a state has adopted to give effect to the provisions of the Convention, and that while CEDAW permits ratification subject to reservation—a formal declaration that the State does not accept as binding on it specific treaty provisions—this is meant to be a temporary measure so that States can take steps to remove obstacles to the implementation of the articles it has reserved. CEDAW's unique clause is Article 28 (2), which precludes any reservation which is incompatible with the Convention's object and purpose, especially its three fundamental principles of Equality, Non-discrimination, and State Obligation. On the latter principle, State Obligation, States Parties are not only obligated to bring their domestic law in line with the Convention but also to ensure the practical realization of rights by undertaking extra measures to implement 'enabling conditions' so that women's capacity to access the opportunities provided is enhanced. In the reports—to be submitted within one year of accession or ratification and thereafter every four years or when the Committee requests—States Parties must indicate the measures they have adopted to give effect to the provisions of the Convention.

Ann Mayer (1991) has shown how Muslim states, among others, ratify UN conventions, but they also register numerous reservations based on their adherence to 'higher laws' that, they claim, 'the international community is powerless to change.' She contends that the goal is to convince the global community that their reservations are compatible with women's equality. But having so many reservations, such as we can see when States signed onto the Vienna Human Rights Convention or the Beijing 'Platform for Action', the original strength and potency of an instrument becomes watered down. CEDAW's own requirements, therefore, are geared to preclude this from occurring.

At issue, in particular, within the Muslim world is the concept of *equality* versus the concept of *equity*. *Equality* is often raised as being a uniquely Western concept. The goals of struggles for gender *equity* are argued to be equitable distribution of power, resources, access and the like. It includes a recognition that peoples and cultures *do* differ from one another, generally *have* some sort of gender-based division of labour but that neither men nor women should enjoy privileges and power denied to the other; that neither men nor women are unduly *valued* over the other; and that each occupies important spaces in their given societies. An example can saliently illuminate this point. A controversial issue that emerged at the 1993 Vienna Human Rights conference was that of inheritance. Americans and most Western European delegates wanted the resolution to state the equal inheritance of sons and daughters. Representatives from predominantly Muslim areas argued that in their societies, there were other social support mechanisms built in, especially within the extended family, that provided benefits that could not be measured in terms of land or capital. Dr Anis Ahmed, Director of the Daw'ah Academy at the International Islamic University in Islamabad, expressed to me that he differentiates between equity and equality in that he sees equity as taking a qualitative approach, equality taking a quantitative one, regarding the needs, requirements and roles of women and men in society. This issue of *equitable* versus *equal* remains under contestation in Pakistan's CEDAW report.[15]

Pakistan became a State Party to CEDAW, the Convention on the Elimination of All Forms of Discrimination against Women, in March 1996, eight months before the PPP government was dismissed by the then President of Pakistan, Farooq Leghari. Many people within and outside of Pakistan are often surprised when they hear that Pakistan has acceded to CEDAW. Why not? It had become a State Party to a number of gender-focused UN human rights instruments as far back as the 1953 Convention on the Political Rights of Women. However, instead of ratifying the Convention on the Consent to Marriage, Minimum Age for Marriage and Registration of Marriage, it promulgated the 1961 Muslim Family Laws Ordinance. While it doesn't go as far as the UN convention in regulating marriage, it does provide economic and legal protection to women by regulating divorce and restraining polygamy.

Pakistan became a State Party to the UN Convention on the Rights of the Child in 1990, the 1993 Vienna Declaration 'which recognized women's rights as human rights,' the 1994 Cairo Population and Development conference's Programme of Action, and the 1995 'Platform for Action' in Beijing.

Since Pakistan ratified CEDAW, the state has been undergoing a process of questioning where and how it can implement and enforce the Convention. Pakistan's 'Instrument of Accession' to CEDAW states that the government of Pakistan would strive to implement the Convention but with the following reservations:

General Declaration: The accession by Government of the Islamic Republic of Pakistan to the Convention on the Elimination of All Forms of Discrimination Against Women is subject to the provisions of the Constitution of the Islamic Republic of Pakistan.

Reservation: The Government of the Islamic Republic of Pakistan declares that it does not consider itself bound by paragraph 1 of Article 29 of the Convention.

This paragraph states that any dispute between two or more States/Parties concerning the interpretation or application of CEDAW which is not settled by negotiation between them can be submitted for arbitration to the International Court of Justice. This is not a dispute with any aspects of CEDAW's *essence*, but rather to counter the prospect of another state's criticism of Pakistan's *implementation* of CEDAW. The state has lodged no objection or reservation that there is a difference between CEDAW's understanding and local understandings of women's rights.

We can see the poignant debate which has emerged regarding what constitutes discrimination against women and what rights women should enjoy in a Muslim context, a debate that I.A. Rehman had despaired has not existed yet in Pakistan. The Ministry for Women's Development has, in practice, melded the process of compiling data for the 'National Plan of Action' (that was done as a follow-up to the Beijing 'Platform for Action') with the process of identifying discriminatory laws, policies and attitudes within each federal ministry in preparation for writing Pakistan's CEDAW report. The Ministry for Women's Development contacted every federal ministry (as well as many provincial ones) asking for feedback on how that ministry is responding to the state's promises to empower women. Despite repeated attempts by the ministry to clarify their questions, responses from the line ministries were mixed, underscoring the confusion that some people had with the very questions being posed. However, I have found it very curious that, in this correspondence, many government officials have retorted that Islam says something about a particular matter but in fact what is claimed is not necessarily true. Indeed, even at the level of federal government ministries, codified traditions are perceived as religious doctrine. This enables such bureaucrats, in practice, to deny recognizing the problems confronting women in various arenas as well as to neglect solutions for women's empowerment along the lines that CEDAW and others recommend.

Thus far, a number of draft CEDAW reports have been written, but the state has determined it necessary to take a step back and first articulate a National Policy on Women. It has been trying to do this in the past year by holding provincial meetings with local stakeholders—government bureaucrats, elected officials, and grassroots activists—to create consensus on key themes to promote women's empowerment. However, the language used in the draft national policy closely resembles CEDAW requirements, such as using the terminology of 'creating enabling conditions', to the extent that it draws the deep commitment of the state somewhat into question.

The key areas of dispute that the Pakistan state has had with CEDAW fall into three categories: co-education, inheritance, and evidence/legal witness. The first category is often framed as being contradictory to those sentiments prevailing in the local culture which largely operate under the ideal of separate spheres for males and females. Interestingly, co-educational schools had been a norm in higher education in Pakistan until its expansion in the 1970s when students from a range of social, economic and religious backgrounds began to attend high schools and universities; it was dismantled nearly everywhere during the waning years of Ziaul Haq's regime a decade later.

The latter two categories are directly affected by Pakistan's Constitution, which requires that no laws can be in contradiction to the injunctions of Islam. These two categories of dispute—inheritance and evidence/legal witness—are widely regarded as being derived from the Quran and, as such, are immutable (although both have recently been sites of contestation in Pakistan). The state has contended that Pakistani law cannot grant complete equality in inheritance to men and women given that verse 4:11 in *Sura al-Nisa* is interpreted as stating, 'A male shall inherit twice as much as a female'. The issue of evidence/legal witness is slightly more problematic. Ziaul Haq's controversial Law of Evidence (*Qanoon-e-Shahadat*) was promulgated by the Government of Pakistan based on verse 2:282 in Sura al-Baqr:

> Call in two male witnesses from among you, but if two men cannot be found, then one man and two women whom you judge fit to act as witnesses; so that if either of them commit an error, the other will remember.

However, this has been interpreted in a number of ways, and the current practice in Pakistan does not restrict women's testimony except in certain kinds of financial cases.

One point that many people believe is an issue in Pakistan—but legally is not—concerns consent and guardianship at the time of marriage. Pakistani case law until recently was ambiguous on this, as it has sometimes ruled in favour of a father who had opposed a daughter's marriage (on the basis that he is her *wali*), other times ruling in favour of the new bride and her husband. But in the Saima Waheed and Humaira Butt cases in the late 1990s,[16] the ruling was clear: based on Islam, once a child is legally considered to be an adult, the only consent necessary to obtain for a marriage to occur is that of the man and woman entering into the marriage. Consequently, a parent's objection to a marriage is not relevant to the law (albeit it is preferred within the culture). The ruling noted that the issue has been raised in Pakistan repeatedly more because of *rivaj* than because of its legal foundations within Islamic jurisprudence. As an extension of this interpretation, of a woman's rights as a legal adult, the nationality law has been revised so that a Pakistani woman's children can 'inherit' her nationality, irrespective of her husband's nationality, although her husband still cannot.

In its draft CEDAW Report, the Pakistan government identifies a number of obstacles, quite forthrightly, that it faces in eliminating discrimination against women and in implementing the Convention, notably prevailing socio-cultural norms, the existing patriarchal system, legal guarantees that are often not translated into concrete actions, and the society's feudal values.[17] It argues that most of the substantive challenges lie in implementation, especially at the grassroots level, due to locally-perceived cultural restrictions and political necessities to appease certain groups.

However, the 1997 ground-breaking 'Report of the Commission of Inquiry for Women' identified a number of specific laws and criminal procedures, in addition to traditional customs and social practices, that are discriminatory toward women in Pakistan. It makes explicit recommendations as to how Pakistan can remove such discrimination and redress inequities toward women. The Report also expresses concern that the state has taken contradictory positions on eliminating discrimination against women by acceding to CEDAW but *not* reversing those existing discriminatory laws.

The 'Report of the Commission of Inquiry for Women', suggests that to experience real and meaningful progress, the Pakistan state must adopt a new vision,

> which regards any acceptance of equality not as a favour or indulgence granted but as a prolonged and cruel injustice at last undone; which treats affirmative action as a necessary means of reversing centuries of discrimination and imbalance, not as a privilege or concession; which redefines the concept of

equality keeping in mind the special needs of women as their right; and which explores fresh and imaginative strategies to make the vision a workable reality.[18]

How this vision can become metabolized within the state's machinery and among Pakistanis is the clearest challenge it faces, as codified traditions are often perceived as religious doctrine. This has long enabled bureaucrats, in practice, to deny recognizing the problems confronting women in various arenas as well as to neglect solutions for women's empowerment along the lines that CEDAW and others recommend. Policies of former governments have been inconsistent, shifting between those promoting women's empowerment and those which have diminished it. An unforeseen consequence of such actions is that they fuel the 'culture wars' between different groups, for the state is not playing a mediating role but rather a provocative one.

CONCLUSION: THE EVOLVING PROCESS

Indeed, many of the laws enforced during Ziaul Haq's Islamisation programme, begun in 1979, exacerbate prevailing culturally sanctioned violence. Power relations between men and women, while being renegotiated in private spheres, are not on the agenda at the national level.[19] Due to the tendency to censure the victims of domestic abuse or to risk being charged with zina for claiming abuse, women are often reluctant to discuss violent acts of abuse that occur within the family. A common fear among women is that if they flee from their homes (as victims of abuse), they may be charged with adultery. Whether the charge can be proven or not is irrelevant; women often have little knowledge of the functioning of the penal system, and often languish for long periods of time under detention. In the event a woman is raped, she often fears to press charges because if she cannot prove the allegation, she can in turn be charged with adultery and imprisoned. Most people assume that if a woman is in prison, she must have done something wrong, and therefore her life is now ruined as she is considered contemptible. Additionally, a woman will often be separated from her children who, under shariah law, are to be remanded to a father's custody under most circumstances.

In response to such conditions, the 'Report of the Commission of Inquiry for Women' makes a strong demand for the state to redress such inequities and repeal these kinds of discriminatory laws. The Report makes the point that to do so is not only to create more equitable circumstances within Pakistan, but also to raise Pakistan's stature in the international arena. That the Pakistan state has signed various international accords, including CEDAW, further energizes the internal argument to create more equitable conditions for women. The authors of the Report recognize that the contradictory positions of the state—acceding to CEDAW but *not* reversing existing discriminatory laws and practices—are aggravating the divides between the various camps' sentiments regarding women's rights in the country. Such cleavages also exist within the bureaucracy, among the government workers whose responsibility it is to carry out the decisions made by the state. Many of these workers, however, subscribe to Islamist or traditionalist sentiments and see no reason why women should be given 'new' rights which they also perceive as being in conflict with Islamic tenets.

For Pakistan to follow through on its decision to become a State Party to CEDAW requires that the state play a greater leadership role in implementing the stance it takes at the international level in domestic policy and processes. It needs to mobilize government workers to raise their awareness of *why* the state has reached the conclusion that it is for the betterment of the country and all of its people to regard women as equal with men. The Report argues that in order for Pakistan to experience real and meaningful progress, it must adopt a new vision,

> which regards any acceptance of equality not as a favour or indulgence granted but as a prolonged and cruel injustice at last undone; which treats affirmative action as a necessary means of reversing centuries of discrimination and imbalance, not as a privilege or concession; which redefines the concept of equality keeping in mind the special needs of women as their right; and which explores fresh and imaginative strategies to make the vision a workable reality.[20]

How this vision can become metabolized within the state's machinery and among Pakistanis is the clearest challenge it faces. One way of legitimizing it is to place this vision into an Islamic context, which would enable some of its opponents to accept it. The Council for Islamic Ideology (CII), a constitutional body whose mandate in Article 230 (1a) is to make recommendations to the state so that 'the Muslims of Pakistan [may] order their lives individually and collectively in all respects in accordance with the principles and concepts of Islam as enunciated in the Holy Qur'an and Sunnah' has recently taken up the Commission's Report, to ascertain where it is or is not consistent with Islam. In September 2001, when I pressed the CII Chairman for a copy of their report (which I had heard had been released in draft form in Urdu), he admitted that it would not be finalized for some time to come. At least there is a recognition that the state must now tread lightly on this path.

It is clear that this was not the case when we analyze the contradictory actions of the former Nawaz Sharif government: On the one hand, writing the 'National Plan of Action', undertaking the writing of the CEDAW Report, and revisiting other UN human rights treaties to consider if Pakistan might ratify them, while on the other, *not* implementing key recommendations of the Report of the Commission of Inquiry for Women, especially the recommendation to repeal laws they assessed as being discriminatory toward women or to reinstate reserved seats for women. Policies of past governments have been inconsistent, for some appear to promote women's empowerment while others appear to diminish it. An unforeseen consequence of such actions is that they fuel the 'culture wars' between the different groups, for the state is not playing a mediating role but rather a provocative one. A salient example is the controversy that erupted over the Nawaz Sharif government's proposed 15th Amendment that it introduced in August 1998. The protection of women's rights—ensured in the Constitution at this point—would have become arbitrary if the Amendment had passed, as all 'constitutionally secured rights and freedoms may be superseded by the executive's directives, dependent only on the executive's interpretation of *Shariah* and their assessment of what is "right" for women' (Amnesty International, 1998: 2). A Pakistani opposition politician explained to me, at the time, that the Nawaz government was not intent on repealing the Hudood ordinances and proposed legislation such as the 15th Amendment because they were, 'apologists who are terrified of the militant orthodoxy raising its head in the country'.[21] The result of such actions was the furthest the state could get from consensus building as it increased tensions between and among various groups in the country, and served to increase the alienation they already identified they had with others' viewpoints. Indeed, these dilemmas drew the state further into the discourse of defining women's rights through the institutional structures it supports. An example is seen in its consideration of the role of the *wali*. The Criminal Law Amendment Act, passed as an Act of Parliament in 1997 with limited discussion, lays out the method for distribution of *qisas* and *diyat* in the event of a murder. The 'Report of the Commission on the Status of Women' interprets this Act as making criminal offences 'a private matter rather than treating them as crimes against society.' While the *wali* is defined in gender-neutral terms, in both language and examples, in practice the *wali* is always a male. For the state to contend that the *wali need not necessarily* be a man would be to invalidate longstanding local patriarchal interpretations of men's responsibilities vis-à-vis women.

An official in the foreign Ministry offered that most of the flaws that Pakistan has faced regarding CEDAW lie in implementation, not legislation, especially at the grassroots level because of political necessities to appease certain groups. The Report of the Commission of Inquiry for Women identified certain areas—laws, customs, practices, criminal procedures—that are discriminatory toward women, and made recommendations on how Pakistan can remove this discrimination. It made three important, albeit controversial key recommendations:

(1) to legalize abortion;
(2) to abolish the Federal Shariat Court, as it is not required as other courts can do the same things; and
(3) that since Hudood laws haven't achieved their objectives they should be repealed.

For example, it suggested that the government repeal the *zina* law relating to 'unlawful fornication', which contravenes constitutional safeguards and various provisions of CEDAW that laws should not discriminate between men and women. The issue of evidence and the evidence law was also taken up here, as a woman can be found guilty of *zina* by virtue of becoming pregnant while a man cannot. The Report notes that since the *zina* law was promulgated, the numbers of women in Pakistani prisons have risen dramatically, and while nearly two-thirds have been accused of *zina*, hardly any of the charges have been proven. Most women are ultimately released, underscoring that while in theory there are checks against false accusation of *zina,* in practice it happens very frequently. However, no action was taken in any of the three suggested arenas, although a proposal does now exist to abolish the Federal Shariat Court. It would, of course, take a great deal of political will to do so.

The challenges to navigating such uncharted paths as promoting the rights of women in Pakistan are substantial, but nothing compared to the risks and lost opportunities *not* to do this. In the recent past, the Musharraf government sought to bypass the question of religion and forge on to ensure representation. In preparation for the June 2000 Beijing +5 conference at the UN headquarters in New York, Musharraf pledged that from that point forth, all so-called 'honour killings' would be considered as crimes of murder, once and for all, and would receive no special consideration. While his government reinstated reserved seats for women, one-third in local government elections, and reserved an unprecedented sixty seats for women in the October 2002 national elections, it did not repeal the draconian *hudood* laws. Neither did it, however, seek out opportunities to implement them, either. The question remains whether the present government is indeed committed to revisiting the kinds of laws passed two decades ago in the name of Islam, and get input from civil society groups into repealing or at least revising them. It is hoped that it will go as far as the government in Tunisia has begun to do: Conduct *ijtihad* in its 'progressive reading of the Quran' as it creates new programmes that support the empowerment of women while framing them in an Islamic context.[22] Yet one thing is decidedly clear: how the state in Pakistan frames its modernity project and incorporates women and women's groups into that process will certainly open up new arenas for discourse concerning the relationship between Islam and women's status, rights, and empowerment in Pakistan. This is a process that women will no longer allow to be delayed.

GLOSSARY

madrassahs	religious schools
shariah	religious law
Qisas and *Diyat*	Retaliation and Blood Money
izzat	honour
sharafat	respectability
wali	guardian
rivaj	tradition

NOTES

1. This is part of an in-progress book, *Interpreting Islam, Modernity and Women's Rights: Implementing CEDAW in Pakistan, Tunisia, and Malaysia*.
2. National Assembly of Pakistan, *The Constitution of the Islamic Republic of Pakistan (as modified up to 28 July 1991)* Islamabad 1993, p. 6.
3. Ibid., p. 7.
4. For further elaboration on Zia's Islamisation programme's effects on women, refer to Anita M. Weiss, 1986 and 1996, and Jehangir and Jilani, 1990.
5. Commission of Inquiry for Women, *Report of the Commission of Inquiry for Women in Pakistan,* Islamabad. August 1997, ii.
6. Ibid., xi.

7. For further elaboration of this point in the example of the walled city of Lahore, see Anita M. Weiss *Walls within Walls: Life Histories of Working Women in the Old City of Lahore,* 2nd edition, Oxford University Press, 2002.
8. For further elaboration, see Weiss 2002.
9. Government of Pakistan, Planning Commission, *Ten Year Perspective Development Plan 2001–11 and Three Year Development Programme 2001–04,* Printing Corporation of Pakistan Press, Islamabad, September 2001, p. 211.
10. National Assembly of Pakistan, op. cit., 1993, p. 137.
11. As quoted in 'People's Government Fulfilling an Agenda for Change: Social Sector' November 1994, pp. 20–21.
12. As reported by Beena Sarwar 'Women: Muslim Legislators Conference sets the tone for Beijing' *Inter Press Service,* 7 August 1995.
13. Address by Benazir Bhutto, [former] Prime Minister of the Islamic Republic of Pakistan, at the Fourth World Conference on Women, Beijing, 4 September 1995.
14. Ibid.
15. This assessment is based on the draft report issued by the Government of Pakistan, Ministry of Women Development, Social Welfare & Special Education. 1999.
16. 1997 and 1999, respectively.
17. These are stated thus: (i) A number of sociocultural norms influence women's status and perception of self in the community and are a hindrance in the implementation of laws safeguarding women's status and enjoyment of basic human rights; (ii) [the] prevailing patriarchal system, cultural norms and feudal values in the society continue to influence the role of women in the community; (iii) the legal guarantees often do not get translated into concrete actions, due to prevalent social and cultural norms/practices in the society; and (iv) domestic affairs are considered a private matter and incidents of family/domestic problems are usually hushed up; community conciliatory committees have been set up; trained case workers have been posted in different localities to provide initial marriage and family counselling services.
18. Report, pp. xiii.
19. For further discussion of the renegotiation of gender relations within the family and local institutions in Pakistan, refer to Weiss 1994: 127–140.
20. Report, pp. xiii.
21. Based on confidential, personal communication in Pakistan in early 1999.
22. This was conveyed to me by Emna Aouij, Tunisia's representative on the CEDAW panel of experts, as well as by representatives of the Ministry of Women and Family Affairs in Tunisia, as part of field research conducted for a project, *Interpreting Islam, Modernity and Women's Rights: Implementing CEDAW in Pakistan, Tunisia, and Malaysia.*

CHAPTER 4

Religious Education and the Rhetoric of Reform: The Madrassahs in British India and Pakistan

MUHAMMAD QASIM ZAMAN

The madrassah is one of the many institutions which have seen recurrent attempts at reform in Muslim societies during the nineteenth and twentieth centuries. Since the eleventh century, when it first emerged as the principal institution of higher Islamic learning, the madrassah has undergone many changes, adapting in varying degrees to local cultures and changing times.[1] Given the centrality of this institution in the preservation and production of knowledge as well as in the formation of the religious elite, the madrassah is crucial to the construction of religious authority. Profound changes in Muslim societies in modern times have not necessarily marginalized this institution, but such changes have frequently raised questions about the position and function of the madrassah in society and of the ulama reared in it, about whether this institution ought to be reformed, and if so, to what end, how, and by whom.

Debates on such questions have received some scholarly attention with reference to several Muslim societies.[2] South Asian Islam has hitherto been much neglected in this regard, and though the role of the madrassah as an agent of religious change—that is, the reform of local social and religious practices through the madrassah—have begun to be studied,[3] the significance of the initiatives towards reforming the madrassah itself remains to be appreciated. A variety of efforts towards reforming the madrassah were, in fact, undertaken during the colonial period, both by British administrators and by Muslim reformers; and attempts have likewise been made to reform madrassahs in Pakistan. This study draws attention to the importance of these initiatives and of the reactions they have called forth in shaping not only competing visions of the madrassah itself but also some of the ways in which Islam has come to be viewed and located in society and the position and authority of the ulama is visualized.

I hope to show in the following study how particular concepts and categories of colonial analysis have shaped and continued to persist in much of the debate on the reform of the madrassah in modern South Asia. What these categories connote differs quite markedly for different people engaged in or affected by the debate, as indeed does the very meaning of reform. Yet all modern discussion of reform not only presupposes these categories (even as many of those engaged in it deny their value or validity), the problem of madrassah reform also raises fundamental questions about what religious education consists of, about the usefulness of such education, and ultimately, about the place of religion in Muslim society. I will try to indicate how the initiatives towards reform, no less than the opposition to them, have fostered views of religion as occupying a distinct sphere in society. Such a conception of religion is distinctly modern, so far as Muslim societies are concerned. Yet, it is striking that this conception is favoured even by many ulama, that is, by the very people who are known to deny in principle that religious matters comprise, or that they are limited to, a separate, or separable, sphere of life.

MADRASSAH REFORM: BRITISH PERCEPTIONS, CATEGORIES, INITIATIVES

In their effort to understand and regulate the systems of education prevalent in India, to relate them to their own ideas of how education ought to be imparted and to what end, and to reform the local systems in view of their own perceptions, colonial officials routinely invoked what to them were familiar and often self-evident concepts and categories. These were not peculiar to colonial analyses of the educational systems in India, though we shall consider them here only with reference to education. The significance of these categories lies not only in their defining the British understanding of Muslim (and Hindu-Sanskrit) education but also in their subsequent influence both on the ulama and on initiatives by successive governments of Pakistan to reform the madrassah.

The most important of categories that have shaped all discussion of the madrassah, as indeed of many other institutions of Indian society, is the notion of religion itself. As Talal Asad has argued, developments in modern Europe, and especially the impact of the Enlightenment, have led not merely to the subordination of religion to the state or the confinement of the former to the sphere of 'private' life but also to 'the construction of religion as a new historical object: anchored in personal experience, expressible as belief-statements, dependent on private institutions, and practiced in one's spare time. This construction of religion ensures that it is part of what is *inessential* to our common politics, economy, science, and morality.'[4]

In India the British constantly encountered situations and institutions where no clear distinctions between the religious and the secular or non-religious were made. To many, this situation was reminiscent of Europe's own medieval history, where such distinctions were frequently blurred, often to the advantage of the Church. For all the horrors that this parallel suggested, viewing India as dominated, or determined, by religion meant that the Indians could be seen as not only different from post-Enlightenment Europeans but also inferior to the colonial rulers and therefore in need of the latter's enlightened governance and liberating reform.[5] There was, however, much ambivalence on whether all life was in fact governed by religion in India or, conversely, that Indians only thought (or were made to believe by a devious religious elite) that it was. Either way, it was imperative for sound practical administration—and in the interest of reform and improvement—to make a distinction between the religious and the non-religious, the personal and the public or general.

Such distinctions were commonly made in the British handling of the Muslim endowments (*waqf*),[6] but no less in matters of education. In government schools, a policy of religious neutrality was adopted, which meant excluding all formal instruction in religion from the school curriculum.[7] This policy suggested that religion could be confined to a definite sphere, which in turn ought to be excluded from the course of general education. Conversely, if indigenous education was perceived to be suffused with a religious ethos, then reform meant, among other things, taking education out of the religious sphere. The first Director of Public Instruction in the Punjab had little doubt about how to effect a separation of the religious and the secular. 'I [have] ordered all village schools to be removed from the precincts of mosques and other buildings of a religious character,' he wrote in June 1858. 'Native subordinates informed me that no other buildings were available. I then ordered that the schools should be closed rather than held in such buildings.... I [have also] directed the disuse of all books of a religious character in the schools.'[8]

The madrassahs were, of course, regarded as religious institutions and in many cases, especially in the aftermath of the Revolt of 1857, were abolished. At best, their existence was effectively jeopardized for that reason.[9] Yet many also continued to be administered or financially supported by the government. What concerns us here is only the fact, however, that familiar distinctions between religious and secular learning continued to be invoked in colonial analyses of the madrassahs, quite as much as in that of other educational institutions. Even in institutions defined as religious, British policy favoured the patronage of what was deemed to be secular learning. Thus 'indigenous religious schools…[were] entitled to a grant from the Government…so long as they teach secular subjects in a satisfactory manner.'[10] However reform was conceived, the distinction between the religious and the non-religious was central to that project.[11] As we shall see, this distinction has remained a constant theme of all discussion on the reform of the madrassah; it is, however, a modern distinction, with little precedent in earlier Muslim societies.[12]

Medieval Muslim scholars often distinguished between the 'traditionally transmitted' (*naqliyya/manqulat*) sciences—such as morphology and syntax, Quranic studies, *Hadith* (the traditions attributed to the Prophet Muhammad [PBUH]), law (*fiqh*), principles of jurisprudence (*usul al-fiqh*), theology, and so forth—and the 'rational' ('*aqliyya/ma'qulat*) sciences, for example, logic, philosophy, astronomy, and arithmetic. The rational sciences were also studied in madrassahs, whereas the study of the 'transmitted'—or for that matter, any other—sciences was not confined only to these seminaries.[13] The standing of the sciences relative to one another was frequently discussed, and many scholars were opposed to the study of such 'foreign', rational sciences as Aristotelian logic and philosophy; there were also complaints that the sciences which are worth studying 'for their own sake', such as Quran, Hadith, and law, were sometimes given less attention than ancillary disciplines like morphology and syntax, which were meant only to assist in the study of the former.[14] Yet discussions on madrassahs as representing, and guarding, the 'religious' sphere in society; on what is 'purely religious' in the curriculum of the madrassah; or on religion as occupying a distinct sphere in society—discussions which have continually occupied reformers of the madrassah in the nineteenth and twentieth centuries—are eminently *modern* debates with little precedent in medieval Islamic societies.

Another fundamental category of education was the criterion of what was called useful instruction. The English Utilitarians were most emphatic in invoking the notion of what was called useful learning, though not unique in their commitment to it. Addressing the question of the allocation of funds by the East India Company for the advancement of education in India, the influential Utilitarian thinker and historian James Mill (d. 1836) had written in February 1824:

> The great end should not have been to teach Hindoo learning, or Mahomedan learning, but useful learning.... In professing, on the other hand, to establish Seminaries for the purpose of teaching mere Hindoo, or mere Mahomedan literature, you bound yourself to teach a great deal of what was frivolous, not a little of what was purely mischievous, and a small remainder indeed in which utility was in any way concerned.[15]

In his evidence before the Punjab Education Commission of 1884, G.W. Leitner, a Hungarian Orientalist and principal of the Government College in Lahore, provides the following, somewhat sarcastic illustration of education in government schools in terms of the notion of 'useful learning':

> After leaving the middle school, a boy...knows arithmetic, Urdu and Persian, if not a little English, all of which may be said to be "useful" to him, whilst he has acquired some information regarding history, geography, and elementary science, which, also, cannot be affirmed to be "useless." He has also learnt the elements of mensuration, which is a "practical" acquirement for him, especially if he wishes to become a sub-overseer, overseer, or engineer. He has also, if he has studied English, read Cunningham's Sanitary Primer, and if he has practiced the lessons contained in it, that knowledge too is 'practical'.[16]

But Leitner goes on to note that by the time a student completes high school, 'he has more information [but]...is rather less suited for a "useful" and "practical" career, than when he passed the middle school. His distaste to all physical exertion, except to that of the pen, has grown, and he is more unwilling than before to return to his father's shop.'[17]

Given constructions of usefulness such as James Mill's, the religious sciences studied in madrassahs were scarcely useful, which meant that it was deemed inappropriate for the East India Company to support such institutions at all or without first reforming their 'inefficient' condition. But many British officials of the early nineteenth century had a different view of useful learning. They did not, of course, deny the utility of English and the European arts and sciences but they did affirm the value of Oriental learning and the need for its patronage by the British. The disagreement between the Orientalists and the Anglicists over what constituted useful knowledge was settled in the 1830s in favour of the Anglicists;[18] the notion of useful knowledge continued, however, to define British approaches to problems of education in India, and specifically for our purposes, their negative perception of madrassah education and the need to reform it.

The notion of useful knowledge (*al-'ilm al-nafi'*) also figures prominently in the Islamic tradition, where it refers primarily (but not exclusively) to knowledge which assists in salvation and is consequently used to facilitate virtuous acts.[19] The very activity of imparting or receiving knowledge was frequently also described in medieval texts as useful or as a benefit (*naf', fa'ida, mufid*).[20] The modern ulama's defence of madrassah education as useful owes its inspiration to Utilitarian notions of useful learning far more than it does to the medieval 'ilm al-nafi', however. The useful learning that colonial officials spoke of left little room for religion in general, let alone for the learning acquired in the madrassah. It was precisely in response to this challenge that the ulama argued for the usefulness of madrassah education, and as we shall see, for religion as comprising a distinct sphere in society.

British initiatives at reform were limited to those madrassahs which had either been established by them, such as the Calcutta Madrassah founded by Warren Hastings in 1781, or which they financially supported. Even among the latter, however, not all madrassahs were reformed or reformed in the same measure. Colonial policies were often confused and contradictory, the more so because of the hesitation with which they were implemented;[21] and education was no exception. Though the idea of reform remained paramount, precisely how it was conceived or carried through varied at different times or in case of different madrassahs. The reform of the Madrassah-i A'zam of Madras, found in a 'very inefficient condition' according to the Education Report of 1858–59, may be taken to represent one end of the spectrum:

> The amount of useful instruction imparted was extremely limited. The business of the Institution, like that of its namesake at Calcutta, was teaching the Arabic and Persian languages, and the doctrines of the Mahommedan religion. All this has been altered. An efficient Master [sic] has been placed at the head of School; and the teachers, generally, have been replaced by more competent ones.[22]

The Calcutta Madrassah, on the other hand, was treated less severely. The Madrassah had begun by following the *Dars-i Nizami*, a list of authoritative texts the study of which was in vogue in most other madrassahs of the subcontinent too.[23] But only a decade after its inception, the first of several efforts at reforming the Madrassah was already thought to be necessary; and among other things, changes were introduced in the curriculum. A major reorganization was also effected in 1850, when the Madrassah was divided into two separate departments, the Arabic (or Senior Department) and the Anglo–Persian (or Junior Department). The latter was modelled on other 'Anglo–Vernacular' government schools and was termed 'a complete success' in government reports.[24] Much ambivalence continued, however, to characterize efforts to reform the former—to substitute 'a more modern and rational system of instruction in the Arabic language and in the principles of Mohammadan Law for the antiquated and faulty system of the Indian Moulvies.'[25] There was resistance to radical reform from the Muslims, and more decisively perhaps, from many British officials themselves. Though some saw the Madrassah as not merely useless but also politically subversive,[26] government support for it continued. So also did uncertainties about reform. The 'Moulvies' were occasionally reminded that the Madrassah was a 'Government Institution…and it is the Government and not the Professors who are responsible for the nature of the education given to its Mahommedan subjects therein.'[27] Yet the Calcutta Madrassah (and in particular its Arabic Department) was usually exempted from having to teach the useful subjects introduced in most of the other government madrassahs of Bengal.[28]

British ambivalence on the question of reform seems to have been due primarily to two factors: lingering uncertainties, despite the success of the Anglicists against the Orientalists, about the usefulness of Oriental learning; and apprehensions that drastic measures of reform might provoke a hostile reaction on the part of Muslims.[29] In 1873, the government of Bengal even took the initiative (to the dismay of many, including some Muslims)[30] of establishing three new madrassahs, to 'realize the Muslim ideals of liberal education.' Lest this measure be seen as a reversion to the discredited Orientalist stance, it was emphasized that 'the encouragement of the study of oriental literature for its own sake was a very subsidiary part of the plan.'[31] These new institutions were, in all likelihood, 'reformed' madrassahs, where useful instruction was to be imparted together with the teaching of authoritative Islamic texts. The latter was deemed desirable, if only because it appealed to Muslim ideals and was worth patronizing for that reason.

British administrators were aware of the prestige many madrassahs enjoyed[32] and were conscious that drastic changes, even in madrassahs they had themselves established, provoked deep resentment. For all their uncertainties about the efficacy of oriental learning, British administrators saw themselves as preserving tradition, not doing away with it.[33] In the case of madrassahs they established or took over and administered, the British usually thought of reform as the addition of useful learning to the Islamic sciences taught in the madrassahs, not—as at the Madrassah-i A'zam of Madras—reforming Oriental learning out of existence in these institutions. The extent to which useful learning was introduced in madrassahs varied. This meant that, as in Bengal, a spectrum of reformed, semi-reformed, and unreformed government madrassahs, in addition to those which the government neither recognized nor supported, existed side by side, posing a constant challenge to the energies of the government committees which were periodically constituted to suggest ways to reform them.[34]

REFORM AND THE ULAMA IN BRITISH INDIA

The decline of the madrassah is a familiar theme in modern Muslim analyses of the decline of Islam. Sayyid Abu'l-Hasan 'Ali Nadwi, an influential religious scholar of contemporary India, suggests, for instance, that the decline of the madrassah—the beginnings of which he dates to the sixteenth century—reflected and exacerbated a pervasive intellectual and cultural decadence of Muslim societies everywhere. The authoritative writings of the earlier masters were gradually eliminated from among the list of texts which were commonly studied, to be replaced by the glosses and abridgements of uncreative pedants. According to Nadwi, an obscure, allusive, convoluted style, characterized by 'an extreme economy in the use of paper', took the place of the clear and readily intelligible ('*am fahm*) style of writing characteristic of the 'ancients'.[35] Nadwi belongs to an institution of learning which, as we shall presently see, had sought to break with the styles of education prevalent in most madrassahs of the nineteenth century. But even those who continued to affirm the efficacy of existing styles of learning agreed at least that the madrassahs of modern times no longer produced figures comparable to the intellectual giants of medieval Islam.[36]

It is not clear when, or where, the idea first originated that at some point in medieval Islam the madrassah had undergone a thorough decline and that a lack of creative thinking, manifested in the tradition of writing glosses and commentaries on earlier works, reflected that decline. Recent scholarship on medieval Islamic law has suggested new ways of looking at the role of glosses and commentaries, however. As Brinkley Messick has argued, medieval works ought to be seen as 'open texts' which, by 'internal discursive construction,' required constant interpretation and commentary: 'The written literature of shari'a jurisprudence, for example, developed largely by means of [such] interpretive elaborations on basic texts.'[37] Though the provenance of notions of Muslim intellectual decline cannot be explored here, it is tempting to speculate that the influence of modern, Western ideas of useful learning, of creative, and conversely, of degenerate thinking, exercised some influence. There is much in laments of Muslim intellectual decline that echoes Gibbon's characterization of Roman intellectual life, for instance, as one of 'blind deference' to authorities of the past, of 'cold and servile imitations,' with 'a cloud of critics, compilers, and commentators darken[ing] the face of learning.'[38] Modern Muslim efforts to reform madrassahs do often presuppose such analyses of decline.

The texts studied at present in most madrassahs of India and Pakistan comprise what is known as the 'Dars-i Nizami', a corpus whose introduction in madrassahs is attributed (somewhat questionably) to the influence of Mulla Nizam al-din Muhammad (d. 1748), the founder of the Farangi Mahal family of scholars in Lucknow in northern India. Many of these texts were being taught in Indian madrassahs long before Nizam al-din's time, however; and several others were added considerably after his death.[39] The texts themselves were, in most cases, composed between the ninth and the eighteenth centuries C.E. largely by scholars of Iranian, Central Asian, and Indian origin. The precise textual content of the Dars-i Nizami was subject to considerable fluidity until after the middle of the nineteenth century. Only in the latter half of the nineteenth century, and as Farhan Nizami has suggested, possibly in response to a certain measure of influence exercised by Western styles and institutions of education in British India, did the Dars-i Nizami acquire a more or less standardized form and was widely adopted as a 'curriculum' by madrassahs of the Indian subcontinent.[40] Yet madrassahs have continued to differ in their versions of this curriculum, and the latter has scarcely been impervious to change. The single most important of such changes concerns the relative prominence that the study of Hadith has come to have in the Dars-i Nizami from the late nineteenth century onwards.

The primary emphasis of the Dars-i Nizami is on the 'rational sciences' (*ma'qulat*), as distinguished from the 'transmitted sciences' (*manqulat*).[41] Already in the eighteenth century, the north Indian reformer Shah Wali Allah (d. 1762), had introduced in his own madrassah in Delhi a style of learning which gave special importance to works of Hadith.[42] Though his curriculum did not become widely prevalent, Wali Allah's ideas have continued to exert a powerful influence on later reformists, in particular on those associated with the madrassah of Deoband.

The movement associated with the madrassah of Deoband in Northern India (established in 1867) represents perhaps the most prominent instance on the Indian subcontinent of inviting people to conform to the 'true' Islam of authoritative religious texts, as defined by an urban, madrassah-based, religious elite. The reformist ideology of this madrassah soon acquired a sectarian dimension, with these Deobandis distinguishing themselves (and their madrassahs) from such other sectarian groups as the Barelawis and the Ahl-i Hadith, all of which (along with many others) emerged in India in the second half of the nineteenth century and still constitute the most significant sectarian affiliations among Sunni Muslims of the Indian subcontinent.[43] My concern here is not with reform in this sense, however, or with the madrassah as an agent of religious change but with the reform of the madrassah itself (though the latter may, of course, itself be conceived of as a means, or a prelude, to other forms of reform). Deoband's aspirations signified more than weaning the masses away from their inherited, customary beliefs and rituals. In the perception of the ulama of Deoband, these purposes necessitated a revival of those aspects of the Islamic intellectual heritage, such as Hadith, which were thought to be most authoritative and best suited to providing religious guidance to Muslims. That is, some reform of the madrassah was thought to be required too.

While the texts of the Dars-i Nizami continued to be studied at Deoband (as indeed they were at most other Islamic seminaries), the study of Hadith was given an importance much greater than it had previously enjoyed in most other madrassahs.[44] Thus, rather than the *Mishkat al-Masabih*, a compendium of Hadith based on selections from the six classical Hadith collections deemed authoritative in Sunni Islam, the latter collections themselves came to be studied.[45] As Barbara Metcalf has shown, Deoband was also different from its predecessors in 'emulating the British bureaucratic style for educational institutions.' Deoband—and soon madrassahs everywhere in the Indian subcontinent—came, for instance, to have a set curriculum, separate classes for students of different levels, an academic year, annual examinations, and networks of affiliated madrassahs.[46]

The texts studied in this new institutional setup have remained, with the exception of a more extensive emphasis on Hadith, the same as those of the Dars-i Nizami. The primary concern at Deoband—and most other madrassahs—has always been the conservation of the classical Islamic texts and sciences as studied in madrassahs, not textual innovation. Unlike Deoband, the movement of the Nadwat al-ulama, launched towards the end of the nineteenth century to bring Muslim religious scholars of various persuasions together, concerned itself from the outset, self-consciously and even ostentatiously, with the reform of the madrassah.[47] The revival of the Muslim community depended, in the view of the Nadwa's founders, on infusing the ranks of the ulama with fresh vigour and on broadening the scope of their activities and their role in the Muslim community. To achieve these goals, it was deemed imperative to reform the prevalent styles of learning. The existing madrassahs were seen as lacking in intellectual creativity and as being equally indifferent to changes in Muslim societies and to the challenges facing them.[48] As Mawlana Muhammad 'Ali Mongiri, one of the founders of the Nadwat al-ulama, emphasized at its annual session of 1896, the Nadwa's proposed curriculum sought to produce religious scholars capable of providing guidance and leadership to the community in a wide range of spheres: in law and theology, in *adab* (belles-lettres), in philosophy, and in 'matters of the world.'[49] As part of the initiative to unite the ulama, it was proposed to have all the existing madrassahs adopt the curriculum that the Nadwa promised to devise. It was not long before it became clear, however, that not many among the ulama were willing to merge their differences into a common curriculum, or to accept the Nadwa's reformers as arbiters of their differences.[50] Consequently, the founders of the Nadwa established a new madrassah (the Dar al-'Ulum) of their own, where they could hope to experiment with their reforms.

Those associated with the Nadwa have frequently complained of a duality in the system of education 'between the old and the new, the religious and the secular,' a duality they trace to colonial rule in India.[51] Yet even as they lamented this compartmentalization and pledged, in striving for a new curriculum, to do away with it, the Nadwa's founders often spoke and wrote in terms which pre-supposed precisely the same distinctions. Religion or matters religious continued to be defined as comprising a distinct sphere, albeit one which was assigned the first importance. The early leaders of the Nadwa were also keen to allay all British suspicions about this institution by insisting on its strictly apolitical character. This entailed presenting the Nadwa as an exclusively religious forum. It also meant laying claim to exclusively represent the Muslim community in all matters religious. As Mawlana Shibli Nu'mani

(d. 1914), a major Muslim intellectual who was prominent among the leaders of this movement, suggested at the annual session of 1912, the Nadwa ought to become the voice of the entire nation in religion on par with the All-India Muslim League, which sought recognition as the representative of the Muslims' political interests.[52] Abu'l-Hasan 'Ali Nadwi (d. 1999), the late rector of the Nadwa, has likewise noted that the basis of the movement which culminated in the establishment of the Nadwat al-ulama was 'purely religious', unlike that of many other, contemporary reformist movements.[53]

In discussing the establishment of a new madrassah under the aegis of the Nadwa, Shibli Nu'mani lamented that 'there is not even one *purely religious* madrassah in the whole of India, no institution worthy of being considered the "great madrassah" in terms of its all-embracing concern [with the religious sciences] and its grandeur.'[54] The implication here seems to be that the existing madrassahs were spending far more time teaching 'ancillary sciences' like morphology and syntax or the 'rational sciences' like logic and philosophy, rather than the 'purely religious sciences', such as Hadith, law and legal theory, and the Quran and its exegesis. The madrassah of Deoband and its affiliates had tried to redress this perceived imbalance by emphasising the study of Hadith in the curriculum, but the Nadwa wanted to go further. Striking here is the sense, which the ulama of the Nadwa had possibly imbibed from colonial analyses of educational and other institutions, that religion was a distinct sphere of life. They denied that religion was a private matter, divorced from public life, yet had little trouble speaking of a 'purely religious' institution and of the religious sphere as clearly distinguishable from all others.

Paradoxically, however, the founders of the Nadwa also attacked the madrassahs from another perspective which was quite incompatible with the one outlined above. The existing madrassahs were out of touch with the world in which they existed, it was said, hence they were incapable of providing leadership to the community. 'A major reason for the decline in the ulama's influence in the country', Muhammad Ali Mongiri wrote, 'is the popular perception that they have withdrawn into their cells and know nothing about the state of the world, so that in worldly matters their guidance is entirely unworthy of attention.'[55] On this view, even if the madrassahs were academically sound—which they were deemed not to be—and even if they were purely religious institutions, they would still not be fulfilling what was required of them. In fact, to be purely religious was precisely what a madrassah ought not to be if it were to meet modern challenges to Islam. In its initial years, therefore, the Nadwa had sought to bridge medieval and modern disciplines—a goal whose implications bitterly divided the leaders of this movement and which, as it turned out, was never to be achieved.[56]

The ambivalence in the Nadwa's goals points, among other things, towards an inability to arrive at an acceptable definition of religion itself and how to reform it.[57] At issue in the enterprise of devising a new curriculum was nothing short of determining what an Islamic education—and, by extension, Islam itself—signified, how to teach it, and how to make that education useful to the Muslim community.

As in the reports and recommendations of British policy makers on education, there was much in the Nadwa's reformist rhetoric on useful education.[58] The reformers of the Nadwa did not mean quite the same thing by the notion of useful education, though all agreed on the ultimate goal of creating a new generation of ulama fit to lead the Muslim community. Some other attributes of this type of education, as enunciated by the Nadwa's leaders, are also worth noting here. The study of commentaries and glosses was deemed detrimental to creative thinking, for instance, as we have noted earlier; useful Islamic education meant, rather, the study of the original and authoritative works of the 'ancients'. Learning to write and converse in the Arabic language, which was said to be beyond the abilities of most graduates of the Indian madrassahs, was another accomplishment the Nadwa sought. Products of its curriculum were to be not only aware of modern challenges to Islam but also able to defend Islam against them and to engage actively in proselytization. An intimate knowledge of Arabic would assist them in these purposes as well as in establishing a rapport with scholars elsewhere in the Muslim world; the Arabic language would also serve as the basis of the study of literature, a subject 'the neglect of which was tantamount to neglecting the religious sciences.'[59] Much emphasis was also laid on 'moral' instruction, of which the study of certain classical Sufi texts were to be a medium.[60] Finally, there was a recognition that some practical skills ought to be imparted to students so that they would be able to earn a respectable living.[61]

In general, not just the notion of useful education but also of what such usefulness consists of shows the influence of colonial analyses, and perhaps, a desire to make the Nadwa's education look useful to colonial authorities. The emphasis on moral instruction—which British officials thought was lacking in Indian systems of education;[62] on literature, which in government schools had come to substitute for formal instruction in religion;[63] on practical skills; on fostering a generation of ulama who would be more in touch with, and hence, according to British notions, more 'representative' of the people;[64] on bridging medieval and modern education; and, not least, on an intimate knowledge of Arabic, which to many colonial officials was one of the 'classical languages of India',[65] and hence a mark of cultural authenticity and religious authority—are all interpretable as responses to ideas much in vogue in late nineteenth century British India.

Though the existing madrassahs served as the foil against which the Nadwa's goals were defined, there was serious disagreement over the extent to which it was deemed appropriate to break with the madrassahs' prevailing intellectual styles. To have many a religious scholar agree that the choice of texts and subjects needed revision was one thing; to have a consensus on precisely what changes were to be brought about and how was quite another. That the ulama would agree to substitute the books which they had studied for long and from whose mastery they derived their religious authority proved to be an unrealistic expectation.[66] The Nadwa had initially aspired to have a reformed curriculum introduced in all the madrassahs; but even in its own Dar al-'Ulum, a century after the movement of the Nadwat al-ulama began, change has only been partial as well as controversial. Aristotelian logic and philosophy came to be given much less importance than they were in other madrassahs; and scriptural exegesis, Hadith, history, and Arabic literature are prominent in the curriculum.[67] Yet key texts in law and legal theory, theology, even logic and philosophy (which had especially been the object of criticism by the Nadwa's founders)[68] have remained substantially the same as those in other madrassahs.[69] In general, the Nadwa's curriculum has continued to be very much under the shadow of the Dars-i Nizami. Contrary to the rhetoric of some of the Nadwa's founders, the teaching of English and the question of the students' exposure to Western learning have also remained thorny and divisive issues.

A major factor militating against initiatives towards reform was the frustrating realization that the graduates of Nadwa's Dar al-'Ulum were not usually (though with some important exceptions) accorded the same deference by the ulama, or as ulama, that the students of madrassahs such as Deoband were. If being one of the ulama meant that one was reared on certain texts (rather than others), then to deny their authority or to replace them with others, as attempted at the Nadwa, was to be marginalized in the structures of authority sustained by reverence for such texts. Moreover, as noted, the Nadwa had sought not only to combine medieval with modern learning but also to create a favourable impression on the colonial government. In 1908, the latter had even approved a monthly grant for the promotion of secular education (*dunyawi ta'lim*) at the Nadwa.[70] During the nearly 100 years of the school's existence, scholars of the Nadwa have often looked for alternate sources of influence: the Tablighi Jama'at, a respected proselytizing movement with a worldwide network,[71] Sufism, and perhaps most distinctively, recognition in the Arab world.[72] But they have also tried to minimize their differences with the other ulama, to become (and thus to be recognized as) one of them.

The Nadwat al-ulama's rhetoric regarding the need to reform the madrassah curriculum has no parallel among non-governmental reformist initiatives in British India. Yet the question of madrassah reform has continued to be much discussed—in both post-independence (1947) India and Pakistan—and in terms not dissimilar to those familiar in British India. Much of the discussion in Pakistan has revolved around government initiatives towards reforming madrassahs, and it is these initiatives and reactions to them which I now propose to discuss.

MADRASSAH REFORM IN PAKISTAN

Pakistan did not inherit most of the better-known madrassahs which had been active in the colonial period and many of which have continued in existence in post-independence India.[73] One notable exception was the Calcutta Madrassah which, as its historian says, 'migrated' to Dhaka at the time of the partition of India.[74] Significantly, this migration was also a partition for the Madrassah itself and along lines in keeping with familiar categories of colonial analysis. Thus, it was decided, in August 1947, that of the two departments which comprised the Madrassah, the Anglo–Persian Department, which had borne the brunt of government reforms and experiments in usefulness, would stay in Calcutta, while the Arabic Department, concerned with the classical texts, would move to Dhaka in what was to become East Pakistan (now Bangladesh).[75] It was thought fitting perhaps that only the purely religious side of the Madrassah ought to become part of a state established in pursuit of the Muslim community's Islamic aspirations.

The subsequent history of the Calcutta Madrassah will not occupy us here. While other prominent madrassahs of British India did not migrate to Pakistan, religious scholars associated with many of them did; together with scholars native to the areas which comprised Pakistan, they came to play a considerable role in the religious and political life of the newly established state and fostered the growth of new madrassahs. The modern school system has everywhere come to dominate education, yet the madrassahs have not only survived but shown quite a phenomenal growth. There were 137 madrassahs in what is now Pakistan (the former West Pakistan) at the time of the establishment of the state in 1947; in early 1994, there were estimated to be more than 2,500 in the Punjab alone, the most populous of Pakistan's four provinces.[76]

Of the various government efforts to reform and regulate the affairs of this institution, two deserve special notice.[77] The first dates to the early 1960s; and the second, to the late 1970s. Reports comprising recommendations on madrassah reform were produced on both occasions by committees which included some prominent religious scholars, though bureaucratic officials outnumbered the ulama in the first committee and were marginally fewer than the ulama in the second and neither committee was headed by a religious scholar.[78]

Some of the major issues with which policy makers and reform committees had grappled in British India have continued to be prominent in both reports, while certain other themes are conspicuously new. Of the latter, the single most important theme, a refrain throughout these two reports, is the assurance of Pakistan's continuing commitment to Islam. As the Report of 1962 puts it, 'No doubt it was Islam which gave birth to Pakistan and more than anything else it is Islam which will guarantee its future greatness. The importance of religious education is therefore obvious in a country like Pakistan.'[79]

Yet, a nagging uncertainty about precisely what religious education means, or worse still, what is religious in the education imparted in madrassahs, continues to persist. The Report of 1962 explains that it refers to religious learning ('Deeni Uloom') and non-religious learning ('Duniavi [literally, worldly] Uloom') 'only as convenient expressions and not…to convey the impression that Duniavi Uloom are something outside religious education.' Yet repeated reference to 'basic Islamic studies,' 'strictly religious subjects,' and to the need to expunge 'unnecessary non-religious subjects from the existing syllabus' suggest just the opposite: that is, the positing of a basic dichotomy of the religious and the secular, and a dichotomy not just in society but in the madrassah itself.[80] In the Report of 1962, reform seems primarily to mean two things: to restore the purity of religious learning to the madrassah by eliminating all that is perceived as unnecessary, non-religious, or both; and at the same time, to introduce 'essential non-religious disciplines comprising modern knowledge'[81] in its curriculum. The latter is, of course, the useful instruction that colonial initiatives at reform so assiduously sought. The Report does not do away with the dichotomy between the religious and the non-religious but, rather, reinforces it. The sphere of the non-religious stays intact in the madrassah, with the only (and for the reformers, fundamental) difference being that 'essential' non-religious disciplines are to occupy the space which is to be vacated by the 'unnecessary' non-religious ones.

The Report of 1962 does not deny that the religious disciplines are useful but only that everything usually taught in the madrassah is religious. Logic and philosophy are subjects of particular emphasis in the Dars-i Nizami curriculum of the madrassahs. In the past, these disciplines have been considered fundamental to the study of legal theory and jurisprudence (*usul al-fiqh*) and of theology ('*ilm al-kalam*). Expertise in them was taken to make many of the other disciplines accessible, as madrassah texts even on morphology and syntax, rhetoric and disputation, often presume an intimate acquaintance with logic. The Report of 1962 recommends, however, that logic and philosophy be 'drastically cut down' for 'frankly speaking these are not essential in achieving the objective of religious education.'[82] That objective is taken primarily to consist of making ordinary people, who are 'generally religious-minded, though they have very little knowledge of Shari'ah,' better acquainted with Islam.[83] But inculcating 'true religious values' presupposes that those charged with the task are themselves possessed of it and that in turn requires that the religious learning must only be based on 'undisputed sources of knowledge'. For the latter alone would assure both the usefulness of the madrassah's learning and the fact that it will indeed be properly religious.

Medieval Arabic 'rational sciences' are, in short, deemed to deserve less attention than they have received in the past; while Qur'anic studies, Hadith, and early Islamic history are deemed to require greater emphasis.[84] Other implications of exercising this criterion of 'undisputed sources' are not stated. But, given that much of what is taught in the madrassah is considered not to be based on such undisputed sources, it can hardly escape notice that, in purifying and Islamicizing the sphere of religious learning, the recommendations of the Report also restrict that sphere and, to the extent it is restricted, that of modern knowledge will be enlarged in the madrassah.

The concern to form a precise definition and thereby delimit the sphere of the religious accords with the strong distrust of the religious elite characteristic of the Ayub Khan era during which the Report of 1962 was produced. That concern is much less in evidence in the Report of 1979. The latter is part of the campaign of Islamization launched by General Muhammad Ziaul Haq early in his eleven-year rule (1977–88).[85] Courting the support of the religious scholars was a major concern of Ziaul Haq's policy; the Report of 1979, produced by a committee he had appointed to review the state of the madrassahs and suggest reforms regarding their functioning, leaves little doubt about the regime's efforts to co-opt the ulama. The Report credits the madrassahs with preserving Muslim identity in British India[86] and goes on to describe their position in Pakistan as that of 'an anchor which holds the entire society together.'[87] Yet, no less than earlier governments, Ziaul Haq's regime sought to bring madrassahs under government supervision, even as it paradoxically disclaimed any intention 'to interfere' in their affairs. It was not without reason that many sceptics saw some incongruity between the government's initiatives to reform madrassahs, and integrate them into the mainstream of education,[88] and disclaimers about any interference in their affairs.

The rhetoric justifying the integration of the madrassah into the educational mainstream—a major concern of the Reports of 1962 and 1979, as indeed it was of the reform committees in British India—has had many expressions but is perhaps best illustrated with reference to the Report of 1962. In terms with which the ulama could have had little to quarrel, the Report begins by characterizing Islam as an all-encompassing religion, which it takes to mean that religious education ought to 'cover all aspects of human life.'[89] Such a conception of Islam seems to contrast sharply with the effort to define and restrict the sphere of religion, which we have noticed earlier. But the contrast is apparent only. That Islam regulates all aspects of life, this worldly as well as other-worldly, only supports the case for the reform of the madrassahs; for reform alone would enable the ulama to better participate in modern life—to play an active role in matters of the world, as Islam itself enjoins upon them. The ulama should not, moreover, have anything against the introduction of the modern sciences in madrassahs, since Islam recognizes no distinction between the religious and the non-religious. But precisely because the latter is the case, not only should the modern disciplines be made part of the madrassahs education, but (a point only implied) the latter should itself be integrated into the general system of education.

Neither the Report of 1962 nor that of 1979 actually says that madrassahs should therefore cease to exist, but both do recommend that religious education be somehow brought within, and be regulated by, concerns similar to those of the general stream of state-sponsored education. Whether the sphere of religion is so delimited as to create greater space for the modern disciplines or, conversely, is so extended as to become indistinguishable from other areas of life, the independence of the madrassah and the authority of its ulama seems to be called into question or, at least, to be reshaped in ways which are not of the latter's own choosing. Even the Report of 1979—which offered the ulama many perquisites (financial aid to madrassahs, scholarships, and various other amenities to students, government recognition of the degrees awarded by madrassah and hence the prospect of government employment) should they consent to the reform of their madrassahs, and was, in general, more favourable to them than any previous government initiative—was nevertheless a challenge to their autonomy.

Though few ulama would have failed to perceive that challenge, few were as stringent in their response as Mawlana Muhammad Yusuf Ludhianawi in his detailed critique of the Report of 1979.[90] Ludhianawi, a prominent religious scholar and polemicist, taught at the Jamiat al-'Ulum al-Islamiyya, a major Deobandi madrassah in Karachi, where he was also the editor of its monthly journal. Though the ulama of different sects (and even of the same sect) sometimes differed among themselves in their criticism of the governmental initiatives, I shall confine myself in this chapter to some aspects of the Deobandi critique. This critique, and others, will be discussed in the next section, but one point deserves attention here. Taking it as a given that the system of education established in India by the British was meant to undermine Muslim identity and culture and that it remains largely intact in Pakistan, Ludhianawi musters all his polemical zeal to argue that to integrate madrassahs with this educational system can only mean destroying Islam itself—that the government of an Islamic state would thereby achieve what the British never could.[91] The madrassahs are the 'defenders of the religious sciences' in society, he says; their integration with the state-sponsored system of education signifies nothing but to 'prevent them from their *purely religious services* and to subordinate them to [literally: make them the servants of] the modern [read: Western] sciences. Though in other contexts Islam's 'worldliness,' encompassing life in all its fullness, is a major theme in the ulama's religious discourse, it becomes necessary to deemphasize this worldliness in the face of the madrassah's reform. From this viewpoint, the madrassahs guarantee the preservation of religion in society. That is, there is a separate and independent sphere of religion to be so preserved; and only the independence of the madrassahs can assure its continued existence.

REFORM AND RELIGIOUS AUTHORITY

Mawlana Yusuf Ludhianawi's critique of the Report of 1979 makes explicit an issue which is central to all discussion of madrassah reform: the question of religious authority. Any attempt at reform which is perceived to threaten the identity and the authority of the ulama is by definition suspect. The Report of 1979 had attempted to devise a curriculum which would be acceptable equally to all sectarian affiliations— to the Deobandis, Barelawis, and Ahl-i Hadith among the Sunnis, as well as to the Shia; the establishment of a national board of madrassahs was also visualized, and all sects were to have equal representation on it. But if the authority of a religious scholar is based, in part at least, on his sectarian identity and on his ability to appeal to (and foster) that identity in his audience, then a mixed or hybrid (*makhlut*) curriculum can scarcely be acceptable. Further, as Ludhianawi puts it, any equality between the sects is conceivable only 'in the purely worldly sphere; but no convergence is possible from the point of view of religion'.[92]

The Report's insistence that madrassahs open themselves to the modern sciences, and more generally, that religious education be integrated into the educational mainstream, is likewise unacceptable, as we have seen, but not only because the latter is a legacy of the British and therefore detrimental to Islam. A mixed curriculum, with something from both the religious and the modern sciences, will not produce men who 'combine the medieval and the modern...[Rather], the products of such a system would be useless equally for religion and the world'.[93] What the reform seeks to create is not ulama, Ludhianawi concludes, 'only loyal government servants.'[94]

That government reform diminished a madrassah's standing in society had already been clearly recognized in British India. Though reformed madrassahs of British Bengal had the privilege of government recognition, which meant that they might receive financial support and their graduates were eligible for government service as well as for admission in government educational institutions and universities, they were seen, even by the official reforming committees, to lack the prestige or authority that the unreformed, non-government madrassahs enjoyed. Thus, even as the Harley Committee of 1915 insisted, for instance, that only by being reformed could madrassahs 'play their part in the various activities which go to make up the public life of India', it had recommended that the Calcutta Madrassah 'be reserved for studies *on the orthodox lines*...[and]

the kind of teaching which made the madrassahs in Upper India centres of Islamic learning for the whole of India.'[95]

In British India, it did not perhaps take much imagination for the ulama to see government initiatives to reform madrassahs as a conspiracy to undermine Islam and to do away with the ulama. But, as Ludhianawi's criticism of the Report of 1979 shows, similar suspicions have continued to be expressed in Pakistan.[96] He is in no doubt that the content of the proposed reform subverts the purpose of the madrassah and the position of the ulama, and he is not alone in such suspicions. The ulama have often defended their madrassahs by pointing to the prestige, influence, and authority of some of the most distinguished of religious scholars educated in them. If madrassahs can produce such scholars, then, the argument goes, there can hardly be anything wrong with their system of education; and those who insist on changes in the curriculum can have no purpose but to undermine the madrassah, to prevent the role this institution has historically played in the life of Muslims.

The justification for reform offered by government committees is thus turned on its head: Madrassahs can continue to play the role they have played in Muslim societies of the past not by undergoing reform but rather by resisting it.[97] That reform can and does connote a variety of things in modern Muslim societies comes out strongly here. Many religious scholars, and madrassahs like Deoband, are reformist in the sense of seeking change in existing styles of religious beliefs and practice. It can be argued, in fact, that their claim to religious authority is rooted, in part at least, on their reformist credentials.[98] But reform in this context does not mean striking out a new, uncharted path; rather, it signifies changes that would bring religious doctrine and practice, as interpreted by these reformers, into conformity with whatever is conceived of as true or original Islam—the Islam of the pious forbears. Reform in the sense of actively integrating modern with classical knowledge is suspect to many, however; for it is perceived as undermining the unity and integrity of madrassah education and as devaluing the credentials of those trained in it. Such sentiment is, of course, not peculiar to the Indian subcontinent. Shaykh 'Abd al-Rahman al-Shirbini, the rector (1905–09) of Egypt's al-Azhar—one of the oldest and most prestigious institutions of Islamic learning in the Muslim world—had argued, for instance, that this institution had been established 'for nothing but the preservation and propagation of *religion and the religious sciences.*' He demanded of the government therefore to 'leave it as it is—as a fortress of religion.... If reform is sought at all, then let it be limited to better arrangements for health, comfort, and good food for the students. As for [modern] philosophy and the modern sciences, let the government introduce these in its own numerous colleges.'[99]

Notwithstanding al-Shirbini's reticence, the Egyptian government did carry through large-scale changes in al-Azhar, though these need not be discussed here.[100] It is worth mentioning, however, that the ulama of Pakistan have sometimes pointed to experiments with madrassah reform in other Muslim countries to caution that scholars of any standing have ceased to appear in those societies as a result of such initiatives; conversely, the madrassahs of the Indian subcontinent, thanks to their having resisted reform, can still boast of many distinguished scholars.[101] In question here is not only the problem of religious authority—those reared on a hybrid (religious and non-religious) education would not be 'real' ulama—but also useful knowledge. In a book on 'the syllabus and the system (*nizam*) of the madrassahs,' Mufti Jamil Ahmad Thanawi (d. 1995), the leading jurisconsult at the Jami'a Ashrafiyya, a prominent Deobandi madrassah of Lahore, had listed thirty(!) useful purposes that madrassahs fulfill in society. To him, as also to Ludhianawi, the only useful knowledge for the madrassah is religious knowledge, and anything less, or more, is detrimental to the madrassah's *raison d'etre*: the maintenance of religion in society.[102]

Ideas such as those of Ludhianawi and Thanawi resonate in the writings of many others on the question of reform. There are, however, other shades of opinion.[103] Though the association representing the network of Deobandi madrassahs rejected the Report of 1979, many prominent Deobandi (as well as non-Deobandi) scholars do, in principle at least, recognize the need for some kind of reform. Mawlana Muhammad Yusuf Banuri (d. 1978), the founder of the Jami'at al-'Ulum al-Islamiyya of Karachi, conceded, for instance, that many of the texts which are studied in madrassahs are sometimes 'barely intelligible' without extensive commentaries and glosses. He held such texts to be 'obscure' because they were written and introduced into madrassahs during a period of Muslim intellectual decline in the later middle ages. For someone reared on the long tradition of studying—and writing—glosses and commentaries, this is a striking observation.[104] Yet Banuri's purpose here was not to subvert the madrassah's learning but ultimately to salvage it. The texts conventionally used in madrassahs ought to be replaced, he wrote, but only by *earlier* ones: These are simpler, clearer, and more authoritative. 'We do not want to do away with the traditional sciences, but seek only to create greater competence in them through the introduction of better books. We do not want modernism (*tajaddud*) but rather to go further back (*taqadum* [in search of authenticity]).'¹⁰⁵ Nevertheless, in viewing commentaries and glosses as impeding innovative and useful learning rather than making for 'interpretive dynamism' and the construction of the interpreters' religious authority,¹⁰⁶ Banuri's comments do show the influence of colonial and modernizing analyses of the madrassah.

Yet Banuri, like many other scholars, also recognized the need for the introduction of new subjects (for example, modern philosophy, a 'new scholastic theology,' economics) in the madrassah;¹⁰⁷ and major Barelawi as well as Deobandi madrassahs now include courses from the modern school system as part of their curriculum—a measure, no doubt, of the influence exerted by government reform committees.¹⁰⁸ But it is noteworthy that, in contemporary Pakistani madrassahs, subjects from the government school system are typically treated as a distinct and separate segment of their education—a segment that students are expected to deal with as a barely legitimate, almost quarantined prelude to their real vocation, the Dars-i Nizami. However they are understood, purely religious studies occupy an exclusive space even within the madrassah. Rather than mitigating this sense of exclusivity, the presence of new elements from the government school system rather serves, ironically, to reinforce it.

THE ULAMA'S RELIGIOUS SPHERE: DIMINUTION OR GROWTH?

In the epilogue to his history of the Calcutta Madrassah published in 1959, Mawlana 'Abd al-Sattar, a lecturer in the Madrassah, vigorously emphasizes the importance of this institution in the preservation of Islamic learning and in the Islamicization of society. But with equal vigour, he also laments the declining fortunes of the Madrassah, and more generally, of religious education in all its forms. He cites several reasons for this decline, emphasizing in particular the hostility towards madrassahs on the part of those who are reared in the English system of education. It is odd, he says, that while specialization is valued in all fields of modern knowledge, madrassahs are criticized—and deemed harmful for 'national interests'—precisely because they train their students to specialize in the Islamic sciences. 'What this means is that...though the preservation and welfare of our society requires farmers, blacksmiths, tailors, and clerks, it needs no religious ulama.' 'Times have changed,' he says. 'Religion (*madhhab*) no longer has any importance for the nation (*qawm*). Religion has become the pastime (*mashghala*) of the idle. In such circumstances, what use can the nation have for those who occupy themselves with the religious sciences?'[109]

At issue for 'Abd al-Sattar is evidently not simply the madrassah and the usefulness of its learning but the broader question of the place of religion in society. Several others among the ulama who have written on the question of madrassah reform have likewise insisted that the debate on the madrassah is a debate on the status and future of Islam itself, for the madrassah is both the bastion of Islam and its guardian. This equation between Islam and the madrassah is not just a polemical—and to some, doubtless, a persuasive—argument against reform, it is also an argument for the separation of religion from other areas of life and its autonomy in society.

The question here is not a separation of religion and state, or of society and state—which, some have argued, had come about in Muslim societies from the first centuries of Islam[110]—but rather a recognition, by the ulama themselves, of greater differentiation within society, with religion occupying a distinct, inviolable, autonomous sphere. Such a view of religion on the part of many ulama in Pakistan has close parallels with developments in modern Muslim societies elsewhere, and not only in the matter of madrassah education. For example, in the face of modernizing reforms of the nineteenth century, the sphere of Islamic law, of 'the pure Shari'a in its traditional form,' came to be increasingly restricted all over the Muslim world to laws of personal status that governed the family and matters of inheritance. The ulama left the rest to modernizing legal reformers, complaining only when this restricted sphere of law was threatened.[111] In education, likewise, the ulama left it to government initiative to devise new forms of education, resisting governmental efforts only when the madrassahs—which they had increasingly come to define as their own sphere—were made the object of change or were otherwise directly threatened.[112] In turn, this differentiation increasingly led the ulama, as Serif Mardin has observed with reference to late nineteenth century Ottoman Turkey, 'to focus on the primarily religious aspect of their vocation. Religion thus became more of a subject matter or a field of specialization than a pervasive social function.'[113]

In one sense, making religion a distinct sphere represents a diminution of the more pervasive influence it enjoyed in Muslim societies in the past; and though they themselves define it as such, none is more conscious of this diminution than the ulama themselves. In his criticism of the 1979 'Report of the National Committee on Madrasas', Mawlana Yusuf

Ludhianawi bitterly complained, as have many others before and since, that those educated in the English system of education, and under their influence almost everyone else, did not even count graduates of the madrassah among the educated. Ludhianawi also recalled an incident when a bus conductor snubbed a madrassah student's request for a reduced bus fare but accepted a reduced fare from students of an English school, for the latter, he said, were 'really students' and therefore entitled to that special concession.[114] The point of this seemingly trivial anecdote is to draw attention to the decline in the ulama's social standing, and from the ulama's perspective, in the deference accorded to religion in society.

Laments on an inexorable decline comprise a familiar topos in Muslim literature.[115] However, as Jonathan Berkey and Michael Chamberlain have shown for medieval Cairo and Damascus, respectively, the social status of the ulama and the prestige accorded to religious learning was apparently quite different from what it is in many modern Muslim societies.[116] Berkey shows, for instance, that in medieval Cairo, no firm barriers existed between education and religious devotion and between the scholars and the non-scholars so far as people's interest in Hadith and the religious sciences was concerned; he also shows how various (otherwise external) segments of society—the Mamluk military aristocracy, women, and ordinary people—could all come together to participate in sessions where Hadith was heard and transmitted.[117] Though some even then had reservations about sharing religious knowledge with all and sundry, popular participation in Hadith sessions was nevertheless a mark of reverence for such knowledge and for those—the ulama—who had more than a casual interest in it. In many Muslim societies, much of the intellectual life had continued to be dominated, if not virtually monopolized, by the ulama until the early decades of the twentieth century.[118] The situation has changed in modern societies in more than one way, however. New, modern forms of education introduced during the colonial period have seriously restricted the usefulness of madrassah education and its prestige, even in the eyes of those who lack any formal education in modern schools. On the other hand, modern education as well as exposure to other forms of information through, inter alia, the impact of print on Muslim societies has meant that the ulama's interpretations of religion can be challenged or even ignored by people who can and do have independent access to religious texts. Muslim societies have seen the emergence, during the nineteenth and twentieth centuries, of what some scholars have characterized as the 'new' religious intellectuals: Individuals whose understanding of Islam is not derived from the ulama or from formal education in madrassahs and who, more often than not, are sceptical of the usefulness of the ulama and their institutions of learning.[119] It is not surprising, then, that the ulama should seek to preserve their autonomy from bureaucratic reform committees, no less than from the new religious intellectuals. To do so entails for them defining religion as a distinct sphere and claiming to be its exclusive guardians and representatives.

If we ought to take the ulama's laments about their decline seriously, we cannot also be oblivious to the fact that the decline in question has proven to be less severe than the rhetoric of many ulama would have it. To claim a separate sphere for religion does not signify its privatization, still less its diminishing appeal, as predicted by theorists of secularization.[120] Pakistan's successive constitutions have assigned Islam a prominent place in public life, and many among the ulama have remained active in the effort to define an Islamic identity for Pakistan.[121] The total number of madrassahs has grown, not diminished in Pakistan during the fifty years of the state's existence; and despite the emergence of the new religious intellectuals, madrassahs primarily sustain the structure of religious life (for example, in supplying prayer leaders and preachers in mosques, as well as in providing education to many who never make it to government schools or drop out from them) in Pakistan.[122] The number of madrassah students in the Punjab have increased from 24,822 in 1960; to 81,134 in 1979; to a startling 218,939 in 1995—that is, this number has increased nearly nine times since 1960.[123] Unlike, say, Morocco, as described by Dale Eickelman, the ranks of the madrassah-educated scholars are anything but being diminished in Pakistan.[124] The situation may be similar in some other Muslim countries as well. For instance, predictions about the decline of al-Azhar of Egypt[125] have proved premature. According to Malika Zeghal, the primary and secondary institutes run by the Azhar had '89,744 students at the beginning of the 1970s and more than 300,000 at the beginning of the 1980s.... Nearly a million students between the ages of 5 and 19 were in charge of the Azhar at the beginning of the 1990s.'[126]

Nor indeed are the madrassahs of Pakistan quite as impervious to change as the rhetoric of many ulama on the one hand and that of government reform committees on the other would have one believe. Many madrassahs now provide for the teaching of certain subjects prescribed in government schools, as already noted; and a small but growing proportion of the ulama associated with madrassahs are said also to have had some form of education in the modern school system.[127]

Whether or not those associated with the madrassahs realize or admit this, the very effort to preserve the madrassah, and Islam, unchanged in a rapidly changing world involves considerable redefinition of what Islam means, where to locate it in society, and how best to serve its interests. As we have seen, one way to do so is to define Islam as occupying a distinct sphere in society and to equate the autonomy of this sphere and the authority and identity of the ulama with an ideally invariant corpus of purely religious texts. For all its novelty, at least for the ulama, such a view of Islam and of its place in society is meant to claim for themselves the prerogative to define—if often in terms patently borrowed from colonial and post-colonial bureaucratic analyses—what constitutes useful education for the madrassah and what (if anything) needs to be reformed or how. The ulama seek to extend their influence in society, to refashion all else, if not in their own image then at least according to their prescription. Yet the effort to do so has come increasingly to be predicated on the prior existence of, and firm boundaries between, their sphere of religion and the rest of society, not on the blurring of such boundaries.

Author's Note: This article was first published in *Comparative Studies in Society and History*, vol. 41, no. 2 (1999). Apart from some typographical and other minor corrections, no change of any substance has been made in reprinting this article.

NOTES

Research for this essay was made possible by a grant from the Triangle South Asia Consortium Residency Program, funded by the Rockefeller Foundation and administered by Duke University, Durham, North Carolina. An earlier version was presented at the workshop on 'The Transformations of the South Asian Islamicate Community in the 19th and 20th centuries', University of North Carolina, Chapel Hill, 23–26 May 1996. I wish to thank the participants in the conference, and especially Professors Carl W. Ernst, David Gilmartin, Bruce B. Lawrence, and John F. Richards, for their comments and encouragement.

1. On the madrassah in medieval Islam, see George Makdisi, *The Rise of Colleges* (Edinburgh: Edinburgh University Press, 1981); Jonathan Berkey, *The Transmission of Knowledge in Medieval Cairo: A Social History of Islamic Education* (Princeton: Princeton University Press, 1992); Michael Chamberlain, *Knowledge and Social Practice in Medieval Damascus 1190–1350* (Cambridge: Cambridge University Press, 1994).
2. See J. Heyworth-Dunne, *An Introduction to the History of Education in Modern Egypt* (London: Luzac, 1938), especially 1–84; A.L. al-Sayyid Marsot, 'The Beginnings of Modernization among the Rectors of al-Azhar, 1798–1879,' in *Beginnings of*

Modernization in the Middle East, W.R. Polk and R.L. Chambers, eds. (Chicago: University of Chicago Press, 1968), 267–80; A. Chris Eccel, *Egypt. Islam and Social Change: al-Azhar in Conflict and Accommodation* (Berlin: Klaus Schwarz Verlag, 1984); S. Akhavi, *Religion and Politics in Contemporary Iran: Clergy-State Relations in the Pahlavi Period* (Albany: State University of New York Press, 1980), 117–58; Brinkley Messick, *The Calligraphic State: Textual Domination and History in a Muslim Society* (Berkeley: University of California Press, 1993).

3. See, most notably, Barbara D. Metcalf, *Islamic Revival in British India: Deoband 1860–1900* (Princeton: Princeton University Press, 1982).
4. Talal Asad, *Genealogies of Religion: Discipline and Reasons of Power in Christianity and Islam* (Baltimore: The Johns Hopkins University Press, 1993), 207 (emphasis in the original). On the evolution of the modern notion of 'religion', see Peter Harrison, *'Religion' and the Religions in the English Enlightenment* (Cambridge: Cambridge University Press, 1990).
5. Thomas R. Metcalf, *Ideologies of the Raj* (Cambridge: Cambridge University Press, 1994), 4ff, 66–112, and passim; cf. Barbara D. Metcalf, 'Too Little and Too Much: Reflections on Muslims in the History of India,' *Journal of Asian Studies*, 54 (1995), 956.
6. See Gregory C. Kozlowski, *Muslim Endowments and Society in British India* (Cambridge: Cambridge University Press, 1985), on the British distinction between public and private endowments.
7. For a discussion of the debate on this policy, see Gauri Viswanathan, *Masks of Conquest: Literary Study and British Rule in India* (New York: Columbia University Press, 1989).
8. Education Report from the Director of Public Instruction, Punjab to the Financial Commissioner, Punjab, 25 June 1858, section 18; extracts in G.W. Leitner, *History of Indigenous Education in the Punjab since Annexation and in 1882* (Patiala: Languages Department Punjab, 1971 [first published in 1883]), Appendix, vi, 20.
9. See Leitner, *History,* 71–72 and passim; also see F.A. Nizami 'Madrasahs, Scholars and Saints: Muslim Response to the British Presence in Delhi and the Upper Doab 1803–1857' (unpublished Ph.D. dissertation, University of Oxford, 1983), 42–58.
10. Extracts from Parliamentary Report (1874, C. 1072-II, part III) in Leitner, *History,* vii.
11. Cf. T. Metcalf, *Ideologies,* 36–37.
12. I do not intend to suggest, of course, that British categories of analysis were the only source of such distinctions in colonial India, only that the former seem to have substantially contributed to them. Factors other than the impact of colonial rule may have played some part, and even the influence of colonialism had many different manifestations.
13. Cf. Berkey, *Transmission,* passim; Chamberlain, *Social Practice,* 69–90.
14. Ibn Khaldun, *The Muqaddimah: An Introduction to History,* F. Rosenthal, trans. (New York: Pantheon Books, 1958), III, 299–300; Hajji Khalifa, *Kashf al-zunun 'an asami al-kutub wa'l-funun,* G. Fluegel, ed. (Leipzig: Oriental Translation Fund, 1835), I:114–5.
15. James Mill, Revenue Department dispatch, 18 February 1824, Bengal, E/4/710, para. 83, India Office Library and Records, British Museum, quoted in Lynn Zastoupil, *John Stuart Mill and India* (Stanford: Stanford University Press, 1994), 32–33. Also see the despatch of the Court of Directors to the Bengal Government, 24 October 1832, in *The Correspondence of Lord William Cavendish Bentinck,* C.H. Philips, ed.

(Oxford: Oxford University Press, 1977), 933–4 on some of the content of useful learning.
16. *Report by the Panjab provincial Committee with evidence taken before the committee and memorials addressed to the education commission* (Calcutta: Superintendent of Government Printing, India, 1884), 369.
17. Ibid., 370.
18. On this controversy, see David Kopf, *British Orientalism and the Bengal Renaissance: The Dynamics of Indian Modernization 1773–1835* (Berkeley: University of California Press, 1969), 7–8, 241–52, and passim; Viswanathan, *Masks of Conquest*, 29ff., 101ff., and passim.
19. Cf. A.J. Wensinck et al., *Concordances et indices de la tradition musulmane*, IV [Leiden: E.J. Brill, 1962], 330; Franz Rosenthal, *Knowledge Triumphant: The Concept of Knowledge in Medieval Islam* (Leiden: E.J. Brill, 1970), 243; Hajji Khalifa, *Kashf al-zunun*, I:48–52.
20. Chamberlain, *Social Practice*, 111–3.
21. Cf. Javed Majeed, *Ungoverned Imaginings: James Mill's The History of British India and Orientalism* (Oxford: Clarendon Press, 1992), 196ff.
22. Quoted in A.M. Monteath, *Note on the State of Education in India*, 1862, in *Selections from Educational Records of the Government of India*, vol. I: *Educational Reports. 1859–71* (Delhi: National Archives of India, 1960 [hereafter *SERGI*, I]), 45–46.
23. For the history of this Madrassah, see 'Abd al-Sattar, *Tarikh-i* Madrasa-i *'Aliya*, 2 vols. (Dhaka: Research and Publications, Madrasa-i 'Aliya, 1959). On proposed or actual reforms in the Madrassah, see ibid., I:47ff. and passim. On the *Dars-i Nizami,* see note 39, below.
24. *SERGI*, I:21.
25. Ibid., I:21.
26. 'Abd al-Sattar, *Madrasa-i 'Aliya*, I:119–20, 129, 134.
27. *SERGI*, I:23.
28. See the revised curriculum introduced in 1871 in 'Abd al-Sattar, *Madrasa-i 'Aliya*, I, 171–2. Most of the texts which comprise the curriculum are the same as those in the *Dars-i Nizami.*
29. For such apprehensions, see for instance 'Abd al-Sattar, *Madrasa-i 'Aliya*, I:55, 140–1.
30. Cf. Sayyid Amir 'Ali's evidence before the Education Commission of 1882, quoted in *Report of the Muslim Education Advisory Committee*, 1934, in M.S.A. Ibrahimy, *Reports on Islamic Education and Madrasah Education in Bengal (1861–1977)*, 5 vols. (Dhaka: Islamic Foundation Bangladesh, 1987 [hereafter: Ibrahimy, *Reports*]), III:141.
31. Quoted in the *Report of the Madrasah Education Committee*, 1941, in Ibrahimy, *Reports*, III:335.
32. See, for instance, William Adam, *Reports on the State of Education in Bengal (1835 and 1838)*, A. Basu, ed. (Calcutta: University of Calcutta Press, 1941), II:153.
33. On the contradictions in this 'preservationist ideal,' see T. Metcalf, *Ideologies*, especially 66–92.
34. For the recommendations of the various madrassah-reform committees in nineteenth- and twentieth-century Bengal, see Ibrahimy, *Reports*, passim.
35. Abu'l-Hasan 'Ali Nadwi, *Insani dunya nar musalmanon key 'uruj wa zawal ka athar*, 5th ed. (Lucknow, 1966), 226; cf. Ibn Khaldun, *The Mucaddimah*, III:290–1.
36. Cf. Mawlana Muhammad Zakariyya, *Ta'rikh-i Mazahir*, I (Saharanpur: Kutub khana-i isha'at al-'ulum, 1972 [written in 1916]), I:144.

37. Messick, *Calligraphic State*, 30–36, at 30.
38. Edward Gibbon, *The History of the Decline and Fall of the Roman Empire*, David Womereley, ed. (London: Allen Lane, 1994), vol. I:ch. ii, 84. Also see the remarks of James Mill on traditional Islamic education in India: *The History of British India*, 5th ed. (New York: Chelsea House Publishers, 1968 [1858 edition]), I:52ff.
39. On Mulla Nizam al-din, see Muhammad Rida Ansari, *Bani-yi Dars-i Nizami* (Lucknow: Nami Press, 1973); *The Encyclopaedia of Islam*, new ed. (Leiden: E.J. Brill, 1960–) s.v. 'Nizam al-din, Mulla' (F. Robinson); on the Farangi Mahal, F. Robinson, 'Problems in the History of the Farangi Mahall Family of Learned and Holy Men,' *Oxford University Papers on India*, I:pt. 2 (Delhi: Oxford University Press, 1987), 1–27; on the *Dars-i Nizami*, see 'Abd al-Hayy al-Hasani, *al Thaqafa al-Islamiyya fi'l-Hind*, 2nd ed. (Damascus: Majma' al-lugha al-'Arabiyya bi-Dimashq, 1983), 9–17; Akhtar Rahi, *Tadhkira-yi Musannifin-i Dars-i Nizami* (Lahore: Maktaba-yi Rahmaniyya, 1978); Nizami, 'Madrasahs, Scholars and Saints,' 24–32, 279–81; Jamal Malik, *Islamische Gelehrtenkultur in Nordindien* (Leiden: E.J. Brill, 1997), 151ff., 522ff.
40. Nizami, 'Madrasahs, Scholars and Saints,' 30–32.
41. For some of the major texts of this curriculum, see Nizami, 279–81; Malik, *Islamische Gelehrtenkultur*, 522ff.
42. On the style and substance of learning in Wali Allah's madrassah, see S.A.A. Rizvi, *Shah WaliAllah and his Times* (Canberra: Ma'rifat Publishing House, 1980), 382–86.
43. On Deoband, see B. Metcalf, *Islamic Revival*, passim; on other contemporary sectarian movements, ibid., 264–314. On the Barelwis, see Usha Sanyal, *Devotional Islam and Politics in British India: Ahmad Riza Khan Barelwi and his Movement 1870–1920* (Delhi: Oxford University Press, 1996).
44. B. Metcalf, *Islamic Revival*, 100ff.; cf. Gilani, *Nizam-i Ta'lim*, I:240ff., 289.
45. These six collections of Hadith are: the *Sahih* of al-Bukhari (d. 870); the *Sahih* of Muslim (d. 874); the *Jami'* of al-Tirmidhi (d. 892); the *Sunan* of Ibn Maja (d. 886); the *Sunan* of Abu Da'ud (d. 888); and the *Sunan* of al-Nasa'i (d. 914–15).
46. B. Metcalf, *Islamic Revival*, 87–137, at 93.
47. On the Nadwat al-ulama, see Muhammad Ishaq Nadwi and Shams Tabriz Khan, *Tarikh-I Nadwat al-ulama*, 2 vols. (Lucknow: Nizamat Nadwat al-ulama, 1983–84 [hereafter TNU]); Sayyid Muhammad al-Hasani, *Sirat-i Mawlana Sayyid Muhammad 'Ali Monairi. bani-yi Nadwatal-ulama* (Lucknow: Maktabat Dar al-'Ulum Nadwat al-ulama, 1964 [hereafter Sirat]); Abu'l-Hasan 'Ali Nadwi, *Karwan-i Zindagi*, 5 vols. (Karachi, 1983–94), passim; B. Metcalf, *Islamic Revival*, 335–47; Jamal Malik, 'The Making of a Council: The Nadwat al-ulama,' *Zeitschrift der deutschen morgenlandischen Gesellschaft*, 144 (1994), 60–90.
48. For various criticisms of the traditional madrassahs, see *TNU*, I:63–79.
49. Ibid., I:139–42.
50. For some aspects of the opposition to the Nadwa, see Muhammad al-Hasani, *Sirat*, 143–4, 170ff.; Sanyal, *Devotional Islam*, 217–26; B. Metcalf, *Islamic Revival*, 342ff.
51. TNU. I:57; cf. ibid., I:125, 249.
52. See Shibli's speech on this occasion in *Khutbat-i Shibli*, ed. Sayyid Sulayman Nadwi (A'zamgarh: Dar al-Musannifin, 1941), 128.
53. TNU, I:59, citing Abu'l-Hasan 'Ali Nadwi, *Hayat-i 'Abd al-Hayv* (Lucknow: Majlis-i-tahqiqat wa nashriyyat-i Islam, 1970), 130.
54. *Maqalat-i Shibli*, ed. Sayyid Sulayman Nadwi (A'zamgarh: Dar al-Muannifin, n.d.; reprinted Lahore: National Book Foundation, 1989), VIII:91 (emphasis added).

55. Quoted in Muhammad al-Hasani, *Sirat*, 147–8; *TNU*, I:79.
56. See TNU, II, 32–81 passim; Muhammad al-Hasani, *Sirat*, 204ff., 260–90.
57. Contrast Malik, 'Making of a Council,' especially 87ff., for an interpretation of the differences among the Nadwa's leaders in terms of their different social origins and cultural orientations.
58. Cf. Muhammad al-Hasani, *Sirat*, 71, 82, 119, 167 etc.; TNU, such as I:147, 238; II, 110, 180, 219, 240, 294, 318f. Indeed, as Sayyid Sulayman Nadwi noted in his speech at the annual session of 1915, disquisitions on the necessity (*darurat*) and usefulness (*fawa'id*) of the Nadwa's Dar al-'Ulum were a constant feature of all its annual sessions. Ibid., II:110–11.
59. As Shibli put it in his speech at the annual session of the Nadwat al-ulama in 1894: see *Khutbat-i Shibli*, 19. On the importance of literature (*adab*) in the Nadwa's curriculum, see *TNU*, I:147. 60Cf.*TNU*, I:148, 218.
60. Cf. *TNU*, I:148, 218.
61. For the goals of the Nadwa as enunciated on various occasions during its early years, see ibid., I:55ff., 139ff., and passim.
62. Cf. Adam, *Reports*, II:147, II:151; *Report of the Punjab Education Commission*, 411.
63. Viswanathan, *Masks of Conquest*.
64. On British notions of representation, see Farzana Shaikh, *Community and Consensus in Islam: Muslim Representation in Colonial India* (Cambridge: Cambridge University Press, 1989).
65. Cf. Leitner, *History*, vi, vii.
66. The following (unattributed) verses celebrating the authority of the *Hidaya*, a compendium of Hanafi substantive law which dates to the twelfth century and has long been studied in madrassahs, indicates the authority certain texts in the madrassah enjoyed: 'The *Hidaya*, like the Qur'an, has abrogated whatever books had been written on law; so persist in reading it and carefully attend to its recitation, for thereby will your speech become free of waywardness and falsehood.' Quoted in Gilani, *Nizam-i Ta'lim*, 313.
67. Cf. *Khutbat-I Shibli*, 57,88.
68. Cf. ibid., 18; *Maqalat-i Shibli*, III:127.
69. Abu'l-Hasan 'Ali Nadwi, *Karwan*, I:199–226, especially 200, 225f.
70. TNU, II:53. This grant was finally discontinued, at the Nadwa's own initiative, in 1920. Ibid., 272.
71. On the Tablighi Jama'at, see B. Metcalf, '"Remaking Ourselves": Islamic Self-Fashioning in a Global Movement of Spiritual Renewal,' in Martin Marty and R. Scott Appleby, eds., *Accounting for Fundamentalisms* (Chicago: University of Chicago Press, 1994), 706–25.
72. On this aspect of the Nadwa's pursuit of recognition, see Muhammad Qasim Zaman, 'Arabic, the Arab Middle East and the Definition of Muslim Identity in Twentieth Century India,' *Journal of the Royal Asiatic Society*, series 3, vol. 8 (1998), forthcoming.
73. On madrassahs in post-independence India, the study of which is beyond the scope of this essay, see Kuldip Kaur, Madrassah *Education in India: A Study of its Past and Present* (Chandigarh: Centre for Research in Rural and Industrial Development, 1990).
74. 'Abd al-Sattar, *Madrasa-yi 'Aliya*, II:114ff.
75. Ibid., II:114.
76. For figures on the growth of madrassahs between 1947 and 1971, see Hafiz Nadhr Ahmad, *Ja'iza-yi madaris-i 'arabiyya-yi Maqhribi Pakistan* (Lahore: Muslim Academy,

1972), 691-2; for the growth of madrassahs in the Punjab in more recent years, see *Zindagi* (Lahore), 17 February 1995, p. 39; *The News* (Islamabad), 7 March 1995. Recent figures for the country as a whole are not available to the present writer.

77. Recommendations for the reform of madrassahs in East Pakistan (now Bangladesh) were also made at various times between 1947 and 1971. See Ibrahimy, *Reports*, vols. 4-5, passim. These will not be discussed in this essay.

78. For a list of members comprising each committee, see *Report of the Committee set up by the Governor of West Pakistan for Recommending Improved Syllabus for the various Darul Ulooms and Arabic Madrasas in West Pakistan* (Lahore: Superintendent, Government Printing West Pakistan, 1962 [hereafter *Report* {1962}]), p. i; *Report Qawmi Committee bara-yi Dini Madaris-i Pakistan* (Islamabad: Ministry of Religious Affairs, 1979), hereafter *Report* (1979), 3-7. For a discussion of the two reports and the reactions to them, see Jamal Malik, *Colonialization of Islam: Dissolution of traditional institutions in Pakistan* (Delhi: Manohar, 1996), 123-8, 132-9. I am much indebted to Malik's pioneering work, though his study, in being primarily concerned with the effects of state-sponsored Islamization (between 1977 and 1984) as a vehicle of increasing state control over 'autochthonous institutions,' has a focus different from mine. As will be observed, I am concerned here not with such encroachment by the state, but rather with the emergence of a distinct religious sphere as a response to categories of colonial analysis. Though he claims to discern the continuing existence of, *inter alia*, the 'colonial' sector in Pakistani society, Malik pays scant attention to the shaping of religious discourse in terms of colonial categories, either in British India or in Pakistan

79. *Report* (1962), 3.
80. For these phrases, see ibid., 5, 7, 9, 12, 14, passim.
81. Ibid., 11.
82. Ibid., 22-23.
83. Ibid., 4.
84. Ibid., 19-30, and Appendix IV (pp. 1-51 of the Urdu text).
85. On some aspects of Zia ul-Haq's Islamization, see Anita M. Weiss, ed., *Islamic Reassertion in Pakistan: The Application of Islamic Laws in a Modern State* (Lahore: Vanguard, 1987); Rudolph Peters, 'The Islamization of Criminal Law: A Comparative Analysis,' *Die Welt des Islams*, 34 (1994), 246-74, especially 256ff. Malik, *Colonialization of Islam*.
86. *Report* (1979), 44.
87. Ibid., 50.
88. Ibid., i, 8-9. The terms used are *marbut karna* (p. i: literally, to integrate), *ham-ahang [karna]* (p. 8: to harmonize) 'with the general system of education in the country', and to establish *yaksaniyyat awr yakjahti* (similarity and uniformity) 'between the curriculum and system of examinations' of the madrasa and general education).
89. *Report* (1962), 7.
90. For Ludhianawi's detailed critique of the Report of 1979, see *Bayyinat* (the journal of the Jami'at al-'Ulum al-Islamiyya), 38:2 (January 1981), 2-28. Also see idem, in *Bayyinat*, 47:1 (May 1985), 35-63. The Report of 1979 was also rejected by the Wifaq al-Madaris, the network of Deobandi madrassahs. For the text of the latter's resolutions in this regard, see *Bayyinat*, 38:2 (January 1981), 4-5; *Bayyinat*, 47:1 (May 1985), 45. Also see Malik, *Colonialization of Islam*, 136-8.
91. Ludhianawi, 'Basa'ir wa 'ibar', in *Bayyinat*, 38:2 (January 1981), 12-13. Emphasis added.

92. Ibid., 17. The reference to a 'mixed' curriculum is meant, of course, to be contemptuous.
93. Ibid., 16. For a very similar argument, see Mufti Jamil Ahmad Thanawi, *Nisab wa Nizam-i Dini Madaris* (Lahore: Nashiran-i Qur'an Limited, n.d.), 59–60.
94. Ludhianawi, 'Basair,' in *Bayyinat* (January 1981), 27. It is worth noting here that making government servants out of the madrassah educated does not everywhere carry the stigma it does in the foregoing statement. For instance, many of the scholars calling for the reform of the Azhar of Egypt in the late nineteenth and early twentieth century sought the introduction of modern subjects there precisely to enable graduates of the Azhar to compete with others in the quest for government jobs. Eccel, *Egypt. Islam and Social Change*, 313–4.
95. Quoted in *Report of the East Bengal Educational System Reconstruction Committee. 1949–52*, in Ibrahimy, *Reports*, IV:40, emphasis added.
96. The ulama's reluctance to associate with those in power may also have something to do with their resistance to governmental reform of the madrassah, though the implications of such distrust should not be exaggerated. For if some ulama have always insisted on maintaining their distance from the ruling authorities, there has never been a dearth, in Muslim societies, of those who were willing to be actively involved in the administration.
97. For this argument, see, for instance, Thanawi, *Dini Madaris*, 66–71. Cf. Gilani, *Nizam-i Ta'lim*, I:252–316 and passim.
98. I am grateful to Professor David Gilmartin for elucidating this point to me.
99. Quoted in Muhammad Rashid Rida, *Tarikh al-ustadh al-imam al-shaykh Muhammad 'Abduh* (Cairo: Matba'at al-Manar, 1931), I:504; emphasis added.
100. On these reforms, see Marsot, 'The Beginnings of Modernization,' 267–80; Daniel Crecelius, 'Nonideological Responses of the Egyptian Ulama to Modernization,' in Nikki R. Keddie, ed., *Scholars, Saints, and Sufis: Muslim Religious Institutions in the Middle East since 1500* (Berkeley: University of California Press, 1972), 167–209; Eccel, *Egypt. Islam and Social Change*.
101. Cf. Thanawi, *Dini madaris*, 66–68.
102. Ibid., passim.
103. See, for instance, the proceedings of the seminar on 'the education system of madrassahs,' organized in November 1986 by the Institute of Policy Studies, Islamabad: Muslim Sajjad and Salim Mansur, *Dini madaris ka nizam-i tatlim* (Islamabad: Institute of Policy Studies, 1987; reprint, 1993).
104. Banuri is the author of a six-volume commentary in Arabic on the *Jami' of al-Tirmidhi*, one of the major Sunni collections of Hadith. This commentary (entitled *Ma'arif al-Sunan*) is, in turn, based on the lectures on the *Jami'* by his teacher, Mawlana Anwar Shah Kashmiri (d. 1933), the sometime principal of the madrassah at Deoband
105. See, for instance, Mawlana Muhammad Yusuf Banuri, 'Dars-i Nizami: Chand tawajjuhtalab pahlu,' in *Jaridat al-Ashraf* (Journal of the Jami'a Ashrafiwa Sukkur. March-April 1994), 26–52; the quotation is from p. 32.
106. Messick, *Calligraphic State*, 34.
107. Banuri, 'Dars-i Nizami,' 31.
108. For instance, see the curriculum issued by the network of Barelwi madrassahs: *Nisab-i ta'limi tanzim al-madaris (Ahl-i Sunnat) Pakistan* (Lahore: Markazi dafter tanzim al-madaris Pakistan, 1412 A.H. [1991]); and cf. Malik, *Colonialization of Islam*, 164–76.
109. 'Abd al-Sattar, *Madrasa-i 'Aliya*, II:146–47. Compare Asad, *Genealogies*, 207.

110. For example, Ira M. Lapidus, 'The Separation of State and Religion in the Development of Early Islamic Society,' *International Journal of Middle East Studies*, 6 (1975), 363–85. Also see idem., 'The Evolution of Muslim Urban Society,' *Comparative Studies in Society and History*, 15:1 (1973), 21–50, especially 28ff.; idem, *A History of Islamic Societies* (Cambridge, 1988), especially 120ff. Closer analysis of religious and political trends in early Islam, and especially of early 'Abbasid history—on which Lapidus' findings are primarily based—reveals, however, that there is little evidence to suggest the 'separation of state and religion' that he posits: see Muhammad Qasim Zaman, *Religion and Politics under the Early 'Abbasids* (Leiden: E. J. Brill, 1997).
111. N.J. Coulson, *A History of Islamic Law* (Edinburgh: Edinburgh University Press, 1964), 149–225; the quotation is from p. 154. Also cf. Messick, *Calligraphic State*, 61f.
112. Cf. Crecelius, 'Nonideological Responses,' 187–8; Richard L. Chambers, 'The Ottoman Ulema and the Tanzimat', in Keddie, ed., *Scholars, Saints. and Sufis*, 33–46, especially 41, 45.
113. Serif Mardin, *Religion and Social Change in Modern Turkey* (Albany: State University of New York Press, 1989), 112.
114. Ludhianawi, 'Basa'ir', in *Bayyinat* (January 1981), 22–23.
115. Cf. Berkey, *Transmission*, 182ff.; idem., 'Tradition, Innovation and the Social Construction of Knowledge in the Medieval Islamic Near East,' *Past and Present*, 146 (1995), 38–65.
116. Berkey, *Transmission*; Chamberlain, *Social Practice*.
117. Berkey, *Transmission*, 128–218.
118. Dale F. Eickelman, *Knowledge and Power in Morocco: The Education of a Twentieth-Century Notable* (Princeton: Princeton University Press, 1985), 5–6; Green, *The Tunisian Ulama*, 53.
119. In characterizing such individuals as '"new" religious intellectuals,' I follow Dale Eickelman and James Piscatori, *Muslim Politics* (Princeton: Princeton University Press, 1996). On the impact of print in Muslim societies, see Francis Robinson, 'Technology and Religious Change: Islam and the Impact of Print,' *Modern Asian Studies*, 27 (1993), 229–51; Adeeb Khalid, 'Printing, Publishing, and Reform in Tsarist Central Asia,' *International Journal of Middle East Studies*, 26 (1994), 187–200; Messick, *Calligraphic State*, 115–31.
120. For a recent critique of theories of secularization, see José Casanova, *Public Religions in the Modern World* (Chicago: University of Chicago Press, 1994); on notions of public and private religions, see ibid., 40–66.
121. For an analysis of the ulama's early efforts in this regard, see Leonard Binder, *Religion and Politics in Pakistan* (Berkeley: University of California Press, 1961).
122. At the level of primary education, the ratio of dropouts among boys was calculated in 1994–95 to be 43 per cent in the urban areas of Pakistan and 78 per cent in the rural areas. For girls, the ratio was 59 per cent and 88 per cent, respectively. See *The News* (Islamabad), 27 June 1995, p. 2. Such dropouts appear to form an increasingly greater proportion of contemporary madrassahs, though many still come without any exposure to government schools. Figures naturally vary, and for a variety of possible reasons, from one madrassah to another. An official of the Khayr al-Madaris, a prominent Deobandi madrassah of Multan, in the Punjab province, with about 2,500 students, reported to the present writer in August 1995 that there were 'very few' students who were illiterate at the time of their admission to the madrassah. Conversely, the Jami'at Anwar al-'Ulum, a Barelwi madrassah also in Multan (with

about 800 students) reported in July 1995 that the proportion of those who were illiterate prior to admission in the madrassah was about 55 per cent. Precisely how to account for such differences remains to be studied.

123. Figures based on: Nadhr Ahmad, *Ja'iza*, 695; *Report* (1979), 198; *Zindagi* (Lahore), 17 February 1995, p. 39.
124. Eickelman, *Knowledge and Power*, 167–8.
125. See, for example, Crecelius, 'Nonideological Responses,' 167–209.
126. Malika Zeghal, *Gardiens de l'Islam: Les ulama d'al-Azhar dans l'Egypte contemporaine* (Paris: Presses de la fondation rationale des sciences politiques, 1995), 279 (author's translation). Also cf. the remarkable increase in the number of mosques in Egypt, 'by 100 per cent between 1961 and 1979, leaping from 17,000 to 34,000', and to 50,000 by 1984. See Patrick D. Gaffney, *The Prophet's Pulpit: Islamic Preaching in Contemporary Egypt* (Berkeley: University of California Press, 1994), 15.
127. See Ministry of Education, Government of Pakistan, *Pakistan ke dini madaris ke ulama-yi kiram ki directory* (Islamabad: Higher Education Research Cell, 1986), 476.

CHAPTER 5

Reforming Mysticism: Sindhi Separatist Intellectuals in Pakistan

OSKAR VERKAAIK

This chapter examines the revival of Sufism and mysticism by the Sindhi separatist movement in the South of Pakistan. It explores the emergence of a network of young intellectuals from a rural and mostly peasant background, and focuses on two pioneers of Sindhi nationalism and Sufi revivalism: G.M. Syed and Ibrahim Joyo. Influenced by Gandhian as well as Marxist ideas on social reform and national identity, these two leaders transformed the annual *urs* celebration at local shrines into commemorations of the martyrs of Sindh. The study traces their relationship as well as their pioneering role as political leaders, educational reformers, and teachers. Analysing their ideas as a particular form of Islamic reform, it discusses the way they adapted and innovated existing cultural ideas on Islamic nationalism, ethnicity, and social justice.

In the late 1960s and early 1970s a rebellious movement emerged in Sindh, the southern province of Pakistan, which protested against the military regime, and later, after the first democratic elections in the history of Pakistan, called for the independence of Sindh. Although Pakistan is now widely associated with radical Islamist movements and authoritarian military regimes, this Sindhi movement did not fit in this picture at all. Its two main ideologues were a neo-Gandhian wearing white clothes while writing treatises on the meaning of mysticism, and a Marxist struggling for the moral and social elevation of the local peasant population. The name of the former was G.M. Syed, the latter was called Ibrahim Joyo. The former was a well-known politician during the time of Independence and a member of an aristocratic landlord family. The latter was the son of a peasant and one of the very few of his generation who had gotten the opportunity to pursue higher education. They had several things in common, for instance, their physical appearances, which resembled the humble, homespun fashion of a disciplined vegetarian cultivated by Mahatma Gandhi. Both of them were concerned with the place of Sindh within Pakistan and together they located the basis of the province's unique position in Pakistan in a reformed Sufism for which they were themselves responsible. Their reformulation of Sufism was a radical break with traditional Sufism, just as most forms of Islamic reform radically differ from tradition. This contribution focuses on these two intellectuals, the peculiar form of Islamic reform they developed, as well as the context in which they operated.

I take Islamic reform as a response to a globalizing trend that starts with European colonialism and imperialism and continues after decolonialization.[1] Part of this globalizing trend is the distribution of ideas, often in modern educational institutions. Islamic reformists have made use of these ideas while rejecting or criticizing them and they continue to do so.[2] While there is increasing academic consensus on these general views, less work has been done on the emergence of intellectual networks or milieus,[3] which critically engage with the influx of new ideas and ideologies. In this study I am especially interested in the emergence of new networks of political activists and Islamic reformists in relation to the introduction and spread of secular education.

This chapter is structured as follows: after some introductory remarks about the relationship between secular education and new forms of contentious politics framed in the language of Islam, I briefly discuss the setting of my case study, which is the province of Sindh in Pakistan. I introduce the various forms of Islamic reform in Pakistan and how these are related to the discourses of nation and ethnicity in Pakistan, and particularly in Sindh. Next, I look at the secularisation of education during the colonial period. The next sections focus on the main leaders of the Sindhi separatist movement, namely G.M. Syed and Ibrahim Joyo. By way of short life stories, based on written sources and interviews I had with Joyo, relatives of G.M. Syed, and followers of both men, I illustrate how these men formulated a reformed notion of Sufism, which radically differed from the folk Sufism of the rural areas, and which became the basis of a Sindhi separatist movement that gained much influence among the Sindhi population in the 1960s and 1970s. Throughout these life stories I will pay specific attention to how these two men used and reformed education as part of their political struggle.

ISLAMIC REFORM IN PAKISTAN

Of crucial importance for the rise of Sindhi separatism[4] was the introduction and spread of secular education. In that respect, it resembled the development of other forms of Islamic reform. Indeed, secular education, as a major vehicle for modernization, has had many unexpected consequences, including the rise of political Islam. As Oliver Roy has argued for recent trends in Islamic reform, 'the cadres of the Islamist parties are young intellectuals, educated in government schools following a Western curriculum'.[5]

The link between Islamic reform and secular education is not new. The success of Islamism in universities and other institutions of higher education in countries like Egypt, Algeria, Pakistan, and Turkey is rather the most recent manifestation. In fact, this is not surprising, since one of the main aspects of Islamic reform is the democratisation of religious authority. Throughout the Muslim world, Islamic reform since the nineteenth century has been initiated by intellectuals not belonging to the milieu of the traditional *ulama*, that is, the body of lettered men who dominated education and intellectual production in theological schools and universities known as *madrassahs*. Whereas these ulama adhered to one of the four established legal schools (Shafii, Malik, Hanafi, and Hanbali), Islamic reformists in the nineteenth century called for the right to individual interpretation (*ijtehad*) of the founding texts of Islam (Quran and the Sunnah) without regard to the tradition of these four legal schools. Reformists were equally critical of the Sufi brotherhoods (*silsilah*), which to them also constituted traditional authoritative bodies responsible for the decline of Muslim power and culture. Islamic reform, then, generally took place only outside the madrassahs and the brotherhoods. Its main protagonists were intellectuals educated in modern educational institutions.

The study of Islamic reform in Pakistan primarily focuses on two such traditions. First, the interpretation of Islam as an essentially progressive religion, which, in its truest form, promotes Muslim nationalism, social equality, and scientific inquiry, and has become highly influential in the Pakistani intellectual, political, and military elite. This tradition harks back to the Muhammadan Anglo-Oriental College, later University, of Aligarh in North India, established in 1875, and also to the works of Muhammad Iqbal, the intellectual founder of Pakistan. Second, the interpretation of Islam as essentially opposed to nationalism and securalism has informed anti-elitist, Islamist groups and parties, calling for the sovereignty of the shariah and for Islam as a total way of life. Although intellectual developments are never unilinear, this tradition is influenced by the theological academy (*dar-ul-ulum*) of Deoband, North India, established in 1867, and by the writings of Abul Ala Maududi, the founder of the Jamat-i Islami.[6]

However, it is often overlooked that Pakistan has produced a third variety of Islamic reform, which is the reform of mystical traditions, or Sufism. Although Sufism is notoriously difficult to describe—it has been labelled as the 'esoteric' dimension of Islam, as well as the 'folk' tradition of Islam—Sufism in South Asia mostly relates to brotherhoods (*tariqa*) connected to the shrines of holy men, which have been, and still are, important centres for popular piety.[7] As such, Sufism is widely seen as juxtaposed to the reform and modernization of Islam. Yet, precisely in the process of defining Sufism as the quintessential tradition of South Asian Islam, Sufism ceased to be merely a religious practice and became an object of intellectual activity. This intellectual trend, then, rejects the two other forms of Islamic reform as foreign, and looks instead for an indigenous, folk, sometimes ethnic form of Islam. Downplaying the transnational character of Sufi brotherhoods, such an indigenous Islam is found in reformed Sufism.[8]

In the 1960s and 1970s, this reformed Sufism was a powerful ideological force behind left-wing and ethnic movements that protested the modernizing and centralizing policies and ideologies of the state, including the independence movement in East Pakistan that led to the founding of Bangladesh in 1971.[9] In order to prevent the fragmentation of Pakistan in various ethnic groups, the central government during the early decades of Pakistan's existence deemed it necessary to actively promote a modernized form of Islam as the basis for a national identity. Hence, the infamous 'One Unit Scheme', which brought the provinces directly under the rule of the central government, and went hand in hand with efforts to purify Islam from what was condescendingly seen as regional folk traditions, superstition, and non-Islamic elements. Particularly the well-known institution of the *pir*—that is, the descendents of the founders of Sufi brotherhoods, who embody the mystical powers attributed to these founders—was seen as a hindrance to the spread of a modern Islamic mentality. These pirs, often claiming descendancy from the Prophet Muhammad (PBUH), often held powerful positions as spiritual leaders as well as landlords. In order to undermine their authority, the modernizing elites condemned the spiritual and healing practices of the pirs as backward and impure forms of Islam. The Sindhi turn to folk

Islam, then, was partly a matter of reversing the stigma of backwardness. In the process, however, folk Islam was no longer seen as primarily connected to the power of the pirs, but reformed and refashioned into a deep-running inclination towards mysticism and Sufism.[10]

In the late 1960s, the combination of ethnic identity and Sufism proved to be attractive for student activists and others critical of the military regime. The flirtations with the folk, the traditional, and the mystical formed a powerful critique of the modernism and authoritarianism of the central government. The Sindhi movement was one of the main contributors to the popular protest that led Pakistan into a major crisis, resulting in the first democratic elections in 1970 and the foundation of Bangladesh in 1971. Following the model of the Bengalis, the Sindhi movement led by G.M. Syed called for the independence of Sindh in 1973. Confronted with similar ethnic movements in other parts of the country, the winner of the 1970 elections, the Pakistan People's Party headed by Zulfiqar Ali Bhutto, acknowledged ethnic identity as a legitimate form of loyalty within the context of Pakistan, partly giving in to the demands of the ethnic movements. This was a break with earlier state discourse in which ethnicity and Islam were seen as incompatible.[11] In this respect, the Sindhi movement has remarkably influenced state ideology, even though the separatist parties have never managed to win real power.

The Sindhi separatist movement represents a particular form of Islamic reform because its main proponents were popular intellectuals. That is to say that they neither belonged to the ranks of traditional religious leaders nor to the mainly city-based middle class intellectuals who had been engaged in earlier forms of Islamic reform. Furthermore, the Sindhi separatist intellectuals emerged on the scene after independence, when Islamic reform, itself developed in reaction to European colonialism and orientalism,[12] had left its mark on the dominant ideology of Pakistani Muslim nationalism. Sindhi separatist intellectuals therefore had to frame their protest within the limits set by Muslim nationalism. Even in rejecting Pakistani Muslim nationalism, the Sindhi separatist intellectuals adhered to the notion that Islam constitutes the basis for national identity. Within these restrictions, however, they designed their own version of Islam, which allowed them to argue for a separate Sindhi national identity based on Sindh's unique experience with Sufism.

In terms of the themes central in this volume, this chapter looks at how Sindhi separatist intellectuals appropriated certain aspects of official state discourse in order to pursue their own anti-state activities. Whereas dominant Muslim nationalism left no room for ethnic identity within the Pakistani nation, the Sindhi intellectuals challenged this view not by rejecting the importance of Islam in political discourse as such, but by interpreting Islam in terms of mystical traditions, subsequently linking this mysticism with loyalties of homeland and kinship. Besides appropriating state discourse they also used and transformed various other discourses present in South Asia, notably Gandhian or theosophical notions on the shared core of all religions, as well as vaguely Marxist notions on feudalism and class struggle. In doing so, they also became cultural innovators producing a new language of ethnic politics eventually adopted by the Pakistani state. As most of these popular intellectuals were educated at institutions of secular education, I will now look at the modernization of the educational system in Sindh.

THE SECULARISATION OF EDUCATION

When the British conquered Sindh in 1843, they found that the *syeds* played a crucial role in education as men of learning and education.[13] The syeds[14] claim descendency from the Prophet's grandsons Hasan or Hussein. Syeds had an extraordinarily powerful position as religious specialists and men of learning in Sindh. The status of the syed community had been enormously enhanced in the eighteenth century when the Mughal influence in Sindh was on the decline and Balochi kings took over power. These kings relied heavily on the support of the syeds and pirs and granted them various privileges in return.[15] For this reason, the syeds and pirs enjoyed a much higher status as religious specialists than the ulama did. The latter are associated with theological seminaries, of which there were only a few in Sindh prior to the British rule.

Before the colonial conquest, the syed community ran the madrassahs where Arabic and Persian—the latter being the language of administration—were taught. In total, there were six of these madrassahs, which were the apex of the Sindhi educational system. Apart from these madrassahs, there were Muslim primary schools, teaching the Quran, as well as Hindu primary schools, where Khudawadi, the language of commerce, was taught. In addition, many landlords employed private tutors for their children, of which some of the village children could also benefit. Private tutorage and primary education were often funded privately by local landlords and notables and they generally survived the British takeover of power. However, the madrassahs were state-funded and these funds stopped soon after the British conquest. After five years of British rule,

Sir Richard Burton, who then worked as an official interpreter for the British colonial government, remarked that 'it is a matter of regret to me that under our enlightened rule, we should have suffered the native places of education to become all but deserted for want of means to carry on the system'.[16]

By the time Sindh was conquered, the controversy about the language and education policy in British India had already been decided in favour of those who preferred English, rather than an oriental classical language, as the language of administration and higher education. A new education system was introduced based on the Bombay tradition, meaning that primary education was in the vernacular, while higher education was in English. As a result, Persian lost its status as the language of administration and learning. However, the British did little to promote higher education in Sindh. It was left to the missionaries to establish English schools—which they reluctantly did, particularly in Karachi, a colonial city that was hardly accessible for most Sindhis. As a result, students who wanted to pursue higher education were forced to travel to Bombay.

Thanks to local initiatives, this situation gradually improved. In 1885, a Sindh Islamic Madrassah was founded in Karachi on the model of the Muhammadan Anglo-Oriental College in Aligarh. Although the school was for Muslim students only and its name may suggest a traditional Muslim curriculum, in practice it was meant to promote modern secondary education in English. Many of the teachers were, in fact, Hindu, from Sindh as well as from Gujarat and Bombay. Nonetheless, Sindhi students still had to travel beyond the borders of Sindh for higher education. Till Independence it was common practice for Sindhi students to finish their education either in Bombay, the Muslim princely state of Junagadh in neighbouring Gujarat, or in Aligarh.

As the highest place of education in Sindh, the Sindh Madrassah played an important role in the creation of a new group of intellectuals who would form the core of the left-wing Sindhi separatist movement in the 1960s and 1970s. They were the first generation of students from a non-elite village background who acquired modern education. These students came from Muslim families who had benefited from social transformations during the colonial period. Some had fathers or uncles who had been hired as village government servants (*tapedars*) by the colonial government. Others were from families who had recently managed to purchase some land, often from Hindu traders and moneylenders. Thirdly, the sons of village headmen (*wadero*), who acted as intermediaries between the landlords and the peasants, also got access to modern education. All of these village boys started their education at the village level, sometimes receiving private education from a local Hindu schoolteacher or at a village mullah school (*makhtab*). If they were lucky, there was a primary school in the vicinity where they could go to, where they received education in Sindhi up to seven years. To be able to go to the Sindh Madrassah in Karachi from there on, it was essential to have good contacts with traditional patrons such as landlords and syeds. As a result, only a few students who were not from high class (*ashraf*) family background managed to make it to the Sindh Madrassah prior to independence, but of those who did several would join the Sindhi movement that emerged after 1958.

After the British conquest Sindh had been ruled from Bombay, but in 1936 Sindh gained provincial autonomy, with the result that the education system and opportunities in Sindh improved. This continued after independence, despite the fact that many Hindu teachers left for India. Primary education was made compulsory in 1940. More primary and secondary schools were opened throughout the province. In 1947, a few months before independence, a university was opened. Originally located in Karachi, the Sindh University was moved to Hyderabad in 1951.

The establishment of the Sindh University was a major step in the secularisation of education, a process that had started with the British conquest that destroyed the local education system in which the syed community played a crucial role. As the West Pakistan *Gazetteer* of 1968 remarked, 'throughout [the colonial period] the [local] mullah schools or makhtabs were treated very much as the Cinderellahs (sic) of the educational world'.[17] The syed-run madrassahs or places of secondary education also suffered from a lack of funds. Instead, a secular system based on the British model was established, a task for which the British-colonial government showed little interest, leaving it to the Sindhi cultural elite to set up new schools and colleges. For this reason, the reconstruction of the educational system along secular lines was only seriously taken in hand between 1936 and 1947, when Sindh was no longer ruled from Bombay. The secularisation of the educational system continued after independence when the British system of education became the model for the new educational system introduced throughout Pakistan.

As the following sections show, the institutions of secular education would become meeting places of new intellectuals, relatively independent of the traditional political and religious elite. They would adopt and reinterpret ideas about freedom, social equality, and social reform, which prevailed throughout South Asia, turning these ideas into a new and powerful frame of contentious politics, which consisted of a combination of Sindhi nationalism, Sufi reform, and Marxism.

G.M. SYED

Let me now turn to the main figure in this study, which is Ghulam Murtaza Syed—generally known as G.M Syed in Sindh and Pakistan. He was in many ways a remarkably productive, original, and largely autodidactic intellectual, creating his own personal interpretation of Islam out of a range of intellectual influences such as nineteenth-century Islamic reform, Darwinian evolution theory, theosophy, eighteenth-century Sindhi poetry, Marxism, classical Sufism, German idealism, and probably more. He successfully managed to present this eclectic mix of ideas as the authentic and age-old Sindhi tradition of Islam. At the same time he was an experienced politician, at some point the main protagonist of the Muslim League in Sindh, while later becoming the most vocal and radical critic of Pakistan nationalism. But he became the intellectual leader of a rather small group of intellectuals from a village background—an avant-garde or vanguard to some of its members—who, often thanks to G.M. Syed's patronage, were the first of their generation to pursue higher education outside their village or district, and who belonged to his most loyal supporters.

When he died in 1995 at the age of ninety-one, he had become Pakistan's most controversial political figure. He had published books and interviews in which he had called Pakistan a mistake. He had argued that Islam acknowledged no borders between Muslims; therefore Islam could never be the basis of a modern state. However, he continued, it is a natural fact that Muslims are divided in historically and geographically determined cultures, but the advocates of Pakistan have not accepted this natural fact. He had criticized the founding fathers of Pakistan—Muhammad Iqbal and Muhammad Ali Jinnah in particular—for their un-Islamic behaviour. He had condemned animal sacrifice, circumcision, and the circumbulation of the Kaaba that is part of the annual pilgrimage to Makkah as pagan practices that had perverted the original message of the Prophet. He had called Islam a stage in the evolution of human spirituality rather than the final word of God. He had accepted Buddha, Christ, Gandhi, Jalalludin Rumi, and the eighteenth-century Sindhi poet Shah Abdul Latif as prophets of mysticism (*tasawwuf*), which he considered the final stage of this spiritual evolution. Passages from the

Quran, the Bhagavad Gita, the Bible, the Torah, and the *Shah-jo-risalo* (the collection of verses of Shah Abdul Latif) were read at his funeral. He had been arrested many times and had spent twenty-eight years under house arrest without trial, including twenty-two years between 1973 and his death in 1995. In the Sindh Museum, located on the campus of the Sindh University near Hyderabad, he is remembered as one of the most important figures in the history of Sindh.

According to Hamida Khuhro, a leading historian of Sindh and at some point a political ally of G.M. Syed, 'syedism' was his first and most constant ideology. G.M. Syed was born in 1904 as the son of a syed landowner in a village known as Sann on the west bank of the Indus. After his father died when he was two years old, he was brought up with the idea that a syed is a spiritual leader to his people, that is, the peasants (*haris*) working for him. Rather than the people of flesh and blood working on his fields, however, he soon took the hari as an abstract or imagined category including all landless Muslim peasants in Sindh. He saw the haris as an exploited and backward people, who needed to be freed and uplifted. To him, this was the main task of the syed. The organic bond that he felt existed between the syed and the hari was grounded in a shared spirituality rooted in the soil. This reinterpretation of the syed's task from a local patron to a social reformer was enhanced further when he met Gandhi in 1921, who had come to Sindh to campaign for the Khilafat Movement, expressing solidarity with the Turks in their fight against the European powers. Gandhi advised the seventeen-year-old Syed to wear *khaddar* (home-spun cloth) and identify with the local people, as Gandhi himself did with the *harijan* ('untouchables'). Another role model was Khan Abdul Ghaffar Khan, often called the Frontier Gandhi, who led a campaign of civil disobedience mixed with social reform in the rural and tribal areas of the North West Frontier Province.[18] As a junior politician and a member of the Congress Party, G.M. Syed had access to these anti-colonial leaders.

The Khilafat Movement meant his entrance into anti-colonial politics. But true to his 'syedism', his first political act was to found a Syed Committee to urge his fellow syeds to take their leading tasks seriously. Next, he founded a Hari Committee to protect the peasants from exploitation from Muslim landlords and Hindu moneylenders. At that time, Sindh administratively belonged to Bombay and in 1928 a movement was launched to call for provincial autonomy for Sindh. This movement was crucial for fostering a Sindhi political identity. As initially both Hindus and Muslims were involved in this movement, which was supported by the Congress Party and the Muslim League alike, the arguments raised to prove Sindh's cultural uniqueness were not based on Islam. One rather referred to Arabic historical sources that identified the Indus delta as a separate country between Persia and *Hind* (India).[19] The archaeological discovery in 1926 of the remains of the Indus Valley Civilization in a site known as Mohenjo-Daro were also presented as proof of Sindh's historical uniqueness as the land of the Indus. In other words, a Sindhi nationalism already existed prior to the introduction of Muslim nationalism in the late 1930s and 1940s. This influenced G.M. Syed's notion of Pakistan when he allied himself with the Muslim League in 1938. For him, Pakistan was the restoration of a historical–geographical entity, a *Greater Sindh*, which he argued had once existed on the borders of the Indus and its tributaries.[20]

Sindh won its provincial autonomy in 1936. Muslim–Hindu riots first occurred in Sindh in 1939. G.M. Syed was arrested for being the leader of the rioting Muslim population of Sukkur, a town in Upper Sindh. Later, he became the minister of education in the provincial government of Sindh and a leading figure in the Muslim League. He also established a school, including a boarding house for students, in his home village, which became the first Anglo-vernacular school in the vicinity, where both English and Sindhi were used as languages of instruction. Over time, however, he became more of a politician than a social reformer. In his autobiography, which he wrote in the form of a deposition for the court, he mentions several mentors who warned him not to forget his task as a social reformer and spiritual leader. But he admits that he did not yet listen.[21] In 1945, he left the Muslim League, but he remained part of the Sindhi political elite. This elite almost exclusively consisted of landlords, syeds, and pirs, together with a few representatives of the up and coming Muslim trading communities (Memon, Khoja, Bohra) who had settled in Karachi—the port city, established by the British, isolated from the province's heartlands by desert areas.

It was in 1958 that G.M. Syed, in his own words, left party politics behind and returned to his true 'faith'[22] of spiritually and economically liberating the rural poor. For some commentators, the incentive for this came from the memory of an unhappy love affair with a Turkish woman known as Mademoiselle Taraki, whom he had met in Bombay. G.M. Syed himself indeed often told his visitors that he learnt his first lessons about true love (*ishq*) from her, subsequently sublimating this worldly kind of love (*ishq-i mijazi*) into a higher state of love (*ishq-i haqiqi*) for Sindh and the divine. He gives a more profane explanation in his autobiography.

The military takeover in 1958 banned all political activities, and several politicians, including G.M. Syed, were put under detention. For seven and half years, he was under house arrest. In retrospect, he considered this a blessing in disguise as it made him leave 'the thorny field of politics'.

He made a study of the history of Sufism in Sindh, which resulted in the publication in 1967 of a book called *Religion and Reality*—originally written in Sindhi, but translated into English and Urdu. In this book he presents an evolutionary theory of religion, distinguishing various stages such as Hinduism, Buddhism, Christianity, Islam, 'Science', and finally mysticism (*tasawwuf*) or 'natural religion', which fully acknowledges the oneness of being (*wahdat ul-wajud*). In his interpretation, mysticism goes beyond doctrine and ritual. Hence, there is a mystical core in any religious tradition that remains essentially the same. Mysticism, being universal and eternal, can never be the basis of nationalism. Religious nationalism in any form is a mistake and creates false communities. Although the love for mankind as a whole is the truest form of love, akin to the love for God, mysticism accepts loyalty to one's family and homeland as genuine incarnations of love. Naturally, nations are based on a shared love for the homeland. Sindh is, therefore, a natural nation, but Pakistan is an artificial nation. Moreover, he calls Sindh the cradle of mysticism with a long history of religious tolerance and revolt against the tyranny of the ulama and mullahs. In other words, it is Sindh's vocation to protest false nationalism and promote mysticism.[23]

The book caused a scandal and met with several *fatwas* as well as legal persecution. Nonetheless, it became the basis for the Sindhi revolt against the military government in the 1960s, when groups of students and intellectuals took to the streets to call for free democratic elections. After G.M. Syed was released from detention in 1966, he continued his political activities by promoting Sindhi literature, culture, and language. It was a threefold campaign. On 'the cultural front' he founded the Sufi Society of Sindh (*bazm-i sufia-i Sindh*). He also initiated a foundation to promote Sindhi language and literature (*Sindhi Adabi Sangat*). Finally, he tried to arouse 'political and social awareness' among Sindhi students. He noted that 'nations had been defeated politically and economically but their intellectuals, working from the fastness of civilisation, literature and culture, not only converted political and economic defeat into victory but also overcame their victors'.[24] These intellectuals, whom he called his 'friends',[25] did not belong to the political establishment. They were rather the first generation of students from peasant and artisan backgrounds educated in the new secular educational institutions for which G.M. Syed himself was partly responsible. A central figure in this network of young intellectuals was Ibrahim Joyo.

IBRAHIM JOYO AND THE YOUNG SINDHI INTELLECTUALS

Ibrahim Joyo was born in 1915, twenty miles from the village where G.M. Syed was born. His father was a peasant but also acted as a middleman between the landlord and the other peasants. On top of this, he owned some land of his own. This gave him an important position in the village where the peasants and artisans were Muslims, and shopkeepers and traders were Hindus. The landlord, a syed, was also the spiritual leader. However, Joyo's father died when Ibrahim was two years old. Ibrahim nonetheless got the opportunity to go to the primary school in the village. After five years, he went to the school G.M. Syed had founded in his home village. G.M. Syed also arranged a scholarship for him that enabled him to go to the Sindh Madrassah in 1932. There he stayed for two years, living in G.M. Syed's house in Karachi, known as Hyder Manzil. This house became a meeting place for students connected to G.M. Syed, and later, after 1958, it would become a centre of the Sindhi movement emerging around G.M. Syed and Ibrahim Joyo.

It became Joyo's ambition to become a teacher at the Sindh Madrassah himself and he managed to get another scholarship to do his bachelor in teaching in Bombay. During the two years he spent in Bombay, he got in touch with Marxist journalists and writers, writing in English, most of them from Bengal. They were opposed to both the Congress Party and the Muslim League. This was an important influence on Joyo's thinking. He became a critic of communal politics, that is, the religious identity politics that pitted Hindus against Muslims, and vice versa. True to Marxist doctrine, he considered religion an instrument of class politics and economic exploitation. For him, the main struggle was a class conflict, but capitalists as well as landlords used the religious sentiments of the people in order to keep the underprivileged masses divided. When he returned to Sindh, he became a teacher at the Sindh Madrassah. He also started a magazine called *Freedom Calling*, which argued for supporting the British during the Second World War in return for independence.

In 1947, he published a little book called *Save Sind, Save the Continent (From Feudal Lords, Capitalists and their Communalisms)*, with a foreword by G.M. Syed. In this book he condemns the landlords (*zamindar*) and pirs for exploiting the peasants. He condemns the peasants for living like slaves, while on their part tyrannizing their women. 'The only duty they know is to work like bullocks for their landlords and money-lenders, to touch the feet of their Zamindar-Masters and Pirs, and worship them literally as living gods, and lastly to instruct their children to do likewise'.²⁶ This is particularly pitiful, he goes on, because these peasants are Muslims and Islam is a liberating religion. He thus gives his own twist to the notion, widespread among reformists of various kinds, that the true message of Islam has been forgotten with the result that the Muslims live in misery. For Joyo, however, the main fight is not one with European powers. The main fight is against oppressive landlords, backward spiritual leaders, and Hindu moneylenders, a fight that can only be won if the Muslims return to the Islamic message of social justice and equality.

Besides, Joyo argues in his book, the recent Punjabi settlers, who came to Sindh after the completion of the irrigation works in the 1930s that turned vast desert areas into agricultural lands, are to blame for the misery of Sindh's peasants. He blames these settlers for being ignorant of Sindhi culture and especially of the eighteenth-century poet Shah Abdul Latif, who was the first poet to sing in the Sindhi language. He also blames them for obstructing the cultural decolonialization of Sindh after Sindh's provincial autonomy in 1936. He writes:

> Poor G.M. Sayed, when he was the Education Minister, had issued or was on the point of issuing orders that every non-Sindhee in Sind must learn *Sindhee* within a stipulated period of time. This, at that time, raised such a vehement noise everywhere among the circles concerned, as if somebody was asking them for giving up their religion.²⁷

The 'circles concerned' were of course the Punjabi settlers.

In short, in Joyo's analysis the notion of class struggle, Islamic revivalism, and early Sindhi nationalism come together in an optimistic belief in 'the river of Progress',²⁸ in which the Sindhi Muslim peasants constitute the progressive potential, struggling against the reactionary forces of landlords, traditional religious specialists, and recent Punjabi immigrants. Recognizing the class and national differences between Muslims, he also criticizes Muslim nationalism, saying that '[t]o talk of Muslim nationalism would be as meaningless and self-contradictory as to talk of world-Nationalism, for Islam represents Universalism, and can be embraced by any one of the hundred and one Nations of the world'.²⁹

At the time of publication the book failed to get much attention in Sindh as the group of leftists was still very small. Joyo saw it as his first task to form a revolutionary vanguard of young Sindhi students and intellectuals. 'It is to their youth,' he writes, 'more specially their student community, and to their middle class Intelligentsia, that a people always turns for rescue, in times of danger, sorrow or distress. In this respect, the people of Sind appear to be a little unfortunate'[30] as there was as yet hardly a Sindhi student community to speak of. His ambition to be a teacher was therefore ideologically informed. At the Sindh Madrassah in Karachi, and later at the Sindh University in Hyderabad, he left his ideological mark on several Sindhi students from peasant and artisan backgrounds. One of them was Hyder Bakhsh Jatoi, who became the president of the Hari Committee in 1948. He was also a poet, writing poems in Sindhi in praise of the great river Indus or *Sindh*. Another student of Joyo was Rasul Bakhsh Palijo, who graduated from the Sindh Madrassah in 1948. He became a schoolteacher in the town of Thatta and later became a lawyer defending Sindhi students and separatists in many controversial court cases. In the 1960s, Palijo was one of the most radical leaders of the Sindhi movement protesting against the military regime of General Ayub Khan. A third vocal leader of the Sindhi movement was Jam Saqi, leader of the Sindhi student movement in the late 1960s, who later became the leader of the Communist Party. Both Jam Saqi and his father had been students of Ibrahim Joyo—the father at the Sindh Madrassah in Karachi, Jam Saqi himself at the Sindh University near Hyderabad. Like G.M. Syed's house in Karachi, Joyo's residence in Hyderabad became a meeting place of Sindhi separatists and leftists from the 1960s onwards.

MYSTICISM AND MARXISM COMBINED

Till the mid-1960s, G.M. Syed's ideas about mysticism and Joyo's Marxism still seemed incompatible, as Joyo, a self-declared materialist,[31] had little patience with mysticism. Despite their close mentor–pupil relationship, the two men certainly did not agree on everything. Joyo was diametrically opposed to the 'syedism' of his G.M. Syed. Like other reformists such as Muhammad Iqbal and Maulana Maududi, he condemned the devotion to spiritual leaders as a form of idol worship (*shirk*). On a personal level, however, Joyo always remained loyal to the man who had made his higher education possible. Joyo's admiration for G.M. Syed was made easier because G.M Syed himself dismissed the uncritical commitment to the spiritual leader as wrong. His reform of mysticism was a radical one, leading to the rejection of the various Sufi brotherhoods. As Joyo told me in an interview, 'G.M. Syed accepted no guides, only books.' In his personal conduct, however, he continued to behave like a syed, wearing white clothes to express his purity and detachment from worldly matters. Till the end of his life, the peasants working on his lands would touch his feet asking for favours. This was unacceptable for Joyo.

When in 1966 his house arrest was lifted, however, G.M. Syed turned to Joyo's group of young Sindhi students in order to return to politics. This turned out to be mutually beneficial. G.M. Syed gave to his new friends his charisma as a syed, a social reformer, and a political leader. In return he received the revolutionary enthusiasm and street power of the young intellectuals. This was the beginning of a new twist to Sindhi nationalism, which combined both G.M. Syed's reformed Sufism and Joyo's interpretation of Marxism, resulting in a powerful and attractive ideology for many young Sindhis.

G.M. Syed encouraged his new friends and 'comrades' not to restrict their activities to the university campus and schools. He sent them to the many shrines of local holy men in the rural areas, especially on the annual *urs* celebration, when the holy man's release from this world is celebrated in colourful festivals that attract many pilgrims. These events were important for several reasons. New intellectuals went back to the rural areas from where they originated, bringing with them a new way of looking at these places of pilgrimage. In the interpretation of G.M. Syed and his group, the holy men were martyrs for the cause of mysticism, Sindh, and the liberation of the peasant. Jam Saqi, the student leader, for instance, wrote a book on one of these local holy men, the eighteenth-century Shah Inayat of Jhok, calling him somewhat anachronistically a 'Socialist Sufi'. In Saqi's reading, Shah Inayat had been the leader of a commune of liberated peasants, for which he was beheaded. This reinterpretation of holy men as social reformers was a potential threat to many local landlords, pirs, and syeds, who often claimed to be the descendents (*sajjada nishin*) of holy men, who had inherited part of their miraculous powers (*barakat*). In Sindh, as elsewhere in South Asia, traditional Sufism consists of various brotherhoods of holy men (*pir*), their descendents (*sajjada nishin*), and their followers (*murid*). As the sajjada nishin are often landlords, traditional Sufism is related to patron–client relations. By way of speeches, songs, and discussions with fellow-pilgrims, however, G.M. Syed and his group criticized this hierarchical structure of spiritual authority based on inherited charisma. They condemned the patron–client relations that were ritually confirmed and reproduced during the traditional urs. Instead, they tried to turn the local holy men into historical heroes of Sindh and prophets of mysticism, with whom the disciples could get in touch through the traditional practices of music and dance. In these mystical encounters they would be able to find the spirit to free themselves from their oppressors, that is, the landlord families, most of whom supported the military government.

Although these activities probably did spread some awareness among pilgrims and peasants about the causes for social inequality, the main effect of these activities was a deeper engagement with mysticism and Sindhi separatism among the Sindhi students and intellectuals themselves. The trips to the rural shrines became important rituals for the Sindhi left. Identifying with the rural fakir and other mystical figures who are so absorbed in the love for God that they are indifferent to pain and fear, they derived from these trips a romantic sense of passion and belonging, which was apparently more compelling than Ibrahim Joyo's belief in the inevitability of Progress.

Zulfiqar Ali Bhutto, also a Sindhi, recognized the potential of this reformed Sufism when he founded the Pakistan People's Party to contest the elections of 1970. He, too, went to the rural shrines, sat down to talk to the peasants and pilgrims, and called himself a fakir. However, whereas G.M. Syed called for the independence of Sindh, Bhutto's ambition was to rule Pakistan, and when he did, he turned some of the shrines in Sindh into places of national, rather than provincial, importance. Attracted by Bhutto's rhetoric of socialism and mysticism, some of the Sindhi left-wing intellectuals joined Bhutto, but most of them were soon disappointed and returned to the Sindhi separatist movement of G.M. Syed. In 1973, the latter founded the Jeay Sindh Movement, which, two years after the foundation of Bangladesh, called for an independent Sindhudesh. From then on, G.M. Syed spent most of his life under house arrest. This seriously damaged the Sindhi movement. However, the notion of Sindh's unique identity rooted in a history of mysticism was spread widely. Today, it is commonly understood in Pakistan that Sindh is a place of religious tolerance and mysticism.

A brief note, then, on the question of why Bhutto could successfully use the reformation of Sufism for his own project, while the separatist movement of G.M. Syed failed. Due to the Anglo-Saxon system of democracy, in which people vote in districts according to the winner-take-all principle, people in Pakistan tend to vote for local power brokers rather than along ideological lines. In this way landlord families have become the most powerful political class in Sindh. The Pakistan People's Party, in particular, relied for many years on the brokerage of local landlords within their districts. It is mainly for this reason that Sindh's new intellectuals and radical politicians have not been able to become an important political factor, even though many people in Sindh were sympathetic to their dual agenda of social reform and the revival of mysticism. Till recently, it was not uncommon for Sindhis to have a portrait of G.M. Syed in their house, often alongside a portrait of Zulfiqar Ali Bhutto or his daughter Benazir. The former was widely admired as a true syed. When it came to voting, however, most people opted for his rivals, the Bhutto family of the Pakistan People's Party. After one of the many elections he lost, G.M. Syed remarked about the people of Sindh: 'They sing and dance for me, but they don't vote for me.'[32]

The lack of electoral success may have been the reason why the Sindhi separatist movement fell apart in various smaller parties from the 1970s onwards. Nonetheless, the Pakistan People's Party adopted the discourse of peasant liberation and mysticism, for which G.M. Syed and Ibrahim Joyo were largely responsible. In the hands of the Pakistan People's Party, however, this discourse, once meant to bring to power an up and coming class of new intellectuals within an independent Sindhudesh, served to confirm the political power of landlord families within Pakistan.

CONCLUSION

The new intellectuals I have described called themselves secularists because of their rejection of Muslim nationalism. Following G.M. Syed's distinction between religion and mysticism, they rejected the political relevance of religion, that is, religious doctrine and ritual, as well as the authority of the ulama, the mullahs, and the pirs and syeds. I have nonetheless called their ideology a specific form of Islamic reform or revival. Whereas some Islamic reformers revived the tradition of *ijtehad* or the individual interpretation of Islamic sources, and others returned to the sovereignty of the shariah or Islamic law, the Sindhi movement built upon the Sufi notion of *wahdat ul-wajud* or the oneness of being. Like the other variations of Islamic reform, the claim was to return to the original meaning of the concept, to rationalize it, and to purify it from the corruption of later innovations (*bidat*). In practice this meant an attack on the hierarchy of religious authority. Whereas other forms of Islamic reform undermined the authority of the ulama and the mullahs, the Sindhi form criticized the Sufi brotherhoods and their leaders, that is, the pirs and syeds who claimed to be the descendents of the founder of the brotherhood. In Sindh, the pirs and syeds used to be the most powerful religious specialists, more important than the ulama.

In this chapter I have focused on the network of new intellectuals responsible for this peculiar form of Islamic reform. For want of space I have not analyzed the wider debates on Islam, nationalism, and ethnicity as they have evolved after independence in the process of nation and state building.[33] Like most other Islamic reformists, the students, teachers, lawyers, journalists, poets, and social workers who joined the Sindhi movement received their education in secular educational institutions. Most of them were among the first of their social milieu to be trained in these institutions. Their secular education took them out of their environment and into the city—the Sindh Madrassah in Karachi, and after independence, the University of Hyderabad. Moreover, they did not only benefit from new educational opportunities, they also actively promoted secular education as a means to reform society. Apart from politicians and intellectuals, they also were—and self-consciously wanted to be—teachers, founders of schools and boarding houses, and educational reformers.

Secular education enabled them to look at the villages from which they came in a new way. It also gave them the tools to develop their own kind of Islamic reform. Of particular importance was the reformation of the urs celebration at local shrines. For the new leftist intellectuals, the urs no longer was an occasion in which the authority of the landlord *qua* pir or syed was confirmed. For them, it rather became an event to commemorate the martyrs of Sindh and its peasants.

Although critical of the state and the state ideology of Muslim nationalism, the Sindhi intellectuals were influenced by other forms of Islamic reform as well as the discourse that links the nation to the religious community. In their own unique ways they were searching for the essence of Islam, finding it in mysticism, and defining the distinct character of the Sindhi nation on the basis of this mystical essence of Islam. They were, in Gramsci's term, on the defensive, that is, responding to a dominant discourse of religious nationalism, appropriating it to argue for the uniqueness of the Sindhi people within Pakistan. They did so in opposition to an authoritarian regime, initially a military government, followed by a democratically elected regime that was hardly less oppressive than the military rule that preceded it—witness G.M. Syed spending years under house arrest.

However, state oppression was not the main factor that rendered the Sindhi movement powerless. Paradoxically, the movement suffered more from the gradual incorporation of its ideas into official nationalism. In the 1970s, the Pakistan People's Party under the leadership of Zulfiqar Ali Bhutto managed to cut the grass from under the feet of G.M. Syed and his followers by reconciling the latter's ideas on ethnicity and mysticism with the notion of religious nationalism. This perhaps shows how close G.M. Syed and Ibrahim Joyo remained to the dominant discourse of Muslim nationalism and Islamic reform, despite their efforts to show that Pakistan was a mistake and despite the uniqueness of their interpretation of Islamic reform. In their opposition to state discourse they remained inextricably connected to it.

NOTES

1. See François Burgat, *Face to Face with Political Islam* (London, 2003). which analyses today's political Islam as a phase in a continuing process of decolonialization. See John Gray, *Al Qaeda and What It Means to be Modern* (London, 2003) for a provocative analysis of political Islam and today's globalization.
2. See Partha Chatterjee, *Nationalist Thought and the Colonial World: a Derivative Discourse?* (London, 1986) and *The Nation and its Fragments* (Princeton, 1993) for an analysis of how Indian nationalism criticized colonial rule while using and reshaping liberal and Orientalist traditions. Chatterjee's work is especially relevant in my case as Indian nationalism and Islamic reform mutually influenced each other, leading to Muslim nationalism and the demand for an independent Pakistan. Olivier Roy, *The Failure of Political Islam* (Cambridge, MA, 2001), Gilles Kepel, *Jihad: The Trail of Political Islam* (London, 2002), Seyyed Vali Reza Nasr, *The Vanguard of the Islamic Revolution: the Jama'at-i Islami of Pakistan*, (London, 1994), and others have emphasized the influence of Marxism and Leninism on today's Islamism as well as how these influences have been turned into a critique of Marxism.
3. I prefer the terms network and milieu to community here because the connotation of the term community as a boundaried social unit is not entirely adequate. Although the term community may be useful in the case of militant political organizations—see David Apter, *The Legitimization of Violence* (London, 1997)—the intellectual circles connected to these organizations are networks or milieus rather than communities or organizations.
4. The Sindhi movement emerged as one of the most vocal parties in the popular uprising against the military regime at the end of the 1960s. It consisted of several organizations, including political parties, student organizations, and labour unions. It took part in demonstrations and strikes against the government. In the late 1960s and early 1970s, and again in the late 1980s, several Sindhi groups regularly clashed violently with so-called Muhajirs, migrants from India who constitute the second-largest ethnic group in Sindh since the time of the Partition. For a fuller discussion of this polarization between Muhajirs and Sindhis, see Oskar Verkaaik, *Migrants and Militants: Fun and Urban Violence in Pakistan* (Princeton, 2004). After the 1971 national elections, the Sindhi movement grew more radical, calling for an independent Sindhi homeland under the name of Sindhudesh in 1973. Although most Sindhi ethnic and/or separatist organizations have refrained from political violence, other

groups have occasionally opposed the central government with violence, especially during the 1983 uprising of the Movement for Restoration of Democracy (MDR).
5. Roy, *The Failure of Political Islam*, p. 49.
6. See David Lelyveld, *Aligarh's First Generation: Muslim Solidarity in British India*, (Princeton, 1978) and Barbara Dale Metcalf, *Islamic Revival in British India: Deoband, 1860–1900*, (Princeton, 1982) for the various nineteenth-century educational centres in Muslim South Asia.
7. Katherine P. Ewing, *Arguing Sainthood: Modernity, Psychoanalysis, and Islam* (Durham, 1997), and Pnina Werbner & Helene Basu, *Embodying Charisma: Modernity, Locality and the Performance of Emotion in Sufi Cults* (London, 1998).
8. See Burgat, *Face to Face with Political Islam* for a related argument on the Maghreb.
9. Asim Roy, *The Islamic Syncretistic Tradition in Bengal* (Princeton, 1983).
10. Verkaaik, *Migrants and Militants: 'Fun' and Urban Violence in Pakistan*, chapter 1.
11. Oskar Verkaaik, 'Ethnicizing Islam: 'Sindhi Sufis', 'Muhajir Modernists' and 'Tribal Islamists' in Pakistan', (Paper presented at Columbia University, New York, 2003).
12. See Peter van der Veer, *Religious Nationalism: Hindus and Muslims in India* (Berkeley, 1994) and Carol A. Breckenridge & Peter van der Veer, *Orientalism and the Postcolonial Predicament: Perspectives on South Asia* (Philadelphia, 1993).
13. E.H. Aitken, *Gazetteer of the Province of Sind* (Karachi, 1986), p. 472, and H.T. Sorley, *Shah Abdul Latif of Bhit: His Poetry, Life and Times* (Karachi, 1968), p. 675.
14. Note that there are various ways of transliteration. Syed can also be spelled as sayad, sayyad, sayyid, seyyid, etc.
15. Sorley, *Shah Abdul Latif of Bhit*, pp. 154–162.
16. Quoted in Hamida Khuhro, *The Making of Modern Sind: British Policy and Social Change in the Nineteenth Century* (Karachi, 1978), p. 260.
17. Sorley, *Shah Abdul Latif*, p. 680.
18. G.M. Syed, *The Case of Sindh: G.M. Sayed's Disposition for the Court* (Karachi, 1995), p. 18.
19. The most elaborate treatise arguing for Sindh's separate identity is a pamphlet called *A story of the sufferings of Sind*, first published in 1930 by Muhammad Ayub Khuhro in Hamida Khuhro (ed.), *Documents on Separation of Sind from the Bombay Presidency*, (Islamabad, 1982), pp. 196–254. This text was an early expression of the notion of Sindh as the victim of a series of invasions—Arab, Mughal, British, Punjabi, Muhajir—which is an important trope in Sindhi nationalism.
20. Riaz Ahmad, *Foundations of Pakistan, Volume II* (Islamabad, 1987), pp. 442–3.
21. Syed, *The Case of Sindh*, pp. 47–49.
22. Ibid., p. 34.
23. G.M. Syed, *Religion and Reality* (Karachi, 1986).
24. Syed, *The Case of Sindh*, p. 160.
25. Ibid., 159.
26. Ibrahim Joyo, *Save Sind, Save the Continent* (Karachi, 1947), pp. 103–4.
27. Ibid., p. 131.
28. Ibid., p. 139.
29. Ibid., p. 45.
30. Ibid., p. 133.
31. Personal communication with Ibrahim Joyo.
32. Personal communication with Hamida Khuhro.
33. See Verkaaik, 'Ethnicizing Islam' and *Migrants and Militants* for an elaboration of these debates.

CHAPTER 6

Flagellation and Fundamentalism: (Trans)forming Meaning, Identity, and Gender through Pakistani Women's Rituals of Mourning

MARY ELAINE HEGLAND

In July 1991, I was able to return to my Fulbright position in Peshawar after a six-month evacuation necessitated by the Gulf War. My euphoria was blemished by my discomfort at being an American and thus inevitably connected with American foreign policy. Knowing how distressed my friends in Peshawar had felt about the possibility of an American war against their fellow Muslims in Iraq, I apprehensively wondered how I would be received.

It was the month of Muharram, Americans reminded me during my Islamabad stopover. During this Arabic lunar month, Shia Muslims commemorate the AD 680 martyrdom of Imam Hussein, grandson of the Prophet Muhammad.[1] I should stay in the capital for the next several days, these Americans suggested; business would be closed down in Peshawar, and violence might erupt. As I had concentrated on Muharram rituals and politics in earlier research in Iran, however, I was delighted with this inadvertent timing and at once made plans for a flight to Peshawar.

During the process of the 1978–79 revolution in Iran, the meaning and political implications of the Muharram rituals had been transformed (Hegland 1986). Before the revolution, Iranians had viewed Imam Hussein's martyrdom as the source of holy mediating power for those who pleased him, a perspective that suggested the currying of political favour with the this-worldly powerful as well. In the months leading up to the revolution on 11 February 1979, however, many Iranians had begun to see Imam Hussein's self-sacrificing willingness to confront tyranny as a model for emulation (Hegland 1983a, 1983b). With this revised interpretation, the Iranian Muharram processions of December

1978 were turned into rituals of revolution, and marked the shift of majority support from the Shah's regime to the revolutionary forces. Shortly thereafter, the Shah fled the country, his government was overthrown, and Ayatollah Khomeini flew into Teheran to proclaim the Islamic Republic.

> *In addition to the expansion of their ritual involvement resulting from the growth of religious transnationalism, Shia Muslim women in Peshawar, Pakistan have increasingly faced restrictive ritual constructions of femininity and fundamentalist ideology. In mourning rituals they have encountered symbolic complexes that reinforce men's role as repositories of holy power and succour and remind them of their own unworthiness to shed blood on behalf of Imam Hussein and his cause. Because of binding ties to family, religious group, and representatives of the sacred, the women have not been inclined to protest overtly against male authority and dogma. Rather than denying or contradicting symbolic and verbal deprecations of femininity outright, they have devoted themselves to the commemorative rites for the Sh'a martyr, Imam Hussein. They have used these rituals to develop their own self-confidence, performance abilities, entertainment, fame, and social support, disclosing through the performative aspects of their ritual activity their agency and transformative achievements. When we examine what individuals make of religion and rituals in practice, self-flagellation and religious fundamentalism may present potential for agency and individual creativity together with renewal of cultural and power structures.* [gender, ritual performance, Pakistan, Shia Muslims, the body, agency, fundamentalism, religious transnationalism]

I was curious to see whether a similar reworking of symbolic meaning might be taking place in Pakistan. In Peshawar I discovered that many Shia found the analogy of Imam Hussein's small seventh century band—aligned against the much larger forces of the corrupt and unjust Caliph—relevant at several political levels: Pakistani Shia as a mistreated and threatened minority, Iraqi Shia as beleaguered by the brutal Saddam Hussein, and in general Muslims under attack by the West. Muharram mourning rituals became a means to rally Peshawar Shia of various ethnic and linguistic backgrounds into a more united front, as well as to connect them with the national and transnational fundamentalist Shia community.

At the same time, dawning changes in the attitudes and activities of females in Peshawar were beginning to emerge in ritual participation. Women contributed significantly to the season of mourning, despite the fact that Peshawar women—in the heartland of the gender-conservative Pukhtun ethnic group—were heavily secluded. In separate men's houses or rooms with separate entrances, men could entertain male guests away from household womenfolk. Girls, thus carefully secluded, had no opportunities to meet young men. Their marriages were arranged by their families. Expected to stay in the house, they could go out only for compelling reasons. Then they had to cover themselves with enveloping veils hiding the face or all but the eyes, and be chaperoned by their husbands or other male relatives. Women did not go to mosques. For most females, schooling did not disrupt their seclusion either: only some three per cent of females in the North-West Frontier Province were literate. Students at the University of Peshawar's sex-segregated College of Home Economics, and even women's faculty, came to campus in a sex-segregated bus, or were driven to the walled-in college by watchful husbands or brothers. Only after they had passed through the heavy gates opened by armed guards did they unveil.

Fearing harm to their reputations or well-being, Peshawar females were generally reluctant to venture outside the home even when their male supervisors gave them permission. Kidnapping and rape of opponents' womenfolk are part of the history of Pakistani political competition. Perpetrators of such violence against women need not fear legal repercussions. In order to secure a conviction for rape, a prosecutor must produce four male eyewitnesses to testify that the sexual encounter was indeed rape—and not consensual; otherwise, the female victim will be punished.[2] The atmosphere for women in Peshawar is conveyed by the ominous Pukhtun saying about women's rightful place: 'Women—either the house or the grave.' For women, then, home is both fortress and cage.

The dominant Pukhtun culture in Peshawar influences the lives of even non-Pukhtun women. Pukhtun men, with their conservative expectations about a proper female's comportment, populate Peshawar's streets. Women who dress or behave inappropriately are subject to penetrating stares and worse. Because of the war in Afghanistan and the presence in Peshawar of so many Afghan Pukhtun refugees and warring political factions, Peshawar women experience discomfort and fear away from home. Several nurses were kidnapped by an Afghan political group shortly after my arrival in Peshawar.

Given these attitudes and concerns, Shia women's daily travels around the city to attend a round of Muharram rituals took me by surprise. Particularly astounding were the competitive and loudly energetic commemorative performances by young, educated women. Among them shone Shahida (a pseudonym), a MS student from my social science classes at the University's College of Home Economics.

Faced with Peshawar's restrictive gender boundaries, Shia women found in their Muharram rituals a means for self-expression, self-definition, and personal empowerment, and for implicitly questioning gender ideology. The contradictory implications for women's power in the 1991 Muharram religious rituals were striking. In these rituals men ordered, admonished, and berated, while women alternately complied, ignored, or discreetly contradicted views of women's roles. Because of their binding attachments to patriarchal family, religious community, and Shia spirituality, Peshawar Shia women were unable to voice resistance through direct verbal discourse. Rather, they developed and expressed gender resistance implicitly through the body, and specifically through its engagement in ritual activity. Through Shia ritual practices, in conjunction with changing conditions and perceptions, women formed, transformed, and subtly contested meaning, identity, and gender.

THE SHIA, THEIR MUHARRAM RITUALS, AND POLITICAL PROCESS

The Shia have become well-known on the world stage through the 1978–79 Iranian Revolution and the subsequent creation of the Islamic Republic. Iran is the only nation where Shia form the political majority and control the government.[3] Estimates of the Pakistani Shia population vary according to the source. A reasonable estimate is 15–20 per cent of the total population of roughly a hundred million (see Ahmed 1987). Many studies on the Shia are available,[4] although information about Pakistani Shia is scarce.[5] Most literature about Shia mourning rituals relates men's activities.[6] Inquiries into women's lamentations are much harder to find.[7] In this study I hope to provide new insights into how Pakistani Shia women have used mourning rituals to develop agency and identities that subtly contest gender regulations.

Shia rituals commemorating the passion of Imam Hussein have often furnished sites for contestation over power and change. Gustav Thaiss, analyzing religion and politics among Tehran's religious clerics and bazaar merchants during the late 1960s, found that the symbolic multivocality of Hussein's passion provided 'an idiom for the communication of conflicting claims over resources and power particularly under conditions of social change' (Thaiss 1972:111,119).[8]

As David Kerzter (1988) points out, rituals can provide political impetus to support an existing regime or to rebel against a centre of control. With its potential for conveying powerful political connotations, the Muharram paradigm has often been efficacious in bringing about political outcomes. Political leaders may bolster their political legitimacy by sponsoring and controlling commemorative rituals. Dissenters may use the rituals to question an incumbent's political legitimacy. Most dramatically, the 1978–79 Iranian Revolution followed the recasting of the December 1978 Muharram processions from rituals of mourning into rituals of revolution (Chelkowski 1980; Fischer 1980; Hegland 1983a, 1983b; Thaiss 1973).

Although scholars have investigated connections between Muharram rituals and political process, no attention has been given to the Imam Hussein commemorations as sites of gender contestation. In Peshawar I found that contradictory messages about femininity were available in Muharram rituals, permitting women to resist negative lessons by foregrounding their own positive ritual practice experiences. In addition to the multiple and nuanced meanings in ritual symbolism noted by Thaiss, meanings created through personal experience and social interaction in ritual practice also lend themselves to the divergent aims of different groups and individuals.

SHIA WOMEN'S MOURNING RITUALS IN THE 1991 PESHAWAR SETTING

Peshawar, site of my research on the women's *majles* (plural, *majales*), is the capital of the Pukhtun-dominated North-West Frontier Province of Pakistan,[9] close to the Khyber Pass leading to neighbouring Afghanistan. Peshawar's population is approximately three million. Rather than declining, as they had been in modernizing Iran of the 1960s and early 1970s (Hegland 1983a; Thaiss 1973), Peshawar Muharram rituals in general were becoming more numerous and larger. More families were constructing home *imambargah,* shrine-rooms dedicated to Imam Hussein.[10] Men and women attended Shia rituals outside their own neighbourhoods, and even travelled to other villages or towns for majales. Particularly noteworthy was the crossing of ethnic lines among those who attended majales. Peshawar Shia—a diverse group including Muhajir, Pukhtun, and Persian-speaking Qizilbash—were in the process of constructing a common tradition, identity, and community.[11] The flourishing Muharram rituals were connected to a growing sense of Shia identity internationally and to the desire of Shia—a minority in Pakistan—for a cohesive network to defend Shia interests.

This intensification of Shia sensibility and unity was linked to the intensification of Shia fundamentalism. Seyyed Vali Reza Nasr (1994, 1995) has argued that many aspects of current Islamic fundamentalism originated during the partition process of Pakistan from India. Nasr credits Pakistani theologian and ideologue Mawlana Maududi with developing a Muslim fundamentalist perspective to safeguard the interests of Muslims within the Muslim state of Pakistan. At partitioning, religious identity was emphasized rather than ethnic. The process is repeating itself in Pakistan as religious dichotomization between Sunni and Shia (Hegland 1997b).[12]

Women, as is so often the case (Moghadam 1994), were central as symbols and means in this process of Shia religious and cultural assertion. Peshawar women's deepening involvement in the majles was part of a larger Shia pattern of religious nationalism and transnationalism. Realizing their political usefulness, Shia leaders commented positively on Peshawar women's ritual performances and encouraged their mourning gatherings.

During their majales, Shia women lamented the suffering and death of Imam Hussein—the Shia community's third imam after the Prophet's death in AD 632. Imam Hussein and some seventy of his male followers were killed on the Karbala plains, south of Baghdad in present-day Iraq, in battle against the reigning Caliph's army in AD 680. The band's womenfolk were then taken as captives to the Caliph's seat of power at Damascus. According to tradition, the courageous lamentations and recounting of the Karbala tragedy by the captive Zaynab, sister of Imam Hussein, initiated the mourning commemorations of weeping, telling stories about the Karbala martyrs, and acting them out in passion plays.

Nothing had prepared me for the intense dedication of many Peshawar women to the contemporary mourning rituals modeled on Zaynab's grieving. Commonly, married women in Shahida's neighbourhood rose early to rush through housework before beginning a remarkable extended round of majales at different homes, attending five-to-eight rituals, each lasting one or two hours. At night, women might sit behind a curtain for the men's longer majles at the community imambargah or *Husseiniyyah*. Women's involvement in these communal mourning rituals during the Muslim months of Muharram and Safar was increasing when I conducted my 1991 Peshawar research. In addition to the growing number of imambargah and majales in their own neighbourhoods, women's new custom of attending majales in other city sections, ethnic groups, and even other cities made their ritual schedules all the more hectic. Before

1991, according to informants, unmarried girls might attend a majles three times throughout the whole Shia mourning season. By 1991, they attended as many as four or five a day for the entire two-and-a-half months of mourning.

At a home majles, the gathered women and girls sang *marsia*, listened to a female preacher outline their obligations as pious Muslim women and recited the Karbala tragedy, beat their chests in grief while chanting *noha*, and prayed (Hegland 1995, 1997a, 1997b). After the formal proceedings, the hostess often served refreshments, conceived as offerings to the Karbala martyrs, while the women conversed.

Through these assemblies, the fundamentalist messages of female segregation, modesty, and obedience were reaching ever more women. As their ritual involvement expanded, however, Peshawar Shia women still managed to disregard many messages inherent in the Muharram rituals about female inferiority, dependency, and disruptiveness. Paradoxically, instead of taking these messages to heart, further concealing their bodies and restricting their behaviour, some women used the gatherings as a medium for assertiveness and self-expression, a vehicle through which they could excel, and an arena for building self-affirmation, and female as well as Shia solidarity. In spite of overwhelming gender constraints, some female participants created from majles practices definitions of valuable female religious contributions and strong self-concepts as gendered agents. As actors and audience simultaneously, the Shia women muffled disparaging ritual pronouncements about women by devising more vital communications from their own ritual experiences.

TASU'A (THE NINTH) OF MUHARRAM, 1991

The following is an account of the first women's majles that I attended: a large Tasu'a gathering and procession at the Husseiniyyah Hall in Peshawar's Sadar Bazaar area. 21 July, the date of my arrival in Peshawar, was also the eighth day of the month of Muharram. The ninth (Tasu'a in Arabic) was commemorated by Shia Muslims as the eve of the tragic Battle of Karbala. Attending Tasu'a rituals confronted me with dramatic and unfamiliar ritual behaviour, my own awkward irresolution about how to comport myself at rituals, my shame about the American devastation of Iraq, and my fear of entering spaces potentially filled with extremist Shia distraught about the fate of Iraqi Shia following the US bombing of Iraq.[13]

I went with Shahida, who was dressed in black *shalwar*, *kamiz*, and *dupatta*. Shahida gave me a large black dupatta embroidered with coloured dots to drape over my black shalwar and kamiz. She put on her black chador and lent me a black chador edged with rust-coloured embroidery. Then we started out for the Husseiniyyah, the public complex in the Sadar Bazaar area for mourning Hussein. As a Shia woman, she would not be allowed to watch the men's procession, Shahida told me, but if I wished I could do so.

At the Husseiniyyah, Shahida's father was busy managing paperwork and collecting contributions at a table just inside the gate with several other men. She pointed out her brothers, mother's brothers, and mother's father, all central figures in administering this large gathering. Women and children, most clothed in black, streamed into the women's section. Mothers carried their babies, also dressed in black. People did not pay much attention to me, I noted with relief. We stood waiting in the doorway of a side room, instead of following the roped-off path into the segregated women's rooms. When men rushing by told us to move back into this room, Shahida ignored them and even shooed other women further inside to afford us a better view.

Finally the men's procession began. Men handed the *alams*, long bamboo poles, each topped with a metal hand and wrapped with many women's dupattas, to the other males coming out of the courtyard in front of us and moving through the passageway toward the street. Strings of flowers hung from the tops of the alams. Chanting and slapping their chests vigorously, men in black marched by us, some holding little boys, also in mourning clothes, by the hand.

When the men had all gone out to the street, we walked straight ahead into the emptied courtyard. Shahida told me to remove my chador. The rooms designated for women were now opened up to the courtyard, and we stepped in. I was pleased to spot another of my former students and watched as Shahida and Nasreen beat their chests—right hand to left side, and left hand to right side—in time to the chanting. With the reassuring presence of Shahida and Nasreen and recalling my years of residence and research in Shia Iran, I began to feel more comfortable. Shahida acted confidently and as though in charge. Nasreen was quieter, more easygoing, and less managerial.

Feeling foolish as the sole exception, I told Nasreen at my right in the circle of flagellants that I wanted to learn to do *sineh-zani* and, when she nodded, began to imitate her. In the middle of our circle of flagellants, a mother sat cross-legged on the floor, beating her chest and chanting while nursing her child. A young woman at our left started calling out chants in a loud voice, the girl next to her holding a booklet up for both of them. The girls in our circle gave the answering verses forcefully, and others in the area joined in too. We seemed to be competing with the older woman and her group toward the right. The girls prevailed and others started joining our chant.

Shahida arranged for her grandfather to take me outside to the procession. Policemen were all around, some holding up the rope barriers surrounding the entire procession area. Lifting the rope for me to pass, the grandfather brought me into the parade area. Reins in hand, Shahida's father and uncle stood formally at either side of the horse representing Imam Hussein's steed, Zuljinnah. Offerings of orange, yellow, and white blossoms and bright-hued, frothy women's dupattas were piled high on his neck and saddle. People bestowed loving attention on the horse. One young man held an umbrella to shade his head and another kept lifting the white battle dress spotted with imitation human blood, fanning the horse's body underneath. Two teenagers splashed water, cooled by chunks of ice, from a pail onto the horse, the hot pavement, and mourners' bare feet. Women—probably Sunni Muslims, covered with light-coloured chadors[14]—crowded around the horse, touching and kissing it, and extending their open palms toward it in prayer and supplication.

Further on, different circles and rows of men, bared to the waist, were energetically beating themselves on the chest in rhythm with their chanting. They stayed in place for some time and then moved up a short way before stopping again. Whenever the sound of clanging metal arose, people ran in the direction of the noise to see men striking their backs with chain flails ending in knives, for the few moments before others forced them to quit their bloody self-mortification. As men cut away at their backs, blood ran down, soaking their shalwar sometimes even to the ankles and showing up in striking red contrast against their pure, white cotton pants.

When I made my way back to the Husseiniyyah, my two students were holding hands with other young women to form a barrier around a side doorway in the courtyard. Young unmarried men, excused from purdah restrictions for majles service, carried out several layers of stainless steel trays at a time, tan-coloured rice pushed down flat on each. Standing behind the young women's barricade, they handed trays to the outstretched arms of impatiently waiting women. The young people looked as if they were enjoying themselves distributing the food.

Shahida's brothers were among the men distributing the trays of rice. Dressed in blood-stained white shalwar with black kamiz, they had clearly performed *zangir-zani* not long before. They looked vigorous and active and never winced while they worked. Flagellants were not to supposed to show any discomfort; in fact, one girl told me, they do not feel pain.

Some women struggled to get the trays of rice. One obviously poor older woman complained that no one would give her any rice. 'These people,' one of the girls commented, 'put the rice in their bags and take it home.'

Instead of eating at the Husseiniyyah, we walked to Shahida's uncle's home, climbing a narrow stairway to a room where women were eating around a tablecloth spread on the floor. We greeted the hostess and sank down at the space carved out for us. Soon word reached us that another contingent of women was arriving and, to make room for them, we returned to the Husseiniyyah.

There, Shahida's aunt (MZ) was delivering a sermon. Nearing the end of the emotional story of martyrdom, she rasped out a phrase, stopped to gasp a breath, and then rasped out another. At the final tragic conclusion, her voice reached a sobbing crescendo and then abruptly stopped. Shahida took a central role in directing the subsequent activities of the women.

We stood and began chanting and beating our chests. Shortly, a great commotion erupted to our left and the horse was brought in. The entrance of the horse was a recreation of the AD 680 return of Zuljinnah to the encamped women, the empty saddle on his back testifying to the death of his master, Imam Hussein. In response, the women started rapidly hitting their heads with their hands in agitation. They cried out their distraught grief to Zuljinnah in verse with louder voices. The reverberation of their fists knocking their heads rang out sharply, replacing the hollow sound made by the thump, thump, thump of hundreds of palms whacking chests. Several times the horse's handler led him to stand just in front of the shrine, effecting a poignant pilgrimage to the replica of his master's tomb, then rushed him to the left again through the frantically sorrowing women. Women tried to touch the horse while also staying clear of his tumbling hoofs. The whole room was tense with excitement. Finally, the horse was taken through the doorway in front of us, back to the room from where he had first emerged. Facing the doorway through which the horse had departed, the women chanted their grieving farewells while beating themselves. We continued chanting and striking our chests, calming down gradually. At one point the flagellation mode changed back from head to chest beating. Slowing down little by little, the beating and chanting finally ended. We stood there a while. More water and sweetened drinks were distributed. Some Pukhtun women came up and spoke to me; they liked it that I had worn black and beaten myself. Shahida, evidently unhappy at my talking to the Pukhtun women, led me away. The streets were quiet and calm now. On the way hack through the bazaar I heard one shopkeeper say to another, 'There go the Shia.'

THE MAJALES AND LIMITING MESSAGES ABOUT FEMININITY

Male domination over sermons, process, and symbols: Through ritual participation, Shia women faced a deluge of messages about female dependency and religious, social, and physical inadequacy. Ritual sermons disseminated messages of male authority and advised greater restrictions for women. Male preachers at the men's rituals—which women attended in silence behind doors or curtains—and female preachers at the women's rituals exhorted women to follow Islamic laws, cover themselves strictly, obey their husbands completely, and stay away from unrelated men.

As well as permeating ritual sermons, male dominance pervaded ritual process. Men took positions as ritual masters, while women assumed positions as ritual managers. Women conducted their own rituals, but with male approval and encouragement. Men took over whenever they were present. Although women planned, administered, and performed in their own rituals, they remained out of sight when attending male rituals. There, they were not to chant or pray aloud or even weep or strike themselves loudly enough to be heard by men. Women's inability to participate visibly or audibly in male rituals demonstrated their inferior position.

Among the most ritually active women were female relatives of male officers in the Shia organizations. Shireen, the female *rozahkhwana*, was the wife of a central figure, who was also a rozahkhwan. An outstanding marsia reciter—the mother of Shahida—and Mahreen, the female preacher, were sisters of the president of the local Shia organization. Outstanding female performers had been encouraged and taught by male relatives. Shireen, the rozahkhwana from the Old City, which was home to many Shia descendants of Persianized Anatolian Qizilbash, had been trained by her husband. When other female rozahkhwana could no longer sing owing to their advanced age, he had told her that she should replace them. Mahreen was encouraged by her brother, the president of the Peshawar Shia organization. He had written a speech for her when she was a student. It had been a very good speech, he told me, but she had not been able to deliver it at school. She was disappointed. 'Never mind,' he told her. 'You can give it at the Husseiniyyah Hall.' She did, and so was launched on her preaching career. Realizing what useful resources female majles activists were for their own power struggles, male leaders supported their female dependents' prominence in majales.

In spite of the avowed unity and equality of all Shia, these male politicians were contending for power, not only with the Sunni government and demographic majority, but also within the Shia population. The well-to-do Mohajir and Qizilbash Shia, successful merchants and financiers, dominated Shia political organizations and ritual activity alike. Although they attempted to curb these attitudes in public, Mohajir and Qizilbash Shia looked down on Pukhtun Shia. These Shia, a minority among the otherwise Sunni Pukhtun, were of rural origin and lacked the sophistication, education, and—most often—wealth of the Mohajir and Qizilbash Shia.

Shia women and, more obviously, Shia men competed with each other for ritual and political prominence, which was closely related to economic success. Sponsoring rituals was expensive but necessary for Shia political power. For Shia political leaders, having a good number of female relatives active in majales was a prerequisite for success. These female relatives enjoyed advantages that made their ritual preeminence possible. They had the space and money for hosting many majales, class-induced self-confidence, and the literacy necessary for preparing sermons, conducting ritual readings, and transcribing and learning all the new marsia and noha in order to have the largest, most up-to-date ritual repertoires.[15]

As these women were crucial political resources, the men took care to control them. Gossip suggested that Mahreen's brother had refused all her suitors in order to keep her outstanding preaching abilities under his own management. He owned the courtyard and rooms where she lived with her two unmarried sisters and where she held her many majales. Whenever he was in Mahreen's courtyard, he took charge. One evening after a women's majles, the sisters and I were sitting in the calm of the courtyard enjoying the evening, drinking tea, and chatting with the small group of women who had stayed on. Their brother brusquely ordered us into the curtained-off rooms; men were starting to arrive for the men's majles to follow. We did as we were told.

When Mahreen hosted women's majales at her home, this brother and other male relatives carried in the huge kettle of food. In a display combining cooperation and control, they dished it into platters distributed by women and unmarried girls. Their physical strength in carrying the heavy kettle, financial power in funding the meal, and social and cultural authority in monitoring women's behaviour highlighted female subordination and dependency.

Even among themselves, women did not escape supervision. Women served as agents of patriarchal authority. They pressured others to attend majales, forming effective social control units. If one missed a meeting, her relatives were queried. The absentee was also directly interrogated at the next opportunity. Pressure did not stop at prodding others to attend majales. Older women monitored self-flagellating zeal and were quick to reproach lethargy. During one all-night majles, after hours of beating my sore chest, I slapped a thigh in time to the marsia instead. When that thigh started to sting, I slapped the other thigh. Finally, I just sat, exhausted; it was two in the morning. One of the informal leaders came by, picked up my hand, stretched it high into the air, and then slammed it back against my chest. The message was clear; I numbly started thumping my chest again. The group of women who spent so much time together for two-and-a-half months exerted social control as well as social support.

In addition to ritual sermons and ritual process, men controlled the most significant symbolic complexes. As a climax to the majales dedicated to Hazrat-e Abbas (younger half-brother of Hussein), one or more alams were brought from the shrine room into the assembly. The females cried out in sorrow, and their self-flagellation grew more frenzied. A number of alams also headed men's mourning processions watched by less strictly secluded women. The alams represented the battle flag held by Hazrat-e Abbas when he was martyred at Karbala. Hazrat-e Abbas had been a protector of women, I was told; this was why women's dupattas were tied to his alams.

When Imam Hussein died in battle, his horse, Zuljinnah, was wounded. According to legend, the riderless horse returned to the waiting womenfolk, thereby announcing his master's martyrdom and throwing the women into paroxysms of grief. A white horse representing Zuljinnah, decorated with flowers and women's scarves, walked in each male procession. Men trained the horses taking this role; women could not handle Zuljinnah, I was informed. After processions, one or two men brought him into the large room or courtyard, bringing the waiting women to a climax or sorrow. Women crowded around the central symbolic complexes of the mourning rituals—both of them male—

touching or clinging to them in hopes of spiritual help in their suffering and adversity.

Bloodshed: male martyrs—female filth and frailty: Women devoted far more time than men to meritorious mourning—because they had nothing else to do, both women and men told me. The most dramatic, painful, and therefore, meritorious mourning practices, however, belonged to men. To conclude the large majales for men, some men bared their upper bodies upon the entrance of Zuljinnah and lashed their backs with chains ending in knives (zangir-zani). In anticipation of this event, women jockeyed on hidden balconies or behind curtains for good vantage positions, then pushed and shoved to see the flaying arms, clanging metal, and naked backs streaming with blood, the scene ending after a few short moments of pandemonium.

Before she and her brother left me at the door of such a gathering, a student friend—herself prevented from attending by her strict family—warned me to pull no punches in elbowing and jostling my way to the front of the women's balcony to get a good view of the men's zangir-zani: 'Being polite will get you nowhere!' At processions in the Old City's narrow alleyways, my Qizilbash companions crowded in, craning their necks. They urged me into a well-placed corner to view the retiring flagellants striding past to go and rinse off their backs, awash in bright red blood.

Mothers did not express concern about their flagellant sons but were heartened by their manly courage. One afternoon, as I sat with Shireen, the Qizilbash rozahkhwana, during the intermission of her relatives' ritual, she called to her sons in the courtyard, proudly drawing the curtain aside to let them enter. They had just rendered zangir-zani. Stepping in, they turned around at her request to display their bloody backs.

Boys begin swinging the chain-and-knife scourges at an early age. I saw boys as young as five or six grasp a wooden handle and awkwardly jerk the scourge in a half-circle to fling the chains toward their backs. The knives fastened to the end links cut at their young shoulders for a few moments before older boys brought the novice flagellants' session to a close. Teenagers and young men more vigorously whipped the scourges around one side and then the other, knives fleetingly slicing their backs, new dribbles of blood sprouting with each stroke. After friends forced an end to their frenzied devotion, they bathed and donned white tunics. When they reappeared, the red stains slowly spreading over the backs of their snowy clean garments were dramatic badges telling of sacrifice and spiritual zeal.

After about 40 years of age, men no longer possess the vitality for the arduous zangir-zani practiced by virile youth, but their backs still carry the marks of the severe thrashing. When I left the Sadar Bazaar Husseiniyyah to watch the 1991 Tasu'a men's street procession, a circle of middle-aged men beat their bare chests with one fist and then the other in time to mourning chants as I walked by. On the bared backs turned in my direction I could see long, slashing, crisscrossing scars, notarizing years of zangir-zani. The jagged blazes, sculpted in raised welts, were ineradicable, embodied testimony to their Shia identity and devotion.

But women are not allowed the meritorious zangir-zani. Because of modesty requirements, women cannot bare their backs for zangir-zani, as they patiently explained. Also, they claim that menstruation makes women too weak to lose more blood. Thus, women are disqualified from the most laudable and spectacular manner of veneration.

Male bloodshed is a precious gift to the Imam and a sign of readiness for martyrdom, but repositories of sacredness, by contrast, abhor feminine bloodshed. When the white horse entered the assembly of women, re-enacting Zuljinnah's telling riderless appearance at the Karbala camp, menstrual bloodshed would be despicable to him. Zuljinnah would become angry with any menstruating woman in the crowd, my students told me, and would try to strike her with his hoofs. She should not have exposed his holy presence to her pollution.

The body as site of the power of resistance: women's unworthiness: The body is generally seen as the ultimate site for the demonstration of political might. Dorinda Outram calls the physical body 'the most basic political resource' (1989:1). The ability to control another's body, to mark it, act in violence against it, or force it to go through prescribed motions, is the most effective sign of power. Whereas the oppressor subjugates the other's body and denies it autonomous subjectivity, the latter grasps at even small opportunities to retain subtle 'objectionable' viewpoints, minute behavioural deviations, or a modicum of self-control over the body.

Through self-flagellation, Shia Muslims are in a sense reinterpreting past, present, and potential violence against themselves, construing it to signify their ability and willingness to suffer bodily harm. They are sending messages, written on their very flesh, to Imam Hussein about their loyalty and reverence, to other Shia about their credentials and adherence, and to enemies about their courage and conviction.[16] By striking themselves, Shia men pre-empt oppressors' blows to their bodies, acting out their strength and resolution in the face of possible assault. Nothing done to their bodies will defeat them. Quite to the contrary, even in death they will find life; they are prepared to follow in the footsteps of Imam Hussein, to become martyrs for him and his cause of defeating tyranny and pursuing justice.

Shia Muslims' self-mortification reminds us that the body is not only a site for inscription of oppressors' messages; it is also a site for self-inscription of messages by rebels and resisters.[17] It is thus a site for contestation over meaning and power. Shia men, through zangir-zani, took back their bodies from present or potential oppressors and used them to convey their own meanings. By carving badges of blood and crisscrossing scars on their bodies, they transformed their very bodies into units of communication. Through self-inscription with scourges, they testified to their capacity and willingness to be martyred, should there be the call.

In contrast to men's zangir-zani, Peshawar women's self-flagellation seemed more a sign of readiness for suffering and grieving for the dead than a readiness to face death as martyrs themselves. Women's Muharram practice of beating their chests with their hands and weeping and moaning fits a more general idiom of mourning for the dead in the Middle East and South Asia. The lack of demand for their blood paralleled the assumption that women were unqualified to become martyrs. Shia men, by inscribing bloody badges and scars on their bodies through self-flagellation, could turn their bodies into 'words' (de Certeau 1982:149) of consummate spiritual meaning, thereby earning the greatest reward. Women, although embodying holy meanings of willingness to suffer loss, were not able to convert their bodies into signs of martyrdom in imitation of Imam Hussein.[18]

Ironically, perhaps, the prohibition against women shedding blood and scarring flesh through scourging their backs as an offering to Imam Hussein served as yet another powerful message about their lack of worth. Yet they managed to turn the Muharram majles, the source of so much subduing imagery and commentary on femininity, into a forum for developing self-worth. Women's weak, menstruating bodies and expected self-abnegation were symbols of their religious unworthiness and dependency. Yet on this occasion when the men, through bodily practice, also expressed self-abnegation, the women could achieve a sense of redemption—and agency—through parallel bodily practices.

RESTRAINTS ON AGENCY: THE TIES THAT BIND

Ties that bind—family affiliation: Peshawar Shia women were in no position to dispute these oppressive ritual statements on femininity in any overt manner. The family, religious, and spiritual attachments they perceived as vital for their well-being affected their agency, quieted frank protests, and limited their methods of resistance to experiential, practical, or artful assertions.

Unlike other oppressed groups, women are generally on intimate terms with their oppressors, sharing family ties, love, sexual relationships, economic and political interests, religious beliefs and affiliation, residence, and long years of personal history with those who most directly dominate them. Women are therefore reluctant to relinquish relationships tarnished by gender-based subordination (see also Hochschild 1990; Zavella 1990). Such is particularly the case in Middle Eastern countries, where some women often feel so family-connected that they do not report sensing an autonomous identity. A Middle Eastern woman generally understands separation from family—her source of security if also of bondage (Joseph 1982)—to be nearly impossible.[19] Pakistani women similarly tend to judge it best to accept the 'patriarchal bargain' (Kandiyoti 1988) of dependency in exchange for protection, economic support, and social legitimacy.[20]

Ties that bind—religious affiliation: construction of community and evolution of religious transnationalism: The threatened, minority status of Pakistani Shia and their related political mobilization significantly affected Shia women's agency as well, deterring open revolt against male privilege and power. Pakistani Shia were becoming more politicized and conscious of Shia identity as well as discrimination and violence against Shia. With easy transportation, contacts with Shia communities in India were common. Peshawar Shia traveled to Iran as well. The great majority with whom I spoke were delighted with the Iranian revolution of 1978–79 and its subsequent developments. They were devoted to the memory of Ayatollah Khomeini. Women spoke to me enthusiastically of their pilgrimages to shrines in Iran and their guest visits, accompanied by male relatives, at the 1991 commemorations of Ayatollah Khomeini's death. Shia anguished over the violence against Muslims in Kashmir, an area controlled by India although populated by a Muslim majority. After the Gulf War they turned against Saddam Hussein because of his treatment of Iraqi Shia and collected funds to assist the devastated Iraqi Shia.

In addition to the impact of international events, internal politics incensed the Shia community and bound it closer together. People spoke about job discrimination against Shia. Shia told me in distress that they had seen, painted on walls, the words 'Shia are *kafir* [unbelievers].' The unpunished 1988 assassination in Peshawar of the highest ranking Pakistani Shia cleric, Arif al-Hussaini, enraged the Shia community. Said one man, 'You know how people say, 'Live like Ali and die like Hussein'?[21] Now we say, 'Live like Khomeini and die like Hussaini.'

Other Pakistani Shia martyrs were plentiful. Violence against the Shia during Muharram mourning processions was common. The Shia were assaulted during processions in 1991, including some in Parachinar, a Northwest Frontier Province town, who were killed by the very police—members of the Sunni majority—assigned to protect their procession! Elsewhere in Pakistan, Shia were murdered by explosives thrown into ritual gatherings.[22] In the face of growing Sunni extremism and Saudi influence,[23] Shia felt forced to unite and lobby for security during ritual practices.

The Shia found much in current events to make them feel like a besieged minority, reminiscent of Imam Hussein's small band fighting a caliph they considered to be a corrupt interloper.[24] Shia women shared the men's anger, fear, and increased Shia sensibility, and avoided obvious gender-based dissension that might have precipitated a debilitating rift.

Ties that bind—spiritual affiliation: the Karbala morality tale and its experiential portrayals: The battle on the Karbala plains generated the central Shia paradigm, with its profound significance for Shia spirituality and sensibility. Several anthropologists have scrutinized processual paradigms—key enculturated concepts that represent, explain, and order the course of events in human history.[25] Members of a culture distill root paradigm or cultural models and forge the concepts and attached emotions and predispositions into representations or experiential portrayals through ritual—'cultural performances' (Singer 1958) or a culture's 'formal statements' (Ortner 1987:1).

For Shia Muslims, the Karbala myth is a potent processual paradigm, root metaphor, or cultural script. Its ritual representations and enactments—*rozah, ta'ziyeh*, processions, majales, sineh-zani, zangir-zani, marsia*, and *noha*—are fundamental to Shia spiritual, emotional, social, cultural, and political life. For most Shia, Imam Hussein and the Prophet's family and descendants are not only spiritual figures but are also seen as intimate associates or close family members (Betteridge 1985,

1989). The paradigmatic myth of male martyrdom and female captivity at Karbala is not desiccated history but immediate tragedy, suffering, and grief with profound relevance for life today. For devotees, the spiritual world has become one with the physical through this focal parable. By lamenting the Karbala martyrs and captives, Shia connect themselves to the Sacred, the Prophet and his holy family, the cosmos, and all others in the community of believers throughout history who have likewise mourned and remembered. By mourning Imam Hussein, the Shia seek redemption.

Through their ritual performances Shia women are seeking a relationship of reciprocity with spiritual figures, with consequences for both the next world and their cares and wishes in this one.[26] After a mourning ritual, women have told me, they feel spiritually cleansed and purified; they feel lighter. The rituals are an emotional outlet, helping them to release tension. Because of their spiritual and emotional attachments to the Karbala martyrs and root paradigm, Peshawar Shia women would be loath to forego the rituals, nor would they bluntly challenge ritual instructions about the character and place of women. No woman criticized religious pronouncements about gender in my presence.[27]

Women were thus not willing to go beyond permitted parameters to develop their sense of agency and gendered self-worth. Other than the majles, they had virtually no suitable forum for competition and assertiveness, public performance, travel to far-flung neighborhoods, development of a large social network, enjoyable companionship, or the gaining of fame and reputation. Shia women did not forgo the rituals, explicitly deny their gender messages, or question the validity of these beloved rites. Rather, they muffled belittling messages about gender by amplifying their achievements and capabilities in ritual practice.

WOMEN'S RITUAL PRACTICE: AGENCY DESPITE CONSTRAINT

In considering the connections between their ritual performances and the Shia women's gendered agency and subjectivities, I am reminded of Muharram rituals in the Iranian Revolution. In Iran, the Imam Hussein mourning rituals served as a crucible for transforming meaning, subjectivities, and ultimately, political power. In the years leading up to the revolution, increasing numbers of people practiced the same traditional Muharram rituals—but with an evolving meaning, a 'hidden transcript' (Scott 1990) circulated behind the scenes, of the need to imitate Imam

Hussein's courage in struggling against unjust authority. Ultimately the Iranian revolutionaries were able to unveil their opposition—nurtured under the protective curtain of traditional ritual—in open protest during the transformed December 1978 Tasu'a and *'Ashura* (the tenth) processions (Hegland 1983a, 1933b). This strategy or transforming meaning, world-view, and subjectivity under the camouflage of traditional ritual, through bodily rather than verbal discourse, can also be applied to gender politics.[28]

Majles performances: creating meaning through ritual practice: Shia women of Peshawar influenced the meaning of the Hussein root paradigm and its cultural performances for themselves in the only way they could: through their enactment practices. As Schieffelin (1985) and Brenneis (1987) argue, ritual audience members are not passive recipients of a rigid and uniform ritual package but instead are actively involved in the social construction and resulting meaning of a ritual.[29] This argument applies powerfully to majles performers and their creativity. At a majles everyone is both performer and audience. Through their individual actions and the meaning they choose to foreground, all participants influence their ritual experiences and their significance for them.

Although, according to Schieffelin, 'the performance is bound to mean different things to different people' (1985:722), majles participants are not unrestrained in what they can make of ritual texts and symbols.[30] Further, as Catherine Bell points out, 'one might retain one's limited and negotiated involvement in the activities of ritual, but bowing or singing in unison imperceptibly schools the social body in the pleasures of and schemes for acting in accordance with assumptions that remain far from conscious or articulate' (1992:215).

Nevertheless, participants help construct a ritual and its ambience, action, and significance. The meanings and effects from ritual framing, personal input, and interaction among participants can be as influential as, or even more so than, the meanings and effects officially derived from formal majles texts. Action constantly re-creates and modifies cultural structures that simultaneously channel it.[31] All action is marked by the influence of cultural constraints and thus in some ways entails accommodation, serving to reinforce existing structures. At the same time, actions cannot be exact replications of cultural structures. Agency and the consequent possibility of resistance are intertwined, even merged, with accommodation. Enactments of cultural representations thus simultaneously enable (allow agency and creativity) and constrain (channel experience and meaning) (see Coombe 1989:90).[32] While acting out their profound attachment to Imam Hussein through the Muharram rituals, the women simultaneously 'subverted' the rituals for additional aims and meanings.[33]

Social construction of ritual experience: Shia women attempted to use their empowering ritual experiences to contrive a protective shield against gender disdain.[34] Women aimed to attend as many rituals as possible, and were quietly proud of their eminence as performers; a few younger women even boasted of it. They acted on their own and did backstage directing. They gained self-esteem from their capabilities and gifts to Imam Hussein and to Shia unity (Hegland 1997a). Rituals provided women with a legitimate excuse to leave their houses and chores (Hegland 1997b). Men never told them not to go, an older woman claimed, and it was apparent that women relished the two-and-a-half-month social whirl during the mourning season. They appreciated the comfort of singing and chanting long-familiar verses and enjoyed themselves with time to eat, drink, and chat. The older Pakistani women chewed *paan*.

A number of single, childless, widowed, and even divorced women found in ritual an approved outlet for their time and energy. Troubled women could reach out to the holy objects and saints for assistance. They dedicated their mourning activities to Imam Hussein or his younger half-brother Abbas in hopes of succour. Other women sympathized with their heartaches. In addition to the surveillance and social pressure already mentioned, women found group approval for their participation and seemed to sense unity with others in the mourning process.

Women could hold respected leadership roles. Several middle-aged women, who constituted an informal decision-making core, subtly guided rituals, ruling on contested performance slots and regulating the length of each ritual stage. When they determined that the laments should end, one of them chanted *Hussein, Hussein, Hussein* while rapidly pounding her chest. The other women immediately understood her signal to stop offering noha. Shireen, for example, described how others respected her: even her older sisters-in-law deferred to her because of her recitals of Karbala stories and because her face flagellation was more rigorous and painful than the styles performed by other women. Mature women also appreciated these opportunities. Two older women living in the Old City who were close friends held many majales; each attended the ceremonies of the other, looking comfortable and relaxed sitting quietly together.

Even self-flagellation could be appropriated for self-expression, performance excellence, and individuality. A few women engaged in unusually energetic chest-beating, one leaving scabs and others developing bruises of which they seemed quietly proud. I saw several women drop their otherwise ever-present dupattas or scarves and swing from side to side in a chest-beating routine resembling a dance, face uplifted and eyes closed in a trancelike state. Shireen explained her own face flagellation, in which she painfully beat her cheekbones, as showing greater devotion to Imam Hussein. Taught that their female bodies precluded the highest veneration to Imam Hussein, women used those same bodies to attain unusual devotion and to experience and act out their engendered worth. Thanks to the symbolic multivocality of the 'discursive body',[35] they could use their bodies not only to convey Shia religious, spiritual, and political meanings, but also to convey gender meanings, implicitly resisting dominant, patriarchal dogma.

Women gained a sense of power from contact with the Divine and the religious strength thereby gained. Religious permission to enjoy an active life outside their homes brought this-worldly power through social support and freedom from household confinement. One woman, an outstanding performer with a beautiful voice, did not have children. Her Muharram singing was her profession, her calling, another woman explained; her strenuous schedule and highly regarded talent helped fill her childless days. One evening she was sick. Her feet had swollen, the soloist told me, through so much walking from one majles to another. Her husband scolded her, 'You're going to get terribly ill if you don't rest. Don't go tomorrow!' She tossed her head in the midst of telling the story. 'I told him, 'I'm *going.*' And today I got up and got ready and I'm just *fine!*' In this she even implied that, with the Imam's mystical intervention, she did not need to listen to her husband![36]

Shahida's triumph: Shahida's triumphant seizing of a performance opportunity in front of hundreds of women, too, was a delicious illustration of how females can appropriate mourning rituals—which are, after all, to the glory of the Imam—for self-aggrandizement and personal identity formation with complete propriety.

Outstanding performer status brought prestige and honour to a young woman or group of sisters, relatives, or friends. Women eagerly vied for the opportunity to earn a reputation for their excellence at performance. Because of time limits, however, not all who wished to perform were able to do so. At a majles, only three or four marsias could be sung before, and three or four nohas chanted after, the sermon. To seize a time slot, a group had to jump in exactly as the previous group was drawing its marsia or noha to a close. Successful contenders for the opportunity to display their talent early on, or even to perform at all, must be astute judges of timing and shrewd negotiators of etiquette requirements—all in all, formidable strategists.

At a large, multiethnic gathering of Muhajir, Qizilbash, and Pukhtun Shia women in the Old City Husseiniyyah Hall, I watched Shahida and her group ready themselves to sing as the sermon ended. An older ensemble of apparently notable women began a noha, obviously by previous arrangement with the organizers. Holding their ground at the front of the hall, Shahida and her group of friends stood together waiting. Before the conclusion of the first noha, the hostess rushed over to them with the apologetic request to wait until after yet another noha by a group that she did not wish to offend. While another woman led the second noha, Shahida's ensemble concentrated on making sure that no one else would beat them to performing the next noha. They obtained control over the microphone, firmly placing the stand in front of themselves. They positioned themselves with the air of those about to start a race they were determined to win.

A split second after the conclusion of the noha, Shahida's ensemble began singing in blaring voices. Beating themselves with athletic swings to the chest with one hand and then the other, they piously looked up toward the heavens. Clearly, they were not prepared to see or hear any other group that might start a noha; they would not interrupt their singing under any circumstances. Another group did start a noha and kept up a rival song for a number of lines. But there was no contest. Possession of the microphone allowed the voices of Shahida and her friends to flood over the hundreds of women crowded into the Husseiniyyah Hall. Shahida's group had won the performance slot and wider performance fame. The other group conceded defeat.

When I asked her why she was so active in ritual performance, Shahida unabashedly responded, 'I do it for fame!' She smiled with delighted pride as she told me she was the best noha singer in the whole city. Her uncle confirmed her assertions: 'Everyone in Peshawar, Sunni or Shia, knows of her because of her noha recital.' The young woman was assertive and strong, competitive and self-confident—all with the approval of her uncle.

The conservative, seyyid, pir family of another student did not even allow her and her female relatives to attend the segregated women's majales. In sharp contrast to those of the ritual activists, these women's activities and personas suffered considerably. The contrast showed me what a difference the opportunities allowed by a busy ritual schedule can make in the lives of women who would otherwise be confined to their homes.

Shahida's worldview and subjectivity entailed a relatively positive view of feminine contributions, value, and power. More than other women, Shahida expounded on Hazrat-e Zaynab's centrality to the Karbala paradigm, recognizing her courage and strength as no less than a man's in guiding and protecting the other captive women and one ill male, and telling the martyrdom story even at the Caliph's court. Without Hazrat-e Zaynab's speeches and laments, Shahida claimed, the Karbala paradigm could not have survived and 'if there was no Karbala, there is no Islam.'[37]

Shahida's engendered confidence and competence, suggested in her comments about Zaynab's key role in preserving Islam and so apparent in her own dashing ritual performances, carried over into her behaviour elsewhere. Whereas other students displayed shyness in front of me, their professor, Shahida always exuded self-assurance. This young woman, so bold in ritual performance, was also the first to imitate me in wrapping her chador around her body, but leaving her head and hair exposed on our daily bus trips to the women's college. The young women students crowded into our females-only bus tried, as I did, not to stare when, for the first time, and with a toss of her head, she let her chador drop down to her shoulders. Shahida's posture and expression showed her awareness of the splash she was making and her gratification with her own daring. On subsequent trips, a few other students followed Shahida's example—until, worried about anger against the American threats to attack Iraq, I also retracted my self-display and kept my head covered, even on the bus.

Agency and accommodation in Peshawar Shia women's ritual practice: Women's agency is closely related to their subjectivity, which is constantly evolving as the contributing factors to women's worldviews change and interact with each other. As their components changed, Shia women's majles practices continuously evolved, producing ceaselessly unfolding meaning, subjectivity, and social context. In turn, as the ritual practices changed, the components of the practices evolved (see Loeffler 1988:250).

Their attachments to family, religious community, and Shia spirituality had a significant impact on Peshawar Shia women's subjectivity, and thus on their agency. Partly in deference to these bonds, the women were not able to struggle overtly for gender equality in 1991. When open struggle is not feasible, sometimes religious ritual provides a permitted, protected transformative arena in which to develop the experiences, meanings, subjectivities, capabilities, analytical frameworks, and power needed for overt resistance to patriarchal structures. Unable in any significant degree to transcend gender rules or develop agency through direct, confrontational verbal activity, some Peshawar Shia women found in ritual the opportunity to do so through performative action. Thus, finding little indication in explicit verbal discourse, we must read the performative aspects of their ritual activity or the discursive body for implicit evidence of their developing agency.

Perhaps, if and when circumstances permit, this developing power can be utilized to struggle directly for change within a framework that is both confining and all-embracing, or even to venture outside it. Transforming ritual experiences can help prepare participants to take a chance and face the consequences—the likely challenges, traumas, and punishments—in an attempt to bring about more equitable voice, opportunity, and evaluation for themselves and others. While conditions prevent open political activism, ritual practice can enable ritual participants to wield agency, share in creating meaning, and make more of their worlds.

CONCLUSION: FORMING, REFORMING, AND TRANSFORMING EXPERIENCE, MEANING, AND SELF

What women make of their majles ritual experiences is inspired by the ongoing dialectic between themselves and their surrounding social structure (Loeffler 1988). 'Social theory must take into account the contributions agents make in constructing the view of the social world (and thereby in constructing this world) by means of the representational activity that they constantly perform, for it is in such activity that power lies' (Coombe 1989:103).

The Peshawar women found power in majles performances. While enacting mourning rituals, Shia women added their own personal, emotional reasons to the official purposes of the majles meetings. In ritual performance, they attended to their own concerns as gendered agents as well as to the concerns of their wider religious community. Their practices and interactions provided some with more potent meaning about their gendered power than the ritual texts, symbols, and fundamentalist sermons.

Indeed, women in general did not seem to take fundamentalist admonitions very seriously. When the visiting cleric from Karachi rebuked women for their lapses in purdah and in obedience to their husbands during his men's majles sermon, they chuckled quietly in their curtained-off rooms. Their muted laughter—a muffled sign of resistance—indicated how untroubled they were about such alleged deficiencies.

From what I saw in the summer of 1991, their wider arena of ritual activity brought some benefits to the otherwise quite restricted Peshawar Shia women. At the time of my research, Peshawar Shia women managed to blend accommodation and agency so as to construct a world offering some social support, autonomy, and individuation, even as they operated within an ultimately male-controlled framework. Drawing from cultural and religious resources, changing social circumstances, and their own personalities and creativity, they formed, reformed, and—to a degree—transformed ritual experiences, meanings, and subjectivities. Will their proliferating ritual opportunities to develop leadership, self-confidence, social support, and assertiveness gradually enable them to do more? It is hard to imagine the dynamic student Shahida failing to seize any available opportunity. Or, acting as they did within permitted parameters, if their increasingly fundamentalist supervisors curtail those parameters, will the Shia women have to go back to attempting to gestate selves in more restrictive enclosures?

To address this question, we must take more than one level of action into account. An analytical approach informed by practice theory enables us to see the lively agency of Peshawar Shia women in making what they can of a limiting world and finding ways to question those limits without risking too much. Women's agency, however, is not the only force influencing their immuring walls. The majestic audacity of Shahida's gesture of uncovering her head on a bus testifies not only to her agency, but also reveals much about the overwhelming power of larger structures and the attendant difficulty of women's resistance in Peshawar's severely conservative environment.[38] We must recognize the level of confinement that leaves Peshawar Shia women little option but to spend their agency and creativity in attempting to transform self-flagellation, phallocentric rituals, and a fundamentalist movement into constructive incubators for self, gender, and community. With regard to both Shia women's heavy involvement in majles rituals and Shahida's bold move to bare her head, we must 'take into account the brutally restricted *range* of options within which this particular choice is seen as rational and "free" (and, indeed, defiant)' (Seaman 1992:308).

Women's innovative agency is a necessary but insufficient factor for decisive gender transformation.[39] Women's agency in ritual practice may indeed partially transform meanings and subjectivities, and these in turn may further affect agency. When they express their modified worldviews, women make these ingredients available to others (Loeffler 1988). As Loeffler reminds us, however, 'the spread of these "mutations" is then more than anything else a matter of power, access to distribution nets come to be perceived as eminently true' (1988:252). What these Shia women will be able to do with their transformations of oppressive ritual dogma into affirming, self-enhancing experiences and meanings is uncertain. Whether women's agential creativity, effort, and sacrifice will lead to significant gender transformation is not under their sole control. Change also depends on social, economic, and political forces from the local to the international level.

GLOSSARY

black *chador*	large, rectangular veil for maintaining *purdah* or seclusion while outside of the home
dupatta	long rectangular scarf always worn by women as part of their dress
imambargah or *Husseiniyyah*	building for mourning Hussein
kamiz	knee-length tunic
majles	commemorative ritual gathering
marsia	mourning hymns
Muhajir	migrants from India
noha	mourning couplets
paan	a preparation including betel leaf
pir	saint
rozah	narratives
rozahkhwana	reciter of Muharram accounts
seyyid	descended from the Prophet (PBUH)
shalwar	loose pants
sineh-zani	chest-beating
ta'ziyeh	passion plays,
zangir-zani	beating the back with chains

NOTES

Acknowledgements. This article evolved from papers presented at the panel 'Women and Politics: Creating and Criticizing Tradition' at the Middle East Studies Association conference in November 1991 and the invited session on 'Gender and Religious Fundamentalism Cross-Culturally,' sponsored by the Association of Feminist Anthropologists and the General Anthropology Section at the Annual Meeting of the American Anthropological Association in November 1993. The efforts of organizers, chairs, discussants, and other presenters are much appreciated. For funding my research in Pakistan I am grateful to the Fulbright Commission, and for their generosity in allowing me a year of leave and providing me with supplementary research funds, I thank the administration and the members of my department at Santa Clara University. Although their names have been changed to protect their privacy, I owe much to my Peshawar Shia friends for their cordial assistance and fellowship. For their creative, constructive comments, prodding me into further development and enhanced expression of my ideas, I am grateful to Catherine Bell, Sima Fahid, Marilyn Fernandez, Dorothea French, Erika Friedl, Shahin Gerami, Shahla Haeri, Patricia Higgins, Diane Jonte-Pace, Nancy Lindisfarne, Barbara Molony, Carol Mukhopadhyay, Seyyed Vali Reza Nasr, Nayereh Tohidi, George Westermark, *American Ethnologist* editor Michael Herzfeld and the *AE* anonymous reviewers, and especially to Diane Dreher and Jean Hegland who generously gave dedicated support and detailed attention to several drafts. To my wonderful research assistants, Michelle Brunet and Caprice Scarborough, many thanks.

1. Sunni (the majority in most Muslim countries) and Shia are the two main groups of Muslims. Like Catholic Christians, Shia believe in intercession between God and humanity—in this case through the family of the Prophet, Imams (successors to the Prophet), and *imamzadeh* (descendants of the Imams). Like Protestant Christians, orthodox Sunni do not accept mediation or spiritual hierarchy, although many Sunni individuals do.
2. See Ahmed 1994, Haeri 1995b, and Mehdi 1990.
3. Shia are a minority in most other Muslim countries, such as Bahrain, Kuwait, Saudi Arabia, Pakistan, Lebanon, and Afghanistan. Although most Iraqis are Shia (about 55 per cent), the government is controlled by Sunnis. Shia are the majority in newly independent Azerbaijan, formerly a republic of the USSR, although the government is secular. A large minority in Tajikistan is Shia as well.
4. See, for example, Ajami 1986, Cole 1988, Cole and Keddie 1996, Halawi 1992, Hasnain 1999, Keddie 1983, Kramer 1987, Loeffler 1988, Mottahedeh 1985, Nakash 1994, Norton 1989, Pinault 1992a, Ram 1994, Rizvi 1986, Schubel 1993, and Wiley 1992.
5. See Ahmed 1987; Keddie 1993, 1995:183–186, 208, 209; Sagaster 1993; and Schubel 1993.
6. Among the published works on men's mourning processions, gatherings, recited stories, theater productions, poetry, and hymns developed around Imam Hussein's AD 630 martyrdom are Al-Naqvi 1974; Ameed 1974; Ayoub 1978; Beeman 1931; Bogdanov 1923; Cardoza 1990; Chelkowski 1971,1979,1980, 1985; Chelkowski and Korom 1993; Fernea 1989; Fischer and Abedi 1990:11–19; Good and Good 1988; Hjortshoj 1987; Hosted 1993; Korom 1994a, 1994b; Korom and Chelkowski 1994; Lassy 1916; Lindell 1974; Mahdjoub 1988; Moinuddin 1971; Nakash 1993, 1994:141–133; Naqvi 1987; Pelly 1879; Peters 1956, 1972; Pinault 1992a, 1992b;

Riggio 1988, 1994; Schubel 1991, 1993; Thaiss 1972, 1973, 1978, 1994; and Unvala 1927.

7. Information about Shia women's mourning rituals—majales (or *rozeh* as they are called in Iran, and *kraya* in Iraq) is rare because researchers have generally been men with access only to the public men's rituals. Other than some material about Shia women's mourning gatherings in Bard 1996; Dunham 1975, 1996; Fernea 1989; Fernea and Fernea 1978; Friedl 1989; Hegland 1986; Sagaster 1993; and Torab 1996a, 1996b, I have not been able to find more than a few scattered sentences on Shia women's Muharram rituals. For the variety of ritual practices among Shia women, such as pilgrimage and *sofreh* (meals offered up to the saints as thanks or pleas for assistance), see the work of Anne H. Betteridge (1985, 1989) based on fieldwork in the southwest Iranian provincial capital, Shiraz.

3. In addition to Thaiss's sagacious work in prerevolutionary Iran (1972, 1973, 1978), other studies of Muharram rituals commemorating the passion of Imam Hussein as sites of political competition, conflict, or struggle over change are provided by Bogdanov 1923; Chelkowski 1980; Ende 1978; Freitag 1989; Good and Good 1988; Hegland 1983a, 1988b; Jayawardena 1963; Kumar 1989; Peters 1956, 1972; Ram 1994; Richard 1995; Singh 1988; Thaiss 1994; and Yousefi 1995.

9. The Pukhtun, dominant in the North-West Frontier Province of Pakistan, are well known to anthropologists through the writings of Ahmed 1976; Barth 1959; Grima 1992; and Lindholm 1982.

10. Cole 1988, Das 1992, Naqvi 1987, and Pinault 1992a provide additional description and discussion of Shia shrines in India.

11. For elaboration on the earlier divergent ritual practices of the various Peshawar Shia ethnic groups and the influences on the increasing uniformity of Shia rituals, see Hegland 1997a, 1997b.

12. While Pakistani Shia are suppressing ethnic differences to strengthen sectarian unity, other Pakistanis are engaging in ethnic conflict. Violence between natives and immigrants from India (Muhajirs) in Karachi, for example, has produced many casualties.

    Discussion on the applicability of the term *fundamentalism* to Middle Eastern or South Asian Islamic religious movements can be found elsewhere. (See, e.g., Contention 1995a and Contention 1995b) It is, I believe, the best term available to refer to a re-emphasis on religion, including a return to what adherents consider to be the fundamentals or basics of the religion and recognizing the need for their application in this-worldly life and especially to politics. Fundamentalists generally consider standardized behaviour, principles of hierarchy and obedience, and the defined nature of gender and thus the sexual division of labour to be basic to their religion. They claim support for their assertions from holy sources. Fundamentalisms will naturally vary in meaning and character according to situation (and from person to person in spite of the belief that only one version of the truth is valid). Some people prefer the use of the term Islamist for such phenomena in Muslim societies. I find this term to be problematic as well, as it suggests that Muslims who do not adhere to such attitudes are not Muslims.

13. The women's hospitality soon put this fear to rest. The presence of my students also helped calm my anxiety, and the embodied memory of attending similar women's gatherings with close Iranian Shia friends lent me an even greater sense of comfortable familiarity. Because of my many visits to Iran and many close Iranian friends in the United States, my attitude toward people of Shia Muslim background contrasts sharply with that of the majority of Americans.

14. I assumed that these women were Sunnis because Shia women would have been wearing black chadors and would not have been out in a public gathering of this sort.
15. See Hegland 1997b for further discussion of my positioning. See Hegland 1997h for discussion of class, ethnicity, and education as they relate to majles ritual dynamics in Peshawar.
16. See also Peteet's research (1994) showing how oppressed people may resist through reinterpreting the violence perpetrated on their bodies by the politically powerful.
17. See also de Certeau 1988:139–150. Outram 1989 and Peteet 1994 also emphasize the subjectivity of subjected bodies.
18. In a similar case, Peteet (1994), in her study of Israeli beatings of Palestinian youths, found that those few females subjected to imprisonment and violence did not gain the same esteem and access to political leadership as did young males in similar situations.

    I am here pointing out the gender politics of women's exclusion from access to valued activity—*zangir-zani*—and the rationale behind this restriction. I am not indicating regret that women do not practice the bloody self-scourging of their backs.
19. See Arlene MacLeod's perceptive discussion of why lower-middle-class working women in Cairo do not resist openly but rather put on the veil in 'accommodating protest' (MacLeod 1992b:553, 554). See also Al-Khayyat 1990; Altorki 1986; Arebi 1994; Friedl 1994; Jeffery 1989; Joseph 1993, 1994; MacLeod 1992a; Peteet 1991; Rugh 1984; and Tapper 1988–89, 1991.
20. For informative discussion about the situation of Pakistani women, see Eglar 1960; Ewing 1991; Haeri 1993, 1995a, 1995b; Jalal 1991; Mehdi 1990; Mumtaz 1994; Mumtaz and Shaheed 1987; Papanek 1973, 1982, 1984, 1994; Rahat 1981; Ramazahi 1985; Rauf 1987; and Weiss 1985, 1990, 1992.
21. Ali was son-in-law and cousin to the Prophet Muhammad and the Shia community's first Imam or leader after Prophet Muhammad's death. Hussein here refers to Imam Hussein.
22. Sectarian bloodshed has erupted in Pakistan each Muharram since 1991, with the worst in Punjab and then spreading to Karachi. In 1995, the killings began even before Muharram—during Ramadan, the month of fasting for both Sunni and Shia—with yet another massacre at a Karachi Shia mosque on 5 February and two more on 25 February. Karachi turned into a sectarian battlefield, and hundreds of people there and in other Pakistani cities were killed in 1995 alone. Newspapers carried accounts of more mosque and sectarian massacres in 1996, 1997, and 1998.
23. People talked to me about the Saudi funding of Ziaul Haq and his subsequent actions against Shia, including decimation of Shia villages, attacks against their mosques, and even desecration of their Qur'ans. Today, as well, they told me, the Saudi Arabian government was providing funds to anti-Shia groups in Pakistan. For further information on the conflict between Ziaul Haq and the Shia see Ahmed 1987 and Keddie 1993.
24. Of course, not all Shia in Peshawar held the same views or saw the meaning of the Karbala paradigm as instructing political dissension.
25. In her work with processual paradigms, Sherry Ortner has utilized the concept of root paradigms, 'preorganized schemes of action, symbolic programs for the staging and playing out of standard social interactions in a particular culture' (1990:60). In working with this concept, Victor Turner used such phrases as 'root metaphor,' 'root paradigm,' 'subjective paradigm,' and 'dramatic or narrative process model' (Turner 1978).

26. See Betteridge 1989. Richard Flores (1994) has likewise pointed out that South Texan Mexican–Americans enacting 'Los Pastores' (plays about the shepherds going to Bethlehem) see themselves in a relationship of reciprocity with Christian holy figures.
27. An illiterate, poor village woman in Iran confided to Erika Friedl her strong suspicion 'that religion, as preached and practiced, was not made by God but by men in order to suppress women' (Friedl 1989:133). The Shia women in Peshawar, because of their proximity and history with India and their minority status as Shia in largely Sunni Pakistan among other reasons, were probably somewhat less inclined to ponder contradictions between Islamic claims of justice and mistreatment of women or to verbalize any such reflection.
28. My view of Shia women's resistance through ritual practice is in accord with Reed-Danahay's perception of resistance as including fluidity, providing power for the 'weak', and serving not only 'as reactions to (or resistance to) dominance, but as modes for the creation of new cultural meanings' (1993:223).

    Abu-Lughod's caution against 'romanticizing resistance' (1990) and Okely's caution (1997) against taking resistance to document lack of female subordination (instead of subservience) must be applied to research about gender politics. Also, covert resistance has its shortcomings (Hegland 1995). Several social scientists (e.g., Comaroff 1985; de Certeau 1988; Scott 1990; Tiano 1994) have nevertheless pointed out that in overlooking subtle, covert, undeclared, or even unknowing forms of resistance we leave out a vast area of political activity. Specifically, in the realm of gender politics with women tied in so many ways to the mutually reinforcing networks of forces oppressing them, and consequently often able to engage only in circumspect resistance, we must attend to these obscure and ambiguous forms of struggle. Through tiny subversive acts, alternative transcripts, and created worlds of personal meaning and attainment, even within the walls of patriarchal structures, women maintain resilience and may even build their strength, confidence, abilities, and subjectivities. Later, if and when circumstances change, these may be applied in other arenas to serve their interests more specifically (Hegland 1995). Therefore, as Gutmann asserts, 'we must study both overt and covert forms (of resistance) and the relations between them' for 'these forms occur together, alternate, and transform themselves into each other' (7993:76).
29. Researchers have made similar arguments about media: individual consumers do not receive printed or broadcast material passively, but bring to it their own views and reactions. Thus different individuals will construct different meanings and draw different inferences from the same material (see, e.g., Mankekar 1993).
30. Even playing active roles in ritual through self-flagellation, singing, chanting, and grieving does not mean that the women are free to change words or actions or to mould the performance as they wish. Likewise, women operating within a fundamentalist framework can go only so far in creating an autonomous space. For analyses or the dangers fundamentalisms pose for women see Baffoun 1994, Hale 1994, Hardacre 1993, Lawrence 1994, Mazumdar 1994, and Papanek 1994. Seaman (1992) presents similar reservations about the degree of latitude audiences have to interpret media.
31. As Rosemary Coombe states, 'while incorporating experience into our conceptual maps we modify the map' (1989:92). Sherry Ortner also contends that 'actors both manipulate their culture *and* are constrained by it' (1990:63). Ortner has been inspired by Pierre Bourdieu's emphasis on actual practice as reproducing *habitus*—the embodiment of culture in the individual (1977). Deborah Heath writes, 'As Bakhtin

reminds us, domination, complicity, and resistance are all potentially present in every communicative exchange' (1994:99). Some words of Arlene MacLeod are also especially relevant here:

'To continue this effort of detailing the complexities of women's part in power relations, I argue that women, even as subordinate players, always play an active part that goes beyond the dichotomy of victimization/acceptance, a dichotomy that flattens out a complex and ambiguous agency in which women accept, accommodate, ignore, resist, or protest—sometimes all at the same time' (1992b:534).

Reed-Danahay likewise finds that the same action can incorporate aspects of accommodation as well as of resistance—that 'power and resistance can no more be viewed as separate processes than can structure and agency' (1993:222).'

32. Such is the case even for enactments of fundamentalist religious 'cultural representations.' In the words of Diane Jonte-Pace, 'it is perfectly possible to do two things at the same time: live in and experience (and even bolster, I would add) patriarchal oppression and, at the same time, create a realm of freedom, creativity, activity, and agency' (personal communication, 6 July 1994). For other secular and religious examples see Abu-Lughod 1986, 1990; Arthur 1993; Cattell 1992; Guthrie and Castelnuovo 1992; Heath 1994; Holland and Skinner 1995; Ingersoll 1995; Kaufman 1991, 1994; Lawless 1988, 1991; MacLeod 1992a, 1992b; Mankekar 1993; Moore 1993; Oldenburg 1990; Ong 1990; Raheja and Gold 1994; Reed-Danahay 1993; Stacey 1991; and Stacey and Gerard 1990.

33. In speaking of the agency of people unable to confront those in authority openly, de Certeau's concept of 'fundamental inversions' is relevant: 'the Indians often used the laws, practices, and representations that were imposed on them by force or by fascination to ends other than those of their conquerors; they made something else out of them; they subverted them from within.' [de Certeau 1988:32; also quoted in Coombe 1989:95]. See also Comaroff 1985; Comaroff and Comaroff 1991; and Taussig 1980, 1986.

34. Shahin Gerami (1994) found that middle-class Iranian women did not accept all of the teachings of the Islamic Republic officials about females and their place. Women rejected sexual spatial segregation, and with it, the belief that women should not work as they did not belong in public space. Apparently, the Iranian women who answered her survey had also found some means of resisting: umbrellas to shelter them from the deluge of messages falling down on them through the facilities of the Islamic Republic and its supporters.

35. I am indebted to Barbara Molony for this phrase.

36. For a Muslim woman charged with obeying her husband, such a sentiment would be considered insubordinate. Indeed, had the sermon at the majles that she attended been given by Mahreen, the preacher of Indian background, the ritual singer would have heard much about the obligation of a pious woman to submit herself to her husband. Had this been the case, it would have been ironic, for, in essence, the singer would then have defied her husband for the opportunity to hear that she must not defy him. (I owe this observation to Diane Dreher.)

37. Interview with Shahida, 8 August 1991. Fried (1993) has analyzed the contradictions in Iranian Shia women's concepts of Hazrat-e Zaynab and Hazrat-e Fateme, daughter of the Prophet Muhammad and mother of Imam Hussein and Hazrat-e Zaynab.

38. Here, Abu-Lughod's point (1990) about resistance as a useful 'diagnostic' of power rings strikingly true.

39. Elsewhere (Hegland 1995), I discuss further the centrality of women's agency and 'everyday forms of resistance' (Scott 1977, 1985, 1990) for gender transformation.

CHAPTER 7

The Sunni–Shia Conflict in Jhang (Pakistan)

MARIAM ABOU ZAHAB

INTRODUCTION

Although sectarian[1] issues were not prominent in the course of the freedom movement in Pakistan, these identities surfaced soon after independence. Violent clashes were isolated and mostly happened during Muharram when the Shias perform *azadari* in public and take out huge processions. Since the mid-1980s, parties and violent groups, often sponsored by Islamic states, have emerged with a narrow sectarian agenda, and thanks to the easy availability of weapons and to the training facilities in Afghanistan and in Kashmir, the level and intensity of violence has tremendously increased, claiming hundreds of lives. Every region of Pakistan has been affected—Sunnis and Shias have killed each other in the name of religion in the Punjab, in the NWFP, in Karachi and in the Northern Areas of Gilgit and Baltistan—but the conflict has been particularly violent in the Punjab, especially in the south of the province.

Much has been written on the internal and external causes of the emergence of the sectarian conflict in Pakistan at the macro level. Therefore, we will neither insist on Ziaul Haq's politics of Islamization and its consequences nor on the regional dimension of the sectarian conflict fuelled by the Iranian revolution and the Iran–Iraq war which assumed the character of a proxy war between Iran and Saudi Arabia on Pakistani soil (Abou Zahab 2002). Such analyses, although relevant, fail to explain why sectarian violence affected some areas of Punjab more than others.

This chapter focuses on the Sunni–Shia conflict at the micro level with a study of Jhang, a city of central Punjab where the Anjuman Sipah-e-Sahaba (later renamed Sipah-e-Sahaba Pakistan, SSP), an extremist Sunni movement, was founded in September 1985.[2] The case study reveals that a multiplicity of factors, most of them not related to religion, have to be taken into account while analysing sectarianism at the grassroots level.

The aim of this study is to analyse the factors that led to the rise of sectarianism in Jhang. Our assumption is that the sectarian conflict in Jhang is mainly the result of the struggle for political power between the traditional feudal families who are primarily Shia and rural-based and the emergent middle class which is largely Deobandi or Ahl-i-Hadith and urban-based.

This study will examine the religious dimension, which is not the main reason for the conflict but only a pretext which proved to be a powerful means of mobilization in the 1980s. We try to analyse the complexity of the social conflict in Jhang, which is not limited to a class struggle between feudals and the urban middle class but should also be analysed as a conflict between the locals and the Muhajirs and as a conflict inside the Sunni community between two dominant castes or *biradaris*. We will describe the rise of the SSP which emerged as a credible alternative to the feudals and was instrumentalized both by local Sunni landlords and businessmen and by the Muhajir emergent middle class who used it to mobilize the urban youth in the defence of their own interests. Finally, the criminal dimension (the Islamization of criminality) should not be overlooked as it played a major role in the mobilization of the militants and in the persistence of the violence.

GEOGRAPHICAL CONTEXT

Jhang is located about 200 kilometres south of Lahore. It had historically a great politico-strategic importance for two reasons: the Sial dynasty was once powerful and Jhang was situated on the main communication line between Lahore and Multan. Parts of the vast district were taken away by the British and later by the Government of Pakistan when they created new districts. Today Jhang consists of three tehsils: Jhang, Chiniot, and Shorkot. According to the 1998 census, the total population of the district is 2804 million out of which 655,000 (1/5) live in the urban areas. Jhang itself has a population of 292,000 inhabitants.

The municipal area of Jhang is divided into three parts: Jhang City (the walled city known as Jhang Sial), predominantly Hindu before 1947 and where the Muhajirs are in a majority, Jhang Saddar (Jhang Maghiana) with a sizeable Muhajir population (both Sunnis and Shias) and the satellite town with a mixed population. Jhang City and some *mohallas* of Jhang Saddar have also been affected by sectarian violence.

THE SOCIAL STRUCTURE

Jhang is the centre of Punjabi folk culture, the famous epic Hir–Ranjha took place in Jhang where the shrine of Hir attracts many devotees. Many prominent academics and politicians[3] belong to Jhang which was also the home of the Pakistani Nobel prize winner, Dr Abdus Salam, the nuclear scientist who happened to be an Ahmadi.

Jhang is one of the most backward and feudal districts of Pakistan. The feudals—more precisely the Shah Jewna family[4]—and the Pirs have dominated the political set-up of the district since the days of the Raj; the local population is convinced that they have deliberately kept the district backward, refusing the opening of schools and the building of roads. In 1947, a sizeable number of refugees from India, many of them hailing from Panipat, were settled in Jhang;[5] they occupied the properties left by the Hindus and started business activities. The large influx of refugees provoked a negative reaction among the locals, some of whom had occupied the properties of Hindus and Sikhs which were later taken back from them to be distributed to Muhajirs. Contrary to what is generally assumed, even those who settled in the rural areas could never assimilate although they came from East Punjab and shared the same language and culture with the local population. Although they do not identify themselves as Muhajirs, the local population considers them as such. The wounds of Partition have not healed, there is resentment even among those who were born much later, and everybody has a story to tell about who became rich overnight or about the *kammis* who changed their caste during Partition to become Syed. Relations between the communities were always tense, even if violent clashes were few.

THE RELIGIOUS COMMUNITIES

Although the majority of the population is Sunni, Jhang district has a sizeable Shia population, probably around 25 per cent (10 per cent in the city itself) although it is very difficult to make an accurate assessment. Shia communities had moved to Punjab and Sindh after the conquest of Muhammad bin Qasim. Ismaili missionaries were also active in the area. Under the Abbasids, the Governor of Jhang, Umar bin Hafas, was a clandestine supporter of the Fatimid movement and the Batiniya influence spread in Southern Punjab. Then, the Karamats who had established contacts with the Fatimids in Egypt set up an independent dynasty in Multan and ruled the surrounding areas till they were defeated by

Mahmud Ghaznavi.[6] The Karamat movement left a deep impact on the local population. The small Shia Muhajir community settled in Jhang Saddar belongs mostly to the educated middle class, is often Urdu speaking, shares the Sunni hatred for the feudals and has few contacts with the local Shias who are mostly Siraiki speaking and rural-based.[7]

While Muhajir Sunnis are often Deobandis, most of the local Sunnis are Barelvis. The shrine of Sultan Bahu is located in Jhang district and a Qadiri Pir belonging to the Gilani family who was previously settled in Azam Warsak (Waziristan) has moved to Jhang in the early 1980s. According to Pir Syed Agha Kazem Shah Gilani, known locally as Pir Pathan, he chose Jhang because of the central geographical location of the city which makes it much easier for his *murids* to visit him than when he was based in Waziristan.

Jhang has a history of sectarian conflict which goes back to pre-Partition days. After 1947, the relocation of the headquarter of the Ahmadi community from Qadian now in Indian Punjab and the transformation of Rabwah (near Chiniot) to an 'Ahmadi Vatican' attracted militant Sunnis originally from Panipat, Rohtak, and Hisar in Jhang and Chiniot where they opened madrassahs and were active in the anti-Ahmadi movement since the 1950s. Maulana Manzoor Ahmed Chinioti, the head of Tehrik-e Khatm-e Nubuwwat, always took the lead of anti-Ahmadi campaigns. The Muhajirs were also in the forefront of anti-Shia and anti-feudal activity but they were not yet economically powerful and they did not have enough support among the locals to challenge the monopoly of the Shia feudals on politics (Ali 1999). The Muhajirs, whose religious identity had been sharpened by the revivalist movements of the 1920s in East Punjab[8] and by the sufferings experienced during Partition, have always supported religious parties, namely Jamiat-e Ulama-e Pakistan (JUP) and Jamiat-e Ulama-e Islam (JUI).

Elections have been contested on a sectarian basis in Jhang since the 1950–1 provincial elections. Maulana Ghulam Hussain started an anti-Shia crusade in the 1950s; he opposed Colonel Syed Abid Hussain both as a feudal and as a Shia and was utilized by the small Sunni landlords who drew political benefits from this campaign (out of a total of nine seats, Sunni landlords were able to secure four seats in 1951). The elections of 1954 were not fought on a sectarian basis: Syed Abid Hussain won the only seat from Jhang in the National Assembly and became the federal minister. But in 1970, there was an unprecedented mobilization of Sunni ulama against the Shia feudals of Jhang due to violent Sunni–Shia clashes in front of Khewa Gate (renamed Bab-e Umar by the Sunnis) during the procession of seventh Muharram (March 1969) which had caused the death of five Sunnis. Syed Abid Hussain was defeated by Ghulam Haider Bhawana, a Sunni landlord, and the three National Assembly seats were won by Sunni candidates elected on a JUP ticket.[9] The political activism of the ulama was however short-lived, their attention was focused on the Ahmadis and on Islamization and they soon went back to their madrassahs. The Sunni–Shia factor receded to the background for some time, the middle class was still very small and too weak to challenge the political monopoly of the Shia feudals. Sunnis supported Sunni landlords but they had a feeling of betrayal as the Sunni landlords were as indifferent to their interests as the Shia landlords[10] and they were not ready to share power with the emergent Muhajir middle class.

By that time, members of the Sunni business class, both Muhajirs and locals, had entered the municipal committee: Sheikh Iqbal, a local who claimed he belonged to the famous trading *biradari* of the Chinioti Sheikhs and who monopolized municipal politics for many years, became Vice-president of the municipal committee in the late 1960s and later the Chairman, a post which he held for almost 25 years. He was elected to the Provincial assembly on a JUI ticket in 1970 and joined the PPP in 1972. Since then, Sunnis have dominated the municipal committee while the district committee remained, except for a very short period, in the hands of the Shia feudals sometimes associated with the *sajjada nishins* of Sultan Bahu as is the case since the local elections held in 2001 under the devolution plan designed by General Musharraf.

In 1974, the Qadianis were declared non-Muslims by a constitutional amendment and in 1977 Zulfikar Ali Bhutto banned alcohol and declared Friday a weekly holiday. General Ziaul Haq, who took power in July 1977, soon started implementing a programme of Islamization. This emboldened the ulama and in the context of Jhang, the Shias were likely to be their next focus. The consequences of Ziaul Haq's politics of Islamization and the politicization of the Shias after the Iranian revolution and the imposition of *zakat*[11] led to a new phase of sectarianism in Jhang.

The formation of the Tehrik-e Nifaz-e Fiqh-e Jaafria (TNFJ) in 1979, later renamed Tehrik-e Jaafria Pakistan (TJP), with a purely religious agenda in the beginning, was a turning point for the sectarian conflict in Pakistan. This party, whose agenda sounded offensive to Sunnis, became much more militant from 1984 under the leadership of Allama Arif Hussain al Hussaini, a charismatic leader who empowered the Shia community and transformed this religious movement to a political party in July 1987. The young ulama who had been educated in prestigious religious schools in Iran promoted a more rationalized and puritan version of Shiism. They were branded as 'Wahhabi Shias' by the traditional clergy who accused them of destroying the religion, but surprisingly enough, they soon became very popular among the community and their *majlis*, often politicized, attracted crowds.[12] The young ulama opened madrassahs with Iranian support and became an inspiration for the Shia community, especially for the students who joined the militant Imamia Students Organization (ISO). Although the feudals had no influence on these ulama who were financed by Iran, the Sunnis blamed them for the new assertiveness of the Shia community.

It is in this context that the Anjuman Sipah-e-Sahaba was founded on 6 September 1985 in Jhang by Maulana Haq Nawaz Jhangvi (1952–90). There are lots of rumours about the role of the agencies in the creation of the SSP—a parallel can be drawn with the foundation of the MQM in Karachi, both parties being the product of the political vacuum created by Ziaul Haq's regime—and about the financing of the party by Iraq and Saudi Arabia and by zakat money.[13] It is obvious that the SSP was a retaliation to Shia militancy and that Ziaul Haq was too happy to get an opportunity to teach the Shias a lesson. It can also be assumed that Haq Nawaz, who was at that time vice-amir of the JUI for the Punjab,[14] had political objectives as the SSP was created a few months before the lifting of martial law on 1 January 1986.

The SSP's goals are to defend the honour of the Sahaba, to strive against *rafiziyat* by all legal and constitutional means, to proscribe Muharram processions, Shia *azan* and all forms of *azadari* and *matam* in public, to get Shias declared as non-Muslims and Pakistan declared a Sunni state, and to make efforts to unite Sunni sects.[15]

Born in a poor rural family of the Khoja caste of Chela, a village of Jhang district, Haq Nawaz received a madrassah education[16] and, in 1973, he became the *khatib* and *imam* of a Deobandi mosque in the mohalla of Piplianwala in Jhang Saddar. Before he started mobilizing Sunnis against Shias, he had participated in the anti-Ahmadi movement and had also denounced Barelvi rituals.[17] Haq Nawaz, who was a fiery orator, launched a crusade against Iran which he accused of supporting the Shias in Pakistan and of wanting to export its revolution; his attacks were as much directed against Khomeini as against Shia beliefs and rituals. Locally, he particularly targeted the Shah Jewna family and the district administration. Besides appealing to anti-Shia sentiments, Haq Nawaz started addressing social problems, becoming involved in *thana-kutcheri* issues, which made him extremely popular even among local Shias. He emerged quickly as a credible alternative to the feudals and won the support of persons who were not otherwise sympathetic to his personality or ideology[18] as he was much more accessible and more efficient than the feudals to solve people's problems.

The class struggle rhetoric of the SSP was largely borrowed from the JUI which remained closely associated with the SSP at least till 1989. The SSP denounces the Shia *jagirdars* who received lands from the British and the 'black laws'[19] and claims that nothing has changed since the days of the Raj as the poor have simply become the slaves of the 'Brown sahibs', that is those feudals who supported the Raj and were the slaves of the British. With such a rhetoric, the SSP attracted the downtrodden who had voted for the PPP in 1970 and had seen their hopes frustrated.

THE CAUSES OF THE CONFLICT

The conflict has a religious, or rather a cultural, aspect. Although he had denounced Barelvis till the early 1980s, Haq Nawaz was later careful to avoid antagonizing them and he managed to win their electoral support for the SSP to some extent. Haq Nawaz criticized the peasants for their ignorance of 'true' Islam which he linked to the influence of Shiism, he accused them of being devoid of religious identity and wanted to make them aware of the differences between Sunnis and Shias (Zaman 1998) which are quite blurred in the rural Barelvi society. The SSP wants to convert Sunnis to a rationalized Islam, to replace customary practices by the Islam of urban ulama and madrassahs, their struggle is directed as much against local rituals seen as Shiism as against the influence of pirs, both Sunni and Shia. They want to purify Islam from all external influences and their rhetoric often borrows from the reformist literature of the nineteenth century to which they constantly refer to give legitimacy to their anti-Shia campaigns. The SSP preaches a total social boycott of the Shias, relying on famous *fatwas* of the founders of Deoband. It denounces Shias as Zionist agents and as the 'other' responsible for all the problems of the country. The SSP's rhetoric equates local forms of religious beliefs and cultural practices to the influence of Shiism. However, these rituals have hardly anything in common with Shia rituals in Iran or Lebanon, they are a local expression of the tragedy of Karbala which is deeply rooted in the Punjabi culture and often evokes Sikh or Hindu rituals. It is true that up to now Sunnis and Shias, and even Ahmadis, participate in Shia rituals in Jhang, just like the Hindus participated before Partition,[20] because they do not equate *majlis* or processions with Shiism but with their local culture. By assassinating prominent *zakirs*, the SSP militants are destroying part of the Punjabi culture transmitted orally from father to son. Those zakirs are targeted because they are popular with Barelvis who share the same devotion to the *Ahl-i-Bait*; they are seen as more dangerous than the Iran-educated zakirs who preach a rationalized form of Shiism which appeals only to a fraction of the Shia community.

This religious aspect is however not the main reason for the conflict: these themes were not new, the Deobandi madrassahs and ulama had been promoting the same anti-Shia sentiments for many years and they had promulgated anti-Shia fatwas but these ideas never penetrated the society in South Punjab and did not lead to large scale violence.

Religion was only a pretext as anti-Shia rhetoric proved to be a powerful means of mobilization in the mid-1980s and also a way to get support both from the state and from foreign sources. The Sunni emergent middle class, both local and Muhajir, who had been trying to enter the political arena, made full use of this situation and quickly understood the benefits it could draw from supporting Haq Nawaz. Sunni landlords and the emergent under-class of transporters, contractors,[21] intermediaries and shopkeepers benefited from the liberal economic policy of the Zia regime and supported the SSP to further their own political and economic interests. Most of the Muhajir businessmen dealing in animal skins and distributors of ghee, sugar, and flour who had prospered under the Zia regime financed the SSP. Haq Nawaz gained the support, both financial and political, of the rich businessmen of Jhang who wanted access to the political arena and also wanted to break Sheikh Iqbal's monopoly on municipal affairs. Muhajir businessmen and shopkeepers supported the SSP, either directly or through the powerful Anjuman-e Tajiran (Association of Traders). It is not surprising that shops belonging to Sunni Muhajirs were set on fire at the instigation of Shia feudals as retaliation. Those who wanted to stand for the provincial elections against the feudals and could not get a Pakistan Muslim League (PML) ticket also supported the SSP. Sheikh Iqbal[22] and Sheikh Yousaf were competing to support Haq Nawaz. Sheikh Iqbal, who wanted to keep Haq Nawaz away from local politics, discreetly financed his electoral campaign for the national elections of 1988, which ironically gained him the support of the local Shias who shared the same interests.

Sheikh Yousaf, once a small contractor of Jhang settled in Lahore, had become very rich in the 1980s. He now owns Hasnain Construction Company to which the contract of the Islamabad–Lahore motorway, among other lucrative contracts, was awarded. This former MPA, well connected in army circles, was the major financier of Haq Nawaz and of the SSP in general, providing Pajeros and the like and financing the election campaigns. Richer than Sheikh Iqbal, he had the support of all those, Sunnis and Shias, who were opposed to Sheikh Iqbal. Haq Nawaz thus became a pawn in this rivalry between local Sunni businessmen, and his assassination in February 1990 was most probably perpetrated at the instigation of Sunni leaders as they were competing for the same constituency. Some sources argue that Haq Nawaz wanted to stand for the provincial assembly elections against Sheikh Iqbal and that he resented the fact that Sheikh Iqbal had convinced him to rather contest the National Assembly elections in 1988.

After the assassination of Haq Nawaz, Sheikh Iqbal, who was a MPA at that time, made a mistake which contributed to the cycle of violence. The police had wanted to launch an operation against the SSP which was postponed at the request of Sheikh Iqbal. When he refused later to finance the purchase of weapons for the SSP activists, they attacked his home.[23] From that time, Sheikh Iqbal and his family have become the enemy of the SSP and have been the target of many acts of violence perpetrated by the SSP militants.[24]

The social conflict has thus several levels: feudals versus the emergent middle class, Shias versus Sunnis, local Shias versus Muhajir Shias, local Sunnis versus Muhajir Sunnis, Syed (local and Muhajir Shias) versus *julahas* and *kammis* (Sunni Muhajirs), Sheikh biradari (local Sunnis) versus Arain biradari (Muhajir Sunnis), and also competition for power inside the local Sheikh biradari. The local-Muhajir conflict can also be analysed in terms of a conflict between two dominant castes (Sheikh versus Arain).[25]

If the biggest financiers were local, the cadres of the SSP come mostly from the Muhajir community and belong to the Arain biradari as did many of the settlers who migrated from East Punjab to the Canal Colonies at the end of the nineteenth century. Many of them have fought in Afghanistan and most of the terrorists who caused a lot of bloodshed between 1990 and 1993 in Jhang were Muhajirs.[26] The SSP militants belong to the emergent 'under-classes', semi-urban, often unemployed, who are at the margin of the middle class, and whom the SSP has empowered by giving them an aggressive Sunni identity (Zahab 2002).

During Haq Nawaz's lifetime, there was not such a high level of violence in Jhang as after his death. This can be attributed to the fact that he was a local. His successors as leaders of the SSP were Muhajirs, outsiders imported in Jhang,[27] and it can be said that the SSP thrived on the death of Haq Nawaz. The criminalization of the sectarian conflict in Jhang, which could be observed since the creation of the SSP, became much more obvious after the death of Haq Nawaz thanks to the weaponization of society and to the power of the local mafias.[28] Muhajir *goondas* who had joined the SSP—Anwar alias Gaddu, Haider Butt, Saleem Fauji[29] to name but a few—played a prominent role in the bloodshed which followed the assassination of Haq Nawaz. They became heroes when they vowed to avenge his death. They got political protection from the SSP and a lot of local drug dealers gave them protection money which means that the SSP utilized them to maintain a certain level of tension in the streets. In exchange for financing the SSP, Sheikh Yousaf is also alleged to having used SSP activists and hooligans to threaten and sometimes kill people.

The sectarian situation was also manipulated by the drug mafia—Jhang is at the crossroads of drug and arms distribution networks. The drug mafia had an interest in maintaining a certain level of tension and resorted to provocations whenever the situation was too calm for its activities. Heroin smuggling became a main commercial activity in Jhang after the onset of sectarian violence[30] and electoral campaigns were financed by the profits of the drug business. Both sides were involved: a Shia feudal who is an ex-MNA is regularly denounced as one of the drug mafia bosses and the SSP apparently controlled the retail sales with the connivance of the police. When Jhang experienced the worst violence in 1992, drug dealers and drug users were the only persons who could move freely between the different parts of the city.

The SSP tried to get rid of the hooligans after Azam Tariq was elected MNA for the first time in a by-election in 1992, and adopted a soft line, insisting on welfare (development projects, Sui gas, etc.) and on the necessity to maintain peace in Jhang. The extremists who felt betrayed, created the Lashkar-e Jhangvi headed by Riaz Basra in 1994 and the violence spread to other districts where it was more terrorist in nature.

Azam Tariq was elected as an independent MNA in October 2002—the authorities tried, so far in vain, to get his election invalidated—he had spent the whole year either in jail or under house-arrest after the SSP was banned in January 2002. Although Shia feudals have lost some of their influence,[31] Faisal Saleh Hayat, a powerful Shia landlord and *sajjada nishin* of Shah Jewna, was rewarded with the Ministry of Interior for having left the PPP to join the PML(Q). Sughra Imam, the daughter of Abida Hussain, was elected MPA and Asad Hayat, a Shia feudal and brother of Faisal Saleh Hayat, was naib nazim of the district. The results of the elections held in August 2001 demonstrated that, at least at the local level, it is power and the traditional Punjabi rivalry between factions which count rather than ideology. The SSP supported Sahibzada Sultan Hamid of Sultan Bahu and Asad Hayat, a PPP-backed panel, against Sughra Imam who was defeated. It shows once again that when the game is about power and money, Shia feudals and Barelvi Pirs are acceptable to the SSP.

Local Sunnis have retained their power at the local level as Sheikh Akram, the brother of Sheikh Iqbal, was elected tehsil nazim despite the efforts of the SSP to take over this seat. Given the enmity between Sheikh Akram and the SSP, there was every reason to fear a new outbreak of violence in Jhang.

CONCLUSIONS

This short study of the many aspects of the sectarian conflict in Jhang demonstrates that sectarianism is linked with the power struggle and that, due to the lack of confidence in the state and the absence of channels of political participation, primordial identities come to the forefront and are instrumentalized by the protagonists to conflicts involving class, biradari, factions, or ethnic identity. It shows that in the context of Jhang the conflict cannot be explained in religious and ideological terms alone and that it is primarily the result of the socio-economic tensions among different classes of the society. Sectarianism can thus be defined in this particular context as a temporary substitute identity and as a vehicle of social change.

GLOSSARY

rafiziyat	Shiism
Khoja	pathfinders
kammis	lower caste people
murids	followers
azan	call to prayer
matam	chest beating
Sahaba	companions of the Prophet
Ahl-i-Bait	the family of the Prophet
goondas	hooligans
azadari	mourning rituals

NOTES

1. In the Pakistani context, sectarianism refers to the conflict between Sunnis and Shias.
2. The SSP was banned by President Musharraf on 12 January 2002, along with four other jihadi outfits but its militants were not really targeted in the crackdown on extremist groups which followed the ban.
3. Among others, Maulana Tahir ul Qadri, a prominent Barelvi leader.
4. In true Punjabi fashion, this prominent political family is divided into two rival factions. The first one was led by the late Colonel Abid Hussain and now by his daughter Abida Hussain (former federal minister in Nawaz Sharif's government and ambassador to the USA), her husband Fakhr Imam and their daughter Sughra Imam who started her political career in December 1998 as Chairman of the district council. The other faction is led by Makhdoom Faisal Saleh Hayat who is the *sajjada nishin* of Shah Jewna. A central leader of the PPP, he defected in 2002 to join the PML (QA), and became the federal minister of Interior. Leaders of both factions contested elections against one another at the local and at the national level in 2001 and 2002.
5. According to the 1951 census, Muhajirs formed 49 per cent of the population of the district and 65 per cent of the population of the municipal area of Jhang.
6. Bilal Zubeiri, *Tarikh-e Jhang*, nd, np.
7. The local Shias blame, for instance, the Muhajirs for having introduced Hindu customs in the Muharram processions while many Muhajirs consider the local Shias as uneducated and ignorant of 'true Shiism'.
8. The Jats of Rohtak were the target of a Shuddi movement launched by the Arya Samaj in the 1920s and was aimed at reconverting them to Hinduism.
9. One of them was Sahibzada Nazir Sultan linked to the Sultan Bahu shrine who defeated Arif Khan Sial.
10. Two of the three Sunnis elected in 1970 had joined the ruling PPP and they contested the election in 1977 on PPP tickets (PPP was very much seen as pro-Shia). The number of National Assembly seats in Jhang was increased from 1 in 1965 to 3 in 1970, 5 in 1977 and 6 in 2002.
11. For more details about the politicization of the Shia community, see Mariam Abou Zahab, 'The politicization of the Shia community in Pakistan in the 1970s and the 1980s' (paper presented at the Conference on Images, Representations and Perceptions in the Shia world, Geneva, October 2002 (forthcoming).
12. This does not mean that the traditional zakirs who often have no formal religious education and who have always been economically dependent on the feudals were marginalized. Both styles of *majlis* coexist in Punjab and attract crowds.
13. There have also been recent allegations about links between the SSP and Al Qaida networks.
14. Haq Nawaz's militancy against Shias annoyed Maulana Fazlur Rehman who did not want to antagonize his sizeable Shia constituency in Dera Ismail Khan and who opposed his election as amir of the JUI for Punjab.
15. *Dastur-e Asasi*, Sipah-e-Sahaba, nd.
16. He graduated in 1971 from Khair ul Madaris in Multan, joined the JUI and started teaching in a madrassah of Toba Tek Singh in 1972.
17. See for more details Maulana Mohammad Ilyas Balakoti. *Amir-e Azimat*. Jamia Usmaniya, Jhang Saddar, nd. This tendentious book is the 'official' biography of Haq Nawaz Jhangvi.

18. Mukhtar Ahmad Ali, 1999.
19. The Punjab Land Alienation Act of 1900.
20. It is often said that the best zakirs of Jhang were Hindus.
21. These two professions are often described as powerful mafias.
22. Sheikh Iqbal's personality is very controversial. In the 1970s, Sheikh Iqbal owned a petrol pump, a hotel, a cinema hall and dozens of buses.
23. A case was falsely registered against Shias who became martyrs in the eyes of the Shia community.
24. Sheikh Iqbal was himself assassinated in March 1995 by the SSP. The only son of Sheikh Iqbal, who is a high civil servant, was designated in the FIR registered after the assassination in January 1991 of Isar ul Qasmi, the successor of Haq Nawaz, in which Sheikh Iqbal's family was in fact not involved. Sheikh Iqbal's brother, Sheikh Akram, was elected tehsil nazim in 2001, defeating the SSP candidate, Zahoor Sajid Janjua, brother of late MPA Riaz Hashmat Janjua.
25. The importance of caste in Jhang can be judged from the fact that our informers always refer to Ibbetson's book 'Punjab Castes' published in Lahore in 1916 and based on the Census Report of 1881. This book is regularly reprinted both in Pakistan and in India and has recently been translated into Urdu.
26. Mukhtar Ahmad Ali, op. cit. Muhajirs, both Sunnis and Shias, are said to be more assertive and to resort quickly to violence because they do not have the same values and family networks as the locals who have many other ways of resolving conflicts before resorting to violence.
27. Isar ul Qasmi was from Samundri and Azam Tariq was settled in Karachi but born in a village near Chichawatni.
28. The Punjab government did not move against the SSP between 1988 and 1993 because the Islami Jamhoori Ittihad (IJI) saw it as a potential ally and because the targets of the SSP, namely Ahmadis and Shias, were seen as supporters of the PPP, their rivals. Benazir Bhutto sought the alliance of the SSP against the PML.
29. Saleem Fauji was killed in a police encounter in 1992. Azam Tariq attended his funeral and pronounced a very provocative speech describing him as a martyr. His death provoked the attack of a police APC with a 17 mm anti-aircraft gun which caused the death of four policemen and provoked a police operation against the SSP.
30. Drug and alcohol trafficking witnessed an increase of 250 to 300 per cent after the onset of sectarian violence. Khalid Hussain, 'Live and Let Die,' *The Friday Times*, 3–9 September 1992.
31. Abida Hussain, her husband Fakhar Imam, and Amanullah Sial were defeated in the elections.

CHAPTER 8

Langar: Pilgrimage, Sacred Exchange, and Perpetual Sacrifice in a Sufi Saint's Lodge

PNINA WERBNER

INTRODUCTION: PILGRIMAGE AND SACRED EXCHANGE

An important feature of pilgrimages, it has been argued, is that the symbolic transformations pilgrims undergo effect a sacred exchange between two symbolic worlds, and mediate the contradictions between those worlds (see R. Werbner 1989:261–262, 296). During pilgrimage, pilgrims shed their mundane person, often through metonymic giving to the poor or at a sacred site, while they return bearing symbolic substances imbued with the sacred power of the ritual centre. Hence, for example, Huichal Indians in Mexico go on annual pilgrimage to their sacred centre of Wirkuta in order to return reborn and bearing with them the peyote needed to revitalize their world (Meyerhoff 1974). In the Kalanga cult of the high god of Mwali, the 'hot' ash of the old year is rubbed on the back of a female klipspringer buck, which is released into the mountains where the rain washes off the ash, bringing coolness. Paralleling this act, Kalanga adepts of the cult bring back from the oracle centre the dust they roll in when 'tied' in possession by Mwali. The dust is only washed off when they reach their natural homesteads, bringing coolness, fertility and prosperity to the earth (Werbner 1989).

A focus on sacred exchange in pilgrimage reveals the limitations of theories which stress merely the experiential dimensions of pilgrimage. Of these theories, that of Victor Turner on pilgrimage as 'anti-structure' and 'communities' powerfully captures an important dimension of the pilgrimage experience, while glossing over the fact that pilgrimage is a highly structured process of metonymic (and not just metaphoric) transformation. The view proposed here is that pilgrimage is both 'anti-structure' and 'counter-structure'. The counter-structural features of pilgrimage refer to the fact that pilgrims expect to undergo not only a spiritual renewal but a renewal of personhood through contact with the sacred, and a renewal of community through the bearing of what has been in contact with the sacred centre home into the structured, mundane world. These transformations of personhood and home often require a highly structured and elaborate series of symbolic acts. Some of these acts may be in the form of transactions with ritually designated persons. Hence in Benares, as Party (1994) has shown, pilgrims must unload their 'sins' in the form of gifts to Brahmins before they can purify themselves.

This type of interested exchange leads Eade and Sallnow to describe metonymic exchanges effected at pilgrimage centres as 'self-interested exchanges between human beings and the divine' (1991: 24). 'This marked ideology', they argue, 'embraces both the miracle and the sacrificial discourses' (ibid.). Although, they recognize, 'lay helpers are enjoined to set an example in self-sacrifice to other pilgrims by giving freely of their time and labour (in the spirit of the 'pure' gift).... For as strongly salvatory religion...it is questionable whether the notion of purely disinterested giving can be anything other than a fiction' (ibid., 25). Hence, Eade and Sallnow refer to this type of 'sacred commerce' (ibid.)

In the spirit of this interpretation, studies of Islamic pilgrimage have repeatedly stressed the intercessionary role of the saint who mediates between supplicants and God. Pilgrims make offerings at a saint's tomb in the name of the saint in order to return imbued with the saint's charisma or *baraka*, containing the curative powers and blessing they desire. This type of sacred exchange seems on the surface to be relatively simple, and has been explained as modelled upon a supplicants' everyday experiences of secular power as being based on patronage (Eickelman 1976).

Sacrifice more generally has also often been conceived of in relatively simple terms as a sacred exchange between humans and God with the victim acting as mediator (Hubert and Mauss 1965). Recent research has, however, begun to explore the extreme complexity of the symbolic transformations involved in animal sacrifice as analysed in particular cultural settings (see de Heusch 1985; R. Werbner 1989: Ch. 3; also Werbner 1990: Ch. 5).

But reduction of processes of sacred exchange in pilgrimage to mere interested reciprocity, however disguised, obscures the highly structured and complex set of symbolic operations which bring about the desired transformation, both in the moral persona of a pilgrim and in his or her acquisition of the desired sacred substances to be taken back on the journey home. Within this process, animal sacrifice is a key moment which has to be set in relation to other symbolic acts.

This chapter argues that the *langar* at a Sufi saint's lodge may be regarded as a form of perpetual sacrifice which is a key symbolic moment of metonymic exchange during pilgrimage to the lodge. As such, it structures both the routine organization of the lodge and the wider organization of the Sufi regional cult focused upon it. In its generative organizing capacity, it also structures gender relations and makes women integral to the process whereby God's blessing is at object at the lodge.

My interpretation of the acts of sacrificial service, and the act of sharing in a sacrificial meal at the lodge, stresses the need to unmask a self-interested discourse in order to reveal the central experience of altruism and humanism which energises Sufism. My argument thus reverses a common sociological tendency to seek material interests beneath the surface of apparent altruism. In Sufism, a discourse of market relations and patronage is used by supplicants to 'explain' their relation to the saint, alive or dead. Given an occidental tendency to seek self-interested motive behind apparently altruistic facades, this Sufi allegory of interested exchange may easily be accepted at face value, as a 'true' explanation of supplicants' motives. Similarly, the occasional unmasking of individual saints as exploitative charlatans or sexually promiscuous seducers of innocent female supplicants, is seen as proof of the manipulative nature of Sufism.

To comprehend fully the Sufi langar, however, it needs to be understood in the context of other forms of Islamic sacrifice, on the one hand, and in relation to the other sacred exchanges accompanying it—of voluntary service, ritual substances, social identification and powerful blessing—on the other.

For Muslims the *hajj* to Makkah is the ultimate pretext for all sacred exchanges during pilgrimage. My research on the hajj was conducted in Manchester through discussions with returning hajjis, who, in telling me of their journey in minute detail, relived the experience of the hajj while reflecting, at my request, on its significance.

Seen as sacred journeys, the counter-structure of the hajj and *umrah* rituals achieves the desired symbolic transformation in the person of the pilgrim through a series of significant alternations and reversals in time. Starting from Mina on the eighth day of the month of hajj, the pilgrims are moved back in time on the ninth day at the valley of Arafat, which is both the beginning and end of time (the birthplace of Adam and the site of the final Day of Judgment). The sacrifice of the Eid, commemorating the binding of Ismail, is followed on the tenth day by the encounter with the devils which leads to the binding of Ismail.

This reversal of the original time sequence of the sacred Qur'anic (and Biblical) narratives is not accidental, in my view, but part of the process through which the pilgrim gradually sheds her or his sins and becomes as pure and innocent as a newborn infant. The pilgrim starts this symbolic journey dressed in two white sheets, likened to the shrouds of the dead; that is, at the end of life. After the sacrifice commemorating the binding of Ismail, his or her head is shaved or clipped and he or she is reborn as a new person.

The hajj ritual is highly elaborate. From the valley of Arafat, where the pilgrims spend a day in the baking sun, they move to the valley of Muzadaliffah, where they spend the night and where they collect forty-nine tiny pebbles. Returning to Mina for the second time on the tenth day, the day of hajj, they cast one lot of seven pebbles onto a single pillar, that of Aqaba. They then perform the *qurbani* or sacrifice of the Eid and eat of the meat. Finally, they shave their heads or clip their hair (in the case of women). Once they have completed the sacrificial meal, they can put on their normal clothes and all taboos are lifted, except the prohibition on sexual intercourse.

On the eleventh day of the hajj, following the sacrifice, the pilgrims move to Makkah to perform the Makkan ritual. This ritual, also performed on its own throughout the year and known then as umrah highlights the time reversal of the narrative even more clearly. The movement during umrah is from *tawaf*, the circumambulation of the house of God which is believed to have been rebuilt by Ibrahim (Abraham) and Ismail after their reunification. In the second phase, the pilgrim moves to the sacred spring, the *zamzam*, which Hajra discovered had sprung from the heel of Ismail as he lay wailing in the sand; here the pilgrim washes and drinks the water. The final stage of the umrah is *sai*, the running back and forth between the two hills of Safa and Marwa, which recalls Hajra's agonized running in search of water for her baby boy, Ismail. The movement is thus backwards from death toward purity like that of a baby.

Having completed the Makkan episode, the pilgrims then return to Mina once more for a final stoning—this time of all three devils. Altogether in the post-Makkan stoning, the pilgrims cast forty-two pebbles, fourteen at each of the pillars (seven times three, on each of two days). The pilgrims start from the pillar farthest from Makkah and end with the Aqaba pillar, which is the nearest. In the original narrative,

Ibrahim (some say Ismail) encountered these three devils *before* the binding of Ismail. During hajj and umrah the multiple stoning of the devils (except for the first stoning) occur *after* the sacrifice, reversing the original narrative. Finally, the pilgrims return to Makkah for another re-enactment of the Makkan ritual.

The hajj is thus a moral allegory which can only be understood in relation to its sacred pretext. The sequence of acts, moreover, brings about a series of identifications with exemplary persons. The key identifications elicited are two: with Ibrahim and the ordeal he faced in having to sacrifice his son, and with Hajra, his wife, and the ordeal she faced in wandering with her son in the desert, with no water to quench his thirst. The mythic narratives of these two exemplary persons are structurally identical. In both, a parent is asked to sacrifice his or her child for the sake of God without losing faith in God. In both, God intervenes miraculously at the final moment to save the child from certain death. The pilgrims enact this dual ordeal during the hajj and umrah.

Islamic traditions stress the voluntarism of these ordeals: Ismail knew in advance, pilgrims told me, God's command. Hajra, too, accepted the edict of God. Hence, one pilgrim explained:

> Mina is where Ibrahim sacrificed Ismail. The pillars are the places where the devil tried to stop him. The first devil was small, the second medium and the third large. Ismail said to Ibrahim: 'Tie my legs and put my face away [from fulfilling God's will].

She explained about Ibrahim's ordeals that 'Whomever Allah likes most he tests more than others.' Hence, Hajra was sent into the desert in order that water be found and the Kaaba, the shrine housing the sacred black stone in Makkah, rebuilt.

The identification with a woman is significant. Hence, a woman pilgrim who had just returned from hajj explained to me that the story of Ismail and Hajra was very important to her as a woman. When she was there and performing *sai*, she said, she reflected on what an effort Hajra as a mother had made for her son. Just as all the pilgrims, both male and female, identify with Ibrahim, a male, so, too, they all identify with Hajra, a female.

The Makkan pilgrimage creates other key identifications. Pilgrims invariably explain that they perform the hajj in this particular order because this is the way the Prophet performed it; they are merely retracing his footsteps. When they visit Arafat, one pilgrim told me, they stand where Adam stood on Jabal (Mount) Rehemat to ask God for forgiveness:

> In Arafat Adam asked in the name of the *kalimah* for forgiveness, so we go there to ask God's forgiveness for our sins. The *hajj* belongs to the Prophet Ibrahim as does the *eid*. There are two sunnas, Ibrahim's and Mohammad's. It moves from Adam to Ibrahim. The Prophet did the same [when he performed the first *hajj*].

Although the transformation effected in pilgrims is fundamentally a spiritual one, nevertheless pilgrims return from hajj bearing with them sacred tokens—bottles of water from the holy spring, the zamzam, as well as dates, rosaries and shawls. They sprinkle this water on people back home, spreading the blessings they received (for similar metonymic transfer in Turkey see Delaney 1990:520).

The making of *qurbani* during the hajj is thus a moment in a sequence of structural transformations which effects the movement of pilgrims on hajj towards blessed innocence, a state embodied in the sacred water and dates they carry home with them. Sacrifice is a key moment of transition in this process. In saints' lodges and shrines in South Asia, this moment is expanded and magnified to become the central trope of the lodge, binding together the moral ideas of mystical Sufism with the organizational agendas of the lodges as centres of far-flung regional cults.

Sacrifice in Islam as performed during the hajj is a moment of ordeal and release, in which a person's faith in God is tested. One of the key features of the Eid sacrifice on the hajj is that both the sacrificial slaughter and the prayers accompanying it are multiplied a thousand times. In explaining the hajj, Sharif Ahmad, a distinguished British *alim* told his congregation:

> When one person asks blessings alone from his God, he shall get the blessing. But if many people ask for blessing all together, they will get manifold blessings. The bigger the congregation is when they ask for blessings, the more blessings Allah will give them, and in the whole world there is no gathering of human beings asking for Allah's blessings as large as that of the hajj. And this gathering only takes place on the Mount of Rehemat and in Arafat, nowhere else. And on the day of hajj millions and millions of people, on the same day and with the same intention, call out to their God. So the blessings of God come running towards them. This state, this atmosphere, and this situation cannot be found on any other day, any other time or any other situation.'
>
> The time of *hajj* is the time of blessing. On that day if a person asks for blessing with a true heart, he will get a river of blessings and will be purified.

Such a person will feel so pure, as though he was just born from his mother's belly.

What is stressed here is mediation with God not by a single person but by the community of believers, united in their intentionality and all focusing on Allah. While for Sufis the mediation of the Prophet and of saints on the Day of Judgment is a cornerstone of their belief, this mediation is itself mediated by the ability of these saints to mobilize the multitude in shared ordeal. Like the sacrifice, the day in the valley of Arafat, exposed to the heat of the sun, is regarded as a test of faith.

To develop this point in relation to sacrifice at saints' lodges in India and Pakistan, let me begin by describing the annual sacrifice as a cultural performance held in Ghamkol Sharif, the lodge of Zindapir, in a little valley outside the town of Kohat in north-western Pakistan.

PERPETUAL SACRIFICE

The annual sacrifice on the *'urs* at Ghamkol Sharif is a major event. In 1990, ninety-five goats, thirteen sheep, and seventeen cattle and buffalo were slaughtered over a three-day period, the equivalent of over 3,000 kg of meat, distributed to some 20,000 or more pilgrims and supplicants. In preparation for this annual feast, local high-class *Sayyid* women of wealthy families who claim descent from the Prophet, along with a large number of women from other respected families throughout Pakistan, clean and scrape thousands of clay dishes, hundreds of flat bread baskets, about twenty or thirty giant clay pots, and an equivalent number of iron chappati stoves (*loh*). The latter accumulate a layer of rust over the year and need to be scraped and polished in readiness for the thousands of chappatis that are to be baked on them during the major three-day festival. Once cleaned, they have to be reinstalled in the earth, and women—again I must stress their wealthy, high-caste origins—use heavy iron picks to dig up the dry earth in order to install the ovens. The women's work is all voluntary, an act of *khidmat*, of public service; or, as the living saint of Ghamkol Sharif, Zindapir, stressed to me repeatedly, it is all done out of *muhabbat*, the love of God. The women explain that they 'work for *sawab*, and for God's forgiveness, *Allah mu'af kare*.'

While the women wash, scrape and polish, the men invest their voluntary labour in piling up vast quantities of wood in preparation for the enormous quantities of food to be cooked.

The occasion of the sacrificial feast is the 'urs, the commemoration of the death/rebirth of Zindapir's Sufi master, Baba Qasim. Every year on the 'urs, the valley of the lodge fills with disciples coming in convoys from all over Pakistan. They bear with them tributary gifts for the saint, known as *nazrana*, and offerings for the langar, the sacred food provided freely at the lodge for all supplicants, disciples and pilgrims who visit it. The food is pure, I was told, because it is cooked by men of pure heart who chant *zikr* as they cook.

The 'urs is the high point of a continuous flow of food provided at the lodge by the saint all year round. This food many be conceived of as a perpetual sacrifice, one that provides an apparently endless supply of sacrificial meat every day throughout the year.

A key feature here is, first, the need to conceptualise the difference between Islamic ritual slaughter (*halal*) and ritual sacrifice, since nominally in Islam every animal slaughtered is a sacrifice (see contributions in Brisbarre and Gokalp 1993). Ritual sacrifices are, however, set apart from routine Islamic slaughter by additional customs related to particular festive occasions—the Eid, *aqiqa* or *sadaqa* (see Werbner 1990). The second question is: how can one speak of perpetual sacrifice, quotidian sacrifice, sacrifice as a routine of daily life?

The key difference between routine ritual slaughter (*halal*) and ritual sacrifice, I suggest, is related to an act of conversion. The conversions from the cash economy to the moral economy, the good faith economy, the gift economy. Unlike ordinary *halal* slaughter, a ritual sacrifice is the slaughter of an animal freely given, removed from the cash nexus of commercial buying and selling. This means that a purchased animal must be transformed through rites of sacralisation before it can be sacrificed or defined as an offering. Among Pakistanis this is usually achieved through a communal reading of the whole Qur'an in a cooperative gathering, or through a special specified prayer of dedication—such as the Eid morning prayer—which takes place before the slaughter of the animal, or the cooking and eating of an offering of vegetarian food known as *tabarruk*.

It is in the light of this that the slaughter of animals at the lodges of Sufi saints in Pakistan can be regarded as perpetual sacrifice. All the animals slaughtered for the langar are freely given by pilgrims, disciples and supplicants—none is purchased. Moreover, the sacrifice takes place in a space which has been sacralised by continuous prayer. Zindapir, the saint of Ghamkol Sharif, is said never to sleep but to spend all his time meditating and praying. The lodge itself is a place of zikr. The sound of zikr—*Allah hu* or *La'illaha il Allah* both individually and communally sung—echoes continuously through the valley. The men who slaughter and cook the animals for the langar do so as a meritorious, freely given act, an act of selfless service. All the labour in the lodge is freely given in the name of God. Hence, the lodge is a space set apart from the commodity economy, and capitalist logic does not hold there. During the 'urs the convoys of trucks and buses coming from the different villages, towns, factories, army barracks or workplaces throughout Pakistan and beyond it, including from Britain, where Zindapir's order extends, bear with them not only animals but sacks of flour, bags of rice, large containers of *ghee* and money donated for the purchase of food for the langar. These staples and animals, like the cash and the voluntary labour, are freely given. Perpetual sacrifice and other forms of offering are in this respect identical.

To understand this further we need also to appreciate that Islamic sacrifice in South Asia, as I have argued elsewhere (Werbner 1990: chs. 5, 8), is framed by a semiotic of inequality characterizing what I call hierarchical gift economies (see Figure 8.1).

Figure 8.1: The structure of sacrificial giving

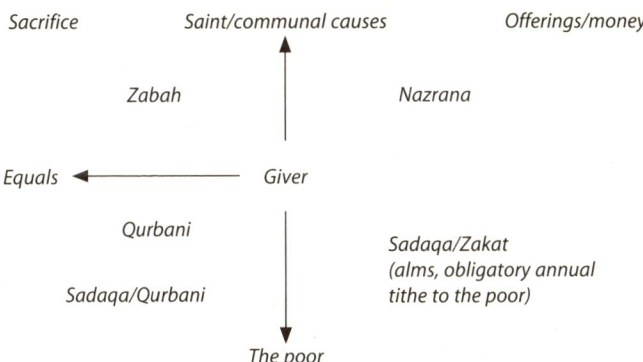

The hierarchical nature of South Asian Islamic gift-giving is clearly expressed in the ideas and practices surrounding sacrificial giving. Gifts to God, including animal sacrifices and offerings of food and money, are always unilateral—gives without expectation of returns. Yet the direction of this gifting is highly significant. Gifts to God are directed either 'downwards', to the poor, in the form of *sadaqa*, or 'upwards', as religious tribute to saints and holy men, whether alive or dead. Alternatively, offerings are made to communal causes such as the building of a mosque or the langar.

Saints, regarded as descendants of the Prophet or his close companions, are almost invariably members of the highest Sayyid or Siddiqi Muslim castes. Members of these castes, I was told, will not accept sadaqa, but only nazrana, a religious tributary gift of money, valuable objects or food given as a mark of respect or in gratitude for a blessing bestowed. The remains of communal meals held after religious gatherings (usually fruit or cooked food) are distributed as *tabarruk* among the people to be taken home; the food is sacrificial and dedicated and hence it cannot be thrown away. Again, I was told the *Sayyids* are not offered and do not usually accept *tabarruk*.

In accord with this distinction between gifts to God via the poor and gifts to God via a superior religious intercessor (a saint), Pakistani Muslims also distinguish between different forms of animal sacrifice: sadaqa is an expiatory gift at the time of extreme danger of a life-threatening kind, in which the victim is given to the poor in its entirety; in qurbani, the Eid sacrifice, a portion is given to the poor and the rest shared among kin and friends conceived of as equals; and in *zabah*, an animal is given as a tribute at a saint's lodge and is usually shared out as langar (see Figures 8.1 and 8.2).

The hierarchical nature of religious giving was made evident to me in Pakistan by Zindapir, the living saint of Ghamkol Sharif. Zindapir described himself as a *faqir*, and he explained: 'A faqir is the friend of Allah. Even if he is offered one lakh [100,000] rupees or nothing to eat for Allah's sake, he would choose to go hungry.' The faqir, he said, denies himself while giving to others: 'This is the way of a faqir. He fasts all day while making sure that everyone else is given food.' Remarkably, the saint gives not just at his own lodge. Hence Zindapir explained: 'I have arrangements to host people wherever I go, all over Pakistan and even all over the world. Wherever I go, whether here [at the lodge] or in Makkah, Allah provides the langar and hospitality for my guests.' Here, Zindapir is referring to his regional cult, the network of satellite lodges distributed throughout Pakistan and Britain which provide langar for visitors. On the annual hajj, Zindapir distributes langar in Makkah. This langar is organized and funded by his vicegerent in Britain—Sufi Abdullah, a saint in his own right, based in Birmingham, itself the centre of a regional cult with satellite centres in nine British cities. The money for the hajj langar is donated by British Pakistanis, while the pots and utensils are kept by disciples of Zindapir living in Makkah who are labour migrants working in Saudi Arabia.

Explaining his remarkable generosity Zindapir told me:

I have to be generous because this [the lodge, or Makkah] is not my house. It is the house of Allah. I, too, am a guest here. It is easy to be generous in someone else's house. If it were my own house, it might be hard for me to part even with a glass of water.

We see in this statement the close identification of the saint with Allah, his proximity to God. But it is also a commentary on the identification between the saint and the community. Commenting on the difference between himself, as a faqir and friend of Allah, and the ulama, the learned doctors who are paid officials, he said: 'Allah will undoubtedly take the ulama to Paradise on the Day of Judgment. But Allah gives paradise to his faqirs on earth. I can give all the blessings of Allah.'

Zindapir repeatedly reminded me of the enormous crowds his langar had just fed during the 'urs festival and the vast number of gifts of money and cloth he had bestowed on his followers and the needy. The 'urs is said, somewhat hyperbolically, to draw 300,000 pilgrims to the lodge, all of whom are fed by the saint. By contrast, ulama are mere employees, Zindapir told me: 'Only yesterday I paid a *maulvi* 400 rupees [about £15] for giving a sermon at the mosque'.

The saint, friend of Allah, most elevated and closest to him, asks for nothing except from Allah. He is the infinite giver through whom flows the bounty of Allah to his followers below him. If he takes, it is only as tribute, a mark of respect and gratitude made towards him by his followers. By contrast the ulama, although undoubtedly pious men, are mere receivers, dependent on human generosity, employees of low status and honour.

Mediation with God is thus achieved either by giving to the poor or, indirectly via a tribute to a saint who, in turn, is expected to use the tribute, if it is a sacrificial animal, for the langar; or by giving directly to the langar, for the sake of the people (*makhluqat*, the community). In Pakistan, and throughout South Asia, most major Muslim shrines and lodges have langar arrangements at festivals and often daily. In Britain, the langar is provided for the celebrations of the 'urs of Abdul Qadir Gilani, regarded as the founder of all the Sufi orders in India. These monthly rituals are known as *gyarvin sharif*, the event of the months, and are held in most of Zindapir's satellite lodges and mosques throughout his regional cult. In addition, during the month of Ramadan, food and offerings are distributed daily at the mosque branches of Zindapir's Sufi order in Manchester and throughout Britain. In all these instances the food is donated and its cooking voluntary. The slaughter of the animals in Britain is, however, entrusted to Pakistani butchers, who slaughter it at the abattoir. There appears to be very little sentimental value attached to the act of personal slaughter, and similarly, people do not appear to attach much value to the appearance of the live animal. The choice of the animal, like the slaughter itself, is entrusted to the butcher.

At Ghamkol Sharif, however, animals are donated by the hoof and one of the disciples slaughters them, assisted by several companions. The same disciple acts as chief slaughterer for the lodge on all major festivals. The langar at Ghamkol Sharif is open twenty-four hours a day all year to all supplicants and pilgrims, from the very poor to the most elevated and powerful in the land. Zindapir is a well-known saint, and he is regularly visited by top civil servants, army brigadiers and generals, and even politicians. All partake of the langar. To partake of the langar is to partake of the blessings of the Sheikh, the divine blessing, *faiz*, which endows him with barkat, and indeed, the langar objectifies this perpetual source of saintly divine spiritual power.

The hierarchical nature of South Asian giving does, however, imbue even the langar with some ambiguity. At Zindapir's lodge there are, in effect, two langars. One is an open, general langar, and the other is run by his son's wife. Many of the most respected guests are fed from this more exclusive langar, although chappati bread usually comes from the central langar. The Sayyid women with whom I spent the *'urs* had brought their own food with them for the festival, and ate almost nothing from the central langar, although they denied that this avoidance had any significance, beyond a matter of taste preferences.

The langar, conceived of as perpetual sacrifice, is the key organizing feature of Sufi lodges in South Asia. Such lodges are centres for the collection and redistribution of food on a vast scale. Virtually all the activity of the lodge is geared to this continuous provision of ritually sacred food. Ghamkol Sharif has its herds of cattle, goats and other livestock, its orange groves and fruit orchards, its vegetable gardens, as well as storage rooms for grains, rice and clarified butter, brought by supplicants or purchased with their donations. Gifts of camels and horses, and of strange and beautiful wild birds and animals, as well as of goats, sheep and buffalo are not unusual. Many are dedicated to the langar and cannot be used for any other purpose.

The saint himself is a vegetarian who eats no meat and regards himself as a protector of all living creatures. Every morning he feeds the ants with the remains of his sweet morning tea. Killing ants and any other creatures, however minute, is prohibited within the lodge area. This is also true of his conduct during the hajj, I was told. A special water trough has been constructed by the saint's son for the wild animals that descend from the hills at night to drink from, while the legends about the Zindapir recount his conquest of the wild. He can cure poisonous snake bites, honey bees are said not to sting, and wild animals do not invade the lodge or attack its inhabitants. The saint is conceived of as the source of natural fertility, and his command over nature is a metaphor for his command over his passionate soul, his *nafs*. He is a source of both infinite nature and infinite love.

Yet his abstention from meat underlines once again the hierarchical logic informing sacrifice. As a perpetual giver he cannot take. The unilateral nature of gifting would be compromised if he took of what was given to him. God is the ultimate source of both food and life, which flow from Him downwards into the world of ephemeral creations.

Sacrifice is a tribute to God just as nazrana is a tribute to the saint. The offerings or tributes are meritorious acts of respect, but neither God nor the saint need the gifts offered to them. Need implies a lack and hence imperfection. The saint is an exemplar of the perfect man, *insaan-e-kamil*. Just as God needs no sustenance from humans, so, too, the saint needs sustenance from God alone. The saint gives generously and accepts tribute, which he himself does not consume but redirects to the langar and hence, ultimately, to the whole community. He fasts all day and is a vegetarian while being the source of meat.

Why do people give to the langar? They do so in fulfilment of a vow (*niyat*) or to seek merit (*sawab*), but also as an act of identification with an unbounded Muslim community, the *umma*. By contrast, the giving of nazrana, even if the expectation is that the tribute will ultimately be redirected to the langar, is much more simply an expression of love and respect for the *sant* by his disciples, or of gratitude, with the added assumption that God loves those who love God's friends, his *awliya*. Although giving nazrana may be constructed as meritorious and efficacious, it is not an act of sacrifice, unless we recognize the identification of the saint, as the exemplary person, within the community. Sacrifice is necessarily mediated either by the poor or by the community. It is an act of expiation and in the case of sadaqa sacrifice of exorcism of afflicting spirits (see Figure 8.2). The poor are not conceived of as scapegoats: since they need the meat for their sustenance and survival, it is assumed it will do them no harm.

Figure 8.2: Sacrifice and offering in the context of migration

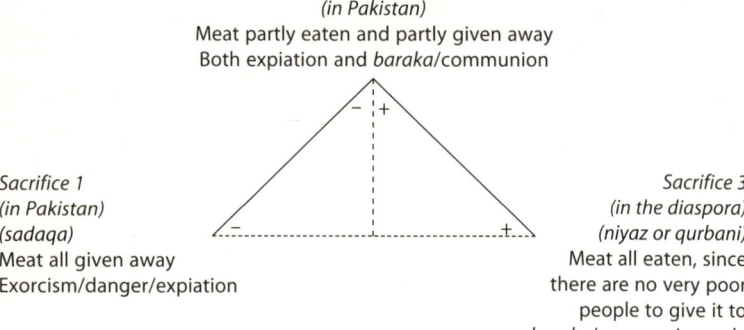

Key:
+ = Positive intervention
− = Expiation or expulsion of evil spirits

THE ENCOUNTER BETWEEN THE GOOD FAITH AND BAD FAITH POLITICAL ECONOMIES

To understand fully, however, why people give to the langar, or why they devote their time and labour to voluntary work at the lodge, we need to recognize the contrast that they and the pir draw between the greed and corruption of the 'world' (*dunya*) and the purity of the lodge as a place of true religion (*din*). The postcolonial reality of contemporary Pakistan is seen by pilgrims as one of mendacious politicians, of greed, selfishness and violence. Even the politicians themselves acknowledge this reality: the celebrations of fifty years of Pakistan's independence, which took place in August 1997, were an occasion for political leaders to beat their breasts in public about the endemic corruption and social divisions afflicting the nation. To lead the good life of a Muslim in this world is, people say, virtually impossible. Only pirs, *awliya*, can therefore guarantee God's forgiveness for their followers on the Day of Judgment.

Hajji Bashir, Zindapir's vicegerent in Manchester and my companion and guide during my 1989 visit to Ghamkol Sharif, told me:

> People believe that on the Day of Judgment they will appear before God as a group and the pirs will speak for them and ask God to forgive them, and they will then be forgiven and go to heaven They know that if they stood alone before God they would definitely not go to heaven.

'Why not?' I asked. 'You are a good man, why should you fear God's judgment?'

'Because this is not an Islamic country and it is very hard to be a good Muslim here.'

Zindapir repeatedly explained that he refused to get involved in elections because, he said, 'God is not elected, and to become a Sufi you don't need to be elected' (that is, a saint is chosen not by the people but by God). He continued:

> Politicians come to me and ask me for my support but I always refuse. Once, a local politician who had cheated in the elections came to me. He wanted to put two of his political opponents in jail. But I said to him: 'Even though you got elected by cheating, now you must do what is good for the people, and you should not put those people who fought against you in jail.' Politicians come to me for *duas* and I pray for them, but still they have the thoughts of politicians by coming to me they are making a public demonstration that they respect me, in order to get the people's support.
>
> 'Why don't you like them? I asked. He replied, 'Because they tell lies [*jhut*]'.

The corruption of politicians and large *zamindars* is associated also with an unbridled hubris: they believe that their wealth can buy anything, even God's approval. Zindapir is fond of telling stories of politicians who have wanted to supply the langar with vast quantities of food or money, and whom he has refused:

> A very great landowner came to see me from Sahiwal district. He offered to provide all the food for the langar for three days if I gave him permission to heal by *dam*. I said to him: 'If I let you provide the langar for three days I will make you a partner with God which would be *shirk*. Indeed, I refused even to make him my *murid*.

In another version of this tale, it was the uncle of the Minister of Finance who made the offer after Zindapir cured him of an incurable disease. Pir Sahab cast *dam* on him and said: 'Let him eat from the langar's food and he will be cured.' Once cured, the minister's uncle offered to supply the langar for three days but was refused. Zindapir told him: 'You will provide for the langar for three days but what will happen after that? I cannot make you a partner (*shirk*) with God.'

The paradigmatic tale which illuminates the place of the lodge as the sole source of God's boundless nature is contained in the founding myth of Ghamkol Sharif. On their first journey to establish the lodge, Zindapir recalled, he saw one of his companions carrying a sack of flour. He told the man: 'What will you eat when the flour is finished? Throw it away and trust in Allah.' This story, like others, stresses the finitude of men's resources, whatever their wealth or power, set against the infinity of God's capacity to feed the world. Wherever he goes, Zindapir regards himself as dwelling in the house of God. On one occasion he was invited by an important Saudi politician to stay at his home in Jeddah, but he replied: 'When I visit the house of God, I am the guest only of Allah.'

On my visit in 1991, I was told confidentially that one of the leading political figures in Pakistan had visited the lodge and had wanted to write Zindapir a cheque for a very large sum of money. The saint refused the donation and instead offered the politician and his entourage food from the langar to eat. If it even crosses the mind of a saint to influence politicians, he told me, then he is no longer a faqir, a man of God.

The evidence for the superiority of saints over politicians is proven, Zindapir repeatedly asserted, by the honour given to saints' shrines after their death:

> The tombs of kings do not get *izzat*; only those of *awliya*. The men whom God gives respect to in their lifetimes, in their death their respect grows and grows. Like Data Ganj Baksh in Lahore [the shrine of the eleventh-century Sufi saint Hujweri]. If you go to the Emperor's [Jahangir's] tomb you will find no people there. But at Data Ganj Baksh there are thousands of people all the time.

In similar vein he recalled: 'When the Viceroy of India visited the shrine of Khwaja Ajmeri [one of the great Muslim saints of India] he saw all the people coming there—Hindus, Muslims, Sikhs. After his visit he said: 'India is ruled by two governments—the British government and the government of Khwaja Ajmeri, and the second one is the greater power because it rules people's hearts.'

Zindapir stresses that he asks no one his name, *badshah* or *gharib*. All are equal. The Chief Minister of Azad Kashmir visited him several times, but Zindapir told me, he never asked his name. When this was commented upon Zindapir responded: 'I have no need to know anyone's name. I know only the name of Allah' (that is, Zindapir needs no favours from those who come to see him; he is a giver, never a taker).

The polar contrast between the world of everyday greed and corruption and the infinite generosity of the lodge are captured by Zindapir in a series of aphorisms: '*Dunya ki laraf pith kare, ton khuda ki laraf munh hote hey*' ('if you turn your back to the world you will face God') and 'The world and religion [*dunya aur din*] are like two sisters. If you marry one, you cannot marry the other.'

In his encounters with politicians, the sheikh presented himself as tough and definite. Politicians who aspire to acquire some of his powers must confront the fact that they cannot compete with the divine spiritual power of God's chosen saints. Again and again, it is the sheikh's ability to provide nurture on a daily and annual basis to all who come, from an unending source, which the morality tales stress. It is this which makes it impossible for politicians to compete with him, and which proves that his following is much vaster than that of any politician. This world of generosity and giving as constructed by the saint, the one pilgrims enter into when they arrive at the lodge, bearing their gifts for the saint and the langar, is what may be conceived of as an imaginative as much as a real journey.

Yet just as he denies the importance of the visits and honours granted him by state officials and politicians, so too, paradoxically, do the visits prove that Zindapir is indeed a great and spiritually powerful *wali* of Allah. And despite the constructed ideological opposition between the lodge and the world, the growth and success of the lodge have profited from official goodwill. Land, telephone lines, water, roads and transport have all been provided free through official channels, and Zindapir takes great care, in reality, not to offend politicians. Moreover, there is a symbolic economy of gifting which pervades pilgrims' and supplicants' relations with the saint.

In exchange for the gifts of money, perfume, flour, animals, rice and clarified butter given to the pir as nazrana, or donated directly to the langar, the saint gives his close disciples white chiffon headscarves, embroidered praying caps and perfumes. These he draws, with the almost magical gesture of a conjurer, out of the treasure house of objects he accumulates in his room, buried in the silk and brocade cushions on which he reclines. He distributes salt and amulets to the supplicants who visit him, along with du'a and dam. He also donates money generously to the poor and needy who come to him with requests for help. I myself was showered with gifts: several clothing outfits, jewellery, perfume and a handbag from the sheikh's son's family; four large bottles of honey collected from the lodge's beehives; a lovely white, finely woven cotton headscarf of a type usually reserved for disciples; a beautiful length of silk cloth; and a box of *mithai*, all to take home with me to England, gifts from the sheikh. My attempts to reciprocate were of little avail. The gifts embodied the saint's generosity but, even beyond that, they proved his supreme elevation above the anthropologist, and indeed, any educated, non-Muslim Westerner.

EXPERIENCING THE GOOD FAITH ECONOMY

We see the limitations of the suggestion put forward by Eade and Sallnow (1991) according to which much of the activity at saints' lodges is a matter of 'sacred commerce'. Such a conception denies, moreover, the experiential dimensions of voluntary labour and sacrifice, particularly in the case of close disciples of the saint. Most of the women who work as volunteers in preparation for the langar of the 'urs say they are seeking merit, but I would argue that the reality of the transformation they experience is both far more immediate and far more complex.

For three weeks before the 'urs both men and women begin arriving at the lodge to contribute their voluntary labour to the preparations for the festival. Much of the building of the lodge takes place during this period, including the extension of water pipes, sewerage and electricity. New hostels are constructed for pilgrims. The women arrive daily, increasing in numbers as the festival approaches. They come from throughout the Frontier and even from Lahore. But a core of women come from neighbouring Jungel Khel, the birthplace of Zindapir himself. Most of the women are, as I mentioned, from the high-ranking Sayyid family which is the largest, wealthiest and most important in Jungel Khel, now a small town of 20,000 inhabitants. Members of this large family are scattered throughout the world, occupying professional positions as doctors, engineers or pilots. They hold, and held in the past, many of the top administrative positions in the town. They own large houses and the women who run these have servants to assist them. Yet these very women are willing to take on the most menial, dirty, unpleasant tasks, hard, tiring, physical labour, and live in crowded conditions, sleeping on mats on the floor if they come from some distance, in preparation for the sacrificial feast of the 'urs. During the 'urs they also help supervise the visits of women supplicants to the saint.

Paralleling the seasonal pilgrimage of organized groups to the lodge on major festivals is a constant daily flow of supplicants seeking healing for their ailments or divine blessings in their jobs, careers and marital fortunes. The healing powers of the saint are grounded in a belief in his ability to see below the surface, to the occult and social causes of illnesses, the thoughts, feelings and accidental transgressions which have brought about pain, chronic illness, infertility, depression, business failures and so forth. As an agent of God, the saint is able to act on these hidden forces and change the course of natural illnesses and social fortunes.

The saint is visited by both male and female supplicants. They sit at some distance from him. Both men and women expose their faces, the women drawing their veils above their heads. The exposure underlines the belief that the saint transcends sexuality. His persona combines male and female qualities—the gentleness, love and tenderness of a woman with the power, authority and honour of a man (see also Kurin 1984).[1] He communicates very briefly with the supplicants, addressing them in short, distant tones. Once they have explained their problem to him, he usually instructs them to perform their daily prayers, sometimes throwing a rolled-up, inscribed paper amulet in their general direction. At other times, he instructs them to collect amulets 'outside'. Once he has heard a whole round of supplicants (he takes in about ten at a time) he raises his hands in du'a. Even in the brief interchanges, however, the symbolic transference appears to be very powerful. One can only speculate that for the supplicants his immense healing power derives precisely from his gendered ambiguity: he combines maternal and paternal qualities: he is a maternal father or paternal mother, protective yet authoritative.[2]

His relationship to the women preparing for the 'urs is radically different. Every day during the weeks of preparing for the 'urs, the saint visits the women at their work. They greet him '*asalam u pir*' ('greetings, saint'). There is no bowing or scraping. He does not allow it. They smile at him, an elderly man limping along slowly since his knees are painful and have been causing him some trouble. It is clear that the women are very fond of the saint.

After work every day the women workers come into the saint's inner sanctum to receive his blessings. During these meetings he prays a du'a for them. The meetings are marked by an atmosphere of intimacy. To most women supplicants the saint is a distant, charismatic figure, fearful and awe-inspiring. His face as he distributes amulets, salts and prayers, is expressionless, his tone matter-of-fact, verging on abruptness. The vast majority of his male disciples treat him with awe and respect. The saint is a remote figure, revered, feared and respected. His commands are instantly obeyed. Grown men tremble at his anger and sink into despair. He is treated as a king or prince. On their visits to his room women supplicants sit behind a low wooden barrier placed there to prevent them from reaching too close to him.

This remoteness contrasts with his relationship with his close disciples, those who work on the preparations for the 'urs. The women disciples who assist in the preparations for the sacrificial meal of the 'urs treat him with the freedom of companions. The *sheikh* clearly enjoys the company of these women, and they entertain him with anecdotes and tales of amusing incidents and gossip, including the ridiculous behaviour of the anthropologist, which he finds particularly amusing. They are an invaluable source of information to him about what goes on behind the confines of the room in which he meditates. They are also privy to a good deal of information about his family and private life to which others have no access. They say they fear him, but in practice, what they mainly express is their fondness for him. During my visit to the lodge in 1991, Zindapir's son's wife was undergoing an operation on her throat in England. On the day of the operation the women visited the saint. Earlier, he had been to pray in the northern guest house for the success of the operation. The women disciples kept trying to comfort him by discussing the details of his daughter-in-law's condition. But he kept sighing and lapsing into long silences, then renewing the conversation. They too would lapse into sympathetic silence. This went on for about forty minutes. As time passed with no news of the operation from England, the whole lodge entered into a state of worried expectation. Eventually, at 9.30 p.m., the telephone message arrived, informing the saint that the operation had been a success.

I tell this story to underline the clear connection between sacrifice and moral amity. If sacrifice in Islam hinges on the existence of inequalities, of a category willing to define themselves as 'poor', it nevertheless also encompasses notions of moral responsibility within a moral community. The langar objectifies the moral community embodied by the saint himself as a figure of infinite generosity. This underlines the fact that in Islam voluntary labour, sacrifice, donations, offering and charity merge. All these acts are vehicles mediating the relationship between person and God. In all, moral space is extended, objectified and personified, while the identification between person and community is revitalized.

It is remarkable that in many ways the langar at Sufi *dar ul ulooms* in Britain differ rather little in organisation and ideology from the langar in Pakistan, except for the fact that, as yet, it is not a perpetual sacrifice. The same discourses and practices characterize both langars. The resemblance underlines the transnational nature of Zindapir's order. British branches of the saint's regional cult, like the branches of the cult in Pakistan, provide langar for the same major Islamic and Sufi holidays and festivals, just as the branches in both countries send tribute to the sheikh himself. The ultimate objectification of the diaspora's transnationalism is through the langar provided annually by the order on the hajj. Members of the cult from Pakistan in the east and from Britain in the west, along with disciples working as labour migrants in the Middle East and Gulf states, meet in Makkah annually for the hajj. From the east comes Zindapir, the source of powerful blessing; from the west Sufi Abdullah, his most trusted and highly ranked *khalifa*. It is, however, Sufi Abdullah who provides the sacrificial offering, the langar (as against the Eid sacrifice) which objectifies the saint's *baraka* and his infinite generosity. This ritual international division of labour produces a perpetual sacrifice at the global centre of Islam. What is evident is that the spread of Zindapir's cult has been associated with contemporary global movements of migrant labour from Pakistan to the West.

The global regional cult which has emerged as a result of this international migration process mediates between the universalism of Islam and the particularism of migrants' networks of associations (see Werbner 1989). The focus on a central lodge and its charismatic saint, and on periodic mobilizations—local, national, and global—brings together a widespread network of disciples from the various branches of the cult for the purpose of sharing in a sacrificial feast.

On the surface, however, the saint's relation to the majority of supplicants is nevertheless based on a calculus of exchange. If we deploy familiar religious terms such as penance and salvation, we may easily mistake the work of women and men for what they explicitly say it is—a calculating act of service before God for the purpose of accumulating merit. So, too, offerings and sacrifices, whether directly to the saint or to the langar, can be understood as they are apparently intended: as acts of reciprocity in which a favour is sought from the saint or from God in return for an offering. The saint's gifts to pilgrims—white cotton scarves and white embroidered hats for his disciples, gowns for his khalifa, amulets and salts for supplicants—may all be seen as items in a simple relationship of reciprocal exchange. If, however, as I believe, these ideological statements tell only a very partial truth, then the need is to consider what the sacred exchange effected in the pilgrimage to the 'urs is. At first glance, there is no elaborate sacred text or metonymic acts in the 'urs which may be said to parallel and comment upon those of the hajj.

Yet the 'urs too has its pretexts. Hence, a key feature of Ghamkol Sharif is its sacred peripherality (Turner 1974). The lodge was built outside any established settlement, very gradually, over many years, in what was previously an uncultivated valley. The men and women who return annually to work for the 'urs have participated in this gradual transformation of the lodge. Each year they retrace the footsteps both of the saint and of themselves in prior years as they move beyond the boundaries of their settled communities. Metaphorically, they move back in time by journeying once again to the lodge in order to be renewed. As they work they often recall the early days of the lodge. The women's gossip during the long working hours is in itself a work of making history, reliving the myth of the lodge's establishment.

The same is true for all the pilgrims who visit the lodge annually. The journey to the lodge is a movement back in time in the sense that it repeats an earlier journey. In his final supplication for the sake of the community, the saint recalls his own first arduous journey to the lodge. Indeed, he repeats the story of this legendary journey almost verbatim every year. The assembled crowd wait for this final du'a, the request for God's blessing, the peak moment of this three-day ritual festival. Yet, as in the hajj, the supplication is more than the voice of a single individual: it is the sum of all the silent prayers of the multitude present, even if it is embodied in the trembling tones of the saint. So, too, the sacrificial feast is perceived to be more than the multiplication of individual acts of sacrifice. It is an achievement of a community that has stepped outside the world. As in the hajj, the pilgrimage to Ghamkol Sharif is a fleeting act of world renunciation in which the pilgrims identify with their saint. In a sermon delivered in Rochdale, UK on the day of the hajj, Ahmad Sharif, a well-known *maulvi*, told his congregation: 'While the real test of faith is faith in the world then...if someone wants to renounce this world, it is possible for him to do so in hajj; a pilgrim, as long as he keeps his *ihram* on is faqir of God.' The food of the langar eaten in this extramundane world differs in every respect from the sacrificial halal meat normally consumed.

This may be taken to imply that the annual pilgrimage to Ghamkol Sharif is a text (in the Ricoeurian sense) enacting Eliade's myth of eternal return to a point of original creation (Ricoeur 1981: 197–221; Eliade 1954). It may also be taken to be a reiteration of Turner's (1974) view that pilgrims both to the hajj and to the 'urs experience a sense of communitas in which the boundaries between the individual and the community are obliterated. The 'urs is a cultural performance which can be analysed from different perspectives (on this see Weingrod 1990). Beyond calculus or communitas, I want to stress a further point:

pilgrimage to the 'urs, and especially the voluntary labour vested in preparation for it, is a text which is both personal and performative: each pilgrim re-enacts his or her own text, her or his annual visit and contribution to the growth of the lodge. Each personal text reflects on all the prior personal texts, as a series of reflexive memorials of positive action. In addition, each personal text also allegorises the shared pretext of the saint's first journey to the lodge, itself an allegory of the texts of the Prophet's migration and return to Makkah, for which Ibrahim's test of faith by sacrifice, and Hajra's ordeal in the desert, searching for water for her infant son, are the ultimate pretexts. Hence also, for example, the text of the 'urs in Britain echoes that at Ghamkol Sharif while being uniquely British. These acts of identification imbue the sacred exchange at a saint's lodge with moral meaning in the world. The gifts, amulets and blessings, charged with saintly charisma, which are carried back from the pilgrimage, have to be understood as tokens of moral renewal, energizing this mundane world of the here and now in which pilgrims live their daily lives.

ACKNOWLEDGEMENTS

This chapter is based on research in Pakistan at the lodge of Zindapir during several weeks in 1989 and 1991, and on research in Manchester among returning pilgrims from hajj during 1988–1989. The research was supported by the ESRC, UK, and Leverhulme Trust, and I am grateful to these foundations for their assistance. The sayings quoted here are from a sermon delivered by Sharif Ahmad at the Blue Mosque in Rochdale on the day of the hajj in 1989. The sermon was in Urdu and was translated by his daughter and son, Nyla and Arshad Ahmed. I would like to thank both Arshad and Nyla for their help. I would also like to thank Hajji Bashir Ahmed, who clarified many of the points about sacrifice at a saint's lodge discussed here. An early version of this chapter was given at Nanterre University in Paris in 1991 to a seminar series on Muslim sacrifice organized by Anne-Marie Brisbarre and Altan Gokalp, of the Laboratories d'Ethonologie et de Sociologies Comparative. I would like to thank the participants at the seminar for their comments.

GLOSSARY

alim	religious scholar or official
aqiqa	on the birth of a child
awliya	friends of God
badshah	king
dam	blew a prayer; healing breath
dar ul ulooms	places of learning
du'a	prayer, supplication
faqir	an ascetic
gharib	poor man
ghee	clarified butter
hajj	annual pilgrimage
ihram	the two sheets the hajji wears
izzat	honour
khalifa	vicegerent
Khwaja	lord, gentlemen
langar	the communal distribution of food at a religious lodge or celebration
maulvi	Islamic preacher
mithai	sweets
murid	disciple
qurbani	sacrifice
sadaqa	alms; sacrifices of exorcism or expiation; gifts to the poor
sant	saint
sheikh	saint, spiritual mentor
shirk	polytheism, blasphemy
tabarruk	blessing, thanksgiving
umrah	pilgrimage to Makkah which can be performed any time of the year
'urs	commemoration of the saint's death
wali	friend
zamindars	landowners
zikr	the remembrance of God, the incantation of God's name

NOTES

1. The belief that this professional distance is abused is widespread, fuelled by tales of the excessive sexual appetite of saints (see Lindholm 1990: 33) and periodic scandals. The power of the cultural ideal of saints as world renouncers is evidenced, however, by the fact the women continue to unveil before the saint. In the case of Zindapir, his reputation was quite immaculate.
2. That helping is achieved through transference is suggested by Kakar (1982:91) and Ewing (1984). Ewing (1993) also suggests a similar view on the saint's qualities.

CHAPTER 9

All-Male Sonic Gatherings, Islamic Reform, and Masculinity in Northern Pakistan

MAGNUS MARSDEN

MUSIC, ISLAM, AND MASCULINITY IN NORTHERN PAKISTAN

In this chapter, I explore the complex opportunities afforded by high-intensity performative events for the instantiation of diverse forms of sociality and masculinity in the mountainous Chitral region of Pakistan's North-West Frontier Province. I focus ethnographically on two types of all-male musical gatherings that are regularly attended by Chitrali Muslims: the *istók* and the *mahfil*. The 'permissibility' of these types of entertainment, according to Islamic authoritative teachings, is a source of considerable debate in the region: Many Chitrali 'men of piety,' who are mostly trained in Pakistani madrassahs and are often affiliated with so-called Islamist political parties, deliver mosque addresses during which they pronounce such gatherings 'impermissible' within Islam. Analysis of the role played by these all-male sonic gatherings in the instantiation of locally contested forms of masculinity furnishes unique insights into the much-debated issue of how Muslims handle and respond to pressures to Islamize. More broadly, I aim to contribute to wider anthropological debates concerning the constitution and significance to everyday life of local theories of aesthetics, emotion, and ethical action. [*Pakistan, Islam, emotion, performance, masculinity, music*]

Some of my most enduring memories of fieldwork in Chitral—a mountainous and relatively remote region in Pakistan's North-West Frontier Province that is populated predominantly by ethnically Chitrali Muslims—are of the many outdoor night time musical programmes that I have attended since first visiting the region in 1995. These are referred to in the language spoken by Chitralis, Khowar, as 'istóks.'[1] This term denotes a wide range of 'playful' activities important in the region, including the intense yet unscripted performance of local forms of music and dance as well as children's games and competitive team sports such as Chitrali polo, football, and volleyball. In contrast to other South Asian settings, in which 'play' may involve carefully plotted dramatic performances (e.g., Seizer 2004), the istóks I explore here are a particular type of gathering that involves Chitrali men dancing to music performed by professional musicians.

These istóks, however, are vigorously criticized by Chitral's 'men of piety' (*dasmanán*), who are educated in madrassahs in Pakistan.[2] They often claim during the course of their mosque addresses that such all-male gatherings are a source of un-Islamic immorality. Such dasmanán say that listening to music poses unique moral dangers: it can lead men to forget God, lose their ability to think rationally, and experience strong feelings of love, which generate sexual desires that, in turn, may lead them to commit one of the greatest sins of all—fornication (*zina*).[3] The political power of the istóks' Islamizing detractors has, moreover, grown in recent years. In October 2002, a coalition of Islamist parties (the Muttahida Majlis-e Amal, or MMA) was elected to power in the North-West Frontier Province government.[4] The MMA's representatives took immediate steps to prevent the holding of musical events, for example, arranging protest marches against planned events.

By pointing toward the complexity of interactions between local systems of aesthetics and global forms of religious transformation, istóks and the dasmanán's attacks on them raise important analytical questions concerning recent anthropological work that focuses on the interactions between performance, emotions, and politics as experienced during everyday life. As intense participatory events, Chitrali istóks afford complex opportunities for the instantiation and experience of diversely constituted forms of sociality, and they do so in the face of attacks made by Islamizing mullahs who label them 'impermissible' (*najáiz*). Much recent work focuses on the ways in which, rather than simply communicating 'meaning', particular performance events have broader 'significance' determined by interactive processes involving 'intention, evaluation, response and effectiveness' (Brenneis 1987:237; see also Herzfeld 1985). The shared expectations and work that audiences bring to performance events, rather than any symbolic meaning inherent in the performance, are what invest the events with their wider significance (e.g., Racy 2003).

Music's fundamentally 'nondiscursive' nature, moreover, has led anthropologists to consider the aesthetic and emotional dimensions of the ways in which people's 'acceptance of and pleasure in particular musical events hinge on their appropriate form and effective or pleasing ways of manipulating it' (Brenneis 1987:238). A wide range of in-depth ethnographic accounts of both sonic and more verbalized forms of performances document the ways in which local systems of 'social aesthetics' are diversely constituted and involve the deployment of 'different orientating values' for the evaluation of 'different kinds of performances' (Brenneis 1987:238). Locally situated social aesthetics that 'infuse' intellectual and sensory criteria for beauty with notions of personhood and emotion (Brenneis 1987:237) may focus on a particular 'focal principle,' such as manhood (Herzfeld 1985), constitute public or intimate 'discrepant discourses' (Abu Lughod 2000), or be embedded within an overarching discourse (Brenneis 1987).

The power of sound and music to invoke 'sensual and bodily registers' (Hansen 2006:200), destabilize 'gendered and sexual conventions' (Stokes 1997), and 'trigger cultural memories' that produce and reproduce power (Stoller 1994:636) is, indeed, something that has been widely noted by anthropologists.[5] Music's power to 'organise collective memories' (Stokes 1994:7) and facilitate the remembering of feelings and habits through sounds, Regula Qureshi argues, invests 'contests over "rules to feel music by"' (2000:810) with their political significance. It would appear relatively straightforward, thus, to characterize all-male sonic gatherings in Chitral, such as istóks, as contested events in which local people openly 'resist' the teachings of the region's politically powerful dasmanán. Yet the musical gatherings I explore in this study, far from being the preserve of a well-defined group of men uninterested in public forms of religious life, are organized and attended by a wide range of Chitrali men, and moreover, it is not surprising to encounter committed supporters of Islamist parties at such musical programmes (Marsden 2005:ch. 5).[6]

More recently, studies have extended the theoretical implications of this body of work by suggesting that the appreciation of sound and music is not simply an 'aesthetic gloss' that is applied to 'discursive content' but, rather, is itself a 'necessary condition' for 'ethical action' (Hirschkind 2006:13). Charles Hirschkind has challenged what he refers to as an Enlightenment-derived 'modernist narrative' that understands practices of audition as leading to the self's 'engulfment' in sound and the concurrent threats that this poses to the 'autonomy of the enlightened liberal subject' (2006:13–14). Hirschkind's ethnography focuses on the practice among men in Cairo of listening to cassette recordings of Islamic sermons. Hirschkind's informants bring 'intentions, goals and ethical attitudes' to audition (2006:35), and in doing so, they play an active role in shaping a 'common substrate of embodied dispositions' on which the Islamic tradition is articulated (2006:88).[7]

Alternatively, therefore, istóks could be considered gatherings central to the instantiation of forms of sensory, aesthetic, or ethical dispositions that are very different from the conceptions of Islamic piety currently being advanced by Chitral's dasmanán. This type of model addresses the ways in which local theories of social aesthetics are diversely constituted and how they may also afford possibilities for persons to move between contrasting embodied dispositions during the course of their daily lives. Yet what I have also recognized during the istóks that I have attended in Chitral is that they are often experienced by participants in ways that point toward complex processes of interaction between contrasting modes of emotional experience and aesthetic judgement, rather than the cultivation of these modes in response to one another. A good musical gathering is described by many of its participants, for example, using the same religious language that the dasmanán deploy in their sermons to attack such events: 'Impermissibly good fun' is how many men I know describe a good evening's musical entertainment.[8] The 'fun' of istóks, thus, is often framed and invested with political and affective significance by participants in a way that creatively builds on the theories of emotion advanced by their Islamist detractors.[9]

In this article, I seek to document the multivalent ways in which Chitrali Muslims experience and enjoy different forms of musical events in relation to a complex and internally dynamic theory of social aesthetics that considers contrasting sounds as appropriate to particular types of performative arenas. Simultaneously, I theorize the broader significance of the different forms of sociality that are instantiated during such events by exploring the expectations that people bring to musical gatherings and by documenting the ways these expectations are shaped by broader processes of political contestation and social transformation important in the region today. In short, musical gatherings are central to the instantiation of diverse yet interconnected types of sociality that give rise to meaningful forms of action and offer vivid insights into the nexus between social aesthetics, emotion, and politics in the region today.

The musical gatherings explored below are almost exclusively male; that is why I explore their significance in relation to the instantiation of masculinity. Much recent anthropological work, within and beyond Muslim-majority states and Muslim communities elsewhere, emphasizes the ways in which masculinity is always 'contingent' and 'dissonant'

(Peletz 1996:137) and constantly refigured by 'modernizing' transformations (e.g., Ghoussoub 2000; Gilsenan 1996:282), political oppression (Peteet 2000), and violent conflict (Mookherjee 2004) as well as in more instrumental ways by state institutions, notably, the military (Altinay 2006).[10] These works have challenged older anthropological accounts that often treated manhood in rural Muslim societies as rigid, inflexible, and defined within unchanging codes of honour and systems of 'patriarchy' (Grima 1991:81; Lindholm 1982).[11] There is also a growing appreciation of the ways in which masculinity and the forms of emotionality with which it is locally associated offer insights into the emergence of new political styles, identities, and boundaries. Movements of Hindu religious reform in India, for example, urge men to refrain from dimensions of life that are overly sensual, calling on them, instead, to retain the vitality of their manhood for more morally virtuous forms of political action (e.g., Banerjee 2006; Hansen 1999).[12] Fewer studies, however, have attempted to understand the ways in which Islamizers and their adherents have sought to reform local forms and conceptions of masculinity as well as the types of social arenas in which these are enacted and embodied. This lacuna in the literature stands in contrast to an expanding body of work on the active role played by women in the inculcation of 'embodied' forms of Islamic ethical sensibility and piety (e.g., Brenner 1996; Deeb 2006; Mahmood 2005).

My aim, in this chapter, therefore, is not simply to document the vibrancy of a multiplicity of masculinities in Chitral to challenge lingering non-Muslim stereotypes of the inherent 'patriarchy' of Muslim societies. I ask, rather, how apparently diverse types of Chitrali masculinity are dynamically connected to one another and interact with broader processes of social, political, and religious transformation. Many accounts typify apparently irreconcilable forms of masculinity as belonging either to 'dominant' or 'subordinate' forms: 'Bravery' and 'assertiveness' are depicted as being 'dominant' or publicly acceptable forms of masculinity (Abu-Lughod 2000; Bourdieu 1977:11; Peteet 2000), whereas homosexuality is delineated as 'subordinate' (Connell 1990). The expression of apparently subordinate forms of masculinity is often depicted as taking place within intimate discourses that are confined to 'alternative' sites divorced from normative forms of 'public' life (Abu-Lughod 2000), such as poetry. This approach reproduces official gendered transcripts, conceals the wider significance of apparently 'illicit' gendered relationships (e.g., Osella and Osella 2006), and renders invisible understandings of manhood that are framed in terms of dynamic and multivalent aesthetic sensibilities.

At first glance, much of what my Chitrali friends say about their understanding of 'manliness' (*mosigári*) appears to fit non-Muslim stereotypes that emphasize the inherent patriarchy of Islamic manhood (e.g., Harris 2005). Almost all daily life in Chitral is characterized by strict forms of sexual segregation. Women, for example, are rarely, if ever, seen in the bazaar. Unlike other places in the North-West Frontier Province, moreover, Chitral does not have a tradition of all-women gatherings of song and dance (Grima 1992). Khowar also has a well-developed vocabulary related to virility and male strength that is frequently deployed during the course of daily life. Mothers call their sons their 'powerful ones', men considered socially weak are said to be 'those who let it in', and the term for a man who commits sodomy is used as a violent insult to disgrace village 'enemies' (*dusmanán*). Male assertiveness is also a feature of displays of manly bravado as enacted by Chitrali men and boys. When asked if they are scared that the village dasmanán will discover that they drink alcohol, men often proudly respond, 'Nobody can catch my penis'. Such displays of male assertiveness in the face of authority are frequently the source of triumphant congratulation by Chitrali men and women. Men who have proven their bravery in dramatic ways are lauded by their fellow villagers for being *serkóti*s, men powerful enough even to 'castrate lions'. Life in the home (*dur*) is also injected with the types of behaviour that, according to Charles Lindholm (1982), inculcate young boys with an early understanding of their social 'superiority'. Young Chitrali boys frequently have their penises touched and kissed by their fathers and they are also encouraged to strut, dance, and laugh before guests in their homes. Girl children, in contrast, rarely dance and are often told by their elder sisters that even laughing makes them appear immoral (*sum*).

By exploring the production of masculinities in diverse types of all-male sonic gatherings, however, I have come to recognize that displays of masculine bravado are not hegemonic to mosigári in Chitral; categorizing the multiple expressions of masculinity that I have encountered in Chitral as either 'dominant' or 'subordinate' in relation to a shared moral code overlooks the ways in which Chitrali social aesthetics value men who demonstrate that they are capable of mastering a range of diverse and apparently irreconcilable yet interlocking masculine registers. In such high-intensity performative events as istóks, forms of masculinity are produced that challenge from different angles the conceptions of manhood advanced by the region's Islamizing dasmanán, and others are actively advanced by a range of authoritative opinion makers in the region, including self-defined local cultural elites, the police, and even the military, who seek to determine the parameters of acceptability.

DANCING, BEARDS, AND THE TALIBAN

Much scholarly and popular writing on Pakistan's North-West Frontier Province focuses on the importance to everyday social life of local conceptions of manhood. Historians, in particular, have debated the extent to which the British colonial regime actively refigured pre-colonial codes of masculinity. Ashish Nandy claimed that, in pre-colonial Indian societies, gender identities were fluid and ideas about bisexuality and androgyny widespread. The British, he argued, juxtaposed the hypermasculinity that was central to the ways they defined themselves in opposition to the femininity of the colonized, thereby expanding the role for martial masculinities within Indian society (Nandy 1983).[13] In her exploration of masculine martial styles in eighteenth century North India, Rosalind O'Hanlon challenges Nandy's formulation: The relationship between colonialism and masculine identities in Indian society, she argues, was more complex—a wider culture of 'imperial masculinity' was an essential feature of pre-colonial life in North India, thereby problematizing the simple categorization of hypermasculinities as colonial 'inventions' (1997:16).[14]

Anthropological perspectives have also played a major role in shaping the nature of these debates between historians. Mukulika Banerjee documents the ways in which, during the first half of the twentieth century, the North-West Frontier Province became the site for 'vigorous contestations' between the 'state and people' over conceptions of male sexuality (2000:208). British colonial officers celebrated Pukhtuns for their manliness, something they contrasted to the 'effeminate' dispositions of Indian Hindus. Yet they saw another, distinctly more dangerous, side to Pukhtun virility, too. Anxieties about interracial homosexual relations between Pukhtuns and British colonial officials form a critical dimension of much colonial writing on Pukhtun society, and the North-West Frontier Province was widely seen by the British as a 'space of irresistible temptation and vice' (Banerjee 2000:39).

Chitral was forcibly incorporated into British India in 1895 as a semi-autonomous kingdom in the Hindu Kush, which it remained until 1969, when it was fully integrated within the Pakistani state. Olaf Caroe famously described Pukhtuns as a people who looked the British 'in the face', making them feel as if they had 'come home' (1996:1) after their interactions with 'effeminate Indians'. Chitralis were depicted in more ambiguous ways by British scholar–soldiers, who saw them and neighbouring peoples in Pakistan's modern-day Northern Areas as white, and therefore, racially similar to themselves (Sökefeld 2006). At the same time, however, Chitralis were said to be 'soft' and feminine in ways the Pukhtuns were not: 'All [Chitralis] have pleasant and ingratiating manners, an engaging light heartedness, free from all trace of boisterous behaviour, a great fondness for music, dancing and singing, a passion for simple minded ostentation, and an instinctive yearning for softness and luxury, which is the mainspring of their intense cupidity and avarice' (Robertson 1899:10).

British writers did recognize that Chitralis were capable of 'manly' forms of violence and 'martial spirit', yet even this ability was represented as proof of Chitralis' oriental capacity for feminine duplicity. According to a 1928 account,

> That there is a good fighting strain in Chitral is proven by the fact that they have been successful when led by competent and brave leaders in repulsing invading herds of Pathans and other tribes along their borders, and thus preserved, in bygone days, the integrity of their country.... They are splendid mountain men, hardy, frugal in their mode of living...and adept at the usage of guerrilla warfare. [Baig 2005:64]

Much scholarly debate today concerns the ways in which gendered stereotypes such as these reflect the role played by 'colonial knowledge' in the establishment of colonial governmentality in India at the turn of the twentieth century. It appears clear, however, that colonial scholar–soldiers sought to depict Chitralis as existing in a complex intermediary position between martial Pukhtun manhood and Indian effeminacy and that this led to an underlying confusion in attempts to document the true cultural essence of the Chitrali people. What is more striking is the resemblance between the ways in which colonial scholar–soldiers categorized their subjects as inhabiting either 'manly', 'effeminate', or intermediate forms of gender identity and more recent attempts by anthropologists to analyze different expressions of manhood in particular social settings as either 'dominant' or 'subordinate.'

Social differences between Chitral and other regions of the North-West Frontier Province are not, however, merely the product of the colonial imagination (cf. Titus 1998). Much anthropological work on so-called segmentary lineage systems is the product of research in the 'tribal' and largely Pukhtun-populated borderlands of northern Pakistan. Chitral, however, was a semi-autonomous princely state within British India and home to a Mughal–Timurid culture of statecraft that was clearly evident in the polite styles of Persianized speech that characterized much social interaction within the region (Parkes 2001b). For British scholar–soldiers, Chitral society was divided into four caste-like categories of people: the ruling family from which the *mehtar*, the ruler of Chitral until the region's full constitutional incorporation into the Pakistani state in 1969, was descended; a lordly class of nobles (*adamzada*, lit. true humans); peasant farmers (the *yuft* or *rayat*); and serfs (*cirmúz*).[15] The British oversimplified the hierarchical form of Chitral society and concealed the fluidity of relationships between the region's hierarchically nested status groups (Parkes 2001a:21–27; Sökefeld 2006). Yet a long-standing distinction between the landowning 'aristocracy' and 'commoner' Chitralis is an important dimension of social stratification in the region and continues to be a contested feature of life there today. Many of Chitral's most powerful 'secular' politicians claim descent from the region's one-time princely family.

What forms do courtly arenas once central to the expression of locally embedded forms of gendered sociality take in the region today? Many studies have argued that 'premodern' cultural forms have been 'sanitized' and rendered apolitical artifacts by the hegemonic designs of the Indian subcontinent's postcolonial 'national cultures' (Ali 2004:3; Reed 2002:250). Other works point to more complex processes in which 'feudal' and 'courtesan' culture and music have become recontextualized (Qureshi 2000:807). I seek to show below that both of these sets of processes are visible in Chitral today. At the same time, however, Chitralis bring many different types of aesthetic and emotional work to one time courtly musical gatherings. Rather than such events being sanitized by the Pakistani state or the North-West Frontier Province's Islamizers, the diversity of expectations brought to them means they hold creative possibilities for the production of multiple forms of political significance.

Historians have invested considerable attention in the study of gendered identities in courtly societies. Building on Norbert Elias 1983, many have argued that, within courtly settings, 'outward bearings and manners' were not simply superficial and external displays of etiquette but central to the livelihoods and social relationships of courtiers (Ali 2004:8). O'Hanlon suggests that in some North Indian political entities, a mastery of 'Persian courtly skills' was blended together with the 'warrior traditions of the central Asian steppe' (1997:6) in a way that forged complex masculine codes. These courtly masculine codes, therefore, did not merely exist in opposition to perceptions of female weakness but were part of an expanding Mughal world (e.g., Gommans 2002; Richards 1996) within which Persian courtly skills were imagined in opposition to more rustic forms of masculine warriorship.

O'Hanlon describes the 'highest inner qualities' expected of courtly men in the North Indian state of Farrukhabad in the seventeenth century as 'purposeful action and heroic striving for the highest ideals, of resolute personal courage tempered by discretion and self-control, of personal honour expressed and safeguarded through dignified personal submission to the legitimate authority of the emperor, who was himself presented as the "perfect man"' (1997:6).

Military service and sporting performance were particularly important for both military training and character building. Young aspirants could catch the emperor's eye and consolidate loyalties and friendships. Sporting contests, especially on the region's polo grounds, were also an important feature of Chitrali court life (see Kennion 1910; Parkes 1996). As elsewhere (e.g., McDevitt 2005), British colonial officials deployed such activities to create a type of 'cultural consensus' in which 'shared values and practices'—such as the British officers' love of polo—could read as a 'British affirmation' of local virtues of manliness (Sökefeld 2006:952). The British, then, cultivated 'courtly' accomplishments and skills like hunting and polo to create commonalities and establish hierarchies with local people (Sinha 1995).

Chitralis remain famous across Pakistan today for their love of music, dance, polo, and hunting—activities that, O'Hanlon (1997:12) argues, provide 'multiplex arenas' for the display of manly inner qualities. In ways strikingly similar to the pre-colonial North Indian courtiers described by O'Hanlon, many Chitralis contrast the nature of life in their 'peaceful' (*sukoon*) and 'sophisticated' society with the 'crude', 'uncultivated', and 'inferior' (*vesirú*) behaviour of neighbouring Pukhtun communities. Such modes of comparison partly derive from colonial validations of Chitrali habits and pastimes. Yet Chitralis are also aware of the historical differences that distinguish them from their Pukhtuns neighbours and often claim that 'wild' (*jangali*) and 'tribal' Pukhtuns are prone to violent revenge feuds (*adal-badal*), unlike Chitralis, who are 'lovers of peace' (*aman pasand*).[16]

There is, however, no 'Chitrali masculinity' embedded within a monolithic 'Chitrali culture'. Neither is there any simple two-way split between forms of Chitrali masculinities that conform to an 'ideal', 'dominant', or hegemonic form of Chitrali manhood and those that are 'subordinate' or 'subversive' in any straightforwardly instrumental sense. Rather, Chitralis work hard to ensure that different, although interactive, types of all-male musical gatherings exist as critical sites within which diverse forms of masculinities invested with meaning in local settings are produced and enacted. Yet these gatherings are fashioned in the context of the growing power of Islamist movements in the North-West Frontier Province, many of which actively seek to 'purify' the practices and comportment of the region's Muslims. This complex process is intimately linked to the ways in which Pakistan's successive military and authoritarian governments have sought to extend (Nasr 2002) and legitimate (Jalal 1995) state authority by deploying multiple forms of Islamic discourses and legislation (Verkaaik 2004), which has also led to the suppression, problematization, or reconfiguration of other oppositional or minority ways of 'being Muslim' (cf. Qureshi 2000:811). These transformations, however, exist alongside the ongoing influence of Chitral's one-time privileged class of noble families, who continue to exert considerable forms of political influence and authority in the region.

THE POLITE GATHERING

During my stays both in Rowshan, a large Chitrali village with a population of about 8,000 Khowar-speaking Ismai'li and Sunni Muslims, and in Markaz, the region's district headquarters, which is home to about 20,000 townspeople, including significant numbers of Dari and Pashto-speaking Afghan 'refugees', I have often seen young Chitrali men crying into handkerchiefs sewn by their 'beloved' girlfriends (*dostán*). The ability to express and convey intimate sentiments of melancholy, emotional failure, and the pain of defeat in romantic encounters to one's fellow villagers is a critical if contested dimension of Chitrali manhood. Such affective expressions are widely cultivated through the savouring of Chitrali *ghazal* music performed in programmes known as 'mahfils', or 'polite gatherings'. Many modern Khowar-language songs are deeply influenced by Persian poetic and linguistic forms, one of the key dimensions of which is ghazal poetry, a genre that seeks to convey the experience of passionate love (*'ishq*), devoted both to humans and to God.[17]

In Chitral, unlike many other Muslim societies in which 'evening gatherings of intimates for music, conversation and food' (Shannon 2003:75) have diminished because of the expansion of mass-mediated music, television, and film, many men continue to attend and organize evening mahfils of music and dance. In contrast to many studies that focus on the role played by modern musical genres in the inculcation of gendered subjectivities (e.g., Osella and Osella 2006), my aim here is to document the ongoing vitality of a type of all-male social event that would be easy to assume had been 'shut down' by sometimes colliding and other times diverging Islamizing and modernizing processes.

The refined display of music and dance characteristic of such gatherings is one way that 'being Chitrali' is enacted in conscious opposition to ethnic stereotypes held by many of the region's people about 'unruly' and excessively 'violent' Pukhtun males. Ethnic stereotypes, in which 'robust' rural Pukhtuns are juxtaposed, for example, to unmanly *muhajir* city boys, are of importance to Pakistan's political culture. Oskar Verkaaik (2004:125–127) recently explored the ways in which young muhajir men in Hyderabad build competitive forms of masculinity to challenge these stereotypes, at the same time mobilizing their 'community' politically.[18] Chitralis who attend mahfils, however, do not seek to recuperate the hypermasculinity of their Pukhtun neighbours but self-consciously define themselves as 'polite' (*sarîf*) and 'soft' (*narum*) in contrast to unruly Pukhtuns. Such local cultural tropes are of considerable political significance because the leadership of Pakistan's Islamist parties is to a large degree dominated by ethnic Pukhtuns (Nasr 2005), and most of Chitral's Islamist leaders have also studied in the largely Pukhtun city of Peshawar. Some of them, moreover, also present themselves to Chitrali Muslims as the only people capable of bringing an end to the influence of princely authority and political influence in the region. The display of distinctly Chitrali forms of soft cultural refinement, self-consciously enacted in contrast to the behaviour of 'hard' Pukhtuns, then, is one way in which the moral authority of the region's Islamizing dasmanán is contested.[19]

I spent a great deal of my time in the field attending mahfils at which local musicians, poets, and comedians performed. They were, without exception, characterized by their tea party-like politeness.[20] Men gathered in a friend's house in the early evening for a meal of roast meats and rice.[21] Depending on the company, sometimes before they ate or listened to the musicians perform, some shared a bottle of home-brewed mulberry spirit. On other occasions, they offered prayers before the entertainment began.

At all gatherings I attended, however, the guests exercised particular care to ensure that men opposed to drinking did not witness the consumption of alcohol, and before the music began, it was also usual for a man to announce that it was being played in an 'environment free from the curse of intoxication'.

The expert musicians who performed at these musical programmes were amateurs: They did not accept payment for their music but, rather, they repeatedly told me, performed because of interest (*sauq, dilcáspi*) and a love of music. Some of these musicians, and more often the evening's hosts (*mezban*), were from quasi-aristocratic lordly families; others were poorer men who owned small shops and were from relatively low-status backgrounds. Yet they were all local celebrities in the region. They played the local four-stringed Chitrali sitar, the *jircæn* (an empty petrol can used as a drum), a large *daf* (tambourine), and twin kettledrums, or *damáma*.[22] The instrumentalists accompanied the group's lead singer, who recited largely modern Khowar love songs written by local poets. Rebecca Bryant notes that Turkish *saz* playing requires a unique masculine strength and confers on the player the status of 'representative of Turkish tradition' (2005:233). The Chitrali sitar player, in contrast, is said to require especially 'delicate' (*názuk*) and 'thin' (*bariki*) fingers, and the male voice is widely considered to be most beautiful when it is so high-pitched that it resembles that of a girl.

As in the case in other Muslim-majority settings, many Chitralis consider the masculinity of Chitrali male amateur musicians in distinctly ambivalent ways (Stokes 1992). The mahfil performers (*fankarán*) are often said to be 'lovers of form' (*husun parast*). They travel around in open jeeps accompanied by 'attractive' (*cust*) young men, which is widely said to be a 'bad' (*sum*) way of behaving in public. The jealousies that inevitably emerge within groups of performers are also widely imputed to be the ignoble cause of their eventual breakups. Such dynamics, which Chitralis say point to musicians' susceptibility to beauty and jealousy, are not secretly enacted in a hidden realm. Musicians, rather, publicly flaunt their power to attract handsome folk into their entourage, even if it courts criticism from other Chitrali folk.

As I have noted above, ghazals are the musical pieces most often performed at mahfils. Love songs recently composed by Chitrali poets draw on old traditions of Persianate Sufi poetry. They describe the pain of the heart (*hardío dard*) caused by separation from a lover, compare a man's broken heart to the shards of glass from a smashed wine bottle, and describe love as a force that makes the 'intellect astonished but the heart compelled.'[23] These love songs are deeply influenced by Persian poetic forms. Chitrali musicians speak of this influence in terms of the sweet and plaintive form of the ghazal songs they compose and perform. The songs are reflections on the spiritual necessity of losing control of the intellect, and of the embodied state of cool rationality the intellect generates, when one experiences heightened emotional states induced through both worldly and divine forms of love.[24] Many musicians and poets, indeed, told me that both their work and their enjoyment of the music were deeply influenced by real-life experience of cross-gender love relationships.

After attending a mahfil, I would sometimes stay with my friends in the rooms they rented in Markaz bazaar for the night. On such occasions they would show me photographs of the girlfriends (*dostán*) of their youth. Sometimes they would pull from boxes that they carried the handkerchiefs that their girlfriends had lovingly embroidered and given to them as gifts. They sighed about the women they had been unable to marry because of parental opposition and commented that, although marriage and love are 'destined' and in God's hands, separation from one's beloved, nevertheless, causes acute forms of pain and distress. During mahfils, some older men remembered and openly reflected on their past experiences of falling in love with women, and younger participants framed their current experience of romantic love by composing and listening to ghazal music.

Men's imaginative horizons in mahfils are not defined solely in terms of longing for unobtainable women. Elegies (*marsiya*) are also written in memory of men who have recently 'left this world': The sounds of the sitar played with ghazals that articulate feelings of abandonment and separation are considered appropriate for the expression of sadness and mourning.[25] One marsiya I heard was composed in honour of a prominent Chitrali lawyer who had suffered a fatal heart attack while playing polo. Other songs were dedicated to friends who had left Chitral to work as labourers in the Gulf States: Audiotapes of the songs are sent to those in the Gulf, who play them as proof of the 'faithfulness' of friends back home. Affective dispositions that nurture cross-sexual and male–male friendships are cultivated at mahfils through a combination of the events' sonic and lyrical dimensions.[26]

Much can go wrong at such gatherings, however, and when it does, the danger of seeing mahfils as simply reflecting the sanitizing designs of their patrons becomes apparent. One of Chitral's long-term musical supporters is a generous businessman who is a known supporter of an important Pakistani Islamist party. One evening, he walked into a room in which some musicians and their friends were enjoying a pre-performance glass of highly potent mulberry spirit. The lawyer had already been held responsible for ruining several mahfils: He had talked too loudly, instructed the musicians to perform at the wrong tempo, and irritated those gathered by insisting that all the men perform congregational prayers before the music began. On this occasion, he once again demonstrated his 'donkeylike' capacity for social sensitivity by rudely barging into a secret gathering. Demonstrating one's ability to be a 'man fit for the mahfil' is complex. The mahfilgoer must be able to understand and express the range of painful emotions that are shaped by firsthand experiences of passionate love and melancholic longing and loss and to connect these sentiments to measured displays of cultural connoisseurship. Failing to meet these standards of social and affective competency can mean being excluded from the next gathering or even the group itself.

Mahfils, thus, emphasize a style of Chitrali male subjectivity that focuses on the cultivation of cultural connoisseurship and taste as well as the nurturing of emotional sensitivity. This emphasis is conveyed by the organized quality of the evening's proceedings, the attentiveness of the audience, and a soundscape that is dominated by a solo voice and a single sitar. Displays of manly assertiveness are toned down, for they disturb the mahfil's delicate balance. Musical groups and their entourages, moreover, have sought to sanitize mahfils and render them 'respectable' in the eyes of both Chitral's Islamizing dasmanán and the well-paid NGO and government officials who are increasingly their most prominent patrons. In what follows, I explore a very different type of Chitrali musical gathering, in which different yet connected styles of masculinity are instantiated in a way that also illuminates contrasting modes of interaction between performers, audiences, Islamizers, and local cultural elites.

Fighting, Courting, and 'Impermissible Fun': The Rowdy Play

The istók, or play, is an event in which a variety of Chitrali men—including many known aficionados of mahfil music—gather to enjoy very different types of music, dance, and fun that characterize the mahfil.[27] It starts early in the morning, lasts late into the night, and if considered a success, may go on for as many as three days. It is far from a gathering of intimates, and most men who attend such a 'rowdy play' (*vesirú istók*) do so out of choice and without an invitation. The istók is held outdoors (*béri*)—usually in somebody's orchard or garden, the local polo ground, or a well-cared-for garden outside a government rest house. The outdoor setting is critical to the form taken by the night's proceedings. In the mahfil, displays of politeness play a significant role in shaping the interpersonal interactions within a small gathering of intimates. These concerns recede in the outdoor world (*berió dunyá*) of the istók, where the 'common pursuit of masculinity' finds freer play (O'Hanlon 1997:16). I now track a diverse range of masculine styles that are both instantiated and invested with wider significance during the course of the play. Plays, like mahfils, bear the imprint of Islamization. Whereas mahfils have been partially sanitized by their organizers in an attempt to render them sufficiently respectable for the more religious minded of the new Chitrali elites who patronize them, those who attend istóks, actively seek to distance the events from Islamic conceptions of piety and personhood, and this intent also bleeds into the types of masculinity and enjoyment experienced during such events.

THE QAZI OF THE PLAY

In almost all Chitrali villages (*deh*), some dasmanán frequently deliver *fatwas* declaring plays un-Islamic: The dictates of such dasmanán are often ignored, however. In one village, known by many Chitralis as deeply influenced by the Islamizing activities of boys studying in down-country madrassahs, a respectable man descended from a one-time lordly family that now lives in Markaz, decided to arrange a play to celebrate his son's marriage. The village dasmanán opposed his decision, and villagers feared that 'bearded men' (i.e., madrassah students and active supporters of Islamist political parties) would attack them with sticks in the night. The istók went ahead, however, and was attended by thousands of villagers, many of whom, my friends informed me, were drunk and all of whom described the evening as 'impermissibly amazing fun' (*najáiz zabardást mazadár*).

In the early afternoon on the day of an istók, drums start beating a rhythm, known as 'ponwár,' once played on the eve before the mehtar was to set off on horseback through his realm. This rhythm triggers cultural memories of the old courtly styles of the Chitrali state (Qureshi 2000: 811; Stokes 1994:7; Stoller 1994: 636) and provokes debates concerning the relevance of the region's courtly heritage for daily life today.[28] Many elderly villagers from relatively high-status family backgrounds remember the 'era of the mehtar' (*mehtáro zamaná*) as a time of order: 'People knew their place,' I was often told, 'unlike today when everyone has their own choice, nobody has affection, and fights are the norm.' In contrast, young and educated men, often descended from lower-status families, say the 'old times' (*qadímo zamaná*) were a period of exceptional 'cruelty' (*zulm*), when no man's wife or daughter was safe from the sexual desires of Chitral's princes, who are widely reputed to have taken into their harems any attractive woman on whom they set their eyes.

Chitral's courtly past is associated by some Chitrali Muslims with immoral, un-Islamic, and secular forms of pleasure. This is one reason why, as elsewhere in Muslim-influenced regions of the Indian subcontinent, music has an 'ambivalent assignation' as a sign of immoral forms of 'emotional excess' (Qureshi 2000:825). Some Chitralis who hold such views about the region's past support Islamist political parties. The connections, however, between music, Chitral's courtly heritage, and Islamism involve more complex social and aesthetic dynamics than represented by a simple division between Muslims who continue to value forms derived from lordly high culture and others who denounce such practices as un-Islamic and turn, instead, to piety-focused forms of Islamic ethical subjectivities. The types of masculinity that are instantiated at istóks simultaneously engage with the Islamizing injunctions of Chitral's dasmanán and the claims to sophisticated cultural authority made by the region's self-defined elite, its one-time 'lords'.

The most prominent man at the play is the *istóko qazi*, or 'judge of the play'. This man's behaviour demonstrates that plays are often framed as events in which normative religious values should be actively forgotten to ensure the quality and uniqueness of the night's entertainment. The Arabic term *qazi* refers in Khowar, as elsewhere in the Muslim world, to a senior dasman who possesses sufficient Qur'anic learning to issue religious legal verdicts based on shariah law. The play's qazi, however, must encourage playgoers to clap their hands, hoot, and dance: He is held responsible if the play is boring and cold (*usak*) or, alternatively, too 'rowdy' (*vesirú*) and out of control. Usually a man in his mid-twenties, he marches around the gathering brandishing a stick that he deploys to cajole playgoers into clapping their hands or to encourage them to take to the dance floor. The use of the term *qazi* to describe the man whose task it is to organize the dancing is one way in which the authority of the region's pious ones is treated in a distinctly playful way by istók-goers.

The atmosphere of 'happiness' (*xosaní*) and 'pleasure' (*mazáh*) that playgoers work hard to create is very different from the melancholy of the mahfil. In contrast to the solo sitar player and single vocalist featured at the mahfil, the professional musicians that perform at plays vigorously beat two types of drums, the *dol* and damáma, whose rhythms accompany the high-pitched sound of a double-reed instrument, the *surnai*, played by two or sometimes more experts. The sound of surnai music joyfully proclaims wedding festivities and other types of exhilarating events, such as sporting tournaments and dances arranged to mark the victory of a village polo team. Unlike the more contained sounds of the mahfil, the sound of the music performed at plays is both non-concealable and inescapable: It is audible in the night air for miles. This is one of the reasons why such music was central to the ways in which the mehtar marked his authority across the region's disparate mountain realms. It is also why Chitral's Islamizing dasmanán conceptualize plays as having the capacity to transform Chitral from an 'abode of Islam' to an 'abode of unbelief' in a way that indoor mahfils do not.

The qazi does more than actively encourage playgoers to forget any lingering preoccupations they may have with the enactment of Islamic piety. He tells men with 'serious' faces to 'lighten up' in the interest of contributing to the collective enjoyment of those gathered. At one play I attended, a drummer (*dolci*) stood up during the evening's proceedings and shouted, 'Neither are you going to Raiwind [the headquarters of the Islamic movement of purification, the Tabligh-i Jama'at] nor are you going on Hajj, so start clapping and enjoying yourselves or else I'm packing my drums and going home.'[29] Plays, thus, are not merely performed in response to old and important debates between Islamic jurists, within and beyond the region, concerning the permissibility of music. Rather, playgoers also conceptualize the significance of these events in relation to the activities of powerful movements of Islamic reform that are an important dimension of Muslim self-understanding in Chitral today. It is also critical to recognize that musicians, like the one just quoted, do not speak to an audience that is homogenously opposed to piety-minded forms of Islam. Many of the playgoers, rather, have intermittently also attended preaching tours organized by committed Tabligh-i Jama'at members in the region.

The message delivered by this musician, the qazi, and other people concerned with ensuring the success of the night's entertainment is this: submit to the shared fun of the play and leave behind any preoccupations you may have with Islamic piety and self-discipline. Istóks, therefore, are public spaces 'framed' in relation to local understandings of sensuality and distanced from conceptions of Islamic piety (Werbner 2002:191). This is one way the istók is different from the mahfil, and this framing points toward the ways in which different forms of sociality, ethical action, and emotional experience adhere to particular types of performance events, rather than forming underlying embodied substrates that permeate all domains of Chitrali Muslim life.

The istók also takes place under the surveillance of the Chitral police. Chitral's police force is now under pressure by the region's MMA legislators to crack down on un-Islamic goings-on in the region. Playgoers attend night time musical programmes in defiance of the edicts of the region's dasmanán, their village adherents, and the local face of the Pakistani state (Navaro-Yashin 2002), whose task it is to implement the MMA's Islamizing legislation. The Chitral police know that many playgoers are in possession of alcohol and hashish, and they are charged with strictly enforcing laws concerning 'un-Islamic' activities, especially the consumption of alcohol. The police are, of course, never a 'monolithic force instrumentally responsive to central command, but always firmly situated within particular social contexts' (Chandavarkar 1998:15). Different Chitrali police officers do, indeed, pursue contrasting policies regarding plays. Farooq, for example, is a high-ranking Chitrali policeman and known music lover who often tells me that he instructs his officers not to interfere with plays. They are, he says, a part of the region's culture that take place only at times of happiness. Other policemen, however, seek to earn reputations for being inflexible men of moral principle (*usul*)—they walk into plays and arrest drinkers on the spot. As a result, playgoers must collectively devise complex strategies to prevent the police from making the play go 'sour'. For example, on their way to plays, they make long and arduous treks along concealed mountain paths and avoid main village roads. Having to do so, however, does not deter Chitrali village men and boys from attending plays. Rather, such subterfuge plays a significant role in shaping the types of expectations that playgoers bring to istóks and adds another layer to the expectation that istóks form a zone within the impermissible.

ROWDINESS CELEBRATED

Istóks, thus, at one level, are a type of gathering that is contested on religious grounds but simultaneously seen as necessary for the instantiation of collective forms of happiness that are critical for distinctively Chitrali forms of communality. Such plays, however, are complex zones in which many if not all playgoers subvert and challenge a range of newer and older types of authority, including conceptions of sophisticated Chitrali sociality held by the region's one-time gentry elite.

Individual men are not invited to plays: Audiences are made up of diverse groups of men from the villages surrounding the home at which the play is to be held. These groups are dominated by Chitral's *naujuwánan,* young men between the ages of 16 and 35. Usually within these groups, however, are at least one or two older men who are known to enjoy plays and who are accomplished dancers (*phonák*). If the play is to be held in a distant village, men must pool funds to book a jeep for the evening. A good play, at which talented musicians perform and that is organized by a Chitrali 'man of respect' (*izzatmán mos*) with a reputation for hosting 'hot' (*garam*) night time musical performances, will draw hundreds of men, many of whom arrive in jeeps from distant villages.

Jeeps are not incidental to the tone of the play; they have wider implications for the types of masculinity enacted at these events. Most men arrive in a shared 'taxi jeep' driven by a neighbour or fellow villager who owns the vehicle or who drives for a 'boss' (*nayik*). Many Chitralis consider driving a low (*past*) profession. Interactions between drivers and passengers are often fraught, with drivers angrily telling their passengers that they, too, are from 'good' family backgrounds and deserve to be treated with greater respect. The widespread availability of alcohol at plays adds to these tensions. Drivers are excluded from drinking sessions on the grounds of safety, although status is a key dynamic in determining which men are invited to stay within a drinking group and which are encouraged to leave. As a result, drivers often 'leave in a sulk' (*kruéik*) and join drinking groups made up of their driver friends before eventually being admonished by their passengers for behaving 'rowdily.' In response to the fraught emotions that emerge between different types of playgoers, some of the event's participants may even seek to sabotage the proceedings of the play completely. One tried and tested way of rendering the play a chaotic farce is for a man to pretend that he has been bitten on his bottom by a scorpion. His scream of distress inevitably leads participants to scuttle on top of one another as they desperately try to escape being bitten.

The role played by status hierarchy in determining the interpersonal relations of Chitralis is a source of great sensitivity in the region today and a domain of life intensified by the emergence of a new elite of Chitrali government civil servants and development professionals, who are often accused by poorer villagers of 'eating' the region's scant resources (cf. Staley 1982). During the course of daily life, villagers consider it improper to openly discuss the status backgrounds of particular families; unspoken tensions are, however, enacted in multiple ways at rowdy plays. One way is through the enactment of competitive masculinity: Men seek to push and pull the play in contrasting directions through momentary outbursts of individualized behaviour. This type of masculinity takes diverse forms and cross-cuts social categories: It may be enacted by the region's youth (*juwanán*) in defiance of the pleas of their elders (*lilótan*) for them to behave in a suitably Chitrali 'polite' and 'respectful' way and by men from low (past) status backgrounds who purposefully act rowdily in the presence of Chitral's lordly men of power, influence, and beauty.

The professional musicians who perform at plays are mostly men descended from a low-status 'conical clan' (Parkes 2001a), known as the *dom*.[30] Male dom members traditionally played music and conducted the circumcision ritual for the region's courtly aristocratic families. Today musicians from dom backgrounds are often employed as performers by the Chitral Scouts—the local wing of the Pakistani army—or the Chitral police. The army's involvement in the organization of plays, indeed, adds another layer of complexity to the form that such events take today. Besides village lords, the police, and the region's Islamizing dasmanán, the premier institution of the Pakistani state—the military—attempts to regulate plays. The musicians often perform at programmes organized by the Chitral Scouts when they host Pakistani VIPs and foreign guests in their forts. A mix of ordinary 'civil' (civilian) villagers, local dignitaries, and Chitral Scouts attend such events. Ordinary Chitrali villagers say that such plays are good fun, but they rarely describe them as 'hot' (garam), like the plays organized by villagers to celebrate the marriage of a village son, at which dom employed by Chitral Scouts also perform. Plays held in Chitral's forts, rather, are considered to be a particular type of spectacle, the defining characteristic of which is the pleasure playgoers take from laughing at the 'proud' and 'arrogant' behaviour of the Chitrali men who serve as *subadars,* junior commissioned officers in the Chitral Scouts. These subadars are said to treat ordinary village people as if they were their 'batmen' (the English military term used to refer to officers' personal valets). They walk around, I am told, with their 'chests puffed out' in the most absurd fashion.[31] The Pakistani army has sought to render plays an apolitical manifestation of Chitrali tradition that is also an acceptable component of Pakistan's military-dominated national culture.[32] Many 'civil' (civilian) Chitralis, however, make jokes about the behaviour of subadars, and the overly brash enactments of puffed-up martial manhood in the context of the istók is what they disapprove of most.

During the course of an istók, the dom play a wide range of musical pieces. These include songs (*basónu*) that narrate ancient Khowar love stories, military battles, and the heroic exploits of historically important Chitrali men and women as well as tunes to which modern Chitrali ghazals are currently performed. Other musical pieces performed by the dom are categorized according to their non-Chitrali origins. Pashto tunes that have been popularized through the sale of commercially recorded audiocassettes are particularly popular. These are referred to generically as 'alyaniwár,' 'Pashto-language' musical pieces; any Pukhtuns present at plays are often encouraged to dance to such music. Most pieces are not categorized according to the tune being played by the surnai player; rather, the accompanying rhythm of the drum categorizes the music performed at plays. There are two main categories of drum rhythm: *Dáni* rhythms are said to be old, heavy, and difficult to dance to, whereas the rhythm of the *sauz* mode is described as fast, light, and easy to dance to (see Nigah Nigah 1996).[33] Dáni rhythms characterize much of the music played during the early part of the evening, whereas sauz music grows in prominence as the event progresses.

This combination of both heavy and light rhythms is mapped onto and instantiated within the different registers of masculinity that are enacted during the istók.[34] Dancing is a central feature of the play. The participants arrange themselves in a circle around the musicians; the empty space in between is lit with lanterns hanging from trees and is where men dance during the evening. In contrast to the slow, solo dance routines of mahfils, men usually dance in groups of three and six, and as the evening progresses, up to 15 boys will take to the floor together. Yet group dancing is criticized by some playgoers, especially high-ranking elders, who say that it is 'un-Chitrali' and that it highlights the unwelcome intrusion of rowdy forms of Pukhtun sociality into the region's 'polite' culture.

Indeed, during the early stages of the play, elaborate, slow, and precise dance routines predominate. These are mostly performed to the sound of the heavy dáni-type drum rhythm, which many of the istók's participants say requires 'expert dancers,' considerable numbers of whom are the descendants of the one-time aristocratic or 'lordly' (*lalei*) families.[35] Such men are described as possessing the ability, gravitas, or, importantly, 'heaviness' (*qahí bik*) to dance to these most exacting dáni rhythms. Both the men and their dances may be described as 'beautiful' (*siéli*). The performances provide an opportunity for an accomplished dancer to publicly demonstrate his lordly beauty and power as well as his capacity to attract people into his affective orbit (cf. Ali 2004).[36] Farhan, for instance, a retired subadar of the Chitral Scouts, one-time captain of

Chitral's polo team, and the descendant of an aristocratic family, is known as an expert dancer and a *zíndadil insan* (a person who is full of life). Being described as such marks a man apart from other elderly villagers, who are said to sit in their homes, grow their beards, and 'make work' out of aging. At one level, tensions between Chitrali elders and the region's youth are expressed during plays. At the same time, however, these events also provide an opportunity for elders to inject themselves into what are referred to as life-sustaining forms of emotion. Publicly attending events with young village men is one of the ways senior Chitrali men generate and experience this emotion.

As the night wears on, however, playgoers increasingly shout out requests to the musicians to play faster and lighter sauz rhythms, which are more popular among the younger men in attendance. The solo dances performed thus far, they complain, are slow, serious, and boring—in short, heavy (*qáhi*)—and many young Chitrali men prefer to dance to the sound of light (*lots*) rhythms with their friends. Younger boys say that, by dancing in groups, they can 'lose their shyness' and 'have fun'. So, some men seek to enact and earn reputations as 'heavy' men of cultural sophistication—something they also embody by maintaining perfectly crafted smiles during their solo dance routines—whereas younger men aim to be 'light', often by laughing while they dance with their friends.[37] Through a complex combination of the temporal unfolding of the event and the imprint of active choice-making processes on the part of the participants, 'heavy' and 'light' styles of masculinity are mapped and instantiated onto the play during the course of the evening. Subtle shifts in musical form and their connected styles of masculinity also play a critical role in investing the event with its distinctive emotional dimensions. As the music speeds up, the dancing area contracts, young men dance in groups, and the hoots of encouragement for the dancers increasingly become shouts, the play is said to become 'hot' (garam). The behaviour of playgoers is also said to be more rowdy (vesirú) than earlier in the evening. There is much swearing, and some men even have reputations for throwing projectiles—usually empty glass bottles—at the dancers. Fights (*janjál*) inevitably ensue. During the course of these fights, some especially aggressive men are said to behave like snow leopards (*phurdúm*)—a mark of respect for their displays of proper manly physical strength; others are merely castigated for being 'drunk' and 'senseless'. One man I knew from a low-status family was a driver who was always warned not to come to plays. He inevitably arrived late and immediately started a fight.

Such disruptive behaviour always plays a critical role in defining plays. Men judge mahfils according to the quality of the music, the abundance of the food, and the presence of well-known, educated, and high-status men. The semi-public forms of status competition that are central to the texture of mahfils render them comparable to Arjun Appadurai's (1986) 'tournaments of value' as does the important role played by their wealthy if not necessarily sophisticated patrons. Whereas mahfil-goers, too, must ensure that mahfils become hot, the heat of the mahfil is very different from that of the play. In the context of the mahfil, heat is a quality of the sensory environment that needs to be created to allow the men gathered to fully appreciate the intensity of emotions of ecstatic love expressed in ghazal music.

The fun of the istók is also judged according to its heat, yet, far from cultivating the emotions necessary for the sophisticated appreciation of music, plays are events in which men rejoice in enacting displays of 'rowdy,' 'irrational,' and 'animalistic' forms of emotional heat (Reed 2002:250). In Chitral, as elsewhere in Pakistan, 'hotness' is associated with life, virility, and procreation (Kurin 1984). During istóks, this ambiguous yet necessary dimension of Muslim personhood is purposefully cultivated in the dispositions of both young men and senior elders.

SEX TALK

The istók is strictly sexually segregated, yet talking openly about sex is an important part of the night's entertainment. Women often watch the goings-on from nearby rooftops and trees, and their physical presence and imagined gaze add another dimension to the ways in which men enjoy the events as 'impermissibly good fun.' In contrast to mahfils, in which ghazal music dwells on the introspective agonies of unrequited love, at plays more sensuous forms of sexuality and masculinity are instantiated and, according to some of my friends, sometimes even enacted. In a region where purdah, the segregation of the sexes, is often strictly enforced but conceptions of romantic love are also a basis for elopement marriage, it would be tempting to see istóks as events in which young men are socially conditioned for the inevitability of heterosexual life and marriage (cf. Osella and Osella 2006). What is striking, however, is that during the course of rowdy plays, a far wider range of sexualities than those associated with heterosexuality are talked about and enacted in public ways.

Some villages in Chitral are widely known for hosting plays that are especially enjoyable because they are watched by many girls. At such events, dancing is not simply a form of competition between men. In addition, the active attempt to impress women also forms a significant dimension of masculine performances during the istók. Playgoers often comment that the boys who are dancing are not doing so for fun but, rather, as 'work' (*kormó bacen*). They are hoping to 'throw a line' to a *top*, an attractive and fashion-conscious village girl. The young women and girls present are shrouded in darkness and seated hundreds of yards away, yet young men squeeze each other's arms and exclaim that they are being watched by 'impermissibly beautiful girls' (*najáiz siéli kumoran*).

Rumours also often circulate about the possibilities for sexual encounters at plays, and these contribute to the types of social relationships that are enacted both within and around plays. Most importantly, they add another layer to the distinctive framework of expectations that villagers bring to such plays. One man who often tells me about the sexuality of plays is a retired subadar of the Chitral Scouts, now in his early fifties. The subadar often tells me that, as a young man, during the course of plays held at the Chitral Scout fort to which he was then posted, he had regularly enjoyed 'relaxing' in a maize field with a village woman who was known for being sexually 'loose'. Although this subadar is widely said to be an 'expert liar' (*cangátu*), many of his fellow villagers listen to his stories with keen interest.

Many of my Chitrali friends, however, told me that they remembered the days when istóks were not all-male gatherings. Khurshid, a man in his mid-thirties with a Master's degree in sociology from Peshawar University, told me that he remembered, as a young child, attending plays organized to celebrate the seasonal wheat harvest, at which men and women had danced together to surnai music. According to Khurshid, it was only during General Zia's Islamizing period of martial rule between 1978 and 1988 that plays had become sexually segregated in the way that they are today. Other Chitralis insisted, however, that although women had once publicly showered male dancers with gifts of walnuts, sweets, and dried apricots, they themselves had not danced at such events. The invisible presence of women at plays today is, thus, a relatively new dimension of such events and demonstrates the intensity of the Islamizing processes that Chitral's Muslims have experienced over the past three decades. More pertinently, it also points to the ways in which the 'fun' that male playgoers experience from 'sensing' the presence of women at plays derives partly from the Islamization of public life in Chitral over the last 30 years: impermissible fun and Islamic piety have shaped one another.

Some younger village women do, indeed, secretly attend plays. They quietly leave their homes at night and listen to the music sitting in trees.[38] On their return, they laugh about the boys they saw dancing and make comments about those who were good dancers and who were 'pretty' (*siéli*) and others who were ugly and 'danced like bears'. Many women, however, are revolted at the thought of attending a play. Those boys who frequent plays, they say, are immoral loafers (*bayólas*) who like to drink, smoke, and look at girls. I am also often told that a girl may even refuse a marriage match because the chosen boy has a reputation for being a committed playgoer: 'Why,' they ask their fathers, 'should I marry a cigarette-smoking bayóla?' Many Chitrali boys respond to these allegations of immorality by ceasing to attend istóks. They worry that being known as a playgoer will lessen their chances of marrying a good, respectable, and educated girl. Young Chitrali men must negotiate a complex range of pressures placed on them to conform to ideal forms of manhood. These emanate from the region's Islamizing dasmanán, who urge them to become pious Muslims, and from senior village elders, who emphasize the importance of the boys' maintaining the reputations of their families and hamlets by being good, polite, and civilized Chitralis. At the same time, the region's young women, many of whom are now educated as far as higher secondary level, have aspirations to live modern lives and be married to educated, clean, and successful breadwinners.

The sexual dangers and potentials of the istók are a source of much anxious discussion for Chitrali wives. Married women attempt to persuade their husbands not to attend plays, which are a domain of village life in which rumours about extramarital cross-sexual liaisons flourish. Many village husbands do, indeed, decide not to attend plays, even in the face of the repeated pleas of their friends and fellow villagers to join them for the fun. By acquiescing to pressure from their wives, men known to enjoy music are subject to accusations of being henpecked by their manlike wives.

The sexually charged atmosphere of the play is invested with a further layer of complexity: Male beauty is openly discussed at these events. Dancers are described as beautiful, especially handsome young men are showered with gifts of money, and older men who dance with beautiful boys are sometimes teased by the crowd for dancing with their 'wives'. On the one hand, the appreciation of male beauty is said to be a marker of 'humanity' (*insániyat*)—it, too, is evidence that a man is not bored and 'awaiting death' but rather, injected with a sustaining 'love of life'. 'All Chitrali men like boys,' I am often told, 'because the appreciation of beauty is a God-given natural thing.' Talk of such attraction is not confined to a concealed or subordinate discourse but, rather, considered central to the proper affective constitution of Chitrali men. On the other hand, older men who are reputed to have openly sexual thoughts about, interests in, and even relations with younger men are not considered 'likers of boys' (*daq xoseiák*) but those who 'play with children' (*bacabáz*), a stinging term of abuse in contemporary Khowar. As in the case of mahfil musicians, public displays of male–male physical attraction are seen by some Chitralis as corrupting the morality of their society and inciting dangerous types of divisive emotion, notably, jealousy. Yet the appreciation of male beauty is considered one further way in which, during the course of appropriate performative events such as plays, men can demonstrate that they are capable of being 'light' and 'lovers of life' rather than 'heavy' and 'bored'.

The play is a dangerous place for people's reputations. Men lose their tempers and are accused of drinking and smoking hashish in defiance of the mullah's sermons. Plays are also the subject of much village discussion—they are spaces in which reputations are broken but also made. During plays, young and older men earn names for being 'heavy' (*qáhi*) and 'attractive' (*siéli*) lords; strong, aggressive, hypermasculine men of snow leopard–like and animalistic bravery who defy both local conventions of politeness and Islamist forms of piety; and light, fun-loving, handsome, and marriageable males. As the evening progresses, the rowdiness becomes more exaggerated and also frequently assumes the form of a defiant masculinity that is enacted despite the injunctions of the region's pious mullahs and 'respectable men' and despite Chitrali traditions of politeness and civility. There is no simple division, thus, between men who choose to inhabit the world of lordly high culture as embodied in plays and mahfils and those who challenge such forms of sociality by embracing 'reform-minded' forms of Islamic piety. Plays, rather, are events at which alternative forms of contrasting yet interconnected types of manly behaviour are creatively enacted and instantiated.

CONCLUSION

In this chapter, I have sought to document a complex nexus between local theories and experiences of performance, masculinity, and emotion in the Chitral region of northern Pakistan. During the course of istóks and mahfils, men must negotiate their way between diverse forms of manhood, including those that value 'hot' (garam) vitality, physical excellence, and the performance of assertiveness and competition. Equally prominent, however, are those emphasizing very different manly arts. The key reference points here are manifestations of taste, cultural connoisseurship, and the cultivation of properly human (*pura insan*) forms of affection (*khuloos*) through the patronage of music and the semi-public performance of longing, sadness, and introspection induced by the experience of ecstatic love ('*ishq*). The ability to move with art and grace between these contrasting registers of masculinity is the true test of manhood for many of my friends in Chitral today.

It is striking that these performative standards are enacted in a region of the Muslim world that has been profoundly affected by many different forms of Islamic activism as well as the persistence of older forms of status distinction and new expressions of class difference. On the one hand, Chitral's politically active Islamists have labelled istóks, in particular, 'impermissible' because they are said to stimulate pernicious feelings that pose unique dangers both to the personal morality of the region's Muslims and to the proper Islamic nature of the society in which they live. On the other hand, by patronizing sanitized performance events such as mahfils, men from Chitral's older gentry and folk from lower-status backgrounds who have benefited from NGO and local civil service employment have sought to remember the imagined luxuries of the courtly past.

From a broader perspective, these musical gatherings offer insights into the interactions between very different forms of sociality, experience, and social aesthetics. On the one hand, they stimulate contrasting forms of sociality. On the other hand, they also trigger alternative cultural memories of the region's courtly past, the shape of which neither Chitral's Islamizing mullahs nor its cultural elite are able to determine. As a result, these high-intensity events form an axis of interaction between theories of emotion held by Chitral's reform-minded Islamizers and forms of sociality derived from the region's courtly past. By drawing anthropological attention to creative forms of performative events that point attention to interactive relationships between contrasting modes of Chitrali Muslim self-understanding and experience, I aim to have highlighted some of the conceptual problems associated with anthropological work that seeks to identify 'common substrate[s] of embodied dispositions' that exist 'beneath the level of expressed belief and opinion' (Hirschkind 2006:88). Chitral's all-male sonic events, instead, elucidate the ways in which Chitrali Muslims bring contrasting modes of judgement to different categories of musical events that are critical to the instantiation of diverse yet interconnected forms of emotional experience and aesthetic standards. This diversity, moreover, is invested with wider social and political potential because of the distinct qualities of emotional work that Chitralis invest in such gatherings in the face of attacks made by the region's dasmanán and the sanitizing designs of the region's new elites as well as of local faces of the Pakistani state. These efforts ensure both the ongoing distinctiveness of the events as well as their wider emotional and political creative significance to everyday life in the region today.

NOTES

Acknowledgements: This chapter would not have been possible without the kindness and help of the many people I have met in Chitral since I first visited the region in 1995. I am especially indebted to the constant support I have received from Mir and Muzzafar Hussein Shah, Hazar Baig, Nizar Wali Shah, and their families. The material on which this chapter is based was collected during an 18-month period of research for my doctoral dissertation in 2000–01 and eight further research visits to Chitral between January 2003 and August 2006. All of this research was made possible thanks to the generous support of Trinity College, the Economic and Social Research Council, and the British Academy. This article has benefited from insightful comment from two *AE* anonymous reviewers, Susan Bayly, Mathew Carey, Shah Hussein, Humeira Iqtidar, and Filippo and Caroline Osella and from ongoing discussions with Peter Parkes. Finally, I am especially indebted to Elena Bashir for help with the transliteration of Khowar terms. All mistakes are my own. I use pseudonyms for people, villages, and small towns in the Chitral region throughout the article.

1. Khowar is an Indo-Aryan language that shows the imprint of Central Asian and South Asian 'linguistic areas' (Bashir 1996:196), but it is especially heavily influenced by Farsi (Endresen and Kristiansen 1981; Morgenstierne 1936). It has a written script that uses a modified version of the Urdu alphabet, although, apart from poetic and other Chitrali forms of literary composition, most of the region's people prefer to write in Urdu, and official business is conducted in both English and Urdu. Khowar is unintelligible to speakers of Urdu, Pakistan's 'national' language, and Pashto, the predominant language spoken in the North-West Frontier Province. Most people in Chitral speak other languages beside Khowar, notably, Urdu, Pashto, English, and Afghan Persian (Dari), although many of the region's older men and women only converse fluently in Khowar. The transliteration system for Khowar used in this article follows that developed by Elena Bashir (e.g., 1996). The special symbols used and their phonetic values are as follows:

   $\check{s}$ voiceless palatal sibilant
   $\check{z}$ voiced palatal sibilant
   $\check{c}$ voiceless palatal affricate
   ṣ voiceless retroflex sibilant
   ṭ voiceless retroflex stop
   ḍ voiced retroflex stop
   x voiceless velar fricative
   γ voiced velar fricative

u<_>sound in English *roof*
æ<_>low front vowel (as in English *cat*)

Persian or Arabic words, for example, *ghazal, marsiya, madrassah,* and *shariah,* that now have accepted or standard English spellings, I have left in the standard English representation.

2. On Pakistan's madrassahs and the complex modes of intellectual and legal reasoning deployed by the country's ulama, see Muhammad Qasim Zaman 2002. As is the case in many other Muslim-majority societies, Chitral's dasmanán are educated in madrassahs that claim adherence to various theological and doctrinal schools. The region's men of learning and piety, thus, hold a very wide range of opinions according to authoritative Islamic legal precepts concerning the permissibility of musical gatherings. Some of the region's madrassah-trained men of learning and piety, moreover, sometimes seek to distinguish themselves from 'hardened' men of piety and earn reputations as 'fully human' and cultured listeners of Chitrali musical traditions (see Marsden 2007a). My central concern in this study, however, is with the ways in which Chitralis have responded to and interacted with the region's politically active dasmanán, most of whom are publicly critical of the types of musical gatherings I document and theorize in this chapter.

3. Islamic views about the permissibility of music are obviously complex and very often ambiguous. Lois Ibsen Al-Faruqi (1985) documents the legal framework within which Muslim jurists perceive music as problematic. For anthropological attempts to explore the ways in which musicians negotiate the ambiguity with which music is regarded in many Muslim-influenced regions of southern and western Asia, see Baily 1988 and Qureshi 1995.

4. The MMA coalition is made up of a diverse range of Islamist parties that wield influence and power in Pakistan's present-day political culture. Chitral, moreover, is an interactive part of a transregional setting, and Chitralis are informed in complex and often firsthand ways about this wider world. For example, their region shares a long and intermittently porous border with Afghanistan, and when all routes in Chitral are closed because of snow, many Chitralis travel to and from their homes by way of an all-season route through Afghanistan. The Taliban's 'prevention of vice and promotion of virtue' police frequently smeared soot on the faces of clean-shaven Chitrali men during these journeys and destroyed the audiocassettes hidden in the glove boxes of Chitrali drivers' minibuses.

5. In an especially rich study of Arebesk music in southwestern Turkey, for instance, Martin Stokes notes that this musical genre's critics label it a 'hybrid Turkish version of popular Arab song' (1998:284) and associate it with two forms of pleasures that are problematic for both Turkish republicanism and Sunni Islam: alcohol and sexuality. Arabesk music is, consequently, associated with feminine 'Arabness' and the corruption of the ideally male national Turkish body (Stokes 1998:284).

6. Among the committed participants in musical programmes I know are educated Chitrali men from high-status families who are well-paid civil servants and NGO officials, officers and troopers in the Pakistani army, small-scale peasant farmers, and Chitrali labour migrants.

7. A wide body of literature explores the ways in which sonic meaning and significance are created through emotional and aesthetic processes that involve the interactive agency of both performers and their audiences (e.g., Qureshi 1995).

8. For anthropological studies of mosque sermons in the Middle East, see Patrick D. Gaffney 1994 and Richard T. Antoun 1989.

9. Alexei Yurchak (2006) has recently addressed this concern in his analysis of the everyday performance of Soviet rituals in 'late socialism'. The performances he explores did not reflect in any simple way the expression of 'constantive meanings' but were, rather, about the capacity of Soviet people to precisely reproduce these rituals (Yurchak 2006:286) and, in doing so, create the possibility for living meaningful lives. The constant enactment of ritualized acts was 'constitutive of Soviet' reality, yet this reality was not one described by the performances themselves. Instead, the ongoing reproduction of Soviet rituals was invested with creative possibilities, as it could lead to the emergence of forms of everyday life that official Soviet texts were unable to determine or describe.
10. For other writing in a similar vein, see Nancy Lindisfarne 1994, Andrea Cornwall and Lindisfarne 1994, and Peter Loizos 1994. Several recent studies have challenged Lindholm's (1982) somewhat one-dimensional approach to the study of gender relations in Pukhtun society. Benedicte Grima 1992 and Amineh Ahmed 2005 challenge Lindholm for his male bias, arguing that Pukhtun notions of honour and independence are also sources of female self-respect. The centrality of acts of male vengeance and manly violence to Pukhtun codes of honour has also been questioned by Banerjee (2000) in her rich account of Abdul Ghaffar Khan and his nonviolent and anticolonial independence movement, the Khudai Khidmatgars (the Servants of God) movement, which was influential in the 1930s and 1940s.
11. Ethnographic accounts of this dimension of life in Pakistan's North-West Frontier Province frequently emphasize the power of relatively one-dimensional codes of honour in which it is the manly performance of control over women and also lesser men that is considered central to the enactment of masculine potency. Lindholm, for instance, argues that in northern Pakistan's Swat valley, boys are 'pampered and trained' into inhabiting their 'superior position' from a very young age (1982:173).
12. Much historical literature traces the ways in which 'muscular' practices were central to the responses of people living under a wide range of colonial regimes (Alter 2004; McDevitt 2005). The authors of such studies argue that colonial regimes sought to depict their subjects as 'effeminate' in comparison to the hypermasculinity of the colonizers, and anthropologists (notably Verkaaik [2004]) suggest that attempts to 'recuperate' lost masculinity have been a vibrant feature of the 'popular' political culture of many South Asian settings as a result of this colonial history.
13. Several studies explore the ways in which colonizers emphasized their masculinity in contrast to the femininity of those they ruled; see, for example, Mrinalini Sinha 1995. Other accounts document more complex interactions between the hypermasculinity of British colonial officials and local frameworks of gendered identity. See Joseph S. Alter 2004, Tanya M. Luhrman 1996, and Patrick McDevitt 2005.
14. Debates about the distinction between 'homosocial' as opposed to 'homosexual' forms of behaviour were particularly significant in early twentieth century Iran; see, Afsaneh Najmabadi 2005.
15. On this historical classification, see J. Biddulph 1972, D. J. T. O'Brien 1895, Parkes 2001a, G. S. Robertson 1899, and John Staley 1982.
16. On Pukhtun society, see Fredrik Barth 1959; Akbar S. Ahmed 1980, 1983; Banerjee 2000; Kaiser 1991; and Lindholm 1982, 1996. Compare Paul Titus 1998.
17. Commercial audiocassette recordings of modern Urdu ghazal music also form a major dimension of South Asia's music industry (Manuel 1991). This body of work also clearly influenced the work of many Chitrali poets (see Marsden 2007b).
18. The term *muhajir* means *refugee* or *migrant* and refers in Pakistan to Muslims and their descendants who migrated to Pakistan from India at the time of Partition.

19. Stokes (1996) has explored the ways in which, in some Muslim contexts, any form of leisure other than physical sport or sexual contact between a husband and wife can be considered morally questionable according to a reading of Hadithic texts.
20. I present a more detailed discussion of the mahfil in chapter five of Magnus Marsden 2005. My aim here is to highlight the differences between the mahfil and the type of musical gathering that forms the central focus of this article, the istók, and to analyze mahfils in relation to the broader arguments I make in this study about the role played by musical performance in the instantiation of diverse forms of masculinity in Chitral.
21. Women never attended a mahfil-type of musical programme, although they did occasionally watch them through windows covered in mosquito netting, and my friends did tell me that, in 'earlier times,' women had formed a part of the audience at such gatherings.
22. The Chitrali sitar is a long-necked, plucked-string instrument that is carved from wood and closely resembles a variety of forms of *dambura* widely found in nearby regions of Afghanistan and Tajikistan (e.g., Slobin 1976:ch. 4). For an analysis of the role played by the dambura in the musical traditions of Badakshan, a province of Afghanistan that borders Chitral, see Hiromi Lorraine Sakata 1983.
23. The content of these songs are explored in detail in Marsden 2005 and Georg Morgenstierne and Wazir Ali Shah 1959. See Marsden 2007b for a more detailed examination and consideration of the significance of cross-gender love relationships in contemporary Chitral.
24. At one level, the dasmanán's attacks on the music performed at mahfils reflects a tension between forms of Muslim self-understanding that build on Sufic forms of devotion associated with the writing of great Persian Sufi poets such as Rumi and Hafiz and other forms influenced by the teachings of 'reform-minded' Islamic doctrinal schools, notably, the Deobandi school, that have become increasingly hostile to Sufi forms of thought and experience over the past 40 years. See Marsden 2005 for a more in-depth consideration of these tensions and the influence that Sufic Persian traditions have on the expectations and experiences of mahfil participants. Barbara D. Metcalf 2004 provides an in-depth historical approach to the understanding of the form taken by such debates in South Asian Islam, more generally. Richard Wolf 2006 explores the significance of very different types of music and dance performed in a major Sufi shrine complex in the Pakistani city of Lahore.
25. The composition of marsiyas, often in honour of the pivotal Shia imams—Ali, Hussein, and Hassan—is considered by many South Asian specialists to be a largely Shia tradition. Some of the musicians who perform at mahfils are Shia Ismai'li Muslims, although many are Sunnis. Marsiyas written as laments for known Chitrali men are, thus, composed and performed by both Sunni and Shia Ismai'li Muslims in Chitral today.
26. Similarities can be seen in Qureshi's consideration of the complex ways in which *sarangi*-playing in the Indian subcontinent is often 'endowed with associations of sadness, loss and mourning' (2000:815).
27. Chitral is also home to approximately 4,000 non-Muslim Kalasha people, who form what Parkes refers to as an 'enclave society' in three valleys in the south of the region. The performance of song and dance is central to various Kalasha ritual seasonal celebrations, although the music is very different from the types of Chitrali music explored in this study: It emphasizes vocal and not instrumental forms of expression (Parkes 1994:164). Parkes analyzes the sequence of performative styles enacted during

the course of Kalasha musical celebrations as an attempt to resolve 'inherent tensions concerning the recognition of interpersonal competition and differential status within a communitarian context of collective enclavement' (1994:158).

28. Some of the older songs performed at both mahfils and istóks also concern the ways in which the region's people experienced the effects of British colonialism. One song, for instance, evokes the pain one lover felt when he was separated from his beloved after being drafted into the Chitral Scouts (a local militia founded by the government of British India and the ruler of Chitral). This song continues to be popular and is widely performed in the region today.

Awá ki lalíman ta custío zor ma díti mudám ma paleés.
Awá asúm iskóta, angrézo bandi, kia wa ma kúra leés?

When I look at you, your beauty will always burn me.
I am in the Scouts, the prisoner of the British, when again will you find me?

29. The Tablighi Jama'at is a worldwide preaching movement of Islamic purification established in the Mehwat region of India in the early 1920s. See Metcalf 1993.
30. See A. Schmid 1997 for an in-depth consideration of the doms' status as falling between social exclusion and cultural power in another region of northern Pakistan, Hunza.
31. On the Scouts, see Charles Chenevix Trench 1985 and Martin Sökefeld 2006.
32. Attempts by the military to sanitize istóks and other Chitrali performative events have recently been prominently displayed at the Shandur Tournament, an event at which polo teams from Chitral and the neighbouring region of Gilgit meet each other annually. In July 2006, for example, the Shandur Tournament was organized under the auspices of Islamabad's Ministry of Tourism. The event was described in an address to local people and foreign dignitaries by its chief guest, President Pervez Musharraf. He emphasized the ways in which the event displayed a positive image of a 'moderate' Pakistan. The istóks organized at the tournament were widely considered dismal failures by the Chitralis in attendance, however. In an attempt to promote 'Chitrali culture' to foreigners and visiting dignitaries, the organizers of these plays invited senior elders to perform old Chitrali songs. The audiences considered these performances wholly inappropriate to the exhibitions of manifest exhilaration expected at plays. The men in attendance eventually became so angry with the organizers that the musical gatherings were abandoned amid threats that the police would be called in to disperse 'rowdy' playgoers, who were accused of damaging Chitral's image as a place of 'hospitable,' 'sophisticated,' and 'peace-loving' people. For a comparative discussion of the changes in the organization and form of polo played at this event, see Parkes 2005.
33. For a detailed consideration by a musicologist of the technical dimension of the patterns, tempo, and rhythms performed at istóks and similar performance events in other regions of northern Pakistan, see Colin Ernst Huehns 1991:365–493.
34. The distinction between 'heavy' and 'light' forms of performance is one widely noted in much ethnographic work on performance (e.g., Brenneis 1987; Cowan 1990). My aim here is to explore the different types of meaning and significance that are attached to these forms by Chitrali male dancers and their audiences.
35. See Tahir Ali 1981 for discussion of the role played by status and descent in the performance of music and dance in another one-time princely state in northern Pakistan, Hunza.

36. Matters of status distinction remain critical for some of the younger men in attendance. Young men from lordly backgrounds often take great pride in earning reputations for being able to perform difficult dance routines.
37. In contrast to my focus on the ways in which both solo dances and the music to which they are performed are widely conceptualized as necessary to make the istók a particular type of event, Jane K. Cowan argues that in contemporary Greece certain types of solo dances, by 'celebrating the isolated individual...tortured by love and anxiety, and acutely self-conscious,' challenge the 'dominant' mode of Greek masculinity, 'the patriarch' (1990:180).
38. Compare Susan Seizer 2004 for an in-depth treatment of the ways in which stigmatized women performers in South India negotiate between self-representation and presentation during their daily lives and are both judged and appreciated by 'respectable women'.

CHAPTER 10

Selves and Others: Representing Multiplicities of Difference in Gilgit and the Northern Areas of Pakistan[1]

MARTIN SÖKEFELD

INTRODUCTION: THE STUDY OF IDENTITIES

The conceptualization of identity and ethnicity has undergone a major change during the last decades. In the human sciences, identity has basically two different meanings, the first of which pertains mainly to psychology and the other to anthropology and other social sciences. In the conventional psychological sense, identity refers primarily to self-identity, the identity of the individual self with itself (e.g. Erikson 1980). In anthropology, in contrast, identity—used for instance in the compound concept of 'ethnic identity'—refers mostly to the identity of an individual with other individuals, that is, to the identity of a group. While the first concept affirms individuality, the peculiarity of the human individual, the second concept tends to negate individuality by stressing those characteristics that an individual supposedly shares with others. In anthropological discourse both meanings of identity are mostly unrelated. A text about 'ethnic' identity does only very rarely refer also to self-identity. But the change in the concept of identity which I want to discuss here engenders a certain (re-)alignment of both meanings.

This change may be indicated by three related terms which together make up a concept of identity: multiplicity, difference, and intersectionality. *Multiplicity* means that identity does not exist in the singular but only as identi*ties*—formed through a plurality of relationships of belonging and otherness. This insight is not entirely new. A hundred years ago, the American psychologist William James wrote that the person 'has as many social selves as there are individuals who recognize him' (James 1890: 294). The postmodern questioning of the unified and universal 'Western' subject, inherited from Descartes, gave new currency to this insight. It stems from the view that identity or self are not original essences of the human being but rather projects and constructions that are reworked, more or less self-consciously, during the whole life-course of an individual, in a great number of different contexts and in juxtaposition to a multiplicity of others.

In a certain sense the concept of *difference* almost replaced the concept of identity in contemporary discourse (Felski 1997). Difference instead of identity emphasises that identity only exists as an always different identity, distinguishing one person from another person, or one group or category from another one. Difference points to the fact that identity is developed in contrast to others. Whereas *identity* stresses the aspect of being identical with others or with the self, *difference* emphasises the contrast which is the necessary premise for establishing such identity. Both aspects cannot be separated; they are two sides of the same coin. But difference, combined with multiplicity, also challenges identity. If identity is based upon difference from others, the self is not simply 'identical'. It is not a singular unity but a 'differing multiplicity' as it differs differently from different others. The self is a bundle of different possible identifications, particular aspects of which may be put to the fore depending on the specific others against which a particular 'identity' is established.[2]

Intersectionality, finally, points to the fact that the different identities (or, in other words: the various differences) which characterize an individual are not unrelated among themselves. Quite the opposite, the different identities embraced by a person may heavily influence each other—not necessarily in the sense that they are mutually trimmed in order to enable a consistent personality, but rather in the sense that they may entail conflict and antagonism, inconsistency and ambivalence. The aspect of intersectionality of identities is frequently related to Jacques Derrida's concept of *différance* (Derrida 1982). Derrida pointed out that the meaning of signs in an ongoing chain of signification can never be finally fixed but that meaning is always affected or changed by the 'environment' of other related signs and meanings—and changes them too. Differences/identities are signs in such interrelated, or, better, interrelating environments of meaning.

Together, these three aspects of a new conceptualization of identity enable that the psychological (individual-oriented) concept of identity and the social or cultural (group-oriented) concept fuse to an unprecedented extent. Rather than negating individuality, social identities contribute to the peculiarity of the individual because each single human being is characterized by a specific combination (multiplicity) of identities (differences) that relate to each other in specific and shifting ways (intersectionality).

This conceptualization of identity/identities was developed from debates of feminism and immigrant identities in the West. Identities that were deemed unproblematic before turned out to be highly disputable: feminists discovered that there was no female identity shared by all women, but only identities of women subject to other differences. Women's experiences are marked differently by differences like class, 'race', nation, etc. What before had been supposed to be a common identity of women turned out to be a specific perspective of some women occupying positions of dominance that allowed them to disseminate their particular view as the perspective of women in general (Crosby 1992; Felski 1997). Indeed, the general category 'woman' became highly questionable. Similarly, identities of immigrants in the diasporas of the West were deconstructed into whole ranges of differing subject positions that made general categories debatable (Brah 1996, Rattansi 1994).

In the light of this critique of identity, anthropological studies of ethnicity have to be questioned for their often simplifying perspective. Mostly they foreground *one* identity (the one which is dubbed as 'ethnic') at the expense of others. Sometimes a number of identities are considered which are represented as fitting into an overall order or taxonomy. Such an order effectively eclipses intersectionality. Put into order, identities neither contradict one another nor produce friction among themselves—that is, they are apparently not subject to *différance*.

A MULTIPLICITY OF DIFFERENCE IN GILGIT

Gilgit, a town of approximately 50,000 inhabitants, is the political, administrative and economic centre of the Northern Areas of Pakistan. Since the beginning of the Kashmir dispute, the Northern Areas—earlier called Gilgit–Baltistan—are under the administration of Pakistan, but legally they do not form a part of Pakistan. The centrality of Gilgit town is due to its strategic position at the intersection of valleys in the high mountain area. Having been alternately a centre of power and a target of attacks by other powers, the population of the place has suffered more than one upheaval. It has faced near extinction as well as waves of immigration from different directions. As a consequence, the present population of Gilgit is characterized by a high degree of difference.

While studying discourses and processes of identity in Gilgit, I analysed mainly five 'dimensions of difference'. These were: religion, *qom*,[3] clan, locality and language. Along each of these dimensions a number of different identities can be distinguished. Within the dimension of religion, for instance, there are Shias, Sunnis, and Ismailis. Within the dimension of *qom*, groups and identities like Shin, Yeshkun, Pashtun and Kashmiri can be distinguished. Locality distinguishes Gilgitwale, Hunzawale, Pashtun and many others. My postulation of these five dimensions of difference is only a heuristic simplification. Most of these dimensions encompass a *disorder* of differences rather than ordered systems. Only in two dimensions, religion and language, is the number of encompassed differences finite. There are three relevant religious groups in Gilgit, and fifteen different mother tongues are spoken. The other three dimensions are rather indefinite. The encompassed differences are very numerous because new differences can always be constructed and because the encompassed differences can themselves be organized into (rather disordered) systems. Locality may distinguish people belonging to different neighbourhoods in Gilgit (*het* or *mohalle*), but also people belonging to different valleys (e.g. Hunza, Nager, Gilgit), subregions of valleys (e.g. Shinaki, Hunza, Gujal) or countries and nations (e.g. Pakistani and non-Pakistani). Identity derived from locality is also structured by the simple dichotomy of people of Gilgit versus people from outside. Finally, not all dimensions are mutually exclusive. Thus, Pashtun can be considered as a *qom* as well as an identity derived from a certain area. Similarly, Hunzawale can be understood as an identity derived from a certain locality as well as a qom.[4]

Drawing on Bourdieu's concept of practice (Bourdieu 1977), I have elsewhere analysed the multiplicity of identities in Gilgit as a system of practical logic that is employed to distinguish between kinds of persons according to specific, practical necessities and for particular purposes (Sökefeld 1997a). A major characteristic of this system is its inherent ambivalence. Such a disordered system cannot be turned into a taxonomically ordered system without completely changing its character.

So far I have described the multiplicity of identities that pertains to the level of groups and congregations of people. But multiplicity also characterizes the identities of every individual. Each person draws identities from each of the above-mentioned dimensions of difference as well as from others like gender, age or class. An individual in Gilgit may be, for instance, a Gilgitwala from the village of Barmas, a Shia, a Shin that belongs to the Shalé-lineage and that speaks the Shina language. A second person may share some of these identities, as he or she may be from the same village, but be a Sunni Yeshkun that belongs to the same lineage of Shalé and that also speaks Shina. Another man may have a completely different set of identities, being, e.g. an immigrant from Hunza that belongs to the qom Dhiramiting and to the Ismailia and who speaks Burushaski. It follows from these examples that the question of whether two persons share an identity or are different cannot be answered easily. Most frequently, persons share only *some* identity but differ by some others. They can be '*both* the same *and* different' (Hall 1990: 227, original italics). Every identity/difference places the individual into a specific discursive space. That is, his or her total repertory of identities entails his or her participation in a number of discursive spaces that may effectively be related by ambivalence, conflict and contradiction. Consider two persons, the first being Shia and Yeshkun, the second Sunni and Yeshkun. According to their religious identity they are antagonists because Shias and Sunnis are divided by history of violent sectarian tensions in Gilgit. On the other hand, by their qom identity, both belong to the same group and it is generally maintained that a high degree of solidarity should be practiced within the qom. Considerable ambivalence arises for social actors from this multiplicity of identities (Sökefeld 1997b). Intersectionality of identities here entails that in certain contexts the two actors may play down religious antagonism in order to emphasize qom solidarity, or the other way round. The meaning of these identities is not fixed for the person who embodies them but is a matter of momentary positioning within the total environment of identities/differences. It follows that it is not always clear whether another person is construed as self or as other. There is a multiplicity of selves, also *within* the individual, to be distinguished from a multiplicity of others. Instead of a dichotomy of self versus other, we should speak of multiple dichotomies of selves and others that are not fixed but that structure momentary relations with particular other persons in a specific environment of differences.

This does not mean that all dichotomies of self versus others share the same degree of relevance within the society of Gilgit. Some are certainly more important than others. In what follows I would like to discuss the difference 'Shia–Sunni' which possessed a very high level of importance during the time of research. After that I will show that despite this salience the religious difference is still subject to multiplicity and intersectionality, and I will explore some examples of how the religious difference is exchanged for other differences.

SHIAS AND SUNNIS IN GILGIT: THE DEVELOPMENT OF ANTAGONISM

The antagonism between Shias and Sunnis is nearly as old as Islam. Still, in Gilgit this difference is said not to have had much significance before the beginning of the 1970s. Accounts of conflict events before 1970 can be heard, but it is generally accepted that only from the early 1970s onwards the difference acquired a salience that effectively divided the town's population into two antagonistic parts.[5] The origin of the dispute in the 1970s is not totally clear, but it seems that some *ulama* (religious scholars) of both sects started at that time to raise the question of whether the members of the other group are really Muslims or not.

Particularly, the special ritual practices of the Shias became a bone of contention between both groups. Most important was the mourning procession on *ashura,* the tenth day of the month of Muharram, in which Shias lament the martyrdom of Imam Hussein and his companions in the battle of Karbala. In Gilgit, the *julus* of *ashura* ended always at the central place of the town, in front of the main Sunni mosque. Here, speeches were delivered to the participants. In the 1960s also many Sunnis would join the procession or assist the Shias who practiced flagellation. They handed them water and pieces of cloth with which the Shias wiped off their blood. On the grounds that the blood-stained cloths that were thrown away defiled the mosque, Sunni leaders demanded in 1972 that the assembly at the end of the *julus* be shifted to another place. But the Shias refused to comply with that demand. Three years later, in 1975, the Shia assembly was shot at from the Sunni mosque. Because of this incident the Sunni *qazi* was arrested. His detention caused great unrest in the Sunni areas of the Indus valley, south of Gilgit, and its side-valleys like Gor, Darel, and Tangir. Sunnis from these regions threatened to attack Gilgit. In the next year the administration demanded that the assembly take place at another location. Again the Shias refused to give up what they considered their habitual right. As a consequence, the *julus* was prohibited for the next two years. Only after that did the Shias concede to move their assembly to another place. Yet the dispute was not solved by this move because now the Sunnis demanded the procession take an entirely different route. A solution that satisfied both opponent parties could not be found and until now Muharram is a time of potential sectarian tension in Gilgit.

The dispute forced the people in Gilgit to increasingly identify themselves either as Sunnis or as Shias. Before, people often repeated, one did not exactly know always to which sect the other person belonged, and Shias and Sunnis frequently prayed together in the same mosque. What reportedly had been only a nominal difference became important in many realms of social life. Since the beginning of the 1970s, there have been no marriages between Shias and Sunnis, in contrast with earlier times in which intermarriage had not been infrequent. In the 1980s the difference entered politics. In the elections of local bodies the appeal to religious sentiment became the most important strategy for winning support and securing votes. In 1988, tensions culminated in a large-scale massacre when Sunni warriors from Kohistan and the Sunni-majority regions of the Northern Areas attacked Shia villages in the vicinity of Gilgit, killing many people and destroying houses, fields and trees. Between 1988 and 1993 many more people became victims of violent tensions.[6]

In the 1980s, another Shia practice was challenged by the Sunni ulama. On festive occasions like the birthday of the Imam Ali, Shias used to light bonfires called *chiraghan* on the mountain slopes surrounding Gilgit. With fire they write words like 'Allah', 'Mohammad' or 'Ali' on the slopes. Again, some Sunni ulama considered this an 'un-Islamic' practice. For them it defiled the names of God and the Prophet because cloths soaked with kerosene were used to write the names. The Sunni ulama demanded an end to the practice of chiraghan, especially on the slopes above Sunni mosques and religious schools. In February 1990, two young men who had lit chiraghan were shot to death from a Sunni *madrassah* when they climbed down a slope.

In 1991, a bomb was found buried in the Sunni *Eidgah* and Shias were accused of having planned the bombing of the whole Sunni congregation during *Eid* prayer. Shias, in return, alleged that they were victims of a conspiracy that aimed at accusing them of fostering tensions. Several persons were killed later that year and the army started to patrol the bazaar area in Gilgit. In May 1992, the assassination of a Sunni youth leader provoked the killing of at least ten more people in revenge and counter-revenge. Curfew was imposed on Gilgit, but this measure could not prevent similar events from occurring again only six weeks later.

Society in Gilgit became effectively polarized by the Shia–Sunni dichotomy. Families living in neighbourhoods where the opposite sect formed the majority moved to majority areas of their own group. Economic cooperation across religious boundaries declined and even commensality between Shias and Sunnis almost ended—especially when it came to having meals containing meat.[7] The Shia–Sunni dichotomy became effectively a premise that structured the perception of the social space.

According to Adam Kuper (1977), polarization of identities implies also a de-pluralization of identities. That is, polarized identities supersede almost all non-polarized identities. This happened in Gilgit too. The religious identity became the most important identity in many contexts, and most persons mentioned their religious affiliation when they were asked their most important identity. Still, this did not mean that multiplicity and intersectionality were eliminated. Instead, it could be observed that in certain contexts people explicitly attempted to foreground other identities at the expense of the religious difference. I would like to present three cases of attempts to replace certain differences that occurred in the beginning of 1993. In two of them, religious difference was traded for other identities (qom and nationality), whereas in the third case the religious difference was emphasized at the expense of locality in a struggle over land rights.

QOM VERSUS RELIGION

In the summer of 1992 two periods of acute tensions occurred within six weeks. Almost twenty people were killed. The first period started when a leader of a Sunni youth organization was murdered and the second began with the assassination of a local politician who happened to be Shia and Yeshkun. The authorities tried to control the incidents by imposing curfew. However, even after the shooting had ended and curfew was lifted, people in Gilgit continued to be very anxious. After dusk, the bazaar area, where tensions mostly started, was deserted. People generally avoided entering the bazaar and restricted their movement to the majority areas of their own sect. Months after the last assassination, public employees did not attend their work if their offices happened to be situated in a majority area of the opposite sect. The threat and fear of further tensions was so strong that people felt very uneasy. In a certain way this fear of new tensions, which was strongly lamented, deepened the rift between the sects because people generally held those of the other sect responsible for the situation. Almost every incident in the town was interpreted within the framework of the conflict between Shias and Sunnis. Polarization prevailed even after acute tensions had stopped.

But in the winter of 1992/93 a discourse emerged among Yeshkun in Gilgit which attempted to foreground qom-identity. I learnt that several Yeshkun were busily organizing an assembly of Yeshkun *motobaran* in

Gilgit irrespective of religious affiliation and locality. At the same time, younger Yeshkun, students and recent graduates, talked about the necessity to hold a similar meeting among themselves. There was an urgent sense that sectarian tensions ultimately endangered the 'identity' of Yeshkun. What I label 'identity' here was represented as both a practice and sentiment of solidarity, belonging and unity among Yeshkun as against other qom, especially Shin.[8] The necessity of an assembly of Yeshkun and the threat that religious antagonism posed to the identity of the Yeshkun was explained in two inconsistent ways. The first explanation considered the forging of unity among Yeshkun irrespective of their religious affiliation an important step to overcome sectarian conflict. Some Yeshkun explained that if they solved the religious antagonism among themselves, and if the Shin did the same, the conflict would almost be finished for want of antagonists. Here, the purpose was to solve the religious conflict, and the first step for that aim was to overcome religious difference among the Yeshkun. The second reasoning was very different. It completely subordinated the religious difference to the difference of qom and declared that sectarian tensions were a conspiracy of the Shin against the Yeshkun. The evidence for this, I was told, was that mostly Yeshkun, both Shias and Sunnis, had been the victims of violent incidents. It was alleged that the Shin, the numerically much inferior qom, had successfully broken the strength of the Yeshkun by disseminating sectarian strife. Some Yeshkun who did not accept the strong version of this thesis conceded that the murder of the Shia Yeshkun politician that had sparked the second wave of tensions in the summer of 1992 had been a Shin–Yeshkun issue rather than a Shia–Sunni matter because the victim had been an important leader of the Yeshkun and his alleged murderer was a Shin.

Although not consistent in their diagnosis, both perspectives argued for the necessity of promoting unity among the Yeshkun and considered the call for a qom-assembly a promising step for that purpose. Further, both opinions converged in the assessment that Shin possessed a much greater internal unity than Yeshkun. Many Yeshkun told me that for themselves religion had become much more important than qom, contrary to Shin for whom qom had always taken first place. As an example, my Yeshkun interlocutors told me that in local body elections Shin gave their support always to other Shin, irrespective of their religious affiliation.[9]

I was also told that similar meetings (both of young and of older men) had taken place earlier but I was unable to find out who had actually taken part and what had been the result of these meetings. Some persons who according to others had taken part in such meetings denied their participation when I inquired about it. All these meetings had been quite clandestine because the Yeshkun did not want to arouse a feeling of threat among the Shin. Further, it seemed that most persons involved were not very eager to talk about these meetings because they obviously contradicted the value of equality and brotherhood among all Muslims, irrespective of descent and similar distinctions. There was no formal organisation of Yeshkun but rather a loose network of men belonging to different places in and around Gilgit, all of them Shina-speakers, who were regarded as important leaders of the qom and who had to take part in such an assembly in order to give it the required vigour.

Some Yeshkun did not only talk about a meeting but were busily engaged in visiting other influential Yeshkun in order to convince them of its necessity. Some of these visits surprised me because they involved very close interaction across the religious divide in spite of the still current strife. For example, a Sunni *lambardar* of a village in one of the Sunni valleys in the south of the Northern Areas stayed for more than a week in the house of a Shia Yeshkun in a purely Shia neighbourhood that had always been a Shia hotbed of sectarianism.[10] From this base he met other Yeshkun in the town in order to get their support for the meeting. In his presence, his host discussed the sectarian issue very frankly with me, although such discussions in the presence of members of the opposite sect were generally avoided in order to prevent emotional exchanges and mutual accusations. Yet the host was a strong advocate of the Shin-conspiracy theory of sectarianism and he articulated the issue within the framework of qom in such a way that his guest did not feel offended.

Still, to organise an assembly of Yeshkun was not an easy matter. I had to leave Gilgit in March 1993 and until then a meeting of Yeshkun had not taken place. First, another period of tensions had seemed imminent[11] and then the beginning of Ramadan intervened. I do not know whether such an assembly took place later. Yet in spite of the fact that the difference of religion seemed to have won over qom in this case, it is clear that both differences and the related issues have to be considered as mutual contexts. No matter whether a qom-assembly of Yeshkun finally took place or not, the issue became pressing for many Yeshkun precisely because of the high degree of religious antagonism. In many contexts, actors drew connections between both differences. For example, one of the motobaran who was very committed to prepare a Yeshkun assembly was at the same time looking for a suitable match for one of his sons. His wife also visited a Shia Shin family in order to ask for the hand of a spouse for her son. The mother of the girl told her: 'I would rather change my religion than give my daughter to a Yeshkun!'[12] Here, too, qom was accorded primacy.

The intersectionality of qom and religion signals a contradiction of ideologies and values. From the point of view of Islam, qom has no positive significance. Islam teaches that all Muslims are brothers and sisters irrespective of ethnicity or any other intervening identity. Some persons in Gilgit therefore explicitly drew the conclusion that in the face of the superior value of religion their belonging to a qom or kinship group was insignificant and that religious affiliation was all that counted. But most persons whom I met admitted the contradiction of values between qom and religion without being able to generally opt for or against one of them. The host of the Sunni lambardar who toured Gilgit in order to win support for a qom assembly put this in the following words: 'Shia or Sunni, this is nonsense. In the Quran there are neither Shias nor Sunnis. And in the last instance also Shin–Yeshkun is nonsense. After all, we are all the children of Adam and Eve.' Yet, this insight did not prevent him from attempting to enhance the importance of qom in the society of Gilgit.

RELIGION VERSUS NATION[13]

The second challenge to religious difference emerged from oppositional politics against the special political status of the Northern Areas. This status results from the entanglement of the Northern Areas in the Kashmir dispute. Since November 1947, the Northern Areas, i.e. the erstwhile Gilgit Agency and Baltistan, are controlled by Pakistan. After an uprising of the local military, the Gilgit Scouts, against the rule of the Maharaja of Kashmir, the local leaders decided to join Pakistan (Sökefeld 1997c). Yet Pakistan did not accept the accession of Gilgit–Baltistan but controlled the area as 'disputed territory', pending the solution of the Kashmir dispute. As a consequence, the region is not a constitutional part of Pakistan and its inhabitants lack a number of constitutional and political rights that Pakistanis enjoy. Many people in Gilgit rejected this political status. In short, they complained that they had opted for Pakistan in 1947 but that Pakistan had not accepted their decision.

In local political discourse the Shia–Sunni conflict is frequently related to this political issue. In 1971, an insurgency against the Pakistani administration occurred in Gilgit that included a general strike, the storming of the police station and breaking of the prison.[14] As it happened, violent sectarian tension started only *after* this upheaval. It is alleged, therefore, that sectarianism was fanned by the Pakistan government as a divide-and-rule strategy against political mobilization. In the subsequent years people in Gilgit were indeed more preoccupied with sectarian conflict than with a struggle for political change, although voices that demanded political and constitutional rights never died out.

Since the late 1980s, Gilgit witnessed the formation of new opposition against the political status of the area. This opposition was increasingly framed in *nationalist* terms. Local activists postulated a nation of the Northern Areas as different from the Pakistani nation. This difference was represented as being based in history, culture and the unique linguistic and geographical conditions of the Northern Areas (Sökefeld 1997a: 296ff., Sökefeld 1999b). Nationalism was a dual strategy as it emphasised not only the difference between the Northern Areas and Pakistan, denying the right of Pakistan to determine the fate of the area, but also affirmed the 'natural' unity of the people of the Northern Areas as a nation. According to the nationalists, to promote this unity which had been endangered by the disruptive strategy of Pakistan was an objective of primary importance. Sectarianism was considered the greatest threat to national unity.

Yet, in the beginning of the 1990s, opposition to the political status of the Northern Areas was clearly marked by the sectarian divide. There were two political projects. The first one demanded the separation of the political fate of the Northern Areas from the Kashmir dispute, questioning that the former Gilgit Agency had ever been a part of Jammu and Kashmir state in a meaningful sense, and favoured the inclusion of the Northern Areas as a regular fifth province into the state of Pakistan. The other project affirmed the historical and cultural relations with Kashmir and demanded the merger of the Northern Areas with Azad Kashmir, and on the long run, with the whole of Jammu and Kashmir.[15] While the activists that endorsed the first project were mostly Shias and Ismailis, although there were also some Sunni supporters, the second project was favoured exclusively by Sunnis, most of them Kashmiris.[16] The sectarian rationale behind the different projects is obvious: Shias and Ismailis feared becoming an insignificant minority in a predominately Sunni State of Jammu and Kashmir whereas Sunnis feared remaining a minority within a province of the Northern Areas in Pakistan.

The nationalist vision of the Northern Areas evolved from the provincial project. But the nationalists who belonged to the small local parties Karakorum National Movement (KNM) and Balawaristan National Front (BNF) envisaged their project in a way that endeavoured to accommodate the Sunnis too. They delimited the projected homeland and territory of the nation of the Northern Areas in a way that would guarantee almost numerical equality of Sunnis and Shias within its population.[17]

The BNF organized a conference on the political status of the Northern Areas which took place on 9 April 1993. Most local parties as well as local sections of Pakistani political parties like the Pakistan People's Party and the Pakistan Muslim League participated. The speeches delivered on this occasion were characterized by a high readiness to cooperate in spite of differing political aims. The conference was remarkable for the fact that it brought together also some local politicians that were at the same time important leaders of the Shia and Sunni communities. The participants expressed the view that internal political differences had to be postponed in order to achieve a change in the political status of the Northern Areas and they argued for unity in opposition to the oppressive grip of the Pakistani bureaucracy.[18] Speakers reiterated the allegation that Pakistan promoted sectarianism in the Northern Areas, and called for sectarian harmony. As a result of the conference, the 'United Front of the Northern Areas' (*Shumali Illaqajat Muttahida Mahaz*) was founded as a body in which different political organizations collaborated for a common cause. This committee organized demonstrations, press conferences and other political events during the following years. Some of these activities were repressed by the authorities. Although violent sectarian tensions in which more than twenty persons were killed swept Gilgit again in August 1993, the United Front of the Northern Areas did not break up but continued its activities.

Here I am not interested in the political success or failure of oppositional political groups in Gilgit but in their reframing of the religious issue by projecting a nation of the Northern Areas. The nationalist groups interpreted sectarianism as an instrument of power employed by the Pakistan government in order to maintain control over the Northern Areas. The alleged divide-and-rule strategy was then countered by a new politics of representation which depicted the people of the Northern Areas as a nation that needed to be united and that was different from Pakistan.

This attempt to replace the difference of religion by a difference of nations occurred in a complex web of overlapping discourses. There was no clear and unequivocal demarcation between 'political' and 'religious' discourses in Gilgit. Especially, Shia activists drew a number of connections between both issues by alleging that sectarianism had to be understood as a disruptive governmental strategy against political commitment and change, and also by representing the political discrimination against the Northern Areas as a discrimination against mainly Shias. The issue was further complicated by the unstable political situation in Pakistan, characterized by frequent changes of governments and policies. As a rule of thumb it can be said that any Pakistani national party exhibited a more sympathetic position towards the Northern Areas as long as it was in opposition, but that it receded from reform schemes as soon as it came into government. As a consequence, even members and activists of Gilgit branches of these national parties participated in political activities against Pakistani control of the Northern Areas.

Certainly, religious discourse and religious antagonism did not become completely replaced by nationalist discourse and the emphasis of national unity. But during the 1990s, Pakistan indeed emerged much clearer as 'the other' of the Northern Areas than ever before.

LOCALITY VERSUS RELIGION

The last case refers to a reverse change of differences: here the attempt was not to supersede the religious divide by some other difference, but religious difference became significant in a conflict about village common lands that arose originally in a framework of locality. This conflict occurred in Manot (a pseudonym), one of the more peripheral *mohalle* of Gilgit. Due to legal uncertainty and a great number of intertwined perspectives the issue is very complicated and can be presented here in an abridged form only.[19]

Because agriculture in Gilgit depends on irrigation, irrigated land (*abadi zamin*) is distinguished from unirrigated land. In the past, unirrigated land was mostly common land of the village (*khalisa-e deh*). The recognised original inhabitants of a village (*muthulfau*) were entitled to use this common land for grazing and other purposes, and they could also take certain portions of it into individual possession. *Khalisa* was thereby turned into *nautor*. Formerly, the usefulness of khalisa was rather restricted and therefore only small portions were appropriated as nautor. In most of the cases this happened only when the irrigation system was extended so that additional land could be cultivated. But for some decades land in Gilgit was in much more demand for construction purposes than for cultivation. The price of land had risen sharply and also unirrigated khalisa that can be turned into nautor had become very valuable. A prescribed procedure had to be followed in order to make pieces of khalisa into nautor. Only muthulfau were entitled for such allotment. Applications for allotment had to be publicized and they needed the approval of both the settlement office and the lambardar.

For a number of reasons land in Manot was very much sought after by newcomers in Gilgit. As it happened, the correct rules of procedure for the allotment of nautor had rarely been followed. In contrast to irrigated land, unirrigated khalisa was relatively abundant in Manot. After the freedom struggle of 1947, khalisa had been allotted as *inam* to non-muthulfau veterans. Because khalisa was plenty and its usefulness quite limited, there had been no local complaints against this practice. Complaints started when during the 1970s and 1980s such effectively illegal allotment continued and the remaining khalisa dwindled.

In the beginning of the twentieth century, only five families had been registered as muthulfau in the settlement records of Manot. All of these were Shias and Yeshkun. At the time of the next settlement, a few more families were registered, among them a Sunni family that had come from Chilas and that was accorded all rights of muthulfau. Other families had given some land in Manot to this Sunni family. One of the original muthulfau families also converted to Sunni Islam. In the 1990s, muthulfau had become a small minority of the population of Manot. Most of the inhabitants were newcomers from Nager, all of whom were Shias, and from Hunza, who were either Shia or Ismaili.

Over the generations, the Sunni family from Chilas became relatively rich and powerful. Contrary to the original Shia muthulfau, they were well-educated. Today, the villages have a dual structure of authority. Although the lambardar has lost most official functions, he continues to be a person of high respect. His 'office' is passed hereditarily from father to son. Since the early 1970s, on the other hand, there are elected 'members' who represent the village in the municipal committee and who are responsible, among other things, for the development of the mohalle. They deal with the administration and wield considerable influence. In some parts of Gilgit, the lambardars have also become members. Not so in Manot. Here, the lambardar family was uneducated and promised little in the difficult negotiations with modern administration. Therefore, members belonged always to influential immigrant families. In 1993, the office of member had been for two electoral periods with the Chilasi family.[20]

Until that year, the muthulfau had become more and more incensed because of the alleged practice of illegal allotment. They pointed out, first, that people from outside that had no right at all had been allotted nautor, and second, that certain persons who had some right to nautor had got much more land than they were entitled to. In the beginning of 1993, the muthulfau of Manot, with the exception of the Sunni immigrant/muthulfau of the village,[21] occupied an area of nautor that in their view had been allotted illegally. They tore down the walls surrounding a few plots, planted some trees there and demanded that the land was re-allotted among the villagers of Manot. But the settlement office confirmed that the previous allotment had been correct and prohibited the irrigation of the newly planted trees which consequentially were about to die from drought.

The muthulfau of Manot lacked the means to defend their rights legally. For seeing through a juridical process on the matter of nautor they required much more resources for advocates and bribes than they could afford. Formerly, their issues had been represented to the judiciary as well as to the authorities by members of the Chilas family, but now the villagers accused this family of having collaborated in and gained from illegal allotment. Therefore, they had to seek other alliances. Already before, they had combined with the inhabitants of the neighbouring village of Haban (a pseudonym) which, situated a little further down the slope, shared the water channel with Manot. The muthulfau of Manot described those of Haban, the majority of who were also Shias, as much more shrewd and skilled in the business of modern local politics. In a similar case which had occurred in the early 1980s, the muthulfau of both Haban and Manot had successfully demanded allotment. At that time also the inhabitants of Haban got some of the khalisa of Manot allotted. Now the Shia muthulfau of Manot were also supported by people from Hunza and Nager who had settled in the village. They participated in the occupation of land. It turned out that all supporters who did not possess any original right to nautor in Manot were Shias like the overwhelming majority of the muthulfau. They had been promised a share of nautor in case of success, whereas the Sunni muthulfau were excluded. Also, people of Haban, who offered their assistance again, were denied a share because, as I was told, there was too little land left.

The Shias did not talk openly about the exclusion of the Sunnis. To the contrary, the persons involved preferred not to mention this fact. Yet the Sunni muthulfau accused the Shias of turning the conflict about nautor into a sectarian issue. The Shias denied that the Sunnis were excluded because of a sectarian rationale and explained that their exclusion was due to the fact that the Sunnis were originally people from outside who had taken advantage of the 'real' muthulfau for much too long.

Here, the religious difference became a base for the recruitment of support. According to their own self-assessment, the Shia muthulfau of Manot were not resourceful enough to defend what they considered their right. They had to win others to support their cause, to contribute funds for the planting of trees and for subsequent legal procedure. These others were not ready to offer assistance without return and had to be baited with the promise of a share of khalisa. Yet, as a consequence of promising land to people not entitled to it, the Shia muthulfau lost part of their legitimacy and became accused of sectarian action. A power strategy of the Shia muthulfau, then, was interpreted as sectarianism by the Sunnis of Manot. The events in Manot can be related to the polarization of society in Gilgit due to the Shia–Sunni conflict. In the context of religious polarization religious affiliation was readily available as a base for recruiting support in an originally unrelated issue.

DIFFERENCE, MULTIPLICITY, INTERSECTIONALITY

All the three cases I discussed here dealt with the redefinition of dichotomies of self versus the other and showed that a choice of others was available in Gilgit for contrastingly crafting selves. Conventional approaches to identity which, for instance, singled out ethnicity as the 'most basic identity' which structures social action (Barth 1969) are challenged by this setting. 'Basic' is indeed the whole environment of differences that provides meaningful contexts for a range of different, and at times, contradicting ways of action. This challenge is taken up by desisting from ascribing any specific content to the opposition of self and other. However, this purely formal, structural dichotomy, which supposes a simple binary relation, still predicates a singularity of identity. Such a singularity is refuted by the multiplicity of identities in Gilgit. The presentation of my three cases showed that identities which no doubt are often supposed by actors as being structured by a singular and basic relation/opposition of self versus the other are strongly challenged by other constructions of that opposition. We observe a multiplicity of relations of selves versus others that in many cases assume singularity but that anyway have to take multiplicity and intersectionality into account. Difference, combined with multiplicity and intersectionality challenges and destabilizes identity. Movements of identity politics take efforts to stabilize a particular identity at the expense of others. Differently defined selves and others contradict and threaten each other with erasure. According to Brah (1996: 124), 'collective identity is the process of signification whereby commonalities of experience around a specific axis of differentiation, say class, caste, or religion, are invested with particular meanings. In this sense, a given collective identity partially erases but also carries traces of other identities. That is to say that a heightened awareness of one *construction* of identity in a given moment always entails a partial erasure of the *memory* or *subjective sense* of internal heterogeneity of a group.'

Even if one difference is supposed to erase another one, traces of the difference-to-erase remain. The foregrounding of qom-identity (being Yeshkun) rather than religious affiliation always reminded of the sectarian divide because it arose precisely in the context of the threat that sectarianism posed to qom. Similarly, the nationalist discourse continually referred to the problem of sectarianism, never stopping to attribute it to nefarious action of the government of Pakistan—that is, to the other in nationalist discourse. By trying to negate the difference of religion through the introduction of the difference of nation, sectarianism was effectively retained *within* that discourse, but its significance was changed from being an essential and violent actuality to being the product of an adverse other.

The nationalism of the Northern Areas can be read as a re-identification and re-construction of an identity/difference that has been eclipsed by Pakistani politics. The alleged production of Shia–Sunni tensions by the government was interpreted as an element of this politics of erasure. Yet it was not the only one. Equally important was that the Northern Areas were deprived of their political agency. The *de facto*—but not *de jure*—inclusion of the Northern Areas into Pakistan implied the area's incapacitation in the political arena which is represented in nationalist discourse as a new colonialism (Sökefeld 2005).

In the political struggle between the Northern Areas and Pakistan the intersectionality of identities/differences becomes most obvious. From the Pakistani perspective, the Northern Areas were 'the other' that had to be accommodated and to come to rest within a shared national identity of Pakistan. But this accommodation could not be realized due to the entanglement of the Northern Areas in the Kashmir dispute. *Différance* is exemplified by the Northern Areas' uneasy and unresolved position as being both part and non-part of Pakistan. At the level of individual political rights this condition is expressed by the inconvenient position of the people of the Northern Areas: Like the people of Pakistan—but unlike the Azad Kashmiris—they were subject to martial law after Ziaul Haq had assumed power in 1977, but they were denied democratic rights when the rest of the country was liberated from dictatorship in 1988.

From the nationalist point of view, the identity of the Northern Areas was threatened both from within by sectarianism and from the outside by the disempowering politics of Pakistan. The threat of sectarianism from within was certainly more dangerous because it shifted the struggle to another site and effectively denied nationality as a fundamental identity by postulating religious affiliation as being more basic. The attribution of this apparent threat from within to the enemy from outside by declaring Pakistan responsible for sectarianism was an ingenious move that turned the threat to nationality into its affirmation. For what had seemed to be fragmenting the 'national' self of the Northern Areas and thereby to question its actuality turned out to be a disruptive strategy of an other (Pakistan) that was aiming at the national self and affirmed it thereby.

In the case of Manot, finally, an important aspect of the conflict was the question of which difference was to be applied to the issue in order to specify its meaning. Was it a matter of Shias versus Sunnis or of muthulfau versus newcomers? The meaning of the dichotomy of self versus other was decisive for the legitimacy of the contested claims.

The multiplicity of identities/differences in Gilgit is obviously not composed of diverse elements that are either situated on an equal level or that are inserted into an uncontested hierarchy of inclusion and exclusion. Instead, these identities/differences are related by continuous struggle, questioning the legitimacy of other differences or reducing them to a subordinate position. Homi Bhabha (1994) distinguishes *diversity* and *difference* as relations between identities, the first being unproblematic, characterized by clear boundaries and derived from a taken for granted universal frame, while the second is characterized by mutual questioning and challenge, that is, by intersectionality. The multiplicity of identities in Gilgit clearly falls into Bhabha's category of *difference*. There is no solution to the contradiction of identities which is acceptable for all and for all time. Nationality can neither be generally subordinated to religious affiliation, nor the other way round. Persons who derive identities from both conflicting differences have to live with that conflict and ambivalence, perhaps by almost 'compartmentalizing' their life and attributing primary importance to either of the differences in shifting contexts. Also, a staunch nationalist values his religious affiliation more than the presumed nationality when it comes to marriage. The possibility to compartmentalize means that the discourses of different identities intersect only at certain, crucial sites.

While discourse can construct social identity in less ambivalent ways, arguing, for instance, unequivocally for the primacy of the nation, personal identity has to be conceived of as a complex chain of identities in which each one necessarily supplements—and partly erases—another identity. We could conceptualize personal identity as a sequence of appendices that explain, specify, reframe, limit, question and restrict one another. Personal identity is subject to the condition of *différance* in that its final and total meaning is always deferred by the intervention of other differences and their social and political predicaments (Sökefeld 1999a).

This was expressed by Mohammad Ali, a student who was active in oppositional politics and in forging qom-identity among young Yeshkun. He tried to explain to me what he was in the following terms: 'At first I am Pakistani. Then I am Gilgitwala because I have been born in this area. And I am Yeshkun; this is very important because this is my blood. But the most important of all is religion because one has to think about what comes after death. Therefore I am Shia in the first place.' For him, each of his identities comes first although this results in an apparently unfeasible, contradictory totality. I recorded his statement at a time when nationalism in Gilgit had only started to develop and when most oppositional activists still opted for the regular accession of the Northern Areas to Pakistan as a fifth province. In the subsequent years Mohammad Ali's political stance might well have changed to a more radical nationalist position resulting in that his being Gilgitwala effectively replaced and erased his being Pakistani.

CONCLUSION: REPRESENTING MULTIPLICITIES OF IDENTITIES

In this chapter I outlined an approach for the conceptualisation of multiple identities in Gilgit town, framing identity within the three dimensions of difference, multiplicity and intersectionality. In the conclusion I would like to outline some consequences of the present approach.

1. Although Gilgit is a place with particular historical and political conditions that generated a social configuration with a high degree of multiplicity, I am of the opinion that this is neither an extraordinary condition nor that other places are necessarily less characterized by multiplicity. I do not know a single village in the Northern Areas that does not display a considerable multiplicity of intersecting differences derived from descent, migration, locality, language, religious affiliation or

other conditions, and I suppose that the same holds true for other regions of the Himalaya as well. If we extend the discussion to other sources of difference, like gender, age or class, it becomes clear that the multiplicity of differences is not a special but rather a general human condition. Anthropological studies of identity, ethnicity or, in general, oppositions of self versus other accordingly should analyse the intersectionality of multiple identities/differences rather than single out a particular difference at the expense of others. We have to explore and acknowledge a plurality of perspectives in analogy to what Nigel Rapport calls 'epistemic diversity':

> Any attempt to force social life into one or other perspective ends in tautology and serves only to destroy the 'reality' under study. To adopt an eclecticism of narrational style, however, is to free one's account from an obsessional Aristotelian combat between battling singularities. And only in such eclecticism—locating human behaviour in more than one frame of reference at once; locating such (often mutually exclusive) frames of reference in conversation with one another—can one escape the notion that, ultimately, epistemic diversity can and should be 'resolved' in terms of a finite limit of possibility (society; structure) or an ultimately determining and integrating code (God; grammar) (Rapport 1997: 183f.).

2. The emphasis on intersectionality also changes the conceptualization of single identities. If we take into account that different differences relate to one another or, more precisely, are related to one another by the actors that embody them, it becomes impossible to conceptualise identities/differences as essences. When, as in the example of Gilgit, nation and qom are employed to challenge religious difference, or when religious affiliation is used to increase power in a conflict originally defined by locality, we see that identities may be employed consciously as strategies to achieve certain ends. They are part of power games in which actors attempt to level out inequality of power by inverting or reframing differences. Essentialism is a strategy itself. Nation or qom are indeed represented as timeless essences that possess almost fathomless historical depth and that are irrevocably anchored in the core and bottom of every human being. There is even a kind of competition for the greatest 'essentiality' among intersecting differences like religion and qom. Essentialism has to be rejected as an analytic approach but it nevertheless remains a powerful topos in the discourses of identity that we study.

3. Being attentive to the intersectionality of multiple differences directs attention to an aspect of human life that largely remains a blind spot in

much of anthropology: individuality, the unique conditions of each human self (Cohen 1992, 1994). From the approach to identities outlined here follows that it is not sufficient to simply sort individual human beings into a grid of groups or collective identities. Rather than being self-evident, the constitution of groups and categories becomes a problem. Every human being occupies a specific and unique subject position within the multiplicity of intersecting differences. Further, not all individuals invest to the same degree into particular identities (Rattansi 1995). This element of choice was most obvious in the question of national identity because not everybody in Gilgit subscribed to a shared nationality of the area. A similar difference of investment into identities also applies to qom and religion. Accordingly, human beings have to be represented as agents who more or less self-consciously act with the differences at hand within the constraints of a specific historical and political setting.[22]

4. The deconstruction of the dichotomy self/other into a multiplicity of selves and others also has consequences for the great 'meta-dichotomy' that provides the fundament for the anthropological approach: the dichotomy of the anthropologist as self versus his/her objects of study as other—a dichotomy which is still sometimes represented as parallel to the (not less questionable) dichotomy of West versus non-West. Critical works, most importantly Fabian (1983), have shown that this dichotomy, too, is not a given but the outcome of a process of other*ing* (and, conversely, self*ing*) which is actively if often unwittingly put into motion by the anthropological approach. Being attentive to the multiplicity and intersectionality of differences demands the dissolution of this unequivocal and unequal dichotomy into a plurality of relations between the anthropologist (as a subject) and the *subjects* he or she studies that can signify both difference and identity. This perspective is put into practice by female and feminist anthropologists who have access to areas of life that, due to the difference of gender, are mostly closed to male researchers. We are required to not only look out for differences but also for continuities between their lives and ours—continuities that, after all, as Tim Ingold (1993) reminds us, are a necessary precondition for the feasibility of the anthropological project.

GLOSSARY

inam — remuneration
julus — procession
lambardar — village headman
motobaran — respected elders
nautor — 'newly broken' land

NOTES

1. This text is a revised version of a paper read at the workshop *Representation of the Self and Representation of the Other in the Himalayas: Space, History, Culture*, Meudon, France, 25–26 September 1998. It is based on fieldwork in Gilgit undertaken from 1991 to 1993.
2. The 'self', too, is a concept with many meanings. In the present context of multiple oppositions of selves and others the self refers more to what I otherwise call 'identity' and not to the 'person' or the 'individual' that embraces and embodies such identities. Relations between both aspects of the self are discussed in Sökefeld 1999a.
3. Qom is a very ambiguous term with a number of significances. Here, I use the term for those groups that in the older literature of the area had been referred to as 'castes' or 'tribes' (e.g. in Biddulph 1971). It is generally maintained that the members of such groups are related by kinship but not necessarily by common descent. Sometimes, these groups are also called 'ethnic groups' but because I see no advantage in replacing one ambiguous term by another one I stick to the local term (Sökefeld 1998b).
4. See Sökefeld 1997a: 38ff. for a more complete exploration of such categories and their pitfalls.
5. The Ismailis form a third religious segment in the population of Gilgit town but because they do not take part in the antagonism they are not considered here.
6. For a more complete and detailed history of sectarian conflict in Gilgit see Sökefeld 1997a: 205ff.
7. Muslims are only allowed to eat meat from animals butchered by Muslims. When people in Gilgit refused to consume meat that was provided by butchers of the other sect, their refusal amounted to the tacit conclusion that the others were *kuffir*, i.e. non-Muslims.
8. As a qom, Yeshkun define themselves first of all in opposition to Shin. Shin and Yeshkun are considered the two important autochthonous qom of Gilgit. The relationship between both groups is not devoid of ambiguities and vacillates between strong rivalry and only casual delimitation (Sökefeld 1994). In the discourse considered here, the relation between the qom was envisaged as antagonism.
9. Some Shin told me the same about Yeshkun.
10. In the religious topography of Gilgit, some neighbourhoods were much more prone to getting involved in sectarian clashes than others. The part of the town to which I refer here had invariably been involved.
11. A Sunni mullah had been killed and this murder was instantly framed as a sectarian incident by Sunnis who openly accused Shias of the crime. Shias, in return, accused Sunnis of fanning sectarianism by holding Shias indiscriminately responsible for all such incidents, without any justification. An outbreak of clashes was prevented by

the strong presence of police and military. Later, it turned out that the victim had been killed by his own son-in-law because of some family issue. The atmosphere in Gilgit, however, remained very tense.

12. This strict reply does not mean that there are no marriages between Shin and Yeshkun. Although both groups are mostly described as endogamous in the literature, intermarriages do occur. Yet it is true that such intermarriages are generally regarded much more critically by Shin than by Yeshkun.
13. Although both quasi-kinship groups like Shin and Yeshkun and political nations are locally referred to as qom, I use the English term for the political nation in order to prevent confusion.
14. See Sökefeld 1997a: 284ff.
15. Azad Kashmir was separated from the rest of Jammu and Kashmir in 1947 by a successful uprising of Kashmiri Muslims who were not ready to accept the expected declaration of accession of the state to the Indian Union. Azad Kashmir has its own government and parliament and is officially independent of Pakistan in internal affairs, but in fact Azad Kashmir is completely controlled by and dependent on the government of Pakistan.
16. These Kashmiri of Gilgit are the descendants of migrants from Kashmir that were already settled in the area in the eighteenth century as artisans and peasants. Today, they form a considerable segment of the town's population and occupy one of its most central mohalle, Kashrot. They all speak the Shina language and have to be distinguished from subsequent migrants from Kashmir that came as merchants only after Gilgit was conquered by Sikh and Kashmiri troops.
17. According to this project, a section of the district Kohistan which is inhabited by Sunnis only and which now forms part of the North West Frontier Province was to be included in the territory of the Northern Areas in order to increase the numerical strength of Sunnis.
18. *Khabrain* (Urdu Daily), 13 April 1993.
19. For a more detailed analysis see Sökefeld 1998a.
20. It is quite questionable to label this family still as 'immigrants' and this already points to a significant change of perspective in the conflict.
21. That is, both the descendants of the immigrants from Chilas that had been registered as muthulfau and the family of original muthulfau that had converted to the Sunnah did not take part in this action.
22. I explored this issue in Sökefeld 1999a.

CHAPTER 11

Islam, the State, and Identity: The Zikris of Balochistan

INAYATULLAH BALOCH

Islam, like other world religions, subscribes to the principle of religious tolerance. Its basic texts emphasize restraint in the use of force in matters of belief. In actual practice, however, the dominant sect of Islam has not always maintained these principles. There are numerous examples in the history of South and South-West Asia of minority Muslim sects which have been persecuted by majority groups as well as by states. The government of Afghanistan's campaigns against the Shias in the nineteenth century is, perhaps, the best-known example. This study focuses on a little-known Islamic sect, the Zikris, which has also suffered due to its heterodox belief system. It takes a historical approach to view relations between the Zikris and other religious and ethnic groups in the region, and to challenge the claim of contemporary opponents of the Zikris that they have always been considered to be heretical by orthodox Muslims.

BACKGROUND

Most Zikris live in southern Pakistan, primarily in Makran and Las Bela in the province of Balochistan and in Karachi in the province of Sindh. Small populations are also found in Iran as well as in the Arab Gulf states. Most of Makran's population is divided between two Muslim sects, known locally as the Namazis (Sunnis) and the Zikris (pronounced Zigris in the Balochi language). The name Zikri is derived from the Arabic word *zikr*.

The current numerical strength of the sect is not known. Before 1947, it was estimated that Zikris formed 50 per cent of the total population of Makran, though some sources now place the Zikri population in Makran at only one-third or one-fourth of the total (BDG Makran 1906:112; India 1913:56; Masson 1843:294). The leaders of the Zikri sect, on the other hand, claim that non-Zikris underestimate their numbers. Census reports published by the government of Pakistan do not provide figures.

The city of Turbat in Kech (Kej) Makran is holy to Zikris. There they have constructed the Koh-e-Murad, which Zikris assert is a shrine but which some orthodox Muslims charge they consider to be a Kaaba akin to the one in Makkah.[1] The principal Baloch sub-groups belonging to the Zikri sect are the Sajdis, the Sangurs, the Rais, the Darzadas, the Meds, and the Koh-Baloch. In addition, some followers of the Zikri faith are also found among the Baloch nomads in the Khuzdar and Kharan regions of eastern Balochistan.[2]

ORIGIN OF THE ZIKRI SECT OR ZIKRISM

The history of the origin of the Zikri sect and its belief system is obscure. The sect was persecuted in the eighteenth century by Mir Nasir Khan the Great, the Sunni Muslim ruler of the Khanate of Balochistan centred in Kalat. At that time nearly all of the sect's religious and historical records were destroyed, and the information which survives is from the few religious works which were preserved, oral traditions, and the writings of non-Zikris. The Zikris claim to be the followers of Syed Muhammad, who they consider to be the Mahdi. The renowned Arab sociologist-historian Ibn Khaldun was the first to study Mahdism systematically and critically. In his major work, *The Muqaddimah*, (1958:156) he wrote:

> It has been well known (and generally accepted) by Muslims in every epoch, that at the end of time a man from the family (of the Prophet [PBUH]) will without fail make his appearance, one who will strengthen the religion and make justice triumph. The Muslims will follow him, and will gain domination over the Muslim realm. He will be called the Mahdi. Following him the anti-Christ will appear, together with all the subsequent signs of the Hour (the Day of Judgment), as established in (the sound traditions of) the Sahih (genuine). After (the Mahdi), Isa (Jesus) will descend and kill the anti-Christ. Or, Jesus will descend together with the Mahdi, and help him kill (the anti-Christ), and have him as the leader in his prayers.

This popular Muslim belief is not supported by the Quran or the authenticated traditions and sayings of the Prophet of Islam (*al hadith*). Nevertheless, the concept of the Mahdi remains part of Muslim traditions, though Shia and Sunni Muslims differ in their formulation of it. There is a long list of individuals in Muslim history who have claimed to be the promised Mahdi. In the fifteenth century, Syed Mohammad Jaunpuri claimed to be the last Mahdi, and scholars generally agree that he or one of his disciples was the founder of the Zikri sect (Bosworth 1981:222; Ahmad 1969:29; Ross 1868:26–7). There is some dissent from this view, however. Some Zikri traditions claim that the Mahdi came to Makran from Attock, for example. Another view was put forward by Haji Nabi of Kabul, who claimed that the Zikri sect was founded by a follower of Bayazid Ansari. This view is not in accord with the teachings of Bayazid Ansari, however, who regarded himself as a 'perfect man' (*mard-e-kamil*) and not the promised Mahdi (Shafi 1961:1121–24).

Syed Mohammad Mahdi was born in 1443 in Jaunpur (in present-day Uttar Pradesh) to a family of Syeds, descendants of the Prophet of Islam (PBUH). Syed Mohammad was a great scholar of Sunni Islam, and toward the end of the fifteenth century he declared himself the Mahdi. He converted hundreds of Muslims (including some prominent rulers) and Hindus to his belief system, but he faced considerable opposition from the *ulama* because of his revolutionary teachings. He migrated to Farah, near Herat in Afghanistan, where he died in 1505 (Bosworth 1981:222). Zikri sources claim, however, that the Mahdi lived in Makran and from there went to Makkah, Medina, Syria, and Turkey, and returned to Kech Makran via Iran. In Makran he spent most of his time in *zikr* at the Koh-e-Murad. According to Zikri tradition, he preached his doctrine, eventually converting the whole of Makran, and then disappeared (Ibrahim 1986). Some followers of the Mahdi of Jaunpur live in India, where they are known as Mahdawi (see Fig. 1), and some Mahdawi migrated to Pakistan in 1947 (Rizvi 1965:68–105).

Figure 1: Muslim sects in south and south-west Asia

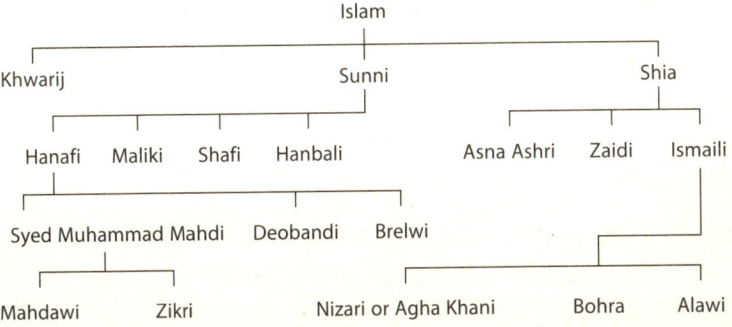

THE ZIKRI DOCTRINES

The principle doctrines of the Zikri faith may be summarized as follows:

1. The mission of Prophet Muhammad (PBUH) was to preach the doctrines of the Quran in their literal sense, but it remained for the Mahdi to further elucidate its meaning. Syed Mohammad Mahdi was in fact the interpreter (*Sahib-e-Tawil*) of the Quran.
2. The Prophet Muhammad (PBUH) is the last prophet and Syed Mohammad is the last Mahdi.
3. The traditional declaration of faith (*kalima*) should be dropped in favour of a new *kalima*, 'There is no God but Allah. Mohammad Mahdi is his messenger.'
4. Instead of prayer (*salat* or *namaz*), people should recite *zikr*.
5. The fast (*som* or *roza*) of Ramadan should be replaced with a monthly seven-day fast.
6. Instead of the Islamic tax on wealth (*zakat*) at the rate of one-fortieth, Muslims should pay a tax on crops (*ushr*) at the rate of one-tenth.
7. The world and the goods of this world should be avoided. People should distribute their wealth among the poor and needy.

Thus, Zikri doctrines deviate from orthodox Muslim belief but Zikris consider themselves to be true Muslims. The Zikris have certain practices in common with another Middle Eastern minority sect, the Alawis, who possess no mosques because of the absence of the prescribed prayers (*namaz*) in their faith (Eickelman 1981:221–9). The Zikris' places of worship, both temporary and permanent, are known as *zikrana* or the *zikrkhanah* (house or place of the zikr). There are two forms of the zikr, the spoken recitations (*zikr-e-jali*), and the recitations repeated inwardly (*zikr-e-khafi*) which are performed six times a day (Qadiri 1967:60–1; Sindhi 1973).

Despite their doctrinal differences there are many Sunni influences on Zikri religious beliefs and practices, and on their socio-political life. Both sects regard the Quran as their holy book and as the final revelation (*wahi*) and actual words (*kalam*) of Allah. Both sects stress the importance of the simple expression of faith in the teachings of the Quran and the traditions (*Iman Mujmal*), and the formal declaration of belief in the six principles of Islamic ideology (*Iman Mufassal*): Allah, the angels, the holy book of Allah, the prophets, the Day of Judgement, and the predestination to good and evil. Zikris also observe the Islamic practices of marriage contracts (*nikah*), divorce (*talaq*), funeral customs (with the exception of *namaz*), and the prescribed method of slaying an animal (*zabah*) without which its flesh is not *halal*. Zikris also believe in the importance of Haj. Above all, both sects believe in the principle of holy war as the war against injustice and exploitation (*jihad*), which is regarded as a major pillar of the Islamic faith. Among the Muslim jurists, Zikris have great regard for Imam Abu Hanifa, the founder of the Sunni Hanafi school of law. In addition, the day-to-day life of Zikris, their names, and their culture are part and parcel of Baloch Muslim traditions.

ZIKRISM AND THE SOCIO-POLITICAL SYSTEM IN MAKRAN

The Mahdi's egalitarian teachings influenced social and political life throughout South and South-West Asia. Mahdawi sources claim that a number of rulers in the region either accepted the Mahdawi faith or were influenced by it. But the Mahdi's message had its greatest and most enduring impact upon the people of southern Balochistan, where the rulers and populace embraced his teachings, and Zikrism was for centuries associated with the area's ruling dynasties. Some scholars contend that Zikrism spread through Makran with the rise of the Boledi dynasty in the seventeenth century. These sources, which have been cited in British official reports, have neglected Zikri works such as the *Dur-e-Sadaf* written by Qadi Ibrahim, a Zikri scholar and judge who lived in the eighteenth century. Ibrahim mentions the conversion of members of the Malik dynasty in the early sixteenth century and describes their services to Zikri Islam (Ibrahim 1986:60–1; see also, Nadeem 1967:67).

Because of Mir Nasir Khan's destruction of Zikri documents and religious records, we have no primary sources of information about the socio-political system of the Zikri state in Makran. Based on the indirect evidence that survived, Ross, a British Political Agent in Makran, has suggested that a proto-federation existed under the Zikri rulers of independent Makran. The capital of the state was situated at Kasrkand-Geh in present-day Iranian Balochistan, while the religious centre was at Turbat (Ross 1868:15, 34; Curzon 1892:260; Qadiri 1967:60–1).

Although it is impossible to tell how they were institutionalized, the doctrines of Syed Muhammad Mahdi are likely to have influenced the socio-political system during the period of Zikri rule. His teachings relating to socio-political life can be summarized as follows (see, Bugti 1967; Qadiri 1967; Baloch 1938:65–7; Mahdi 1982:5–7):

1. Society should be based on egalitarian principles under which private property is abolished, economic resources are distributed equally, and a joint labour system is established.
2. After a person's death his or her personal property should be distributed among the needy members of the community.
3. Followers of the Zikri faith should be treated equally irrespective of their ethnic origin. The criterion for acceptance and success in Zikri society was adherence to Zikrism. This is illustrated by the Gichki clan, which rose to the religious and political leadership of Makran in the early eighteenth century despite its Indian origins. Had ethnicity been the sole criteria for leadership, rather than ideology, it would have been difficult for the Gichkis to rule the Baloch tribes and their country.[3]
4. Mutual help and co-operation were religious duties for Zikris. This concept remains valid among the Baloch of Makran and is known as the *bijar*.
5. Contrary to the practices of orthodox Muslims, women could participate in the community's public socio-religious life. This tradition persists in Zikri society.

Under Zikri rule, Zikri–Baloch culture flourished due to the patronage of the ruling elite. Nadeem (1967) provides a survey of the works of a number of Zikri poets, including Hamal Jihand Hoat and Malik Dinar Gichki, whose war ballads in Balochi throw light on the history of Baloch resistance to the Portuguese and Iranians (see also, Baloch 1977:351–60; Nasir 1977:176–85; Baloch 1986:3–5 and 1987:59–61). Some Zikri rites of worship are conducted in Balochi; in consequence, Zikri poets and religious scholars have enriched Balochi literature. In fact, because they attach religious significance to sites there, the Zikri have developed a special reverence for the land of Balochistan. For them Balochistan, and especially Turbat, is the *Gul-e-Zamin* (Flower of the Earth) (Hashmi 1986:123–4). This patriotic attitude on the part of the Zikri Baloch is the forerunner of modern Baloch nationalism.

EXTERNAL RELATIONS OF THE ZIKRI STATE

In the sixteenth century the major factors shaping the politics of Makran were tensions between Shia Iran and the Ottoman and Mughal empires, and the expansion of Portuguese mercantilists. It should be remembered that the coast and harbours of Balochistan were important strategically and commercially for the Ottoman Caliphate and for Mughal India, which sought to keep the sea trade routes open between south and west Asia and to protect pilgrims to Makkah against Portuguese and Persian attacks (Shedai n.d.:15–17; Farooqi 1989). In the sixteenth century the Ottoman fleet, under the command of the Admiral Sidi Ali Reis was sent by the Caliph Sultan Sulaiman Qanuni to punish the Portuguese and to ensure the safety of the ships of the *hajjis*. According to Sidi Ali Reis, the ruler of Makran, Malik Jalal, and his administration provided the Ottoman fleet with material help, facilities, and ships. The Zikri state acknowledged the supremacy of the Ottoman Caliph and promised further co-operation (Reis 1895). Had the Zikris viewed themselves as a separate religious community they might have co-operated with the Portuguese, as did Safavi Iran. It is important to note that the Zikri belief system went unmentioned in the memoirs of the Ottoman admiral, thus it is unlikely that he regarded them as heretics or infidels.

Zikri relations with other states in the region were generally good. Despite religious differences, relations with Shia Iran were cordial, with the exception of a short period of hostility when the Persian governor of Hormuz made an unsuccessful attempt to occupy Makran (Lorimer 1915:2151). Relations with Oman, ruled by the Khwarij Muslim sect, were also friendly, and the two states were jointly involved in trade with East Africa. Indeed, after the fall of the Zikri state, many Zikris took refuge in Oman, some joining the Sultanate's army where they achieved high rank (Ross 1868).

In addition, relations with Mughal India and its ally, the Mirate (later Khanate)[4] of Kalat, were friendly. Prince Aurangzeb (later the Mughal emperor of India) visited South-West Asia during the reign of his father, Shah Jahan (1628–58). Aurangzeb, known for his orthodoxy, did not denounce the Zikri faith (Baloch 1977:234). Moreover, the Sunni ruling family of Kalat, the Ahmadzai Kambarani, married their daughters to the Gichkis of Panjgur, then followers of the Zikri sect (Nasir 1952b:83). The policy of Kalat's rulers suggests that the authenticity of the Muslimhood of the Zikris was not an issue until the rise of Mir Nasir Khan in the latter half of the eighteenth century.

Mir Nasir Khan the Great (1749–94) was the first Sunni ruler to invade Makran on religious grounds. Balochi traditions, war-ballads, and nationalist writings suggest that Nasir Khan's invasion of Makran was the result of pressure from the religious elite as well as his own expansionist designs. A careful study of the invasion provides us the following insights:

1. Nasir Khan was an ambitious ruler who wanted to unite all the regions of Balochistan under a single political umbrella. To this end he undertook as many as twenty-five military expeditions.
2. The conquest of Makran gave him an opportunity to enrich his treasury through control of commercial routes and the region's fertile oases (ibid.:109–10; Baloch 1987:105).

In order to justify his invasion Nasir Khan played the sectarian card against the Zikris.[5] During the invasion of Makran, Nasir Khan either killed or arrested large numbers of Zikris and defiled the graves of their patron saints. The bones of the latter were exhumed and burnt with horse-manure (Field 1959:62). The invasion of Makran was opposed by the Afghan ruler, Ahmad Shah Durrani. Had it been purely a religious war, it is likely that Ahmad Shah, himself an extremely religious person, and the Afghan ulama, who commanded great influence in the royal court, would have supported Nasir Khan against the Zikri 'apostates' (Ram 1908:108–9; Baloch 1987:104–5). The last Khan of Kalat, Mir Ahmad Yar Khan (1934–48), justified the invasion by his ancestor on religious grounds. He claims that Nasir Khan declared a religious war against the Zikris after he had a dream in which the Prophet (PBUH) instructed him to destroy the sect, and that as a result of the invasion the Caliph in Istanbul rewarded him for his services to Islam.[6] The persecution of the Zikris is a tragic chapter in the history of the Baloch people and one which contrasts with their tradition of tolerance.

Despite this treatment, the Zikris continued to regard themselves as members of the Muslim *ummah*. They fought against the British in support of the successors of Nasir Khan in the early nineteenth century, and took part in the Pan-Islamic movement and other resistance movements in the late nineteenth and early twentieth centuries.[7] In contrast, some Muslim minority sects, notably the Ismailis and Ahmadiyas, co-operated with the British against the anti-colonial struggles of the nations of South-West Asia.[8]

MAKRAN UNDER THE KHANATE OF BALOCHISTAN

To consolidate authority in Makran, Kalat replaced the Zikri political system. Makran was declared a province of the Khanate, and it was administered by a governor (*naib*) appointed by the Khan. A class with vested interests in the new arrangement was created by granting fiefs and other privileges to certain families, as well as by establishing marriage alliances between them and the Khans. Under the new system, Makrani society was divided into the following categories:

1. The nobles or power-elite (*hakimzat*). This class consisted of former and newly-appointed members of the ruling elite, most of whom came from such groups as the Boledis, Gichkis, Nausherwanis, and Bizenjos, as well as the Rais.[9]
2. The tribes (*tumannat*). This group consisted of both the nomadic and settled members of Baloch tribes.
3. The servants (*hizmatgar*). This was the lowest class in the new system and its members were obliged to serve the *hakimzat*. They could be called upon to supply forced labour (*bigar*) for unlimited time at their own expense in any part of the country. In addition, they were forced to pay various kinds of taxes. Slaves were the most oppressed subgroup of the *hizmatgar*. It was a practice among the members of the *hakimzat* to present a slave to a bridegroom, which often resulted in the division of slave families. The *hizmatgar* class was made up of various ethnic groups including the Meds, the Darzadas, the Naqibs, and the Loris.
4. Merchants and traders. Most members of this class were not Baloch but rather Hindus, Afghans (known as Kabulis), or Ismailis.

The majority of the Zikris were members of the servant and tribal categories (Ross 1868:21–6; Pastner and Pastner 1977:121–2).

To minimize the strength and influence of the Zikris, Nasir Khan and his administration introduced Sunni Shariah law and abolished the Zikri legal system, which was based in part on Baloch tribal custom (*riwaj*). The introduction of the Shariah was used to exert pressure on the Zikris in order to bring them into the fold of Sunni Islam. The forced conversion of Zikris to the dominant sect was not the primary goal of Kalat, which sought above all to acquire the economic and commercial resources of Makran (Baloch 1987:105; Nasir 1952b:109–10), but the use of religious chauvinism enabled the attainment of those goals.

After the death of Nasir Khan, successor Khans did not pursue his policy towards the Zikris (see Table 1). The information collected by the British military and political officers provides no evidence of forced conversion of Zikris to Sunni Islam after the death of Nasir Khan or during the period of indirect British rule in Balochistan.[10]

Table 1: Policies of the Khans of Kalat toward the Zikris

Period A (1695–1749)	Mir Ahmad II (1695–1714)	Non-interference; limited control; marriage-alliance; treated the Zikris as Muslim
	Mir Abdullah Khan (1714–34)	
	Mir Mohabat Khan (1734–49)	
Period B (1749–94)	Mir Nasir Khan the Great (1749–94)	Interference; Zikris declared to be apostates; genocide; destruction of the Zikri state
Period C (1794–1933)	Mir Mahmud Khan I (1795–1817)	Non-interference; the policies of Nasir Khan the Great abandoned.
	Mir Mehrab Khan (1817–39)	
	Mir Hassan aka Nasir Khan II (1840–57)	
	Mir Khudadad Khan (1857–93)	
	Mir Mahmud Khan II (1893–1931)	
	Mir Muhammad Azam Jan Khan (1931–3)	
Period D (1933–48)	Mir Ahmad Yar Khan (1933–48)	Discrimination in the judicial system against Zikris; propagation of Sunni Islam among Zikris

IMPERIALISM, BALOCH NATIONALISM, AND THE ZIKRIS

The Baloch nationalist movement was founded in 1929 by a group known as the 'Young Baloch' under the leadership of Mir Muhammad Yusuf Ali Khan Aziz Magassi, the first president of the Anjuman-e-Itehad-e-Balochistan (henceforth the Itehad [Unity] Party). The founding fathers of Baloch nationalism were influenced by the Young Turks, Kemalist Turkey, the Bolshevik Revolution, and the nationalist movement in British India. The influence of these movements and their ideologies can be observed in the programme of the Itehad Party and in the statements and writings of Yusuf Aziz Magassi. To promote nationalism and patriotism Magassi called for the Baloch people to work for the following principles and goals:

1. The unification and independence of Balochistan.
2. A democratic and socialist system guided by Islamic universalism.

3. The abolition of rule by tribal *sardars* (*sardari nizam*).
4. Free and compulsory education for the Baloch people, and equality for Baloch women.
5. The promotion of Baloch culture.

Magassi believed that Baloch unity and the independence of Balochistan depended on socio-political changes in Baloch society (Baloch 1987; 1986:6–9; 1984–5; 1980). His call to promote Baloch culture, including the code of honour (*Balochmayar*), was also linked to principles of social equality and political liberation. In the traditional Baloch code of honour all Baloch were viewed as equal, and a sardar was considered first among equals. Though these egalitarian relations were undermined in Makran in the eighteenth century when Kalat imposed structural changes on the society, they were largely maintained in other parts of Balochistan, especially those in which nomadic pastoralism was the dominant subsistence pattern. During the nineteenth century, British intervention in the civil war between the Khan and the Baloch chiefs paved the way for the Sandeman system (*sardari nizam*), under which government subsidies and military support increased the power of the sardars over the common Baloch. Seeking to transcend tribal boundaries and create a Baloch national identity, Magassi and the Itehad Party opposed the sardars. He accused them and the British of introducing social division and economic disparity in Baloch society (Baloch 1987:151–4).

The Itehad Party also opposed communalism and sectarianism (Magassi 1933), a policy which encouraged minorities such as the Zikris to support it. The Zikris were the most active group in Baloch society in promoting the cause of Baloch nationalism.[11] There are two explanations for this. Firstly, the Zikris were an oppressed people who had lost considerable socio-political status after the middle of the eighteenth century. Secondly, the Zikri religion promotes a socio-economic system which stresses equality and justice.

Throughout the first stage of Baloch nationalism, 1929–48, the movement's leaders were opposed to communalism. They did not often address the issue of sectarianism because it was not a threat to Baloch unity. The situation facing the Zikris was linked with that facing the Baloch nation as a whole, and their belief-system was viewed as a private affair. Neither British official reports nor the Baloch nationalist Press hinted at sectarian rifts in Makran during this time. The first discussion of the history and beliefs of the Zikris to appear in a nationalist newspaper was published in *Al-Hanif* (Jacobabad) in 1938. Entitled 'The Zigris', it was written by a nationalist Islamic scholar, Maulana Abdullah Baloch, a close associate of Magassi. The article mentioned the 'deviant' doctrines of the Zikris which were contrary to the dominant orthodox version of Islam, but it did not depict them as infidels, non-Muslims, or *murtadeen*. The tone and the language of the article was cordial (Baloch 1938:65–7).

Magassi died in the Quetta earthquake of 1935. His death was a great loss for the Itehad Party and the Baloch people. His successors could not keep the party intact, and it split into three (see Table 2).

Table 2: Baloch Nationalist Political Parties (1929–93)

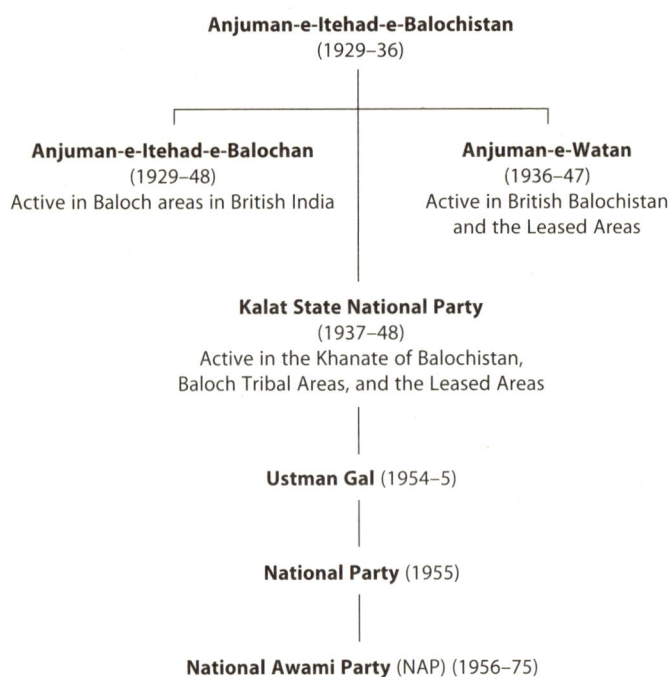

Successor organizations of the NAP

Awami National Party (ANP)
Pakistan National Party (PNP)
Balochistan Liberation Organization (BLO)
Balochistan National Movement (BNM)

The Baloch People's Liberation Front (BPLF) and the Baloch Students Organization (BSO) have also been affiliated with the NAP.

The Kalat State National Party (KSNP) was the successor organization to the Itehad Party in the Khanate, the Baloch Tribal Areas and the Leased Areas. The KSNP also extended its activities into Iranian Balochistan, and it played an important role in the socio-political life of Makran. It actively supported the political demands of the oppressed sections of Makrani society. Several of their demands were implemented through a *farman* of the Khan (Bakhsh 1970:142–4). They included:

1. The abolition of forced labour (*bigar*).
2. The abolition of two taxes, the *zar-e-sar* and *zar-e-shah*, the hakimzat levied upon the subject races. Children and disabled persons were not exempt from these taxes.
3. The abolition of slavery. Although slavery had officially been abolished in Kalat during the reign of Mir Khudadad, it remained in practice.

Among the sardars these reforms created resentment and opposition to the Khan. The confrontation between the modernists and the conservatives resulted in a ban on the KSNP although it continued to work underground in the Khanate (Baloch 1987:154–8). Facing pressure from the sardars, the Khan, Ahmad Yar Khan, established the Ministry of Religious Affairs, with which he sought to promote orthodox religious consciousness. The new ministry established Shariah courts in Kalat and Makran; it also sent Islamic preachers to create greater awareness of Islam (Bakhsh 1970:142, 150–3). Through this ministry the Khan attempted to create a religious lobby in order to pressure the sardars and the British colonial administration. The growing influence of the ulama in Makran was of great concern to the British, who viewed it as a threat to their authority and interests in the region. The sectarian teachings of some of the ulama, particularly those of Maulana Abdul Samad Sarbazi, also alarmed Baloch nationalists in Makran. In 1938, Maulana Sarbazi, a supporter of the Khan who later served as the chief judge (*qadi*) in Kalat, wrote a religious book in which he issued a religious proclamation (*fatwa*) calling for the physical elimination of the Zikris irrespective of their age and sex. Before its distribution, the book came to the attention of Muhammad Hussain Anka, then editor of *Balochistan*, a nationalist newspaper published in Karachi. In a letter to Nawabzada Shahbaz Khan Nusherwani, a former president of the KSNP, Anka warned of the consequences of Sunni–Zikri conflict.

> I want to make an urgent request to you that you draw to the attention of the His Highness [the ruler of Kalat] that Maulana Abdul Samad Sarbazi has recently published a book entitled *Tabara-e-Islam bar Kahur Zigrian*, and has brought it with him. In it he has given the *fatwa* that the killing of the Zikris with all their kith and kin is not only lawful but it is also the order of the Quran and the Hadith. It is a very dangerous book. It will provoke such bloodshed among the Baloch that even the riots of the Hindu–Muslim in India will appear insignificant. It is the wish of the British Government that we fight each other and die so that they rule comfortably. But is it the same wish of Mir Ahmad Yar Khan? If it is not so then he should ban the book and should not allow its distribution in his state. The matter is urgent. A similar type of *fatwa* has produced bloodshed in the area of Sarbaz [Iranian Balochistan] and eight Zikris have been killed. The [owner of the] printing press will not allow me to publish [arguments against it] because the Government of Sind will create trouble for him due to my article.[12]

Nawabzada Nusherwani informed the Khan about the anti-Zikri publication, and the Khan blocked the book's distribution in Kalat State. Maulana Sarbazi was able to distribute a few copies in Karachi which went unchecked by the administration of Sindh, though literature propagating communal or sectarian hatred was banned under the Penal Code of British India.

The Baloch nationalist movement prevented the religious elite from developing sectarianism in Baloch society. British colonial reports (including the Administration Reports and the Fortnightly Reports) provide no evidence of Zikri–Sunni riots in the Khanate, or the forced migration of Zikris from Kalat state.[13]

THE ZIKRIS AND THE CONSTITUTION OF KALAT (1947)

Leaders of fundamentalist and orthodox religious political parties in Pakistan claim that the Zikris had non-Muslim status in the Khanate of Kalat, though their literature fails to provide any documentary evidence in support of their claim. On the contrary, official publications such as the *Gazetteers* and the Census Reports, which were prepared with the knowledge and cooperation of the Khanate of Kalat, treat the Zikris as a heterodox Muslim sect. When Kalat became an independent state under the terms of a constitution promulgated on 1 August 1947, the Zikris were treated as Muslims. The constitution did not define terms such as Muslim and non-Muslim, but by examining the structure of Kalat's parliament, it is possible to determine who was considered to be non-

Muslim. The parliament consisted of two houses, an upper house of tribal lords, the *Dar-ul Umara*, and a lower house of commons, the *Dar-ul Awam*. The upper house consisted of all hereditary chiefs and the lower house of fifty-four members, forty-nine of whom were elected and five of whom were nominated by the Khan.[14] Five seats out of the forty-nine elected seats were reserved for non-Muslims, and these were contested by Hindu candidates. Zikris were included on the Muslim list. There is no written evidence that the Sunni ulama ever demanded parliamentary legislation to establish the non-Muslim status of the Zikris (see, Kalat 1947; Bakhsh 1970:298–305; Nasir 1957:512–16; Creagh Coen 1971:147; Amin 1988:71, 108).

When the state of Kalat celebrated its first independence day on 15 August 1947, the Khan addressed worshippers at the grand mosque in Kalat and in his speech stressed the need to achieve Baloch unity and the establishment of an Islamic state. On the same day (the 27th day of Ramdan), the Zikri Muslims were peacefully performing their religious rituals (*ziyarat*) at the Koh-e-Murad in Turbat. Neither the Khan nor the orthodox ulama made any attempt to forbid the alleged Hajj or to declare the Zikris non-Muslims for performing it.

THE ZIKRIS AND NATIONALIST IRAN

Western Balochistan became part of Iran in 1872 under the Perso–Baloch agreement signed by the states of Kalat and Iran. The demarcation of the Perso–Baloch frontier was supervised by the British representative, General Goldsmid; it resulted in the partition of Makran and thus of the Zikris. The former capital of the Zikri state, Kasrkand, and the region of Sarbaz, inhabited largely by Zikris, became part of Iran. Many Baloch, both Zikris and Sunni, refused to accept the division of their homeland and resisted Persian rule.

In the late nineteenth century, the politics of Persian Balochistan were influenced by Pan-Islamism as propagated by Syed Jamal-ud-Din and Caliph Sultan Abdul Hamid. Their influence led to Baloch revolts against Persian rule and against British control of eastern Balochistan. During the First World War (1914–18) a number of Baloch tribes, irrespective of their beliefs or sectarian affiliation, took part in uprisings which were guided by the Turko–German alliance. The British expected a sectarian rift between Zikri and Sunni Baloch as a result of growing pan-Islamic sentiments, but no such rift developed. Despite the influence of Islamic political movements, most Baloch were largely secular, and the Sunni majority made no effort to impose their belief system on the Zikri minority. In turn, the Zikris supported the cause of their co-ethnics with whom they shared kinship, cultural, economic, linguistic, and historical ties. The subsequent defeat of the Turko–German alliance and disintegration of the Ottoman Caliphate was a set-back to those nationalists of South and South-West Asia who had hoped for moral and material help from the alliance in their struggles for independence (Baloch 1987:143–5; India 1923:5–7; India 1910; von Niedermayer 1925; Griesinger 1916; Nasir 1952b; Curzon 1892; Leghari 1980; Madni 1954; Sindhi 1933).

In 1925, however, the Baloch tribes of Makran under the leadership of Mir Dost Muhammad Khan Baranzai did establish an independent state in Persian Balochistan which lasted until 1928. In 1925, Iran came under the rule of Reza Shah, the founder of the Pahlavi dynasty. He implemented an aggressive policy towards minority ethnic groups aimed at their Persianization and at restricting their autonomy. In 1928, the Iranian army defeated the Baloch forces in western Balochistan. The Shah's rule resulted in the decline of the secular tribal elite in western Balochistan and the migration of Baloch to Kalat, British India, the USSR, and Afghanistan (Baloch 1987:144–5).

The decline of the secular tribal elite in Iranian Balochistan gave rise to an orthodox religious elite, many of whom were trained at Deoband in British India. In the 1930s, Sunni Islam became an important factor in preserving Baloch identity against Iranian nationalism, which was expressly Shia and Persian. The increased influence of the religious elite had a negative impact on relations between Sunni and Zikri Baloch, however. The Sunni elite's efforts to create a homogeneous Sunni culture in order to counter the influence of Iranian national culture led to Sunni–Zikri riots in the Sarbaz region in the 1930s and further migrations of Zikris to eastern Makran (Kalat State). These events did not go unnoticed by the Baloch nationalists in the Itehad Party and the KSNP, and they demanded that Reza Shah's government resettle the refugees and protect the religious rights of Baloch minority sects. Though the government agreed to these demands, most refugees refused to return to Iran out of fear. Most of the Zikris settled near Turbat, while some went to Karachi seeking better economic opportunities (Baloch 1987:143–5).

Iran's current policy toward the descendants of the Zikris who remained is not known. The Islamic Republic of Iran promotes the concept of Muslim unity, therefore it has adopted a cautious policy towards its non-Shia Muslim population. It seems that the Zikris are considered to be part of the Sunni sect. However, some years ago the killing of a Zikri religious leader and some of his followers in Persian Makran were reported in a Zikri publication which blamed the Sunni mullahs of Iran for the murders (Baloch 1979:41–2; Baloch 1991).

THE ULAMA, POLITICAL PARTIES, AND THE ZIKRIS IN PAKISTAN

It has been claimed that the Pakistan movement's goal was to establish an Islamic state, though this view is contested by Muslims with liberal, ethnic-nationalist, and socialist political views. They refer to M.A. Jinnah's speech to the first Constituent Assembly of Pakistan, in which he declared religion a private, individual affair and said that the new state's religious minorities have rights equal to those of the majority (Baloch 1982 and 1989). Since then the history of Pakistan has been characterized by ideological conflict between the two major schools of thought, i.e., modernist Muslims and Islamists. Modernists ruled Pakistan from 1947–77, while the reign of General Ziaul Haq can be classified as Islamist. In the first phase the power elite was opposed to communalism and sectarianism. During this period a number of men, who were not Sunni such as Jinnah, Sir Zafrulla, and General Muhammad Yahya Khan, led the country. Their interpretation of Islam stressed the need for religious harmony, and they envisioned a Muslim welfare-state, instead of a Shariah state (see, Asghar Khan 1985). It is true that in Pakistan's early years sectarian conflict erupted when the predominantly Sunni ulama demanded that the Shariah regulate public life, and that the Ahmadiya sect be declared non-Muslim. These demands were largely ignored by the western-educated elite who were committed to modernization and a re-interpretation of Islam. The ulama continued to agitate against the Ahmadis, and in 1953, anti-Ahmadiya disturbances in Punjab resulted in loss of life and the imposition of martial law (Punjab 1954:231ff).

This situation alarmed other minority Muslim sects, especially the Ismailis and the Bohras (both Shia sects), the Mahdawis and the Zikris. In 1954, leaders of the Zikris and Mahdawis founded the Zikri–Mahdawi Organization, aimed at safeguarding their religious and social rights. The organization issued the following statement accusing *Shariah* courts in Makran, run by the Sunni qadis, of treating the Zikris as non-Muslims:

> The kidnapping of a Zikri female by a Sunni has been justified under the *Shariat-e-Muhammadi*. There are several instances of such practices. Moreover,

the local courts refuse to accept the Zikris as witnesses (*gawah*). The Zikris have been deprived of their rights provided under the Muslim Personal Laws [Mustafai 1955:70].

The state of Pakistan did not respond to the allegations made by the organization, though the authorities continued to regard the Zikris as Muslim in official publications. Political parties in Balochistan such as the Ustman Gal and the National Awami Party viewed the issue as part of the Baloch national question as well as the struggle between communal and secular forces.[15]

In 1974, the Bhutto government passed legislation declaring the Ahmadis to be non-Muslims, a step that paved the way for the rise of sectarianism in Pakistan. When the Bhutto government was overthrown in a military coup led by General Ziaul Haq in 1977, the military junta, which had no popular base in the country, used the call to implement Shariah law to establish legitimacy for its undemocratic rule. Because of its Islamization programme, some Sunni ulama and orthodox religious political parties supported the military regime. In 1978, several religious political parties organized the Tehrik Khatm-e-Nabuat (Movement for the Finality of the Prophethood) in Balochistan and launched an aggressive campaign against the Zikri Muslims. The following are the major assumptions and demands of the fundamentalist ulama and their parties in regard to the Zikris (Haq 1984; Hayat 1974; Baloch 1992):

1. The Zikris are *kafir*, therefore they should be declared non-Muslims by the state.
2. Marriages of Muslims (Sunnis) with Zikris are forbidden in Islam, and existing inter-sectarian marriages stand revoked.
3. Animals slaughtered by Zikris are not *halal* therefore Muslims (Sunnis) should not eat or buy them.
4. Muslims should not help or co-operate with Zikris.
5. Muslims should not attend the festivals and funerals of Zikris.
6. The Zikri shrine at the Koh-e-Murad should be destroyed.

In 1978, General Ziaul Haq responded to the demands of the ulama by promising to appoint a judicial committee to report on the legal status of the Zikris in Islam (Haq 1992:105). Meanwhile, Makran's civil administration asked the local Sunni ulama to submit their views about Zikri doctrines. A study entitled *A Glance at the Zikri Sect* (*Zikri Firqa Par Ek Nazar*) was prepared which concluded that:

1. The Zikris were declared *murtadeen* by Nasir Khan the Great, therefore they are non-Muslims.
2. The Zikris are not followers of Syed Mohammad Mahdi. (This view was asserted because the Sunni ulama accept the Mahdawi as Muslims).
3. The Zikris engage in deviant practices (Hayat 1974).

In 1984, Maulana Abdul Haq of the fundamentalist Jamaat-e-Islami prepared a report on the Zikri sect in which he accused the administration in Makran of being pro-Zikri and demanded that the Zikris be declared non-Muslim. Moreover, the ulama and the religious parties have organized processions, meetings, and other efforts to interrupt Zikri religious ceremonies (Masti Khan 1990; Ahmed 1987).

As mentioned above, General Zia promised the ulama he would appoint a judicial committee to determine the status of the Zikris in Islam. But events such as the revolution in Afghanistan, and demands by some Baloch leaders for a separate homeland, forced him to distance himself from the sectarian conflict in Balochistan. Therefore, a direct confrontation with the Zikris, whose sympathies are generally with the Baloch national movement, was avoided. On the other hand, an indirect anti-Zikri policy was adopted which encouraged the ulama and religious political parties to act against the Zikris.

During the period of Zia's rule, the Sunni ulama and the religious political parties published a vast literature of a communal and sectarian nature on the Zikri sect which went unchecked by law enforcement agencies.[16] On the other hand, scholarly works on human rights were banned under the Press and Publication Ordinance.[17] Janmahmad, a Baloch official in the provincial administration, made the following remarks concerning the government's policy toward the Zikris during this time:

> A systematic campaign against the Zikris was started by the orthodox clergy with official encouragement. The mullas not only incite the people to violence, but openly condemn the Zikri Baloch traditions and their cultural heritage. The Baloch people belonging to any sect, whether Zikri, Sunni, Shia or Ismaili, are secular in their approach; the clergy have started a campaign of vilification against the Baloch in general. All such efforts are guided from outside Balochistan with the active connivance of supporters of world imperialism like Saudi Arabia, which is backing the movement with petro-dollars. Many books and pamphlets have been brought out by the mullas and widely distributed in the area, in which highly objectionable language has been used against the Baloch....

More recently, under active [state] patronage and with Saudi petro-dollars, they [mullas] are becoming more organized and delivering invective harangues against the people. Hundreds of religious educational centres are operating in far-flung areas throughout Balochistan, producing fanatics. The main target is Jhalawan and Makkuran region. Wadh, Panjgur and Turbat have been turned into big mulla camps. Madarasa institutions are operating under foreign guidance with enormous funds. Preachers (*tablighi*) from the Panjab and Sindh are visiting the area more frequently. Their annual gatherings (*ijtimah*), in even remote places such as Wadh in central Balochistan, are attended by Panjabi and Muhajir mullas to preach hatred against the Zikri Baloch. These gatherings are very well organized and financed [Janmahmad 1989:262–3].

These views are not shared by another government official, Akbar S. Ahmed, who was head of Makran's administration during the military regime of Ziaul Haq. He sees the activities of the Baloch Students Organization and tensions between Sunnis and Zikris in the light of super-power rivalry, and does not regard the anti-Zikri ulama as extremist (Ahmed 1987).

The rights of Muslim minorities is an important subject to be discussed in light of Pakistan's on-going programme of Islamization. Supported by the religious elite and financed by foreign governments, this programme has strengthened communalism and sectarianism in the Islamic republic. Under this programme, an educational policy aimed at creating an ideological Sunni Islamic state, and consequently ignoring the cultural rights of the minority Muslim sects, was adopted by the Zia regime. The Ismailis and the Mahdawis, both largely urban-based communities, have been able to promote their interests through private institutions due to their wealth, organizational sophistication, and political alliances. The Ismailis enjoy the support of the international community because of the influence of their religious head, the Aga Khan. The Zikris, in contrast, are an underprivileged and unorganized community. Because their religious beliefs and their history have been ignored in the educational system, their children are open to the influence of foreign ideas, and to conversion to the dominant sect.

In addition to education, Zikris face discrimination and injustice in many other fields in Pakistan. Under the Islamization programme, for example, religious institutions have been financed by the state, but the Zikri Muslims have been denied access to such financial resources. As a consequence, they face obstacles in promoting their cultural and religious rights and in preserving their identity.

BALOCH NATIONALIST PARTIES, THE BALOCH STUDENTS ORGANIZATION, AND THE ZIKRIS[18]

Contrary to the religious political organizations, Baloch nationalist political parties and pressure groups, namely the now-defunct National Awami Party, its successors, and the Baloch Students Organization (BSO) (see Table 2) have defended the rights of Zikris. These organizations advocate secularism and greater autonomy for Pakistan's nationalities, and a majority of the Zikris have associated themselves with them. The most ardent and vocal defender of the religious rights of the Zikris has been the BSO, which was founded in November 1967 with the goal of promoting education in Baloch society and the welfare of Baloch students, a majority of whom come from the lower-middle and working classes. Later, the BSO expanded its objectives, and supported the right of the Baloch to self-determination. Due to the opposition of the fundamentalist forces the BSO suffered heavily at the hands of the administration of General Ziaul Haq. Some of its members were either imprisoned or executed, and others were forced to live in exile. Since 1978, the BSO has been in the forefront of efforts to protect the Zikris from religious persecution at the hands of fundamentalists and their supporters in the governments of Pakistan and the Arab Gulf states.

It would be wrong to suggest that the BSO's support for the Zikris has been the result of Soviet–American rivalry in South-West Asia. In fact, the support of the BSO and other secular forces was based upon their political platforms, which include calls for the separation of state and religion, and a rejection of theocracy. They have organized political rallies to mobilize popular support against sectarianism and communalism in and around Makran. They have also invoked such Baloch cultural principles as Balochness (*Balochiat*) and the Baloch code of honour (*Balochmiyar*), which demand that Baloch defend religious minorities and weak groups. On the intellectual front, the BSO has published and distributed pamphlets and posters explaining the Zikris' passion for the cause of the Baloch nation and Balochistan, as well as their adherence to a Baloch customary law, *nek-wa-bad*, which qualifies a person to be considered a member of a tribe. Despite obstacles created by fundamentalists, and at times, the state, the BSO has been successful in gaining the support of the majority of Makran's Sunni Baloch in defence of the religious rights of the Zikris.

CONCLUSION

Islam advocates religious tolerance and provides a set of laws to deal with relations between Muslims and non-Muslims, but relations between the various sects in Islam have at times been difficult, even bloody. Since there is no single authority to interpret Islamic doctrine, it is open to interpretation and re-interpretation. Liberals, universalists, and extremists have all explained Islam in terms of their own perceptions and interests. Regarding the question of the rights of minority Muslim sects, the ulama who advocate Islamic universalism have opposed sectarianism and communalism. On the other hand, another section of the ulama preaches sectarianism and hatred in order to achieve their social, political, and economic aims. They have been successful when their interests have coincided with those of sections of the ruling classes which have used religious appeals to further their own political and economic interests.

How can the dilemma of sectarianism and ethnic conflict in South and West Asia be resolved? One possibility might be to redefine the political institutions of the region along the lines of the *millat* system developed by the Ottoman caliphate. This system encouraged tolerance and co-existence by granting religious communities (Turkish: *milliyet*) such as Jews, Christians, and Muslims (and various sects within each *millat*) considerable autonomy within the state structure. The *millat* system permitted each community to establish its own courts, schools, and cultural institutions and to use its own language, although Turkish was the language of administration. This system came to an end as a result of the Ottoman's defeat in the First World War and the growing influence of the modern political ideal of nationalism (Baloch 1994).

It is hard to predict the future of the Zikri faith and its followers, but it is certain that their future is connected with the outcome of the struggle between communalists and the nationalist, secular forces in South-West Asia. In this regard it is fitting to quote the advice which Babur, the founder of the Mughal empire, gave to his son, Crown Prince Humayun, which speaks of the responsibility a multi-religious and multi-ethnic state holds for its citizens:

> O my son: People of diverse religions inhabit India; and it is a matter of thanksgiving to God that the King of kings has entrusted the government of this country to you. It therefore behoves you that:
> 1. You do not allow religious prejudices to influence your mind, and administer impartial justice, having due regard to the religious susceptibilities and religious customs of all sections of the people.

2. You should never destroy the places of worship of any community and always be justice-loving, so that the relations between the king and his subjects may remain cordial and there be peace and contentment in the land.
3. The propagation of Islam will be better carried on with the sword of love and obligation than with the sword of oppression.
4. Always ignore the mutual dissensions of Shias and Sunnis, otherwise they will lead to the weakness of Islam.

GLOSSARY

bijar   a Balochi word meaning co-operation and aid
farman   royal order
halal   lawful under Islam
kafir   infidels
murtadeen   apostates
zikr   remembering and recitation; a formula for repeating the various names of Allah

NOTES

1. Abdul Ghani Baloch (1979:24–7), a Zikri, denies that members of the sect perform *hajj* at the Koh-e-Murad. He claims that the Zikris consider the Koh-e-Murad to be a shrine (*ziyarat*). Hittu Ram (1908:669) a native assistant of Sir Robert Sandeman, also described the Koh-e-Murad as the *ziyarat* of the Zikris.
2. Information provided by leaders of the Baloch Students Organization (especially Mr Badal Khan, a former vice-president of the BSO), and Bashir Ahmad Baloch, director of the Balochi Academy in Quetta.
3. See, Ross (1868:35–6) and Maulana Abdul Haq (1992:112). Haq is a leader of the fundamentalist Jamaat-i-Islami party and a member of the Gichki clan.
4. For the distinction between the terms 'khanate' and 'mirate', see, the note on the history of Kalat (in Persian) by Mir Mahmud II, Khan of Kalat. British Record Office, R/1/34/7.
5. Nasir Khan's invasion cannot be treated as an ethnic conflict between Brahuis and Baloch. The army of Nasir Khan the Great consisted of three divisions of both Balochi and Brahui speakers. The army of the Zikris was made up mainly of Balochi speakers although some Brahui-speaking Zikris were also in its ranks. The mother-tongue of the Ahmadzai Khans of Kalat was historically Balochi, though the British political officers categorized them as Brahui.
6. Khan Mir Ahmad Yar Khan has claimed that Nasir Khan the Great was awarded titles by the Caliph in Istanbul for his jihad against the Zikris. The Khan does not provide any documentary evidence to support his claims, and it is more likely that these titles were given to Nasir Khan for his jihad against the Hindus and Sikhs who opposed Mughal rule in India. It is worth noting that the Ottoman Caliphs accepted a number of minority sects as Muslims, including the Alawis, the Yazidis, the Zaidis, and Ashna Ashris. The Alawis and the Yazidis, like Zikris, have no concept of prayers

(*namaz* or *salat*). At one point the first Ottoman Caliph, Sultan Salim I, showed his desire to convert all his subjects to Sunni Islam. That idea was rejected by the *Shaikh-ul-Islam*, who reminded the Caliph that forcible conversion is against the teachings of the Quran. His verdict was accepted by the Caliph.

7. See, Nasir (1952:259–81, 346–7); Sindhi (1933); Leghari (1980); India (1923); Madni (1954).
8. The founder of the Ahmadiya sect denounced the concept of jihad against the British, and his successors supported the British government during the First World War. Sir Aga Khan, the leader (*imam*) of the Ismaili-Shia and a prominent leader of the Pakistan movement, supported Britain against the Ottoman caliphate and instructed his followers in and around Iran to oppose Turko–German interests (see, Kashmiri n.d.:4–15; Baloch 1987:143–5, 260).
9. *Hakom* is a Persian term which refers to a subordinate ruler. The Hoat and Boledi rulers used the titles of *malik* (king in Arabic) and *padshah* (king in Turkish) respectively. These terms signify their independent and sovereign status.
10. Pastner (1978c) claims that numerous Zikris migrated to Karachi due to harassment by their Sunni neighbours in Kalat, though he does not provide any documentary evidence for his claim. In fact, the migration of Zikri and Sunni Baloch took place due to economic pressures, mainly the burden of taxes imposed by the sardars with the support of the British government. The Zikris, like their co-ethnic Sunni Baloch, fought against the British and Persians to liberate Balochistan. Had there been harassment or discrimination on a large scale, it would not have gone unnoticed in the published and unpublished records of the British, who would have exploited it to facilitate their intervention in the Khanate. It should also be noted, however, that the work of the Pastners on contemporary Zikri society provides many valuable insights.
11. Information obtained in interviews conducted in 1977 and 1985 with Mir Ghaus Bakhsh Bizenjo, Nawabzada Mir Shahbaz Khan Nusherwani, and Mir Muhammad Hussain Anka.
12. The letter, dated 20 August 1938, from Mir Muhammad Hussain Anka to Nawabzada Shahbaz Khan Nusherwani (the younger brother of the ruler of Kharan state) has not been published. I am grateful to Nawabzada Nusherwani for providing me the original letter, and to both men for the information they provided in interviews.
13. British Library, I. S. 33, and V/i 0/635.39. *See*, Baloch (1987:260) for a list of unpublished records.
14. Amin (1988) has denied that elections to the lower house of the Kalat parliament were held, though he has not consulted the official records of Kalat State or British India.
15. Information obtained from interviews with Sardar Ataullah Khan Mengal and Mir Ghaus Bukhsh Bizenjo.
16. Some of the sectarian works that distort Zikri history include Hayat (1974); Majid (n.d.); Ahmad (n.d.); Siddiqi (n.d.); Ehtisham-ul-Haq (n.d.); Haq (1992).
17. See, the following Pakistani newspapers and magazines: *Viewpoint*, 26 February 1986, 12 March 1987, and 21 May 1987; *Pakistan Times*, 28 January 1987, 3 February 1987, and 7 May 1987; *Dawn*, 10 February 1985.
18. For details, see, National Awami Party n.d.; Ustman Gal n.d.:13–14; Baloch Students Organization 1967 and n.d.:4; *Balochi Duniya*, June 1973. See also, letter from Mir Bizen Bizenjo to the author dated 28 October 1967.

CHAPTER 12

Sakineh, the Narrator of Karbala: An Ethnographic Description of a Women's Majles Ritual in Pakistan

SHEMEEM BURNEY ABBAS

This chapter consists of an ethnographic account of a women's *majles* (plural *majales*) in Pakistan. The majles will be explored here as a communicative speech event where members of a speech community congregate and participate in an event based on common beliefs, values, and attitudes.[1] The majles will be investigated as an event where speakers and listeners share the knowledge of rules for the conduct and interpretation of speech.[2] The purpose of this study is to provide a sociolinguistic mapping of the women *nowheh*-chanters' discourse in the Pakistani languages using Hymes' model of the ethnography of speaking and how ritual speaking is done in a cultural system.[3] Communicative conduct within a community comprises determinate patterns of speech activity wherein the communicative competence of persons constitutes knowledge with regard to such patterns. I will discuss ways of speaking especially in regard to the Sakineh narratives, focusing on the relationships among speech events, acts, and styles, on the one hand, and personal abilities and rules, contexts and institutions, and beliefs, values, and attitudes, on the other.[4] This is demonstrated through transliteration, translation, and linguistic representation of the order of a women's majles. The transliterations represent the social interactional processes of the majles and the competence of the female *nowhehkhans*. Because of the transliteration methodology, an analytical discussion of the political aspects of these rituals is not given, though these dimensions are manifest in the nowheh texts themselves and the highly politicized opposition that the poetic discourse generates based on the shared rules of performance among the speakers and the listeners. The transliterations are intended to provide the reader with a clearer understanding of the basic structure and style of a women's majles, which is fairly representative of the rituals analyzed in the other chapters.

This account demonstrates how Sakineh serves as the narrator of Karbala in the nowhehs, or mourning songs and chants, at these Shia majales, which are held during the annual Muharram celebrations in Pakistan. The Sakineh myth is concerned with the structural properties of the Karbala story and how it is narrated in the majales.[5] I focus on the dynamic structure of the Sakineh texts by analyzing the stories in relationship to the contexts in which they are performed, in terms of the potential for openness of interpretation and in terms of the ways in which this potential is exploited during Muharram performance and the emotions generated therein.[6] Sakineh is Imam Hussein's daughter; she survived the tragedy of Karbala along with her paternal aunt, Sayyedeh Zaynab. Sakineh's age is not known with any real certainty, but she was a girl-child whose age was probably between five and twelve years. Many of her discourses in the oral tradition are addressed to her sister Sughra, who, according to some *hadith*, was left behind in Medina due to illness. Thus, while Sakineh is the speaker in the stories, Sughra is sometimes the listener to whom the stories are addressed. The nowheh, a song of lament, can be sung as a dyadic unit in which two parties take turns in advancing the story, or it can be chanted as a monologue. Both women and men have participated in the tradition of chanting nowhehs. In a two- to three-hour majles, at least an hour is allocated to reciting nowhehs. Thus, in the chanting of the Sakineh nowhehs, there is a long tradition of mutually understood speech between speaker, hearer, and that which is spoken about, including the political dimensions of the discourse. The mutually shared speech is elaborated in communication theory, linguistics, semiotics, literary criticism, and sociology in various ways.[7]

The nowhehs that are transliterated and translated here, along with the photos provided, were collected during fieldwork in Pakistan during Muharram in 2000. Sakineh embodies grief and evokes a sense of tragic empathy in the assembly of mourners when the nowhehs are chanted in this girl-child's voice. This is a special emotional feature of a Shia majles, according to Hymes' model. Sakineh, as a survivor of Karbala, tells many stories in the aftermath of her father's death. Girl-children are trained to re-enact the stories of Sakineh at Shia majales in Pakistan during ritual Muharram celebrations.[8] These rituals are characterized by the ritualized speech form of nowhehs, which involve linguistic play based on code-switching.[9] Furthermore, the nowhehs have strongly embedded political references: the binaries of a high moral and ethical order versus expediency and moral corruption that led to the Battle of Karbala. Between speakers and listeners in the shared codes of communicative competence the references are mutually shared and interpreted.

The first ten days of Muharram constitute a period of ritual mourning among Shias in Pakistan. Majales are held to lament the martyrdom of Hazrat Imam Hussein in the battle of Karbala in CE 680. During the Muharram celebrations, majales are either held in public Shia *Imambarehs*, which are supported through community funds, or in the private imambarehs that the well-to-do have in their homes in the cities and in rural areas. An imambareh is a public or private space in a Shia community for performing sacred rituals such as prayers, majales, and birth and death rites. The wealthy *sayyeds*, who are descendants of the Prophet Muhammad (PBUH) and typically owners of large landholdings, have private imambarehs in which rituals are enacted in an elaborate manner.[10] Generally, the pattern of the ten-day celebrations in the Muharram majales is as follows:

First to fifth of Muharram: re-enactment of events on a day-to-day basis according to the Karbala tragedy, accompanied with ritual lamentations and self-flagellation (*matam*).

Sixth of Muharram: narratives about Karbala and enhanced matam.

Seventh of Muharram: new rituals are introduced, such as carrying a replica of Ali Asghar's cradle, Qasem's henna ceremony, and Sakineh's nowhehs.[11]

Eighth of Muharram: Hazrat Abbas' *alam*, or standard, raised with the *panjatan*.[12]

Ninth of Muharram: general intense mourning with narratives from Karbala.

Tenth of Muharram: Ashura—the day of Imam Hussein's martyrdom. Pakistani Shias fast on this day, breaking the fast in the late afternoon after noontime prayers. The final activity is the *Sham-e Ghariban* ritual, which commemorates the act of trying to find the corpses of the fallen martyrs.[13]

After Ashura and Sham-e Ghariban rituals, the following are observed:

Soyem: Majales are held on the third day after Ashura and Sham-e Ghariban. These majales celebrate the martyrdom of Hazrat Imam Hussein, his family, and his companions.

Chelum: Majales are held for the same reason on the fortieth day after Ashura.[14]

In between the Soyem and the Chelum, majales are held in the imambarehs according to the schedule of the caretakers. However, there is no set pattern. The period of mourning during Muharram is called *azadari*.[15] The mourners are *azadars*. During this period a part of the home in a Shia household may be temporarily converted into mourning space for the purpose of azadari. The mourning area is called an *azakhaneh*.

The women's majales rituals this researcher observed at imambarehs in Rawalpindi, Wah, and Lahore inform this ethnographic account of speaking as a cultural system. However, the rituals documented here are based on a ritual observed on the seventh of Muharram, 2000, in the Baji Sabira ka imambareh in Chowk Marir Hasan in Rawalpindi, which is popularly referred to as the *zaynabiyyeh*.[16] This imambareh is named after its owner, Ms Sabira Zaidi, who is an émigré from North India and who speaks chaste Urdu.[17] The majales in this imambareh follow the elaborate pattern of Lucknow majales.[18]

The zaynabiyyeh was a 50 x 50 foot square structure built at the far end of Ms Sabira Zaidi's home. The imambareh, compared with the rest of the house, was a newer structure and was carefully crafted after the design of Iranian mosques with arched windows and a handcrafted wooden door with intricate floral filigree carved on it. Inside the imambareh was a large crystal chandelier, perhaps of Turkish or Iranian origin. Outside the imambareh was a large courtyard lined with black marble for women *azadars* to sit when there were more attending, especially on the seventh, eighth, and ninth of Muharram. The courtyard was covered with *chatais* or *duris* during the majales for the azadars to sit on. Across the courtyard was a verandah where there were two bathrooms and a row of faucets for women azadars to perform ablution. The *nazr-niyaz*, which were distributed after the majles and which were typically contributed by the azadars, were set up in the verandah.

Ms Sabira Zaidi, who had been recently widowed, looked after the upkeep of the imambareh herself. Ms Zaidi and her daughters worked to keep the imambareh clean for the azadars. Ms Zaidi called herself the *kaniz*, or the handmaiden of the imambareh. This was evident in the well-maintained environment of the imambareh, as well as the owner's hospitality toward the azadars who had come for the majales. Inside the vast space of the imambareh there were large white sheets for the azadars that covered the carpeting on the floor. The white sheets radiated expansiveness in the space in addition to making the female mourners feel they were welcome in the majles. During Muharram, the white sheets were replaced every day.

Women azadars who participated in the ritual majales were mainly Shia. However, there were also Sunni participants, called *molais*, there because they sympathized with Imam Hussein's cause. Participants at the majles consisted mostly of working-class women such as labourers, maids, factory workers, or housewives from low- or middle-income groups. Among the mourners were also some professionals such as doctors, professors, and bank executives. Since the imambareh was in the army quarters and was centrally located, wives of Shia army officers were also well represented. Ms Sabira Zaidi's imambareh has assumed a high stature due to the sophistication of the majales format and its diverse participants.

In this chapter I apply Hymes' mnemonic speaking model to the women's majles proceedings as recorded at the Rawalpindi imambareh.[19] The sociolinguistic, social interactional model involves the following components:

Setting: imambareh; public or private; morning, afternoon, or evening.
Participants: *zakereh*, *nowhehkhans*, hostess, spokeswomen, female audience.
Ends: lamentation, communication, messaging, demonstration, protest.
Act sequence: story, narratives, responses-ratification, interpretation.
Key: mournfully, grieving, passionately, seriously.
Instrumentalities: rhetorical Arabic, Persian, Urdu; chanted Punjabi and Urdu nowhehs.
Norm of interaction: rhetorical discourse and response; poetic discourse and response.
Genre: majles.

The women's majles reported here was a mutually achieved, mutually ratified speech event between speakers and listeners, performers and audiences. Various speakers took the floor according to a pattern of turn taking. The forms of speech—rhetorical, lament and nowheh chanting, *darud*, *salam*, and *salavat*—were adjacent to each other and within the smaller units of talk, where speakers used the pattern of the adjacency pair as demonstrated in Erving Goffman's work on speech.[20] Briefly, Goffman posits that speech constitutes small units of talk; that talk is socially organized, not merely in terms of who speaks to whom in what language, but as a little system of mutually ratified and ritually governed face-to-face action, a social encounter. Accordingly, the performers of this majles who enacted the lamentation rituals participated on various levels, the highest being the zakereh, who initiated the majles proceedings with a well-researched rhetorical discourse about the moral, political, and ethical issues that led Hazrat Imam Hussein to oppose Yazid.

The zakereh initiated her speech with a verse in Arabic from the Qur'an, followed by the hadith, which are the sayings of the Prophet Muhammad (PBUH) or his family. The zakereh was a trained rhetorician and had been inducted into the discourse traditions from childhood. She patterned her moral and political arguments after Sayyedeh Zaynab, who led Hussein's family after the Battle of Karbala. Sayyedeh Zaynab is said to have been a highly effective orator in Yazid's court, where she articulated the ethical, moral, and political polarities that led to the conflict in Karbala. Thus, the zakereh at a Shia majles often re-enacts Zaynab's oratory, reaffirming Levi-Strauss' approach to analyzing myths across societies and his assertion that such myths or stories have an identifiable underlying or abstract structure.[21] The zakereh's speech invariably referred to the girl-child Sakineh and her infant brother, Ali Asghar, who was martyred in Karbala. The discourse of the entire majles, both the prose of the speakers and the poetry of the nowhehkhans, was loaded with political metaphors; the outcome of Hussein's moral stance was the martyrdom at Karbala. The transliterations demonstrate the political tensions of the conflict: Hussein's rejection of accepting Yazid's caliphate on moral grounds leading to his own death and the death of his supporters, who were male family members and loyal companions. Here one may also draw on Levi-Strauss' symbols of life and death, young and old, and men and women.[22] Each nowheh narrative was immersed in political protest articulated through the subtle chanting of the nowhehkhans. The participants were assumed to know the underlying nuances of the discourse, the deeply rooted metaphors that a nowheh pointed toward, such as a male member like Qasem or Ali Asghar. The participants had grown and matured in the oral Shia traditions; they understood the signification. Thus, while chanting with the nowhehkhans, the participants were able to infuse an emotion into the assembly that resulted in intense lamentation, expressed through chest beating, or matam. The matam is a form of political protest.

During the majles proceedings at the zaynabiyyeh, the zakereh's speech was prompted by the hostess, Ms Sabira Zaidi, who sat close to the *mimbar*, or pulpit, at the feet of the zakereh. The hostess continuously ratified the zakereh's speech. Sometimes she ratified it with the *salavat*, or blessings upon the Prophet Muhammad (PBUH) and his family, in Arabic; sometimes she ratified the speaker's discourse with continued lament through her own weeping and utterances like 'hai, hai'. This was particularly so during emotionally expressive outbursts devoted to Sakineh and the theme of Ali Asghar's thirst at Karbala.[23] Again, one may draw upon Levi-Strauss: historical events or fables are transformed through abstract structures. The performers and participants themselves 'posit underlying structures or meanings in the form of interpretations of the symbolism of the text and its message and—the most important point— they do so as part of its very performance, for an audience to hear, learn from and criticize.' Lamentation was communicated at many levels in the majles.[24]

In addition to the zakereh and the weeping hostess, the key performers of this majles were the nowhehkhans, whose communicative competence was demonstrated in their ability to chant the nowheh with an emotion that brought their listeners to tears. The chanters accomplished this through ritual speech, drama, and vibrant body language, beating their chests in rhythm as they chanted the poetry of the nowheh. The chest beating had percussion qualities that brought out the emotion in the assembly; these elements, put together as text and context, created the majles. The assembled listeners, too, performed their function by ratifying every utterance, every move; they were the ones who understood the ritual-ceremonial discourse of Karbala and who understood the linguistic variety involved.[25]

The women's majles ritual at Ms Sabira Zaidi's imambareh lasted for more than two hours. The speech event constituted the speakers, listeners and participants, and rhetorical and poetic narratives about Karbala. The speech event was a mutually ratified, social interactional context that used text and narratives and the relationships of the linguistic and emotional components. Its basic linguistic and communicative structure was as follows:

- Salavat. Opening of the majles with recital of the darud by Ms Sabira Zaidi, the hostess of the majles: '*Allah homma salli ala Muhammad va al-e Muhammad.*' (O God, may thy blessings be on Muhammad and his family). The participants repeated the *salavat* after the hostess.
- Zakereh. Rhetorical prose majles discourse or sermon, which lasted for thirty-five to forty minutes. It started with an Arabic quote from the

Qur'an. The zakereh's speech was patterned on philosophical discourses related to religious, ethical, social, and political issues.
- Salavat. 'Allah homma Salli ala Muhammad va al-e Muhammad.'
- Darud. 'O God may thy blessings be on Muhammad and his family.' The darud, which was frequently repeated at key points in the discourse, was led by the hostess throughout the zakereh's speech.
- Nowhehs. Punjabi or Urdu chants about Karbala, often in Sakineh's voice.[26]
- Matam. Passionate chest beating for lament, accompanied by nowhehs.[27]
- Salam. Prayers and eulogy in Arabic, Persian, Urdu, and Punjabi for the Prophet Muhammad (PBUH), his family, and the martyrs of Karbala. There was always a reference to Sakineh.
- Ziyarat. Invocation and closure in Arabic, Persian, Urdu, and Punjabi for the Prophet Muhammad (PBUH), his family, and the martyrs of Karbala, again with a reference to Sakineh.

On this particular occasion, which was the seventh of Muharram, 2000, Baji Sabira Zaidi had chosen to dedicate the majles to Qasem, Imam Hasan's adolescent son who was about to be married. Thus, on 7 Muharram, the groom's (i.e. Qasem's) henna ceremony was celebrated. The ritual was a celebration as well as a lament for Qasem. After the zakereh completed her rhetorical speech and the recitation of the salvat and darud that the hostess initiated and that the participants repeated after her, the nowhehkhans moved to the centre of the imambareh, creating a little circle for themselves with the hostess among them. The assembly of participating mourners stood around the group of chanters, ready to join the ritual chanting and the matam. The nowhehkhans chanted the key lines and the assembly repeated the lines after them, establishing the communicative mode. The following Punjabi nowhehs, which have been transcribed and translated, demonstrate the communicative competence of the nowhehkhans, who are inducted into these oral linguistic traditions from childhood. Girl-children chanters took the floor immediately after the women nowhehkhans as a part of their training. The group of women who chanted these nowhehs spoke in the voice of a scribe, probably Sakineh, who writes a letter from Karbala to her sister Sughra in Medina:[28]

1.	*Karbal tun peya likhda*	from Karbala the scribe writes
2.	*hun vaqt reha koi nahin*	now time left none there is
3.	*men keya, men likhan*	I what, what can I write?
4.	*mere Awn-o Mohammad te*	my Awn and Mohammad[29]
5.	*Asghar te javan jeha koi nahin*	and Asghar's youth none matches
6.	*men keya, men likhan*	I what, what can I write?
7.	*Karbal tun peya likhda*	from Karbala the scribe writes
10.	*mor vaqt reha koi nahin*	return, time will not

(Next, lines 6–8 are repeated; followed by lines 3–5; followed by lines 6, 8, and 6)

The nowheh-chanters continued to beat their chests to create rhythm with the poetic text:

9.	*Qasem da je nahin likhiya*	Qasem's news none is written
	(Repeat line 9)	
10.	*hun banara bana betha*	now has adorned himself the groom
11.	*khod sehre saja betha*	himself a crown of flowers has festooned
12.	*khod sagan manan betha*	himself celebrated his own ritual
	(Repeat lines 11–12)	
13.	*mere hun hathan te*	mine now on the hands
14.	*hun rang reha koi nahin*	now henna there is none
	(Repeat lines 6–8)	
15.	*hun ki men likhan*	now what I can write?

The nowhehkhans continued to sing the elegy, in Sakineh's voice in Punjabi, thereby symbolically becoming Sakineh themselves. The audiences ratified the chanting by repeating the nowheh text, line by line after the chanters. The girl-children in the assembly chanted significantly as they beat their chests in harmony with the women, taking the floor independently as performers during a part of the chanting. They sang in Punjabi, leading the performance:

16.	*jag nagar gai ujri*[30]	in the world destroyed
17.	*hun kiyun dukh khani*[31] *tun*	now why grief you swallow?
	(Repeat lines 16–17)	
18.	*ummat ne hai aj lutiya*[32]	the followers have today looted
19.	*Akbar di javani nun*	Akbar's youth[33]
	(Repeat lines 18–19)	
20.	*phupian te mavan vala*	paternal aunts and mothers him to claim
21.	*churche de siva koi nahin*	publicity only there is and nothing else remains[34]
22.	*men kiya men likhan*	I what, what can I write?
	(Repeat lines 20–22)	
23.	*meri behnan de hatan hun*	on my sisters' hand now
24.	*rang koi reha nahin*	henna none remains
25.	*hun ki men likhan*	now what can I write?
26.	*Karabal tun peya likhda*	from Karbala the scribe writes
27.	*hun vaqt reha koi nahin*	now time left none there is
28.	*hun ki men likhan*	now what can I write?

The chanters at the zaynabiyyeh sang another nowheh in Punjabi using Sakineh's voice:

29.	*manzur kiyun na hoiyan*	Why were they not accepted?
30.	*ujri*[35] *di an do_avan*	My prayers, I the shattered one
	(Repeat lines 29–30)	
31.	*kuch bol munh hon*	Akbar Move thy lips and say something O Akbar!
32.	*Sughra nun ja bulavan*	Shall I go and call Sughra?
	(Repeat lines 29–30)	
33.	*Sarvar de dil di halat*	The state of Hussein's heart[36]
34.	*bas rab hi janda he*	Only God alone is aware of
35.	*manzur kiyun na hoiyan*	Why were they not accepted?
36.	*Zaynab da dil he aza*	Zaynab's heart is in lament
37.	*qutbe men parh sunavan*	Shall I read an elegy of it?

Sakineh, the Narrator of Karbala

	(Repeat lines 29–30)	
38.	*Saidanian te barish*	On the *sayyedanis*[37] is wreaked
39.	*pathran di ho rahi he*	The thunder of stones
	(Repeat line 36)	
40.	*Ghazi nun ja bulavan*	Shall I go and call Abbas the Ghazi[38]
41.	*qesmat ne jad milaya*	If fortune favors us and we meet
42.	*Sughra gila kare gi*	Sughra will complain
	(Repeat line 36)	
43.	*Akbar nun sehra lavan*	Shall I put the crown of flowers on Akbar?
	(Repeat lines 29–30)	

The Punjabi nowhehs at the majles, accompanied by the matam, were followed by another general matam led by the hostess, Ms Sabira Zaidi. The communicative patterns of the speech event are illustrated through the following transliteration. This second matam was in Urdu and was characterized by a call-and-response pattern:[39]

H: Hussein Hussein	P: Hussein Hussein
/th/th/th th/(repeating pattern)	/th/th/th th/(repeating pattern)
H: Hussein Hussein	P: Hussein Hussein
H: Ali Mowla	P: Ali Mowla
H: Ali Mowla	P: Ali Mowla
H: Ya Abbas	P: Vali Mowla
H: Hai Sakineh	P: Shir Abbas[40]
H: Hai Sakineh	P: Hai Pias[41]
H: Hussein Hussein Hussein	P: Hai Pias

The communicative dimensions of the majles were evident as I could hear the voices of the girl-children in the background repeating 'Hussein' after the hostess. The text and context established its own relationship on many levels within the same timeframe. The ritual chanting with lamentation, like jazz, was cyclical and not linear; there was much in the performance that was repetitive and generated emotion through linguistic play and verbal art on several simultaneous levels. Following the general lament transliterated above, the participants chanted another nowheh in Urdu, this time using Sayyedeh Zaynab as the mythical narrator. The passion was at its peak in the assembly and weeping could be heard in the background; the hostess, Ms Sabira Zaidi, wept the loudest, her face covered with a white handkerchief. The social interactions were within the established frames of speech and the speech event:[42]

ro ro karti[43] *Zaynab beyn piyasa mar lia*
(Zaynab wept and lamented, 'Thirsty they killed,')
ro ro kati Zaynab beyn piyasa mar lia
(Zaynab wept and lamented, 'Thirsty they killed,')
ya Nabi Kufion ne Hussein piyasa mar lia
('O Prophet, the Kufis killed a thirsty Hussein,')
mera bhai Hussein piyasa mar lia
('My brother Hussein, thirsty they killed')

Intense, emotional matam followed the chanting of this nowheh, which was led by the hostess. Then there was a liturgy of Hussein matam in which the participants chanted: 'Hussein Hussein Hussein' for several minutes, beating their chests in a group self-flagellation ritual. Throughout this matam, I could hear the loud lament and weeping of the hostess, now in the background. She was exhausted and had moved to the back of the assembly; she sat with her back resting against the wall. A different zakereh took over the proceedings in order to recite the salam, which was a prelude to the end of the majles. A calm descended on the participants as the zakereh recited the following salam in poetic narrative in Arabic, Persian, and Urdu.[44] Below are excerpts from this salam, or ziyarat.[45]

al-salam-o alaykom ya ebn-e Fatema	Peace be upon you O Fatemeh,
al-Zahra	the bold
al-salam-o alaykom ya ebn-e Amir-ul-Mo'meneen	Peace be upon you O son of Ali
al-salam-o alaykom shams o shamus	Peace be upon you o sun of the sons
al-salam-o alaykom al-aman	Peace be upon you, may there be
al-aman	peace, grace and mercy
al-salam-o alaykom Ahl-e Bayt-e Haram	Peace be upon you O family of Muhammad

The zakereh recited the salavat/darud:

| Allah homma Salli Ala Muhammad va al-e Muhammad | O God, may thy blessings be on Muhammad and his family |
| Ya Nabi asl-salam-o alaykom | Peace be upon you, O Prophet |

The salavat was followed by a recital of the opening chapter of the Qur'an.[46] The zakereh led the ziyarat and *dua* for the assembly in Urdu:[47]

Ya Khoda	O God
Is qowm ka daman gham-e Shabir se bhur de	Fill this nation's lap with grief for Hussein[48]
Valvala Awn o Muhammad de	Give this nation the valour of Awn and Muhammad
Maon ko mile sani-e Zahra ka saliqah	May mothers have the skills of Zaynab[49]
Behnon ko Sakineh ki do'aon ka asr de	May sisters have the powers of Sakineh's prayers
Mowla tujhe Zaynab ki asiri ki qasam he	O God for the sake of Zaynab's imprisonment
Be jorm yatimon ko rehai ki khabar de	To innocent orphans in prisons, may there be news of freedom[50]
Mowla koi gham na dena de seva gham e Shabir	O God give no other grief except grief for Hussein

For three minutes, the zakereh recited the prayers in Urdu. After the closure of the majles, *nazr* was distributed among the participants. The Pakistani majles described in this chapter reveals that much of the oral history of Karbala tragedy is re-enacted in Sakineh's voice. The nowhehs sung in Sakineh's voice at this majales created '*riqat*,' or ritualized grief, among the female participants. Riqat was created through descriptions of the events at Karbala, from this girl-child's perspective, and in her voice. Both male and female nowhehkhans commonly use this method for emotional effect. Sakineh, therefore, is a metaphor of grief in the folklore built around Karbala. As a vulnerable young girl, Sakineh serves as a highly sympathetic character in the context of the ethical and political issues that led to the Karbala tragedy. Thus, in accordance with Hymes' model, Sakineh serves as the frame for the ethnography of speaking at a Shia majles during the Muharram lamentations.

GLOSSARY

azadars	the mourners or ritual participants
chatais	rush mats
duris	thick cotton mats
darud	prayer for the dead
nazr	food offerings
nazr-niyaz	ritual food offering for the sake of the *imam*
nowhehkhans	chanters
salam	blessings
zakereh	narrator of key sermon

NOTES

1. Dell Hymes, *Foundations in Sociolinguistics: An Ethnographic Approach* (Philadelphia: University of Pennsylvania Press, 1974), 45–46.
2. Ibid., 51.
3. Dell Hymes, 'Toward Ethnographies of Communication: The Analysis of Communicative Events.' In *Language and Social Context*, ed. Pier Paolo Giglioli (New York: Penguin Books, 1972), 21–44.
4. Ibid., 45.
5. Adapted from Joel Sherzer, *Language in Use: Readings in Sociolinguistics*, ed. John Baugh and Joel Sherzer (Englewood Cliffs, N.J.: Prentice-Hall, 1984a), 195.
6. Ibid.
7. Hymes, *Foundations in Sociolinguistics*, 54.
8. Albert B. Lord, *The Singer of Tales* (Cambridge: Harvard University Press, 1960), 21–26. The training of nowheh-chanters in Shia majales is similar to the one that Lord describes among the Muslim *guslars* in Yugoslavia during Ramadan.
9. Collected during a Muharram majles in Pakistan. I apply theoretical and methodological approaches from Richard Bauman, *Verbal Art as Performance* (Austin: University of Texas Press, 1977), and Hymes, 'Toward Ethnographies of Communication.'
10. For instance, the Gilani and Gardezi Sayyeds in Multan and the Makhdooms in Sindh.
11. Ali Asghar, infant son of Imam Hussein, was slain at Karbala. Ali Asghar's cradle becomes a focal point of lament during Muharram rituals. Qasem was the adolescent son of Imam Hasan and a nephew of Imam Hussein. Qasem was about to be married when he was killed at Karbala. Qasem's henna ceremony is celebrated among Shia female mourners in the subcontinent during Muharram majales. All nowhehs may not necessarily be in Sakineh's voice, but a large majority of them are sung as if she were the narrator. Sakineh's narrative creates a passionate lament in the majles assembly.
12. Hazrat Abbas, a half-brother of Imam Hussein, is believed to have inherited Ali ibn Abi Talib's valour. Abbas was martyred at Karbala as he carried the standard of Hussein's forces while attempting to bring water back to the camp from the Euphrates. The flags were green. At the top of flagpoles, there were metal replicas of a human hand, called a panjatan, with each finger representing one of the five most holy persons for Shias. The panjatan include the Prophet Muhammad (PBUH); his

son-in law, Ali; the Prophet's daughter, Sayyedeh Fatemeh Zahra; and the Prophet's grandsons, Imams Hasan and Hussein. Hazrat Abbas is called upon as a protector of children in the Muharram majles.

13. W. and P. Japp Beach, 'Storyfying as Time-Travelling: The Knowledgeable Use of Temporally-Structured Discourse,' in *Communication Yearbook 7*, ed. R. Bostrom, (New Brunswick, N.J.: Transaction Books-ICA, 1983); and A.L. Ryave, 'On the Achievement of a Series of Stories,' in *Studies in the Organization of Conversational Interaction*, ed. Jim Schenkein (New York: Academic Press, 1978). Accordingly, in time travel, it was at zohr, the late afternoon, when all of Hussein's forces were eliminated. Hussein's horse, Zuljenah, returned riderless to the camp. Thus, as part of lament rituals in Pakistan, Zuljenah processions are led by Shia mourners to a local Karbala in the city on Ashura. The evening of Ashura is when the women and children were left alone in the camp with Hussein's ailing son, Ali Zayn al-Abedin. The women's camps were said to have been looted. The evening of Ashura is called the Sham-e Ghariban, or Evening of the Oppressed. According to hadith, Imam Hussein's sister, Sayyedeh Zaynab, was left to assume responsibility for the survivors, including the girl-child Sakineh.
14. In Shia households in Pakistan, Karbala is mourned for fifty days.
15. From the word aza, which means 'to mourn.' The word can also mean 'condolence.'
16. Named after Sayyedeh Zaynab.
17. Out of respect for her grace, the azadars address Ms Sabira Zaidi as 'Baji,' an intimate term for an elder sister. 'Baji Sabira ka Imambareh' means 'imambareh belonging to Baji Sabira.'
18. Meer Hasan Ali, *Observations on the Mussalmans of India* (Karachi: Civil and Military Press, 1973 [1832]), and Abdul Halim Sharar, *Lucknow: The Last Phase of an Oriental Culture*, trans. E.S. Harcourt and Fakhir Husayn (Bolder, Colo.:Westview Press, 1975).
19. Hymes cited in Joel Sherzer, 'Strategies in Text and Context: Kuna kaa kwento,' in *Language in Use: Readings in Sociolinguistics*, eds. John Baugh and Joel Sherzer, 183–197 (Englewood Cliffs, N.J.: Prentice-Hall, 1984b).
20. Erving Goffman, 'The Neglected Situation,' in *Language and Social Context*, ed. Pier Paola Giglioli (New York: Penguin Books, 1972), 61–66. Goffman's theory is that talk is based on small units of speech; utterances and sentences are placed adjacent to each other as speakers take turns to talk. This is demonstrated in some of the transliterations here, e.g., the hostess leading the matam and the assembly of mourners responding with chants of 'Hussein, Hussein.' It is also evident in the photograph of the hostess, Ms Sabira Zaidi, leading the matam proceedings. This is also observed in the 'hai, hai,' utterance that the hostess prompts during the narration of a Sakineh story.
21. Levi-Strauss, cited in Sherzer, 'Strategies in Text and Context'; Aisha Bint al-Shati Mistri, *Karbala ki Sher Dil Khatoon*, trans. Muhammad Abbas (Lahore: Maktaba-e Imamia Trust, 1996).
22. The zakereh uses texts like the following to write her narrative, which she delivers from memory at the majles: Ayub Naqvi Abadi, *Tarjuman-e Karbala: Zaynab Bint e-Ali* (Karachi: Aliya Publications, 1999), and Ibrahimi Ameeni, *Fatima Zehra: Islam ki Misali Khatoon*, trans. Akhtar Abbas (Lahore: Shafaq Publishers, 1405 AH).
23. In Sherzer, 'Strategies in Text and Context,' 195.
24. I adapt this argument from Joel Sherzer's study of the Kuna Indians of Panama; 'Strategies in Text and Context,' 195.

25. Ibid., 189.
26. In Pakistan, nowhehs are sung in languages such as Pashto, Balti, Sindhi, Siraiki, Balochi, and regional dialects according to the speech communities.
27. Catherine Lutz and Lila Abu-Lughod, eds., *Language and the Politics of Emotion* (Cambridge: Cambridge University Press, 1990), and Erving Goffman, *Frame Analysis* (New York: Harper and Row, 1974). Theoretical approaches from these authors are used to interpret the data.
28. According to belief, Sughra, a daughter of Imam Hussein, was left behind in Medina because she was ill and could not travel. The women who chanted the nowheh beat their breasts as they sang. The nowheh can be sung as a dyadic unit in which two parties take turns in the storytelling process. The nowheh can also be chanted as a monologue. The participants stand in a circle for chanting nowhehs and doing matam.
29. Sons of Sayyedeh Zaynab killed in the Battle of Karbala.
30. This is the feminine form of the word meaning 'one who is devastated.'
31. This is the feminine form of the word meaning 'one who swallows.'
32. Ummat means 'sect, people of the same religion.'
33. Akbar was Imam Hussein's adolescent son.
34. Could also mean 'notoriety' in terms of the opposing forces of Yazid.
35. The repetitive use of 'ujri,' or the devastated female Sakineh, is significant.
36. Imam Hussein is called Sarvar here. Sarvar means 'leader' or a 'chief.'
37. Female descendants of the Prophet Muhammad's family.
38. One who fights against infidels, a conqueror, a living hero. Ghazi is embedded in the Islamic concept of jihad, or fight against falsehood.
39. Jim Schenkein, *Studies in the Organization of Conversational Interaction* (New York: Academic Press, 1978), and Harvey Sacks, Emmanuel Schegloff, and Gail Jefferson, 'A Simplest Systemics for the Organization of Turn-Taking in Conversation,' *Language* 50:4 (1974), 696–735. The transcription is based on an adaptation of the conversational analysis system of Sacks, Schegloff, and Jeffersen, also documented in Schenkein.
40. Abbas, the Lion, known for his valour.
41. A reference to Sakineh's thirst.
42. Goffman, *Frame Analysis*.
43. Feminine verb form of 'to do.'
44. The terms are intralingual.
45. Framing of the majles proceedings in this part by the weeping of the hostess in the background.
46. The opening verse of the Quran is also recited for the dead.
47. Ziyarat is a pilgrimage or visit. The hostess continued to weep as the majles was reaching closure through the prayers. The entire ritual was framed in the hostess' weeping and lament, which the participants responded to. Dua is a prayer that can be said in Arabic, as well as in an indigenous code such as Urdu or Panjabi.
48. Fondly called 'Shabbir,' which means a tiger or lion.
49. Also called 'Zahra' or 'Fatemeh the second' for her boldness and oratorical skills.
50. A political reference to current prisoners of conscience in the country.

CHAPTER 13

Al-Huda: Of Allah and the Power-Point

SADAF AHMAD

'Pakistani women socialites embrace Islam: A new breed of scholar is inspiring Islamic study among Pakistan's last bastion of sceptics—the educated female elite' (Ali, 2003, BBC News). Headlines such as this one, describing Dr Farhat Hashmi and her Islamic school for women called Al-Huda, meaning a place of guidance, can easily be found on the Internet and have become a common feature in newspapers and magazines in Pakistan in the last decade (Ahmed, 2002; Alee-Adnan, 2004; Siddiqi, 2004). A school turned social movement, Al-Huda's uniqueness lies in the fact that it has been able to make inroads into the middle and upper classes of the urban areas of Pakistan, a feat other religious groups have been unsuccessful at accomplishing. Its success amongst urban women has contributed to the increase of an exoteric form of Islam in society, and has made it a key player amongst religious groups also interested in *da'wa* or religious outreach. It was in order to understand why an increasing number of middle-and-upper class women were actively engaging with Al-Huda that I spent the months between September 2003 and July 2004 doing fieldwork in Islamabad. This is where Farhat Hashmi, along with her husband Idrees Zubair, established Al-Huda in 1994 in order to:

> equip individuals with authentic knowledge of Qur'an and Sunnah [a collection of sayings and actions attributed to the Prophet Muhammad (PBUH)] so that they may apply it in all aspects of their lives...be better equipped to revive the humanitarian spirit of Islamic teachings and to invite others to Islam in a peaceful and non-aggressive manner...[provide students with counselling] to help them develop their personality, character and self-confidence, and to prepare them for their future roles as wives, mothers, sisters and beneficial members of society (Al-Huda, 2003).

Al-Huda's aim, therefore, is to transform women who engage with its discourse into pious (Mahmood, 2005) or ethical subjects (Foucault, 1997), and it is with this aim in mind that it spreads its ideology into mainstream society through a variety of measures. I suggest, however, that it is not just the discourse itself, but the manner in which the discourse is propagated that has allowed Al-Huda to achieve the success it has, particularly amongst the middle and upper classes of urban Pakistan. Al-Huda's particular pedagogies of transformation have built upon women's faith in Allah and the Qur'an as the word of Allah, and play a critical role in facilitating them to discipline (Asad, 1993) themselves into becoming pious subjects. While the reasons women give for their active engagement with Islam via Al-Huda are many, for 'anything involving large numbers of people will be driven by a variety of motives' (Bruce, 2000:9), I use this space to examine these pedagogies, for they set Al-Huda apart from other religious organisations also interested in religious outreach. It is here that Al-Huda's uniqueness, and subsequent success, largely lies.

I also use this space to illustrate that while Al-Huda's *modus operandi* plays a crucial role in its success, its growth is also facilitated by particular cultural codes—ideologies, values, beliefs—that pre-exist in the socio-cultural landscape of Islamabad. However, as every society is made up of individuals carrying a variety of, often competing, cultural codes, the presence of the latter, particularly if they are very strongly embedded, can also constrain growth and/or produce or accentuate tensions amongst, and dissonance within, individuals associated with the movement. While the presence of a variety of cultural codes and ideological systems in society prevent the dominant religious discourse from creating subjects informed with a unitary consciousness (Ewing, 1997), Al-Huda is attempting to accomplish just that. But before elaborating upon how the school is attempting to do that, it is critical to first place Al-Huda within a larger religio-historical context, and introduce the school turned social movement.

SETTING THE SCENE

Pakistan is a country that is deeply rooted in a pluralistic mindset—where plural truth claims can exist side by side, and where religious and spiritual traditions overlap and borrow from each other and even develop a synthesis (Alvi, 1996; Ahmad, 2005). Yet the major strands of the exoteric, ritualistic part of Islamic discourse that later developed in the subcontinent were quite intolerant; there was no room for doubt, no room for multiplicity of truth claims. Although the roots of such an Islam in the subcontinent can be traced further back (Ahmad, 2000), it was the Deobandi movement that played a significant role in bringing it into the subcontinent. Created in 1867 as a reaction against the British, the Deoband school, which soon turned into a movement, is an illustration of Sunni Orthodoxy heavily influenced by Wahhabism. A common characteristic of the Deobandi, Wahhabi, or the similar minded Ahl-e-Hadith school of thought is that they all consider Islamic thought to be primarily made up of the Qur'an and Sunnah. These movements are characterised by visions of a return to a 'Golden Age' of 'pristine Islam', i.e., that when the Prophet Muhammad (PBUH) and his companions were alive, and they consider any form of religious innovation that took place since that time to be unIslamic (Metcalf, 1984; Werbner, 1996; Al-Munajjed, 1997; Ahmed, 1999). Hence, they oppose practices characteristic of Barailvi Islam[1] and Sufism (Upadhyay, 2003). These include practices such as saint celebration, seeking the help of *pirs* or spiritual guides and faith healers to solve problems, and honouring the Prophet Muhammad (PBUH) through specific rituals and events (Schimmel, 1985; Durrani, 1991; Ali, 1997; Warriach, 1997).

Movements and schools of thought purporting an exoteric form of Islam have steadily increased in influence in Pakistan in the form of a variety of religious groups such as the Tablighi Jama'at (Ahmad, 1991) and Jama'at-i-Islami (Nasr, 1994). The way Islam has developed in Pakistan—where politicians either made harmful policies coated in Islamic rhetoric to secure their powerful position by keeping the religious right happy, and/or by providing an environment where religious groups have been allowed to foster—has contributed to the increase of such an Islam in Pakistan. Stronger links with countries such as Saudi Arabia and the Gulf States also have a direct impact on the kind of Islam being transferred into society, leading to the creation of an environment where a more rigid, ritualistic form of religion is taking root (Ahmad, 2000). Although different on a number of points, these groups share the same rigidity and intolerance that characterises the larger, orthodox strands of Islam, whether it be in following an interpretive framework offered by the Sunnah and a literal translation of the Qur'an, or removing cultural accretion and tradition from society (Nasr, 1994; Ahmad, 2000).

Al-Huda is little different. Its position within the larger umbrella of diverse Islamic thought is clearly manifest in the changes its students undergo. The most visible change is the adoption of the headscarf and *abaya*, a gown worn by women on top of their clothes. Such veiling is a result of both an exoteric approach to understanding the Qur'an and a heavy reliance upon Hadith literature as an analytical frame. Al-Huda's ideology is also manifest in the way women stop listening to music, begin praying five times a day, and actively work towards, as do other such Islamic groups, removing cultural influences from their lives, as well as the lives of those around them. These not only include folk Islamic practices such as saint celebrations and the *chalisvan* ceremony, an event marking the fortieth day of a near one's death, but also includes local cultural festivals such as *basant*, the kite flying festival that marks the advent of spring in the country.

Farhat Hashmi's background helps explain the religious ideology propagated by Al-Huda. Growing up in the small town of Sargodha in Punjab, Farhat Hashmi received her initial religious education from her father, and from accompanying her mother to *dars* or religious study groups offered by the religio-political organization, the Jama'at-i-Islami. Both of her parents were members of the Jama'at, and she herself was active in the Jam'iat,[2] the student wing of the Jama'at, during her college days in the Punjab University in Lahore. She got married shortly after completing her MA in Arabic. After spending a number of years teaching at the Islamic University in Islamabad, both she and her husband left for Glasgow, Scotland, where they both earned their PhD degrees in Islamic Studies, with a specialization in Hadith sciences[3] (a report of the deeds and sayings of the Prophet Muhammad [PBUH]). A specialization in Hadith sciences, along with a former affiliation with the Jama'at-i-Islami, is an indicator of the analytical framework and form of Islam being adhered to; one that is very literal and exoteric in form.

AL-HUDA: A SOCIAL MOVEMENT

What once began as a school in Farhat Hashmi's own home has now turned into what I call a social movement. Al-Huda initially began with roughly a dozen students belonging to the upper classes. The 2003–04 batch in Islamabad had approximately one thousand students, and many had to be turned away because of a lack of space. Al-Huda has had adopted a variety of techniques to expand its audience base over the years. One of the ways it has done so is by offering different kinds of courses. The school's core activity is offering diploma courses to students who have at least completed their tenth grade, covering topics such as the translation and exegetical commentary of the Qur'an, Arabic grammar, Islamic history, Muslim heroes, the biography of the Prophet Muhammad (PBUH), Hadith, the art of Qur'anic recitation, and Islamic jurisprudence. Only one kind of diploma course was offered in its earlier years. It took place over a span of one year, with classes taking place between 7:30 a.m. and 1:45 p.m., six days a week. But the courses offered today also include evening classes for women who have day time commitments, part time courses, and correspondence courses, thus allowing different women with different kinds of responsibilities to have access to its courses.

The presence of a hostel in recent years has meant that girls and women from outside the Islamabad–Rawalpindi areas also have access to the school. Furthermore, the inculcation of the spirit of *da'wa* amongst its students has meant that once they graduate, these individuals make efforts to spread the religious ideology in their own localities, be they in Islamabad, in different parts of the country, or in different countries of the world. These efforts often take the form of Al-Huda graduates opening neighbourhood study groups or establishing small scale Al-Huda branches. Farhat Hashmi was on a tour of the United States and Canada in the summer of 2004, visiting some Al-Huda branches that her former students, who lived in these countries, had opened. Al-Huda itself has opened up central branches in all the major cities of Pakistan in recent years. In addition, the school also relies upon the mass media to disseminate its discourse. Farhat Hashmi's lectures are available both on audio tapes and can be heard on the Internet. She makes frequent appearances on television, as well as the radio.

All these strategies of discourse dispersal have ensured Al-Huda's success in both attracting a large number of students that are no longer limited to the upper classes, and in spreading its ideology even amongst those who do not attend its main branches in the country. It is within this context that I refer to it as a social movement. Social movements are popularly regarded either as a gathering, often spontaneous, of individuals who get together to voice grievances and bring about change, or as an organised collective action to promote a cause in the face of some structural strains (Larana, Johnston & Gusfield, 1994). However, there is no well-defined, closed group against which women affiliated with Al-Huda are reacting, and neither are they joining the school because they feel they are oppressed.

Spreading its ideology into mainstream society through a variety of measures, Al-Huda is committed to infusing the individuals who engage with it with particular 'Islamic' principles so that they can transform themselves into ethical subjects. Many of those who internalise this ideology, regardless of where they are placed or how they hear its message, are taking it upon themselves to spread it further, be it only amongst their family and friends, or amongst larger sections of society. The process continues, taking on a life of its own, as many of those who learn from others also begin spreading the ideology. It is like a domino effect, and it is within this context that I claim that Al-Huda has turned into a social movement, albeit an informal one. Recent literature has focused upon how many Islamic groups have adopted a 'bottom up' approach, encouraging people to 'bridge the gap between religious discourse and practical realities' in their daily lives, hence increasing the 'Islamic' atmosphere in their societies (Ask & Tjomsland, 1999:2). Many women are active participants in contributing to the religious atmosphere in their societies within this larger context, and it is here, within this less formal understanding of social movements (Wiktorowicz, 2004), that I place the women who are engaging with Al-Huda.

Those who are influenced by Al-Huda's ideology or spread it further may not be linked with the institution physically. They may have never been to the main Al-Huda branch. They may not even spread the message in the name of Al-Huda. But they are linked to it through its ideology, and through their individual efforts to transform themselves, and in many cases others, into particular kinds of ethical subjects. The main Al-Huda branches are certainly facilitating the process of da'wa by supporting those who want to spread the message, and societal level changes are visible in women's dress, in the increase in the number of dars offered by Al-Huda graduates in the city, and in the increase in the number of women attending them and the main Al-Huda branch.

Al-Huda's phenomenal success is perhaps not that surprising when one sees how Al-Huda is not functioning in isolation, but rather drawing upon values that already exist to some degree in society, a phenomenon known as frame resonance in social movement theory [McAdam, 1994; Hart, 1996; Benford and Snow, 2000; Wictorowicz, 2004]. The greater the frame resonance, the greater the ease of accepting the discourse. 'Where a movement frame draws upon indigenous cultural symbols, language, and identities, it is more likely to reverberate with constituents' (Wicktorowicz, 2004:16), and this cultural material—also known as cultural codes—includes the 'extant stock of meanings, beliefs, ideologies, practices, values, myths, narratives, and the like' (Benford and Snow, 2000:622). Cultural codes may be altered or transformed by the movement, but they are not a completely foreign import.

Pakistani women, like their counterparts in other parts of the world, are commonly seen as symbols of their national culture (Menon & Bhasin, 1989; Abu-Lughod, 1998; Mankekar, 1999), and this image is reinforced by their roles of wives and mothers, their dress, behaviour, and their affiliation with the private sphere of the home (Chaterjee, 2001). Since Islam is officially considered the *raison d'etre* of the nation, religious ideology has intertwined itself with nationalist ideology, resulting in a hegemonic religio-nationalist discourse, in which women are often used for the 'maintenance of indigenous values and 'cultural authenticity' (Stowasser, 1994:5). An active propagation of this discourse in a society that is already patriarchal to begin with has led to the emergence of a hegemonic discourse about the ideal Muslim woman in Pakistan. Many in Pakistan internalise this discourse simply because that is the reality presented to them as they grow up in Pakistani society. However, there is a difference between this ideal 'Woman' and real 'woman' (Mohanty, 1991:57), as the latter is drawing upon the variety of ideological systems (Hall, 1985) or the larger 'cultural field' (Comaroff & Comaroff, 1991) that is present in any society; her life is not informed by a unitary framework, such as that of religion.

Complex relationships exist between factors such as religion, culture, ethnicity, gender, class, age, and forces of nationalism and modernity (Kandiyoti, 1991; Wadley, 1994; Abu-Lughod, 1998; Saliba, Allen, & Howard, 2002). Growing up in such a context gives rise to an individual whose life is informed by a number of competing identities (Haeri, 2002; Saliba, 2002), and takes us a step beyond the notion of a self that is 'unified, coherent, self-centred…' (Rose, 1996:4). As Clifford Geertz elaborated,

> The Western conception of the person as a bounded, unique, more or less integrated motivational cognitive universe…organised into a distinctive whole and set contrastively both against other such wholes and against its social and natural background, is, however incorrigible it may seem to us, a rather peculiar idea within the context of the world's cultures (1984, as cited in Ewing, 1990:256).

A young girl who believes that listening to music is forbidden in Islam may not listen to it during Ramadan, a time during which her Muslim identity is at its strongest. That does not mean she does not listen to music in everyday life, when she is functioning as a young person living in a culture in which music is a part of normal day-to-day existence. A person may, at any moment, experience her self as a 'symbolic, timeless whole, but this self may quickly be displaced by another, quite different 'self,' which is based in a different definition of the situation' (Ewing, 1990:251). What self an individual projects or what identity is at the forefront is largely context dependant, for identities are often fragmented and multiply constructed. Such a notion of identity can only be understood when rather than being 'reducible to a closed system of signs and relations, the meaningful world always presents itself as a fluid, often contested, and only partially integrated mosaic of narratives, images, and signifying practices' (Comaroff & Comaroff, 1991:27).[4]

Nevertheless, it is through the propagation of a hegemonic discourse that Al-Huda is making attempts to create subjects with a 'unitary' consciousness (Ewing, 1997:19). A danger of viewing subjects as possessing a unitary consciousness is that they are either seen as 'determined by a discourse...or totally outside of that discourse' (Ewing, 1997:18). While this is 'inadequate to capture subjective experience in the face of clash of discourses and the competition of ideologies characteristic of postcolonial societies' (Ewing, 1997:19), it is in line with Al-Huda's core goal, and its activities are working towards bringing those 'outside of the discourse' inside. The extent to which they are successful in creating a unitary subject will determine the extent to which binary dualisms—religious/secular, religious/religious in a different manner—will exist amongst women in society, and the more their success, the less the overlap between them.

AL-HUDA: INITIAL CONTACT

Ninety-eight per cent of the population of Pakistan is comprised of Muslims, and while most may not know what the Qur'an says, or may not follow what are popularly believed to be Islamic injunctions, or even differ in what Islam means to them, most of them do, as I learnt, have faith. Neither familiarity with theological discourse nor possession of a clear cosmic framework is a pre-requisite for having it (Smith, 1962; Asad, 1993).

The women I spent time with grew up learning of, and hence believing in, the existence of Allah, in the Qur'an as the word of Allah, as well as in other basic elements of mainstream Islamic doctrine. They grew up with Islamic Studies as a compulsory subject in both school and college. They also grew up learning that Islam was Pakistan's *raison de etre*, once again, through their school textbooks. This process is significant in contributing towards the construction of a national identity and culture, one that is 'Muslim,' and one that most women have internalised to a certain extent while growing up in Pakistan.

These women's relationship with Islam was not just confined to the level of discourse, but was also a lived experience, as became obvious as I listened to one story after another. While there was some variation with regards to the extent to which Islam was a part of their everyday lives, almost all came from backgrounds in which they fasted in Ramadan, where one or more of their parents prayed, where they would begin praying during times of hardships, such as examinations, and stop as soon as they were over, where they had gone over the Qur'an in Arabic as a child with a *maulvi* or religious teacher, and/or where their parents may have forced them to pray when they were young. This even includes the young woman who spent her teenage years as an atheist: it was, in her own words, a reaction to her mother who had been giving *dars* for 30 years. The presence of faith, no matter how weak or strong, or whether or not it is overtly manifested through religious practices or plays a significant role in ones life, has played a critical role in determining the ease with which women initially join, and later alter their ideology, their behaviour, their dress, and their lifestyle. It leads to their willingness to listen to the discourse, and as Susan Harding claims in her account of Jerry Falwell's fundamentalist movement in the United States, it is this willingness to listen that begins the process of conversion (2001:57).

The beauty of the process lies in the fact that not all women who initially went to Al-Huda shared its ideology, or even knew what its ideology was. A young computer programmer shared her experience of discovering Islam through Al-Huda, and enthused that 'I felt like Harry Potter! Discovering a whole new world that had always existed but of which I knew nothing about.' Only a small proportion of women initially went to the school because their ideology matched that of the school. A larger number of women, however, were those whose pre-disposition towards Islam led them there, but whose ideology altered after they had joined the institute. The phenomenon of ideological conversion following recruitment, rather than preceding it, is well documented in social movement research (Wickham-Crowley, 1992; Brysk, 1995; Clark, 2004), and is certainly applicable in the context of Al-Huda.

Even if women's pre-disposition towards Islamic discourse is not enough in itself to motivate them to join the school, it does make them more amenable to being encouraged to attend it by their friends, acquaintances, or family members. A number of researches illustrate that 'network channel is the richest source of movement recruits' (Snow,

Zurcher, and Ekland-Olson, 1980; Brysk, 1995). I heard of a number of stories like that of Shazia's, a young girl currently studying at Al-Huda at the time I interviewed her, whose neighbour was teaching there and kept urging her to join it. 'I had just given my Matric (tenth grade) exams, and was free, and thought, why not?' If they are hesitant about committing a whole year, short-term options are available as well. Interestingly enough, a large number of girls who now come to Al-Huda for the one year course are those who have recently been exposed to the Islamic discourse in another context, which then whets their appetite for more in-depth knowledge. These contexts include the short summer course, and in many cases a *Daura-e-Qur'an* or 'Journey through the Qur'an' during Ramadan. People who have attended these, or who have even listened to Farhat Hashmi via any form of the media, or been exposed to Islamic lectures by guest speakers in their schools and colleges, have all been made 'structurally available' or structurally pre-disposed to join the one year course (Klandermans and Oegema, 1987:530).

While most girls go to Al-Huda of their own free will—out of a hope to make sense of a personal tragedy in their lives, a desire to increase their religious knowledge, or to find some meaning in their lives—there is also a small proportion of students who go to Al-Huda because their family members forced them to do so, illustrating that individuals who are not part of the mobilizing potential may still end up being exposed to the discourse. The personal desire to learn, however, does soon arise within them. For some the desire to learn more is instant, it hits them like a thunderbolt, as one young woman shared. A guest lecturer in her college was giving a talk on Islam, in which she remarked upon how everything has a purpose, 'a pen has a purpose, a chair has a purpose, but do we know what our purpose is?' This question, its basic simplicity, shook me. This was the moment of truth for me. Once I made the decision to learn more about Islam, I joined Al-Huda,' she shared. For others, especially those whose parents had forced them there, the process is much more gradual. As one former student laughingly shared, 'I slept in the first few classes.' Nevertheless, women's faith and basic connection with Islam does go a long way in easing the path for them. While the different processes they undergo as they interact with the discourse forces us to move away from perceiving them as passive recipients of a hegemonic discourse, the pedagogical techniques employed by the school play a critical role in facilitating this process by initially creating the will to change, and then providing concrete means through which to do so.

PEDAGOGIES OF TRANSFORMATION

Although Al-Huda is increasingly catering to a wider spectrum of women in terms of class, age, and occupation, the fact remains that its increasing popularity amongst the middle and upper classes of Islamabad has been unprecedented. The question that then arises is why they did not avail themselves of the educational opportunities provided by other religious groups functioning in the city. The politico-religious Jama'at-i-Islami, for instance, also focuses on religious education, and their women's wing has been organising dars in different parts of Islamabad since the late 1960s. The Tehrik-i-Islam and Tablighi Jama'at are other organisations that devote themselves to spreading religious knowledge. But the popularity of most of these groups is limited to the lower middle class. Clearly, the mere presence of faith, or a basic connection with Islam was an insufficient motive for further Islamic study for these women. The answer to why Al-Huda has been successful in making inroads into the middle and upper classes when these other religious groups have failed lies in women's stories of their experiences.

One of the reasons middle and upper class urban people have kept formal religious discourse at some distance from their lives is because of its association with the clerics or maulvis of Pakistan. Generally perceived by the masses in general, and women in particular, as uneducated, unkempt, and extremist, particularly when it comes to the rights of women, Islam had largely been associated with them. Therefore it too became infused with a specific meaning, i.e., that of being 'out of date' and backward,' through mere association. It became something that women who prided themselves on being 'modern' did not associate with. So for most of the women, this was the first time they were exposed to the translation and/or explanation of the Qur'an.

Islam is generally perceived as a holistic world view that 'encompasses in it all things material, spiritual, societal, individual, political, and personal' (Eickelman and Piscatori, 1996:46, as cited in Clark, 2004:168), and the Qur'an is popularly referred to as 'a complete code of life'. Yet, despite an unwavering belief in the truth of this statement, usually learnt in Islamic studies in primary school, most women claimed to be vague about how the Qur'an was really relevant to their daily lives. In Pakistan, the cultural emphasis has always been on reading the Qur'an in Arabic, and most children end up doing so with the guidance of a maulvi by the time they are eight or nine; they usually have no idea what they have read. The importance of reading it in Arabic precedes the importance given to decoding the text, a phenomenon found amongst Muslims in other parts of the world as well (Lambeck, 1990), and which also helps explain why most women had not read the translation before.

However, it was not just the fact that they were exposed to the translation, but the manner in which they were exposed that made all the difference. The Qur'an is a difficult text to understand. As Ayesha, a young medical doctor who had lived in the United States most of her life, explained,

> To tell you the truth, I'd pick up the Qur'an, and read *Surah Baqra* [the second Qur'anic chapter titled 'The Cow'], and I would be like it's a story about this cow or whatever, and fine, but so what? I'd feel good that I'd read the Qur'an, but what was the point? I knew that the Qur'an was something holy, it was something I respected...but it truly had no effect here, in my heart.

Al-Huda's gift, many of them claim, is the way each and every verse of the Qur'an is made relevant to their lives. Termed 'experiential commensurability,' this process adds to the relative salience of the frame offered by Al-Huda and makes it more resonant with student's lives (Benford and Snow, 2000). The second chapter of the Qur'an, for instance, devotes a number of verses to the Hypocrites, the individuals who professed to being Muslim in the Prophet Muhammad's (PBUH) time, but who secretly worked against him. After listening to Farhat Hashmi's explanation of those verses in class, the teacher in the large hall we were all sitting in asked the students to make a list of the traits the hypocrites had, and then think about and identify which of those traits *they* had. One of the students sitting there spoke up right there and then that although she was a Muslim, she often lacked the courage to defend Islam when it was made fun of in gatherings of family friends. Some other girls in the hall nodded in what seemed to be a personal recognition of such a shortcoming.

The primary focus in Al-Huda is on self-reflection, looking at one's own behaviour and changing it for the better. The goal is to make individuals what Foucault calls 'ethical subjects,' and one of the essential steps of this process is the 'modes of subjectivation,' that is, 'the way in which people are invited or incited to recognize their moral obligations' (Foucault, 1997:264). 'They make us conscious about the little, everyday things. They tell us to pick up a wrapper that comes up in our way when we are walking; they talk about proper hygiene. They don't make religion superfluous to our lives,' shared a fifty-year-old woman who went to

Al-Huda as a listener for one year. Farhat Hashmi constantly makes her students conscious about what is perceived to be inappropriate normative behaviour, through her *tafsir* and lectures, as is illustrated in an excerpt from one of the talks she gave while visiting the Islamabad branch:

> Where does it say that a bride cannot offer her prayers? People feel embarrassed, are amazed, if they see a bride praying. In war, in sickness, even when you are lying on your death bed but can breathe, you cannot forego your prayers. But we are afraid that we will spoil our makeup on which we spent thousands of rupees…(01.03.04).

She provides her students with a particular 'schemata of interpretation', a frame through which they can judge their behaviour and compare it to the standard provided by the Qur'an and Sunnah (Benford and Snow, 2000:612; Ferree & Merrill, 2000).

Consciousness of behaviour is then ideally followed by 'self forming activities' (Foucault, 1997:265), that is, attempts to modify one's behaviour so that it is in accordance with the guidelines laid out in the Qur'an, which is portrayed and perceived as a divine plan for life. Qur'anic verses are used to provide guidelines regarding how to behave with the opposite sex, how to treat relatives, how to dress, what to eat, how much to give to the poor, how to establish a closer relationship with God, all the do's and don'ts of life. This movement has, what Saba Mahmood (2005:30) refers to as a 'strong individualizing impetus,' in which each individual must fight a constant battle with him/herself in order to become an ethical subject based on hegemonic Islamic guidelines. Talal Asad argues that:

> the formation/transformation of moral dispositions depended on more than the capacity to imagine, to perceive, to imitate—which after all are abilities everyone possesses in varying degrees. It required a particular program of disciplinary practices (1993:134).

These practices are what Foucault termed,

> technologies of the self, which permit individuals to effect by their own means or with the help of others, a certain number of operations on their own bodies and souls, thoughts, conduct, and the way of being, so as to transform themselves in order to attain a certain state of happiness, purity, wisdom, perfection, or immortality (1988:18).

Al-Huda employs a variety of techniques in order to facilitate students' transformation into ethical subjects, hence giving them the means through which they can operate on themselves. The purpose is to provide them with a disciplinary programme that initially brings about consciousness of behaviour, transforms their inner motive, and then connects it to their outer behaviour (Asad, 1993). Daily assignments reinforcing the lessons learnt that day are one example of such a disciplinary programme. Students are urged to take five minutes to reflect upon their day's activities before going to bed every night. They are also required to keep a weekly journal where they record their thoughts, and the process they are going through as they read the Qur'an. Group time is another effective tool. Although most classes take place in the large hall, the students are divided into different groups of about twenty students each. Each group has a 'group in-charge', and she meets her group on a daily basis for forty minutes first thing every morning. This time is spent going over their lessons from the day before, asking students what they had learnt, how they related it to their lives, and answering their questions. Discussions are geared towards practical knowledge rather than more abstract notions. This is illustrated through the following short excerpt from one of my visits to these groups. This particular conversation took place in the English discussion group. Rafia, a young teacher in her mid twenties who grew up in Britain, sits on a chair in the middle of the small room that is normally used as a cloak/staff room during the rest of the day. About fifteen girls sit around her on the carpeted floor. After spending some time testing the girls on the Arabic of the verses they had studied in their Qur'anic exegesis class the day before, she begins the discussion:

> Rafia: [Reading the verses they had gone over the day before] What is the essence of this verse?.... So what does this mean for us?.... Yes, a criteria for friendship. What kind of friends should we have?
> Student 1: Pious?
> GL: But are you always attracted to pious people?
> Student 2: Hardly!
> The class laughs.
> GL: ...you must spent time amongst friends who strengthen your faith.... What happens when you spend time with friends who are not religious? What kind of things do you usually end up talking about?....

As 'interaction and activity are a crucial part of the culture making process' (Hart, 1996:89), a close study of the dynamics that take place within these spaces is key to understanding why students undergo a change as time moves on. Discussions such as these, touching the lived reality of girls' lives, serve to make them conscious of their behaviour when they are outside the school environment as well, so that they, as they explained to me, end up hearing their teacher's voice in their head whenever they are exposed to a situation they had discussed in class, something I too personally experienced as a result of being exposed to the discourse for innumerable hours. The effectiveness of the institution lies in its ability to inculcate within its students a desire to order their own behaviour outside of school, away from the teachers (Foucault, 1995). Accounts such as these also illustrate how disciplinary practices not only create ethical subjects, but also how they remain ethical subjects.

What is important is that suddenly the Qur'an is no longer merely a book that is carefully and respectfully placed on a bookshelf, but something that women are engaging with and thinking about, even when they are not in their classrooms. It is a very intense one-year process. I asked a teenage girl who was in the process of taking the course whether it didn't become too much sometimes, and her reply—'Well, you're doing it for Allah and because you can enter heaven. And for that you have to pay. You have to work your butt off.'—summed up the attitude of most of the women with whom I conversed. This work involved constant self-awareness and disciplining. It required 'honing one's rational and emotional capacities so as to approximate the exemplary model of the pious self' (Mahmood, 2005:31), so that 'one learns to express spontaneously the right attitudes' (Mahmood, 2005:129). This, in many cases, also involves transforming one's discursive consciousness, 'involving knowledge which actors are able to express on the level of discourse,' into practical consciousness, 'tacit stocks of knowledge which actors draw upon in the constitution of social activity' (Giddens, 1979:5, as cited in James, 1996:26). Asad refers to St. Augustine as having claimed that 'the final, individual act of choice must be spontaneous; but this act of choice could be prepared by a long process...' (Brown, 1967, as cited in Asad, 1993:34). Although reference is being made to another faith tradition, the process women undergo through their interaction with Al-Huda is such a process.

Teachers facilitate this process by striving to make their students strong in the face of the resistance they know that they will face from the larger, mainstream society. Parallels were drawn between the students and the

Muslims in the Makkan period, the time when Muhammad (PBUH) was just beginning to spread his message, and all the new converts had to face much criticism and hardship from the rest of society. Such comparisons brought students into the very fold of Muslim history itself, and as some students claimed, motivated them and gave them strength to overcome any criticism or ridicule they might face from their family or friends. Farhat Hashmi also encourages her students constantly: 'When you do the right thing, people's criticism of you is a matter of course. Be patient in the face of difficulties...[those who make fun of you] these are the people who try to present logic so they can get out of following the commands...' (Hashmi, 1).

This encouragement was accompanied by a somewhat novel characteristic of Al-Huda that all the students claimed to love: They were not forced to adopt 'Islamic' behaviour. No one told them that they must cover their head outside of Al-Huda or that they must go home and throw away all their music CDs, or that they must immediately begin praying five times a day. If a listener is sitting listening to the Qur'an in the large hall at Al-Huda with her hair uncovered, no one will come to her and ask her to cover her head. As a teacher remarked, 'our job is merely forwarding the word of Allah. The rest is up to them.'

A standard of 'correct' behaviour is revealed as more and more verses of the Qur'an are read, and the process of transformation is made all the more intense as peers and teachers appreciate students who have 'changed'. Women who change in the face of adversity at home are appreciated even more. There is constant support, affirmation, and encouragement present that helps ease the process of change, both direct and indirect. Countless women told me how they would look at women who had changed, their behaviour, their dress, and would think to themselves that if they can change, so can we. It is also important to remember, however, that the very fact that women who change are appreciated creates a powerful pressure for social conformity (Wickham, 2004), and an argument can be made that such a pressure may end up being more effective than the use of overt force—generously applied in other religious groups—in the long run.

Another characteristic that sets Al-Huda apart from other religious organisations is its 'modern' way of teaching. This is particularly relevant in a social context where Islam has always been closely associated with maulvis, and hence acquired the same negative characteristics prescribed to the latter through association. As a twenty-year-old student at Al-Huda informed me,

I was never interested in religion. There is this mindset, right, that if you go towards religion, people will call you backward. And the maulvis who tell us about religion don't know anything. They don't know where the world is going, what practical life is, or how to make religion practical in today's day and age.

Al-Huda has appropriated the meaning of Islam and presented it as not something that illiterate and ignorant people engage with, but as something very modern. The use of power-point presentations and other audio visual aids contributes to the modern atmosphere of the school, and plays a role in increasing its validity, as does the fact that Farhat Hashmi has a doctorate from abroad. Social movement research clearly indicates that the greater the credibility of the frame articulator, the greater their success at persuading others (Brysk, 1995; Benford and Snow, 2000), a fact Farhat Hashmi is clearly cognizant of. She is often quoted as once having laughingly remarked that the only reason she did her doctorate was so educated people would take her seriously; and as one of her young students affirms, 'my friends don't take what I am doing (course at Al-Huda) seriously until and unless I tell them Dr Hashmi has done her PhD from Glasgow.' Such an attitude is typical of individuals who are 'heirs to the postcolonial legacy, citizens of a nation state' (Haeri, 2002:32), who put great stock in the values of science, rationality, and Western education. The phenomenon of education increasing credibility is a characteristic of an educated class, and is found elsewhere in the world as well. Patricia Horvatich's study of the Islamic reform movement amongst the Sama of southern Philippines illustrates that the Sama are interested in the teachings of the Ahmadiya Movement[5] because it is a movement headed by 'educated elites', and their teachings 'appeal(ed) to their intellect. The Ahmadi do not follow their *imam* blindly. They want to understand the meaning of Islam and the purpose of their activities' (1994:821).

While the students at Al-Huda all believed that faith was the cornerstone of religion, many of them were very vocal about how they were now learning the rationality behind Islamic precepts, and that understanding made acceptance much easier. This is most relevant for the middle class who have more often than not subscribed to the 'high Islam of the scholars and elites…(which) provides a more sophisticated religious interpretation attractive to the growing modernized section of the population' (Ask & Tjomsland, 1998:4), the parallels of which are observed in other faith traditions as well (Schultze, 1993). Although it is false to make an artificial division, with High Islam only considered to be found in urban areas and Low Islam only in rural areas (Ask & Tjomsland, 1998), Ernest Gellner's thesis that the former 'reflects the natural tastes and values of urban middle classes,' such as 'order, rule-observance, sobriety, learning' (Gellner, 1992:11), along with its emphasis on scripture, makes it applicable to the urban women in this study.

The novelty at Al-Huda, therefore, is the space given to rationality. The institution's ideology is not very different from that propagated by the maulvis—Al-Huda too is reinforcing a patriarchal system with gender roles as natural, and man as a head of a household—but it is presenting it in a very different manner, so that women come to realise, for instance, that being made responsible for the house is actually a favour Allah has done on them, as working outside is very difficult on a number of grounds. The novelty lies 'not so much (in) the originality or newness of its ideational elements, but the manner in which they are plied together and articulated, such that a new angle of vision, vantage point, and/or interpretation is provided' (Benford & Snow, 2000:619), with logic and rationality as its bedrock. What comes forth is a dialectic relationship existing between faith and rationality. The presence of the former was clearly not enough to make women engage with religion the way they are doing now, but at the same time, many claimed that they would have found it difficult to accept many religious commands if they did not have that faith.

In a similar vein, Farhat Hashmi's reliance on science and scientific facts also plays a role in paving the way of understanding and acceptance amongst girls. It increases the empirical credibility of the frame, making it more resonant, and hence more acceptable to students (Benford and Snow, 2000). As one of her former students remarked enthusiastically, 'I personally love the way she constantly relies upon science, and brings in science, in her arguments and her explanations. As a former atheist, science was my god, and so logical, scientific explanations have a large impact on me.' Another student, who gave a specific example to illustrate her point, seconded this view:

> One of the things I had always had trouble with in Islam and which I discussed with her [Farhat Hashmi] at length was why, when a person could only do limited good or bad in their world, their stay in heaven or hell is eternal. She used the Chaos theory to explain things to me.... How something like a butterfly fluttering its wings in Australia can, through a chain of events, cause a storm in another part of the world. She used that and explained to me that we never know what kind of impact our deeds, small or big, will have in this

life, and whatever we do will remain and keep on having an impact on our world long after we have gone; and I immediately understood.

The way Farhat Hashmi translates each and every word of the Qur'an, drawing upon rules of Arabic grammar to do so, and brings forth the historical context of Qur'anic verses, not only further increases her credibility in her students' eyes, but also shapes the way they interact with the text. Most students have not studied the Qur'an before. Taking the analytical tools provided by Al-Huda leads them to see the literal, and what is perceived to be timeless, interpretation of the Qur'an as the 'truth', as opposed to seeing it as one of many ways of engaging with the text. Ideological closure occurs in most cases. This is a moment of 'recognition' that occurs when 'the fact that meaning depends on the intervention of systems of representation disappears and we (become) secure within the naturalistic attitude' (Hall, 1985:105). This 'naturalisation' is contrary to Hall's central argument that 'there is no experience outside of the categories of representation or ideology' (1985:105), but in line with the notion of hegemony, which is, after all, 'that part of a dominant worldview which has been naturalized, and having hidden itself in orthodoxy, no more appears as ideology at all' (Comaroff & Comaroff, 1991:25). Al-Huda is involved in creating a hegemonic discourse, which include:

> the order of signs and practices, relations and distinctions, images and epistemologies—drawn from a historically situated cultural field—that come to be taken for granted as the natural and received shape of the world and everything that inhabits it (Comaroff & Comaroff, 1991:23)

Farhat Hashmi's personality also plays a key role in attracting her students. While most of her students would argue that they go to Al-Huda for the Qur'an and not for Farhat Hashmi, almost all would also share how dynamic and charismatic they find her. After listening to her speak, both live and on tape, what comes across repeatedly is how easy it is to understand what she is saying. Her Urdu is a very simple, everyday Urdu, interspersed with analogies, humour, and a knowledge of current events. The everyday examples she draws upon resonate with the lives of the specific classes she is catering to. She gives her points authority by drawing upon the verses of the Qur'an, the Sunnah, and other incidents from Islamic history, subsequently linking them with conditions in contemporary society. All of these strategies combine to make her actual message all the more appealing, illustrating the notion of language as a form of social action (Ahearn, 2001). Other teachers attempt to emulate her and are appreciated by many of their students for their eloquence, knowledge, simplicity in style, and their guidance. Their discourse is all the more effective when it gives practical tips in the course of the exegetical commentary and discussion of Sunnah, tips that directly feed into the lived reality of their lives, such as what verses of the Qur'an to recite to protect oneself from magic, how to increase one's level of faith, what prayers to recite to decrease marital conflict, or what beneficial properties different food items have.

Hence Al-Huda is fulfilling its students on a number of different levels, and its *modus operandi* is playing a significant role in facilitating both ideological and behavioural changes within them. Most women remember the time they spent at the school very fondly. As a former Al-Huda graduate shared:

> I took to Al-Huda like a fish does to water. What I love most about Al-Huda is that it gave me back the Qur'an. They taught me how to read it in Arabic, what that Arabic meant, how beautiful it sounded, just like music. Al-Huda nurtured me emotionally and challenged me intellectually.

COMPETING CULTURAL CODES

One of the key reasons for Al-Huda's success amongst women is that it is not functioning in isolation, but rather in a socio-cultural landscape where pre-existing values—related to both religion and societal norms—facilitate not just their initial entry, but their internal and external transformation as well. But while certain cultural codes may facilitate the movement's growth, other cultural codes can confine it. Social movements, after all, 'belong to a broader social milieu and context characterized by shifting and fluid configurations of enablements *and constraints* that structure movement dynamics' (Wiktorowicz, 2004:13, emphasis added). These constraints exist because 'movement participants and potential adherents are not *tabulae rasae* upon which activists may draw any picture of reality they would like' (Benford, 1993:678). Intra-movement divisions have been known to exist within the school because the actors making up the movement represent the larger society, and as such they come with different backgrounds and different levels of exposure to the larger world. A Pakistani woman's experience and identity is based on myriad factors such as class, education, occupation, rural/urban setting, regional affiliation (Khan, Saigol, & Zia, 1994; Rouse, 1984; Shah, 1986), as well as on how much she has travelled, what kinds of schools she has gone to, whether or not she has ever had a 'secular' job. This difference in background plays out in a number of ways, amongst both teachers and students, whether it be in conflict over pedagogical strategies, or tensions due to issues of language and class.

All the teachers and staff at Al-Huda are Al-Huda graduates themselves. Their ages vary from twenty to fifty years, and they belong to classes ranging from the lower middle to the upper class. Their educational level also varies, with some having an FA [12th grade] degree and some with a Masters degree, be it in business administration, computer sciences, or the arts. Individuals with degrees in computer sciences manage the Al-Huda website and take care of basic office computing. Likewise, those with degrees in art take care of art work within the school. Some teach, and others are in charge of small departments that consist of a number of cubicles in one section of the basement. Each cubicle is a mini department that is in charge of actvities such as networking with other branches, accounts, media, counselling, research, and so on. All teachers and staff members are offered a very modest pay, which some of them give back to Al-Huda as *sadaqah e jariya*.[6]

Despite the fact that all the teachers have studied from Al-Huda, their differences can be a cause of tension between them. One such tension exists between the teachers who teach in Urdu and those who do so in English. Haleema, a thirty-five-year-old Al-Huda graduate, who taught at Colours of Islam at one point, and who had moved to Islamabad from the small town of Sargodha eight years ago, shared that she was not very fluent in English and that she and all the other Urdu-speaking teachers at Colours of Islam felt inferior:

> Whenever I would recommend someone as a new teacher, they [the administration] said that no, she doesn't speak [English] well. I said that how will common people study then. We are so caught up in trying to impress others [i.e. parents] that we will lose touch with our roots. But they were like, no, you should talk in English, because they are English medium children. You should inspire them, impress them.

The majority of the students take the course in Urdu, even many of those who have gone to English medium schools. For instance, only fifteen out of three hundred girls took the course in English in one of the diploma courses in 2003–4. There is some connection between the language that individuals, be they students or teachers, feel comfortable learning/

teaching in, their class, exposure, and general background. For instance, while the teachers using Urdu covered all socio-economic groups, more of them belonged to the lower middle-and-middle class, while those who taught in English only came from the middle and upper classes. Class in turn is related to whether one attends an English medium school or not, which only the more affluent can afford. Students in privately-run English medium schools, particularly those who follow the 'O' and 'A' level route, are trained to critically engage with their subjects, as opposed to the rote memory method followed in most government-run Urdu medium schools. These and other related experiences do have a bearing upon how different women engage with a particular discourse, how much questioning they bring into the learning process, and as I'll illustrate below, how innovative they are in teaching. Although I will only present a couple of examples, they are characteristic of the general differences I found between women based on the interconnectedness of these factors.

Some of the teachers who used to teach the English summer course, Reality Touch, at Al-Huda, shared how many of the Urdu teachers in the administration did not give them enough space to be innovative while teaching. Two of these teachers no longer teach these courses, and do not like associating themselves with Al-Huda. Zarina is one. A young and vibrant person, Zarina teaches the Qur'an from her home in Islamabad and is very popular amongst young, upper class girls. Frequently invited to teach in different cities in Pakistan, as well as abroad, Zarina, shared her experience of a time when she was once invited to teach a summer course in Karachi, and how disappointed she was by the rigidity of the structure.

> I had taken some badminton rackets with me so that the girls could take a break and enjoy themselves, but the other teachers shot down the idea. I also suggested that I take them to the beach for an outing one day, but did not get permission on the grounds that they only had limited time with the girls and they wanted to influence them as much as they could. The girls had a regimented routine, just like a cadet college. But what if you don't feel like praying? What if you're going through a phase and want out from praying for a month? You cannot enforce these things. You have to give girls space to think, to reflect.

Farheen, who also used to be involved with teaching the English summer course at Al-Huda, expressed similar views. These teachers would try out different experimental techniques, using videos and facilitating discussion; in one instance making students watch Malcolm X, to the displeasure of the administration, which complained that it had some 'scenes' [read: sexual ones] in it. As she expressed strongly:

> Fine, so that was wrong Islamically, but the fact is that the girls who come to us are used to seeing much more in the films they watch. This is a transition. It's a level up. Sometimes you have to go down to the level to get to the top.... But Al-Huda follows a certain code of conduct, a certain methodology...and getting permission for anything different is a big headache.

Haleema left Colours of Islam because she could not condone their innovative methods:

> They [at Colours of Islam] had made Islam all fun and games. There would be skits in which children would act out historical scenes, and one in which a student acted the part of the devil. A lot of us were concerned about whether doing role plays of these characters was correct Islamically.

So while all these individuals believe that 'Islam is the solution…there are important divergences over specific tactics and strategies' (Wiktorowicz, 2004:17), and these divergences become a source of tension upon occasion.[7] My intent is not to create any artificial Urdu medium/English medium divisions between women, but simply to illustrate that a person's background influences her *modus operandi*, her way of thinking. Zarina and Farheen got tired of not having full control while teaching, and chose to leave the school. So while one set of cultural codes, a desire to learn about their religion, brought them to this school as students, another set of codes, one related to their way of approaching things—a direct result of their background—made them leave.

Islamabad, like any other place, is made up of actors subscribing to different sets of ideologies. These ideologies cannot be simply put into the religious and secular camp, because not only is there an overlap between them, but also because people are religious in a number of different ways. Students who come to Al-Huda come with pre-existing ideologies, and they have their own ideas about what constitutes right and wrong behaviour. While most students were completely satisfied with their experience at Al-Huda, a very small number were not. They went because of their pre-disposition towards Islam, but felt dissatisfied because the school propagated an ideology that clashed with some of their other pre-existing cultural codes. They either left or chose to focus on what they considered were its good points.

Sadia, a twenty-year-old girl, was one of these students. Enrolled at the school at the time I interviewed her, she began crying while telling me of her experience. A standard of behaviour is set as more and more Qur'anic verses are revealed daily, and those who do not meet up to the standard presented are filled with dissonance. Dissonance is also felt amongst girls who are not changing their behaviour or lifestyle at the rate their peers are. While the dissonance caused by not meeting 'Islamic' standards of behaviour is dispelled over time as women either change themselves, as happens in most cases, or give importance to some commands over others, as happens less frequently, there are some students who seem to be caught between competing cultural codes, i.e., what they feel is right and what they are told is right. Such was Sadia's experience. Her confusion about what is right and wrong comes forth as she talks to me:

> They [Al-Huda] have a concept that if a girl and a boy are friends then there is obviously something fishy going on. They have literally called such friendships *haraam* [forbidden]. I know that it is *haraam*. I agree. But I don't think that if you are talking to someone and if your intentions are pure…I'm not saying that I want to both keep the Qur'an and keep my friendships with male friends. But you decide that you will leave these things slowly. But they make it sound that if you are doing something like this then you are literally doing something bad.

Sadia is a product of a culture that allows her the freedom to interact with the opposite sex, but one that is also permeated with a hegemonic religious discourse that criticizes such freedom. While a person's selves may shift naturally in different contexts, drawing upon different cultural strands when needed, without integrating them as happens in most cases, different instances, such as an interaction with Al-Huda, may bring this lack of integration to the forefront (Ewing, 1990). Efforts are then usually made to achieve some kind of integrated wholeness, something Sadia is attempting to do. Nevertheless, despite her ongoing frustration and confusion, she shares that Al-Huda has allowed her to develop a bond with Allah, and for her that is the most important thing. Clarity on other issues, she claims, will come with time.

While Sadia has chosen to stay on at Al-Huda, Razia, who unlike Sadia, completely submerged herself in Al-Huda and its discourse, chose to leave it and its teachings behind. Razia, who has been working in an international development agency for the last five years, began going to Al-Huda as a listener. 'I soon started feeling that every step of your life you're committing a sin…and the time came when I began thinking that

I'm not going to join any job, I'm just going to stay at home and pray the whole time otherwise I'll be corrupted.' But she did begin a job and she was exposed to the human rights discourse that, she enthused, made so much sense to her. 'Everyone gets importance in a secular environment, no matter what their religion.' The new cultural codes Razia acquired proved to be stronger than her previous ones, particularly because they were, she shared, taught via vibrant role models, and because her work brought her into contact with people in contexts where differences of religion took a back seat in the face of the basic human connection they shared.

For others like Naz, a woman in her late fifties whom I met in one of the dars we were attending, it was simply a matter of Al-Huda not resonating with her religious beliefs. Although she was interested enough to check it out, she left within weeks. Naz came from a Barailvi background in which saint shrines are visited, and where special programmes are held to celebrate the greatness of the Prophet Muhammad (PBUH). As such, she could not condone going to a place where such practices were termed '*biddat*'.[8]

What we see is Al-Huda's success being somewhat constrained by people who are religious, yet who possess competing cultural codes that prevent them from associating with the school. Al-Huda faces even greater criticism from those completely outside the movement, whether they be the secular women's movement, leading human rights groups and NGOs, or even other religiously inclined people. The latter include individuals who believe those at Al-Huda to be extremists, or who see it as propagating an Islam that does not match theirs. Tehzeeb, a twenty-eight-year-old school teacher who began wearing the headscarf a couple of years ago and who has personally studied Islam, argues that:

> People are becoming very judgemental when they leave that place [Al-Huda]. I'm not going to associate Al-Huda with Dr Farhat Hashmi because she is not the only one there. There are many teachers.... You're supposed to be wise once you've studied religion. You are not supposed to stand up and start giving *fatwas*, that this is wrong and that is wrong.... The problem with Al-Huda is that it is catering to young inexperienced girls whose lives had been limited to Mills and Boon. They have not seen the world. They take what is taught as a matter of course and do not ask questions.... It is very isolated from the outside world, it does not inform you of debates on religion going outside in other parts of the world.... The type of girls and the environment is a dangerous combination and is bound to lead to rigidity.... When you go after quantity, the quality is bound to go down.

The 'religiously inclined' people also include some leading clerics who, students claim, feel threatened by the school because they are afraid of losing the power they currently enjoy by holding all interpretations in their hands. Al-Huda is reinforcing a patriarchal system, and highlighting the importance of different gender roles associated with it, with a man being superior to a woman, and a woman being obedient to her husband unless he asks her to do something unIslamic. Yet the school does not, unlike the propensity of many maulvis, ignore the rights women do get in Islam, such as the right to divorce. Although it is something they discourage, and consider to be a very unwelcome and undesirable alternative, they do not gloss over it or ignore it either.

Despite the tensions both within and outside the school, Al-Huda has been quite successful at ensuring that by the time their students graduate, they will have internalised their hegemonic discourse. Hegemony is commonly seen as 'a continuous process rather than a fixed state of affairs' (James, 1996:24) that is always left somewhat incomplete. A particular danger for the school within this context then is that it may gradually lose its influence once students graduate, especially if they have no access to a support system. Aware of this danger, a group leader is given the additional duty to keep in touch with her students even after they have graduated, by calling them up and asking them if they have gotten together recently, keeping them informed of any guest speakers, or special events and activities happening at Al-Huda.

It is imperative to be aware of the constantly shifting relationship that may exist between a hegemonic discourse propagating certain roles and values, and the interpretive agency of subjects (Mankekar, 1999). As Stephen Hart explains, a more useful analysis can occur when it includes the 'culture-making practices and processes by which such codes (discourse) are created, transformed, communicated, applied, and given meaning' (1996: 90). According to this view, meanings arise when individuals interact with a particular body of knowledge; they are 'constructed and transformed in the course of action and interaction' (Hart, 1996: 91). A case in point is Al-Huda's discourse on photography, which, simply put, is forbidden. A parallel is drawn between capturing images on film and idolatry. However, while all students listen to the same explanation by Farhat Hashmi, this prescriptive gets transformed in the process, so that it means different things to different students. While most students truly stop taking or getting their photographs taken, and take down the ones that were displayed in their homes, some may interpret the directive to mean that pictures can be taken but not displayed openly, or that they can be taken if developed by a female or a *mehram,* i.e. a close male kin a woman cannot marry, like her brother or nephew. Still others argue that pictures can be displayed in a room as long as prayers are not offered in them; a clear case of discourse transformation.

Some students also show some behavioural disruptions in discourse. Samira, a twenty-year-old Al-Huda graduate, for instance, says she knows it is wrong for her to talk to *na-mehram,* i.e. men whom she can potentially marry, if there is no need, 'but if I see a friend's brother on the street, and I've known him my whole life, ignoring him and not greeting him seems so rude. So that is still a challenge for me.' She continues on a much lighter note, sharing laughingly, 'My friends call me a nutcase. I call them up to chat, and after half an hour say 'oh, I shouldn't be wasting so much time on the phone,' and then continue talking for another half an hour.' This was a disruption that did not disturb her.

While the instances of discourse transformation and disruption are present amongst Al-Huda graduates, they are not as common as one would expect. Al-Huda students are deliberately cutting their ties with the multiple ideological systems prevalent in society, and making attempts to transform themselves into pious/ethical subjects who are informed with a unitary consciousness. The intenseness of the one year course, the specific pedagogies employed to transform individuals into ethical subjects, the development of a love for and relationship with Allah, accompanied by a fear of the Day of Judgement, all combine to ensure that disruptions become the exception and not the rule. Much of the disruption, when it does occur, is because these women are living in families where not all are religiously inclined in this particular manner, or to this particular extent. That sometimes creates situations where following directives is simply not possible. Disruptions may also be a result of what women term their own personal weaknesses. It becomes important to note that in this context, a disruption in discourse cannot be equated with a disbelief in the discourse. Perhaps a more useful way to see this process is by looking at it *as a process,* where women are struggling to follow Islamic directives on a daily basis. Their struggle may be over getting up for the prayers at dawn, or over controlling their gossip, but their desire is rooted in their faith, in their belief in what they have been taught. Farhat Hashmi is, after all, they claim, spreading Allah's word. You can try to understand it, but you cannot challenge it.

AUDIO TAPE

Hashmi, Farhat 1. *Islam Main Gaana Bajaana* (Music in Islam)

NOTES

1. Barailvi Islam is attributed to Ahmed Reza who founded the religious institution Dar-ul-Ulum Manzar Islam at Bareilly in 1904 to oppose the Deoband movement.
2. Created by the sons of Jama'at workers in 1947, the Islami Jam'iat-e-Tulabah, or Jam'iat as it is popularly called, is the student wing of the Jama'at. Although it was initiated as a *da'wa* movement, it soon took on a life of its own and turned towards violence as a means to crush what it saw as its opponents. Leftist groups headed the list of opponents, and clashes between them became common on campuses. It infiltrated and eventually took over the Punjab University, the intellectual centre of students, in the late 1970s, where today, on their orders, drama, theatre, and musical events are forbidden, and men and women must sit in separate sections of the classroom (Nasr, 1994; Hoodbhoy, 2004).
3. See Berg (2000) for a detailed account of multiple positions taken by different scholars with regards to the reliability of hadith literature.
4. There is a dearth of ethnographic literature on urban Pakistani women, and that present, such as Fouzia Saeed's *Taboo!* (2001) or Anita Weiss's *Walls Within Walls* (2002), deal with women belonging to the lower socio-economic working class. Shahla Haeri's *No Shame For the Sun* (2002) is the only work on women belonging to the urban upper classes in Pakistan. All of these works do, however, bear testament to how women's lives are informed by a number of ideological frameworks.
5. Ahmadis are a Muslim sect founded by Mirza Ghulam Ahmad—who regarded himself as a reformer sent by God to restore Islam—in the nineteenth century, in Punjab. They are now divided into two sub-sects, the Qadianis, who consider their founder to be a Prophet, and the Lahori Jama'at, who consider him to be a reformer (Glasse, 2002). Regarded as heterodox, the Pakistani government under the leadership of Bhutto, in the hope of appeasing the religious parties and securing support amongst the masses, declared Ahmadis non-Muslim in the constitution of 1973.
6. *Sadaqah* refers to 'voluntary charitable giving, (that) is usually distinguished from the more organized almsgiving of *zakaat*' (Newby, 2002:187). *Jariya* refers to something recurring or which continues. Hence the term refers to alms that do not just do immediate good, but continue to benefit people over time. For instance donating books to a library allows innumerable people to get knowledge, who in turn spread that knowledge, or make use of it in ways beneficial to others.
7. It is important to remember that even though Zarina and Farheen chose not to teach at Al-Huda, they are still teaching and spreading a discourse not dissimilar to Al-Huda's. The primary difference lies in their innovative style of teaching, and the way they approach the notion of 'change'. Their methods are attracting girls who prefer their style to that of Al-Huda's. Hence this Islamic discourse continues to spread.
8. *Biddat* (Urdu) or *bid'ah* (Arabic) refers to any religious innovation that may have occurred since the time 'true' Islam was practiced, i.e. from the time when the Prophet Muhammad (PBUH) was alive. Within this context then, different activities that people do in the name of Islam in different cultures—whether it be reaching spiritual heights through dancing, as the whirling dervishes do in Turkey, or making an event out of the Prophet Muhammad's birthday, as is commonly done in Pakistan—are considered *biddat*, and therefore unIslamic, by formal/purist religious schools of thought.

CHAPTER 14

The Rise of Sunni Militancy in Pakistan: The Changing Role of Islamism and the Ulama in Society and Politics

S. V. R. Nasr

The past two decades have witnessed a notable escalation in sectarian violence in Pakistan. Since 1979 doctrinal disputes between Sunnis (who constitute the majority of Pakistan's population) and Twelver Shias (who number between 15 and 25 per cent of the population, and are to be distinguished from Isma'ili, Khoja and Bohra Shias) has given place to full-fledged sectarian conflict. Militant Sunni and Shia organizations have carried out assassinations and bombing campaigns that have killed political rivals as well as children and the innocent at prayer in mosques. In the first seven months of 1997 alone—the year when sectarian conflict reached its apogee—one hundred people died in such attacks in Punjab. The violence escalated further when in the first ten days of August 1997 (immediately preceding the celebration of the fiftieth anniversary of the country's independence) another seventy people were killed in incidents of sectarian violence.[1] Sectarian forces have incited riots (that in 862 incidents between 1989 and 1994 claimed 208 lives and injured another 1,629);[2] and have engaged in armed conflicts (that for instance, in a five-day 'war' in 1996 in Parachinar in North-West Pakistan, in which the combatants used mortars, rocket launchers, and anti-aircraft missiles, claimed the lives of some 200 people).[3] These actions have polarized communities, and undermined civic order and political stability (most notably when a bomb on the eve of the 1997 elections killed nineteen Sunni militant leaders in a courthouse in Lahore) (see Table 2).

Sectarian violence has taken centrestage as militants vie to assert the pre-eminence of their religious communities, gain control of the Islamist discourse and define the nature of state–society relations. Probing the reasons for the rise of sectarian violence can shed much light on changes in the ideology and practice of Islamism in Pakistan. It can elucidate the manner in which changes in the intellectual and social function of traditional centres of Islamic education and the ulama that they produce, have interacted with regional and domestic politics to create a new style of Islamist activism with a different approach to the question of the role of Islam in politics. The probe will also explicate the manner in which interactions between the state and its Islamist and ulama clients since 1977 have precipitated conflicts within Islamist circles and among the ulama over the right to represent Islam in Pakistan. These conflicts have produced new patterns of interaction between ulama and Islamists, and given rise to discourses of power among them which have been important in giving shape to the new style of Islamist activism. This chapter examines these issues with reference to the rising Sunni militancy.

THE ROLE OF MADRASSAHS

The phenomenon of militant sectarianism, especially among Sunnis, is closely associated with the proliferation of madrassahs and *daru'l-'ulum*s across Pakistan, and especially in Punjab. Increasingly, madrassah students and graduates have become active in local and national politics, as well as in the push to Islamize state institutions. More ominously, they have also become prominent in militant movements. Ramzi Ahmad Yusuf's international Islamist network; Harakatu'l-Ansar's (Movement of the Helpers [of the Prophet]) campaign in Kashmir; the Taliban's in Afghanistan, and the anti-Shia crusade of the Sunni Tehrik (Sunni Movement), Tanzim-i Da'wah (Organization of the Call) Lashkar-i Jhangvi (Jhangvi's Army), Sawad-i A'zam-i Ahl-i Sunnat (Majority of Sunnis), Sunni Council, Sunni Jam 'iat-i Tulabah (Sunni Student Association), Pakistan Sunni Ittihad (Pakistan Sunni Alliance), Tahaffuz-i Khatm-i Nubuwwat (Protection of Finality of Prophethood), the Pakistan Shariat Council, and the Sipah-e-Sahabah Pakistan (SSP, Pakistan's Army of the Companions of the Prophet) have all begun in and around militant madrassahs, and recruit from among their students and graduates.

Why and how traditional Islamic educational institutions have become embroiled in militancy and violent activism brings to the fore interesting questions about the changing social and political role of Islamic educational institutions, their relation to the political uses of Islam by the state and the Islamist opposition to it, and the interface between a changing and expanding state and traditional spokesmen of religion. In

1947 there were 137 madrassahs in Pakistan.[4] Today, even the smallest divisions of Punjab have just as many, and Pakistan as a whole has an estimated 8,000.[5] The proliferation of madrassahs belonging to Deobandi, Barelvi and Ahl-i Hadith schools of Sunni Islam, began in the mid-1970s, and has continued at a phenomenal pace since. In Punjab, where the rise in numbers has been most notable (see Table 1), the number of madrassahs increased three and a half times between 1975 and 1996, from over 700 to 2,463.[6] Of the 2,463, about 750 were classed as aggressively sectarian.[7] In Lahore the increase was from 75 to 324, and in Faisalabad, which is today one of the principal centres for militant madrassahs, the increase was from a handful to 112.[8]

Table 1: Madrassahs and their Students in Punjab in 1996[a]

Division	No. of Madrassahs	Deobandi M/S[b]	Barelvi M/S	Ahl-i Hadith M/S	Shi'i	Religious Criminals[c]
Lahore	324	143/17,892	136/18,336	41/5,524	4/373	150
Rawalpindi	169	83/8,367	64/8,307	6/417	16/442	70
Gujranwala	140	36/3,632	87/7,400	13/1,712	4/373	100
Faisalabad	112	47/1,163	39/5,027	18/3,141	8/700	80[d]
Sargodha	149	68/6,158	64/6,427	9/1,318	8/341	na
Multan	325	127/1,888	159/10,798	27/2,620	12/660	140
D.G. Khan	361	133/8,816	174/9,593	24/1,829	30/669	100
Bahawalpur	883	335/32,204	493/29,308	36/2,319	19/746	na
Total	2,463	972/80,120	1,216/95,196	174/18,880	101/4,304	640

a. Source: *Herald* (Karachi) (October 1996), p. 56.
b. M is number of madrassahs and S the number of students.
c. The category is as reported by the police.
d. The 80 were mainly from Jhang.

In its first phase, between 1975 and 1979, the rise in the number of madrassahs was supported by a flow of funds from the Persian Gulf monarchies. Governments of Saudi Arabia and United Arab Emirates had viewed the turn of Pakistan's politics towards the Left in the late 1960s and early 1970s with alarm, and supported all kinds of Islamic activities with the aim of strengthening Islamic institutions and ideology as a bulwark against the Left. By 1973, Prime Minister Zulfikar Ali Bhutto was able to assuage those fears as he cultivated close ties with Persian Gulf rulers and purged his party of its leftist elements.[9] Still, the support for Islamic activism in Pakistan continued unabated, mainly because that support had found its own momentum, and the linkages between Islamic organizations and groups in the Persian Gulf monarchies and those in Pakistan had become entrenched, and operated independently of government control.

This was especially the case when it came to the support of madrassahs and Islamic education projects. Here, links between Saudi and Pakistani ulama, and Sunni activists—as was also the case between Shia madrassahs in Pakistan and Iranian ulama—and their respective educational institutions, were largely voluntary, and produced strong religious and intellectual bonds that became embedded in institutional contacts and networks of patronage. In 1996, of the 2,463 registered madrassahs 1,700 were receiving financial support from outside Pakistan.[10]

The linkages also fitted into Saudi Arabia's larger agenda of controlling Islamic intellectual and cultural life across the Muslim world through such institutions as Rabitah Alam-i Islami (Islamic World League), and to promote its own vision of Sunnism through patronage of Islamic education in the Muslim world. That the recipients of Saudi support in Pakistan were Sunni madrassahs would in time make the patronage also relevant to Saudi Arabia's anti-Iranian regional policy.

RISE OF SUNNI MILITANCY IN PAKISTAN

The Afghan war in the 1980s, too, was important in this regard as it once again raised the prospects of communism reaching the shores of the Arabian Sea. The response of Persian Gulf states was very much the same: providing generous support for all manner of Islamic activities to strengthen Islamic identity in Pakistan, and this time also to help train activists who would be willing to fight in the war.[11] These funds found their way to madrassahs, and as will be seen below, helped create a whole new genre of madrassahs—ones that were equally, if not more, concerned with jihad than with religious scholarship.

TABLE 2
The Worst Instances of Sectarian Violence, 1988–1997[a]

1988	150 Shia killed in Gilgit by vigilante Sunni mobs
1988	assassination of Shia TJP[b] leader, Arif Husaini
1989	assassination of Sunni SSP[c] leader, Haq Nawaz Jhangvi
1990	assassination of Iranian cultural attaché in Lahore
1991	assassination of Sunni SSP leader, Israru'l-Haq Qasimi
May 1991	18 Sunni SSP workers killed in Gilgit
July 1992	15 killed and 40 injured in Peshawar in rioting during Shia Muharram ceremonies
January 1994	6 killed and 21 injured in attack on Shia mosque in Multan
January–5 February 1994	retaliatory assassinations of Shia and Sunni leaders in Punjab
February 1995	20 Shias killed and 17 injured in attack on a Shia mosque in Karachi
February 1995	20 Shia killed in attack on 2 mosques in Karachi
March 1995	12 Shias killed and 28 wounded (including children) in a bomb blast at a mosque. 7 more Shias were killed that night in rioting.
August 1996	12 Sunni SSP workers killed in Karachi
September 1996	Over 200 killed in five days of Shia-Sunni fighting in Parachinar
September 1996	21 Sunnis killed in attack on a mosque in Multan
October 1996	27 Sunnis (mostly children) killed in an attack on a Sunni mosque in Multan
December 1996	assassination of 2 Shia TJP leaders in Lahore and Multan
1996	assassination of Shia SM[d] leader, Murid Abbas Yazdani
January 1997	19 Sunni SSP leaders and workers killed in a bomb blast at a courthouse in Lahore and Multan
January 1997	torching of Iranian cultural centres in Lahore and Multan
January–May 1997	assassination of 75 Shia municipal leaders and prominent community figures in rural Punjab
1–10 August 1997	70 people killed various incidents of sectarian violence in and around Lahore
September 1997	Five Iranian military personnel assassinated in Rawalpindi
January 1998	22 killed and 50 injured in an attack on a Shia religious ceremony in Punjab
March 1998	15 killed in two days of sectarian violence in Hangu, NWFP

a. Source: reports in *Dawn, Herald, Newsline, Takbir, Economist,* and *Far Eastern Economic Review,* 1988–1998.
b. Tehrik-i Ja'fariyah Pakistan (Pakistan's Shia Movement).
c. Sipah-e-Sahabah Pakistan (SSP, Pakistan's Army of the Companions of the Prophet).
d. Muhammad's Army.

In addition, the increase in the numbers of Pakistanis who worked in various Persian Gulf states following the rise in the price of oil in 1974 translated into generous *zakat* and other contributions to madrassahs, or Islamic organizations, preachers, ulama, and lay Islamist activists who would funnel those funds into existing madrassahs or found new ones. There exists a direct link between socioeconomic changes that labour migration brought about and the transformation of the socio-political role of madrassahs.

THE IMPACT OF THE ZIA REGIME AND STATE-LED ISLAMIZATION

The military regime of General Muhammad Ziaul Haq (1977–88) was also instrumental in bringing about changes in both the number and character of madrassahs. The Zia regime was deeply committed to Islamization, and throughout its decade-long rule over Pakistan created numerous Islamic social and political institutions, anchored a good measure of public policy-making in Islamic ideology, and opened various government agencies to Islamist activists.[12] As a part of the Islamization initiative, the government provided financial and other support to madrassahs, and enabled Islamic parties, social groups, and ulama to do the same.[13] Most notably, from 1980 onwards, madrassahs became notable recipients of zakat funds that the government collected. In 1984, for instance, 9.4 per cent of zakat funds went to the support of madrassahs, benefiting 2,273 madrassahs and 111,050 students.[14] Even after some cuts in funding and a crackdown on many madrassahs in 1996, the government was providing $3.5 million a year to various madrassahs.[15]

The Zia regime also encouraged the proliferation of madrassahs by increasing opportunities for employment of their graduates in government agencies and state institutions. Recruitment into government service, however, went hand-in-hand with changing the social and intellectual functions of traditional Islamic education. In 1979, the National Committee on Deeni Madaris produced a report which encouraged madrassahs to reform their curricula in order to be more relevant to the needs of the changing society and economy.[16] The conclusions of the report raised the ire of the traditional ulama who were the first to respond. Maulana Yusuf Ludhianwi, among others, rejected the need to modernize madrassah curricula and emphasized the fact that madrassah education was to be judged in terms of the quality of Islamic scholarship that it produces and not its utility for the modern sectors of society.[17]

In 1982, the government followed on the 1979 report by announcing that it would view madrassah certificates as the equivalent of formal school certificates if madrassahs were willing to undertake certain reforms in their curricula.[18] The announcement opened the door for madrassahs to recruit from a broader spectrum of students, and through them, to play a more central role in society as a whole, as well as in national educational and political institutions.

With the government willing to provide financial support and accommodate their graduates, many madrassahs began to look beyond training ulama to provide the Islamizing state with its new 'Islamic bureaucracy'.[19] The traditional view, and the central role played by the *dars-i nizami*[20] began to give way to a new approach as numerous older and new madrassahs responded to the government's call, and some were actually established to do so. For instance, Barelvis established a new network of madrassahs, the Ziau'l-Qur'an (Light of the Qur'an) in response to the government initiative. The government thus created a new educational arena which the madrassahs were encouraged to dominate.

Various ulama organizations and parties, as well as self-styled Islamist parties, also looked to new madrassahs to help them expand their base of support. A greater role for madrassahs in national education would produce a citizenry that would more likely vote for Islamic parties and consider Islamic ideology an appropriate anchor for the conduct of politics. General Zia may have seen in madrassahs the possibility of changing the character of the Pakistani electorate and strengthening Islamic parties—which were closer to his regime—to the detriment of the secular national parties, such as the Pakistan People's Party, that were likely to oppose his regime. He had hoped that the results of the 1985 elections would bear this out. In those elections Islamic and right-of-centre candidates did well, although not as well as Zia had hoped. While government funding allowed new madrassahs to be created and older ones to be expanded, it was the employment opportunities that the government provided that brought in the students that were needed for making the expansion of madrassah education possible. The number of madrassah graduates jumped from 1,968 in the 1978–80 period (just before the provision of zakat funds and introduction of equivalency certificates) to 3,601 in 1984–85.[21] Whereas 5,611 ulama had been trained in Pakistan in the 1960–80 period, 6,230 were trained in the 1981–85 period alone.[22]

So notable was the impact of the government initiative that Islamist and self-styled Islamic groups—who were predominantly lay members and had received modern education—began to establish madrassahs of their own. The vision of reform and revival (*tajdid'u ihya'*) of Islam that is at the heart of Islamist ideological perspective has taken shape around a disdain for the institution of ulama, and the madrassahs and curricula that has produced them.[23] For instance, the Jama'at-i Islami's (Islamic Party) influential founder and chief ideologue, Maulana Sayyid Abu'l-A'la Maududi (d. 1979), had been particularly critical of the ulama, and had been instrumental in establishing the authority of lay Islamist thinkers.[24] In 1976, the Jama'at opened its first madrassah, the Ulama Academy in Lahore, and in 1980 began to establish a network of madrassahs across Pakistan which by 1990 numbered 75. The Jama'at has also introduced a madrassah for women, the Jami'atu'l-Muhsinat (Society of the Virtuous) to train women preachers—a new religious office that the Jama'at hopes will give it an advantage over the traditional ulama in spreading its influence.[25]

Other Islamic activists such as Israr Ahmad or Muhammad Tahiru'l-Qadri followed this lead and anchored their religio-political enterprises in newly-founded madrassahs. Hence, Ahmad's Khuddamu'l-Qur'an (Servants of the Qur'an) and Qadri's Minhaju'l-Qur'an (Path of the Qur'an) took the form of madrassahs which combine Islamist activism with a traditional style of education.[26] The madrassah model vests the self-styled activists with the trappings of the authority of the ulama, an institution they hope to replace but whose power and social standing they covet.

The Islamist and self-styled Islamic organizations adopted the madrassah model to benefit from generous government funding, and the possibility of infiltrating government agencies and state institutions, and to expand their base of support. More likely, however, they saw in the proliferation of madrassahs the potential for the established schools of Sunni Islam to dominate the Islamic discourse, not only in mosques (where they have been dominant), but in government agencies and in the modern social and intellectual mediums where lay Islamists had set the tone for debates over Islamism and Islamization. By encouraging reform of madrassah curricula and looking to them as a source for its 'Islamic bureaucrats', the state had made the institution of ulama central to Islamization. It had initiated the ulama to the Islamist discourse and by so doing also universalized Islamism as Islam.

The centrality of madrassahs to state-led Islamization meant that the ulama would remain in control of Islamic learning at a time when Islam was poised to define public policy and lay claim to modern sectors of the economy and society. It also meant that they would develop a more prominent role, laying claim to Islamism and its central role in state and society after 1980. The state thus helped create an ulama wing of Islamism, which would increasingly assert itself at the cost of the lay Islamist thinkers and organizations. The proliferation of madrassahs, their reform and new mandate, therefore amounted to a competition between various Islamic and Islamist institutional and intellectual traditions for the control of the Islamization process.

Unable to prevent the entry of ulama into their domain pursuant to the changes in the madrassah curricula, Islamist organizations and groups such as the Jama'at began to challenge the ulama for the control of mosques and their audience—to operate in the domain of the ulama and share in their growing role in Islamization. Consequently, differences between ulama and Islamists have diminished as they have been intruding into each others' territories and adopting the rhetoric, style, and symbolism of authority of the other. As ulama have become Islamists and Islamists have turned ulama, the narrower definitions of their respective religio-political authority, function, and arena of activity have given place to a broader and more all-inclusive Islamic/Islamist conception.

The reform of curricula changed the character of many madrassahs and hence their graduates. The quality of madrassah education declined, the concern for excellence in mastering traditional subjects was no longer important, and instead ideological outlook took over. Although this is not true of the far fewer older and prestigious madrassahs, such as the Deobandi Korangi Daru'l-'Ulum of Karachi, it is generally true of most of the newer madrassahs that cropped up in the 1980s and 1990s, and were instituted and managed by low-ranking preachers or ulama. As madrassahs accepted that training 'Islamic bureaucrats' and activists was more central to their mission than producing veritable ulama they began to modernize and politicize. In the North-West Frontier Province (NWFP) and Balochistan, owing to the proximity of the Afghan war, madrassahs also began to militarize, in many cases combining traditional religious education with a modern military one.

In the late 1980s and early 1990s democratization changed the political climate and slowed the pace of Islamization, and economic recession reduced employment opportunities. As a result, the promised jobs for the graduates of madrassahs did not materialize, leading most to join the ranks of the frustrated unemployed.

Throughout the 1980s the Islamization regime favoured the higher ranking ulama. They received government patronage and occupied high offices. The benefits did not trickle down very far. Lower ranking ulama, preachers, and recent madrassah graduates were not direct beneficiaries of the Islamization process. Their expectations were raised, but never satisfied. When democracy ended the Islamization era in 1988, the lower rungs of the ulama were expected to go back to their traditional functions in managing local mosques and Islamic institutions. Sectarianism began to shape around what Mumtaz Ahmad has termed, the 'revolt of the *petty*-ulama.'[27] Using the rural mosques, madrassahs, and Islamic institutions under their control, and using sectarianism as an Islamic ideology of mobilization, autonomous from the control of the higher-ranking ulama and their institutions and parties, the lower-ranking ulama began to stake out their own claim to power and wealth-satiating appetites for power, status and wealth that Islamization had whetted but left unsatiated.

Since the lower-ranking ulama, and especially those among them who were recent graduates of madrassahs, were less steeped in knowledge and were more political, and many had got their education at new madrassahs that did not offer high standards in traditional education, many would not be able to follow the career path of the traditional ulama, nor were most trained to desire such a career path. If and when they became preachers or ulama, they used the *mimbar* to pursue political agendas. The new breed of ulama and preachers often refused to follow the lead of the established ulama parties or traditional madrassahs, preferring to join smaller militant organizations. For instance, many of the graduates of the Barelvi Ziau'l-Qur'an madrassahs did not join the main Barelvi party, Jami'at-i Ulama-i Pakistan (Society of Ulama of Pakistan, JUP), preferring the militant Sunni Tehrik instead.

The new breed of madrassah graduates were nominally of the ulama, but had a claim to politics and were jihadist in outlook—they had bought into the rhetoric of the Afghan war, and many now view the Taliban's conquest of Afghanistan as the model to follow. In a state with ongoing ethnic, civil, and socioeconomic conflicts, with a preponderance of guns and a 'Kalashnikov culture', this militancy soon turned violent. A prime example here is the escalation of violence in sectarian conflict in the Kurram valley in NWFP; where in the summer of 1996 in Parachinar in a five-day armed conflict some 200 people lost their lives. There had existed socioeconomic grievances between Shias and Sunnis regarding control of fertile land and proceeds from the fecund tomato crop. The manner in which such grievances translated into an outright sectarian war, however, had to do with the fact that the older Shia and Sunni ulama and preachers had been replaced with recent graduates of militant madrassahs, whose activism had served to harden sectarian identities and promote militancy. Sermons had become more vitriolic and mosques were used as arms depots. The proximity of the region to the Afghan conflict had also helped with both the arms build-up by the two sides, and the propensity to use violence.[28]

Many of the frustrated madrassah graduates also quickly became ensnared in the web of criminal activities in Pakistan, from the heroin trade between NWFP and Karachi, to extortion, kidnapping and even robbery in Punjab. Militant activists, *petty*-ulama, and even madrassahs began to receive support from criminals who patronized or joined sectarian organizations, and at times helped establish sectarian madrassahs and armed bands. In return, sectarianism provided a religious cover for criminal activities. Authorities have been hard-pressed to crack-down on criminals who are members of sectarian organizations; for arrests and prosecutions are viewed as harassment of Islamic organizations, and the accused are seen as 'martyrs' in the cause of Islam.

In addition, sectarian groups enjoy the support of the larger mainstream Islamic parties, such as Jami'at-i Ulama-i Islam (Society of Ulama of Islam, JUI), which hail from the same intellectual tradition, or with whom the sectarian forces have been in alliance.[29] The support of the larger parties has in the past translated into immunity from prosecution for all those associated with sectarian activities. That immunity, needless to add, has been a boon for criminal activity.

This process also transformed madrassahs from intellectual institutions into political ones. Madrassahs became the recruiting and training grounds for religio-political activist organizations. In some instances, they also become lucrative financial concerns. This has given a whole new dimension to sectarian posturing. It has made sectarianism a means to a financial end, and militancy a form of 'rent-seeking'. For instance, Saudi and Iraqi sponsorship of sectarianism has led sectarian groups to try to out-do each other in rhetoric and violence in the hope of receiving increasing shares of the flow of funds from the Persian Gulf.

Financial considerations have also influenced internal politics of sectarian movements. The size of the financial endowment of the Sipah-e-Sahaba Pakistan's (SSP) madrassahs has been so great that after the assassination of its first two leaders (Jhangvi and Qasimi) in 1989 and 1991, factional conflicts over the control of the purse and the madrassahs ensued. The losing faction then split, forming a new sectarian organization with its own madrassah(s), and the hope that it would replicate SSP's financial success and political power. Lashkar-i Jhangvi was, for instance, formed in such a manner in 1990 by Riaz Basra, and soon exceeded SSP in assassinations and use of violence. Although the divisions have been real they have not necessarily produced completely separate organizations. SSP has continued to maintain close ties with its splinter groups, some of which have collapsed back into SSP, while others remain only nominally independent.

Patronage of madrassahs went a long way in legitimating the state's Islamization policies just as it extended its control over important and interconnected networks of Islamic education, and local level political authority and social control. Hence, the rise in the importance of madrassahs was part of the dialectics of expansion of state capacity, and in some measure, the indigenization of the postcolonial state in Pakistan. Its consequence, however, was not only to increase the number of madrassahs, but to change their character, bring them into politics, and create a dangerous class of religiously inclined, militant, unemployed, frustrated, and half-educated youth.[30]

Moreover, the reform, politicization and proliferation of madrassahs also created a new axis of conflict with the state. The declining opportunities for madrassah graduates created new pressures on the state and even began to create difficulties in its relations with the various Islamic groups and parties. After the conclusion of the Afghan war the government found it exceedingly difficult to shut down the most militant madrassahs and to demobilize Mujahedin units that were attached to them. The continuation of the Afghan campaign through the Taliban, which are in their entirety madrassah-based, and the dispatch of many fighters to Kashmir, allowed the government to postpone contending with the militant madrassahs. It has, however, further aggravated the situation as the scope of madrassahs' military role has increased. For instance, as part of the Taliban and Kashmir efforts most guerrilla war training bases run by the Jama'at-i Islami or the Afghan leader, Gulbedin Hikmatyar's Hizb-i Islami (Islamic Party), have been handed over to Deobandi Taliban and Harakatu'l-Ansar, thus further entrenching the political and military roles of the madrassahs and their graduates. Furthermore, the very notion of the Taliban (literally, madrassah students) has made madrassahs and their products more central to discussions about Islam's claim to politics and the state, and the ulama's role—as opposed to lay Islamists—in carrying out an Islamic revolution and setting up an Islamic state. The following remark by a mob leader during a recent strike by madrassah students in Karachi is instructive in this regard: 'Do not think of us as weak. We have ousted Soviet troops and infidels from Afghanistan, we can do the same in Pakistan'.[31]

The Zia regime's attempt to extend the state's control over madrassahs by making them dependent on the state for both their finances and employment opportunities for their graduates eventually translated into resistance. Most Islamic groups, parties, and ulama who oversaw madrassahs welcomed state patronage but not the control that came with it.

As the attention of ulama parties, and the Deobandi JUI and Barelvi JUP in particular, has been focused on politics and the struggle for power, they have come to view their religious communities as landlords do their constituencies, as political *jagirs*. This has led the ulama parties to emphasize distinctions between the various schools of Sunni Islam as a means of entrenching religio-political identities, and thereby tightening their hold over their 'jagirs'. Madrassahs play a central role in demarcating the boundaries of the ulama parties' constituencies. Through indoctrination, and by providing the basis for organizational networks, madrassahs have served the political interests of ulama parties, and helped transform their relation to their respective religious communities—from one that is rooted in distinct interpretations of faith to a patron–client relationship. For this reason direct control of madrassahs has been of paramount importance to ulama parties, and they have been willing to defend it tooth and nail against state intrusion—especially when that intrusion was in the name of Islamization.

As early as 1982 various ulama began to complain that reliance on zakat funds, disbursed by the government, had reduced voluntary contributions to madrassahs, which at times exceeded government contributions, and could at any rate jeopardize madrassahs' relations with society. Mufti Mahmud, the influential Deobandi *alim*, and leader of JUI, who was personally close to Zia and his Islamization regime, at one point asked Deobandi madrassahs to refuse zakat funds, lest his party and the Deobandi establishment lose control of their madrassahs to the state.[32] A number of ulama in Sindh declared government funding to be a form of political bribe and hence objectionable. Still others, who sought to shut down altogether the flow of government funds to madrassahs, declared that the funds should not be accepted on religious grounds. For the fact that the state had made zakat donations compulsory and assumed the right to collect the funds, and also that the funds are held in interest-bearing accounts, violates Islamic law.[33]

As the state's control over madrassahs grew, Islamic groups and parties began to show their unhappiness by opposing government policy-making. Since they were hard-pressed to challenge the government's Islamization policies they began to criticize the government on a host of other issues. The result was that the scope of Islamic opposition to the state expanded as did the purview of Islamist groups' political activism. The expansion of state control over Islamic institutions therefore broadened the scope of the state's competition with Islamist parties over policy-making, right to interpret Islam, and control Islamic institution.[34]

REGIONAL POLITICS AND THE RISE OF SECTARIANISM

From the outset the proliferation of madrassahs, and the change in their socio-political role had a sectarian dimension. First, they coincided with the Iranian revolution and greater Shia activism in Pakistan. Zia's Islamization was largely a Sunni affair, and hence viewed Shia activism as a threat.[35] This became apparent when Shias refused to submit to Zia's zakat law, and following large-scale and violent demonstrations by some 25,000 Shia demonstrators from across Pakistan on 5 July 1980—which shut-down the capital, Islamabad—received exemption from it. That Shia demonstrators defied martial law ordinances to rally against the zakat law, and that they increasingly relied on support from Tehran to organize and assert their demands even created certain unhappiness in the military. As a result, the exemption from the zakat law was followed by introduction of a provision to the constitution which made condemnation of the first three caliphs of Islam (Abu Bakr, Umar, and Uthman)—reviled in popular Shia ceremonies—a legal offence. It is, moreover, argued that the martial law administrator of Punjab, General Ghulam Gilani, deliberately turned a blind eye to growing Sunni militancy, and the rise of armed bands centred in madrassahs after 1980, to address the 'problem' of Shia resurgence.[36] The result was anti-Shia militancy and violence, which reared its head first in Karachi in April 1983, when Sunni militants attacked two Shia Imambarahs, precipitating serious clashes.[37]

The state's capitulation to Shia demands was seen by advocates of Islamization as nothing short of constricting the Islamic state and diluting the impact of Islamization. State-led Islamization was in effect being reduced to 'Sunni' Islamization which undermined the universalist claims of the entire process. Many among Sunni Islamist activists argued that Pakistan's Shia were in no position to carp about 'Sunnification' of

Pakistan since Iran had made Shia law into state law with no exemptions afforded to its Sunni minority.

The formation of the Shia Tehrik-i Nifaz Fiqh-i Ja'fariyah (the Front for Defence of Ja'fariyah law, TNFJ) and the Imamia (Shia) Student Organization (ISO) in 1979 (as would also be the case when the militant Sipah-e-Muhammad [Muhammad's Army] was formed in 1991) were seen as signs of hardening of Shia identity—which led Sunni Islamizers to conclude that owing to the Iranian revolution they would not be able to win over Shias and integrate them into their promised Islamic social order.[38] In addition, such actions by Shia activists—emboldened by the Iranian revolution and the prodding of the Islamic Republic's envoys to Pakistan—as demanding the removal of Bab-i Umar (Umar's Gate) in Jhang created antagonisms towards Shias at the local and popular level as well.

The threat to the Islamization process became more palpable as the exemptions led to an increase in the number of Pakistan's Shias. Pakistanis who wished to distribute their inheritance according to Shia law—which favours women more—or avoid paying zakat to the government declared themselves Shias. Many Shia families who had been close to Sunnism gravitated back to their faith for the same reasons. The apparent rise in the number of Shias—and the faith's newly acquired position as a haven from state-led Islamization—was disheartening to General Zia and his Islamist allies. In addition, TNFJ and ISO's adoption of the Iranian model of aggressive oppositional activities was perceived as a threat to both the state and the Sunni establishment. The rise of the charismatic and widely popular Allama Arif Husaini (d. 1988) to the helm of TNFJ also created consternation among many who viewed him as a potential Pakistani 'Khomeini'.[39]

As a result, anti-Shia tendencies began to surface among Sunni Islamist groups and find their way into the ethos of the burgeoning madrassahs. The Zia regime looked to madrassahs to entrench Sunni resistance to the greater assertiveness of Shias.[40] Some argue that the Zia regime was in fact instrumental in organizing madrassah students into militant Sunni organizations in order to counter the rising tide of Shia militancy.[41] One of the first of such organizations was the Anjuman-i Sipah-e-Sahabah (Society of Companions of the Prophet) which later became the Sipah-e-Sahabah Pakistan (SSP). Sectarianism and its institutionalization in madrassahs thus had strategic importance for the state.

Saudi Arabia and Iraq too were concerned about Shia activism in Pakistan and what they saw as Iran's growing influence there. The two

Arab countries were then involved in a bitter campaign to contain Iran's revolutionary zeal and limit its power in the region—since then Saudi Arabia has sought to harden Sunni identity in the countries surrounding Iran, a policy which extends into Central Asia, and which in turn depends on the efforts of Pakistani sectarian groups. As one observer remarked of the pattern of funding of madrassahs in Balochistan and southern NWFP after 1980: 'if you look at where the most madrassahs were constructed you will realize that they form a wall blocking Iran off from Pakistan'.[42]

Pakistan was an important prize in the struggle for the control of the Persian Gulf, as well as for erecting the 'Sunni wall' around Iran. Saudi Arabia and Iraq, therefore, developed a vested interest in preserving the Sunni character of Pakistan's Islamization. In so doing, Saudi Arabia approached its long-standing clients among Pakistan's Islamists, groups such as the Jama'at-i Islami, in the hope of creating a strong anti-Shia Sunni political and organizational front. Islamist parties had always been critical of Shiaism; they had, however, shied away from vitriol against Shiaism, or moving beyond theological disputes to treating Sunni–Shia differences as communal rivalries.

In fact, mainstream Islamists have always refused to be identified as 'Sunni', and had treated Shiaism in the same vein as they treated traditional schools of Sunni thought. For Islamists, the central issue of concern has been Islam versus 'un-Islam' and not Sunni versus Shia.[43] Hence, from Abu'l-Kalam Azad (in his early writings) to Maulana Maududi, to Muhammad Tahiru'l-Qadri and Javid Ahmadu'l-Ghamidi, generations of Islamist thinkers have sought to reinterpret and appropriate—rather than denounce and invalidate—Shia myths and doctrines in a manner that would bring Shiaism into the ambit of their ideological perspectives.[44] Islamism here has sought to be inclusive. Azad approached the martyrdom of Husain ibn Ali (the Shia *imam* who was killed at the Battle of Karbala in 680) with great respect, according it religious and historical significance just as he sought to distance it from the passion and symbolism that the Shia associate with it.[45] Maududi interpreted that martyrdom as a struggle of Islam in the path of justice and for the establishment of an Islamic state. He eviscerated the story of the Battle of Karbala of all the symbolism, myth and meaning that Shias associate with it, transforming it into an Islamist episode that presaged his own. More recently, the influential pro-Islamist Urdu journal, *Qaumi Digest* (National Digest) has followed the same approach in treating the life and thought of the first Shia imam, Ali ibn Abi Talib (d. 661),[46] as has a book by the rector of the Nadwatu'l-Ulama in Lucknow in 1989.[47]

In addition, Maududi, who was a dominant force in Islamist thinking early on, was also critical of the early caliphs, notably Uthman and Mu'awiyah (d. 680). His book, *Khilafat Mulukiyat* (Caliphate and Monarchy, 1966) raised the ire of Sunni ulama and activists, but had the effect of keeping Islamism away from hardened sectarian identity, and open to some elements in Shia interpretations of early Islamic history. In later years, as sectarian tendencies hardened positions on Shiaism, Maududi's treatment of both Shiaism and the early caliphs was denounced, and he was accused of being a closet Shia.[48]

The mainstream Islamists, and the most powerful organization among them, the Jama'at, refused to change course and become embroiled in sectarianism.[49] In fact, since 1988, mainstream Islamist groups have pushed hard for ending sectarian confrontations, arguing that the violence has been damaging to the cause of Islamism. Islamist leaders, for instance, viewed with alarm Benazir Bhutto government's anti-madrassah proclamations in 1994–95, and efforts by her Interior Minister, General Nasirullah Babur, to place restrictions on madrassahs, all in the name of ending sectarian violence.[50] The Jama'at-i Islami's leader, Qazi Husain Ahmad, met with Iran's President Rafsanjani in 1995 before bringing together all Islamist parties under the umbrella of the Milli Yikjahati Council (Council of National Unity) to end sectarian conflict and reconcile SSP and Shia militants.[51]

Saudi Arabia, therefore, looked elsewhere for its anti-Shia front, to self-styled Islamist thinkers such as Muhammad Salahu'ddin or Israr Ahmad,[52] and more important, the Ahl-i Hadith ulama. The Ahl-i Hadith is a puritanical school of Sunni Islam, which, much like Wahhabism, has been strongly opposed to Shiaism.[53] Some Ahl-i Hadith ulama such as Abdu'l-Ghaffar Hasan of Faisalabad, who had taught at the Medina University, had direct ties with Saudi Arabia. In addition, Saudi assistance helped establish new Ahl-i Hadith madrassahs, and to provide an inroad into the Afghan war for the Ahl-i Hadith through such madrassahs as that of Mawlvi Husain Jamalul Rahman in NWFP and southern Afghanistan.[54] Hence, proliferation of madrassahs and the greater power and prominence that comes with it became tied to involvement with the Saudi Arabian sectarian project.

With Saudi encouragement, self-styled Islamist thinkers and the Ahl-i Hadith mounted a strong anti-Shia campaign through publication of books and pamphlets, and magazines such as *Takbir*, sermons in mosques (notably, Israr Ahmad's popular Friday sermons in Bagh-i Jinnah park in Lahore) and activism centred in madrassahs.⁵⁵ Thinkers like Israr Ahmad and Allamah Ihsan Ilahi Zahir, the chief of Jam'iat-i Ulama-i Ahl-i Hadith (Society of Ahl-i Hadith Ulama), formulated the first anti-Khomeini critiques from within Islamist/Islamic circles, but, more important, began to produce a new style and language in criticizing Shiaism, one that depicted that branch of Islam as outside the pale of the religion, and began successfully to transform doctrinal and theological disputes into communal ones.⁵⁶ The line of attack became increasingly focused on Shias as a people and not Shiaism as an interpretation of Islam. Zahir's book, *Shi'is and Shi'ism*, published in Lahore in 1980 and subsequently translated into Arabic and English and distributed across the Muslim world by Saudi Arabia became the most celebrated effort in this genre. Zahir's views continue to appear in Ahl-i Hadith publications, such as *Muhaddith* (Lahore), *Tarjumanu'l-Hadith* (Faisalabad), *Sahifa-i Ahl-i Hadith* (Karachi), *al-Aitisam* (Lahore), *Ahl-i Hadith* (Lahore), and *al-Badr* (Sahiwal), and play a role in fanning the flames of sectarianism.⁵⁷

It became customary for sectarian leaders to name their sons Mu'awiyah and Yazid (d. 683)—the first two Umayyad caliphs whom the Shias hold responsible for the martyrdom of their early leaders, Ali ibn Abi Talib and Husain ibn Ali, and who had not heretofore enjoyed respect among Sunnis either.⁵⁸ In fact, eulogization of the two Umayyad caliphs soon became an important part of the new language of anti-Shiaism, implying that having opposed and killed the two Shia leaders—the first of whom was the fourth caliph and the son-in-law of the Prophet, and the second the Prophet's beloved grandson, facts that are difficult to gloss over for Sunnis who are dedicated to exact emulation of the Prophet's life—they ought to be venerated by Sunnis as defenders of the faith against infidels.⁵⁹ A popular SSP slogan in its campaign during Shia Muharram commemorations was: '*Shi'a kafir...Yazid kay munkir*' (Shias are the infidels, when was Yazid a denier [of truth of Islam]).⁶⁰

The titles of the new genre of anti-Shia books that would dominate the scene from this point on attest to the change in attitudes toward Shias: *Shi'i Hazrat ki Qur'an se Baghavat* (Revolt of Shias Against the Qur'an),⁶¹ *Din Main Ghulluw* (Extremism Within Religion),⁶² or *Shi'i Hazrat ki Islam se Baghavat* (Shias' Revolt Against Islam).⁶³ In 1994, SSP would increase tensions when one of its leaders, A'zam Tariq, would openly assail Shia imams.⁶⁴ This was a new chapter in Sunni polemics against Shiaism, one which is not free of controversy, as many Sunnis hold the family of the Prophet (*ahl al-bayt*) in high esteem. SSP would then introduce the

Namus-i Sahabah (Honour of the Companions of the Prophet) bill in the National Assembly, which sought to add the names of the four Rightly Guided Caliphs (632–661) to the list of those covered by the Blasphemy Law. The intention was greatly to limit the scope of popular Shia commemorations during which aspersions are cast on the first three caliphs (Abu Bakr, Umar, and Uthman), for usurping Ali's right to the caliphate. This was to lay the grounds for declaring Shias as a non-Muslim minority.

The Ahl-i Hadith's anti-Shia campaign eventually precipitated a confrontation with the militant Shia organizations, which soon turned violent. Shia activists sought to silence the Ahl-i Hadith ulama through a number of bomb blasts, most notably one on 23 March 1985 that killed Zahir, who had become the most vocal anti-Shia and anti-Khomeini voice among Ahl-i Hadith ulama. It became evident that the Ahl-i Hadith did not possess the organizational capacity, nor the social base, to confront the more sizeable Shia community and its more formidable organizations. Although Ahl-i Hadith ulama, such as Sajjad Mir, and Ahl-i Hadith students and organizations like Irshad'u Da'wah (Guidance and Call [to Islam]), and its militant off-shoot, Lashkar-i Tayyibah (Army of the Pure), continue to play a prominent role in articulating Sunni sectarianism, the Ahl-i Hadith were soon overshadowed by Deobandi organizations that surfaced to carry on with the anti-Shia campaign.

In 1984, the Deobandi alim, Muhammad Manzur Nu'mani of Lucknow in India, wrote *Irani Inqilab: Imam Khumayni awr Shi'iyyat* (Iranian Revolution: Imam Khomeini and Shiaism).[65] The book, which was prefaced by the popular Indian alim and rector of Nadwatu'l-Ulama of Lucknow and Nu'mani's friend of many years, Sayyid Abu'l Hasan Ali Nadwi (popularly known as Ali Mian), accepted the claims of the Iranian revolution to represent true Shia faith, and Ayatollah Khomeini's to be the undisputed leader of all Shias, although most Indian and Pakistani Shia ulama then were students of Ayatollah Abu'l-Qasim Khu'i of Iraq who flatly rejected the validity of Khomeini's views and the ideology of the Iranian revolution, only to point to the revolution's excesses as proof that Shiaism was outside the pale of Islam. Owing to the high rank of its Deobandi and Nadwi authors, the book quickly made a stir. It was translated into English in India, Arabic, and Turkish; and was soon also published in Pakistan in both Urdu and English. The book made Deobandis central to the ongoing sectarian confrontation in Pakistan.

Nu'mani's views were shaped in the context of Shia–Sunni conflict in Lucknow,[66] and his arguments drew on the tradition of anti-Shiaism in the Deobandi school of thought. Deobandis had always maintained a belligerent attitude toward Shiaism,[67] and in the 1940s the Deoband Daru'l-'Ulum had issued a *fatwa* which declared Shias as infidels (*kafirs*).[68] That fatwa was later endorsed by senior Deobandi ulama in Pakistan.[69] Throughout the 1970s, Deobandi journals in Pakistan, such as *al-Haq* (Akora Khattak), *al-Bayyanat* (Karachi), *al-Balagh* (Karachi), *Tarjumanu'l-Islam* (Lahore), and *Khuddamuddin* (Lahore), printed inflammatory articles against Shiaism, going so far as demanding a separate electorate for Shias.[70] Still, given Nadwi's prominent role in the Saudi Rabitah Alam-i Islami, there was strong suspicion that the Persian Gulf regional politics too, played a role in the writing of the book and the rise of Deobandi interest in the sectarian confrontation.

In Pakistan, politics within the Deobandi community was pushing it in the direction of anti-Shia sectarianism. Competition for power between JUI factions in the early 1980s had grown intense. The protagonists had sought to establish their credentials and claim to power within JUI through acid vituperations against Shiaism.[71] The growing importance of anti-Shiaism to Deobandi politics, and the vacuum created within JUI owing to factional rivalries, opened the door for a rise of militant sectarian organizations from amidst Deobandis.

In 1983, Maulanas Salimu'llah and Isfandiyar of the Deobandi Sawad-i A'zam-i Ahl-i Sunnat launched anti-Shia movements in Karachi with the financial backing of Iraq.[72] These efforts would, however, pale before the SSP which was formed in Jhang, in Pakistan's Punjab, as a semi-autonomous division of the dominant Deobandi political institution, JUI. SSP was formed by Maulana Haq Nawaz Jhangvi (1952–89), a local Deobandi alim of low rank, and the JUI Deputy-Amir (Leader/President) of Punjab.[73] The SSP had close ties with the JUI, and especially with the faction led by Maulana Sami'u'l-Haq. Although the SSP was semi-autonomous, and in 1986 it would completely break with JUI over its advocacy of violence against Shias, they shared—and continue to share—many of their rank-and-file members and office-holders. Still, SSP was developed as an autonomous organization that was dedicated to militant anti-Shia sectarianism.

The SSP proved far more capable and willing to engage the militant Shia organizations. It built on the Ahl-i Hadith rhetoric, demanding that Shias be declared kafirs (infidels). The senior SSP leader, A'zam Tariq, for instance, declared that, '*agar Pakistan main musalman bun kar rahna hey, tu Shi'a ko kafir kehna hey*' (if Islam is to be established in Pakistan, then Shias must be declared infidels).[74] More important, SSP incited violent riots in Jhang, and later in Multan and Kabirwala in southern Punjab, Peshawar (NWFP) and Karachi (Sindh). One of its splinter groups, the Lashkar-i Jhangvi, retaliated for assassinations carried out by Shias with assassinations of its own, the most important of which was that of the Iranian cultural attaché in Lahore in 1990.[75] Although a number of its leaders were killed in its confrontation with Shia militant groups, notably, Maulana Jhangvi in 1989, Maulana Israru'l-Qasimi in 1991and Ziau'l-Rahman Faruqi in 1997 (in a bomb blast that killed 19 and severely injured Faruqi's second in command, A'zam Tariq) the organization has continued to grow in importance and power.[76]

The regional implications of SSP's campaign is reflected in that it has sought to involve Iran directly in the sectarian conflict. When Maulana Jhangvi was assassinated in 1989, SSP chose to retaliate by killing Iran's cultural attaché in Lahore—as opposed to attacking a Pakistani Shia target. Again, in 1997 when a bomb blast killed and injured several SSP leaders and members in a court house in Lahore, the party's response was to set Iranian cultural centres in Lahore and Multan on fire. SSP's actions have been directed at portraying Pakistan's Shias as agents of a foreign country, mobilizing Pakistan's Sunnis against Iran, and complicating relations between Islamabad and Tehran, all of which served Iraqi and Saudi policies in the region. The anti-Iranian aim of Sunni sectarianism became clearer in September 1997 when five Iranian military personnel were assassinated in Rawalpindi. The Iranian and Pakistani governments depicted the assassination as a deliberate attempt to sour relations between the two countries.[77]

With the rise of the Taliban, who like SSP are Deobandis, and who hail from the same madrassah structure and networks—and even training camps in NWFP and southern Afghanistan—the scope of SSP's strategic and political ties with Persian Gulf regional politics has expanded, and its penchant for violent action increased. It is reputed that the Taliban commander, Mulla 'Umar, routinely called on Deobandi madrassahs across Pakistan to provide him with recruits whenever Taliban troops had to be bolstered.[78] The Taliban have in addition strengthened SSP's ideological position and strategic importance, greatly enhancing the significance of the organization and expanding its potential role in Pakistan politics in general and the Islamist circles in particular.

The SSP has complemented its campaign of violence against Shiaism with a drive for a role in provincial and national politics. It has contested in national elections since 1988, and was represented in the national and

Punjab provincial assemblies, and Punjab government between 1993 and 1996.

The rise of SSP has in effect instituted a new form of Islamist politics in Pakistan, one which is more militant, violent, and sectarian—equating Islamization with a 'cleansing' of the society and polity of Shias. It arose in response to Shia assertiveness and owes its prominence to Iraqi and Saudi patronage, but it has gradually found a role and political agenda that is indigenous. It has also helped establish sectarian militancy in the Islamist discourse and praxis in Pakistan. Anti-Shia violence is meant to serve as a trigger mechanism, mobilizing Pakistani public opinion, militating political choices, and strengthening Islamic tendencies. Militant Sunni groups have so far failed to realize these aims. They have, however, succeeded in creating a specific consciousness about the 'Shia problem' in popular Islamic piety, as well as in the Islamist discourse—thus hardening attitudes about Shiaism.

SECTARIANISM AND THE SUNNI MIDDLE CLASSES

Although Persian Gulf regional politics served as an important impetus in the rise of Sunni militant organizations, local socio-political factors have become equally important in explaining their growth and influence. The SSP was formed in the Jhang district of Punjab, and since 1986, urban centres in that region: Jhang city, Sialkot, Sargodha, Gujranwala, Chiniot, and especially Faisalabad have been the centres for militant madrassahs, and the scene of most of the sectarian violence.

Jhang politics has long been dominated by Shia landed families whose constituencies have included both Shias and Sunnis. Rural politics here has largely worked through the clientelist ties between the landlords and the peasants, and has not until recently reflected sectarian identities. Throughout the late 1970s and the 1980s—owing to population pressure and labour-remittances from the Persian Gulf—the urban centres of Punjab grew in size, and also quasi-urban areas developed on the edge of agricultural lands. Urbanization has meant changing patterns of authority, especially because these urban developments have been dominated by Sunni middle classes and bourgeoisie—traders and merchants who are tied to the agricultural economy but are not part of the rural power structure. The Sunni middle classes in the burgeoning urban centres in the region from the 1970s on—and especially with the greater prominence of the post-partition migrants from India,[79] who do not have the same ties with the landed elite—have looked for a say in local politics.

With this the feudal hold over Jhang has come under pressure. Increasingly, the Sunni middle classes and bourgeoisie have emphasized sectarian identity as a means of loosening the hold of the Shia landed elite over Sunni peasants. In the first national elections in Pakistan in 1970, in Jhang, opposition to the popular Shia landlord, Colonel Sayyid Abid Husain, who was running as an independent, sought to make political capital out of his faith. From that point on, the Shia identity of the landed elite became a factor in Jhang politics. It did not, however, significantly change the calculus of the region's politics until the late 1980s.

The SSP and its founder Maulana Jhangvi built on the earlier anti-Shia tendencies in Jhang politics. SSP fashioned itself as a champion of Sunni peasants, fighting oppressive Shia landlords, who control close to 65 per cent of the land in the district.[80] SSP combined sectarianism with populism in the context of local politics to create a base of support for itself in Jhang. The party's strategy here is reminiscent of the Anjuman-i Ahrar-i Islam's (Society of Free Muslims) in the 1950s.[81] The Ahrar then combined socialist rhetoric with anti-Ahmadiya vitriol, arguing that the minority community—and its alleged wealth and prominence—was responsible for the misery of the poor.[82] The Ahrar succeeded in fomenting anti-Ahmadiya riots in Punjab during 1953–54 which initiated the marginalization of that community in Pakistan.[83]

Whereas nationally SSP fought for an Islamist cause, in Jhang it was posing as the vanguard force for the frustrated urban Sunni middle classes, which could see in sectarianism a powerful tool with which to break the hold of the Shia landed elite over Jhang's politics. The growth in the size of urban centres in and around Jhang by the mid-1980s had made the urban Sunni middle classes claim to power stronger.

Maulana Jhangvi started off his organization with the proclamation that Jhang was in the hold of landlords who abused their peasants and lived licentious lives. The landed elite were able to perpetuate their domination because of the prevalence of obscurantist practices (*rusum-i jahiliyyat*)—Shiaism in general, as well as those Sunni customs and mores that may lead to acceptance of Shiaism by Sunnis. This refers to Sunni participation in Muharram commemorations, and also to socio-political institutions that can tie Sunni peasants to Shia landlords. For instance, the prominent Shia landlord of Jhang, Faisal Salih Hayat (against whom SSP have contested elections), is also a *makhdum*—an institution that wields great authority among Sunnis as well. The status of makhdum gives Hayat certain control over Sunni peasants. In contending with Hayat, therefore, weaning Sunnis away from following makhdums and pirs in general—and denouncing those institutions as rusum-i jahiliyyat—has been just as important as denouncing Shiaism. Emancipation from feudalism has gone hand-in-hand with discovery of 'true' Islam and exposing the 'falsehood' of Shiaism.[84]

The opposition to the feudal elite was also evident in SSP's decision to use the assassination of Maulana Jhangvi to mobilize public opinion against the Shia rural elite. Jhangvi was killed by militant Shia activists who followed the TNFJ or one of its factions, and not the landed elite; and ultimately SSP itself pointed the finger at Iran. Initially at least, however, the party organized a strong campaign against the prominent Shia landed elite of Jhang at the time, Faisal Salih Hayat (a Pakistan People's Party member of the National Assembly from Jhang and a minister in Benazir Bhutto's cabinet), Sayyidah Abidah Husain (Colonel Husain's daughter, who was then an independent member of the National Assembly allied with the Islamic Democratic Alliance), Amanu'llah Siyal, and Sardarzadah Zafar Abbas. SSP was hoping to use the anger over Jhangvi's death to weaken the Shia landed elite regardless of the fact that they had no complicity in Jhangvi's assassination. An important implication was that all Shias (and especially those in positions of authority) were guilty.

Two years after the formation of SSP, in 1988, Maulana Jhangvi ran in national elections against Sayyidah Abidah Husain; Jhangvi lost by 8,000 votes. In the elections of 1990, SSP did better, winning one of the five seats from Jhang to the National Assembly and one of the ten seats from the district to the Punjab Provincial Assembly. In the 1993 elections SSP fielded candidates as a part of the Mutahhidah Deeni Mahaz (United Religious Front) coalition, winning one seat each in the national and Punjab provincial assemblies (it then joined the Punjab government when its member of the provincial assembly, Shaikh Hakim Ali, became a provincial minister). SSP did not participate in the 1997 elections.

It was apparent that SSP's power in Jhang city was not disputed, but its weak performance in other Jhang constituencies showed that its influence had not spread beyond the urban centres. In 1993, SSP won 46.8 per cent of the Jhang City (NA-68) seats that it contested, but tallied 6.3 per cent, 4.9 per cent, and 3 per cent in other Jhang contests. In fact, SSP has since done better in other urban centres in Punjab, and notably southern Punjab—where Sunni middle classes compete for power with Shia landlords—and has been able to show its presence in Peshawar and Karachi more than in rural Jhang. Its ability to end the Shia feudal hold has therefore been limited; a fact which attests to the resilience of traditional structures of authority in the face of Islamist challenges.

Still, the spread of its influence to other urban centres of Punjab shows that its promise of empowering urban Sunni middle classes is popular. The Sunni urban middle classes and bourgeoisie have been a strong source of financial support for SSP's activities and especially the madrassahs that produce the foot soldiers in the sectarian conflicts. For instance, the Anjuman-i Tajiran (Association of Merchants) in Punjab and also in NWFP has supported SSP, and their activities have overlapped.[85]

The middle class base of support is complemented by the urban poor and new migrants, among whom SSP has been active, providing them with services and an ideology and common bond that can sustain them in their new urban setting.[86] It is for this reason that Faisalabad, the fastest growing urban centre in Punjab—which is now the second largest in that province after Lahore—is also the seat of the most militant madrassahs. As such, SSP and its politics have spearheaded the Sunni middle classes' struggle for empowerment, just as they have provided a new language of politics for the rapidly growing urban centres through which migrants can be integrated into urban social life.

PROLIFERATION OF MADRASSAHS AND THE DEOBANDI ASCENDANCY

The increase in the number of madrassahs since the mid-1970s has been evident among all schools of Sunnism, and in some cases and periods more among the Barelvis than others. Nor have the Deobandi madrassahs been the only ones to engage in sectarianism; for instance, JUP leader, Maulana Shah Ahmad Noorani, was one of the most notable anti-Shia voices in Sindh in the 1970s, and the militant Sunni Tehrik (Sunni Movement) which is Barelvi, and the Ahl-i Hadith as a whole have lent support to anti-Shia activism. Still, the rise in the number of Sunni madrassahs, and especially their role in militant sectarianism has become enmeshed with an ongoing and much older struggle for power within Sunnism, and is tied to the larger phenomenon of Deobandi ascendancy in Pakistan and beyond.

Before the Partition, the most prominent Deobandi political organization, Jam'iat-i Ulama-i Hind (Society of Indian Ulama, JUH) and its leader, Maulana Husain Ahmad Madani (d. 1957), supported the Congress party and opposed the creation of Pakistan.[87] As a consequence, Deobandi ulama were not prominent in the Pakistan movement, and the movement as a whole—and by extension, the institution of the ulama—have had a difficult relationship with Pakistani nationalism. In 1945, a group of Deobandi ulama who were not active in JUH formed the Jam'iat-i Ulama-i Islam (JUI)[88] in order to preserve their influence over their followers in the future state of Pakistan. The leader of this breakaway faction was Maulana Shabbir Ahmad Uthmani (d. 1952) who would become the don of Pakistani ulama in the early years of the state, and would leave his imprint on debates over an Islamic constitution.[89]

The emergence of JUI and Uthmani's leadership gave the impression that Deobandis in Pakistan were all followers of Uthmani, and that the Deobandi establishment in Pakistan were in their entirety following JUI's lead. That facile conclusion obfuscated the complexity of the Deobandis' relations to politics as a whole, and their place in Pakistan. To begin with, owing to JUH's activist role in Indian politics, a fissure had surfaced in the ranks of the Deobandis in the 1940s over the extent and nature of ulama's involvement in politics.[90] Those who favoured an active role in politics in support of the Congress party and who were close to JUH, came to be known as the 'Madani group'—after JUH's leader, Husain Ahmad Madani. Those who eschewed political activism in favour of greater attention to scholarship and involvement in the religious life of the community, or supported only a limited role for politics in the religious mission of the Deobandi school, came to be known as the 'Thanvi group' after the eminent Deobandi alim, Ashraf Ali Thanvi (d. 1943).[91] The Thanvi group was not altogether insouciant toward politics as its members to varying degrees dabbled in politics, and some later helped form JUI, and took part in Partition politics, and later Pakistani politics.[92] Thanvi group's politics would, however, remain subsumed under the greater attention that it paid to purely religious and scholarly concerns, and would not dominate its vision of an Islamic order. For the Thanvis, unlike the Madanis, politics never became a vocation, nor an integral component of their religious practice and mission, nor did they view the realization of their religious aims to be predicated on success in the political arena,[93] although they did favour a state in which Muslims could live according to Islamic law—which led them to support the Pakistan movement.[94] The Madanis have been closer to Islamism in that for them politics plays a central role in their conception of their religious mission, and control of the political domain has come to dominate their definition of the ideal Islamic order.

Uthmani had been close to the Thanvi group, as had many of the important figures in the JUI in its early years. In fact, that Uthmani had little involvement in JUH owing to his aversion to politics is what enabled him to form JUI and create a Deobandi base of support for the Pakistan movement, and hence keep Deobandis relevant to the new state.

It is important to note, however, that Madani had enjoyed wide support among many Deobandi ulama and their followers in the territories that would become Pakistan. Many of his students were in Punjab, Sindh, and NWFP, where they did not support the cause of Pakistan, and fought against it in such watershed events as the referendum over the future of the NWFP in 1947. In fact, so strong had been Madani's popularity among the Deobandis of NWFP that, when the current leader of the Jama'at-i Islami, Qazi Husain Ahmad, was elected to his office in 1987, the Jama'at made much of the fact that his father had been a devotee of Madani and had named Qazi Husain Ahmad after Husain Ahmad Madani.[95]

The pro-Madani Deobandis assumed a passive role after the creation of Pakistan. They, however, remained influential in Deobandi madrassahs and gradually became active in JUI. In fact, those Deobandi madrassahs in Pakistan that were controlled by the Madani group, such as the Binori madrassah in Karachi, remained closely associated with Deobandi madrassahs in India, and continued to follow the leadership of Madani and JUH, although not openly. That they were politically inclined meant that they could not remain apolitical in Pakistan, even though they had opposed its creation. That the Madani group was more keen on politics than the Thanvi group meant that it would eventually consolidate its hold over political activities and organizations of Deobandis.[96] By the 1970s, this had come to pass. Maulana Mufti Mahmud, the powerful leader of JUI in the 1970s and the 1980s—who oversaw the party's greater politicization during that period—had been a student of Madani, as was his second-in-command at the time, Maulana Ghulam Ghaus Hazarwi—as was the father of the other important JUI leader of the post-1970s period, Maulana Sami'u'l-Haq. The leadership and much of the rank and file of both factions of the JUI today are classified as members of the Madani group, and militant expressions of Deobandis from the SSP to the Taliban to the Harakatu'l-Ansar, too, are offshoots of the Madani group.

The ascendancy of the Madani group in Pakistan coincided with its greater prominence in India in the 1970s. In 1957, Qari Muhammad Tayyib succeeded Husain Ahmad Madani at the helm of the Deobandi establishment. Tayyib was close to the Thanvis in that he emphasized scholarship over political activism in Deoband's conception of its socio-religious role. In the late 1970s, Qari Tayyib's position came under attack from Madani's son, Maulana Asad Madani, who was active in Indian politics and wanted to consolidate his hold on the Deobandi establishment in order to further his interests in the political arena. Asad Madani challenged Qari Tayyib's authority, and finally, with the help of the Indian government, and after receiving support from Maulanas Mufti Mahmud and Sami'u'l-Haq (who came from Pakistan to mediate the dispute), Asad Madani formally took over the management of the Deoband madrassah, and with that, the Deobandi establishment.[97] With this victory the more political Madani perspective once again dominated Deobandi madrassahs and institutions in India, thus supporting the ascendancy of the Madani group in Pakistan as well.

Although Husain Ahmad Madani and JUH had opposed the creation of Pakistan, and had denounced it in the strongest religious language, their followers were eager to participate in Pakistan's politics. Mufti Mahmud is reputed to have argued to his followers that, 'We are fortunate that we had no role in the sin of creation of Pakistan, but being here we have every claim to its politics and future.'[98]

Still, that line of reasoning may have gone over more easily within the walls of Deobandi madrassahs than in the public arena. The legacy of JUH's politics made it difficult for its followers to participate openly in Pakistan's politics.

The Madani group's entry into Pakistani politics therefore followed a circuitous route. It was premised on a two-tier strategy; first, to create a space in the political arena in which it could become active; and second, a drive to dominate the Islamic discourse as well as Islamic institutions and structures of authority in Pakistan. The two strategies are separate although interrelated.

Uthmani and his followers became involved in politics only reluctantly and then over general discussions about the Islamic constitution. In so doing they established links with Islamist forces such as the Jama'at-i Islami, and were even content with following their lead in creating an 'Islamic' space in the political arena. The Madani group refused to follow the lead of Islamist groups like the Jama'at. Bitter altercations between Maududi and Madani before the Partition cast their shadow on the relations between the Jama'at and the Madani group;[99] but more importantly, their penchant for political activism led them to covet the Islamists' position. In addition, issues of importance to the Madani group were not always the same as those that gathered the interest of other Islamist parties. For instance, in the late-1960s when the Jama'at-i Islami and its ilk were fighting against the Left, and focused on the demand for the Islamic state, many in the Madani group supported Zulfikar Ali Bhutto's campaign for power, because his anti-imperialism and populism were in tune with JUH's politics in the years leading to the Partition.

The Madani group also chose not to become directly involved in the debate over the Islamic constitution—which could have put its own record on Pakistan on trial—but to focus instead on the role of minorities in Pakistan, turning it into a wedge issue that would gain entry for them into the political arena, but which would not place them in the position of directly laying claim to the state—which they did not deem it prudent to do at this point.

The Shia and Ahmadiya communities—and the Barelvis among the Sunnis—had been far more involved in the Pakistan movement than Deobandis. Many of the Muslim League's early leaders and patrons such as Muhammad Ali Jinnah, M.A. Ispahani or the Raja of Mahmudabad were Shias; as were M.A. Bogra, Huseyn Shaheed Suhrawardy, I.I. Chundigar—all prime ministers—and Iskandar Mirza, both of whom were governors-general, and the latter also president.[100] The numbers of Shias among various ranks of bureaucrats, Muslim League activists and leaders were far more numerous. The Ahmadiya, too, were prominent among Muslim League supporters and the bureaucracy that founded the new state. The most notable Ahmadiya among the leadership of the Pakistan movement was Sir Chaudhry Zafaru'llah Khan, a senior Muslim League leader and Pakistan's first foreign minister.

The Madani group looked to the role of the Ahmadiya in Pakistan as the issue with the use of which it could mobilize support and find a political base. The campaign was led by the Anjuman-i Ahrar, which was by and large a Deobandi organization, and which, like JUH, had been allied with the Congress party and opposed Pakistan, at least until 1947. Popular Ahrar spokesmen such as Maulana Ahmad Ali Lahori of the old city of Lahore were notable local Deobandi ulama. In the new state, the Ahrar found anti-Ahmadiya activism as the only means of finding a role in politics.

The minority issue was useful in that it shifted focus from what had been the role of Madani group leaders in the creation of Pakistan to what was the role of 'non-Muslims'—how the Ahrar characterized the Ahmadiya—in Pakistan. By shifting focus from their own political legacy to the 'Islamicity' of the state and its leaders, the Madani group was hoping to alter the balance of relations between Pakistani nationalism and those Deobandis who had opposed Pakistan, and to change the central questions in Pakistan's politics to their own advantage, and therefore to be able to appropriate the fruit of the struggle that they had opposed. The concern for the Islamic purity of the state would rehabilitate the Madani group. For it may not be entitled to a role in a state whose creation it had opposed, but it was certainly entitled to participate in an Islamic cause—against the Ahmadiya—which transcended questions of nationalism and loyalty to Pakistan. In effect, the Madani group was saying that the Ahmadiya (and later Shias) may have helped create Pakistan, but because Pakistan is to be an Islamic state, they cannot possibly have a central role in its affairs, and conversely the ulama—the Madani group to be precise—must dominate its cultural, social and political life, because they are the most qualified to do so, regardless of the legacy of their pre-Partition politics. Hence, the status of minorities (and later Shias) appropriately served the greater political objectives of the Madani group.

The Ahrar had a history of anti-Ahmadiya activism. What made its campaign successful was, however, the fact that Deobandi ulama as a whole had been among the Ahmadiya's strongest opponents. For instance, Uthmani himself had written a book against the Ahmadiya in 1924. In fact, the generally apolitical Thanvi group was more likely to become embroiled in a political campaign if it involved the Ahmadiya than one which was for an Islamic state—for the former was an 'Islamic' issue concerning 'who is a Muslim,' whereas the latter was a more directly political one. This allowed the Madani group to take the lead in Deobandi politics. Deobandi ulama, and soon also Barelvis, joined the fray, and the campaign to Islamize Pakistan was reduced to relegating the Ahmadiya to the status of a non-Muslim minority, all under the leadership of the Madani group.

Jama'at-i Islami's Maulana Maududi tried without success to retain control of Islamist politics by arguing that the anti-Ahmadiya campaign was unnecessary because the Islamic constitution would deal with minorities and the Ahmadiya among them, and in the meantime the riots were likely to damage the campaign for an Islamic constitution. Not only did Maududi fail to persuade Uthmani of this, but he was unable to restrain the Deobandis within the Jama'at-i Islami, such as Shaikh Sultan Ahmad. It was only after Maududi realized that he was losing control of the Islamist movement that he decided to join the anti-Ahmadiya campaign.[101]

With the anti-Ahmadiya campaign the Madani group managed to marginalize an important religio-political community—which was finally declared a non-Muslim minority in 1974—rehabilitate itself politically, find a strong presence in JUI and Deobandi politics in Pakistan, and shift the Islamic and political discourse in a manner that would allow former opponents of the state to now lay claim to it. By making the ideology of the state—to be gauged through the role of minorities in it, rather than its constitution, as the Jama'at argued—a central political issue, and by posing as the protectors of Pakistan's Islamicity, the Madani group ensconced itself in Pakistan's politics. It is important to note that many in the leadership of sectarian groups, Maulana Jhangvi included, had been involved in the anti-Ahmadiya campaign, especially in the early 1970s.[102]

Through sectarianism the Madani group and its various offshoots are now extending their claim to the state. SSP is serving the same function that the Ahrar did in the 1950s, mobilizing popular support against a minority, all in the name of preserving the Islamic essence of the state, but in effect to consolidate further the position of the Madani Deobandis in Pakistan's politics. Sectarianism is, therefore, a continuation of the anti-Ahmadiya campaign in that it serves the same function for the same religio-political group.

At face value, the focus of the Islamization process during the Zia period was on state institutions, law, and constitutional issues. At a more fundamental level, however, Zia and his allies sought to take over structures of authority—especially at the local level—through Islamization. This meant defining Pakistan as a Sunni state, which in turn meant charging sectarian forces to penetrate rural structures of authority. In the Zia regime, therefore, the Madani group found a patron and an ally in its drive for power.

By 1996, the rising power of the SSP was complemented with the rise of the Deobandi Taliban in NWFP and Afghanistan and the Harakatu'l-Ansar in Kashmir, all of which replaced older Islamist guerrilla groups tied to the Jama'at-i Islami. The Jama'at viewed the prominence of these groups and their replacement of the pro-Jama'at groups in Afghanistan and Kashmir, as a mark of the increasing Deobandi domination of the Islamist scene, a conclusion that was also shared by Barelvi leaders.[103]

One Barelvi response was the Sunni Tehrik, which was perhaps an attempt at stymieing the Deobandi onslaught by becoming involved in sectarianism. The dominant Barelvi establishments, those under the leadership of Maulanas Shah Ahmad Noorani—who had earlier led anti-Shia movements in Karachi—and Abdus Sattar Niyazi, however, joined hands with Qazi Husain Ahmad of the Jama'at-i Islami, and the leadership of Tehrik-i Ja'fariyah Pakistan (the old TNJF) to form the Milli Yikjahati

Council. Under the guise of bringing about sectarian peace, the Jama'at, Barelvis, and Shias were hoping to form an anti-Madani group coalition. The Milli Yikjahati Council also appealed to remnants of the Thanvi group among the Deobandi ulama for support. The Thanvis, although not active in the political scene, have shown some concern with the radicalization of Deobandi madrassahs. When Maulana Muhammad Manzur Nu'mani of Lucknow issued a fatwa, declaring Shias as infidels, the Korangi Daru'l-'Ulum madrassah in Karachi refused to accept the fatwa as valid.[104]

Sectarianism and the proliferation of madrassahs has also been an aspect of rivalry between Deobandis and Barelvis for control of rural areas, especially in Punjab. In NWFP and northern Balochistan, Deobandis have always been strong, and with the exodus of Afghans into those regions—and with the help of the Saudi and Pakistani intelligence agencies—their hold over those regions has become further consolidated. In Punjab and Sindh, however, Barelvis and Shias have been more prominent in the rural areas, as have traditional religious leaders affiliated with rural shrines-pirs and sajjadah-nishins. The sectarian campaign has been directed at the Shias and has aimed to teach the masses the 'true' faith. As Muhammad Qasim Zaman observes, SSP's anti-Shia campaign is also an articulation of a distinct interpretation of Sunnism.[105] Denunciation of Shiaism goes hand-in-hand with propagation of 'true' Sunnism, which is in effect directed at undermining the Barelvis and the pirs. SSP's journal, *Khilafat-i Rashidah* (Rightly Guided Caliphate), seeks to rationalize and reform rural Sunnism, weaning it away from its traditional beliefs and practices and anchoring it in a Deobandi world view. Furthermore, as Sunnism is defined in terms of anti-Shiaism, then those most active against the Shias—the SSP and Deobandis—should lead and define Sunnism. In effect, SSP is a means of augmenting the power of Deobandi ulama and extending their reach into areas where they have traditionally been weak, rural areas of Sindh and Punjab.[106]

Since 1996, SSP has pursued a more concerted drive at penetrating rural Punjab. It has begun systematically to eliminate Shias from positions of authority at the municipal level in the province, as well as those who enjoy positions of prominence in small divisions and towns. In this campaign, between January and May 1997, SSP assassinated seventy-five Shia figures.[107] The assassinations mark a turning point in SSP's campaign of violence. Until recently, SSP attacked only TJP or SM (Sipah-e-Muhammad) leaders and workers, Shia mosques, and other Shia communal facilities. Government officials were not targets of SSP's attacks. Now the party has begun systematically to eliminate Shias from positions of authority in Punjab. There is little doubt that SSP's campaign is now directed at the state—the party has taken upon itself to rid governmental institutions of Shias. In many regards this policy resembles the drive to eliminate the Ahmediya from government positions in the 1950s.

The SSP's challenge to the state fits the general posture of the rising Deobandi activism in Pakistan. On 15 February 1998, Maulana Fazlur Rahman, a leader of JUI—whose father, Mufti Mahmud was a student of Madani—responded to the possible government attempts to shut down madrassahs in the following manner:

> A particular ruling class who has been ruling over the people for the last 50 years has usurped the right of Pakistan as a sovereign state. This ruling class is a carry-over of the British masters, and has turned Pakistan into its own fiefdom. Speaker of the National Assembly welcomed the Queen Elizabeth, saying, 'Like my forefathers, I, too, am loyal to the British Crown'. Prime Minister Nawaz Sharif, whose forefathers were not in the picture at that time, thanked the Queen for bestowing freedom to Pakistanis. This ruling class had divided the country and one of its representatives, Nawaz Sharif says Pakistan was created in the name of Islam, but its rulers have failed in enforcing it in the country.[108]

Not only is the sharp edge of Fazlur Rahman's vitriol directed at the state, but his reference to the British legacy, and its ties to the creators of Pakistan, echoes Husain Ahmad Madani's anti-British rhetoric and characterization of the leadership of the Pakistan movement.

The electoral performance of SSP indicates that its impact on rural areas has been limited. Still, its campaigns do mobilize Sunnis, and as such, purport to change relations between Shias and Sunnis on the one hand, and alter the structure of rural authority, on the other. In this, it threatens other Sunni schools of thought and traditional Muslim leaders. The rise of the Taliban and the Harakatu'l-Ansar in recent years has suggested that, in fact, the SSP and its role in Punjab are mere pieces in a larger picture. There appears to be a region-wide radical Deobandi resurgence in the making—something akin to the Wahhabi explosion in the eighteenth-century Arabian peninsula—extending in the form of an arc from India through Pakistan and Afghanistan into Central Asia. It is closely tied to Saudi Arabia both intellectually and financially. Its influence, however, extends further. In one Deobandi madrassah alone in Faisalabad in 1996 this author encountered seventy Malay students—

mostly from Kelantan, Terengganu, and Kedah provinces in Malaysia, and some from the Pattani region in Thailand, and Java and Sumatra in Indonesia—who are being trained as ulama. Their interest in a Deobandi education has no doubt been kindled by the example of Nik Abdu'l-Aziz, the chief minister (Mentari Besar) of the Malaysian state of Kelantan—a leader in the ulama-based Partai Islam Se-Malaysia (Islamic Party of Malaysia, PAS)—and a Deobandi alim trained in India. The Deobandi education that the young Malays will go through in Faisalabad is, however, quite different from the one that Nik Abdu'l-Aziz received in India.

CONCLUSION

The rise of Sunni militancy in Pakistan has followed fundamental changes in the role of religious education, as well as the role of ulama in society and politics. These changes occurred in the context of the Zia regime's Islamization initiative and the increasing tensions between Shias and Sunnis owing to the stand-off between Iran and its Arab neighbours in the Persian Gulf. They, however, purport to more. Sunni militancy has become a constituent element in the struggles of domination in rural districts between the traditional elite and the rising middle classes on the one hand, and in the attempt to integrate new migrants into the social fabric of the growing urban areas, on the other. At a different level, Sunni militancy has become a facet of the greater prominence of the Deobandi tradition—and one wing of it in particular—in Pakistan. This process began in 1947 and has gone through many stages, and adopted many forms. In sectarianism it has found a powerful tool to further its cause, to dominate the Islamist discourse at the cost of lay Islamist parties such as the Jama'at-i Islami, and to constrict its rival Sunni traditions, the rural religious leadership, and Shias. This has in turn instituted a particular discourse of power—one which is predicated on demands for religious and communal purity—in Islamist circles. This discourse is likely to continue to determine relations between Sunnis and Muslim as well as non-Muslim minorities. Most recently, the sharp edge of Sunni militancy has turned against Pakistan's Christian minority.[109]

The socio-political functions of sectarianism among Sunnis, and its implications for changing the nature of religious education, the role of Islam as well as that of the ulama in state and society, and the direction that Islamism is likely to take from here on, all point to the complex nature of relations between the Islamist discourse, the varied Islamic/

Islamist traditions that are prevalent in Pakistan, the state, and the dominant social structure of the country.

GLOSSARY

dars-i nizami	a syllabus for the education of the ulama that has been widely used in madrassahs since the eighteenth century
*daru'l-'ulum*s	Islamic seminaries
Deeni Madaris	Religious Schools
fatwa	religious decree
imam	infallible leader
Imambarahs	Shia place of worship associated with commemoration of martyrdom of Shia Imams
Ja'fariyah	Shia
jagirs	fiefdoms
jihad	holy war
makhdum	a hereditary keeper of a shrine
mimbar	pulpit
Shariat	Islamic law
Umar	the second Muslim caliph, much maligned by Shias
zakat	alms tax

NOTES

Acknowledgements: I would like to thank the Harry Frank Guggenheim Foundation, the American Institute of Pakistan Studies, and the Faculty Research Grant fund of the University of San Diego for their support; Israr Ahmad, Mumtaz Ahmed, Zafar Ishaq Ansari, Karar Husain, Khalid Habib, S. Faisal Imam, Khurshid Ahmad, Nadim, S. Mushahid Husain, Maulana Muhammad Ajmal Qadri, Suhayl Mahmood, Ahmed Rashid, and Muhammad Suhayl Umar for their comments and help with locating the pertinent sources; Muhammad Qasim Zaman for his careful reading of an earlier draft of this chapter; and finally the political leaders and activists from various national parties and Shia and Sunni organizations, government officials, and officers in the police and the military who agreed to extensive personal interviews with this author.

1. *The International Herald Tribune,* 16–17 Aug. 1997, p. 1.
2. *The Nation* (Islamabad), 1 Sept. 1994.
3. The official death toll was 95; the actual number according to eye-witness estimates stood at 200. *Newsline* (Karachi) (Oct. 1996), p. 72.
4. *Herald* (Karachi) (Sept. 1992), p. 34.
5. *The News* (Islamabad), 2 March 1995, p. 1.
6. *Zindagi* (Lahore), 15 Feb. 1995, p. 39; and *Herald* (Oct. 1996), p. 56.
7. *Herald* (Oct. 1996), p. 56.
8. Ibid.

9. Anwer H. Syed, *The Discourse and Politics of Zulfikar Ali Bhutto* (New York: St Martin's Press, 1992), pp. 205–24; Stanley Wolpert, *Zulfi Bhutto of Pakistan* (New York: Oxford University Press, 1993), pp. 214–29; and Seyyed Vali Reza Nasr, *The Vanguard of Islamic Revolution: The Jama'at-i Islami of Pakistan* (Berkeley: University of California Press, 1994), p. 179.
10. *Herald* (Oct. 1996), p. 54.
11. On Arab support for the Afghan war, see: Barnett R. Rubin, *The Fragmentation of Afghanistan: State Formation and Collapse in the International System* (New Haven: Yale University Press, 1995), pp. 196–7; idem, 'Arab Islamists in Afghanistan,' in John L. Esposito (ed.), *Political Islam: Revolution, Radicalism, or Reform?* (Boulder: Lynne Rienner, 1997), pp. 179–206.
12. On the Zia regime's Islamization policies, see: Afzal Iqbal, *Islamization in Pakistan* (Lahore: Vanguard Books, 1986); Shahid Javed Burki and Craig Baxter, *Pakistan Under the Military: Eleven years of Zia ul-Haq* (Boulder, CO: Westview Press, 1991); Charles Kennedy, 'Islamization and Legal Reform in Pakistan, 1979–89,' *Pacific Affairs*, 63:1 (Spring 1990), pp. 62–77; Mumtaz Ahmed, 'Islam and the State: The Case of Pakistan,' in Matthew Moen and Lowell Gustafson (eds.), *The Religious Challenge of the State* (Philadelphia: Temple University Press, 1992), pp. 239–67; Anita Weiss (ed.), *Islamic Reassertion in Pakistan: Application of Islamic Laws in a Modern State* (Syracuse: Syracuse University Press, 1986); Seyyed Vali Reza Nasr, 'Islamic Opposition to the Islamic State: The Jama'at-i-Islami 1977–1988,' *International Journal of Middle East Studies*, 25, 2 (May 1993), pp. 261–83.
13. S. Jamal Malik, *Colonization of Islam: Dissolution of Traditional Institutions in Pakistan* (New Delhi: Manohar, 1996), pp. 85–119.
14. *Idem*, 'Islamization in Pakistan 1977–1985: The Ulama and their Places of Learning,' *Islamic Studies*, 28, 1 (Spring 1989), p. 13.
15. *Economist*, 28 Jan. 1996, p. 37.
16. Malik, 'Islamization,' pp. 9–10.
17. Muhammad Qasim Zaman, 'The Reform of the Madrassah in British India and Pakistan,' unpublished paper presented at the Rockefeller Foundation, Duke University, University of North Carolina, Chapel Hill, and North Carolina State University's 'Transformations of the South Asian Islamicate Community in the 19th and 20th Centuries' conference in May 1996.
18. Malik, 'Islamization,' pp. 11–12.
19. The government also established the International Islamic University in Islamabad with the financial assistance of Saudi Arabia for this very purpose.
20. On the *dars-i-nizami*, see Barbara Metcalf, *Islamic Revival in British India: Deoband, 1860–1900* (Princeton: Princeton University Press, 1982), p. 31; and Shaikh Muhammad Ikram, *Rud-i Kawthar*, reprint (Lahore: Idarah-i Thaqafat-i Islam, 1988), pp. 605–9.
21. Malik, 'Islamization,' p. 16.
22. Ibid., p. 12.
23. See, for instance, Maryam Jameelah, *A Manifesto of the Islamic Movement* (Lahore: Mohammad Yusuf Khan, 1969), and *idem, Islam in Theory and Practice* (Lahore: Mohammad Yusuf Khan, 1973).
24. On Maududi's views on the ulama, see Seyyed Vali Reza Nasr, *Mawdudi and the Making of Islamic Revivalism* (New York: Oxford University Press, 1996), pp. 110–22.
25. *Ijtima 'se ijtima 'tak* (1963–1974): Proceedings of the Jama'at-i Islami of Pakistan (Lahore: Jama'at-i-Islami, 1989); Jan Muhammad Abbasi, *Ulama convention ki rudad*

(Proceedings of the Ulama Convention) (Lahore: Jama'at-i-Islami, 1989); and *Herald* (Sept. 1992), pp. 32–3.

26. Seyyed Vali Reza Nasr, "Organization' in Islamic Revivalist Movements, in Charles H. Kennedy and Rasul B. Rais (eds.), *Pakistan 1995* (Boulder: Westview Press, 1995), pp. 61–82.
27. Mumtaz Ahmed, 'Revivalism, Islamization, Sectarianism and Violence in Pakistan,' in Craig Baxter and Charles H. Kennedy (eds.), *Pakistan 1997* (Boulder CO: Westview Press, 1998), pp. 101–21.
28. *Newsline* (Oct. 1996), p. 75.
29. *Herald* (June 1994), p. 30.
30. Olivier Roy refers to this class as the 'lumpen intelligentsia', Olivier Roy, *The Failure of Political Islam* (Cambridge, MA: Harvard University Press, 1994), pp. 89–106.
31. *Herald* (Dec. 1997), p. 64.
32. Jamal Malik, 'Dynamics among Traditional Religious Scholars and their Institutions in Contemporary South Asia,' *The Muslim World*, 87, 3–4 (July–Oct. 1997), pp. 216–17.
33. *Idem*, 'Islamization,' pp. 22.
34. Nasr, 'Islamic Opposition to the Islamic State,' pp. 261–83.
35. On the confrontation between Shia and Sunni Islamism, see Roy, *The Failure of Political Islam*, pp. 123–4, and Chibli Mallat, 'Religious Militancy in Contemporary Iraq: Muhammad Baqer as-Sadr and the Sunni-Shi'i Paradigm,' *Third World Quarterly*, 10, 2 (April 1988), pp. 699–729.
36. *Herald* (Aug. 1992), p. 67.
37. On 12 April 1983 the Sunni activists attacked Markazi Imambarah in Liaquatabad, producing clashes that led to the arrest of 135 people by the police. On 15 April there was another attack on an Imambarah in Golimar; cited in Syed M. Zaidi, 'Shi'i Activism in Islam: An Overview,' unpublished manuscript, p. 36.
38. On Shia politics in Pakistan, see Nikki Keddie, *The Shi'a of Pakistan: Reflections and Problems for Further Research*, Working Paper 23 (Los Angeles: The G.E. von Grunebaum Center for Near Eastern Studies, University of California, Los Angeles, 1993); Saleem Qureshi, 'the Politics of the Shia Minority in Pakistan: Context and Developments,' in D. Vajpeyi and Y. Malik, *Religious and Ethnic Minority Politics in South Asia* (Delhi: Manohar, 1989), pp. 109–38; Afak Haydar, 'The Politicization of the Shias and the Development of the Tehrik-e-Nifaz-e-Fiqh-e-Jafaria in Pakistan,' in Charles H. Kennedy (ed.) *Pakistan 1992* (Boulder: Westview Press, 1993), pp. 75–93; Maleeha Lodhi, 'Pakistan's Shia Movement: an Interview with Arif Hussaini', *Third World Quarterly* (1988), pp. 806–17; Muhammad Qasim Zaman, 'Sectarianism in Pakistan: the Radicalization of Shi'i and Sunni Identities,' *Modern Asian Studies* 32, 3 (1998), pp. 687–716; and Munir D. Ahmad, 'The Shi'is of Pakistan,' in Martin Kramer (ed.), *Shi'ism: Resistance and Revolution* (Boulder: Westview Press, 1987), pp. 275–87.
39. Many Pakistani Shias in fact believe that Husaini was assassinated by the powers-that-be for that very reason.
40. Zia still sought to placate Shias and Iran through symbolic gestures. For instance, between 1985 and 1988 the Speaker of the National Assembly was a Shia, S. Fakhr Imam; and throughout the 1980s, Shia generals held prominent positions in the military, albeit none were placed in charge of sensitive operations.
41. This charge is often levelled by Shia community leaders, and is echoed by some of my interlocutors in the military as well.
42. *Herald* (Sept. 1992), p. 34.

43. For a general discussion of recent Shia–Sunni polemics, see Hamid Enayat, *Modern Islamic Political Thought* (London: Macmillan, 1982), pp. 18–51.
44. Sayyid Abu'l-A'la Maududi, *Shahadat-i Imam Husain* (Imam Husain's Martyrdom) (Lahore: Islamic Publications, 1984), and Muhammad Tahiru'l-Qadri, *Shahadat-i Imam Husain* (Imam Husain's Martyrdom) (Lahore: Idarah-i Minhaju'l Qur'an, 1989).
45. Abu'l-Kalam Azad, *Shahid-i A'zam* (the Grand Martyr) (Lahore: Maktabah-i-Adab-i Islami, 1981).
46. *Qaumi Digest*, Ali Number (Aug. 1988).
47. Abu'l-Hasan Ali Nadwi, *Al-Murtza* (Lucknow, 1989).
48. I am indebted to Mumtaz Ahmed for this information which he had gathered through numerous interviews with ulama and Sunni activists.
49. Personal interview with Jama'at leaders, Qazi Husain Ahmad, Khurram Murad, Khurshid Ahmad, and Chaudhry Aslam Salimi.
50. *Herald* (June 1995), p. 46.
51. On the council see *Herald* (June 1995), pp. 46-50. When Qazi Husain Ahmad arrived at the funeral of SSP leaders killed in a bomb blast in Lahore in January 1997, he was manhandled by the crowd and branded a sell-out for having sought to bring about a reconciliation between the SSP and the Shia militant organizations.
52. See, for instance, Israr Ahmad, *Sanihah-i Karbala* (The Karbala Tragedy) (Lahore: Maktabah-i Markazi Anjuman Khuddamu'l-Qur'an, 1983).
53. On the Ahl-i Hadith see Barbara Metcalf, *Islamic Revival in British India: Deoband, 1860–1900* (Princeton: Princeton University Press, 1982), pp. 268–80.
54. Rubin, 'Arab Islamists', p. 187.
55. The government has begun to view stopping the dissemination of this literature as central to ending sectarian strife; *Nawa'-i Waqt* (Lahore), 29 Aug. 1997.
56. See, for instance, Maulana Abdu'l-Ghaffar Hasan, *Din Main Ghulluw* (Extremism within Religion) (Karachi: Ribatu'l-'Ulum'u'l-Islamiyah, 1983).
57. Ahmad, 'Revivalism,' p. 17.
58. For instance, both Israr Ahmad and Maulana Haq Nawaz Jhangvi name their sons Mu'awiyah and Yazid, and Israr Ahmad insisted on celebrating his daughter's wedding on the Shia day of mourning for Husain ibn Ali, Ashura (tenth of Muharram).
59. See, for instance, Maulana Muhammad Tayyib, *Shahid Karbala awr Yazid* (Martyr of Karbala and Yazid) (Lahore: Idarah-i Islamiyat, 1976).
60. *Herald* (Aug. 1992), p. 66.
61. Azhar Nadim, *Shi'i Hazrat ki Qur'an se Baghavat* (Revolution of Shias Against the Qur'an) (Lahore: Tehrik-i Nifaz Fiqh-i Hanafiyah, nd).
62. Hasan, *Din*.
63. Azhar Nadim, *Shi'i Hazrat ki Islam se Baghavat* (Shias Revolt against Islam) (Jhang: Anjuman-i Sipah-e-Sahabah Pakistan, nd).
64. *Herald* (May 1994), p. 46.
65. Muhammad Manzur Nu'mani, *Irani Inqilab: Imam Khumayni awr Shi'iyyat* (Iranian Revolution: Imam Khomeini and Shiaism) (Lahore: Imran Academy, nd).
66. On Shia–Sunni conflict in Lucknow, see Theodore P. Wright, 'The Politics of Muslim Sectarian Conflict in India,' *Journal of South Asian and Middle Eastern Studies*, 3 (1980), pp. 67–73; and Imtiaz Ahmad, 'The Shia–Sunni Dispute in Lucknow, 1905–1980, in Milton Israel and N.K. Wagle (eds.), *Islamic Society and Culture: Essays in Honour of Professor Aziz Ahmad* (New Delhi: Manohar, 1983), pp. 335–50.
67. Metcalf, *Islamic Revival*, pp. 40–2.

68. Muhammad Munir, From Jinnah to Zia (Lahore: Vanguard Books, 1979) p. 46.
69. Ahmad, 'Revivalism,' pp. 14–15.
70. Cited in ibid., p. 13.
71. Ibid., p. 15.
72. *Aghaz* (Karachi), 26 March 1983.
73. See a biographical sketch of Jhangvi in *Herald* (March 1990), pp. 39–40.
74. *Herald* (March 1995), p. 36b.
75. *Herald* (Jan. 1991), pp. 69–70.
76. Conflicts over local power structures and land are also at the heart of sectarian conflict in Kurram valley in NWFP. The Parachinar confrontation of 1996 was directly tied to disputes over land, and the fact that the most fertile land in the Kurram valley belongs to the Shias who profit far more from tomato production in the region: *Newsline* (Oct. 1996), p. 75.
77. *Dawn* (Karachi), 20 Sept. 1997.
78. *Herald* (Dec. 1997), p. 66.
79. Zaman, 'Sectarianism in Pakistan,' p. 705.
80. Ibid., p. 19.
81. Nasr, *Vanguard*, pp. 131–7.
82. Ibid., pp. 132–3.
83. Ayesha Jalal, *The State of Martial Rule: The Origins of Pakistan's Political Economy of Defence* (Cambridge: Cambridge University Press, 1990), pp. 144–51; and Syed Ahmad Nur, *From Martial Law to Martial Law: Politics in Punjab, 1919–1958*, Craig Baxter, ed., Mahmud Ali, trans. (Boulder: Westview Press, 1985), pp. 315–16.
84. Maulana Iliyas Balakuti, *Amir-i Azimat: Hazrat Maulana Haqnawaz Jhangvi* (Leader of the Movement: Honourable Maulana Haq Nawaz Jhangvi) (Jhang, nd), pp. 20–5.
85. *Herald* (Aug. 1992), p. 68.
86. Zaman, 'Sectarianism in Pakistan,' pp. 705–14.
87. Ziya-ul-Hasan Faruqi, *The Deoband School and the Demand for Pakistan* (Bombay, 1963); and I.H. Qureshi, *Ulema in Politics: A Study Relating to the Political Activities of the Ulema in South Asian Subcontinent From 1566 to 1947* (Karachi: Ma'aref, 1972), pp 351–3.
88. On JUI see Charles Kennedy, 'Jami'iyatul Ulama-i Islam' in John L. Esposito, *The Oxford Encyclopedia of the Modern Islamic World* (New York: Oxford University Press), 1995, pp. 365–5.
89. Leonard Binder, *Religion and Politics in Pakistan* (Berkeley: University of California Press, 1961), pp. 111–234.
90. In religious circles in Pakistan today the division among Deobandis is widely acknowledged, and the terms 'Madani group' and 'Thanvi group' are used with frequency by Deobandis themselves as well as members of other religious organizations and traditions.
91. For an exposition of Thanvi's views on politics, see Maulana Muhammad Taqi Uthmani, '*Hakimu'l-ummat ke siaysi afkar*' (Political Ideas of the Sage of the [Islamic] Community [Ashraf Ali Thanvi]), *Al-Balagh* (Karachi) (March 1990), pp. 23–53. It has also been argued that 'Thanvi group' refers to Maulana Ihtishamu'l-Haq Thanvi who was Shabbir Ahmad Uthmani's close associate after Partition; Kennedy. 'Jami'iyatul Ulama-i Islam', pp. 364–5. Still, popularly the term 'Thanvi group' draws legitimacy by claiming connection to Ashraf Ali Thanvi rather than Ihtishamu'l-Haq Thanvi, who at any rate belonged to Ashraf Ali's school of thought.
92. Mushirul Hasan, *Legacy of a Divided Nation; India's Muslims since Independence* (London: Hurst, 1997), p. 95.

93. Uthmani, '*Hakimu'l-ummat ke siaysi afkar*', pp. 23–53.
94. Hasan, *Legacy of a Divided Nation*, p. 95.
95. Khurram Badr, *Qazi Husain Ahmad* (Karachi: Saba Publications, 1988), pp. 1–2.
96. The Thanvi group has continued to criticize the overt political activism of the Madani group; see, for instance, Thanvi, '*Hakimu'l-ummat*,' pp. 23–53.
97. I am indebted to Mumtaz Ahmad for the details of this episode.
98. Cited in two separate interviews with Deobandi ulama who chose to remain anonymous.
99. On Maududi and Madani's debates over support for Congress see Nasr, *Mawdudi*, pp. 32–3; Qureshi, *Ulema in Politics,* pp. 330–9.
100. Chief Martial Law Administrator between 1969 and 1971, General Yahya Khan; and prime ministers, Zulfikar Ali Bhutto (1971–77), and Benazir Bhutto (1988–90 and 1993–96) can be added to this list.
101. For a discussion of this issue see, Nasr, *Vanguard*, pp. 131–41.
102. Zaman, 'Sectarianism in Pakistan,' p. 692.
103. Interviews.
104. Interviews.
105. Zaman, 'Sectarianism in Pakistan,' pp. 699–705.
106. It is interesting to note that from 1942 on, the Muslim League, too, had sought to develop political control in Punjab by entering the rural areas and wresting control of its power structure from the landed elite and pirs. In its bid to convert local power structures into Muslim League ones it used *biraderi* networks and local factional divisions; Ian Talbot, *Freedom's Cry: The Popular Dimensions in the Pakistan Movement and Partition Experience in North-West India* (Karachi: Oxford University Press, 1996), pp. 85–6.
107. *Economist*, 10 May 1997, p. 34.
108. *Dawn*, 16 Feb. 1998.
109. In May 1998, following a Christian bishop's self-immolation in protest against the treatment of Christians in Pakistan, some fifty activists attacked a Christian neighbourhood in Faisalabad, burning houses and shops; see *Dawn* between 9 and 13 May 1998.

CHAPTER 15

The Poetics of 'Sufi' Practice: Drumming, Dancing, and Complex Agency at Madho Lal Husain (and Beyond)

RICHARD K. WOLF

THE POETICS OF 'SUFI' PRACTICE

I develop an approach to the 'poetics' of music and movement, vis-à-vis language, in the context of popular Sufism in South Asia. Bringing Michael Herzfeld's notion of 'social poetics' into creative dialogue with Katherine Ewing's notion of the experiencing subject as a 'bundle of agencies,' I attempt to cope with the problem of 'meaning' in a highly heterogeneous event, the *'urs* in Lahore, commemorating the death of the Sufi saint Shah Husain. My pragmatic approach to navigating through an excess of meanings is to focus on what I call 'common terms of understanding.' The analysis illuminates how Islam is popularly grounded in South Asia, more generally, and is suggestive of how music and movement might be construed as forms of religio-political 'embodiment.'
[*poetics, Sufism, music, agency, South Asia, ritual, identity*]

The Punjabi poet Shah Husain (Madho Lal Husain, CE 1539–1600) practiced a heterodox, ecstatic, musical, and homoerotically charged version of Islam, which has left an enduring, if problematic, legacy. Drummers and dancers draw on Shah Husain's life history, his poetry, and his associations with related saints when they participate each year at the end of March in the lively, fiery, sense-filling 'urs commemorating his death (see Photograph 1). This chapter is an exploration of the 'poetics' of this 'urs and a contribution, more generally, to the notion of 'poetics' or what Michael Herzfeld (1997) terms 'social poetics' as it applies to music and dance. I observed a broad range of ritual contexts for vibrant drumming and dancing over about two and a half years (1996–99) while doing the initial fieldwork on this project; I have followed up with additional field visits and interviews.

Photograph 1. Devotees gather at the shrine of Madho Lāl Husain as the festival's inauguration approaches, March 2005. Photo by R. Wolf.

That Pakistan is an Islamic republic does not inhibit its citizens from holding differing ideas of what constitutes Islam, how Islamic practice should be controlled by the state, what the role of religious authorities should be, and how 'music' fits into religious practice. But many Pakistanis do share what I call 'common terms of understanding': structures, themes, or scenarios that are in clear currency—either redundant, passed down from generation to generation, or acute, achieving relevance at particular historical moments. Many subjects filter or shape their understandings through commonplaces drawn from Sufi poetry, stories about saints and 'urses, and spiritual interpretations of music and movement. The music–dance form called 'dhamal', a focus of this study, engages all these areas of social, spiritual, and musical activity.

When social actors in Pakistan receive and manipulate such 'common terms', they engage in 'social poetics'. This 'creative deformation of structures and normative patterns' (Herzfeld 1997:141) draws attention to relationships among cultural form and performance and implicates wider social and political configurations (see also Galaty 1983:363).[1] I explore the analytic potential of social poetics here by showing how some intersubjective forms of coming together and drawing apart at the 'urs implicate processes of social joining and division at encompassing geopolitical and religious levels. These processes are of particular interest here because 'urses are, ideationally, 'weddings' of the spirit of the saint to God. Some of the more engaged participants seek, through ecstatic corporeal practices and music, a spiritual transcendence that recapitulates the saint's union with God. These attempts at union are thoroughly implicated in a politics of who gets included in the category of 'Muslim' in Pakistan. The link between poetics and politics is strong.

I begin by laying ethnographic groundwork—presenting a scene from the 'urs. Then I introduce one drummer, Pappu Sain, who creatively alternates subject positions according to local terms of discourse and behaviour. Katherine Ewing's Gramsci-informed work on Sufism in the Punjab provides a useful perspective on the fragmentary and unpredictable effects of hegemony (e.g., modernism, Islam, and the state) on the individual in this context. Gradually integrating models of how individuals and collectivities apprehend and interpret their world, I analyze what it means for individuals at an 'urs to 'belong' to social categories (to be a 'kind of Muslim,' 'Pakistani,' 'musician,' etc.) in terms of different kinds of joining and dividing. Poetics lies at the nexus of an individual acting in the world—embracing, disassociating from, and deforming categories—and collective forces (or historical trajectories) that make these categories seem fully formed. Hence, I deliberately emphasize a tension concerning the role of the individual agent as he or she negotiates among various interpretive, or associative, possibilities. This emphasis is registered ethnographically in a discussion that returns to the drummers' case study several times and tacks back and forth between what shrine-goers had to say about the shrine, the saint, and his followers in 2003–4, local memories of what was happening at Madho Lal Husain's 'urs in 1997, and my own observations at both points in time.

I conclude by moving to locations beyond the 'urs where specific drum patterns and verbal forms appear in significant transformations. These patterns and their transformations, which index national and international expansions of Sufi shrine practices, have served as points of departure for different kinds of regional identity. The poetics of local action in this last case links worldly and spiritual weddings with values of unity and primordialism in Islam.

Our story starts in Lahore, where, in 1997, perched precariously in a banyan tree, I began to videotape parts of the 'urs of Madho Lal Husain. In describing the following scene from the videotape (see Video 1 at www.aesonline.oeg, 32/2 issue archive page), I have attempted to convey impressions of the diverse participants and their interactions with one another and with their environment. Images of fire and colour, forms of repetition and cyclicity, and simple tenets of Sufi philosophy are all common terms by which Pakistanis understand what happens during an 'urs. My emphasis on the geography of performance is meant to highlight processes of coming together, drawing apart, and mediation. Lahore, where the 'urs is held, is the capital of Punjab province, Pakistan's second largest city, and a long time site of Islamic political and religious significance.

1997: A SCENE FROM THE 'URS

At the 'festival of lamps' (*mela chiraghan*), as this 'urs is sometimes called, drummers Shahid Ali and his uncle Niamat Ali focused intently on the dancers before them, skilfully striking the *dhamal* pattern on their *dhol*, barrel drums. The broad tree stump that someone had turned into a fire pit (*chiraghdan*) that year was still smoking, flaming, and spewing out coals. A bearded dancer with long gray hair, clad in long red robes, approached and receded from the churning embers, irresistibly evoking the ubiquitous Sufi image of a mystic lover as a moth attracted to a candle's flame.

In his passion (*jazbah*), the dancer raised his outstretched arms and slowly whirled, his hair billowing out. Facing the burning chiraghdan, he crouched low to the ground and shook his head right and left, synchronizing his shallow footsteps and the vertical movements of his bent forearms with the drum pattern's duple meter. A break. Then, facing the drummers, his back briefly to the flame, he swirled his hair, which seemed to propel his torso around. His feet followed with tiny steps, tracing narrow circles. A dhol player followed suit, spinning with increased intensity and velocity, his heavy drum visibly tugging at his neck; he did not miss a single beat (see Photograph 2). These forms of musical and kinaesthetic synchronicity, coming together, are critically valued from the artistic perspective of some participants.

Photograph 2. Punjabi dhol players have perfected the technique of spinning while they play. Madho Lāl Husain 'urs, March 1997. Photo by R. Wolf.

The dancer, in this case, was a *malang*, a type of Sufi mendicant. He was directing his attention to the burial place of the saint, who is respectfully addressed as 'lord' or 'master' (*sarkar*). Through the configuration of their performance, such dancers create a 'place' (*than*) for themselves. Those watching the video in 2003 made the 'locational' interpretive move (see Feld 1984:8 and discussion below) of noting how this dancer marked his territory by picking up glowing embers in his bare hands and strewing them at his feet. The dancer, through the 'somatic mode' (Csordas 1993) of his own ecstatic dance and by paying close attention to the contours of the drumming pattern, was drawing himself closer to the saint and to God. He was also creating a formal barrier between himself and other people—much as he does as a malang in everyday life.

Many nucleated centres of attention, circles of drummers, dancers, and those focused on them gave human form to the shrine complex's milling throngs. The central shrine, graveyard, burning lamps and bonfires (*mac*), and large pots of communal food provided fixed points around which visitors squeezed their bodies. Marginalized, waiting their turn just inside the shrine's walls, were a few dhol players in search of patrons; as yet, these lesser drummers were being ignored, barely holding their own as people streamed by. Crowds poured out into the surrounding gullies and narrow lanes of fishmongers, knife sharpeners, and vegetable hawkers of the Baghbanpura neighbourhood.

INTERPRETING MOVES

Anyone attending the Madho Lal Husain 'urs carries with him or her a complex personal history and is likely to encounter a confusing array of sensory data. What are the poetics by which an attendee apprehends music and movement in such an array? An experiencing subject might engage in what Steven Feld (1984) calls 'interpretive moves' to negotiate various 'dialectics' in his or her encounter with dhamal. The 'locational' interpretive move of relating a heard 'object...to an appropriate range within a subjective field of like items and events or unlike items and events' (Feld 1984:8) describes well some of the motivations of musicians, dancers, and listeners when they move and listen. Acting and responding via 'somatic modes of attention' (Csordas 1993), key participants are charged with channelling certain activities (genres, dance types, etc.) to the centre and others to the periphery. Drummers play rapid, repetitive rhythms for dancers near the shrine while reserving more complexly structured patterns for smaller gatherings of connoisseurs on the periphery (see Photograph 3). Dancers respond to the movements and the sounds of drummers and attend 'to and with' their bodies in their surroundings (Csordas 1993:138), which include other persons as well as elements of the physical environment (such as fire).

Photograph 3. Drummers travel together from different parts of Pakistan and camp at peripheries of the shrine complex, March 2005. Photo by R. Wolf.

THE MULTIPLE AGENCIES OF A PERFORMER

I shall take a performer as an example of an individual motivated by what Ewing calls a 'bundle of agencies' (1997:5). In Ewing's model, the experiencing subject is differentially and unpredictably influenced by prevailing discourses in different social–cultural realms. As they move through time, as they assume different subject positions, subjects may associate themselves with or dissociate themselves from different social categories—or deform those categories—thereby engaging in a kind of social poetics.

Consider Zulfiqar Ali, also known as Pappu Sain, a local celebrity in Lahore, who attends the Madho Lal Husain 'urs every year. As a malang, he is ideologically removed from many mundane forms of order and discipline. Yet, by identifying with this category of mendicants—notable in Pakistan for their tattered robes, beads, and distinctive jewellery—he conforms sartorially to a type. Honorifically called 'sain' (lord or master), many malangs carry walking sticks, sport dreadlocks, and gather at Sufi shrines to dance to qawwali music or to the sound of the drums (see Photograph 4). Pappu Sain, unique among them as a drummer (rather than merely a follower), stretches the limit of, deforms, what a malang can be.

Photograph 4. Two prominent malangs, having watched the 'urs video, dress in finery for interviews and photographs. Madho Lāl Husain shrine, December 2003. Photo by R. Wolf.

When Pappu plays and verbally represents himself as a musician, he conveys the image of one controlled by a disembodied agency—the saint. But when he talks technically about music, religion and mysticism fall by the wayside: He studied music with a recognized master of the classical tabla drums and can articulate how he has adapted their rhythms to his large, barrel-shaped drum, the dhol. (Participating in the modern musical world by choice, he is not bound by ascription to a drumming community (an erstwhile 'caste'). Yet he also perpetuates the legacy of his father, a drummer who was devoted to his Sufi preceptor (*pir*). Pappu technically belongs to the Shia Muslim sect, which often represents itself in opposition to Sunnis. But to me, in 1997, he politely disassociated himself from an identity politics of division and embraced the Sufi ideology of unicity. Finally, Pappu has been caught in a crossfire of managers, promoters, tour organizers, and music fans, the motivations of whom remain difficult to reconcile with Pappu's stated goal of using the dhol to propagate the faith.

Knowing enough about an individual, one could presumably identify the subjective categories with which the person chooses, shiftingly, to identify. Among those attending the 'urs or, for that matter, making any weekly Thursday visit to the shrine, the most striking example of this identity shifting occurs in the case of what one consultant called a 'part-time malang,' that is, the person who adopts the persona of the malang during shrine visits and appears rather more ordinary at home or work.

BELONGING

In the case of Pappu and the part-time malang, the theme of unity and division implicates the politics, and the timing, of belonging. Although it remains important for Muslims to assert across time and space that they remain essentially unitary, communities and their leaders often foreground or background differences among sects, offshoots, and sub-communities. One way of mitigating this tension is to limit those who are 'truly' Muslim to a select few, and thereby, define unity by reference to a limited community. Another solution, which draws on some forms of Sufi thought, is to efface differences among Muslims and among humans, more generally. Those who engage in some Sufi disciplines attempt to take this process of union further by trying to dissolve that which separates humans from the divine.[2] But like any ideology, the Sufi ideology of effacing differences can itself be put to political use (see Ewing 1997:72 ff.).

The question of who 'belongs' at an 'urs such as that for Madho Lal Husain might elicit the catholic response 'anybody.' But actors maintain ideologies of unicity at the same time that they promote possible lines of cleavage associated with language identity and provincial politics. Although this point cannot be developed here in detail, Madho Lal Husain's shrine has been, post-colonially, a strong symbol of Punjabiness as against other linguistic and regional–cultural affiliations. Actors continue to use such examples of linguistic difference to produce ideologically a 'diagram' of social difference (Woolard and Schieffelin 1994:60)—Punjabis versus Sindhis or Punjabis versus native Urdu speakers.

As actors adopt possible social models of togetherness or emphasize regionality and difference, they objectify moments in their own history of cultural production. They produce 'texts' (cultural objects) of their own, which they then receive, transmit, and manipulate. What Michael Silverstein and Greg Urban (1996) call 'entextualization' and 'contextualization' are critical stages in the enactment of a poetics: For any structure to be 'deformed,' it must first be constituted, or 'entextualized' and then manipulated, or 'contextualized.'

A good example of such poetics concerns my central musical case, the dhamal genre, which has come to be known (entextualized), synecdochically, by a few distilled encapsulations of the drum groove; simply put, a 'groove' is how a rhythm is felt and danced.[3] As I detail below, actors contextualize these encapsulations in explicit verbal forms, which are made to be iconic with the drum pattern. The indexical relationship of the verbalized texts to their ritual contexts raises questions as to what subjectivities the generators and receivers of these signs are creating and how these subjectivities associate with social–political categories in modern South Asia. Dhamal has regional origins in worship at the shrine of the saint Lal Shahbaz Qalandar in the province of Sindh. Yet this 'residue of past social interaction' (Silverstein and Urban 1996:5) merely adds another layer—be it a pan-Pakistani, pan-Sufic, or specifically Sindhi layer—to what is, for many, still a symbolically Punjabi event and place.

Linguistic and regional associations are some of the broad terms by which 'urs participants may construct an understanding of themselves as Muslim, Punjabi, or Pakistani in relation to the event. More specific interpretations draw from a pool of images in Sufi poetry. Those whose themes are joining and dividing are my concern here.

JOINING AND DIVIDING IN SUFI POETRY

In Sufi (and other) poetry of South and West Asia, love and longing of an individual for another person is understood analogically as the craving of the human for the divine. The eroticism of male dancing during the 'urs is connected with this larger spiritual love theme. The form and content of poetry often combine forces to create an aesthetic in which the listener or reader experiences a multileveled tension (or alternation) among different kinds of joining and dividing. Connoisseurs in the traditional Urdu poetry reading (*mushaira*) could, for instance, frequently anticipate the conclusion of a *ghazal* couplet, which often hinged on a metaphor connecting human with divine love.[4] The momentary social union in which multiple expectations were fulfilled—when audience members might deliver the conclusive words in chorus, along with words of praise—was different from the symbolism of union or separation in the poem itself but was part of a larger aesthetic in which elements of form and content merged.[5] The convergence of multiple forms of union was, socio-culturally, part of the poetics of poetry recitation.

The notion of spiritual union has also been thematized in different phenomenological forms. In seventeenth and eighteenth century Deccan folksongs, for example, circular motions mimicking the grinding of food grains and the spinning of threads were used to create an 'ontological link' between the individual, his or her spiritual leader, and God (see Eaton 1974). The songs implicated entrancing Sufi spiritual exercises, called *zikr* (lit. remembrance; see Qureshi 1994:505ff.), which often consist of such simple phrases as 'God is one'. Zikrs are repeated until they become virtually a part of the utterer's inner constitution. Linking bodily practice to philosophical themes remains common in Sufi songs and poetry in many regions to the present day. When Punjabi drummers spin while playing, they may reinforce the Sufi theme of cyclicity, and more importantly, achieve transcendence in a manner consistent with the process of reciting zikrs. Such virtuosity has the potential to resonate with poetic images when contextualized in a Sufi setting such as the 'urs of Madho Lal Husain.[6]

The motion of the long-gray-haired and bearded malang dancing by the flames at the 'urs formally reproduces one of the most ubiquitous allegories in Sufi poetry and philosophical writings, that of the moth fluttering about the flame of a candle. The devotee, drawn by his or her love of God, approaches closer and closer, despite the danger; the attraction is sustained as long as moth and flame remain apart. But just as a mortal can never entirely apprehend God while retaining a human existence, so, too, the moth is immolated at the moment of contact with the flame.[7]

The flames around which much significant activity was focused in the 'urs, along with their red colour (which they share with some malangs' robes), contain rich metaphorical potentials for union and division in poetry and everyday life.[8] The poetics of fire are suggested by its possible forms: A flame can encompass two flames or be divided without losing its integrity.[9] A flame can incorporate by incineration or deter by the threat of burning. Red is a colour of love, union, and fertility. Brides and grooms (not only Muslims) wear red in many parts of the South Asian subcontinent, and sexuality is implied in the red garb of the *faqir*, a kind of Sufi mendicant, dancing before the shrine of the 'red' saint, Lal (red) Husain.

Although a broad pool of Sufi images is shared across different languages and regions, one might expect knowledgeable participants in the 'urs of Madho Lal Husain to be motivated, in particular, by this saint's poetry, which combined the esoteric philosophy of Sufism with common folk themes in the vernacular (Schimmel 1975:384, 388). Devotees become familiar with Shah Husain's epigrammatic poems, called *kafis*, by listening to South Asian devotional songs, instrumental melodies, and film songs and by participating in didactic reading sessions with experts.[10]

A shrine frequenter with whom I spoke recited (his version of) his favourite Shah Husain kafi for me.[11] Its building blocks enduringly contribute to the family of features found in all Sufi poetry: the emotions of love and pain, the representation of separation, the images of smoke and redness, and the implications of fire. These compose part of the 'familiar background' for ordinary shrine frequenters, not just scholars or mystics.[12] This version also presents unintentional if not creative deformations, such as the substitution of 'the bread of happiness' for what was supposed to be 'the bread of sadness':

> Oh mother! To whom can I tell
> The condition of pain that separation has caused
> The smoke of my teacher (master) descends
> and when I look it's red inside
> The bread of happiness; the broth of the gallows
> and the tinder of my sighs

Fire, lurking unmentioned in this poem, could be wisdom, knowledge, the 'self,' or the divine—perhaps all of these. One makes inferences about the fire via the qualisign of redness and the indexes of 'smoke' and 'tinder'. Is this the smoke of an inhaled intoxicant? Is the 'smoke' the teacher himself or the knowledge he attempts to convey? What for the ordinary person is sustenance—bread and broth—is equated with that for which the Sufi craves: suffering and death, annihilation (*fana*). In a higher sphere, these are forms of life: merging one's self with the divine. Even manifestations of human feeling, like sighs, are tinder for consumption. The imagery combines to express that existential pain that all Sufis feel while on this earth—a pain that may be felt, after all, as a kind of burning.

Verbal symbolism and vivid imagery of uniting and dividing form a significant component of the 'linguistic habitus' (Hanks 1987) of most Pakistanis who would attend an 'urs—any 'urs, not just that of Shah Husain. This habitus grounds the ways 'urs goers 'interpret' moves. In Peircian semiotic terms, signs in Sufi poetry are rhemes, signs of possibility, for 'objects' of embodied practice (Peirce 1955:103; Turino 1999:229). So, too, are received histories of the lives of Sufi saints, in general, and Shah Husain, in particular.

SHAH HUSAIN: LOVE, INCLUSION, AND SOCIAL CATEGORIES IN LAHORE

Sufism was already well established in Lahore in the sixteenth century when Shah Husain was actively fashioning a heterodox Punjabi face for the body of Sufi literature that had hitherto been dominated by Persian. A barely concealed sexual side of the saint's transgressiveness is implied in Shah Husain's other name, Madho Lal Husain. Shah Husain shares his burial place with a Brahmin boy, Madhu, with whom he is said to have been deeply in love. The inseparable joining of their two names and resting places resonates with the many forms of union performed at the shrine. Punjabis commonly associate the homoerotic theme in Shah Husain's life narrative with well-known incidents in the life of the saint Bulleh Shah (1680–1758). After losing favour with his music-loving pir, Bulleh Shah is said to have apprenticed for 12 years with women in a *kanjar* community of courtesans, musicians, and dancers. He later adopted the persona of a dancing girl and drew the pir to him with his newly acquired art. The partial iconicities among different kinds of union (of human lovers, disciple and pir, and human and God), inclusion (the unity of the Muslim community and of the diverse attendees of an 'urs), and phenomenological joining (tight synchronization of intersubjective bodily movements) remain unstated but, for the most part, obvious to 'urs goers.

Since at least the nineteenth century, the Madho Lal Husain 'urs has been regarded as a kind of spring festival, not limited to the religious observances of one particular community. Maharaja Ranjit Singh, the nineteenth century Sikh ruler of the Punjab who had patronized a spring festival at Husain's tomb, was instrumental in making the festival of lamps an occasion for drawing pilgrims from many religious backgrounds, including Sikh, Hindu, and Christian. This drawing together and association with springtime also has roots in life-historical accounts of the saint. An association between the 'urs and the Hindu holiday of *holi*, during which traditional societal restrictions between classes and sexes are suspended or reversed, may have originated from hagiographies that depicted Husain frolicking with Madhu during this ludic Hindu springtime festival (see Kugle and Behl 2000).

The notion that this 'urs is an event in which 'people of Lahore rub...shoulders regardless of class or communal backgrounds' (Jalal 1995:86) is now a nostalgic one. By the mid-1990s, the 'urs at this shrine had already become 'merely an occasion for the lower strata of the city's teeming millions to congregate and partake of the celebration' (Jalal 1995:86). In accounting for the distancing of middle and upper classes, Ayesha Jalal points out that conservative Islamist ideologues in Pakistan decried such practices as worshiping at saints' tombs and beliefs in the intercessory powers of saints. Although Pakistan's elites continue to resist the pressures of religious conservatism, the rising bourgeoisie apparently find association with the folksy culture of 'urs-goers distasteful. Disentangling the religious from the class issue here is difficult, because 'folk Islam', as it were, is linked to class. Yet shrine Sufism and dancing and drumming hold a rather New Age appeal for young members of the Lahore elite. In the late 1990s, students, especially from the trendy National College of Arts, found it fashionable to hang out at the Shah Jamal shrine and listen to Pappu Sai<u>n</u> play dhamal. Dhamal is a common term for understanding Sufism in the public sphere, but the reception of this term—mediated verbally and through the body—is a matter of poetics.

SOCIAL POETICS AND THE DEFORMATION OF A DRUM GROOVE

The drum groove associated with 'urses, dhamal, has come to be known by a simplified version, which can easily be remembered by a series of drum syllables or words. When faqirs attach the text '[Husain provides] refuge [for the] faith [of Islam]' (Din panah) to this pattern, they find meaning linked to their social group while subtly reworking, or deforming, the drum mnemonics employed by classically trained musicians (see discussion of Figure A7). The key pattern is an entextualization, an abstracted version of the dozens of repetitions and variations characteristic of any performance. The faqirs' act of contextualization, of deformation, indexes their social category and encodes insider knowledge.

The notion that certain kinds of knowledge, people, and, indeed, God, may be manifest (*zahir*) or hidden (*batin*), is important in Sufi and Shia theology. The significance of this alternative 'reading' of dhamal is not manifest in the drummers' inflection of the rhythmic groove but is, rather, constitutive, covertly, of faqir subjectivity.[13] In this simple example, then, the deformation of a received structure, a common term, an entextualization, is made socially significant, albeit musically hidden.

Pappu Sain temporarily stepped out of his persona as malang, a category of person that overlaps significantly with that of faqir, to tell me what 'the faqirs' do. At that moment, he identified as the practiced musician who could recognize and convey the reworked mnemonics to me. As Ewing (1997:22–23) stresses, as an individual moves from one social context to another, different kinds of 'background understandings', possibly mutually inconsistent, come into play, which relate to the different social groups to which the actor simultaneously belongs (also see Gramsci 1999). Such an outwardly verbalized 'interpretive move' on Pappu's part would be unthinkable at the Shah Jamal shrine on Thursday nights, when Pappu conveys the persona of one in trance (except for odd, spell-breaking moments when he motions for someone to put away a video camera).

Recognizing and creating resemblances (iconicities)—for example, Pappu identifying the faqirs' textualizations and the faqirs taking up a pattern for their own devices—are mutually constitutive acts. They define certain kinds of belonging in socially, politically, religiously, and artistically defined groups—which is not to say that each of these is necessarily separate from the others. In Herzfeld's formulation, poetics is 'an analytical approach to the uses of rhetorical form' (1997:142).

Recognizing and creating resemblances are 'rhetorical' acts not because they reify perfect fits—between, say, the structure of an act and the expectations of a social group—but because they redefine the nature of fits, they 'deform,' reform, or transform patterns.[14] The process Ewing describes, whereby the individual strategically adopts different, sometimes conflicting, discursive positions, precisely describes social poetics when those actions involve manipulation of common structures, resignification of well-known phenomena in local culture, and inflection of the local in some significant respect with regard to broader encompassing discourses. How, then, does the man or woman dancing dhamal participate in this poetics?

DANCING DHAMAL

> *Dhamal:* jumping into, or running through fire (a practice of faqirs or qalandars…).
> —John T. Platts, *A Dictionary of Urdu, Classical Hindi, and English*

The bearded, red-robed malang dancing dhamal at the 'urs engaged in several levels of self-identificatory potential or modalities of 'subjunctive mood' (Turner 1982: 83). Strewing fire, he temporarily occupied the role of an individual marking territory. In anchoring his actions around, and thereby, somatically attending to the bonfire, he was indexing for others, and stimulating in his own consciousness, an indeterminate array of Sufi fire tropes. As a pious follower of Shah Husain, he was willing to be 'burned', separated, or, in Sufi terms, annihilated (*fana*), completely 'lost in the contemplation of God' (Platts 2000:784).[15] Fire also embodies continuity—unity as self-sameness in time—in the form of an eternal flame. Fire iterates spiritual presence when thousands of pilgrims burn lamps and place them around the shrine compound in Shah Husain's honour.[16] One devotee I encountered attributed a Punjabi couplet to Shah Husain: 'Neither of the rich nor of the poor, the lamps are lit only for the faqir' and burn forever. In this man's view, the big, centralized bonfire (mac) was an enormous communal lamp, taking the place of the thousands more lamps visitors might have brought. These verbal commentaries convert some of the signs of fire from rhemes to dicents, from possibilities to asserted actualities (Peirce 1955:103; Turino 1999: 229).

Pakistanis recognize dhamal in terms of dance movements and drumming patterns. Serious *dhamali*s dance to achieve *hal*, a higher spiritual state (cf. Qureshi 1994:503ff.). They strive to replicate the 'urs's archetypal form: the spiritual marriage. Locational attention is guided by this overarching goal. Drummers show their respect for the saint by facing the shrine, but they also must watch the dancers for whom they are drumming, and the dancers themselves must face the shrine. So drummers sometimes stand between shrine and dancer and try to pay heed to both. Because the responsibility of such a role requires skill and concentration, dhol players are rarely able to engage in ecstatic practices themselves—for they might fail both as musicians and as ritual functionaries.[17]

As a musician playing for the dancers and as a devotee dissolving his being in Shah Husain, Pappu skilfully bridges this divide by alternating subject positions. In achieving *hal* while continuing to play competently, Pappu seems to have 'sustain[ed] mediated states of multiple or diffuse awareness' (Lewis 1995:231), 'dwell[ing] in states of being that are intermediate—between consciousness of bodily presence and unconsciousness as bodily absence' (Lewis 1995:235). Some, however, have expressed scepticism of his ability to manage both. Let us now take a closer look at the contours of embodiment as musicians shift from one rhythm to another, occupy one place or another, or bond with some dancers and avoid others.

DRUMMING PATTERNS AND DANCE MOVEMENTS

The spiritual aspirations of the drummers Niamat Ali and Shahid Ali are less lofty than Pappu's. These drummers are not malangs, but neither did they express the anxiety regarding the status of their drumming vis-à-vis Islam that I found among some other drummers (who denied their drumming had any connection with Islam). The pair were excellent drummers and had no trouble engaging in a musical conversation. They described playing four drum patterns, dhamal, *bhangra*, *tintara* (*tintal*), and *lahra*, during the public parts of the 'urs, which are appropriate mainly for their brisk tempo.[18] Because dancers recognize common structures across the different duple-meter patterns, they can easily transfer their primary steps or body movements from one groove to another. To invert my theme slightly, as the dancers retain their steps, the drummers deform the pattern beneath the dancers' feet. This reorientation may constitute a slight shift in subjectivity for the dancers simply because it feels different to dance with one's primary steps subdivided in different ways.

The Poetics of 'Sufi' Practice   383

Niamat and Shahid told me that dhol players also perform for one another in small assemblies (*mehfil*) away from the central 'urs activities, in which they may play any pattern at all, express aesthetic appreciation for the entire range of the dhol repertoire, and compete with one another. This geography of performance is both a result and a cause of interpretive moves regarding location. Drummers join in a higher-level musical discourse with other drummers in the shrine periphery. At the centre, musical complexity is backgrounded in favour of attention to dancers and the shrine, the former attention (usually) resulting in synchronicity with the dancers, the latter resulting (all hope) in emotional closeness with the saint.[19]

In the public arena, drum grooves organized around odd patterns of three or seven counts are avoided because they do not fit the dances. In the simpler patterns, drummers create interest for the dancers by inserting breaks (*tora*) and tripartite cadences (*tiya*s) as well as other patterned gaps in the otherwise thick texture of strokes. The better dancers anticipate and respond to these articulations with sudden, stylized movements of the head, arms, or legs. Drummers, when they create breaks, also respond to dancers' movements, working articulations musically into the flow of their drumming, resuming a duple groove at the original tempo. From this perspective of mutually rapid response, unicity is a matter of tight intersubjective bonding, an awareness of one another's movements to the point of being able to anticipate them (cf. Berliner 1994:390).

Niamat provided the syllabic representation (*bol*s) of dhamal that appears in Figure 1 (see Audio 2 at www.aesonline.org, 32/2 issue archive page). The numbers are 'counts,' or, in Hindustani classical terms, *matra*s (measures). The counts are subdivided into four parts, each indicated by a syllable or an empty square.[20]

1				2				3				4			
dhīn		di	nā		di	na	tān			ta	nā			ta	na

Figure 1. Syllabic representation of dhamal bols.

Dancers tend use these counts to anchor their leg, arm, and head movements. Such syllabic representations, or bols, often used as mnemonics or for teaching, are always incomplete abstractions, or entextualizations. Played on the drums, contextualized, dhamal is more complicated and exists in many variations (see Appendix, Figure A1). The basic pattern (*naghma*) serves as a foundation (*bunyad*) over which dhol players perform variations, insert rapid patterns, and create changes in density. The Punjabi term *phiran*, which Pappu used in referring to this process, is spatially evocative: 'to turn, to return, to go back, to ramble, to make a circuit, to walk; to abandon one's intentions, to bend, to be awry or crooked' (Punjabi English Dictionary 1983:911).

Such kinds of 'rhetorical' play around standardized forms are common in many musical genres and have many names (like *improvisation*). In Punjabi dhol playing, recognitions of sameness and difference and deformations of structure are implicated at other levels of musical perception as well. The difference between dhamal and bhangra, for instance, is not dramatic, and thus, may escape those who are not musically attuned.[21] Both patterns consist of four (or two) counts (see Appendix, Figures A3 and A4 and discussion at Audio 1–4 at www.aesonline.org, 33/2 issue archive page).

DRUMMING TEXT

Drummers and lay persons sometimes call dhamal 'mast qalandar' because they recognize the common zikr 'dam a dam mast qalandar' in the drum groove. It encodes Sufi ideas: 'With each and every breath' [dam-a-dam], the Sufi qalandar—one who has attained an advanced stage on the spiritual path—will become increasingly intoxicated (be mast) and, thereby, spiritually elevated. The phrase 'dam-a-dam', used in everyday speech to mean 'continuously', here also references 'breath' (dam): the mystic's life breath and the repeated inhalations of cannabis, hashish, or opium through which he augments his ecstasy. This phrase's significant rhyming counterpart, *'ali da pahla 'number'* (*number* is in English), means that 'Ali is literally 'number one', the first in the hierarchy. This well-known zikr is semiotically overdetermined, indexing a variety of musical and philosophical phenomena in the modern world (see Appendix, Figures A5 and A6). Those (not just faqirs or malangs) who chant the phrase while Pappu is playing at Shah Jamal may not be preoccupied with its semantics.

In Pappu Sain's words, this 'mast qalandar' drumbeat is the 'call to prayer' (*azan*) for qalandars at the shrine of Lal Shahbaz Qalandar. In Pappu's view, the first dhamal was danced by the Prophet's son-in-law, 'Ali, himself. 'Ali circled three times to rejoice after the Prophet raised 'Ali's hand and said 'for whom I am sarkar (lord), 'Ali is also sarkar', thus, establishing the key principle of succession followed by Shias and by many

Sufis.[22] Pappu retains 'residues' of several different entextualizations clearly in his consciousness: the extraction of dhamal from the shrine in Sindh and its reduction to simplified versions. He developed the 'connotation' (in Roland Barthes's [1970:90 ff.] sense) further by pointing out that 'Ali is not 'first' but, rather, he stands above the system of succession as 'the one who assigns the numbers'.

Not all drummers or listeners reduce the pattern to 'mast qalandar', yet the phrase remains a common term of understanding. Trained drummers, especially, would rather represent the rhythm with bol (syllable) patterns, as ability to abstract renditions of rhythms in the manner of a classical musician is a marker of high musical knowledge. In the more recondite textualization by which faqirs give voice to their social group (to which I alluded above), 'din panah' is followed by semantically nonreferential syllables, 'da na.' *Din panah* means 'faith refuge': Husain, the grandson of the Prophet Muhammad (PBUH) and son of 'Ali, provided safe haven for Islam through his act of self-sacrifice at Karbala. The 'classical'-like, abstract bol pattern (top line of Appendix, Figure A7) is close to the meaningful one (bottom line), although twice the length. Perhaps complete immersion in the act of reciting the phrase 'refuge in the faith' as a zikr itself constitutes the act of taking refuge in the faith, and thereby, produces the self-altering affect William M. Reddy (2001) has ascribed to 'emotives' in language, which in this instance might be described as a social poetics of the self.

RECOGNIZING RESEMBLANCES

To analyze the iconicities of drum patterns, dance steps, and verbal abstraction requires some attention to the processes by which actors make these connections, recognize resemblances, and associate (or deform) patterns. Some aspects of these processes must be inferred, whereas others are verbally indexed. In 1997, Pappu called knowledge (*'ilm*) of music the only thing (*kam*) that is really true (*saca*): When one is playing a rhythmic pattern (*thekah*), another person must match it. Music admits no falsehood (*jhut*); one cannot simply 'throw something in'. Pappu compared this musical truth with that of the dhol player playing dhamal with intoxication (*masti*). Completely absorbed in spirituality, the drummer matches his own being with that of the sarkar, and by extension, with God. The drummer, whose performance is coloured by his temperament (*tabi'at*) or who plays with his eyes open or with money in mind, is lacking such truth. By the same token, Pappu views 'mast qalandar' as a z̲ikr motivated by the saint Shah Jamal, who enters Pappu's heart during a performance and causes his lips to utter the phrase. This, in turn, causes listeners to recite the z̲ikr with the drums. Pappu's remarks creatively link a musical form of truth testing with a spiritual one: Playing in unison is morally equivalent to dissolving one's being in the love of God. This is poetics as musical–spiritual ideology.

Dhamal is the preferred Sufi groove in certain Pakistani shrines; this is the common term. Yet several other patterns are also common and in reality many 'urs-goers cannot differentiate closely related patterns, nor do they need to, to dance.[23] Whereas dhamal's appropriateness is grounded in profound associations with spiritual transcendence and union, the appropriateness of bhangra (and some other grooves) is grounded in regional identity and associations with weddings or other joyous occasions. 'Punjabi culture is bhangra,' as Pappu put it, using the English word *culture* with apparent comfort. With the international circulation of bhangra (as a dance and a world-music genre), such a remark might be expected from youths in Britain or the United States as well.[24]

Dhamal and bhangra, as two kinds of 'urs-appropriate drum genres, one more serious than the other, roughly reproduce the distinction between those who are considered more serious or pious in their dancing for the saint and those who are just fooling around. Interpretations of what constitutes proper movement in these genres are not clear-cut.[25] Moreover, disambiguating personal, transnational, and regional elements is difficult because some regard the setting as a veritable free-for-all. Multiple agencies, for example, may motivate dancers to spin. Spinning has always held a wide potential for signification because of its ubiquity in poetry, folk songs, and philosophy. Now, I am told, whirling Sufi dancers (see Photograph 6) are more commonplace in Pakistan, possibly resulting from more widespread exposure of ('whirling') Mevlevi dervishes to Pakistanis via the media and Islamic arts festivals.[26]

The larger effect of these 'recognized resemblances' on the structure of the Madho Lal Husain event as a whole is that dhamal and, to a lesser extent, bhangra get, literally, centre stage, and the dances at the centre begin to look even more 'Sufi' (because of the whirling) from a global perspective.

Photograph 6. Malang spins while dancing dhamāl to the drumming of Pappu Sāi̱n at the Shah Jamāl shrine, December 2003. Photo by R. Wolf.

2003: REFLECTIONS BACK ON THE 'URS OF 1997

Accompanied by the anthropologist Adam Nayyar, I showed the 'urs video to two audiences in December 2003. One was a diverse group of five or six men; the other was a group of malangs (see Photograph 7). Devotees commenting on the video judged the dancing according to their understanding of the dancers' piety and somatic attention to the shrine, not by movements marked as 'dance' alone. The devotees knew or had seen these dancers at the shrine for many years and used this background knowledge in their evaluative statements. One viewer described how easy it is to ascertain the true dhamali. 'Such a person', he said (in Punjabi), 'will have *lagan* (attachment) and will show attention to the sarkar. He will be mast (intoxicated) in his attachment to the saint and…turned to the saint. He who makes "drama" for himself will do a "disco",' a bit of this and a bit of that. Straight upside down, right side up…a true malang, in his ecstasy, will keep on turning…until he falls down unconscious.'

The dhamali's actions are repetitious, relatively self-same over time; the fraud draws attention to himself, performs variations seen to lack depth or traditionality. A formal parallel can be drawn with Pappu Sain's characterization of a drummer performing with masti and the one whose performance is coloured by his temperament.

Photograph 7. Malangs suggested the laptop be placed in the area reserved for lamps. Viewers (in ordinary clothes) watch and discuss one of three showings, December 2003. Photo by R. Wolf.

Dancers perceived as dancing frivolously—what locals called 'disco'—as being improperly dressed, or otherwise behaving improperly are often ushered out of a dancing arena. Seriousness is marked by the excellence of the drummers, the dancers' proximity to the shrine, and the respect the various participants and onlookers give the dancers. The videotape showed a few boys dancing behind two dhol players, away from the centre area in front of the shrine. Their moves were dismissed by viewers as 'disco', confirming my own suspicion that these boys could exercise relative freedom because they were sidelined from the central shrine area.

For those who are not sidelined, the issue of merging and remaining separate hinges on the relationship between drummer and dancer. The drummer provides driving rhythms to help dancers achieve their spiritual goals corporeally. As dancers get into the groove, their leg and body movements normally coordinate with principal drum strokes. But, according to a range of devotees, the true dhamali is one who can eventually break the bonds of the beat. Synchrony between drummer and dancer is not a direct measure of either the dancer's skill or his or her ingenuousness. This slippage between agents who are cooperating but not 'keeping together in time' (McNeill 1995) is noteworthy in light of much writing on public music making, which emphasizes the role of temporal coordination in group cohesiveness (see Becker 2004:121 ff. and passim; Feld 1988; Turino 1999:241; Wolf 2000:96). Here, lack of coordination between drummer and dancer could index a poor sense of rhythm on the dancer's part, but it may also be a symptom of his or her successful spiritual union. Again, unity and division as phenomenological forms remain only signs of possibility until they are made explicit through speech indexicals or undeniable manifestations of physical transformation.

Whether or not drummers and dancers are synchronized on any given occasion, many opportunities exist for particular drummers to work with individual dancers, develop personal and kinesthetic relationships, 'tune in', in the words of Alfred Schutz (1977).27 The embodied communication between some dancers and drummers belongs to a broader class of intersubjective engagement associated with the ways in which followers of the Sufi path receive instruction from their spiritual master, or pir. Consider the pir Rashid Sain (see Photograph 8), for instance, who used to attend the Madho Lal Husain 'urs with his disciples every year. In 1997, the bald, crippled master sat at the foot of a tree wearing a geometrically patterned sweater of azure, rust, and white. Toothlessly grinning, he kept focus on the eyes of the two boys, aged about ten. Baba Rashid's garland of yellow flowers dangled as he leaned back and made wavelike patterns with his fingers, flicking his wrist up and down, and attending to each boy. They rapidly shook their heads up and down in time to the drumming, following their master's hand movements (see Video 1 at www.aesonline.org, 33/2 issue archive page). Rashid Sain was 'dancing dhamal with his hand', as my video-watching consultants put it, manually impressing the discipline into the children's bodies, constituting the intersubjective master–disciple domain via the transmission of bodily techniques (Farnell 1999:343). Later, when one of the head-shaking boys became overwhelmed—a dicent sign for approaching spiritual union—others in his group lifted him off the ground to rein in his ecstasy. These are the poetics whereby drumming, dancing, and embodied spiritual knowledge are made to converge.

Photograph 8. Bābā Rashīd Sāī<u>n</u> and his disciples at the Madho Lāl Husain 'urs, March 1997. Photo by R. Wolf.

MULTI-LEVELLED MIMESIS

When is the phenomenology of 'urs practices obvious and when is it recondite? Where are the 'structures' to which social actors adhere or from which they depart? Moth–flame and similar analogies remain signs of possibility, which may get activated by word or deed at any point (see, e.g., Tambiah 1985:156 ff.).[28] Iconicities of similar-sounding names pave the way for semantic slippages and the agglutination of identities. The prefix *lal* (red) in Madho Lal Husain's popular name, refers to the saint's colourful garb, which he wore while dancing to the drums, singing, and drinking. The prefix links the name with that of the saint Lal Shahbaz Qalandar, who also, reportedly, wore red robes. The name of a third saint, Jhule La'l of Sindh, tends to appear with those of the first two in songs, chants, and ecstatic outbursts. *La'l*, so spelled in Persian and Arabic, means 'ruby' or 'gem'. It has also become the preferred spelling for *red* in

Pakistani public venues (signs and newspapers), for the Arabic letter 'ain (denoted here by ') marks the word as Islamic (i.e., less Indian).

All three (now) 'red' saints have been revered by both Hindus and Muslims; all three are associated with musical practices.[29] The homonyms are conduits for a bundle of associations whereby 'urs participants commune with all these related saints when they wear red robes and dance. Their colour coding does not activate a core meaning because the implications of red are multiply determined by context. Rather, it participates in a set of parallel associations: Red may evoke fire, light, wisdom, divinity, and annihilation as well fertility and sexual union.

Such multileveled mimesis is extremely important in Sufi behaviour. When malangs at Madho Lal Husain's 'urs dance, swivelling their hips seductively, they foreground the homoerotic implications of Husain's life narrative and index the aforementioned story of Bulleh Shah. Popular histories of both saints spill over into the phenomenology of action at the 'urs of Madho Lal Husain. Overflowing even further into the social life of Lahore, Madho Lal Husain is reportedly something of a patron saint for Lahore's gay community as well as for courtesans of Lahore's red-light district, Hira Mandi (lit. diamond market).[30] The malang's feminine dances attract the saint's gaze. While metaphorically conveying the desire for union, the very same act also articulates a hierarchy that separates the two. Feminine dancing, here, is an act of humility that indexes the devotee's status as a mere prostitute before the saint.

These well-known phenomenologies of the dance are controversial; and so, Husain's transgressiveness has resulted in his isolation. Associations with eroticism, ecstatic dancing, and intoxication help explain why Shah Husain's image was missing from a popular poster of important Pakistani saints and why some Pakistani school books, and the broader institutions of which they form a part, deny Shah Husain's status as a Muslim (Jalal 1995). The question of Shah Husain's inclusion in larger moral units in modern Pakistan also implicates language, in as much as his folk poetry is so strongly Punjabi. Indeed, after a 1954 demonstration to recognize Punjabi as an official language, Punjabi writers began to use Shah Husain's 'urs as the platform for rallying support for such recognition. The national language, Urdu, does not belong to any Pakistani region and is, in this respect at least, more neutral and inclusive.

POETICS OF INCLUSION

Matters of regional and national inclusiveness may be debated on a local level as well as manipulated by the government. Ewing has documented the ways in which the Ayub Khan and Zulfikar Ali Bhutto governments, inspired by Muhammad Iqbal's vision of a Muslim democracy as filtered through the writings of his son Javid (Iqbal 1959), attempted to neutralize the power of individual religious figures by nationalizing the Sufi shrines. In some governmental rhetoric, '"caste, creed, and geographical factors" [were identified as] major sources of disruption in the effort to build Pakistan as a nation' (Ewing 1997:72).[31] Countering this, Ewing implied, government pamphlets had emphasized certain saints' association with the concept of '*wahdat al wujud*', 'the unity of being', 'the transcendence of categories', or 'the blurring of borders between the external religious forms' (Schimmel 1975:267, 286), a controversial Sufi doctrine developed by thirteenth century Andalusian philosopher Ibn 'Arabi (CE 1165–1240) (Ewing 1997:72).

Such refined philosophy appears distant from everyday politics; yet this philosophical doctrine is relevant to two characteristic dhamal gestures of a malang: dancing on one leg and raising a single finger in the air. For several Pakistani shrine frequenters, these gestures are dicent-indexical signs of oneness or, in more elevated language, wahdat al wujud. Before returning to Lahore in December 2003, I was sceptical that the iconic form of these dance gestures could convey such persuasive meaning. Even if they did, I wondered how agents' recognition of iconicity (their willingness to 'deform' patterns and see them as 'the same') might have been affected by influential writers and politicians who were preoccupied with questions of national unity. My doubts could not be reconciled easily, but one observation struck me as significant on Christmas night 2003, at Shah Jamal, as Pappu Sain was performing dhamal. One dancer, bald headed, concentrating his attention on the shrine, had been reiterating a deliberate move for several hours: Slowly raising his finger in the air, he was shouting, 'Yaktai,' a Persian (and Punjabi) word that means literally 'oneness'—as in oneness of purpose, oneness of mind, or, in this case, the singularity of God—and that is conventionally used in Iran to mean God.

The apparent obviousness of meaning here left me with a series of unanswered questions. Had this kind of physically embodied Sufi philosophy been more or less in a dancer's repertoire for centuries? Was this a kind of aesthetic posturing, adopting of a malang fashion or style?

Was it a move inherited from those inspired by the religio-political rhetoric of unity in the 1960s and 1970s? Neither of these alternatives need be regarded as absolute or as having any bearing on the spiritual status of the dancer himself, who was judged to be sincere. The same question could be asked of the many rapidly spinning, (possibly) Mevlevi-inspired malangs, whose circular movements have philosophical implications in Sufi thought (and resonate with images in poetry) but appear to be innovations in the local dance.

ON THE SIGNIFICANCE OF ONENESS

If verbal and gestural expressions of 'oneness' amounted to performances of spiritual unity in these contexts, uttering 'ali da pahla "number"' ('Ali is number one) in the context of the zikr connected with dhamal gave prominence to human difference: the social and spiritual hierarchy that is part and parcel of Sufism.[32] Expressions of togetherness and difference are simultaneous in dhamal. The mystical phrase that underlies 'ali da pahla "number"' articulates the principle of religious and political succession beginning, after the Prophet, with 'Ali. But it is also a phrase with a 'ring' to it: Easy to remember, it appears in many places; the transformative potential of this and other zikrs has at least as much to do with rhythmic organization, repetition, and the aesthetic feeling of the sounds (see Sapir 1925) as it does with meaningful content.

Merely to think or utter the paired phrases 'dam-a-dam mast qalandar—'ali da pahla "number",' however, does not mean one is on the Sufi path. Neither does the ubiquity of the phrases index the extension of Sufism. Exploring these phrases in a final illustration, we join a drumming group and electronic organ player at a Muslim wedding in Barkas, Hyderabad, Andhra Pradesh in South India (see Video 2 at www.aesonline.org, 33/2 issue archive page). Their first piece conforms, rhythmically, to bhangra. When I ask the name of this metrical framework (tal), their response, 'Qawwali', puzzles me. One drummer elaborates (in Urdu):

> What we just presented is called 'Dam-a-dam mast qalandar.' It's qawwali. This is played among Muslims. It's there at the very beginning, as a foundation (*usul*). Its histories come down to us through the ages; that's why we play qawwali first. That's the original thing (*asal bat*). Then later comes the 'filmi system' and so forth. That's all wrong (*ghalat*).

This calls for some explanation. The Sufi vocal genre called 'qawwali', prevalent largely in North India, Pakistan, and Muslim areas of South India such as Hyderabad, is stylistically and textually recognizable.[33] What this group played, however, conformed to qawwali merely in a nominal sense. Many texts and melodies can be rendered in different genres, using different styles; hence, text alone (or melody alone) is musically insufficient for genre identification.[34] Clearly, a different sort of claim is being made.

For one thing, this group (others use this terminology too) has entextualized the qawwali genre synecdochically, somewhat parallel to the way in which Pakistanis did with respect to dhamal—via the phrase 'dam-a-dam mast qalandar'. Just as dhamal has strong connotational meaning in shrine Sufism of Pakistan, so, too, does qawwali in many regions of South Asia, including Hyderabad.[35] The connection between the two has been fostered by the mass media, which is responsible for disseminating the phrase 'dam-a-dam mast qalandar' across the Indian subcontinent. The eponymous folk song, also called 'Lal Meri Pat', was recorded, instrumentally at least, as early as the 1950s (Jogi 1997:track 4), made famous by the singer Reshma in the 1960s (Abbas 2002:25ff.) and later performed internationally by qawwali singers such as the Sabri Brothers (1991:track 4).

Today, the qawwali version of the song 'Dam-a-dam mast qalandar' is the most well-known and imitated across the Indian subcontinent, downloaded as cell-phone ringtones and piped as insipid background music in express trains. Disseminated as fodder for variously passive or active aesthetic consumption, the song carries very little of its earlier symbolic import. In its associations with Sufi shrines and qawwali, the song has generalized 'Muslim' connotations, but even these have been watered down. Young people hearing the popular melody via multiple media seldom have the tools to connect the song with its source as a mystical phrase associated with a shrine in Sindh. I could not even recognize the popular melody of 'Dam-a-dam mast qalandar' in the Hyderabad performance, so if what I heard was a version of the popular piece, it had been multiply transformed. The only 'residue of past social interaction' (Silverstein and Urban 1996:5) that adhered to the piece as played was a generalized sense of Muslim identity in a diverse South Asian context, the sense that this piece should always be played first and that it is foundational even though performers may not quite know why.

The Hyderabad group accompanied the piece with bhangra (although they chose not to identify it as such), which is somewhat ironic because they do know a pattern called 'dhamal'. Members of the group were unaware of the close connection between the specifically Sufi phrase 'dam-a-dam mast qalandar' and the drum rhythm of dhamal as played in Pakistan. The bhangra drum rhythm has become absolutely generalized as a kind of South Asian groove and carries the sense of Punjabiness only weakly. The powerful vehicle for creating Muslim musical identities across the subcontinent is not the individual drummers in shrines but the popular recording artists who disseminate their musical styles and play a role in influencing local musical tastes.

The phrase 'Ali da pahla "number",' which rhymes with and follows 'dam-a-dam mast qalandar,' has significant Sufi (and Shia) connotations in its emphasis on 'Ali as the first link in the spiritual 'chain' following the death of Prophet Muhammad (PBUH). In the Hyderabad example, 'Dam-a-dam mast qalandar' had been, in effect, generalized from its multiple origins. Re-inscribed as a propitious ritual beginning, it had come full circle: This music provided a link between a worldly wedding and the spiritual wedding, or 'urs, of Sufi saints. 'Dam-a-dam mast qalandar' has become a point of departure for different kinds of regional identity that, at the same time, plug into national and international expansions of shrine practices in Sindh province.

One need not agree with Charles Keil's well-known assertion that music must be 'out of time' and 'out of tune' to be 'personally involving and socially valuable' (1994:96) to accept the idea that music's social character can be read in the ways in which elements of a performance work together. I have focused here on forms of coming together and drawing apart that are acted out in 'urs participants' interactions and referenced through specific gestures and esoteric drum rhythm meanings. When poets, politicians, musicians, and others envision what it means to belong to a particular social group, whether defined by Islam, language, region, or affiliation to particular saints or shrines, they manipulate a common set of themes and symbols (and, from time to time, they probably create new ones). Many draw on the philosophical potentials in Sufi thought for bringing moral unity in the face of empirical forms of difference.

From a 'poetics' perspective, my focus has been on ways in which social actors connect and disconnect formal structures with one another—most broadly, those having to do with the moving body in space and the ambiguous potential of coordination among parts to embody forms of 'truth' (as Pappu put it). Because the range of possible ways in which participants act, generate, and receive meanings at complex events such as 'urses remains elusive in its complexity and magnitude, it remains difficult to move much beyond the potential shiftiness of individuals and their 'multiple subjective modalities' (Ewing 1997:35; see also Gramsci 1999). Yet commonplace names, gestures, and meanings remain useful points of departure for examining the ways in which individuals create subjectivities and situate them within something larger.

NOTES

Acknowledgments: This research was funded in part by a postdoctoral fellowship from the American Institute of Pakistan Studies (1997). The ideas leading to the development of this chapter were born during my fellowship year at the Radcliffe Institute for Advanced Study (2002–03). I also received support that year from an American Council of Learned Societies–Social Science Research Council–National Endowment for the Humanities International and Area Studies Fellowship. I am grateful to all three institutions. Versions of the chapter have been presented at the Ohio State University (May 2003); the Barbara Stoler Miller conference, Columbia University (February 2004); the Society for Ethnomusicology (Atlanta, November 2005); and Harvard University Department of Music (March 2006). I would like to thank the following persons who provided helpful comments on oral and written drafts: Sabir Badalkhan, Amy Bard, Aditya Behl, Stephen Blum, Katherine Brown, Katherine Ewing, Michael Herzfeld, Adam Nayyar, Gibb Schreffler, Susan Slyomovics, and three anonymous readers for *American Ethnologist*.

1. Although the term *poetics*, as Herzfeld notes, derives from a Greek root meaning 'action,' in wider academic usages, the term often indexes a focus on aesthetics and language and is, therefore, sometimes avoided when the focus is on issues of embodiment or music (Brenneis 1987:248). The whole question of 'language' and how it is related to human activities that are 'not language' rests on a problematic bifurcation of the two (Hill and Mannheim 1992:382); but beginning with the assumption that something exists in music and movement that lies beyond the grasp of direct language, without foreclosing language's larger role, leaves open rich avenues for exploring the nuances of human communicative activity.
2. Embodying an 'excess of meanings' (Ewing 1997:45), Sufism is notoriously difficult to define. It refers both to a diversity of practices actors enact at shrines and to the specific philosophies associated with particular religious and social orders. Its members range from iconoclastic individualists—Madho Lal Husain was one—to communally oriented practitioners with restrictive interpretations of Muslim law (*shariah*). Many of those who follow what is called 'the Sufi path' share the belief that an individual can become closer to and gain a better understanding of God through experiential means. Some seek forms of self-awareness and transcendence that do not directly implicate notions of the divine. Important experiential means include intensive love (*'ishq*), reiterative physical or verbal regimens (*zikr*), and the internalization of mystical insights. Although the more internationally visible followers of the Sufi path are known for their ecstatic dancing (*raqs*), love of music, and consumption of intoxicants, several Sufi orders do not support these ways. (Naturally, one would not expect to find drumming at shrines associated with such orders.)

3. James Kippen defines *grooves* as 'regularly repeating accentual patterns rooted in bodily movement (i.e. dance)' (2001:1). Kippen argues that certain *tals* (metrical configurations) in Hindustani classical music now played on the tabla derive from the folk grooves played on drums such as the dhol.
4. The ghazal, originally a genre of Arabic poetry whose themes were love and intoxication, accrued mystical dimensions beginning in the eleventh century when the form was taken up in Persia. See Pritchett n.d. See also Barbara Herrnstein Smith's landmark study, *Poetic Closure: A Study of How Poems End*, which discusses with sophistication and elegance closural properties of repetition in, among other things, rhymed couplets (1968:70ff.).
5. Judith Becker points out, however, that 'the distinction [between the message and its medium] is crucial to the Sufis' (2004:81; Qureshi 1986:121).
6. See the related issues of 'indeterminacy' raised by Thomas J. Csordas (1993:149 ff.), which apply to this and other examples of 'signs of possibility' in a Peircian framework; I find Csordas's category of 'indeterminacy' rather ill defined, whereas the Peircian concept is well framed within a semiotic model.
7. The noted historian of Islam G. S. Hodgson highlighted the combined force of the moth and flame as a symbol, 'that interresonance of disparate points of experience which, through some common structural character, serve to illuminate one another and to enrich one another's implications' (1964:222). This much-exploited image appears not only ubiquitously in world literatures of the present day but can be found in early Hindu and Sikh sources as well (Brockington 1977:448; Fenech 2001:24).
8. Fire, in Sherry Ortner's (1979) terms, is an elaborating symbol, and redness, in Charles Sanders Peirce's (1955) terms, is a qualisign, a quality that serves as a sign when embodied.
9. Nancy D. Munn (1974:580) has emphasized the importance of the sign vehicle's form to the message carried.
10. In December 2003, singing sessions were held on Sundays and readings on Thursdays.
11. The scope of this chapter does not permit a detailed comparison of his version with more authoritative versions or analysis of variations in his own rendition of the same stanza. I relied on Adam Nayyar for the translation from Punjabi presented here.
12. 'Familiar background' is an allusion to William Hanks's discussion of discourse genres (of which Sufi poetic tradition is one) as both formal structures and 'orienting frameworks, interpretive procedures, and sets of expectations' (1987:670–671) that form an integral part of a speech community's linguistic habitus. Hanks emphasizes the Bakhtinian notion that 'no element can enter...without importing its value coefficients with it. Actors take these values for granted, as a familiar background... against which their acts are intelligible' (1987:671).
13. Presumably some faqirs chant 'din panah' aloud as well, thereby communicating this textualization to Pappu, who conveyed it to me.
14. This is common in jazz and many world traditions of musical improvisation. See, for example, descriptions of jazz performers deforming one another's patterns in Berliner 1994:362, 390. See also Julian Gerstin's (1998:144 and passim) wonderfully detailed phenomenological description of dancer–drummer interactions, especially in negotiating imprecisions, in Martinican Bèlè.
15. Whether the history of Sufic uses of fire metaphors has any bearing on the origin of fire practices at 'urses is difficult to determine; multiple continuities exist with ancient Hindu and Zoroastrian fire rituals.

16. Fire is also used in a common metaphor for Islamic dynastic succession. Safavid ruler Shah Ismail (1487–1524) invoked it when he declared himself to be 'descended from the seventh imam...and the bearer of the divine [pre-eternal] fire...that preceded the Quran and the creation of the universe' (Lapidus 2002:234).
17. The same might be said of other musicians who provide music for others' transcendent experiences, such as performers of qawwali, a Sufi vocal and instrumental genre (Qureshi 1986). See also Becker 2004:82.
18. Niamat and Shahid played dhamal at 130 counts per minute at the 'urs.
19. Also note here the local emphasis on difference in form, played out in degrees of complexity, for drumming repertoire marked as religiously functional; similar kinds of formal differentiation characterize religious from nonreligious language (Keane 1997:52).
20. Important to both this bol pattern (see also Appendix, Figure A2) and to parallel practices in the Hindustani concert tradition (to which many dhol players have access), is the contrast between the aspirated, voiced syllable (*dhin*) on the first count and the unaspirated, unvoiced one on the third (*tan*). The aspirated, voiced bol is iconic of a resounding bass articulation on one side of the drum (left or right; this varies according to performer). The unaspirated, unvoiced syllable corresponds to a stressed treble stroke on the opposite side of the drum; the last pulse of the unvoiced count is marked by a damped bass stroke (see Appendix, Figure A1).
21. In her discussion of jazz and zouk rhythmic textures, whose components are named rhythmic grooves, Ingrid Monson notes that 'while the full range of patterns combine to form the dynamic whole of the rhythmic feel, some layers play a more significant role in defining that sound' (1999:45). In this way, similar components of a larger rhythmic configuration may migrate from a layer of one named unit to a layer of another, and this may or may not have implications for how that rhythm is identified. In the case of dhamal, bhangra, and some other grooves, there is room for temporary overlap or mixing, which would necessarily add ambiguity to the classification.
22. Presumably Pappu is referring to the *hadis* 'man kunto maula fa 'ali-un-maula' [whoever accepts me as master, 'Ali is his master too]. This is also a foundational text used in qawwali, in which it is termed the 'qaul' (see Qureshi 1986:20–21 and passim). Shias commemorate the Prophet Muhammad's (PBUH) utterance of this hadis on the 18th of Zil Hijjah in the Muslim calendar. The holiday is called ' 'Eidul Ghadir.'
23. Other rhythmic configurations possess their own potentials, as, for instance, tintal, which Pappu Sain claims caused fire to erupt behind him and his partner Jhura Sain when they were performing at the shrine of Pir Pak Farman. Pappu Sain, articulating system-level knowledge, once insisted that dhamal was the only pattern that could induce masti with the saint or God in the dancer. Later, in response to queries about his own practices at Shah Jamal shrine, he admitted that *punjabi lava* (the name of a particular rhythmic pattern) could have the same effect and, for that matter, so could any rhythm played on the dhol—a good example of the kind of position-shifting discussed by Ewing.
24. See Leante 2004 for an excellent musical investigation of bhangra in Britain. Some Punjabis in Pakistan, who insist that bhangra is more Sikh than Punjabi, dissent on the matter of bhangra being essentially Punjabi. To them, the *luddi* dance is emblematic of the region; luddi is also danced at 'urses but bears no particular relationship to Sufism. Whereas such markers of identity and distinction are male, women on both sides of the India–Pakistan border dance their own characteristically

Punjabi dance, *giddha*, by clapping, singing and stepping in and out of a circle (see Middlebrook 2000:652–654).
25. Some say that 'real' dhamal dance involves more emphasis on lower body moves, whereas bhangra emphasizes upper body movements.
26. This was, in any case, the observation of the journalist Sarwat Ali and the anthropologist Adam Nayyar, as we discussed changes we had observed at Shah Jamal over the years. We had attended Pappu's performance together that Christmas night (2003) at the shrine.
27. Over and above the common reference to musical togetherness as a sign, or instantiation, of social togetherness, some scholars have become interested in naturalistic and biological models to explain what it means to be in synch. Ongoing research on the phenomenon of 'entrainment,' whereby two oscillating bodies (machines, insects, etc.) begin somehow to coordinate with one another, is beginning to be explored by ethnomusicologists and music cognitivists. See, for instance the ongoing activities of the 'Entrainment Network,' organized by Martin Clayton (Open University, Milton Keynes, UK) and Udo Will (Ohio State University), and Judith Becker's recent book, which develops the concept of 'structural coupling' (2004:121 ff. and passim), the ways human brains and bodies, and other organisms, become 'linked through repeated interaction'. Becker uses the notion of 'structural coupling' to explore the kinds of interactions listeners and dancers experience with musicians under the larger rubric of 'trance.'
28. Although dancers are not likely to carry images such as that of a moth attracted to a flame in their consciousness while they dance near a fire, everyday images have played an important role in music and quotidian life to transmit aspects of Islamic thought and culture (Eaton 1974).
29. The term *lal* also means 'dear', 'son', or 'precious one'. These associations of endearment infiltrate the meanings of these saint names for Pakistanis.
30. A fine article by Scott Kugle (2000) explains some of the bowdlerization of the Husain narrative in the historical record.
31. See also Iqbal's recent discussion of regional and ethnic forces 'which were not anticipated or even contemplated by the founding fathers...[and which] superseded the spirit of Muslim nationalism' (2003:361).
32. Such hierarchies are found in the separation of master from disciple, the various 'stages' through which the Sufi novice passes, and the ranked offices, spiritual and administrative, in a shrine.
33. The genre name *qawwali* may also get attached to non-Muslim song styles, as it is common for genre names, even *dhamal*, to travel semi-independently from their musical referents or for song styles to change dramatically while retaining their names. See, for instance, the case of *Bhajan kavvali*, the didactic Hindu genre performed by diasporic Indians in Fiji (Brenneis 1987)
34. In Lahore, the same piece may be rendered, for instance, in kafi style or qawwali style.
35. Non-Muslim styles and commercial, seemingly religion-neutral versions of qawwali do exist on the subcontinent. But, as Sharilee Johnston (2000:52) put it, Sufi performances of qawwali in the old city of Hyderabad are still considered *mazhabi* (religious, authentic, proper) despite variations in style; she suggests that the term *mazhabi* 'becomes an ideological trope for its Muslim participants when used in distinction to a Hindu-ized and commercialized cultural milieu' (Johnston 2000:53).

APPENDIX

One of the principal dhamal patterns as played on the dhol is illustrated in Figure A1.

x			x			x	x	•	x		x			x
X		X			X					o		X		

Figure A1. A basic version of dhamāl as demonstrated by Nazir Ahmed (Multan, 27 March 1997 [see Audio 4 at www.aesonline.org, 33/2 issue archive page]). M.M. (tempo) = 160. Top line (treble): x= stressed stroke; x = lighter stroke; • = very light stroke. Bottom line (bass): X = open, resonant stroke; o = closed/damped stroke. All strokes are played with sticks.

The syllabic representation of the rhythm prioritizes some strokes and ignores others. Moreover, the bols under a given rubric may vary from time to time as uttered by a single performer or by a range of performers. Pappu Sai<u>n</u>'s more skeletal, qualitatively contrasting pattern, uses slightly different vowels and consonants (see Figure A2).

| dhāg | | | da | nāg | | din | | tāg | | | da | nāg | | din | |

Figure A2. One of Pappu Sāi<u>n</u>'s representations of dhamāl (7 February 1998).

Regarding the distinction between dhamal and bhangra, see Figures A3 and A4 and discussion below. Pappu Sai<u>n</u> (see Audio 1 at www.aesonline.org, 33/2 issue archive) used these vocal representations of drum patterns to illustrate the limited 'scope of the dhol' (*dhol ka maqsad*) compared with that of the classical tabla, on which his dhol playing is modelled.

A

1			2			3			4		
dhā		ga	nā		ga	nā		ga	dhī		ga

B

1			2			3				4			
dā		ga	nā		din	na	trā			ga	nā		din	na

Figure A3. Two 'unadorned' (*sadāh*) or 'simple' (*sīdhe*) bol patterns for bhangrā.

A

1			2				1			2		
dhen		da	na	ka	din	na	dhen		da	na	ka	din	na

B

x		x	x			x	x		x	x		x	
X					X		X				X		

Figure A4. Bhangrā bols spoken and played on the dhol by Nazir Ahmed (Multan, 27 March 1997 [see Audio 3 at www.aesonline.org, 33/2 issue archive page]). M.M. = 174.

The bol patterns of some dhamal and bhangra versions are virtually identical; bhangra counts may be subdivided into three (see Figure A3, A) as well as four (see Figures A3, B; and A4, A and B) pulses, and some dhamal variations (not shown here) also exploit triple subdivisions. What differentiates the two patterns? Superstructural patterns played on the bass side of the drum. In bhangra, key bass strokes are on counts one and four (or, counted differently, one and two-and-a-half, and three and four-and-a-half; see bottom line in Figure A4, B; and bols in bold in Figures A3, A and B; and A4, A).

Such emphasis in the bass distinguishes bhangra from other duple grooves, including dhamal. Further contrasts with bhangra appear in bass variations, such as those that combine treble and bass stroke components of basic dhamal (see Figure A5).

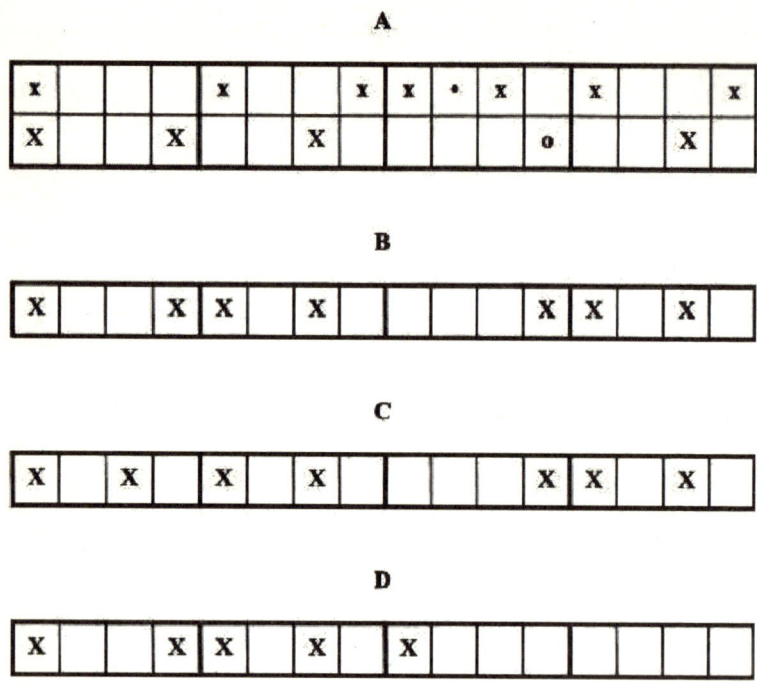

Figure A5. Basic dhamāl pattern (A) compared with bass variants (B–D).

Some of the phrases and their corresponding drum patterns can be repeated fragmentarily. Bass drum pattern B in Figure A5, which corresponds to 'dam-a-dam mast qalandar,' can be played or verbally chanted independently; pattern C, which corresponds to 'ali da pahla "number",' tends to be verbalized only after phrase B but can be deployed independently as a rhythmic pattern on the drums. Pattern D, which corresponds to 'mast qalandar mast', perhaps the smallest unit that represents dhamal as a whole, can both be chanted and played. The texts line up with the principal counts in Figure A6.

Phrase 5D:

x		x	x	x		x					
mast		qa	lan	dar		mast					

Phrase 5B:

x		x	x	x				x	x		x
mast		qa	lan	dar				dam	ā		dam

Phrase 5C (phrase 5B text in parentheses):

x	x	x	x			x	x		x
(mast		qa	lan	dar)			a	li		dā
pah	la		nam	bar			(dam	ā		dam)

Figure A6. Correspondences between bass-drum patterns and zikr chants commonly heard as listeners interacted with Pappu Saīn on Thursday nights at Shah Jamāl. Casually observed 1997, 1998 (see Audio 5 at www.aesonline.org, 33/2 issue archive page), 2003 (Phrases 5B–D refer to Figure A5 B–D).

Figure A7 depicts faqirs' vocalization of dhamal. The top line is the abstract bol pattern; the lower line is a phrase meaning 'refuge [for the] faith.'

dhīn		di	nā	di	na	tān		ta	nā	ta	na
dīn		pa	nāh	da	na	dīn		pa	nāh	da	na

Figure A.7. Faqīrs' refiguration of dhamāl (according to Pappu Saīn).

Bibliography

Abbas, S.B. *The Female Voice in Sufi Ritual: Devotional Practices of Pakistan and India*. Austin: University of Texas Press, 2002.

ABC News. 'Suicide Bombing in Pakistan kills Twenty' (http://abcnews.go.com/International/wireStory?id=7976 65). 27 May 2005.

Abdul H.S. *Lucknow: The Last Phase of an Oriental Culture*. E.S. Harcourt and F. Husayn trans. Boulder: Westview Press, 1975.

Abou, M.Z. 'Sectarianism as a Substitute Identity: Sunnis and Shias in Central and South Punjab in Pakistan.' *The Contours of State and Society*. S. Mumtaz, J.L. Racine and I.A. Ali (eds.). Karachi: Oxford University Press, 2002, 77–95.

Abou, M.Z. 'The Regional Dimension of Sectarian Conflicts in Pakistan.' *Pakistan: Nationalism without a Nation?* C. Jaffrelot (ed.). Delhi: Manohar, 2002, 115–28.

Abu-Lughod, L. 'Introduction: Feminist Longings and Postcolonial Conditions.' *Remaking Women*. L. Abu-Lughod (ed.). Princeton: Princeton University Press, 1998, 3–25.

Abu-Lughod, L. 'The Romance of Resistance: Tracing Transformations of Power through Bedouin Women.' *American Ethnologist* 17 (1990): 41–55.

Abu-Lughod, L. *Veiled Sentiments: Honor and Poetry in a Bedouin Society*. Berkeley: University of California Press, 1986.

Ahearn, L.M. 'Language & Agency.' *Annual Review of Anthropology* 30 (2001): 109–37.

Ahmad, K. *Exploring Dimensions and Challenges of Pluralism in Pakistan*. Islamabad: Centre for Peace and Pluralism, 2000.

Ahmad, Kamran. 'Mental Blocks,' in Political Economy. *The News on Sunday*. Pakistan. 3 April 2005.

Ahmad, M. 'Islamic Fundamentalism in South Asia.' *Fundamentalisms Observed*. M.E. Marty and R.S. Appleby (eds.). Chicago: The University of Chicago Press, 1991.

Ahmad, M. 'Revivalism, Islamization, Sectarianism, and Violence in Pakistan.' *Pakistan: 1997*. New York: Westview Press, 1998.

Ahmad, R. *Foundations of Pakistan, Volume II*. Islamabad, 1987.

Ahmed, A. 'Bringing About *Change*, Without Causing Much *Rage*.' *Elegant Pearls: Jaihoon*. Retrieved from http://www.jaihoon.com/pearls/farhathashmi.htm, 10 December 2002.

Ahmed, A. 'Death and Celebration among Muslim Women: A Case Study from Pakistan.' *Modern Asian Studies* 39.4 (2005): 929–980.

Ahmed, A.S. *Millennium and Charisma among Pathans: A Critical Essay in Social Anthropology.* London: Routledge and Regan Paul, 1976.

Ahmed, A.S. *Pukhtun Economy and Society.* London: Routledge and Kegan Paul, 1980.

Ahmed, A.S. *Religion and Politics in Muslim Society: Order and Conflict in Pakistan.* London: Routledge and Kegan Paul, 1983.

Ahmed, I. 'South Asia.' *Islam Outside the Arab World.* Westerlund, D. and Svanberg, I. (eds.). New York: St. Martin's Press, 1999.

Ahmed, M.D. 'The Shi'is of Pakistan.' *Shi'ism, Resistance, and Revolution.* M. Kramer (ed.). Boulder: Westview Press, 1987, 275–287.

Ahmed, N. *Pakistan: Rape Laws against Women.* WIN News 20:34, 1994.

Aijaz, S.Z. *Muslim Children—How to Bring up?* Karachi: International Islamic Publishers Ltd., 1989.

Aitken, E.H. *Gazetteer of the Province of Pakistan.* Karachi, 1986.

Ajarni, F. *The Vanished Imam: Musa al Sadr and the Shia of Lebanon.* Ithaca: Cornell University Press, 1986.

Alee-Adnan, E. 'Hijab: The Big Debate.' *She Magazine.* March Edition (2004): 94–96.

Al-Faruqi, L.I. 'Music, Musicians and Muslim Law.' *Asian Music* 17.1 (1985): 3–36.

Al-Huda. Retrieved from http://alhudapk.com, 2003.

Ali, A.A. '*The Role of Faith Healers in Resolving the Socio-medical Problems of the Village Naniyan.*' Unpublished Masters Thesis. Anthropology Department. Quaid-e-Azam University, Islamabad, 1997.

Ali, D. *Courtly Culture and Political Life in Early Medieval India.* Cambridge: Cambridge University Press, 2004.

Ali, M.A. *Sectarian Conflict in Pakistan: A Case Study of Jhang.* Colombo: Regional Center for Strategic Studies, 2002.

Ali, M.A. *Sectarian Conflict in Pakistan: A Case Study of Jhang.* Colombo: Regional Center for Strategic Studies. June 1999.

Ali, M.H. *Observations on the Mussalmans of India.* [1832]. Karachi: Civil and Military Press, 1973.

Ali, S. 'Pakistani Women Socialites Embrace Islam.' *BBC News. World Edition.* Retrieved from http://news.bbc.co.uk/2/hi/south_asia/3211131.stm, 6 November 2003.

Ali, S.S. *Gender and Human Rights in Islam and International Law: Equal before Allah, Unequal before Man?* The Hague; Boston: Kluwer Law International, 2000.

Ali, T. 'Ceremonial and Social Structure among the Burusho of Hunza.' *Asian Highland Societies in Anthropological Perspective.* C.F. Haimendorf (ed.). Delhi: Sterling Publishers, 1981, 231–244.

Al-Kaysi, M.I. *Morals and Manners in Islam: The Guide to Islamic Adab.* Leicester: The Islamic Foundation, 1986.

Al-Khayyat, S. *Honor and Shame: Women in Modern Iraq*. London: Saqi Books, 1990.
Al-Munajjed, M. *Women in Saudi Arabia Today*. New York: St. Martin's Press, 1997.
Al-Naqvi, A.N. *A Historical Review of the Institution of Azadari for Imam Husein*. Karachi: Peermahomed Ebrahim Trust, 1974.
Alter, J.S. 'Indian Clubs and Colonialism: Hindu Masculinity and Muscular Christianity.' *Comparative Studies in Society and History* 46.3 (2004): 497–534.
Altinay, A.G. *The Myth of the Military Nation: Militarism, Gender, and Education in Turkey*. London: Palgrave Macmillan, 2006.
Altorki, S. *Women in Saudi Arabia: Ideology and Behavior among the Elite*. New York: Columbia University Press, 1986.
Alvi, S.S. 'Islam in South Asia.' *The Muslim Almanac: A Reference Work on the History, Faith, Culture, and Peoples of Islam*. A.A. Nanji (ed.). New York: Gale Research Inc., 1996, 55–72.
Ameed, S.M. *The Importance of Weeping and Wailing*. Karachi: Peermahomed Ebrahim Trust, 1974.
Anderson, J.N.D. *Islamic Law in the Modern World*. New York: New York University, 1959.
Antoun, R.T. *Muslim Preacher in the Modern World: A Jordanian Case Study in Comparative Perspective*. Princeton: Princeton University Press, 1989.
Appadurai, A. 'Commodities and the Politics of Value.' *The Social Life of Things: Commodities in Cultural Perspective*. A. Appadurai (ed.). Cambridge: Cambridge University Press, 1986, 3–63.
Appadurai, A. 'Is Homo Hierarchicus?' *American Etghnologist* 13.4 (1986): 745–61.
Apter, D. *The Legitimization of Violence*. London, 1997.
Arebi, S. *Women and Words in Saudi Arabia: The Politics of Literary Discourse*. New York: Columbia University Press, 1994.
Arthur, L.B. 'Clothing, Control, and Women's Agency: The Mitigation of Patriarchal Power.' *Negotiating at the Margins: The Gendered Discourses of Power and Resistance*. S. Fisher and K. Davis (eds.). New Brunswick: Rutgers University Press, 1993, 43–65.
Asad, T. *Genealogies of Religion*. Baltimore: John Hopkins University Press, 1993.
Asim R. *The Islamic Syncretistic Tradition in Bengal*. Princeton, 1983.
Ask, K. and M. Tjomsland. 'Introduction.' *Women and Islamization*. K. Ask and M. Tjomsland (eds.). Oxford: Berg, 1998, 1–16.
Ayoub, M. *Redemptive Suffering in Islam: A Study of the Devotional Aspects of Ashura' in Twelver Shi'ism*. The Hague: Mouton, 1978.
Ayub N.A. *Tarjuman-e Karbala: Zaynab Bint e-Ali*. Karachi: Aliya Publications, 1999.

Baffoun, A. 'Feminism and Muslim Fundamentalism: The Tunisian and Algerian Cases.' *Identity Politics and Women: Cultural Reassertions and Feminisms in International Perspective.* V.M. Moghadam (ed.). Boulder: Westview Press, 1994, 167–182.

Baig, R.K. *Chitral: A Study in Statecraft.* Karachi: International Union for the Conservation of Nature, 2005.

Baily, J. *Music of Afghanistan: Professional Musicians in the City of Herat.* Cambridge: Cambridge University Press, 1988.

Banerjee, M. *The Pathan Unarmed: Memory and Opposition.* Oxford: James Currey, 2000.

Banerjee, S. *Make Me a Man! Masculinity, Hinduism, and Nationalism in India.* Albany: State University of New York Press, 2006.

Bard, A. 'From *"Elegiac Lament"* to *"Heroic Masterpiece":* The Urdu Marsiyah Re-examined.' M.A. Thesis. Columbia University, 1996.

Barth, F. 'Introduction.'. *Ethnic Groups and Boundaries.* F. Barth (ed.). Boston: Little, Brown & Company, 1969, 9–39.

Barth, F. *Political Leadership among the Swat Pathans.* London: Athlone Press, 1959.

Barthes, R. 'Elements of Semiology.' *Writing Degree Zero and Elements of Semiology.* [1964]. A. Lavers and C. Smith Trans. Preface by S. Sontag. Boston: Beacon Press, 1970.

Bashir, E. 'The Areal Position of Khowar: South Asian and Other Affinities.' *Proceedings of the Second International Hindu Kush Cultural Conference.* E. Bashir and Israr-ud-Din (eds.). Karachi: Oxford University Press, 1996, 167–179.

Becker, J. *Deep Listeners: Music Emotion and Trancing.* Bloomington: Indiana University Press, 2004.

Beeman, W.O. 'A Full Arena: The Development and Meaning of Popular Performance Traditions in Iran.' *Continuity and Change in Modern Iran.* M.E. Bonine and N. Keddie (eds.). Albany: State University of New York Press, 1981, 285–305.

Bell, C. *Ritual Theory, Ritual Practice.* New York: Oxford University Press, 1992.

Benford, R.D. 'Frame Disputes within the Nuclear Disarmament Movement.' *Social Forces* 71.3 (1993): 677–701.

Benford, R.D. and D.A. Snow. 'Framing Processes and Social Movements.' *Annual Review of Sociology* 26 (2000): 611–39.

Berg, H. *The Development of Exegesis in Early Islam.* Richmond: Curzon Press, 2000.

Berliner, P.F. *Thinking in Jazz: The Infinite Art of Improvisation.* Chicago: University of Chicago Press, 1994.

Betteridge, A. 'The Controversial Vows of Urban Muslim Women in Iran.' *Unspoken Worlds: Women's Religious Lives.* N.A. Falk and R.M. Gross (eds.). Belmont: Wadsworth, 1989, 102–111.

Betteridge, A. 'Ziarat: Pilgrimage to the Shrines of Shiraz.' Ph.D. Dissertation. University of Chicago, 1985.

Bhabha, H.K. 'The Commitment to Theory.' *The Location of Culture*. London: Routledge, 1994, 19–39.

Biddulph, J. *Tribes of the Hindu Kush*. [1880]. Lahore: Ali Kamran, 1972.

Biddulph, J. *Tribes of the Hindoo Koosh*. [1880]. Graz: Akademische Druck-und Verlagsanstalt, 1971.

Boddy, J. *Wombs and Alien Spirits: Women, Men and the Zar Cult in Northern Sudan* Madison: University of Wisconsin Press, 1989.

Bogdanov, L. 'Muharram in Persia: Some Notes on Its Mysteries and Ceremonies.' *Visva-Bharati Quarterly* 1 (1923): 118–127.

Bourdieu, P. *Outline of a Theory of Practice*. R. Nice trans. Cambridge: Cambridge University Press, 1977.

Bowen, J.R. *Muslims through Discourse: Religion and Ritual in Gayo Society*. Princeton: Princeton University Press, 1993.

Brah, A. *Cartographies of Diaspora: Contesting Identities*. London: Routledge, 1996.

Breckenridge, C.A. and P.V.D Veer. *Orientalism and the Postcolonial Predicament: Perspectives on South Asia*. Philadelphia, 1993.

Brenneis, D. 'Performing Passions: Aesthetics and Politics in an Occasionally Egalitarian Community.' *American Ethnologist* 14.2 (1987): 236–250.

Brenner, S. 'Reconstructing Self and Society: Javanese Muslim Women and "the Veil".' *American Ethnologist* 23.4 (1996): 673–697.

Brisbarre, A.M. and G. Altan (eds.). *Islamic Sacrifice: the spaces and Occasions of Ritual*. Paris: CNRS, 1993.

Brockington, J.L. 'Figures of Speech in the Ramayana.' *Journal of the American Oriental Society* 97.4 (1977): 441–459.

Brown, D. *Rethinking Tradition in Modern Islamic Thought*. Cambridge: Cambridge University Press, 1996.

Bruce, S. *Fundamentalism*. Malden, MA: Polity Press, 2000.

Bryant, R. 'The Soul Danced into the Body: Nation and Improvisation in Istanbul.' *American Ethnologist* 32.2 (2005): 222–238.

Brysk, A. '"Hearts and Minds": Bringing Symbolic Politics Back In.' *Polity* 27.4 (1995): 559–85.

Buehler, A.F. *Sufi Heirs of the Prophet: The Indian Naqshbandiya and the Rise of the Mediating Sufi Shaykh*. Columbia: University of South California Press, 1998.

Cardoza, R. 'The Ordeal of Moharram: Shiites in India Mourn Their Savior.' *Natural History* 99 (1990): 50–57.

Caroe, O. *The Pathans*. London: Macmillan, 1996.

Cattell, M.G. 'Praise the Lord and Say No to Men: Older Women Empowering Themselves in Sarnia, Kenya.' *Journal of Cross-Cultural Gerontology* 7 (1992): 307–330.

Cavell, S. 'Declining Decline: Wittgenstein as a Philosopher of Culture.' *This New Yet Unapproachable America: Lectures after Emerson after Wittgenstein.* Chicago: University of Chicago, 1989, 29–77.

Cavell, S. 'The Argument of the Ordinary: Scenes of Instruction in Wittgenstein and in Kripke.' *Conditions Handsome and Unhandsome: The Constitution of Emersonian Perfectionism.* Chicago: University of Chicago Press, 1990, 64–101.

Cavell, S. 'The Uncanniness of the Ordinary.' *Quest of the Ordinary: Lines of Skepticism and Romanticism.* Chicago: University of Chicago Press, 1988, 153–78.

Cavell, S. *The Claim of Reason: Wittgenstein, Skepticism, Morality, and Tragedy.* London: Clarendon Press, 1982.

Chandavarkar, R. *Imperial Power and Popular Politics: Class, Resistance, and the State in India.* [c.1850–1950]. Cambridge: Cambridge University Press, 1998.

Chatterjee, P. 'The Nationalist Resolution of the Women's Question.' *Postcolonial Discourses: An Anthology.* G. Castle (ed.). Oxford: Blackwell, 2001, 151–65.

Chatterjee, P. *Nationalist Thought and the Colonial World: a Derivative Discourse?* London, 1986.

Chatterjee, P. *The Nation and its Fragments.* Princeton, 1993.

Chelkowski, P. 'Dramatic and Literary Aspects of Ta'zieh-Khani—Iranian Passion Play.' *Review of National Literature* 2 (1971): 121–138.

Chelkowski, P. 'Iran: Mourning Becomes Revolution.' *Asia* 3 (1980): 30–37, 44, 45.

Chelkowski, P. 'Shia Muslim Processional Performances.' *The Drama Review* 29.3 (1935): 18–30.

Chelkowski, P. and Korom F.J. 'Moharram in Trinidad: A Festive Mourning.' *The India Magazine of Her People and Culture* 13.2 (1993): 54–63.

Chelkowski, P. *Ta'ziyeh: Ritual and Drama in Iran.* New York: New York University Press, 1979.

Clark, J.A. 'Islamist Women in Yemen: Informal Nodes of Activism.' *Islamic Activism: A Social Theory Movement Approach.* Q. Wicktorowicz (ed.). Bloomington: Indiana University Press, 2004, 143–63.

Cohen, A.P. 'The Future of the Self: Anthropology and the City.' *Humanising the City? Social Contexts of Urban Life at the Turn of the Millennium.* A.P Cohen and K. Fukui (eds.). Edinburgh: Edinburgh University Press, 1992, 201–221.

Cohen, A.P. *Self Consciousness: An Alternative Anthropology of Identity.* London: Routledge, 1994.

Cole, J.R.I. and N.R. Keddie. *Shilsin and Social Protest.* New Haven: Yale University Press, 1986.

Cole, J.R.I. *Roots of North Indian Shi'ism in Iran and Iraq: Religion and State in Awadh, 1722–1859.* Berkeley and Los Angeles: University of California Press, 1988.

Comaroff, J. and J.L. Comaroff. *Of Revelation and Revolution: Christianity, Colonialism, and Consciousness in South Africa.* Vol. 1. Chicago: The University of Chicago Press, 1991.

Comaroff, J. *Body of Power, Spirit of Resistance: The Culture and History of a South African People.* Chicago and London: University of Chicago Press, 1985.

Commission of Inquiry for Women. *Report of the Commission of Inquiry for Women in Pakistan Islamabad.* August 1997.

Connell, R.W. *Masculinities.* Cambridge: Polity Press, 1990.

Contention. 'Comparative Fundamentalisms: I. Comparative and General Considerations'. *Contention* 4.2 (1995): 19–73.

Contention. 'Debates on Fundamentalism.' *Society, Culture, and Science* 4.3 (1995): 15–221.

Coombe, R.J. 'Room for Maneuver: Toward a Theory of Practice in Critical Legal Studies.' *Law and Social Inquiry* 14 (1989): 69–121.

Cornwall, A. and N. Lindisfarne. 'Dislocating Masculinity: Gender, Power and Anthropology.' *Dislocating Masculinity: Comparative Ethnographies.* A. Cornwall and N. Lindisfarne (eds.). London: Routledge. 1994, 11–47.

Coulson, N.J. *Conflicts and Tensions in Islamic Jurisprudence.* Chicago: University of Chicago Press, 1969.

Cowan, J.K. *Dance and the Body Politic in Northern Greece.* Princeton: Princeton University Press, 1990.

Crapanzano, V. *Tuhami: Portrait of a Moroccan.* Chicago and London: University of Chicago Press, 1980.

Crosby, C. 'Dealing with Differences.' *Feminists Theorize the Political.* J. Butler and J.W. Scott (eds.). New York: Routledge, 1992, 130-143.

Csordas, T.J. 'Somatic Modes of Attention.' *Cultural Anthropology* 8.2 (1993): 135–156.

Das, N. *The Architecture of Imambaras.* Lucknow: Lucknow Mahotsava Patrika Samiti, 1992.

Das, V. 'Language and Body: Transactions in the Construction of Pain.' *Social Suffering.* A. Kleinman, V. Das and M. Lock (eds.). Berkeley, Los Angeles, and London: University of California Press, 1997.

Das, V. 'Masks and Faces: An Essay on Punjabi Kinship.' *Contributions to Indian Sociology* 10.1 (1970): 1–30.

Das, V. 'Voice as Birth of Culture.' *Ethnos* 60.3–4 (1995): 159–79.

Das, V. 'Voices of Children.' *Daedalus* Fall (1989): 263–94.

Das, V. 'Wittgenstein and Anthropology.' *Annual Review of Anthropology* 27 (1998): 171–95.

David Lelyveld. *Aligarh's First Generation: Muslim Solidarity in British India.* Princeton, 1978.

Dawood, N.J. (Translator). *The Koran.* Penguin Books, 1986.

de Certeau, Michel. *The Practice of Everyday Life.* S. Rendall Trans. Berkeley: University of California Press, 1988.

de Heusch, L. *Sacrifice in Africa: A Structuralist Approach*. Bloomington: Indiana University Press, 1985.
Deeb, L. *An Enchanted Modern: Gender and Public Piety in Shi'i Lebanon*. Princeton: Princeton University Press, 2006.
Delaney, C. 'The *Hajj*: Sacred and Secular.' *American Ethnologist* 17.3 (1990): 513–530.
Deleuze, G and F. Guattari. *A Thousand Plateaus: Capitalism and Schizophrenia*. B. Massumi Trans. Minneapolis: University of Minnesota Press, 1987.
Deleuze, G. and C. Parnet. *Dialogues II*. H. Tomlinson and B. Habberjam Trans. New York: Columbia University Press, 2002.
Deleuze, G. *Difference & Repetition*. P. Patton Trans. New York: Columbia University Press, 1994.
Deleuze, G. *Essays Critical and Clinical*. D.W. Smith and M.A. Greco Trans. Minneapolis: University of Minnesota Press, 1997.
Deleuze, G. *The Logic of Sense*. M. Lester Trans. New York: Columbia University, 1990.
Dell, H. 'Toward Ethnographies of Communication: The Analysis of Communicative Events.' *Language and Social Context*. P.P. Giglioli (ed.). New York: Penguin Books, 1972.
Dell, H. *Foundations in Sociolinguistics: An Ethnographic Approach*. Philadelphia: University of Pennsylvania Press, 1974.
Derrida, J. *Margins of Philosophy*. Chicago: University of Chicago Press, 1982.
Devji, F. 'Gender and the Politics of Space: The Movement for Women's Reform, 1857–1900.' *Forging Identities: Gender, Communities, and the State*. Z. Hasan (ed.). New Delhi: Kali for Women Press, 1994.
Devji, F. *Landscapes of the Jihad: Militancy, Morality, Modernity*. Cornell: Cornell University Press, 2005.
Dunham, M.F. 'Selections from *Jarigan*, the Folk Epic of Muslim Bengal.' *Journal of South Asian Literature* 11.1–2 (1975): 147–155.
Dunham, M.F. *Jarigan: Muslim Epic Songs of Bangladesh*. Dhaka: University Press, 1996.
Durrani, A. 'Role of Shrine in Solving Psychological Problems Among Females.' Unpublished Masters Thesis. Anthropology Department, Quaid-e-Azam University, Islamabad, 1991.
Eade, J and M.J. Sallnow. 'Introduction.' *The Anthropology of Christian Pilgrimage Contesting the Sacred*. J. Eade and M.J. Sallnow (eds.). London: Routledge, 1991, 1–29.
Eaton, R.M. 'Sufi Folk Literature and the Expansion of Indian Islam.' *History of Religions* 14.2 (1974): 117–127.
Eglar, Z. *A Punjabi Village in Pakistan*. New York: Columbia University Press, 1960.
Eickelman, D. *Moroccan Islam: Tradition and Society in a Pilgrimage Centre*. Austin: University of Texas Press, 1976.
Eliade, M. *The Myth of Eternal Return*. (1948). New York: Bollingen, 1954.

Elias, N. *The Court Society*. Oxford: Blackwell, 1983.
El-Zein, A. 'The Evolution of the Concept of the Jinn from pre-Islam to Islami.' Ph.D. Dissertation. Georgetown University, 1996.
Encyclopedia of Islam (EI). CD-Rom. Leiden: Brill Publishers, 2003.
Ende, W. 'The Flagellanons of Muharram and the Shi'ite 'Ulama.' *Der Islam* 55 (1978): 19–36.
Theil E.R and K. Kristiansen. 'Khowar Studies.' Monumentum Georg Morgenstierne. *I. Acta Iranica*, 21. Leiden, the Netherlands: E.J. Brill, 1981, 210–243.
Erikson, E. *Identity and Life-Cycle*. New York: Norton and Company, 1980.
Ernst, C.W. *Words of Ecstasy in Sufism*. Albany: SUNY Press, 1995.
Erving G. 'The Neglected Situation.' *Language and Social Context*. P.P. Giglioli (ed.). New York: Penguin Books, 1972.
Erving G. *Frame Analysis*. New York: Harper and Row, 1974.
Ewing, K.P. 'Can Psychoanalytic Theories Explain the Pakistani Woman? Intrapsychic Autonomy and Interpersonal Engagement in the Extended Family.' *Ethos* 19.2 (1991): 131–160.
Ewing, K.P. 'The Dream of Spiritual Initiation and the Organization of Self Representations among Pakistani Sufis.' *American Ethnologist* 17.1 (1990a): 56–74.
Ewing, K.P. 'The Illusion of Wholeness: Culture, Self, and the Experience of Inconsistency.' *Ethos*. 18.3 (1990b): 251–278.
Ewing, K.P. 'The Modern Businessman and the Pakistani Saint: The Interpretation of Worlds.' *Manifestations of Sainthood in Islam*. G.M. Smith and C. Ernst (eds.). Istanbul: Editions Isis, 1993, 69–84.
Ewing, K.P. 'The Sufi and the *Mullah*: Islam and Local Culture in Pakistan.' Paper presented at the American Institute of Pakistan Studies conference, 'Pakistan at 50.' 28–31 August. Winston-Salem: Wake Forest University, 1999.
Ewing, K.P. 'The Sufi as Saint, Curer and Exorcist in Northern Pakistan.' *Contributions to Asian Studies* XVIII (1984): 106–114.
Ewing, K.P. *Arguing Sainthood: Modernity, Psychoanalysis and Islam*. Durham: Duke University Press, 1997.
Fabian, J. *Time and the Other: How Anthropology Makes its Object*. New York: Columbia University Press, 1983.
Farnell, B. 'Moving Bodies, Acting Selves.' *Annual Review of Anthropology* 28 (1999): 341–373.
Feld, S. 'Aesthetics as Iconicity of Style, or 'Lift-Up-Over Sounding': Getting into the Kaluli Groove.' *Yearbook for Traditional Music* 20 (1988): 74–113.
Feld, S. 'Communication, Music, and Speech about Music.' *Yearbook for Traditional Music* 16 (1984): 1–18.
Felman, S. 'Turning the Screw of Interpretation.' *Literature and Psychoanalysis* (ed.). Baltimore: The Johns Hopkins University Press, 1980.
Felski, R. 'The Doxa of Difference.' *SIGNS* 23 (1997): 1–21.

Fenech, L. 'Martyrdom and the Execution of Guru Arjan in Early Sikh Sources.' *Journal of the American Oriental Society* 121.1 (2001): 20–31.

Fernea, E.W. (ed.). *Children in the Muslim Middle East*. Austin: University of Texas, 1995.

Fernea, E.W. *Guests of the Sheik: An Ethnography of an Iraqi Village*. New York: Anchor Books, Doubleday, 1989.

Fernea, R.A. and E.W. Fernea. 'Variation in Religious Observance among Islamic Women.' *Scholars, Saints, and Sufis: Muslim Religious Institutions since 1500*. N.R. Keddie (ed.). Berkeley: University of California Press, 1978, 385–401.

Ferree, M.M. and D.A. Merrill. 'Hot Movements, Cold Cognition: Thinking about Social Movements in Gendered Frames.' *Contemporary Sociology*. Vol. 29 (2000): 454–62.

Fischer, M.M.J and A. Mehdi. *Debating Muslims: Cultural Dialogues in Postmodernity and Tradition*. Madison: University of Wisconsin Press, 1990.

Fischer, M.M.J. *Iran: From Religious Dispute to Revolution*. Cambridge: Harvard University Press, 1980.

Flores, R.R. '"Los Pastores" and the Gifting of Performance.' *American Ethnologist* 21 (1994): 270–285.

Foucault, M. 'Technologies of the Self.' *Technologies of the Self*. L.H Martin, H. Gutman and P.H Hutton (eds.). Amherst: The University of Massachusetts Press, 1988, 16–49.

Foucault, M. *Discipline and Punishment: The Birth of the Prison*. New York: Vintage Books, 1995.

Foucault, M. *Ethics: Subjectivity and Truth*. P. Rabinow (ed.). New York: The New Press, 1997.

François B. *Face to Face with Political Islam*. London, 2003.

Freitag, S.B. 'State and Community: Symbolic Popular Protest in Banaras's Public Arenas.' *Culture and Power in Banaras: Community, Performance, and Environment, 1800-1980*. S.B. Freitag (ed.). Berkeley: University of California Press, 1989, 203–228.

Freitag, S.B. *Collective Action and Community: Public Arenas and the Emergence of Communalism in North India*. Berkeley and London: University of California Press, 1989.

Friedl, E. 'Islam and Tribal Women in a Village in Iran.' *Unspoken Worlds: Women's Religious Lives*. N.A. Falk and R.M. Gross (eds.). Belmont: Wadsworth, 1989, 125–133.

Friedl, E. 'Legendary Heroines: Ideal Womanhood and Ideology in Iran.' *The Other Fifty Per cent: Multicultural Perspectives on Gender Relations*. M. Womack and J. Marti (eds.) Prospect Heights: Waveland Press, 1993, 261–266.

Friedl, E. 'Sources of Female Power in Iran.' *The Eye of the Storm: Women in Post-Revolutionary Iran*. M. Afkhami and E. Friedl (eds.). Syracuse: Syracuse University Press, 1994, 151–167.

Fyzee, A.A.A. *Outlines of Muhammadan Law*. Oxford: Oxford University Press, 1974.

Gaffney, P.D. *The Prophet's Pulpit: Islamic Preaching in Contemporary Egypt.* Berkeley: University of California Press, 1994.

Galaty, J.G. 'Ceremony and Society: The Poetics of Maasai Ritual.' *Man* (n.s.) 18.2 (1983): 361–382.

Gellner, E. *Postmodernism, Reason and Religion.* London: Routledge, 1992.

Gerami, S. 'The Role, Place, and Power of Middle-Class Women in the Islamic Republic.' *Identity Politics and Women: Cultural Reassertions and Feminisms in International Perspective.* V.M. Moghadam (ed.). Boulder: Westview Press, 1994, 329–348.

Gerstin, J. 'Interaction and Improvisation between Dancers and Drummers in Martinican Bèlè.' *Black Music Research Journal* 18.1–2 (1998): 121–165.

Ghoussoub, M. 'Chewing Gum, Insatiable Women, and Foreign Enemies: Male Fears and the Arab Media.' *Imagined Masculinities: Male Identity and Culture in the Modern Middle East.* M. Ghoussoub and E. Sinclair-Webb (eds.). London: Saqi Books, 2000, 227–235.

Gilles K. *Jihad: The Trail of Political Islam.* London, 2002.

Gilsenan, M. *Lords of the Lebanese Marches: Violence and Narrative in an Arab Society.* London: I.B. Tauris, 1996.

Glasse, C. *The New Encyclopedia of Islam.* Walnut Creek: Alta Mira Press, 2002.

Gommans, J. *Mughal Warfare.* London: Routledge, 2002.

Good, M.J.D.V and B.J. Good. 'Ritual, The State, and the Transformation of Emotional Discourse in Iranian Society.' *Culture, Medicine and Psychiatry* 12 (1988): 43–63.

Government of Pakistan, Ministry of Women Development and Youth Affairs. 'Pakistan National Report: Fourth World Conference on Women, Beijing.' Islamabad: Printing Corporation of Pakistan Press, 1995.

Government of Pakistan, Ministry of Women Development, Social Welfare & Special Education. 'Report on the Implementation of CEDAW.' Islamabad. November 1998.

Government of Pakistan, Ministry of Women Development, Social Welfare & Special Education. 'Report on the Implementation of CEDAW.' Islamabad. September 1999.

Government of Pakistan, Ministry of Women Development. 'National Plan of Action (NPA).' Islamabad: September 1998.

Government of Pakistan, Planning Commission. 'Ninth Five Year Plan (1998–2003): Report of the Working Group on Women's Development.' Islamabad: Printing Corporation of Pakistan Press. August 1997.

Government of Pakistan, Planning Commission. 2001. Ten Year Perspective Development Plan 2001–11 and 2001–11 and Three Year Development Programme 2001–04.' Islamabad: Printing Corporation of Pakistan Press, September.

Gramsci, A. *Selections from the Prison Notebooks of Antonio Gramsci.* Reprint. Q. Hoare and G.N. Smith (eds.) and Trans. New York: International Publishers, 1999.

Gray, J. *Al Qaeda and What It Means to be Modern.* London, 2003.

Grima, Benedicte. 'The Role of Suffering in Women's Performance of *Paxto*.' *Gender, Genre and Power in South Asian Expressive Traditions.* A. Appadurai, F.J. Korom and M.A. Mills (eds.). Philadelphia: University of Pennsylvania Press, 1991, 81–101.

Grima, Benedicte. *The Performance of Emotion among Paxtun Women.* Austin: University of Texas Press, 1992.

Gupta, A. 'Reliving Childhood? The Temporality of Childhood and Narratives of Reincarnation.' *Ethnos* 67.1 (2002): 33–56.

Guthrie, S.R. and S. Castelnuovo. 'Elite Women Bodybuilders: Models of Resistance or Compliance?' *Play and Culture* 5 (1992): 401–408.

Gutmann, M. 'Rituals of Resistance: A Critique of the Theory of Everyday Forms of Resistance.' *Latin American Perspectives* 20 (1993): 74–92.

Haeri, S. 'Obedience versus Autonomy: Women and Fundamentalism in Iran and Pakistan.' *Fundamentalisms and Society: Reclaiming the Sciences, the Family, and Education.* The Fundamentalism Project, 2. M.F. Marty and R.S. Appleby (eds.). Chicago: University of Chicago Press, 1993, 181–213.

Haeri, S. 'Of Feminism and Fundamentalism in Iran and Pakistan.' *Contention: Debates in Society, Culture, and Science* 4.3 (1995a): 129–149.

Haeri, S. 'The Politics of Dishonor: Rape and Power in Pakistan.' *Faith and Freedom: Women's Human Rights in the Muslim World.* M. Afkhami (ed.). Syracuse, NY: Syracuse University Press, 1995b, 161–174.

Haeri, S. *No Shame for the Sun: Lives of Professional Pakistani Women.* Syracuse: Syracuse University Press, 2002.

Halawi, M. *A Lebanon Defied: Musa al-Sadr and the Shi'a Community.* Boulder: Westview Press, 1992.

Hale, S. 'Gender, Religious Identity, and Political Mobilization in Sudan.' *Identity Politics and Women: Cultural Reassertions and Feminisms in International Perspective.* V.M. Moghadam (ed.). Boulder: Westview Press, 1994, 145–166.

Hall, S. 'Cultural Identity and Diaspora.' *Identity: Community, Culture, Difference.* J. Rutherford (ed.). London: Lawrence and Wishart, 1990, 222–237.

Hall, S. 'Signification, Representation, Ideology: Althusser and the Post-Structuralist Debates.' *Critical Studies in Mass Communication* 2.2 (1985): 91–114.

Hanks, W.F. 'Discourse Genres in a Theory of Practice.' *American Ethnologist* 14.4 (1987): 668–692.

Hansen, T.B. 'Sounds of Freedom: Music, Taxis and Racial Imagination in Urban South Africa.' *Journal of Public Culture* 18.1 (2006): 185–208.

Hansen, T.B. *The Saffron Wave: Democracy and Hindu Nationalism in Modern India.* Princeton: Princeton University Press, 1999.

Hardacre, H. 'The Impact of Fundamentalisms on Women, the Family, and Interpersonal Relations.' *Fundamentalisms and Society: Reclaiming the Sciences, the Family, and Education. The Fundamentalism Project* 2. M.E. Marty and R.S Appleby (eds.). Chicago: University of Chicago Press, 1993, 129–150.

Harding, S.F. *The Book of Jerry Falwell: Fundamentalist Language and Politics.* Princeton: Princeton University Press, 2001.

Harris, Colette. 'Desire versus Horniness: Sexual Relations in the Collective Society of Tajikistan.' *Social Analysis* 49.2 (2005): 78–95.

Hart, S. 'The Cultural Dimensions of Social Movements: A Theoretical Assessment and Literature Review.' *Sociology of Religion* 57 (2006): 87–100.

Hashmi, F. *Islam Main Gaana Bajaana (Music in Islam)*. Audio Tape.

Hasnain, N. *Shias and Shia Islam in India: A Study in Society and Culture.* New Delhi: Harnam Publications, 1988.

Heath, D. 'The Politics of Appropriateness and Appropriation: Recontextualizing Women's Dance in Urban Senegal.' *American Ethnologist* 21 (1994): 88–103.

Hegland, M.E. 'A Mixed Blessing: The *Majales*—Shi'a Women's Rituals of Mourning in North West Pakistan.' *Mixed Blessings: Gender and Religious Fundamentalism Cross Culturally.* J. Brink and J. Menchers (eds.). New York: Routledge, 1997a, 179–196.

Hegland, M.E. 'Imam Khomeini's Village: Recruitment to Revolution.' PhD dissertation. SUNY-Binghamton, 1986.

Hegland, M.E. 'Ritual and Revolution in Iran.' *Culture and Political Change. Political Anthropology Series* 2. M.J. Aronoff (ed.). New Brunswick: Transaction Books, 1983a, 75–100.

Hegland, M.E. 'Shi'a Women of Northwest Pakistan and Agency through Practice: Ritual, Resistance, Resilience.' *Political and Legal Anthropology Review* 18.2 (1995): 1–14.

Hegland, M.E. 'The Power Paradox in Muslim Women's *Majales:* North-West Pakistani Mourning Rituals as Sites of Contestation over Religious Politics, Ethnicity, and Gender.' *SIGNS* 23.2 (1997b): 391–428.

Hegland, M.E. 'Two Images of Husain: Accommodation and Revolution in an Iranian Village.' *Religion and Politics in Iran: Shi'ism from Quietism to Revolution.* N.R. Keddie (ed.). New Haven: Yale University Press, 1983b, 218–235.

Herzfeld, M. *Cultural Intimacy: Social Poetics in the Nation-State.* New York: Routledge, 1997.

Herzfeld, M. *The Poetics of Manhood: Contest and Identity in a Cretan Mountain Village.* Princeton: Princeton University Press, 1985.

Hill, J.H. and B. Mannheim. 'Language and World View.' *Annual Review of Anthropology* 21 (1992): 381–406.

Hirschkind, C. 'The Ethics of Listening: Cassette-sermon Audition in Contemporary Egypt.' *American Ethnologist* 28.3 (2001): 3–34.

Hirshkind, C. *The Ethical Soundscape: Cassette Sermons and Islamic Counterpublics.* New York: Columbia University Press, 2006.

Hjortshoj, K. 'Shi'i Identity and the Significance of Muharram in Lucknow, India.' *Shi'ism, Resistance, and Revolution.* M. Kramer (ed.). Boulder: Westview Press, 1987, 289–309.

Hochschild, A.R. and A. Machung. *The Second Shift.* New York: Avon Books, 1990.

Hodgson, G.S. 'Islam and Image.' *History of Religions* 3.2 (1964): 220–260.

Holland, D. and D. Skinner. 'Contested Ritual, Contested Femininities: (Re)forming Self and Society in a Nepali Women's Festival.' *American Ethnologist* 22 (1995): 279–305.

Holy Quran, The. The King Fahd Complex for the Printing of the Holy Quran. Medina, Saudi Arabia.

Hoodbhoy, P. 'Schools or Zealot Factories.' *The Friday Times.* Islamabad, Pakistan, 25 June–1 July 2004.

Horvatich, P. 'Ways of Knowing Islam.' *American Ethnologist*, 21.4 (1994): 811–26.

Hubert, H. and M. Mauss. *Sacrifice.* (1898). London: Cohen and West, 1964.

Huehns, C.E. 'Music in Northern Pakistan.' PhD dissertation. Faculty of Music. University of Cambridge, 1991.

Hughes, T.P. *A Dictionary of Islam.* (reprinted n.d.) Lahore: Kazi Publications, 1885.

Husted, W.R. 'Karbala' Made Immediate: The Martyr as Model in Imami Shi'ism.' *The Muslim World* 83.3–4 (1993): 263–278.

Ibrahim J. *Save Sind, Save the Continent.* Karachi, 1947.

Ibrahimi A. and F. Zehra. *Islam ki Misali Khatoon.* A. Abbas Trans. Lahore: Shafaq Publishers, 1405 AH.

Ingersoll, J.J. 'Which Tradition, Which Values? 'Traditional Family Values' in American Protestant Fundamentalism. *Contention* 4.3 (1995): 91–103.

Ingold, T. 'The Art of Translation in a Continuous World. *Beyond Boundaries: Understanding, Translation and Anthropological Discourse.* G. Pálsson (ed.). Oxford: Berg, 1993, 210–230.

Iqbal, J. *Islam and Pakistan's Identity.* Lahore: Iqbal Academy: Vanguard Books, 2003.

Iqbal, J. *The Ideology of Pakistan and Its Implementation.* Lahore: Ghulam Ali, 1959.

Jaffrelot, C. (ed.). *Pakistan: Nationalism without a Nation?* New Delhi: Manohar, 2002.

Jalal, A. 'Conjuring Pakistan: History as Official Imagining.' *International Journal of Middle East Studies* 27.1 (1995): 73–89.

Jalal, A. 'The Convenience of Subservience: Women and the State of Pakistan'. *Women, Islam, and the State.* D. Kandiyoti (ed.). Philadelphia: Temple University Press, 1991, 77–114.

Jalal, A. *Democracy and Authoritarianism in South Asia: A Comparative and Historical Perspective.* Cambridge: Cambridge University Press, 1995.

James, A. and A. Prout (eds). *Constructing and Reconstructing Childhood: Contemporary Issues in the Sociological Study of Childhood.* London: Falmer Press, 1997.

James, B. *Demons and Development: The Struggle for Community in a Sri Lankan Village.* Tuscon: University of Arizona Press, 1996.

James, Henry. *The Turn of the Screw.* New York: Augustus M. Kelley, 1971.

James, W. *Principles of Sociology.* New York: Holt, 1890.

Japp, P. and W. Beach 'Storyfying as Time-Travelling: The Knowledgeable Use of Temporally-Structured Discourse.' *Communication Yearbook* 7. R. Bostrom (ed.). New Brunswick: Transaction Books-ICA, 1983.

Jayawardena, C. 'Ideology and Conflict in Lower Class Communities.' *Comparative Studies in Society and History* 10 (1968): 413–446.

Jeffery, P. *Frogs in a Well: Indian Women in Purdah.* London: Zed Books, 1989.

Jehangir, A. and H. Jilani. *The Hudood Ordinances: a Divine Sanction?* Lahore: Rhotas, 1990.

Jilani, H. *Human Rights and Democratic Development in Pakistan.* Lahore: Human Rights, 1998.

Jogi, I. *The Passion of Pakistan.* Compact disc. Previously released by Olympic Records [ca. 1950s]. Salem: Tradition, 1997.

Johnston, S.M. *Poetics of Performance: Narratives, Faith and Disjuncture in Qawwali.* Ph.D. Dissertation. Department of Anthropology. University of Texas at Austin, 2000.

Joseph, S. 'Brother/Sister Relationships: Connectivity, Love, and Power in the Reproduction of Patriarchy in Lebanon.' *American Ethnologist* 21 (1994): 50–73.

Joseph, S. 'Connectivity and Patriarchy among Urban Working-Class Arab Families in Lebanon.' *Ethos* 21.4 (1993): 452–484.

Joseph, S. 'The Family as Security and Bondage: A Political Strategy of the Lebanese Urban Working Class.' *Towards a Political Economy of Urbanization in Third World Countries.* H. Safa (ed.). New Delhi: Oxford University Press, 1982, 151–171.

Kakar, S. *Shamans, Mystics and Doctors.* Chicago: University of Chicago Press, 1982.

Kandiyoti, D. 'Bargaining with Patriarchy.' *Gender and Society* 2 (1983): 274–290.

Kandiyoti, D. 'Introduction.' *Women, Islam and the State.* D. Kandiyoti (ed.). Philadelphia: Temple University Press, 1991, 1–21.

Karim, Maulana F. *Al-Hadis: An English Translation and Commentary of Mishkat-ul-Musabih.* Four Volumes. Delhi: Islamic Book Service, 1989.

Kaufman, D.R. 'Paradoxical Politics: Gender Politics among Newly Orthodox Jewish Women in the United States.' *Identity Politics and Women: Cultural*

Reassertions and Feminisms in International Perspective. V.M. Moghadam (ed.). Boulder: Westview Press, 1994, 349–366.

Kaufman, D.R. *Rachel's Daughters.* New Brunswick: Rutgers University Press, 1991.

Keane, W. 'Religious Language.' *Annual Review of Anthropology* 26 (1997): 47–71.

Keddie, N.R. (ed.). *Religion and Politics in Iran: Shi'ism from Quietism to Revolution.* New Haven: Yale University Press, 1983.

Keddie, N.R. 'The Shi'a of Pakistan: Reflections and Problems for Further Research.' Working Paper No. 23. The G.E. von Grunebaum Center for Near Eastern Studies. University of California, Los Angeles, 1993.

Keddie, N.R. *Iran and the Muslim World: Resistance and Revolution.* London: Macmillan Press, 1995.

Keil, C. 'Participatory Discrepancies and the Power of Music.' *Music Grooves.* C. Keil and S. Feld. Chicago: University of Chicago Press, 1994, 6–108.

Keiser, L. *Friend by Day, Enemy by Night: Organized Vengeance in a Kohistani Community.* Fort Worth: Holt, Rinehart and Winston, 1991.

Kennion R.L. *Sport and Life in the Further Himalaya.* London: William Blackwood and Sons, 1910.

Kertzer, D. *Ritual, Politics, and Power.* New Haven: Yale University Press, 1988.

Khan, N. 'Grounding Sectarianism: Islamic Ideology and Muslim Everyday Life in Lahore, Pakistan.' Ph.D. Dissertation. Columbia University, 2003.

Khan, N. 'The Construction of the "*Jahil Maulvi*": An Instance of Religious Debate in Contemporary Pakistan.' Paper Presented at the Summer Institute on Public Spheres and Muslim Identities. Wissenschaftskolleg zu Berlin, Germany, July 2001.

Khan, N. 'Trespasses of the State: Ministering to Theological Dilemmas through the Copyright/Trademark.' *Bare Acts: Sarai Reader 5.* L. Liang (ed.). Delhi: The Sarai Programme, 2005.

Khan, N.S., R. Saigol, and A.S. Zia. 'Introduction.' *Locating the Self: Perspectives on Women and Multiple Identities.* N.S Khan, R. Saigol and A.S. Zia (eds.). Lahore: ASR Publications, 1994.

Khuhro H. *The Making of Modern Sind: British Policy and Social Change in the Nineteenth Century.* Karachi, 1978, 260.

Khuhro, H. (ed.). *Documents on Separation of Sind from the Bombay Presidency.* Islamabad, 1982.

Kippen, J. 'Folk Grooves and Tabla Tal-s.' *Echo: A Music-Centered Journal* 3.1. Electronic document, http://www.humnet.ucla.edu/echo, accessed 26 November 2005 (2001).

Klandermans, B. and D. Oegema, 'Potentials, Networks, Motivations, and Barriers: Steps Towards Participation in Social Movements.' *American Sociological Review.* 52 Aug. (1987): 519–31.

Korom, F, and P. Chelkowski. 'Community Process and the Performance of Muharram Observances in Trinidad.' *The Drama Review* 38.2 (1994): 150–175.

Korom, F.J. 'Memory, Innovation, and Emergent Ethnicity: The Creolization of an Indo-Trinidadian Performance.' *Diaspora* 3.2 (1994a): 135–155.

Korom, F.J. 'The Transformation of Language to Rhythm: The Hosay Drums of Trinidad.' *The World of Music: Journal of the International Institute for Traditional Music* 36.3 (1994b): 68–85.

Kramer, M. (ed.). *Shi'ism, Resistance, and Revolution.* Boulder: Westview Press, 1987.

Kugle, S. and A. Behl 'Haqiqat Al-fuqara: Poetic Biography of Madho Lal Hussayn (Persian).' *Same-Sex Love in India: Readings from Literature and History.* R. Vanita and S. Kidwai (eds.). S. Kugle commentary and translation and A. Behl poetic translations. New York: St. Martin's Press, 2000, 145–156.

Kumar, N. 'Work and Leisure in the Formation of Identity: Muslim Weavers in a Hindu City.' *Culture and Power in Banaras: Community, Performance, and Environment, 1800–1980.* S.B. Freitag (ed.). Berkeley: University of California Press, 1989, 147–170.

Kurin, R. 'Morality, Personhood and Exemplary Life: Popular Conceptions of Muslims in Paradise.' *Moral Conduct and Authority: The Place of Adab in South Asian Islam.* B.D. Metcalf (ed.). Berkeley: University of California Press, 1984, 196–220.

Lambek, M. 'Certain Knowledge, Contestable Authority: Power and Practice on the Islamic Periphery.' *American Ethnologist,* 17.1 (1990): 23–40.

Lambek, M. 'Spirits and Spouses: Possession as a System of Communication among the Malagasy Speakers of Mayotte.' *American Ethnologist* 7.2 (1980): 318–331.

Lapidus, I.M. 'Adulthood in Islam.' *Daedulus* 105 (1976): 93–107.

Lapidus, I.M. *A History of Islamic Societies.* 2nd edition. New York: Cambridge University Press, 2002.

Larana, E., H. Johnston and J.R. Gusfield. 'Identities, Grievances, and New Social Movements.' *New Social Movements: From Ideology to Identity.* E. Larana, H. Johnston and J.R. Gusfield (eds.). Philadelphia: Temple University Press, 1994, 3–35.

Lassy, I.J. *The Muharram Mysteries among the Azerbaijan Turks of Caucasia.* Helsingfors: Lilius and Hartzberg, 1916.

Lawless, E.J. 'Rescripting Their Lives and Narratives: Spiritual Life Stories of Pentecostal Women Preachers.' *Journal of Feminist Studies in Religion* 7.1 (1991): 53–71.

Lawless, E.J. *Handmaidens of the Lord: Pentecostal Women Preachers and Traditional Religion.* Philadelphia: University of Pennsylvania Press, 1988.

Lawrence, B.B. 'Woman as Subject/Woman as Symbol: Islamic Fundamentalism and the Status of Women.' *Journal of Religious Ethics* 22.1 (1994): 163–185.

Leante, L. 'Shaping Diasporic Sounds: Identity as Meaning in Bhangra.' *World of Music* 46.1 (2004): 109–132.

Levi-Strauss, cited in Sherzer. 'Strategies in Text and Context' *Karbala ki Sher Dil Khatoon*. Aisha Bint al-Shati Mistri. M. Abbas Trans. Lahore: Maktaba-e Imamia Trust, 1996.

Lewis, J.L. 'Genre and Embodiment: From Brazilian Capoeira to the Ethnology of Human Movement.' *Cultural Anthropology* 10.2 (1995): 221–243.

Lindell, D. T. 'Muharram in Hyderabad.' *Al-Basheer* 3 (1974): 14–29.

Lindholm, C. 'Validating Domination among Egalitarian Individuals: Swat, Northern Pakistan and the USA.' *Person, Myth and Society in South Asian Islam*, special issue of *Social Analysis* 28. P. Werbner (ed.). University of Adelaide, 1990, 26–37.

Lindholm, C. *Frontier Perspectives: Essays in Comparative Anthropology*. Oxford: Oxford University Press, 1996.

Lindholm, C. *Generosity and Jealousy: The Swat Pukhtun of Northern Pakistan*. New York: Columbia University Press, 1982.

Lindisfarne, N. 'Changing Marriage Ceremonial and Gender Roles in the Arab World: An Anthropological Perspective.' *Arab Affairs* 8 (1988-89): 117–135.

Lindisfarne, N. 'Variant Masculinities, Variant Virginities: Rethinking 'Honour' and 'Shame'.' *Dislocating Masculinity: Comparative Ethnographies*. A. Cornwall and N. Lindisfarne (eds.). London: Routledge, 1994, 82–96.

Lindisfarne, N. *Bartered Brides: Politics, Gender and Marriage in an Afghan Tribal Society*. Cambridge: Cambridge University Press, 1991.

Loeffler, R. *Islam in Practice: Religious Beliefs in a Persian Village*. Albany: State University of New York Press, 1988.

Loizos, P. 'A Broken Mirror: Masculine Sexuality in Greek Ethnography.' *Dislocating Masculinity: Comparative Ethnographies*. A. Cornwall and N. Lindisfarne (eds.). London: Routledge, 1994, 66–81.

Lord, A.B. *The Singer of Tales*. Cambridge: Harvard University Press, 1960.

Luhrman, T.M. *The Good Parsi: The Fate of a Colonial Elite in a Postcolonial Society*. Cambridge, MA: Harvard University Press, 1996.

Lutz, C. and L. Abu-Lughod (eds.). *Language and the Politics of Emotion*. Cambridge: Cambridge University Press, 1990.

MacLeod, A.E. 'Hegemonic Relations and Gender Resistance: The New Veiling as Accommodating Protest in Cairo.' *SIGNS* 17 (1992b): 533–557.

MacLeod, A.E. *Accommodating Protest: Working Women, the New Veiling, and Change in Cairo*. New York: Columbia University Press, 1992a.

Mageo, J.M. and A. Howard (eds.). *Spirits in Culture, History, and Mind*. New York: Routledge, 1996.

Mahdjoub, M.D. 'The Evolution of Popular Eulogy of the Imams among the Shia.' *Authority and Political Culture in Shi'ism*. Said Amir Arjomand (ed.). J.R. Perry Trans. Albany: State University of New York Press, 1988, 54–79.

Mahmood, S. *Politics of Piety: The Islamic Revival and the Feminist Subject*. Princeton: Princeton University Press, 2005.

Malik, J. *Colonialization of Islam: Dissolution of Traditional Institutions in Pakistan.* Delhi: Manohar Publications, 1996.

Mankekar, P. 'National Texts and Gendered Lives: An Ethnography of Television Viewers in a North Indian City.' *American Ethnologist* 20 (1993): 543–563.

Mankekar, P. *Screening Culture, Viewing Politics.* Durham: Duke University Press, 1999.

Manuel, P. 'The Popularization and Transformations of the Light Classical Urdu *Ghazal*-Song.' *Gender, Genre, and Power in South Asian Expressive Traditions.* A. Appadurai, F.J. Korom and M.A. Mills (eds.). Philadelphia: University of Pennsylvania Press, 1991, 347–161.

Marsden, M. 'Islam, Political Authority and Emotion in Northern Pakistan.' *Contributions to Indian Sociology* (2007a).

Marsden, M. 'Love and Elopement in Northern Pakistan.' *Journal of the Royal Anthropological Institute* 13.1 (2007b): 91–108.

Marsden, M. *Living Islam: Muslim Religious Experience in Pakistan's North West Frontier.* Cambridge: Cambridge University Press, 2005.

Masud, M.K. (ed.). *Travellers in Faith: Studies of the Tablighi Jamaat as a Transnational Islamic Movement for Faith Renewal.* Leiden: Brill Academic Publishers, 2000.

Mazumdar, S. 'Moving Away from a Secular Vision? Women, Nation, and the Cultural Construction of Hindu India.' *Identity Politics and Women: Cultural Reassertions and Feminisms in International Perspective.* V.M. Moghadam (ed.). Boulder: Westview Press, 1994, 243–273.

McAdam, D. 'Culture and Social Movements.' *New Social Movements: From Ideology to Identity.* E. Larana, H. Johnston and J.R. Gusfield (eds.). Philadelphia: Temple University Press, 1994, 36–57.

McDevitt, P. 'Muscular Catholicism: Nationalism, Muscularity and Gaelic Team Sports, 1884–1914.' *Bodies in Contact: Rethinking Colonial Encounters in World History.* T. Ballantyne and A. Burton (eds.). Durham: Duke University Press, 2005, 201–218.

McNeill, W.H. *Keeping Together in Time: Dance and Drill in Human History.* Cambridge: Harvard University Press, 1995.

Mehdi, R. 'The Offence of Rape in the Islamic Law of Pakistan.' *International Journal of Sociology of Law* 18 (1990): 19–29.

Menon, R. and K. Bhasin. 'Borders and Boundaries: Recovering Women in the Interests of the Nation.' *Borders and Boundaries: Women in India's Partition.* New Delhi: Kali for Women, 1998.

Metcalf, B.D. 'Islamic Reform and Islamic Women: Maulana Thanawi's Jewelry of Paradise.' *Moral Conduct and Authority: The Place of Adab in South Asian Islam.* B.D. Metcalf (ed.). Berkeley: University of California Press, 1984, 184–195.

Metcalf, B.D. 'Living Hadith in the Tablighi Jama'at.' *The Journal of Asian Studies* 52.3 (1993): 584–608.

Metcalf, B.D. *Bihisti Zewar: Perfecting Women.* Maulana Ashraf Ali Thanawi's Bihisti Zewar, A Partial Translation with Commentary. Lahore: Idara-e-Islamiat, 1997.

Metcalf, B.D. *Islamic Contestations: Essays on Muslims in India and Pakistan.* Oxford: Oxford University Press, 2004.

Metcalf, B.D. *Islamic Revival in British India: Deoband, 1860–1900.* Princeton: Princeton University Press, 1982.

Meyerhoff, B. *Peyote Hunt: The Sacred Journey of the Huichol Indians.* Ithaca: Cornell University Press, 1974.

Middlebrook, J. 'Punjab.' *The Garland Encyclopedia of World Music.* Vol. 5: South Asia: The Indian Subcontinent. A. Arnold, (ed.). New York: Garland, 2000, 650–657.

Moghadam, V. (ed.). *Identity Politics and Women: Cultural Reassertions and Feminisms in International Perspective.* Boulder: Westview Press, 1994.

Mohanty, C.T. 'Under Western Eyes: Feminist Scholarship and Colonial Discourse.' *Third World Women and the Politics of Feminism.* C.T. Mohanty, A. Russo and L. Torres (eds.). Bloomington: Indiana University Press, 1991, 51–80.

Moinuddin, K. *A Monograph on Muharram in Hyderabad City.* Andhra Pradesh: Indian Administrative Service, 1971.

Monson, I. 'Riffs, Repetition, and Theories of Globalization.' *Ethnomusicology* 43.1 (199): 31–65.

Mookherjee, N. 'My Man (Honour) Is Lost, but I Still Have My Man.' *Asian Masculinities: Contexts of Change; Sites of Continuity.* R. Chopra, C. Osella and F. Osella (eds.). Delhi: South Women Unlimited, 2004, 335–363.

Moore, E.P. 'Gender, Power, and Legal Pluralism: Rajasthan, India.' *American Ethnologist* 20 (1993): 522–542.

Morgenstierne, G. 'Iranian Elements in Khowar.' *Bulletin of the School of African and Oriental Studies* 8 (1936): 657–671.

Morgenstierne, G. and W. Ali Shah. 'Some Khowar Songs.' *Acta Orientalia* 24 (1959): 29–58.

Mottahedeh, R. *The Mantle of the Prophet: Religion and Politics in Iran.* New York: Simon and Schuster, 1985.

Mufti, A.R. 'Towards a Lyric History of India.' *Boundary 2* 31.2 (2004): 245–74.

Mumtaz, K. 'Identity Politics and Women: 'Fundamentalism' and Women in Pakistan.' *Identity Politics and Women: Cultural Reassertions and Feminism in International Perspective.* V.M. Moghadam (ed.). Boulder: Westview Press, 1994, 228–242.

Mumtaz, K. and F. Shaheed. *Women of Pakistan: Two Steps Forward, One Step Back?* London: Zed Books, 1987.

Munn, N.D. 'Symbolism in a Ritual Context: Aspects of Symbolic Action.' *Handbook of Social and Cultural Anthropology.* J.J. Honigman (ed.). New York: Rand McNally, 1974, 579–612.

Najumabadi, Afsaneh. 'Mapping Transformations of Sex, Gender and Sexuality in Modern Iran.' *Social Analysis* 49.2 (2005): 54–77.

Nakash, Y. 'An Attempt to Trace the Origin of the Rituals of 'Ashura.'' *Die Welt des Islams* 33 (1993): 161–181.

Nakash, Y. *The Shi'is of Iraq.* Princeton: Princeton University Press, 1994.

Nandy, A. *The Intimate Enemy: Loss and Recovery of Self under Colonialism.* Delhi: Oxford University Press, 1983.

Naqvi, S. *Qutb Shahi 'Ashur Khanas of Hyderabad City.* Hyderabad: Bab-ul-Ilm Society, 1987.

Nasr, S.V.R. 'National Identities and the India–Pakistan Conflict.' *The India-Pakistan Conflict: An Enduring Rivalry.* T.V. Paul (ed.). Cambridge: Cambridge University Press, 2005, 178–201.

Nasr, S.V.R. Communalism and Fundamentalism: A Reexamination of the Origins of Islamic Fundamentalism. *Contention: Debates in Society, Culture, and Science* 4.2 (1995): 121–139.

Nasr, S.V.R. *Islamic Leviathan: Islam and the Making of State Power.* Oxford: Oxford University Press, 2002.

Nasr, S.V.R. The Rise of Sunni Militancy in Pakistan: The Changing Role of Islamism and the Ulama in Society and Politics.' *Modern Asian Studies* 34.1 (2000): 139–80.

Nasr, S.V.R. *The Vanguard of the Islamic Revolution: The Jama'at-i Islami of Pakistan.* Berkeley: University of California Press, 1994.

National Assembly of Pakistan. *The Constitution of the Islamic Republic of Pakistan.* (as modified up to 28 July 1991). Islamabad, 1993.

Navaro-Yashin, Y. *Faces of the State: Secularism and Public Life in Turkey.* Princeton: Princeton University Press, 2002.

Newby, G.D. *A Concise Encyclopedia of Islam.* Oxford: Oneworld Publications, 2002.

Nigah, N.M. 'Khowar Music and Songs.' *Proceedings of the Second International Hindukush Conference.* E. Bashir and I. Din (eds.). Karachi: Oxford University Press, 1996, 209–216.

Norton, A.R. *Amal and the Shi'a: Struggle for the Soul of Lebanon.* Austin: University of Texas Press, 1988.

O'Brien, D.J.T. *Grammar and Vocabulary of the Khowar Dialect (Chitrali), with Introductory Sketch of Country and People.* Lahore: Civil and Military Gazette Press, 1895.

O'Hanlon, R. 'Issues of Masculinity in North Indian History: The Bangash Nawabs of Farrukhabad.' *Indian Journal of Gender Studies* 4.1 (1997): 1–19.

Okely, J. 'Defiant Moments: Gender, Resistance, and Individuals.' *Man* 26 (1991): 3–22.

Oldenburg, V.T. 'Lifestyle as Resistance: The Case of the Courtesans of Lucknow, India.' *Feminist Studies* 16.2 (1990): 258–287.

Ong, A. 'State versus Islam: Malay Families, Women's Bodies, and the Body Politic in Malaysia.' *American Ethnologist* 17 (1990): 258–276.

Ortner, S.B. 'Patterns of History: Cultural Schemas in the Foundings of Sherpa Religious Institutions.' *Culture through Time: Anthropological Approaches.* A.O Tierney (ed.). Stanford: Stanford University Press, 1990, 57–93.

Ortner, S.B. *Sherpas through Their Rituals.* Cambridge: Cambridge University Press, 1987.

Ortner, S. 'On Key Symbols.' *Reader in Comparative Religion: An Anthropological Approach* (4th Edition). W.A. Lessa and E.Z. Vogt (eds.). New York: Harper and Row, 1979, 92–98.

Osella, F. and C. Osella. *Men and Masculinities in India.* London: Anthem, 2006.

Outram, D. 'The Body and the French Revolution: Sex, Class, and Political Culture.' New Haven: Yale University Press, 1989.

Pandey, G. *The Construction of Communalism in Colonial India.* Delhi: Oxford University Press, 1998.

Pandolfo, S. 'The Thin Line of Modernity: Some Moroccan Debates on Subjectivity.' *Questions of Modernity.* T. Mitchell (ed.). Minneapolis and London: University of Minnesota Press, 2000.

Papanek, H. 'False Specialization and the Purdah of Scholarship—A Review Article.' *Journal of Asian Studies* 44.1 (1984): 127–148.

Papanek, H. 'Purdah in Pakistan: Seclusion and Modern Occupations for Women.' *Separate Worlds: Studies of Purdah in South Asia.* H. Papanek and G. Minault (eds.) Columbia: South Asia Books, 1982, 190–216.

Papanek, H. 'Purdah: Separate Worlds and Symbolic Shelter.' *Comparative Studies in Society and History* 15 (1973): 289–325.

Papanek, H. 'The Ideal Woman and the Ideal Society: Control and Autonomy in the Construction of Identity.' *Identity Politics and Women: Cultural Reassertions and Feminisms in International Perspective.* V.M. Moghadam (ed.). Boulder: Westview Press, 1994, 42–75.

Parkes, P. 'Alternative Social Structures and Foster Relations in the Hindu Kush: Milk Kinship and Tributary Alliance in Former Mountain Kingdoms of Northern Pakistan.' *Comparative Studies in Society and History* 43.1 (2001a): 4–36.

Parkes, P. 'Indigenous Polo and the Politics of Regional Identity.' *Sport, Identity and Ethnicity.* J. MacClancy (ed.). Oxford: Berg, 1996, 43–67.

Parkes, P. 'Indigenous Polo in Pakistan: Game and Power on the Periphery.' *Subaltern Sports: Politics and Sport in South Asia.* J.H. Mills (ed.). London: Anthem, 2005, 61–82.

Parkes, P. 'Personal and Collective Identity in Kalasha Song Performance: The Significance of Music Making in a Minority Enclave.' *Ethnicity, Identity and Music: The Musical Construction of Place.* M. Stokes (ed.). Oxford: Berg. 1994, 157–188.

Parkes, P. 'Unwrapping Rudeness: Inverted Etiquette in an Egalitarian Enclave.' *An Anthropology of Indirect Communication.* J. Henry and C.W. Watson (eds.). London: Routledge, 2001b, 232–251.

Parry, J.P. *Death in Banaras*. Cambridge: Cambridge University Press, 1994.
Peirce, C.S. *Philosophical Writings of Peirce*. J. Buehler (ed.). New York: Dover, 1955.
Peletz, M. *Reason and Passion: Representations of Gender in a Malay Society*. Berkeley: University of California Press, 1996.
Pelly, L. *The Miracle Play of Hasan and Husain, Collected from Oral Tradition, I, II*. London: The India Office, 1879.
Peteet, J. 'Male Gender and Rituals of Resistance in the Palestinian Intifada: A Cultural Politics of Violence.' *American Ethnologist* 21 (1994): 3–49.
Peteet, J. *Gender in Crisis: Women and the Palestinian Resistance Movement*. New York: Columbia University Press, 1991.
Peters, E.L. 'A Muslim Passion Play: Key to a Lebanese Village.' *The Atlantic Monthly* 198 (1956): 176–180.
Peters, E.L. 'Shifts in Power in a Lebanese Village.' *Rural Politics and Social Change in the Middle East*. R. Antoun and I. Harik (eds.). Bloomington: Indiana University Press. 1972, 165–197.
Pinault, D. 'Shi'a Muslim Men's Associations and the Celebration of Muharram in Hyderabad, India.' *Journal of South Asian and Middle Eastern Studies* 16 (992b): 33–62.
Pinault, D. *The Shiites: Ritual arid Popular Piety in a Muslim Community*. New York: St. Martin's Press, 1992a.
Platts, J.T. *A Dictionary of Urdu, Classical Hindi, and English*. Reprint. New Delhi: Munshiram Manoharlal, 2000.
Pritchett, F. N.d. Overview of the [ghazal] genre Electronic document, http://www.columbia.edu/itc/mealac/pritchett/00ghalib/about/x_genre_overview.html, accessed 22 November 2005.
Punjabi English Dictionary. *The Punjabi English Dictionary*. [1895]. Lahore, Pakistan: Vanguard Books, 1983.
Qureshi, R. 'Exploring Time Cross-Culturally: Ideology and Performance of Time in the Sufi Qawwali.' *The Journal of Musicology* 12.4 (1994): 491–528.
Qureshi, R. 'How Does Music Mean? Embodied Memories and the Politics of Affect in Indian Sarangi.' *American Ethnologist* 27.4 (2000): 804–838.
Qureshi, R. *Sufi Music in India and Pakistan: Sound, Context and Meaning in Qawwali*. Chicago: University of Chicago Press, 1995.
Qureshi, R. *Sufi Music of India and Pakistan: Sound, Context, and Meaning in Qawwali*. Cambridge: Cambridge University Press, 1986.
Racy, A.J. *Making Music in the Arab World*. Cambridge: Cambridge University Press, 2003.
Rahat, N. 'The Role of Women in Reciprocal Relationships in a Punjab Village.' *The Endless Day: Some Case Material on Asian Rural Women*. T.S. Epstein and R.A. Watts (eds.). Oxford: Pergamon Press, 1981, 47–81.
Raheja, G.G. and A.G. Gold. *Listen to the Heron's Words: Reimagining Gender and Kinship in North India*. Berkeley: University of California Press, 1994.

Ram, H. *Myth and Mobilization in Revolutionary Iran: The Use of the Friday Congregational Sermon.* Lanham: University Press of America, 1994.

Ramazani, N. 'Islamization and the Women's Movement in Pakistan.' *Journal of South Asian and Middle Eastern Studies* 8.3 (1985): 53–64.

Rapport, N. 'Edifying Anthropology: Culture as Conversation: Representation as Conversation.' *After Writing Culture.* A. James, J. Hockey and A. Dawson (eds.). London: Routledge, 1997, 177–193.

Rattansi, A. '"Western" Racisms, Ethnicities and Identities in a "Postmodern" Frame.' *Racism, Modernity and Identity: On the Western Front.* A. Rattansi and S. Westwood (eds.). Cambridge: Polity Press, 1994, 15–86.

Rattansi, A. 'Just Framing: Ethnicities and Racism in a 'Post Modern' Framework.' *Social Postmodernism: Beyond Identity Politics.* L. Nicholson, and S. Seidman (eds.). Cambridge: Cambridge University Press, 1995, 250–286.

Raul, A. 'Rural Women and the Family: A Study of a Punjabi Village in Pakistan.' *Journal of Comparative Family Studies* 18 (1987): 403–415.

Reddy, W.M. *The Navigation of Feeling: A Framework for the History of Emotions.* Cambridge: Cambridge University Press, 2001.

Reed, S.A. 'Performing Respectability: The Berava, Middle-Class Nationalism, and the Classicization of Kandyan Dance in Sri Lanka.' *Cultural Anthropology* 17.2 (2002): 246–277.

Reed-Danahay, D. 'Talking about Resistance: Ethnography and Theory in Rural France.' *Anthropological Quarterly* 66 (1993): 221–229.

Reetz, D. 'The Busy World of the Tablighi-Jamaat: An Insight into their System of Self Organization (*intizam*).' Paper presented at the 17th European Conference for Modern South Asia Studies. Heidelberg. 9–13 September 2002.

Reynolds, P. *Childhood at Crossroads: Cognition and Society in South Africa.* Cape Town, South Africa: David Philip, 1989.

Reynolds, P. *Traditional Healers and Childhood in Zimbabwe.* Athens: Ohio University Press, 1996.

Richard, Y. *Shiite Islam: Polity, Ideology, and Creed.* Cambridge: Blackwell, 1995.

Richards, John F. *The Mughal Empire.* Cambridge: Cambridge University Press, 1996.

Ricoeur, Paul. *Hermeneutics and the Social Sciences.* J.B. Thompson Trans. Cambridge: Cambridge University Press, 1981.

Riggio, M.C (ed.). *Ta'ziyeh: Ritual and Popular Beliefs in Iran.* Hartford: Trinity College, 1988.

Riggio, M.C. 'Ta'ziyeh in Exile: Transformations in a Persian Tradition.' *Comparative Drama* 28.1 (1994): 115–140.

Ring, L. '(En)gendering tension: Anger, Intimacy and Everyday Peace in Karachi (Pakistan).' Ph.D. Dissertation. Chicago: University of Chicago, 2003.

Rizvi, S.A.A. *A Socio-Intellectual History of the Isna 'Ashari Shi'is in India, I, II.* Canberra: Ma'refat Publishing House, 1986.

Robertson, G. S. *Chitral: The Story of a Minor Siege*. London: Methuen, 1899.
Rose, N. *Inventing Ourselves*. New York: Cambridge University Press, 1996.
Rothenberg, C.E. 'Spirits of Palestine: Palestinian Village Women and Stories of the Jinn.' Ph.D. Dissertation. Toronto: University of Toronto, 1998.
Rouse, S. 'Women's Movements in Contemporary Pakistan: Results and Prospects.' Working paper 74. Michigan State University, 1984
Roy, O. *The Failure of Political Islam*. Cambridge, MA, 2001.
Rugh, A.B. *Family in Contemporary Egypt*. Syracuse: Syracuse University Press, 1984.
Ryave, A.L. 'On the Achievement of a Series of Stories.' *Studies in the Organization of Conversational Interaction*. J. Schenkein (ed.). New York: Academic Press, 1978.
Sabri Brothers. 'Musiciens Kawwali du Pakistan: *Le Frères Sabri.*' *Musique Soufi, Vol. 3*. Compact disc. F. Gründ Notes. ARN 64147. Paris: Arion, 1991.
Sacks H., E. Schegloff and G. Jefferson. 'A Simplest Systemics for the Organization of Turn-Taking in Conversation.' *Language* 50.4 (1974)
Saeed, F. *Taboo: The Hidden Culture of a Red Light Area*. Karachi: Oxford University Press, 2001.
Sagaster, U. 'Observations Made during the Month of Muharram, 1989, in Baltistan.' *Proceedings of the International Seminar on the Anthropology of Tibet and the Himalaya*. C. Ramble and M. Brauen (eds.). Zurich: Ethnological Museum of the University of Zurich, 1993, 308–317.
Sakata, H.L. *Music in the Mind: The Concepts of Music and Musician in Afghanistan*. Kent: Kent State University Press, 1983.
Saliba, T. 'Introduction: Gender, Politics, and Islam.' *Gender, Politics, and Islam*. T. Saliba, C. Allen and J.A. Howard (eds.). Chicago: The University of Chicago Press, 2002, 1–14.
Sanyal, U. *Devotional Islam and Politics in British India: Ahmad Riza Khan Barelwi and his Movement, 1870–1920*. Delhi: Oxford University Press, 1996.
Sapir, E. 'Sound Patterns in Language.' *Language* 1.2 (1925): 37–51.
Schacht, J. *An Introduction to Islamic Law*. Oxford: Clarendon Press, 1964.
Schenkein, J. *Studies in the Organization of Conversational Interaction*. New York: Academic Press, 1978.
Schieffelin, E. 'Performance and the Cultural Construction of Reality.' *American Ethnologist* 12 (1985): 707–724.
Schimmel, A. *And Muhammad is His Messenger: The Veneration of the Prophet in Islamic Piety*. Chapel Hill: University of North Carolina Press, 1985.
Schimmel, A. *Mystical Dimensions of Islam*. Chapel Hill: University of North Carolina Press, 1975.
Schmid, A. *Die Dom zwischen sozialer Ohnmacht und kulturella Macht: Interethnische Beziehungen in Nordpakistan*. Stuttgart: Franz Stenier Verlag, 1997.
Schubel, V. 'The Muharram Majlis: The Role of a Ritual in the Preservation of Shi'a Identity.' *Muslim Families in North America*. E. Waugh, S.M. Abu-

Laban, R.B Qureshi, (eds.). Edmonton: University of Alberta Press, 1991, 118–131.

Schubel, V. *Religious Performance in Contemporary Islam: Shii Devotional Rituals in South Asia.* Columbia: University of South Carolina Press, 1993.

Schultze, Q. 'The Two Faces of Fundamentalist Higher Education.' *Fundamentalisms and Society.* M.E. Marty and S. Appleby (eds.). Chicago: University of Chicago Press, 1993, 490–535.

Schutz, A. 'Making Music Together: A Study in Social Relationships.' *Symbolic Anthropology: A Reader in the Study of Symbols and Meanings.* J.L. Dolgin, D.S. Kemnitzer and D.M. Schneider (eds.). New York: Columbia University Press, 1977, 106–119.

Scott, J.C. 'Protest and Profanation: Agrarian Revolt and the Little Tradition.' *Theory and Society* 4.1 (1977): 1–38 and 4.2 (1977): 211–246.

Scott, J.C. *Domination and the Arts of Resistance: Hidden Transcripts.* New Haven: Yale University Press, 1990.

Scott, J.C. *Weapons of the Weak.* New Haven: Yale University Press, 1985.

Seaman, W.R. 'Active Audience Theory: Pointless Populism.' *Media, Culture and Society* 14 (1992): 301–311.

Seigel, J. *The Rope of God.* Ann Arbor: University of Michigan Press, 2003.

Seizer, S. *Stigmas of the Tamil Stage: An Ethnography of Special Drama in South India.* Durham: Duke University Press, 2004.

Sen, A. *Development as Freedom.* Oxford University Press, 1999.

Shah, W.A. *The Conclusive Argument from God: Shah Wali Allah of Delhi's Hujjat Allah Al-Baligha.* Circa 1800. M.K. Hermansen Trans. Islamabad: Islamic Research Institute, 2003.

Shah, N.M. *Pakistani Women.* Islamabad: Pakistan Institute of Development Economics, 1986.

Shannon, J.H. 'Emotion, Performance and Temporality in Arab Music: Reflections on *Tarab*.' *Cultural Anthropology* 18.1 (2003): 72–98.

Sherzer, J. 'Strategies in Text and Context: Kuna kaa kwento.' *Language in Use: Readings in Sociolinguistic.* J. Baugh and J. Sherzer (ed.). Englewood Cliffs: Prentice-Hall, 1984b, 183–197.

Shurreef, J. *Qanoon-e-Islam or The Customs of the Mussalmans of India.* Reprinted 1973. G. A. Hercklots Trans. Lahore: Al-Irshad, 1832.

Siddiqi, K. 'Dars of Pakistan.' *Stringer Story: raccontie storie dall'Asia.* Retrieved from http://www.stringer.it/Stringer%20Schede/STORY/Stringer_story_karachi2.hm, 31 August 2004.

Silverstein, M. and G. Urban. 'The Natural History of Discourse.' *Natural Histories of Discourse.* M. Silverstein and G. Urban (eds.). Chicago: University of Chicago Press, 1996, 1–17.

Singer, M. 'The Great Tradition in a Metropolitan Center: Madras.' *Traditional India.* M. Singer (ed.). Philadelphia: American Folklore Society, 1958, 141–182.

Singh, B. 'Inhabiting Civil Disobedience.' Forthcoming *Political Theologies*. H. Vries and L. Sullivan (eds.). New York: Fordham University Press.

Singh, K. *Bloodstained Tombs: The Muharram Massacre of 1884*. London: Macmillan Publishers, 1983.

Sinha, M. *Colonial Masculinity: The 'Manly Englishman' and the 'Effeminate Bengali' in the Late Nineteenth Century*. Manchester: Manchester University Press, 1995.

Slobin, M. *Music in the Culture of Northern Afghanistan*. Tucson: University of Arizona Press, 1976.

Smith, B.H. *Poetic Closure: A Study of How Poems End*. Chicago: University of Chicago Press, 1968.

Smith, Daniel. 'Introduction: "A Life of Pure Immanence": Deleuze's "Critique et Clinique" Project.' *Essays Critical and Clinical* by Gilles Delueuze (1997).

Smith, W.C. *The Meaning and End of Religion*. New York: The Macmillan Company, 1962.

Snow, D.A., L.A. Zurcher and S. Ekland-Olson. 'Social Networks and Social Movements: A Microstructural Approach to Differential Recruitment.' *American Sociological Review*. 45 Oct. (1980): 787–801.

Sökefeld, M. 'Discourse and Action: Unequivocalness and Ambivalence in Identifications.' *Perspectives on History and Change in the Karakorum, Hindukush, and Himalaya*. I. Stellrecht, I.M. Winniger (eds.). Köln: Köppe, 1997b, 101–117.

Sökefeld, M. 'Balawaristan and Other Imagi*Nations*: A Nationalist Discourse in the Northern Areas of Pakistan.' *Ladakh: Culture, History, and Development between Himalaya and Karakoram*. M. van Beek, K.B. Bertelsen and P. Pedersen (eds.). Aarhus: Aarhus University Press, 1999b, 350–368.

Sökefeld, M. 'Debating Self, Identity and Culture in Anthropology.' *Current Anthropology*, 1999a.

Sökefeld, M. 'From Colonialism to Postcolonial Colonialism: Changing Modes of Domination in the Northern Areas of Pakistan.' *Journal of Asian Studies* 64.4 (2006): 939–974.

Sökefeld, M. 'Jang Azadi: Perspectives on a Major Theme in Northern Areas' History.' *The Past in the Present: Horizons of Remembering in the Pakistan Himalaya*. I. Stellrecht (ed.). Köln: Köppe, 1997c, 61–82.

Sökefeld, M. 'On the Concept, Ethnic Group.' *Karakorum-Hindukush-Himalaya: Dynamics of Change* I. Stellrecht (ed.). Köln: Köppe, 1998b.

Sökefeld, M. 'Sīn und Yeśkun in Gilgit: Die Abgrenzung zwischen zwei Identitätsgruppen und das Problem ethnographischen Schreibens.' *Petermanns Geographische Mitteilungen*, Bd. 138. Gotha, 1994, 357–369.

Sökefeld, M. *Ein Labyrinth von Identitäten in Nordpakistan: Zwischen Landbesitz, Religion und Kashmir-Konflikt in Nordpakistan'*. Köln: Köppe, 1997a.

Sökefeld, M. 'The People Who Really Belong to Gilgit: Perspectives on Identity and Conflict in Theory and Ethnography.' *Transformations of Social and*

Economic Relationships in Northern Pakistan. I. Stellrecht and H.G. Bohle (eds.). Köln: Köppe: 1998a, 94–224.

Sorley, H.T. *Shah Abdul Latif of Bhit: His Poetry, Life and Times.* Karachi, 1968.

Stacey, J. 'Global Ministries of Love and New Wave Evangelicalism.' *Brave New Families: Stories of Domestic Upheaval in Late Twentieth Century America.* New York: Basic Books, 1991, 113–146.

Stacey, J. and S.E. Gerard. '"We Are Not Doormats": The Influence of Feminism on Contemporary Evangelicals in the United States.' *Uncertain Terms: Negotiating Gender in American Culture.* F. Ginsburg and A.L. Tsing (eds.). Boston: Beacon Press, 1990, 98–117.

Staley, J. *Words for My Brother: Travels between the Hindu-Kush and the Himalayas.* Karachi: Oxford University Press, 1982.

Stetkevych, J. *Muhammad and the Golden Bough: Reconstructing Arabian Myth.* Bloomington and Indianapolis: Indiana University Press, 1996.

Stokes, M. '"Strong as a Turk": Power, Performance and Representation in Turkish Wrestling.' *Sport, Identity and Ethnicity.* J. MacClancy (ed.). Oxford: Berg, 1996, 21–42.

Stokes, M. 'Imagining the 'South': Hybridity, Heterotropias and Arabesk on the Turkish-Syrian Border.' *Border Identities: Nation and State at International Frontiers.* T.M. Wilson and H. Donnan (eds.). Cambridge: Cambridge University Press, 1998, 263–288.

Stokes, M. 'Introduction.' *Ethnicity, Identity and Music: The Musical Construction of Place.* M. Stokes, (ed.) Oxford: Berg, 1994, 1–27.

Stokes, M. 'Voices and Places: History, Repetition and the Musical Imagination.' *Journal of the Royal Anthropological Institute* 3.4 (1997): 673–691.

Stokes, M. *The Arabesk Debate: Music and Musicians in Modern Turkey.* Oxford: Oxford University Press, 1992.

Stoller, P. 'Embodying Colonial Memories.' *American Anthropologist* 96.3 (1994): 634–648.

Stowasser, B.F. *Women in the Quran, Traditions, and Interpretation.* New York: Oxford University Press, 1994.

Syed, G.M. *Religion and Reality.* Karachi, 1986.

Syed, G.M. *The Case of Sindh: G.M. Sayed's Disposition for the Court.* Karachi, 1995.

Tambiah, S.J. *Culture Thought and Social Action: An Anthropological Perspective.* Cambridge: Harvard University Press, 1985.

Tambiah, S.J. *Leveling Crowds: Ethnonationalist Conflicts and Collective Violence in South Asia.* Berkeley, Los Angeles and London: University of California Press, 1996.

Taussig, M.T. *Shamanism, Colonialism, and the Wild Man: A Study in Terror and Healing.* Chicago: University of Chicago Press, 1986.

Taussig, M.T. *The Devil and Commodity Fetishism in South America.* Chapel Hill: University of North Carolina Press, 1980.

Thaiss, G. 'Contested Meanings and the Politics of Authenticity: The 'Hosay' in Trinidad.' *Islam, Globalization and Postmodernity.* A.S. Ahmed and H. Donnan (eds.). New York: Routledge, 1994, 38–62.

Thaiss, G. 'Religious Symbolism and Social Change: The Drama of Husain.' Ph.D. Dissertation. Washington University, St. Louis, 1973.

Thaiss, G. 'Religious Symbolism and Social Change: The Drama of Husain.' *Scholars, Saints, and Sufis: Muslim Religious Institutions since 1500.* N.R. Keddie (ed.). Berkeley: University of California Press, 1978, 349–366.

Thaiss, G. *Unity and Discord: The Symbol of Husayn in Iran.* Iranian Civilization and Culture. C.J. Adams (ed.). Montreal: McGill University, Institute of Islamic Studies, 1972, 111–119.

The Holy Quran. Medina: King Fahd Holy Qur-an Printing Complex.

Tiano, S. *Patriarchy on the Line: Labor, Gender, and Ideology in the Mexican Maquila Industry.* Philadelphia: Temple University Press, 1994.

Titus, P. 'Honour the Baloch, Buy the Pashtun: Stereotypes, Social Organisation and History in West Pakistan.' *Modern Asian Studies* 32.3 (1998): 689–716.

Torab, A. 'Piety as Gendered Agency: A Study of Jaleseh Ritual Discourse in an Urban Neighbourhood in Iran.' *Journal of the Royal Anthropological Institute* 2 (1996): 735–753.

Torab, A. 'Piety as Gendered Agency: A Study of Women's Prayer Meetings in Iran.' Ph.D. Dissertation. University of London, 1996.

Trench, C.C. *The Frontier Scouts.* London: Cape, 1985

Turino, T. 'Signs of Imagination, Identity, and Experience: A Peircian Semiotic Theory for Music.' *Ethnomusicology* 43.2 (1999): 221–255.

Turner, V. 'Pilgrimages as Social Processes.' *Dramas, Fields, and Metaphors: Symbolic Action in Human Society.* Ithaca and Cornell: Cornell University Press, 1974.

Turner, V. *Dramas, Fields, and Metaphors: Symbolic Action in Human Society.* Ithaca: Cornell University Press, 1978.

Turner, V. *From Ritual to Theatre: The Human Seriousness of Play.* New York: Performing Arts Journal Publications, 1982.

US Department of State. 'Pakistan: Country Reports on Human Rights Practices—2001.' Released, 2002.

United Nations, Division for the Advancement of Women. 'Convention on the Elimination of All Forms of Discrimination against Women.' Entered into force, 1981.

Unvala, J. M. 'The Moharram Festival in Persia.' *Studie Materiale di Storia Delle Relegioni* 3 (1927): 82-96.

Upadhyay, R. 'Islamic Institutions in India: Protracted Movement for Separate Identity?' *South Asia Analysis Group.* Paper no. 599 (2003).

Veer, P. *Religious Nationalism: Hindus and Muslims in India.* Berkeley, 1994.

Verkaaik, O. 'Ethnicizing Islam: 'Sindhi Sufis', 'Muhajir Modernists' and 'Tribal Islamists' in Pakistan.' Paper presented at Columbia University. New York, 2003.

Verkaaik, O. 'The Captive State: Corruption, Intelligence Agencies, and Ethnicity in Pakistan.' *States of Imagination: Ethnographic Explorations of the Postcolonial State* T.B. Hansen and F. Stepputat (ed.). Durham: Duke University Press, 2001, 345–64.

Verkaaik, O. *Migrants and Militants: Fun and Urban Violence in Pakistan*. Princeton and Oxford: Princeton University Press, 2004.

von Grunebaum, G. and R. Caillois (eds.). *The Dream and Human Societies*. Berkeley: University of California Press, 1996.

Wadley, S.S. *Struggling with Destiny in Karimpur, 1925–1984*. Berkeley: University of California Press, 1994.

Warriach, A.I. 'An Ethnographic Study of the Shrine of Madhu Lal Husain Shah.' Unpublished Masters Thesis. Anthropology Department. Quaid-e-Azam University, Islamabad, 1997.

Weingrod, Alex. *The Saint of Beersheba*. Albany: State University of New York Press, 1990.

Weiss, A.M. (ed.). *Islamic Reassertion in Pakistan: the Application of Islamic Laws in a Modern State*. Syracuse University Press, 1986.

Weiss, A.M. 'Benazir Bhutto and the Future of Women in Pakistan.' *Asian Survey* 30.51 (1990): 433–444.

Weiss, A.M. 'Challenges for Muslim Women in a Postmodern World.' *Islam, Globalization and Postmodernity*. S. Akbar and D. Hastings (ed.). London and New York: Routledge, 1994.

Weiss, A.M. 'Women's Position in Pakistan: Sociocultural Effects of Islamization.' *Asian Survey* 25.8 (1985): 863–880.

Weiss, A.M. 'The Slow Yet Steady Path to Women's Empowerment in Pakistan.' *Islam, Gender and Social Change*. Y.Y. Haddad and J. Esposito (ed.). New York: Oxford University Press, 1996.

Weiss, A.M. *Walls within Walls: Life Histories of Working Women in the Old City of Lahore*. Karachi: Oxford University Press, 2002.

Werbner, P and H. Basu. *Embodying Charisma: Modernity, Locality and the Performance of Emotion in Sufi Cults*. London, 1998.

Werbner, P. 'The Making of Muslim Dissent: Hybridized Discourses, Lay Preachers, and Radical Rhetoric Among British Pakistanis.' *American Ethnologist*, 23.1 (1996): 102–22.

Werbner, P. *Imagined Diasporas amongst Manchester Muslims: The Public Performance of Pakistani Transnational Performance*. Oxford: James Currey, 2002.

Werbner, P. *The Migration Process: Capital, Gifts and Offerings among British Pakistanis*. Oxford: Berg, 1990.

Werbner, R. *Ritual Passage, Sacred Journey: The Process and Organization of Religious Movement*. Washington DC: Smithsonian Institution Press, 1989.

Westermarck, E.A. *Ritual and Belief in Morocco*. In Two Volumes. London: Macmillan and Co., Ltd., 1926.

Wickham, C.R. 'Interests, Ideas, and Islamist Outreach in Egypt.' *Islamic Activism: A Social Theory Movement Approach*. Q. Wicktorowicz (ed.). Bloomington: Indiana University Press, 2004, 231–49.

Wickham-Crowley, T.P. *Guerrillas and Revolution in Latin America*. Princeton: Princeton University Press, 1992.

Wiktorowicz, Q. 'Introduction: Islamic Activism and Social Movement Theory.' *Islamic Activism: A Social Theory Movement Approach*. Q. Wicktorowicz (ed.). Bloomington: Indiana University Press, 2004, 1–33.

Wiley, J.N. *The Islamic Movement of Iraqi Shi'as*. Boulder: Lynne Rienner, 1992.

Wolf, R.K. 'Embodiment and Ambivalence: Emotion in South Asian Muharram Drumming.' *Yearbook for Traditional Music* 32 (2000): 81–116.

Wolf, Richard. 'The Poetics of 'Sufi' Practice: Drumming, Dancing, and Complex Agency at Madho Lal Husain (and Beyond).' *American Ethnologist* 33.2 (2006): 246–268.

Woolard, K.A. and B.B. Schieffelin. 'Language Ideology.' *Annual Review of Anthropology* 23 (1994): 55–82.

World Bank. *World Development Report 2000/2001: Attacking Poverty*. New York: Oxford, 2001.

Yousefi, N. *Religion and Revolution in the Modern World: Ali Shariati's Islam and Persian Revolution*. Lanham: University Press of America, 1995.

Yurchak, Alexei. *Everything Was Forever until It Was No More: The Last Soviet Generation*. Princeton: Princeton University Press, 2006.

Zaman, M.Q. 'Sectarianism in Pakistan: The Radicalization of Shii and Sunni Identities.' *Modern Asian Studies* 32.3 (1998): 689–716.

Zaman, M.W. *The Ulama in Contemporary Islam: Custodians of Change*. Princeton: Princeton University Press, 2000.

Zavella, P. *Women's Work and Chicano Families: Cannery Workers of the Santa Clara Valley*. Ithaca: Cornell University Press, 1990.

Zia, S. and F. Bari. *Women's Participation in Political and Public Life in* Pakistan, 1999.

Zwemer, S.M. *Studies in Popular Islam: A Collection of Papers dealing with the Superstitions and Beliefs of the Common People*. London: The Sheldon Press, 1939.

Notes on Contributors

Anita M. Weiss, Professor of International Studies at the University of Oregon, received her PhD in Sociology from the University of California at Berkeley. Her current research concerns alternative visions on women's rights in Pakistan, part of a larger work-in-progress which addresses how Muslim states are grappling with articulating their views on women's rights. She has published four books and numerous articles on social development and gender issues in Pakistan, including *Walls within Walls: Life Histories of Working Women in the Old City of Lahore* (2nd edition, Oxford University Press, 2002) and with Zulfiqar Gilani (co-editor), *Power and Civil Society in Pakistan* (Oxford University Press, 2001). She is a member of the editorial boards of two journals, *Citizenship Studies* and *Globalizations*, is on the editorial advisory board of Kumarian Press, and now serves as the Treasurer of the American Institute of Pakistan Studies.

Dr Inayatullah Baloch obtained his BA from Peshawar University and MA in political science, from the University of Punjab, Lahore. He was granted postdoctoral fellowship by the Center of Middle East, University of California, Berkeley. He received his PhD in history from the University of Heidelberg, Germany. He teaches at the South Asia Institute, University of Heidelberg. His work *The Problem of Greater Balochistan: A Study of Baloch Nationalism*, has been published under the auspices of the University of Heidelberg. He has published several articles on history and politics of southwest Asia in international journals. His research interests are ethnic and religious conflicts, and political Islam.

Katherine P. Ewing is an Associate Professor at Duke University. She received her PhD in Anthropology from the University of Chicago. Her areas of specialisation include globalisation, identity, migration and psychological anthropology in South Asia and the Middle East, with field research in Pakistan, Turkey, and among Muslims in Europe. Her books include *Arguing Sainthood* (1997), which examines the Sufi mystical tradition as a focus of religious and political controversy in Pakistan, and *Stolen Honor: Stigmatizing Muslim Men in Berlin* (2008). Other publications include the edited volumes *Shariat and Ambiguity in South Asian Islam* (1988) and *Being and Belonging: Muslims in the US since 9/11* (2008), as well as numerous articles. Her current research is focused on South Asian Muslims in the United States and Turkish Muslims in Germany.

Magnus Marsden has been conducting ethnographic research in Chitral since 1995. His ethnographic work in Chitral has focused on the ways in which village and small town Muslims in the region have responded to the growing influence of reform-minded forms of Islam, including those associated with the Taliban. Marsden's book, *Living Islam: Muslim religious experience in Pakistan's North-West Frontier* (Cambridge, 2005), and a series of other publications, explore the ways in which Chitralis set to the task of 'being Muslim' in this world of political uncertainty and transformation. Since the publication of *Living Islam*, he has been expanding his interests, both ethnographically and conceptually and has been conducting research in the regions of Tajikistan and Afghanistan over the past two years.

Mariam Abou Zahab, a specialist on Pakistan, is a researcher affiliated with the Centre d'Etudes et de Recherches Internationales (CERI) and a lecturer at the Institut d'Etudes Politiques (IEP) and at the Institut National des Langues et Civilisations Orientales (INALCO), both in Paris. Her research interests focus on sectarianism and on jihadi movements, as well as on Pashtun society in Pakistan. Her publications include *Islamist Networks: The Afghan-Pakistan Connection* (with Olivier Roy), Hurst, London/Columbia University Press, New York, 2004, and a number of articles on Pakistan and Afghanistan.

Martin Sökefeld received his PhD from the University of Tübingen, Germany, after doing fieldwork on ethnicity and conflict in Gilgit. Subsequently he was an assistant professor at the University on Hamburg and did research on the Turkish Alevi diaspora in Germany and in transnational space. Since 2005, he has been an assistant professor at the Institute of Social Anthropology of the University of Berne, Switzerland, and works, among other things, on the political mobilization of Kashmiris in Britain. His main areas of interest are political anthropology, identity politics and the theory of identity, migration, diaspora and transnationalism. Selected publications: *Struggling for Recognition: The Alevi Movement in Germany and in Transnational Space* (Oxford, Berghahn Books, 2008); 'Mobilizing in Transnational Space: A Social Movement Approach to the Formation of Diaspora', *Global Networks* 6, 2006: 265-284; 'From Colonialism to Postcolonial Colonialism: Changing Modes of Domination in the Northern Areas of Pakistan', *Journal of Asian Studies* 64, 2005: 939-974; 'Alevism Online: Re-Imagining a Community in Virtual Space', *Diaspora* 11, 2002: 85-123; 'Rumours and Politics on the Northern Frontier: The British, Pakhtun Wali and Yaghestan', *Modern Asian Studies* 36, 2002: 299-340; 'Debating Self, Identity and Culture in Anthropology', *Current Anthropology* 40, 1999: 417-447.

Mary Elaine Hegland's fieldwork has focused on the Middle East and South Asia: Iran, Turkey, Pakistan, Tajikistan, and Afghanistan specifically. She has also worked among Iranian Americans in the Bay Area of California. Dr Hegland's publications deal with the Iranian Revolution of 1978–1979; women and gender in religion and politics in Iran; change and continuity in an Iranian village; and women and gender in Shia Muslim rituals in Pakistan. Currently, Dr Hegland is conducting research about aging and the elderly in Iran and among Iranian Americans in California's San Francisco Bay Area and about women and education, and about social and cultural change in the area of Shiraz, Iran. She also plans to study women and gender and family hierarchy and dynamics as related to aging and the elderly in Tajikistan.

Muhammad Qasim Zaman is a Niehaus Professor of Near Eastern Studies and Religion at Princeton University. He is the author of *The Ulama in Contemporary Islam: Custodians of Change*; *Religion and Politics under the Early Abbasids*; and *Ashraf Ali Thanawi: Islam in Modern South Asia*.

Naveeda Khan is an assistant professor at the Department of Anthropology at Johns Hopkins University. She received her Master's degree in anthropology from The New School for Social Research in 1995 and earned her doctorate in anthropology from Columbia University in 2003, writing her doctoral dissertation on how sectarian violence is folded into everyday life in urban Pakistan. She is the recipient of numerous research grants from foundations such as the Social Science Research Council, National Science Foundation and Wenner-Gren Foundation for Anthropological Research, American Institute for Peace Studies, and the American Philosophical Association. Her articles have been published by journals such as *Cultural Anthropology* and *Social Text*. She has recently completed an edited book titled *Crisis and Beyond: Pakistan in the 20th Century* to be published by Routledge India and is in the process of completing a manuscript titled 'The Passage of a Promise: Muslim Perfectionism and Sectarianism in Pakistan.'

Oskar Verkaaik is a journalist and anthropologist who has conducted extensive research in Pakistan over the past twenty years. He was awarded a PhD with distinction at the University of Amsterdam. He is currently Assistant Professor at the Research Centre for Religion and Society at the University of Amsterdam. Verkaaik has researched ethnicity, nationalism, migration and religion in Pakistan, concentrating on aspects of violence, gender, and age and has published two books in English on these issues: *A People of Migrants: Ethnicity, State and Religion in Karachi* and *Migrants and Militants: 'Fun' and Urban Violence in Pakistan*. He has also published various books in Dutch on Pakistan. He has been research fellow of the Globalization Project of Professor Arjun Appadurai at the University of Chicago and the coordinator of the International Institute for Asian Studies in Amsterdam.

Pnina Werbner is an urban anthropologist who has studied Muslim South Asians in Britain and Pakistan, and more recently, the women's movement and the Manual Workers Union in Botswana as part of the ESRC programme on Non-Governmental Public Action. She is a professor of social anthropology at Keele University. Her two most recent books, *Imagined Diasporas among Manchester Muslims*, and *Pilgrims of Love: the Anthropology of a Global Sufi Cult*, are the second and third in the Manchester Migration Trilogy, a series of three single-authored books tracing the processes of Pakistani migration, community formation, religious transnationalism and diaspora over a period of fifty years. The series as a whole interrogates the translocation of culture—its dislocation, transplantation and translation in the course of migration. Collectively the three books form the most comprehensive body of ethnography about any immigrant community in Britain.

Richard K. Wolf, Professor of Music at Harvard University, is an ethnomusicologist who has devoted his career to the interdisciplinary study of South Asian musical traditions. Wolf has written broadly about classical, folk and tribal musical traditions in South India as well as on musical traditions associated with Shiism and Sufism in North India and Pakistan. Wolf's recent publications include 'Doubleness, *matam* and Muharram drumming in South Asia' (2007) and the book *The Black Cow's Footprint: Time, Space, and Music in the Lives of the Kotas of South India* (2005 and 2006), which was awarded the Edward Cameron Dimock, Jr. Prize in Humanities. He has been the recipient of numerous grants and fellowships, recently including those from the Radcliffe Institute for Advanced Study, the American Council of Learned Societies, the Social Science Research Council, the National Endowment for the Humanities, and the American Institute of Pakistan Studies. In an effort to promote a study of South Asian music that transcends conventional boundaries of geography and discipline, Wolf is editing a book entitled *Theorizing the Local: Music, Practice and Experience in South Asia and Beyond* (under contract with Oxford University Press, New York), which stems from an International Council for Traditional Music colloquium and Radcliffe Advanced Seminar. He is also completing his own monograph entitled *Reciting Remembrance: Resonances of Popular Islam in South Asia* (under contract with the University of Illinois Press).

Roger Ballard has a long-standing interest in the religious traditions of South Asia, and the role that they have played in the reconstruction of diasporic communities. His interest in religion was sparked off during the course of his doctoral research, when he conducted an ethnographic study of a Hindu village in Himachal Pradesh. It developed still further during the course of his subsequent explorations of the internal dynamics of Hindu, Sikh, and Muslim transnational networks which have emanated from both East and

West Punjab during the course of the past half century. Editor of *Desh Pradesh: the South Asian Presence in Britain* (London: Hurst and Co. 1994), he has also published numerous articles exploring the cultural, familial, political, and economic dimensions of the global Punjabi diaspora.

Sadaf Ahmad is currently an assistant professor at the School of Humanities and Social Sciences at The Lahore University of Management Sciences. She completed her PhD in Cultural Anthropology from Syracuse University in 2006. She received her MA in Gender, Anthropology and Development from Goldsmiths College, University of London, in 2001, and has a Master's degree in Psychology from Quaid-e-Azam University, Islamabad, Pakistan. A native of Pakistan, Sadaf has always been interested in working on gender issues, and has done so both practically—for instance, by working at a crisis centre, offering women self defence classes, and doing street theatre on gender issues for a number of years—and academically, as exemplified through research and writing. Her doctoral research, for example, sheds light on how its techniques of expansion and pedagogies of persuasion have allowed Al-Huda, an Islamic school for women established in Islamabad in the early 1990s, to turn into a social movement. Her work also illustrates the manner in which Al-Huda aims to create subjects with a 'unitary' consciousness by propagating a particular kind of hegemonic religious discourse amongst them, and highlights the multiple reasons urban Pakistani women have for engaging with and internalising such a discourse. Apart from studying social movements and themes surrounding gender and religion, her research interests also include food and culture, body politics, identity issues, and gender based violence.

Seyyed Vali Reza Nasr is an Iranian–American academic and scholar, as well as professor of International Politics at the Fletcher School of Law and Diplomacy of Tufts University. He is an expert in contemporary Middle Eastern affairs and Islam and politics. In January 2006, Nasr was named the Adjunct Senior Fellow for Middle Eastern Studies at the Council on Foreign Relations, a non-partisan think-tank focusing on foreign policy. He is also a Senior Fellow with The Dubai Initiative, Belfer Center for Science and International Affairs at the Kennedy School of Government at Harvard University. He was named the Carnegie Scholar in 2006. He has authored *The Shia Revival*; *The Islamic Leviathan*; *Democracy in Iran*; *The Vanguard of the Islamic Revolution: The Jama'at-i Islami of Pakistan*; *Mawdudi and the Making of Islamic Revivalism*; *Forces of Fortune*, and others.

Shemeem Burney Abbas is the author of *The Female Voice in Sufi Ritual: Devotional Practices of Pakistan and India*, published by the University of Texas Press in 2002 and Oxford University Press in 2003. Her research is on women's rituals in Islamic societies. 'Sakineh; the narrator of Kerbala,' is her chapter in *The Women of Kerbala*, published by the University of Texas Press, 2005. Abbas's latest publication is an article, 'Risky Knowledge in Risky Times: Political Discourses of Qawwali and Sufiana-kalam in Pakistan-Indian Sufism,' in *The Muslim World*, Blackwell 2007. In 1993, UNICEF published Abbas' *Qissa Khwan*, (Storyteller) a collection of short stories for girls. Her other publications focus on teaching the English language in South Asia. She is currently working on a novel set in Kashmir; she is additionally working on a book about postcolonial laws in Afghanistan and Pakistan in the post cold-war period. Abbas launched the largest graduate teacher-training programme in English as a Foreign Language for South Asia, through the Allama Iqbal Open University in Islamabad.

Index

A

Abaya (gown), 302
Abbas, Hazrat-e, 144, 152, 285
Abbas, Sardarzadah Zafar, 350
Abbasids, 166
Abdullah, Sufi, 186, 197
Abu Bakr (RA), 340, 345
Abu Hanifa, Imam, 263
Adab (belles-lettres), 86
Adam (Prophet), 7, 10, 179, 182, 245
Adeeb (Farooq sahib's son), 4, 8, 11, 13, 15, 22
Afghan war (1980s), 330, 335, 337–8, 343
Afghanistan, 134, 136, 164, 172, 259, 261, 274, 277, 328, 339, 343, 347, 357, 359
Afghans (known as Kabulis), 266–7; political group, 134; Pukhtun refugees, 134, 211
Aga Khan, The, 278
Ahl-i Hadith (Lahore, journal), 344
Ahl-i Hadith, 13–4, 85, 95, 165, 343, 345–6, 351; school, 301, 329
Ahl-i-Bait, 171, 344
Ahmad, Israr, 334, 343–4
Ahmad, Mumtaz, 336
Ahmad, Qazi Hussain, 343, 353, 357
Ahmad, Sadaf, 299
Ahmad, Shaikh Sultan, 356
Ahmad, Sharif, 182, 198
Ahmadi Vatican, 167 *see also* Rabwah
Ahmadiya/Qadian (sect), 166–8, 170, 266, 275, 315, 355–6, 359; declared as non-Muslim minority in 1974, 168, 356; movement, 315
Ahmed, Akbar S., 278
Akbar (librarian), 13
Akram, Sheikh, 174
Aladdin and the magic lamp, 23
Al-Aitisam (Lahore), 344
Alam (standard), 285 *see also* Abbas, Hazrat-e

Alawis (sect), 262
Al-Azhar University, 96, 101
Al-Badr (Sahiwal), 344
Al-Balagh (Karachi), 346
Al-Bayyanat (Karachi), 346
Algeria, 113
Al-Hanif (Jacobabad), 269; wrote about 'The Zigris' in 1938, 269
Al-Haq (Akora Khattak), 346
Al-Huda (estb. 1994), 299, 302–4, 306–9, 310–9, 320–1, 323–4; as a social movement, 304, 318; audio visual aids, 315; diploma course of, 302–3, 319; graduates, 304, 319, 325; ideology of, 302, 304; mass media, 303; 'modern' ways of teaching, 314; *modus operandi*, 300, 318, 321; use of power-point presentations, 315;
Al-Hussaini, Arif, 149, 168, 341; viewed as potential 'Pakistani Khomeini', 341; was assassinated in 1988, 149
Ali (Farooq sahib's son), 15
Ali (RA), 9, 10, 149, 241, 342, 344–5, 384–5, 393
Ali da pehla number, 384–5, 393, 395
Ali, Mohammad (a student), 254
Ali, Mukhtar Ahmad, 10
Ali, Niamat, 370, 382–3
Ali, Shahid, 370, 382–3
Ali, Shaikh Hakim, 350
Ali, Zulfiqar, 373
Aligarh, 113, 117
Alim, 15, 182, 345; Deobandi, 360
Al-Qaeda, 1
Al-Sattar, Mawlana 'Abd, 98–9
Al-Shirbini, Shaykh 'Abd al-Rahman, 96–7; as rector of Al-Azhar university, 96
Alyaniwar (musical pieces), 222
American(s), 37, 42, 49, 132, 138, 155, 235; government, 45
Amil, 4, 15, 17–8, 22
Amliyat, 15

Anarkali, 3
Andalusian, 392
Andhra Pradesh, 393
Anglicists, 80–2
Anglo-vernacular school, 121
Anglo-Vernacular, 82
Anjuman Sipah-e-Sahaba (later Sipah-e-Sahaba Pakistan, SSP), 164, 169, 170–4, 337, 341, 346
Anjuman-e Tajiran (Association of Traders), 171, 351
Anjuman-e-Itehad-e-Balochistan (Itehad [Unity] Party), 268–9, 270, 274; split into three groups, 270
Anjuman-i Ahrar-i Islam (Society of Free Muslims), 349, 355–7; are Anti-Ahmadiya, 349, 355–6; is a Deobandi organization, 355
Anka, Muhammad Hussain, 271
Ansari, Bayazid, 261
Anthropology, 235, 256
Anti-Ahmadiya: movement, 167, 275, 355–7; riots (1953–4), 349
Anti-British rhetoric, 359
Anti-colonial politics, 120
Anti-imperialism, 355
Anti-Iranian, 347
Anti-Khomeini critiques, 344–5
Anti-Madani group coalition, 358
Anti-madrassah proclamations (1994–95), 343
Anti-Shia crusade, 328, 340, 342–3, 345; in 1950, 167; in 1983, 340
Anti-Shia *fatwas*, 171, 346; rhetoric, 10, 169, 170–1, 341, 344–6, 349
Anti-Shia movement, 346–8, 351, 357–8
Anti-Shiaism, 344–7, 358
Anti-Zikri, 272, 277–8
Appadurai, Arjun, 224
Aqaba pillar, 180
Aqida, 4, 21
Aql, 8
Arab world, 90, 342, 360
Arabian Nights, 23
Arabian Peninsula, 359
Arabian Sea, 330
Arabic language, 81–2, 88–9, 116, 217, 259, 287–9, 290, 294, 302, 307, 312, 318, 344–5, 390–1; as one of 'classical languages of India', 89; grammar, 302, 317; literature, 89, 121
Arafat, 179, 180–3
Arain *biradari*, 172
Aristotelian logic/philosophy, 79, 89, 255
Asad, Talal, 77, 311, 313
Asghar, Ali (RA), 288–9
Ashura (tenth) procession, 10, 151, 169, 240, 285
Asia, 77
Asian steppe, 210
Attock, 261
Aurangzeb, Prince (later Mughal Emperor), 265; did not denounce Zikri faith, 265
Australia, 316
Authoritarianism, 115
Awliya, 189, 192
Ayesha (doctor), 310
Azad Kashmir, 192, 246, 252
Azad, Abu'l Kalam, 342
Azadari, 164, 169
Azadars (mourners), 286; women, 287
Azakhaneh, 286
Azam Warsak (Waziristan), 167
Azan (the call to prayer), 3, 384
Aziz, Nik Abdu'l-, 360

B

Bab-i Umar (Umar's Gate), 341 *see also* Khewa gate
Babur (Mughal Emperor), 280
Babur, Naseerullah, 343
Baghdad, 137
Baji Sabira ka imambareh, 286, 289
Baksh, Data Ganj, 192
Balawaristan National Front (BNF), 246–7
Baloch nationalism, 264, 268–9; first stage 1929–48 of, 269
Baloch Students Organization (BSO), 278–9
Baloch Tribal Areas, 271; tribes, 264, 267, 273–4; tribal custom (*riwaj*), 267
Baloch, 269, 270, 272–3, 277, 279; are secular, 273; chiefs (*sardars*), 269, 271; culture, 269, 279; customary law (*nek-wa-bad*), 279; kings, 116; migration to Kalat, 274; nation, 269, 279; national identity, 269, 276; nationalist movement, 268, 271–2, 274, 277; nationalist

political parties, 279; nationalist Press, 269; resistance/revolt, 264, 273; society, 269, 272, 279; traditions, 265; unity, 273; women, 269
Baloch, Inayatullah, 259
Baloch, Maulana Abdullah, 270
Balochi language, 259, 264; literature, 264
Balochistan (newspaper), 271
Balochistan, 259, 260, 263–4, 266–9, 276–9, 335, 342, 358
Balochistan, Khanate of, 260, 266, 271–2 *see also* Kalat, Khan of
Baltistan, 164, 245
Banerjee, Mukulika, 207
Bangladesh, 114–5, 127
Banuri, Mawlana Muhammad Yusuf (d.1978), 97–8; founder of Jami'at al-'Ulum al-Islamiyya, 97
Barailvi Islam, 301, 323 *see also* Barelvis
Baraka, 178 *see also* miraculous powers
Baranzai, Mir Dost Muhammad Khan, 274
Barelvi(s), 12–4, 17–8, 85, 95, 98, 167, 170–1, 351, 355–8; madrassah, 98, 329, 333; Pirs, 174
Barelwism, 12
Barkas, 393
Barmas, 238
Basant, 302
Basher, Hajji, 190
Basra, Riaz, 173, 338
Batiniya influence, 166
Bell, Catherine, 151
Benares, 178
Benefit (*naf, fa'ida, mufid*), 81
Bengal, 82–3, 123
Bengalis, 115
Berkey, Jonathan, 100
Bhabha, Homi, 253
Bhagavad Gita, 120
Bhangra, 382, 384, 386, 393–5
Bhawana, Ghulam Haider, 168
Bhoots, 15
Bhutto government (1974), 276
Bhutto, Benazir, 9, 128, 343, 350
Bhutto, Zulfiqar Ali, 115, 127–8, 130, 168, 330, 355, 392
Bible, The, 120, 180
Biddat, 323
Bihar, 43
Binori madrassah (Karachi), 353

Biradaris, 165, 168, 174
Birmingham, 186
Bizenjos, 267
Blasphemy Law, 10, 345
Bogra, M.A., 355
Bohras, 121, 275, 327
Boledis, 263, 267
Bolshevik Revolution, 268
Bombay, 117–8, 120–1, 123
Bonfires (*mac*), 371, 381
Bourdieu, 238
Brah, 251
Brahmins, 178
Brenneis (1987), 151
Britain, 185–8, 196–7, 199, 312, 386
British Bengal, 95
British colonial government, 79, 90, 95, 117–8, 192, 271–2; official report of, 263, 272
British India, 84, 89, 90–1, 93, 95–6, 117, 207, 209, 268, 272, 274
British Pakistanis, 186
British: 37, 76–8, 80–3, 86, 89, 94–5, 116, 118, 123, 165, 170, 182, 199, 207–9, 263, 266, 269, 271, 273, 301, 359; administrators, 82–3, 88–9, 210; cities, 186; colonial period, 100, 102, 112, 206–7; policy, 79; Raj/rule, 116, 166, 170, 267; scholar-soldiers, 208–9
Brotherhoods (*tariqa*), 114
Bryant, Rebecca, 213
Buddha, 119
Buddhism, 122
Bureaucratic model, 36–7, 39, 48, 101; of British, 85; post-colonial, 102
Bureaucratic officials, 91, 355; of Pakistani, 247
Burton, Sir Richard, 117
Burushaski language, 239
Butt, Haider, 173

C

Cairo, 100, 203
Calcutta Madrassah (1781), 81, 90, 95, 98; divided into two departments, 82; the Anglo-Persian (Junior Department), 82, 90; the Arabic (Senior Department), 82, 90
Calcutta, 81, 90

Canada, 303
Canal Colonies, 172
Caroe, Olaf, 207
Census of 1998, 165
Census Reports, 260, 272
Central Asia, 342, 359
Central Asian, 84
Chalisvan ceremony, 302 *see also chelum*
Chamberlain, Michael, 100
Chatais, 286
Chela, 169
Chelum, 285–6
Chilas, 249
Chilasi family, 249, 250
Chilla, 15
Chiniot, 165, 167, 348
Chinioti Sheikhs, 168
Chinioti, Maulana Manzoor Ahmed, 167
Chitral police, 219
Chitral Scouts, 221–2, 224; *subadars*, 221, 224
Chitral, 201, 203, 205, 209, 212, 217–8, 220–1, 224, 228; full constitutional incorporation in Pakistani state, 209; incorporated in 1895 in British India, 207
Chitrali *ghazal*, 211, 213, 222, 224
Chitrali language, 201
Chitrali masculinity/manhood, 205, 209, 210–1, 214–6, 220–1, 224, 227–8
Chitrali men, 202–6, 211, 213, 215, 219, 220–4, 226–8; likers of boys (*daq xoseiák*), 226; play with children (*bacabáz*), 227
Chitrali musicians, 213–5; sitar, 213, 217
Chitrali Muslims, 201, 204–5, 212, 217, 219, 225–6, 228
Chitrali polo, 202, 214–5; teams, 223
Chitrali women, 206, 222, 224, 226
Chitrali(s), 208–9, 210–2, 214, 217, 220, 224–7, 229; as 'lovers of peace' (*aman pasand*), 210; as polite (*sarif*), 212, 221–2; as soft (*narum*), 212; court life of, 210; culture of, 211; elders (*lilótan*), 221, 223–4, 227–8; form of Communality, 219; government civil servants, 220; man of respect (*izzatman mos*), 220; social aesthetics, 206, 219, 229; society, 209; state, 216; tradition, 227; villagers, 221; villages (*deh*), 216,

224; youth (*juwanán*), 221, 223–5, 227
Chowk Marir Hasan, 286
Christ, 119
Christianity, 122
Christians, 280; of Pakistan, 360, 379
Chundigar, I.I., 355
Churail/witch, 17, 19
College of Home Economics, 134
Colonial: knowledge, 208; policies, 81, 88, 92
Colonialism, 252
Colours of Islam (institute), 319, 321
Communalism, 269, 278–9, 280
Communism, 330
Communist Party, 125
Congress Party, 120–1, 123, 351–2, 355
Conical clan (*dom*), 221
Constituent Assembly, 275
Contextualization, 375, 380, 383
Corruption, 37, 41, 43, 49, 190–2, 285
Cult, 196 *see also* Zindapir
Cunningham, 80
Curriculum: mixed/hybrid (*makhlut*) 95, 97

D

Da'wa (religious outreach), 299, 303–4
Dādā murshid, 47–8
Damascus, 100, 137
Dancers (*phonák*), 220
Dar al-'Ulum madrassah (founded by Nadwa Ulama), 86, 89
Darel, 240
Dari language, 211
Dars, 15, 302, 304, 307, 309, 323
Dars-i Nizami, 81, 84–6, 89, 92, 98, 333
Daru'l-'ulums (of Pakistan), 328, 346
Dar-ul Awam, 273 *see also* Kalat state parliament
Dar-ul Umara, 273 *see also* Kalat state parliament
Darwinian evolution theory, 119
Darzadas (Baloch group belonging to the Zikri sect), 260, 267
Das, Veena, 2
Daura-e-Qur'an, 308
Deccan folksong, 376
Decolonialization, 112, 124
Delhi, 12, 14, 17, 84

Democracy, Anglo-Saxon system of, 127
Democratization, 113
Deoband madrassah (estb. 1867), 85–6, 89, 96, 114, 170, 274, 301, 346, 352–4
Deobandi Korangi Daru'l-'Ulum (Karachi), 335, 358
Deobandi madrassah (of Pakistan), 94, 97–8, 169, 171, 329, 339, 347, 352–3, 358–9; organizations, 345
Deobandi Sawad-i A'zam-i Ahl-i Sunnat, 346
Deobandi Taliban, 338, 347, 357
Deobandi ulama, 85, 351–3, 355–6, 358
Deobandi(s), 4, 12–5, 18, 21, 85, 94–5, 97, 165, 167, 339, 345–6, 351–2, 355–6, 358; activism, 359; are strongest opponents of Ahmadiyas, 356; education, 360; journals, 346; movement, 301; politics, 356–7; resurgence of, 359; traditions, 360
Deobandism, 12
Derrida, Jacques, 236
Descartes, 236
Dhaka, 90
Dhamal (music-dance form), 368, 370, 372, 375, 379, 380–1, 383–6, 392–5
Dhamalis dance, 381, 388; achieve *hal*, 381, 387
Dhiramiting *qom*, 239
Dhol (barrel drums), 370, 373–4, 380, 383; players, 384–5, 388
Dictionary of Urdu, Classical Hindi, and English, A, 381
Différance, Concept of (Derrida), 236–7, 252, 254
Difference, dimension of, 238, 252–6; clan, 238; locality, 238; language, 238
Din Main Ghulluw (Extremism within Religion), 344
Din panah (faith refuge), 380, 385
Din, Syed Jamal-ud-, 273
Divide-and-rule strategy, 247
Divorce, rights of, 324
Doctrinal disputes, 327, 344
Drug mafia, 173
Drumming patterns, 371–2, 381–2, 385, 389, 395; *bhangra*, 382, 384; *dhamal*, 382, 384; *lahra*, 382; *tintara* (*tintal*), 382

Drums rhythm, 216, 218, 222, 375; *damáma*, 218; *dáni*, 222; *dol*, 218; *ponwar*, 216
Du'as, 181, 198
Dua, 295
Dur-e-Sadaf, 263
Duris, 286
Durrani, Ahmad Shah, 266

E

Eade, 178, 194
East Africa, 265
East India Company, 80
East Pakistan (now Bangladesh), 90, 114
East Punjab, 166–7, 172
Eastern Balochistan, 273
Education (system), 77–8, 80, 88–9, 91, 93–4, 112–3, 117, 129; of British India, 88; of British/English, 80–1, 85, 94, 98, 100, 117–8; of Hindu-Sanskrit, 77, 80; of Madrassah, 81; of Muslim/Islamic, 77, 80, 88; of Pakistan, 37
Education Report of 1858–59, 81
Egypt, 96, 101, 113, 166
Egyptian government, 97
Eickelman, Dale, 101
Eid, 182, 184, 186, 241
Elections 1970, 127
Elections 1985, 333
Elections 1988, 172, 347, 350
Elections 1993, 350
Elections 1997, 350
Elegies (*marsiya*), 214
Eliade, 198
Elias, Norbert, 209
Elizabeth, Queen, 359
Endowment (*waqf*), 78
England, 41, 193, 196 *see also* Britain
English language, 80, 89, 117, 121–3, 312, 319, 320–1, 344–5, 386
English Press, 18
English school, 100, 319, 320
English Utilitarian, 79
Enlightenment (age of), 77
Entextualization, 375, 380, 383
Epistemic diversity, 255
Eroticism, 376, 391
Essentialism, 255

Ethnicity, 111–2, 129, 130, 235, 237, 251, 255, 264, 305
Ethnography, 6, 283, 286, 295, 369
Europe, 77–8
European colonialism, 112, 115
European(s), 35, 120, 124; arts, 80; Post-Enlightenment, 78; sciences, 80
Eve (Prophetess), 10, 245
Exorcism, 20

F

Fabian, 256
Faisalabad, 329, 343, 348, 351, 359, 360
Faiz Qalandar's shrine, 39
Falsehood (*jhut*), 385
Falwell, Jerry, 307
Fana-e-rasul, 12
Faqir (Sufi mendicant), 186, 192, 377, 380, 385
Farah (place), 261
Farah, 8, 16
Farangi Mahal (Lucknow), 84
Farhan, 222
Farheen, 320–1
Farooq (Urdu teacher), 3–7, 9, 10–2, 14–9, 20–3; as calligrapher, 11–2
Farooq, 219
Farrukhabad, 210
Faruqi, Ziau'l Rahman, 347
Fatimid movement, 166
Fatimids (in Egypt), 166
Fatwas, 122, 170, 216, 271–2, 323, 346, 358
Fauji, Saleem, 173
Feld, Steven, 372
Felman, 19
Feminism, 237
Fenichel, 47
Festival of lamps (*mela chiraghan*), 370
Feudal(s), 35, 165–7, 169, 170
Feudalism, 116
Final revelation (*wahi*), 262
Finance, Minister of, 191
Fiqh-e Hanafiya, 15 *see also* Islamic law
Fire pit (*chiraghdan*), 370, 376–7, 381; break (*tora*), 383; tripartite cadences (*tiyas*), 383
First World War (1914–18), 273, 280

Flagellants, 139, 141, 145, 152 *see also matam*
Fornication (*zina*), 202
Foucault, 310–1
Foundation (*bunyad*), 384
Freedom Calling, 123
Freedom movement, 164
Frontier Gandhi, 120 *see also* Khan, Khan Abdul Ghaffar
Fulbright, 132
Fundamentalism, 133
Fundamentalist movement (USA), 307

G

Gaddu, Anwar alias, 173
Gandhi, Mahatma, 112, 119, 120
Gandhian, 111, 116
Gasht, 15
Gazetteer (of 1968), 118
Gazetteers, 272
Gellner, Ernest, 316
German idealism, 119
Ghamidi, Javid Ahmadu'l, 342
Ghamkol Sharif, 183–4, 186, 188, 190, 192, 197–9
Ghazal, 376 *see also* Chitrali *ghazal*
Ghaznavi, Mahmud, 167
Gibbon, 84
Gichki clan, 264, 267
Gichki, Malik Dinar, 264
Gilani family, 167
Gilani, Abdul Qadir, 187
Gilani, Ghulam, 340
Gilani, Pir Syed Agha Kazem Shah, 167
Gilgit Scouts, 245
Gilgit, 164, 237–9, 240–9, 251, 253–6
Gilgit-Baltistan, 237
Gilgitwala, 238, 254
Girlfriends (*dostán*), 211, 214
Glance at the Zikri Sect, A (*Zikri Firqa Par Ek Nazar*), 276
Glasgow, 302, 315
Globalization, 112
Goffman, Erving, 287
Goldsmid, General, 273
Gor, 240
Government College (Lahore), 80
Government of Pakistan, 77, 91, 99, 165, 247, 252, 260, 279, 347; special notices

of madrassahs reforms in 1960s and 1970s, 91
Government of Sindh, 272
Government school system, 98–9, 101, 113
Governor (*naib*), 266
Gramsci, 129, 369
Greater Sindh, 121
Gujal, 238
Gujarat, 117
Gujranwala, 348
Gulf states, 197, 214, 259, 279, 301
Gulf war, 132, 148
Guru, 44
Gyarvin sharif, 187

H

Haban (a pseudonym), 250
Hadith, 5, 8–9, 20, 22, 45, 79, 84–5, 87, 89, 92, 100, 113, 260, 272, 284, 288, 302; *Sirah*, 13
Hafas, Umar bin, 166
Hagiographic literature, 10, 379
Hajj, 179, 180–2, 186, 197–8, 218, 263
Hajjis, 265
Hajra (RA), 180–1, 199
Haleema, 319, 321
Hall, 317
Hamid, Caliph Sultan Abdul, 273
Hamid, Sahabzada Sultan, 174
Haq, Maulana Abdul, 277
Haq, Ziaul, 9, 93, 164, 168–9, 225, 252, 275–9, 332–3, 339, 340–1; his eleven year rule (1977–88), 93, 171, 339, 357, 360
Haraam (forbidden), 322
Harakatu'l-Ansar (Movement of the Helpers [of the Prophet]), 328, 338, 353, 357, 359
Harding, Susan, 307
Hari Committee, 120, 125
Harijan (untouchables), 120
Harley Committee of 1915, 95
Hart, Stephen, 324
Hasan, Abdu'l Ghaffar, 343
Hasan, Imam (RA), 116
Hashmi, Dr Farhat, 299, 302–3, 308, 311, 314–7, 323–5; early education, 302;

founded Al-Huda, 302; received doctorate from Glasgow, 302, 315
Hasnain Construction Company, 171
Hastings, Warren, 81
Hayat, Asad, 173–4
Hayat, Faisal Saleh, 173–4, 349; is also a *makhdum*, 349
Hazarwi, Maulana Ghulam Ghaus, 353
Herat, 261
Heroin trade, 337
Herzfeld, Michael, 367, 380
Hidden (*batin*), 380
High class (*ashraf*) family, 118
Hikmatyar, Gulbadin, 338
Himalaya, 255
Hind (India), 121
Hindu Kush, 207
Hinduism, 45, 122
Hindu-Muslim riots, 272
Hindus, 44, 117–8, 123, 165, 166, 170, 192, 261, 267, 273, 379, 391; moneylenders, 117, 120, 124; primary schools, 116; religion, 204; teachers, 118; traders, 117, 123
Hindustani classical terms, 383
Hira Mandi (lit. diamond market), 391
Hir-Ranjha (an epic), 166
Hirschkind, Charles, 203
Hisar, 167
Hizb-i Islami (Islamic Party), 338
Hoat, Hamal Jihand, 264
Holi (Hindu holiday), 379
Home (*dur*), 206
Honour code of (*Balochmayar*), 269, 279
Hormuz, 265
Horvatich, Patricia, 315
Hosts (*mezeban*), 213
Huichal Indians, 177
Hujweri, 192
Humayun (Mughal Emperor), 280
Hunza, 238–9, 249, 250
Hunzawale, 238
Husain, Colonel Sayyid/Syed Abid, 167–8, 349
Husain, Madho Lal, 367, 372, 375, 378–9, 381–2, 386, 390, 391; his epigrammatic poems, 377; urs of, 369, 370, 372–3, 376–7, 379, 389, 391
Husain, Sayyidah Abida/Abidah (Colonel Husain's daughter), 173, 350

Hussain, Maulana Ghulam, 167
Hussein (RA), Imam, 10, 116, 132–3, 135–7, 139, 140–1, 144, 146–7, 149, 150–3, 240, 284–5, 287–8, 290, 293–4, 342, 344, 385
Hussein, Saddam, 133, 148
Husseiniyyah Hall, 138–9, 140–1, 143, 145, 154
Husseiniyyah, 137 see also *Imambarehs; Imambargah*
Hyder Manzil, 123, 125
Hyderabad (India), 393–4
Hyderabad (Pakistan), 118, 120, 125
Hyderabad University, 129
Hymes model, 283, 287, 295

I

Ibadat, 4, 21
Iblis/devil, 7
Ibn' Arabi (CE 1165–1240), 392
Ibrahim (Abraham), 180–2, 199
Ibrahim, Qadi, 263
Identity, conceptualization of, 235–7, 242–3, 252–6
Ihtekaf, 15
ijtimah (annual gatherings), 278
ilm', 45, 385
Imam, 22, 315
Imam, Sughra, 173–4
Imambarehs, 285–7, 290, 340; social interactional model of, 287, 289
Imambargah, 136–7
Imamia Students Organization (ISO), 169, 341
Imatio Muhammadi, 12, 14
Immoral (*sum*), 206
Immoral loafers (*bayólas*), 226
Imperialism, 112
Impermissible (*najáiz*), 202, 228
India, 9, 12, 14, 17, 77–8, 80–1, 83–7, 90, 95–6, 118, 137, 148, 166, 183, 187, 192, 205, 208, 261, 272, 280, 345, 353, 359, 360
India, Viceroy of, 192
Indian government, 354
Indian Hindus, 20; family, 47
Indian madrassahs, 88 see also Madrassahs
Indian Moulvies, 82

Indian Muslims, 44, 77, 82–3, 85–6, 88, 117, 119, 121, 123; landlords, 120–1; trading communities, 121
Indian Punjab, 167
Indian Subcontinent, 82, 84–5, 96, 209, 301, 377, 394–5
Indian(s), 1, 46, 78, 84, 345; effeminate, 207–8; politics, 352, 354; society, 77, 207; visa, 17
Indonesia, 360
Indus (river), 120–1, 125
Indus Valley Civilization, 121
Indus valley, 240
Inferior (*vesiru*), 210, 223
Infidels (*kafirs*), 276, 346, 358
Ingold, Tim, 256
Innovations (*bidat*), 4, 128
Insaan-e-kamil, 189
Intelligible ('*am fahm*), 83
Interest (*sauq, dilcáspi*), 213
Internalization, 48
Internet, 299, 303
Interpretation (*ijtehad*), 113, 128, 315
Interpreter (*Sahib-e-Tawil*), 262
Intersectionality, 236, 239, 245, 251–5
Intoxication (*masti*), 385
Iqbal, Muhammad (poet), 44, 113, 119, 125, 392
Iqbal, Sheikh, 168, 171–2, 174
Iran, 132, 136, 148, 150, 164, 169, 259, 261, 273–4, 340–3, 347, 350, 360, 392; Sunni mullahs of, 275; with no exemption to Sunni minority, 341; made Shia law into state law, 341
Irani Inqilab: Imam Khumayni awr Shi'iyyat (Iranian Revolution: Imam Khomeini and Shiaism), 345
Iranian Balochistan, 263, 270, 272, 274
Iranian cultural centers, 347
Iranian nationalism, 274
Iranian Revolution 1978–79, 132, 135–6, 148, 150–1, 164, 168, 340–1, 345
Iranian(s), 11, 84, 264, 286; assassination of cultural attaché, 347; assassination of military personnel, 347; government, 347; mosques, 286; Muharram processions of December 1978, 132–3, 136; national culture, 274; revolutionaries, 151; ulama, 330
Iran-Iraq war, 164

Iraq, 10, 132, 137–8, 155, 169, 345
Iraqi Shias, 133, 138, 148
Iraqi, 337, 347–8
Irrigated land (*abadi zamin*), 248
Irrigation system, 248, 250
Irshad'u Da'wah (Guidance and Call to Islam), 345
Isa (Jesus), 260
Isfandiyar, Maulana, 346
Ishq (true love), 121, 211, 228
Ishq-i haqiqi (higher state of love), 121
Ishq-i mijazi (worldly kind of love), 121
Islam, 2, 6–7, 9, 14, 22, 34–5, 37, 39, 40, 76, 83, 85, 88, 91–3, 95–6, 99, 100, 102, 112–6, 119, 120, 122, 124, 129, 155, 170, 182, 196–7, 201, 218, 240, 245, 259, 266, 270–1, 275–7, 280–1, 299, 301–2, 305–7, 309, 310, 314–6, 321, 323–4, 328, 334, 337–8, 340, 342, 344–5, 350, 359, 360, 367–8, 370, 382, 385, 395
Islamabad, 1, 299, 302–3, 309, 311, 319, 320–1, 340, 347
Islamabad-Lahore motorway, 171
Islamic Democratic Alliance, 350
Islamic education, 328, 330, 332, 338; ethics, 205; sciences, 83, 98, 100
Islamic history, 92, 98, 261, 302–3, 314, 317; Shia interpretation of, 343
Islamic law/shariah (*fiqh*), 79, 83, 89, 276, 280, 339, 352; legal authorities, 113; of Shafii, 113; of Malik, 113; of Hanafi, 113, 263; of Hanbali, 113; jurisprudence, 303
Islamic Republic of Iran, 274, 341; adopted cautious policy towards non-Shia Muslim population, 274
Islamic state, 94, 164, 273, 275, 278, 338, 340, 342, 355–7; as welfare state, 275
Islamic University, 302
Islamic: activism, 228, 328, 330, 332, 334, 340, 344; arts festival, 386; bureaucracy, 333–4; constitution, 354–6; fundamentalism, 137; groups/organizations, 332–9, 340, 343; ideology (*iman mufassal*), 262, 300, 304, 330, 332–3, 336; manhood, 206; nationalism, 111; principles/doctrine, 8, 20, 40, 303, 306; reform, 111–5, 119, 128–9, 130, 315; Republic, 133, 135, 278, 368; revivalism, 124, 128; revolution, 338; ritual slaughter (*halal*), 184–5, 188, 197, 263, 276; societies, 79; studies/learning, 91, 96, 98, 299, 302, 306, 309, 334; traditions, 11, 22, 81, 85, 204, 360–1
Islamicity, 355, 357
Islamism, 113, 217, 328, 334–5, 342–3, 352, 360
Islamist movement, 211, 332, 349, 356; Deobandi domination of, 357
Islamist parties, 1, 113, 201, 203, 212, 215, 228, 272, 276–7, 332–3, 337, 341–2, 354, 356, 360 Islamist thinkers, 342–4
Islamist(s), 328, 332–5, 338, 342–3, 351; guerrilla groups, 357; politics of, 348; ideologues, 379
Islamiyat, 3, 11
Islamization, 93, 98, 164, 168, 216, 225, 228, 276, 278, 328, 332–6, 338–9, 340–2, 348, 357, 360
Ismail, 180–1
Ismailis/Ismailia, 166, 211, 238–9, 246, 249, 266–7, 275, 277–8, 327
Ispahani, M.A., 355
Istanbul, 266
Istók language, 201
Istóko qazi! judge of the play, 217
Istóks (musical gathering), 201–6, 218–9, 222, 224–7, 229; beautiful (*sieli*), 222, 227; fights (*janjál*), 223; heaviness (*qahi bik*), 222–3, 227; held outdoors (*beri*), 215; labelled as impermissible, 228; songs (*basónu*), 221, 223

J

Jabal (Mount) Rehemat, 182
Jaffrelot, Christophe, 10
Jagirs, 339
Jahalwan, 278
Jahangir, Emperor, 192
Jalal, Ayesha, 379
Jalal, Malik, 265
Jam'iat (student wing of Jama'at-i-Islami), 302
Jam'iat-i Ulama-i Ahl-i Hadith (Society of Ahl-i Hadith Ulama), 344
Jam'iat-i Ulama-i Hind (Society of Indian Ulama, JUH), 351–3, 355; opposed the creation of Pakistan, 351–2, 354

Jama'at-i Islami, 114, 277, 301–2, 309, 334, 338, 342–3, 353–4, 356–8, 360; women's wing, 309
James, Henry, 19
James, William, 235
Jami'a Ashrafiyya, 97
Jami'at al-'Ulum al-Islamiyya, 94, 97; as major Deobandi madrassah in Karachi, 94
Jami'atu'l-Muhsinat (Society of the Virtuous), 334
Jamiat-e Ulama-e Islam (JUI), 167–9, 170, 337, 339, 346, 352–3, 357, 359; links with Deobandi 339, 352–3
Jamiat-e Ulama-e Pakistan (JUP), 167, 336; linked with Barelvi, 339
Jammu, 246
Janmahmad, 277
Jatoi, Hyder Bakhsh, 125
Jaunpur, 261
Jaunpur, Mahdi of, 261 *see also* Mahdi, Syed Muhammad
Java, 360
Javid, 392
Jeay Sindh Movement, 127
Jeddah, 192
Jews, 280
Jhang City (Jhang Sial), 165, 348, 350
Jhang Saddar (Jhang Maghina), 165, 167, 169
Jhang, 164–6, 168–9, 170, 173–4, 341, 346–9, 350; Shia Muhajir community of, 167; social conflict in, 172; worst violence in 1992, 173
Jhang, Governor of, 166
Jhangvi, Maulana Haq Nawaz, 169, 170–3, 346, 349, 350, 357; as a candidate in elections of 1988, 350; early life, 169; his assassination, 172–3, 337, 347, 350
Jhok, sufi saint Shah Inayat of, 126
Jihad, 263, 330
Jihadist, 336
Jinnah, Mohammad Ali, 119, 275, 355
Jinns, 2, 4–9, 10, 13–9, 21, 23
Journey through the Qur'an, 308 *see also Daura-e-Qur'an*
Joyo, Ibrahim, 111–2, 123–8, 130
Jungle Khel, 194
Jurisprudence, principles of (*usul al-fiqh*), 79, 92

K

Kaaba, 119, 181, 260
Kabirwala, 347
Kabul, 261
Kafis (epigrammatic poems), 377
Kakar, 37, 46–7
kalam (actual words), 262
Kalanga cult, 177
Kalashinkov culture, 336
Kalat State National Party (KSNP), 271, 274
Kalat state parliament, 272–3; consisted of two houses, 272
Kalat state, 260, 266–7, 269, 271–4; Sunni ruling family of, 265
Kalat, Khan of, 265–7, 269, 272; *farman* of, 271
Kambarani, Ahmadzai, 265
Kammis, 166
Kanjar community, 378
Karachi, 14, 94, 97, 117–8, 121, 123, 125, 129, 157, 164, 169, 259, 271–2, 274, 320, 337–8, 340, 346–7, 350, 357–8
Karakorum National Movement (KNM), 246
Karamat movement, 167
Karamats (dynasty), 166
Karbala, Battle of, 10, 137–8, 144, 146, 149, 150, 152, 154, 170, 240, 284–5, 288–9, 290, 295, 342, 385
Karim, Maulana Fazlul, 22
Kashmir, 148, 164, 328, 338, 357; dispute, 245, 252
Kashmir, Maharaja of, 245
Kashmiris, 238, 246
Kasrkand-Geh, 263, 273
Kech (Kej), 260–1
Kedah, 359
Keil, Charles, 395
Kelantan, 359, 360
Kemalist Turkey, 268
Kerzter, David, 135
Khaddar (home-spun cloth), 120
Khaldun, Ibn, 260
Khalifa, 197
Khalisa, 248–9, 250–1
Khan, Field Marshal Ayub, 92, 125, 392
Khan, General Muhammad Yahya, 275
Khan, Khan Abdul Ghaffar, 120

Index

Khan, Mir Ahmad Yar (1934–48), 266, 271–2
Khan, Mir Nasir (1749–94), 260, 263, 265–7; his death, 267
Khan, Sir Chaudhry Zafaru'llah, 355
Kharan, 260
Khawja Ajmeri shrine, 192
Khewa gate (Bab-i Umar), 167
Khidmat, 183
Khilafat movement, 120
Khilafat Mulukiyat (Caliphate and Monarchy), 343
Khilafat-i Rashidah (Rightly Guided Caliphate), 358, 345
Khoja, 121, 327
Khomeini, Ayatollah, 133, 148–9, 169, 345
Khowar language, 201, 206, 211, 213, 217, 221, 227
Khu'i, Aatollah Abu'l-Qasim, 345
Khudadad, Mir, 271
Khudawadi (language of commerce), 116
Khuddamu'l-Quran (Servants of the Qur'an), 334
Khuddamuddin (Lahore), 346
Khuhro, Hamida, 120
khuloos (affection), 228
Khurram valley, 336
Khurshid, 225
Khuzdar, 260
Khwarij Muslim sect, 265
Khyber Pass, 136
Klipspringer buck, 177
Kohat, 183
Koh-Baloch (Baloch group belonging to Zikri sect), 260
Koh-e-Murad, 260–1, 273, 276
Kohistan, 241
Kuper, Adam, 242

L

Labour (*bigar*), 267, 271
Lagan (attachment), 387
Lahore District Census Report, The (1961), 34
Lahore, 2–3, 10, 12, 14–6, 18, 22, 42, 45, 80, 97, 165, 171, 192, 194, 286, 302, 329, 334, 344, 347, 351, 355, 367, 370, 373, 378–9, 391–2

Lahori, Maulana Ahmad Ali, 355
Lal (red), 377, 390–1
Lal Meri Pat (folk song), 394
Lambardar, 249
Landlords (*zamindar*), 123–4, 127–8, 191, 339
Langar, 179, 184–9, 190–1, 193, 196–8; British branches, 196; Eid sacrifices, 197
Las Bela, 259
Lashkar-e Jhangvi (Jhangvi's Army), 173, 328, 338, 347
Lashkar-i Tayyibah (Army of the Pure), 345
Latif, Shah Abdul, 119, 124
Leased Areas, 271
Lebanon, 170
Leitner, G.W., 80; as a Hungarian Orientalist, 80
Levi-Strauss, 288–9
Lindholm, Charles, 206
Loeffler, 158
Longing, state of (*shauq*), 41–5
Lordly (*lalei*) families, 222
Loris (Baloch clan), 267
Lucknow, 84, 343, 345, 358; *majales*, 286
Ludhianawi, Mawlana Muahmmad Yusuf, 94–7, 99, 100, 332; critique of 1979 Report, 95, 100

M

Madani group, 352–7; in Pakistan, 354 *see also* Jam'iat-i Ulama-i Hind; Deoband madrassah
Madani, Maulana Asad, 354
Madani, Maulana Husain Ahmad (d.1957), 351, 353–4, 359
Madras, 81, 332
Madrassah Curriculum, 89, 90, 91, 96, 98, 101, 332, 334–5; reforms in, 333
Madrassah-i A'zam (Madras), 81, 83
Madrassahs, 3, 76–7, 79, 80, 82–4, 86–7, 89, 91–2, 94–6, 98–9, 113, 116, 167–8, 358; decline of, 83, 87–8, 97; reforms of, 90; Sunnis, 241
Magassi, Mir Muhammad Yusuf Ali Khan Aziz, 268–9, 270; his death, 270
Mahdawis, 261, 263, 275, 277–8
Mahdi, 260–1

Mahdi, Syed Muhammad, 260–2, 277; considered by Zikris as Mahdi, 260; teachings of, 263
Mahdism, 260
Mahfil (musical gathering), 201, 211–6, 218, 224, 227–8
Mahmood, Saba, 311
Mahmud, Maulana Mufti, 339, 353–4, 359; opposed the creation of Pakistan, 354–5
Mahmudabad, Raja of, 355
Mahreen, 142–3
Majles (plural, *majales*), 136–8, 143, 147, 149, 150–1, 155–6, 169, 171, 285–9, 293, 295; of women, 138, 143–4, 153, 157, 283–4, 287, 290
Makkah/Mecca, 16, 119, 179, 180–1, 186–7, 197, 199, 260–1, 265; period, 314
Makkuran region, 278
Makran, 259, 260–1, 264–7, 269, 271, 273–5, 277, 279; as Zikri state, 263, 265, 273; civil administration, 276, 278; divided into two sects, 259
Makrani society, 267
Malang (Sufi mendicant), 371, 373–4, 376, 382, 387, 391–3
Malay, 359, 360
Malaysia, 359
Malik dynasty, 263
Mamluk, 100
Manchester, 179, 187, 190, 199
Maneri, Shaikh Sharfuddin (15th century Indian Sufi), 43–4
Manliness (*mosigári*), 206
Manot (a pseudonym), 248–9, 250–1, 253
Mardin, Serif, 99
Markaz (district headquarter), 211, 214, 216
Markaz, 15 see also Tablighi
Marsden, Magnus, 201
Marsia, 138, 142–4, 149, 153–4
Marwa, 180
Marxism, 119, 125–6
Marxist, 111, 116, 123
Maryam, 7–8, 11, 16–7, 19, 20–1
Masjid (mosque), 3, 101, 134, 201, 334, 3444; used as arms depot, 337
Mast qalandar (*dhamal*), 384–6, 393–5
Matam, 169, 285, 288, 290–1, 293–4

Matras (measures), 383
Maududi, Maulana Sayyid Abul Ala (d.1979), 34, 114, 125, 137, 334, 342–3, 356; as fundamentalist reformists, 34
Maulvis, 187, 307, 309, 314–6, 324
Mazars, 3
Medina University, 343
Medina, 3, 12–3, 261, 284, 290
Meds (Baloch group belonging to the Zikri sect), 260, 267
Mehram, 325
Mehtar, 209, 216, 218
Memon, 121
Merit (*sawab*), 189
Messick, Brinkley, 84
Metcalf, Barbara, 85
Metrical framework (*tal*), 393
Mexico, 177
Middle East, 147, 197, 262
Middle Eastern women, 148
Militant Shia organization, 327, 337, 345–6
Militant Sunni organization, 327–8, 337–8, 340–1, 348 see also Sunni militancy
Military government, 129, 211, 332; coup of 1958, 122; coup of 1977, 276
Mill, James (d.1836), 80
Millat system, 280
Milli Yakjahati Council (Council of National Unity), 343, 357–8
Mimbar (pulpit), 289, 336
Mina, 179, 180
Minhaju'l-Qur'an (Path of the Qur'an), 334
Ministry of Religious Affairs, 271
Minority Muslim sects, 259, 266, 275, 278, 280
Mir, Sajjad, 345
Miraculous powers (*barakat*), 126, 178
Mirate (later Khanate of Kalat), 265
Mirza, Iskandar, 355
Miskhat-ul-Masabih, 22, 85
Modern education, 117–8, 334; school system, 91, 98, 100–1, 112, 117
Modern science/disciplines, 93–5
Modernism (*tajaddud*), 98–9, 115, 368
Modernists, 275
Modernization, 34, 99, 113–4, 275, 315
Mohalle (of Gilgit), 248–9
Mohammedan Law, 82 see also Islamic law

Mohenjo-Daro, 121
Molais, 287
Mongiri, Mawlana Muhammad 'Ali, 86–7
Morocco, 101
Morphology, 79, 87, 92
MQM, 169
Mu'awiyah (d.680), 343–4
Mughal: Empire, 37, 210, 264, 280; India, 265
Mughals, 116
Mughal-Timurid culture, 209
Muhaddith (Lahore), 344
Muhajir-Punjabi Sunni family, 2
Muhajirs/Mohajirs, 9, 10, 136, 143, 154, 165–8, 171, 212; population in Jhang, 165, 172; Sunnis, 167, 171; *goondas*, 173; mullahs, 278
Muhammad (PBUH), Holy Prophet, 3, 5–6, 8–9, 10–4, 20–1, 79, 114, 119, 132, 137, 150, 182–3, 186, 241, 260–2, 285, 288–9, 290, 301–3, 310, 314, 323, 344, 384–5, 393; birthday (*Milad-un Nabi*) of, 13
Muhammad, Mulla Nizam al-din (d.1748), 84
Muhammadan Anglo-Oriental College (later University, estb. 1875), 113, 117
Muharram (Islamic month), 10, 13, 132–3, 135–9, 147, 149, 150, 164, 168, 240, 285–7, 290, 295; rituals, 136, 140–1, 144–7, 149, 150–6, 284–5, 349 see also Ashura
Mujahedin, 328
Mullah, 122, 128, 227–8, 277–8 see also Indian Moulvies
Multan, 14–6, 165–6, 347
Multiplicity, 235–7, 239, 251, 253–6
Muqaddimah, The, 260
Murids, 167, 191
Murshid, 47–8
Murtaden, 270, 277 see also Zikris
Musharraf, Pervez, 1, 168
Musical events, 201–3, 212, 215, 228 see also *Mahfil*; *Istóks*
Musical-spiritual ideology, 386, 389, 395
Muslim Children—How to Bring up?, 8
Muslim League, All-India, 87, 355; of Sindh, 119, 121, 123
Muslim(s), 4, 6–7, 9, 12–3, 15, 21–2, 35, 37, 40, 49, 124, 132, 148, 190–2, 201, 224, 244–5, 260–1, 272, 280, 310, 314, 352, 360, 369, 374, 377, 391, 393; communities, 204, 379; connotation, 394; curriculum, 117; democracy, 44, 392; fundamentalists, 137, 279; identity, 305; jurists, 263; literature, 100; nationalism, 113, 115–6, 121, 124, 128–9, 130; Personal Law, 276; political power of, 34, 113, 352; primary schools, 116, 118; societies, 2, 76–7, 79, 83, 86, 96, 98–9, 100, 204, 212; world, 49, 88, 96, 113, 228, 330, 344
Muslim/Islamic reformers, 76, 96, 112–3; *see also* Nadwi, Sayyid Abu'l-Hasan 'Ali
Muslim-Hindu riots, 121
Mutahhidah Deeni Mahaz (United Religious Front), 350
Muttahida Majlis-e Amal (MMA), 202, 219
Muzadaliffah, 180
Mwali, 177
Mysticism (*tasawwuf*), 111, 115, 119, 122, 125–9, 130, 374

N

Nabi, Haji, 261
Nadeem, 264
Nadwat al-ulama, 86–9, 90, 343, 345; annual session of 1896, 86; annual session of 1912, 87; founders of, 86, 89; its rhetoric to reform madrassah curriculum, 89, 90
Nadwi, Sayyid Abu'l-Hasan 'Ali, 83, 345–6; rector of Nadwat al-ulama, 87
Nafs, 7, 189
Nager, 238, 249, 250
Namazis (Sunnis), 259
Namus-i Sahabah (Honour of the Companions of the Prophet) bill, 345
Nandy, Ashish, 207
Naqibs (Baloch clan), 267
Nasr, 43–4
Nasr, S.V., 327
Nasr, Seyyed Vali Reza, 137
Nasreen, 139
Nation (*qawm*), 98, 246, 254–5
National Assembly, 10, 167–8, 172, 345, 350, 359
National Awami Party, 276, 279

National College of Arts, 379
National Committee, 332
Nationalism, 113, 122, 124, 129, 130, 246, 252, 254, 268, 280, 305, 356
Naujuwánan, 220
Nausherwanis, 267
Nautor, 248, 250
Nayyar, Adam, 387
Naz, 323
Nazrana, 186, 188
Nazr-niyaz, 286, 295
New Age, 379
NGO, 215, 228, 323
Niyazi, Abdul Sattar, 357
Nizami, Farhan, 84
Nobles, class of (*adamzada*, lit. true humans), 209
Noha, 138, 149, 154
Nomadic pastoralism, 269
Non-Zikris, 260
Noorani, Maulana Shah Ahmad, 357
North India, 113, 207, 209, 210, 286, 394
North West Frontier Province (NWFP), 120, 134, 136, 164, 194, 201, 206–8, 211, 335–7, 342–3, 347, 351, 353, 357–8; Islamizers, 209, 226
North West Frontier Province government, 202
Northern Areas, 164, 208, 237, 241, 245–8, 252–4
North-West Pakistan, 327
Nowheh, 284, 289, 290, 295; *darud*, 287, 289, 290; of Punjabi language, 290–1, 293; of Urdu, 287, 294; *salam*, 287, 290, 294; *salavat*, 287, 289, 290, 295 *see also Noha*
Nowheh-chanters, 283–4, 287, 289, 290, 291 *see also Noha*
Nowhehkhans, 283, 287–9, 290–1, 295; women, 290, 295
Nu'mani, Mawlana Shibli (d.1914), 86–7
Nu'mani, Maulana Muhammad Manzur, 345, 358
Nusherwani, Nawabzada Shahbaz Khan, 271–2

O

O'Hanlon, Rosalind, 207, 209, 210

Obscurantist practices (*rusum-i jahiliyyat*), 349, 350
Oedipus, 46
Old City, 142, 145, 152, 154
Oman, 265
Omayyad, 10
One Unit Scheme, 114
Organizational model, 35–6
Oriental learning, 80, 82–3
Orientalism, 115
Orientalist(s), 80, 82
Orthodox Muslims, 259, 262, 264, 273; Sunnis, 301
Ottoman: Caliphate, 265, 274, 280; fleet, 265; Turkey, 99, 264
Outram, Dorinda, 146

P

Pahlavi dynasty, 274
Pakistan Army, 221
Pakistan movement, 275, 351, 355, 359
Pakistan Muslim League (PML), 171, 247
Pakistan nationalism, 119, 129, 352, 355
Pakistan People's Party (PPP), 115, 127–8, 130, 168, 170, 173–4, 247, 333, 350
Pakistan Shariat Council, 328
Pakistan Sunni Ittihad (Pakistan Sunni Alliance), 328
Pakistan, 1–2, 9, 10, 12–3, 15, 23, 34, 36, 38, 84, 90–1, 93–4, 96, 101, 111–5, 118–9, 121, 127–9, 130, 133, 137, 164, 168–9, 183–4, 186–7, 196–7, 199, 201, 207, 209, 210, 212, 224, 227, 237, 245–8, 252–4, 259, 261, 272, 275–6, 278–9, 283–5, 299, 300–1, 305–7, 309, 328–9, 330, 333–4, 338–9, 340–2, 345–6, 348–9, 351, 353–7, 359, 360–1, 368–9, 370, 373, 379, 386, 392, 394; authoritarian regime of, 129, 211; constitutional amendment of 1977, 168; independence, 190, 353; Islamic identity for, 101, 137, 330; national identity, 306
Pakistani madrassahs, 90–2, 95, 100–2, 201, 216, 278, 328, 330, 332–4, 336–8, 351; as militant organization, 328–9, 338, 351; foreign funds, 330, 332; funding of, 342; government *zakat* funds, 333, 339; graduates, 328–9,

332–3, 335–8; growth of, 91, 101, 329, 333, 335, 338; modern education made part of, 93, 334; recipients of private *zakat* funds, 332, 339; reforms, 91–3, 95–8, 333–5; restrictions on, 343; shut down of, 359; state control increase of, 340; structural changes during Zia regime, 332; students, 328–9, 332 *see also* Report of 1962; Report of 1979

Pakistani Shias, 11, 133, 136–7, 143, 148–9, 285, 340–1, 347; population, 135

Pakistani ulama, 97, 100, 240, 330, 352, 355; demand to proclaim Zikris as *kafirs*, 276

Pakistani women, 148, 152, 157, 205, 299, 302, 305–6, 310, 318; Muslim, 305

Pakistani: languages, 283; Muslim nationalism, 115; politics, 354, 356–7; shrines, 386, 392; society, 305; state, 209, 219, 229

Pakistanis, 2, 18, 35–7, 40, 42–4, 48, 184, 188, 215, 245, 252, 254, 332, 341, 359, 368, 370, 375, 378, 381, 386, 394; administration, 245; businessmen, 35, 44, 47–8; disciple, 44–6; Muslims, 186; professionals, 35, 37, 41, 44, 48; public venues, 391; schools, 391

Palijo, Rasul Bakhsh, 125

Panipat, 166–7

Pan-Islamic movement, 266

Pan-Islamism, 273

Panjatan, 285

Panjgur, 278

Panjgur, Gichkis of, 265

Parachinar, 149, 347, 336

Partai Islam Se-Malaysia (Islamic Party of Malaysia, PAS), 360

Particularism, 197

Partition, 9, 12, 90, 166–7, 171, 355

Party (1994), 178

Pashto language, 222

Pathans, 208

Patriarchy, 204, 316, 324

Pattani, 360

Pattern (*naghma*), 384

Peasant farmers (*yuft or rayat*), 209, 348

Peasants (*haris*), 120, 124, 126, 129

Penal Code, 272; section 295, 10

Perfect man (*mard-e-kamil*), 261

Performers (*fankaran*), 213; 'lovers of form' (*husun parast*), 213

Persia, 121

Persian Balochistan, 273–4 *see also* Iranian Balochistan

Persian Gulf, 329, 330, 332, 337, 342, 346–8, 360

Persian, 265, 274, 378; courtly skills, 210; language, 43, 80–1, 116–7, 136, 211, 287, 290, 294, 390, 392; poetry, 214; Makran, 275; Sufism, 44; rule, 273

Persianized, 209, 210, 274

Perso-Baloch frontier, 273

Peshawar Shias, 133, 136, 142, 145–6, 150, 154–5; organization, 142

Peshawar women, 133–5, 137, 147, 156; Shias, 138–9, 140, 142, 148, 151, 157

Peshawar, 132–8, 149, 154, 157, 212, 347, 350

Peyote, 177

Phallocentric rituals, 157

Philippines, 315

Phiran (Punjabi term), 384

Piety, Chitrali men of (*dasmanán*), 202, 204, 206–7, 212, 215–7, 219, 226, 229

Piplianwala, 169

Pir Pathan, 167 *see also* Gilani, Pir Syed Agha Kazem Shah

Pirs, 37–9, 40–4, 46–9, 114–6, 121, 124, 128–9, 154, 166, 190

Place (*than*), 371

Platts, John T., 381

PML (Q), 173

Political Islam, 113, 328

Populism, 355

Portuguese, 264–5

Post-colonial, 102, 209, 338

Post-independence (1947), 90, 348

Power-elite (*hakimzat*), 267, 271

Pre-Partition days, 167

Press and Publication Ordinance, 277

Primordialism, 370

Pro-Madani Deobandis, 353

Properly human (*pura insan*), 228

Provincial elections 1950–1 and 1954, 167

Pukhtun, 133, 136, 142, 207–9, 210, 212, 222, 238; are prone to revenge feuds (*adal-badal*), 210; as wild (*jangali*), 210;

considered violent, 212; culture, 134; Shia, 143, 154
Punjab, 9, 10, 91, 101, 164, 169, 275, 278, 302, 327–9, 337, 340, 346, 348–9, 350–1, 353, 358–9, 369, 370, 379; Education Commission (of 1884), 80; government, 348, 350; Provincial Assembly, 348, 350; University, 302
Punjabi, 124, 174, 375, 378, 381, 391; culture, 170–1, 386; *dhol* playing, 384; drummers, 376; folklore, 166; language, 287, 290–1, 384, 387, 391–2; poet, 367; poetry, 45
Purdah, 8
Pushto language, 211

Q

Qadiri Pir, 167
Qadri, Muhammad Tahiru'l, 334, 342
Qalandar, Faiz (pir), 39
Qalandar, Sufi saint Lal Shahbaz, 375, 384, 390
Qanuni, Sultan Sulaiman, 265
Qasem (RA), 288, 290
Qasim, Baba, 184
Qasim, Muhammad bin, 166
Qasimi, Maulan Israru'l, 337, 347
Qaumi Digest (National Digest), 342
Qawwali, 393–4
Qazi/ Qadi, 217; Sunni, 240, 275
Qizilbash *rozahkhwana*, 145
Qizilbash Shia, 136, 143, 145, 154
Qizilbash, Anatolian, 142
Qom, 238–9, 242–5, 252, 254–6 *see also* Difference, dimension of
Quetta, 270; earthquake of 1935, 270
Qur'an se Baghavat (Revolt of Shias Against the Qur'an), 344
Quran, The Holy, 5, 7, 113, 116, 120, 180, 184, 245, 260, 262, 272, 288, 290, 294, 299, 300–2, 306–7, 310–4, 317–8, 320, 322; studies, 79, 92; sura Al-Jinn, 5; sura *Baqra*, 310; verses, 322
Qurbani, 182

R

Rabitah Alam-i Islami (Islamic World League), 330
Rabwah (near Chiniot), 167
Rafia, 312
Rafiziyat, 169
Rafsanjani, President, 343
Rahima *baji*, 4, 7, 12, 15–8, 23
Rahman, Maulana Rahman, 359
Rahman, Mawlvi Husain Jamalul, 343
Rais (Baloch group belonging to the Zikri sect), 260, 267
Raiwind, 218
Ramzan/Ramadan (Islamic month), 15, 187, 244, 262, 305, 307–8
Rapport, Nigel, 255
Rational sciences (*'aqliyyal ma'qulat*), 79, 84, 87, 92; such as, arithmetic, 79; astronomy, 79; logic, 79, 87, 92; philosophy, 79, 87, 92
Rawalpindi, 286–7, 303, 347
Razia, 322–3
Reality Touch (English summer course), 320
Reddy, William M., 385
Reis, Admiral Sidi Ali, 265; of the Ottoman fleet, 265
Religion (*din/madhhab*), 98, 100, 190, 193
Religion and Reality, 122
Religious dichotomization, 137
Religious differences, 238, 245, 248, 251 *see also* Difference, dimension of; sectarian conflict
Religious learning/education ('Deeni Uloom'), 91, 93
Religious nationalism, 122, 129, 130, 137
Report of 1962 (West Pakistan), 91–3
Repot of the National Committee on Madrasas of 1979, 93–9, 332–3
Reshma (singer), 394
Revival (*tajdid'u ihya'*), 334
Revolt of 1857, 79
Reynold, Pamela, 19, 20
Rhythmic pattern (*thekah*), 385, 395
Rightly Guided Caliphs, 345 *see also* Khilafat-i Rashidah
Riqat (ritualized grief), 295
Rochdale, 198
Rohtak, 167
Roman life, 84
Rowshan, 211
Roy, Oliver, 113
Rozah, 149

Index

Rozahkhwana, 142
Rumi, Jalaludin, 119

S

Sabri Brothers, 394
Sadaqa, 185–6, 189
Sadaqah e jariya, 319
Saddar Bazaar area (Peshawar), 138–9, 145
Sadia, 322
Safa, 180
Safar (Islamic month), 137
Safavi Iran, 265
Sahaba jinn, 9, 11
Sahaba, 9, 10; defaming the, 10
Sahifa-i Ahl-i Hadith (Karachi), 344
Sahiwal, 191
Sai, 180
Sain, Pappu, 369, 373–4, 379, 380, 382, 384–6, 388, 392, 395
Sain, Rashid, 389
Saint/religious intercessor, 185–6, 189, 196–8
Saints/pirs-disciples relationship, 34, 38, 41, 44–9, 127
Sajdis (Baloch group belonging to Zikri sect), 260
Sajjada nishin, 39, 126, 168, 358
Sakineh (RA), 283–4, 288–9, 290–1, 295
Salahu'ddin, Muhammad, 343
Salam, Dr Abdus, 166
Salimu'llah, Maulana, 346
Sallnow, 178, 194
Sama, 315
Samara, 325
Sami'u'l-Haq, Maulana, 346, 353–4
Sandeman system (*sardari nizam*), 269
Sandha, 3, 14
Sangurs (Baloch group belonging to Zikri sect), 260
Sanitary Primer (Cunningham's), 80
Sann, 120
Saqi, Jam, 125–6
Sarbaz region, 273–4
Sarbazi, Maulana Abdul Samad, 271–2; later served as chief judge (*qadi*), 271
Sargodha, 302, 319, 348
Saudi Arabia, 164, 169, 186, 277, 301, 329, 330, 341–4, 359; its anti-Iranian regional policy, 330, 347–8; petro dollars, 277–8; sponsorship, 337
Saudi Arabian sectarian project, 343, 348
Saudi Rabitah Alam-i Islami, 346
Saudi, 149, 192, 348; ulama, 330
Sauz, 222–3
Save Sindh, Save the Continent (From Feudal Lords, Capitalists and their Communalism), 123
Sawad-i A'zam-i Ahl-i Sunnat (Majority of Sunnis), 328
Sayyids, 183, 186, 188, 194, 285 *see also* Siddiqi Muslim caste; Syeds
Schieffelin (1985), 151
Schimmel, 45
Schultz, Alfred, 389
Scotland, 302
Second World War, 123
Sectarian conflict, 164–5, 167, 174, 240, 243, 265, 273, 277, 327, 329, 336, 343, 346–7, 351
Sectarian groups, 336–7, 342
Sectarian violence, 327–8, 331, 343, 348; of August 1997, 327
Sectarianism, 1–3, 23, 95, 164–5, 168, 174, 244, 246–7, 251–3, 269, 272, 275–6, 278–9, 280, 328, 336–7, 341, 343–6, 349, 357–8, 360
Secular/non-religious education (*dunyawi ta'lim*), 90–1, 94, 112–3, 118, 129, 319
Secularism, 113, 279
Secularization, 34, 101, 112, 118
Self-flagellation (*matam*), 133, 144–7, 157, 240, 285, 289, 294; of face, 152–3
Serfs (*cirmūz*), 209
Serkoitis, 206
Servants (*hizmatgar*), 267
Seyyid, 154
Shah Jahan (Mughal Emperor, 1628–58), 265
Shah Jamal shrine, 379, 380, 384, 386, 392
Shah Jewna family, 166, 169, 173
Shah, Reza (Shah of Iran), 133, 274; his regime, 133, 274 *see also* Pahlavi dynasty
Shah, Saint Bulleh (1680–1758), 378, 391
Shahida (a pseudonym), 134, 137, 139, 140–2, 153–5, 157; student of social science (course), 134

Shah-jo-risalo (collection of verses of Shah Abdul Latif), 120
Shakh o shubha (doubts), 21
Shalé-lineage, 239
Shalwar Kameez, 15
Sham-e Ghariban ritual, 285
Shariah courts, 271, 275
Shariah/Shari'a jurisprudence, 84, 92, 114, 128, 267
Shariat-e-Muhammadi, 275 *see also* Mohammadan Law
Sharif, Nawaz, 9, 359
Shazia, 308
Shi'i Hazrat ki Islam se Baghavat (Shias' Revolt against Islam), 344
Shi'is and Shi'ism, 344
Shia women, 135, 143–8, 150–3, 155, 158 *see also* Peshawar women
Shia(s), 1–2, 9, 10–1, 13, 17, 95, 132–3, 135, 138, 146–7, 149, 150, 156, 164, 165–9, 170, 172, 238–9, 240–1, 243–4, 246–9, 250, 253–4, 259, 260, 274, 277, 281, 284, 286–7, 295, 336, 341–3, 344–8, 350, 355–6, 358–9, 360, 374, 384; activism, 340–1; activists, 341, 345, 350; *alim/ulama*, 11, 330, 337, 345; army officers, 287; as community, 148–9, 168–9, 171, 247, 285, 345, 355; as non-Muslims minority, 345; *azan*, 169; communal facilities, 358; faith, 345; feudal/rural elites of Jhang, 167–8, 348–9, 350; feudals/ *jagirdars*, 168, 170–1, 173–4; fundamentalism, 137, 157; identity of, 341; imam, 342; Iran, 139, 265–6; landlords, 173, 348–9; law, 341; madrassah, 330; men, 143, 145, 147; militancy, 341, 343, 347; mosques, 358; *muthulfau*, 249, 250–1; political organization, 143, 148; refused zakat laws, 340; Shin family, 244; theology, 380; tradition, 288; Yeshkun, 239, 242–3
Shiaism, 342–9, 350, 358
Shia-Sunni conflict, 1–2, 9, 17, 164, 167–9, 239, 240–1, 243, 245, 251–2, 340, 345 *see also* sectarian conflict
Shiism, 11, 13, 169, 170–1, 179
Shin, 238, 242–4
Shina language, 239, 244
Shinaki, 238

Shin-Yeshkun issue, 243, 245
Shireen, 142, 145, 152–3
Shirk (idol worship), 4, 125, 191
Shorkot, 165
Sial dynasty, 165
Sialkot, 348
Siddiqi Muslim caste, 186
Sikhs, 166, 170, 192, 379
Silverstein, Michael, 375
Sindh (Hyder Bahksh Jatoi), 125
Sindh Islamic Madrassah (1885), 117–8, 123, 125, 129
Sindh Museum, 120
Sindh University, 118, 120, 125, 129
Sindh, 9, 111–2, 116, 118–9, 120, 122–9, 166, 259, 272, 278, 339, 347, 353, 358, 375, 385, 390, 394; conquered by British in 1843, 116–8; gained provincial autonomy in 1936, 118, 120–1, 124; its historical uniqueness, 121
Sindh, Sufi saint Jhule La'l of, 390
Sindhi Adabi Sangat, 122
Sindhi poetry, 45, 125; of eighteenth-century, 119
Sindhi(s), 9, 114, 116–7, 124–9, 375; cultural elite, 118, 121; culture, 121–2, 124; educational system, 116–8; language, 121–2, 124; literature, 122; Muslims, 124; national identity, 115; nationalism, 111, 119, 121, 124, 126; revolt against military government in 1960s, 122; separatism, 113, 127; separatist movement (since 1958), 111–2, 115, 117–8, 123, 125, 127–9; student movement, 125
Sindhudesh, 127–8
Sineh-zani, 139, 149
Singh, Maharaja Ranjit, 379
Sipah-e Hanafiya, 15
Sipah-e-Muhammad (Muhammad's Army), 341, 358
Sipah-e-Sahaba, 10, 15
Sipah-e-Sahabah, Pakistan (SSP, Army of the Companions of the Prophet, Pakistan), 328, 337–8, 341, 343, 347–9, 350–1, 353, 357–9; anti-Shia slogans of, 344; assassinated seventy-five Shia figures, 358; increase attack on Shia Imams, 344; participated in elections, 350

Siraiki speaking, 167
Siyal, Amanu'llah, 350
Small assemblies (*mehfil*), 383
Snow leopards (*phurdúm*), 223, 227
Social: justice, 111, 113, 118, 124; movement theory, 304; movement, 302–3, 315; poetics, 367–9, 372, 380–1, 390; sciences, 134, 235
Socialism, 127
Sociology, 225
Sodomy, 206
Somatic mode, 371–2
South Asia, 7, 13, 34, 116, 119, 126, 147, 182, 187, 259, 263, 265, 274, 280, 367, 375–6
South Asian, 36, 41, 44, 46, 185, 188, 202; devotional songs, 377; groove, 395; hierarchical authority, 35–6, 39, 40, 49; Islam, 76, 185; subcontinent, 377; Sufis, 43; Sufism, 45, 114, 367, 394
South India, 393–4
South West Asia, 259, 263, 265–6, 274, 279, 280, 376
Southern Punjab, 165–6, 171, 347, 350
Soviet troops, 339
Soviet-American rivalry, 279
Soyem, 285–6
Spiritual Aristocracy, 44, 120 *see also Syeds*
St. Augustine, 313
Sufi *Dar ul uloom* (of Zindapir), 196
Sufi music, 367–9, 372, 376, 380; dancers, 371–2, 381–3, 386, 388–9; drummers, 370–3, 382–5, 388–9, 393, 395; Punjabi drummers, 376; theme of cyclicity, 376
Sufi(s), 34–6, 38, 44–5, 48, 183–4, 191, 378, 385, 392; allegory, 179; annihilation (*fana*), 378, 381; brotherhoods (*silsilah*), 113–4, 128–9; death, 378; doctrine, 392; groove, 386; idea/notion, 47, 128, 384; ideology, 374, 380; insight (gnosis), 45; literature, 38, 41, 43, 45–6, 88, 378; of unicity, 374–5; path, 389; pirs/master, 34–6, 38, 43, 184, 374, 389; poet, 45, 119; poetry, 368, 375–8, 393; reforms, 119, 126; revivalism, 111; saint's lodge, 179, 190; shrines, 369, 373–4, 392, 394; Society of Sindh (*bazm-i sufia-i Sindh*), 122; spiritual exercise, 376, 390; suffering, 378; thought, 394–5
Sufism, 12, 34–5, 37, 42, 48–9, 90, 111–2, 114–5, 119, 122, 126–7, 179, 182, 367, 369, 377–9, 393–4; reformulation of, 112
Sughra (RA), 284, 290
Suhrawardi, 39, 40–1
Suhrawardy, Huseyn Shaheed, 355
Sukkur, 121
Sulayman (the jinn), 11, 16–7, 21–3
Sultan Bahu, 174; shrine, 167–8
Sumatra, 360
Sunnah (collection of Holy Prophet's sayings), 299, 301, 311, 317–8
Sunni(s), 1, 9, 10, 13–5, 17, 21, 85, 95, 137, 149, 154, 164, 166–9, 170, 172, 174, 211, 238, 240–1, 243, 246–7, 251, 253, 260, 262, 273, 275, 277–8, 281, 287, 327–8, 336, 340, 344, 347–9, 355, 359, 360, 374; activists, 340, 343; Baloch, 260, 263, 273–4, 279; bourgeoisie, 348–9, 351; community, 165, 247; Council, 328; culture, 274; *Eidgah*, 241; extremism, 149; family, 249; government of, 143; Hanafi School, 263; identity, 342; immigrants, 250; Islam, 12–3, 85, 249, 261, 267, 274, 329, 334, 339, 343; Islamist groups, 341–2; Jam'iat-i Tulabah (Sunni Student Association), 328; Jhang candidates, 168; *lambardar*, 244–5; landlords, 165, 167–8, 171; *madrassahs*, 241; madrassahs, 330, 351; middle classes, 348–9, 351; militancy, 328, 340, 351, 360; militant sectarianism in, 328; militants, 340; mosques, 241; movement (1985), 164; *muthulfau*, 250; peasants, 348–9; political groups, 342; Pukhtun, 143; religious schools, 241; school of thought, 359; sectarianism, 347, 351, 360; Shariah Law, 267; state, 246, 357; Tehrik (Sunni Movement), 328, 336, 357; traditions, 360; Ulama, 167, 241, 273, 275–7, 330, 337, 343; valleys, 244; Wall, 342; women, 140; Yeshkun, 239; youth organization, 241–2
Sunnification, 340
Sunnism, 330, 341, 351, 358

Sunni-Zikri conflict, 271–2, 274, 278
Surnai, 218, 225
Syed Committee, 120
Syed, G.M. (Ghulam Murtaza), 111–2, 115, 119, 122–9, 130; his death, 119; under house arrest, 120, 122, 127, 129; founded the Syed and Hari Committees, 120; became a leading figure in Muslim league, 121; became minister of education, 121, 124; was for *Greater Sindh*, 121; left Muslim League in 1945, 121; was part of Sindhi political elite, 121; left party politics in 1958, 121; became a spiritual mentor, 121; freed from detention in 1966, 122, 126
Syedism, 120, 125
Syeds, 116, 118, 120–1, 128–9, 166, 261; descendents of Holy Prophet, 116; community, 116 see also Sayyids
Syllabic representation (*bols*), 383, 385
Symbolism, 136, 289, 335, 342, 376, 378
Syntax sciences, 79, 87, 92
Syria, 261
System (*nizam*), 97

T

Ta'ziyeh, 149
Tabara-e-Islam bar Kahur Zigrian, 272
Tabarra, 10
Tabarruk, 184, 186
Tabla (drums), 374
Tabligh-i Jama'at/Tablighi Jamaat, 4, 90, 218, 301, 309; *sathis*, 15, 22; the *dawa* branch of Deobandi, 4
Tabriz (Sun poet), 43
Tafsir, 311
Tahaffuz-i Khatm-i Nubuwwat (Protection of Finality of Prophethood), 328
Takbir, 343
Taliban, 328, 338, 347, 353, 359
Tangir, 240
Tanzim-i Da'wah (Organization of the Call), 328
Taqadum, 98
Taraki, Mademoiselle, 121
Tariq, Azam, 173, 344, 346
Tarjumanu'l Islam (Lahore), 346
Tarjumanu'l-Hadith (Faisalabad), 344
Tasu'a gathering, 138, 151

Taxonomy, 237
Tayyib, Qari Muhammad, 353–4
Tehran, 133, 135, 340, 347
Tehrik-e Nifaz-e Fiqh-e Jaafria (TNFJ), 168, 341, 350; branded as 'Wahhabi Shias', 169
Tehrik-e-Khatm-e Nubuwwat, 167, 276
Tehrik-i Ja'fariyah Pakistan (old TNFJ, TJP), 357–8
Tehrik-i-Islam, 309
Tehzeeb, 323
Temperament (*tabi'at*), 385, 388
Terengganu, 359
Texturalization, 385
Thailand, 360
Thaiss, Gustav, 135–6
Thana-kutcheri, 169
Thanawi, Mufti Jamil Ahmad (d.1995), 97
Thanvi group, 352–3, 356, 358 see also Jam'iat-i Ulama-i Hind; Deoband madrassah
Thanvi, Ashraf Ali (d.1943), 352
Thatta, 125
Theology ('*ilm al-kalam*), 92, 380
Theosophy, 116, 119
Thraldom, 44
TJP, 358 see also Tehrik-i Ja'fariyah Pakistan
Torah, The, 120
Traditionally transmitted sciences (*naqliyyal manqulat*), 79, 84
Traditions (*iman mujamal*), 262
Transnationalism, 137
Tribal *sardars* (*sardari nizam*), 269
Tribes (*tumannat*), 267
Turbat, 260, 263–4, 273–4, 278; as the *Gul-e-Zamin* (flower of the Earth), 264
Turkey, 113, 182, 261
Turkish, 121, 213, 280, 286, 345
Turko-German alliance, 273–4
Turks, 120
Turn of the Screw, The, 19
Turner, 198
Turner, Victor, 177
Twelver Shias, 327 see also Shias

U

Ulama (religious leaders/scholars), 8, 10, 14, 76–7, 79, 81, 86–9, 91, 93–6, 99,

100–2, 113, 122, 240, 261, 271, 276, 280, 328, 332–6, 339, 360; parties, 339; political activism of, 168, 327, 352–4
Ulama Academy, 334
Ulama-e salih, 14
Umar (RA), 340, 344
Umar, Mulla, 347
Ummah (Muslim community), 189, 266
Ummayid Caliphs, 344
Umrah, 179
United Arabs Emirates, 329
United Front of the Northern Areas (*Shumali Illaqajat Muttahida Mahaz*), 247
United States, 1, 23, 41, 303, 307, 310, 386; foreign policy of, 132; devastation and bombing of Iraq, 138, 341–2, 346
Universalism, 124, 197, 268, 340
University of Peshawar, 134, 225
Upper: India, 96; Sindh, 121
Urban, Greg, 375
Urbanization, 348
Urdu, 3, 11–2, 80, 122, 167, 286–7, 290, 293–4, 317, 319, 320–1, 342, 345, 375, 391; bazaar, 3; poetry reading (*mushaira*), 376; Press, 18
Urs celebration, 1, 34, 111, 126, 183–4, 187–8, 194–5, 197–9, 367, 374–6, 378, 380–3, 386–7, 390, 395–6
Useful knowledge (*al-'ilm al-nafi'*), 81
USSR, 274
Ustman Gal, 276
Uthman (RA), 340, 343, 345
Uthmani, Maulana Shabbir Ahmad (d.1952), 352, 354, 356
Utilitarians, 80
Uttar Pradesh, 261

V

Village government servants (*tapedars*), 117
Village headmen (*wadero*), 117
Village mullah school (*makhtab*), 118
Village, inhabitants of (*muthulfau*), 248–9, 250, 253
Village, land of the (*khalisa-e deh*), 248
Voice as Birth of Culture (1995, Das), 2
Voluntarism, 181, 196
Vow (*niyat*), 189

W

Wadh, 278
Wah, 286
Wahabbi, 301, 359
Wahabbism, 301, 343
Wahdat ul-wajud (oneness of Being), 122, 128, 392
Wali Allah, Shah (d.1732), 4, 84–5
WAPDA, 39
Waziristan, 167
Weaponization, 173, 327
Werbner, Pnina, 177
West Pakistan, 118
West, 41, 133, 197, 237, 256
Western Balochistan, 273–4
Western, 35–7, 49, 84; curriculum, 113; education, 315; learning, 89, 94; organizational model, 35–6, 40, 48
Westerners, 36, 40, 42, 194
Whirling Mevlevi dervishes, 386, 393
Wirkuta, 177
World (*dunya*), 190, 193

Y

Yaktai (oneness), 392
Yazid (d.683), 10, 288, 344
Yeshkun *motobaran*, assembly of, 242, 244
Yeshkun, 238, 242–5, 249, 252, 254
Young Baloch (group), 268
Young Turks, 268
Yousaf, Sheikh, 171, 173
Yusuf, Ramzi Ahmad, 328

Z

Zabah, 186, 263
Zahab, Mariam Abou, 164
Zahir, Allama Ihsan Ilahi, 344; assassination of, 345
Zaidi, Ms Sabira, 286–9, 290, 293–4
Zakat, 168–9, 262, 332, 339, 340
Zakereh, 287–9, 290, 294–5
Zakirs, 171 *see also* Barelvis; Shias
Zaman, Muhammad Qasim, 76, 358
Zamzam, 180, 182
Zangir-zani (chains ending in knives), 141, 145–7, 149
Zar-e-sar (tax), 271

Zar-e-shah (tax), 271
Zarfrulla, Sir, 275
Zarina, 320–1
Zaynab, Sayyedeh (sister of Imam Hussein), 137, 155, 284, 288, 294
Zaynabiyyeh, 286, 288
Zehgal, Malika, 101
Zezuru Turn of the Screw: On Children's Exposure to Evil, 19
Zezuru, 19, 20
Ziau'l-Quran (Light of the Qur'an), 333, 336
Zigris, 259 *see also* Zikris
Zikr, 184, 259, 261, 376, 384–6, 393
Zikrana, 262
Zikr-e-khafi, 262
Zikri Baloch, 264, 273–4, 276, 278
Zikri Islam, 263
Zikri Muslim, 276, 278
Zikri publication, 275
Zikri rule, 264
Zikri society, 264
Zikri(s), 259, 260–3, 265–7, 269, 271–9, 280; abolishment of its legal system, 267; declared as non-Muslims, 272, 276; denied rights under Muslim Personal Law, 276; doctrine of, 262, 270, 276; Islamic practices of, 263; migration to Makran, 274; population of, 259, 260; religious persecution of the, 266, 279; rites of worship of, 264; socio-political life of the, 263–4
Zikri-Baloch culture, 264, 277
Zikri-Mahdawi Organization, 275
Zikrism, 263–4
Zikrkhanah (house or place of the zikr), 262
Zimbabwe, 19
Zindapir, 183–9, 190–7, 199; described himself as *faqir*, 186, 192; gifts to pilgrims, 193, 197, 199; lodge of, 186–8, 192–4, 196–9; spreading of the cult of, 196–7; Sufi order of, 187, 196
Zionists, 170
Ziyarat, 290, 294–5
Zubair, Idrees, 299
Zuljinnah, 140–1, 144–6